Promises to Keep

Promises to Keep

Decline and Renewal of Marriage in America

EDITED BY

David Popenoe
Jean Bethke Elshtain

AND

David Blankenhorn

ROWMAN & LITTLEFIELD PUBLISHERS, INC.

ROWMAN & LITTLEFIELD PUBLISHERS, INC.

Published in the United States of America
by Rowman & Littlefield Publishers, Inc.
4720 Boston Way, Lanham, Maryland 20706

3 Henrietta Street
London WC2E 8LU, England

British Cataloging in Publication Information Available

Library of Congress Cataloging-in-Publication Data

Promises to keep : decline and renewal of marriage in America / edited
by David Popenoe, Jean Bethke Elshtain, and David Blankenhorn.
p.   cm.
Includes bibliographical references and index.
1. Marriage—United States. 2. Divorce—United States. 3. Single
parent family—United States. 4. United States—Social conditions.
I. Popenoe, David, 1932–   . II. Elshtain, Jean Bethke, 1941–
III. Blankenhorn, David.
HQ536.P76   1996   306.8'0973—dc20   96-7003   CIP

ISBN 0-8476-8230-7 (cloth : alk. paper)
ISBN 0-8476-8231-5 (pbk. : alk. paper)

Printed in the United States of America

∞ ™ The paper used in this publication meets the minimum requirements of
American National Standard for Information Sciences—Permanence of
Paper for Printed Library Materials, ANSI Z39.48–1984.

Contents

Part Three: Rebuilding a Marriage Culture

Part IV: Marriage in America: A Report to the Nation

Acknowledgments

The editors wish to thank the Board of Directors and financial supporters of the Institute for American Values for supporting the work of the Council on Families in America of which this book is a result. In particular we wish to express our gratitude to the William H. Donner Foundation, the JM Foundation, and the Philip M. McKenna Foundation for their generous support of the Council's work.

Members of the Council worked long and hard, over a period of several years, on this investigation of marriage in America. We are pleased with the results and honored by our association with these good colleagues and friends. We are also grateful to Brandeis University, and to the Brandeis House in New York, for hosting all of the meetings of the Council.

In addition to the authors whose essays appear in this book, we are grateful to Carol Browning, Pamela Couture, John Demos, Elizabeth Gill, Richard Gill, T. Grandon Gill, Amy Kass, the late Christopher Lasch, Dana Mack, William R. Mattox, Jr., Vesna Neskow, Father Richard John Neuhaus, Christine Winquist Nord, the late Lee Salk, Louis W. Sullivan, Ann Swidler, and Nicholas Zill for their important participation in our discussions and for their valuable comments on these essays.

For their work on the "American Family Panel" research project that greatly assisted and informed the work of the Council, we are grateful to Research Director Norval D. Glenn, Field Director Benjamin Zablocki, Don S. Browning, Gloria Cook, Grace De George, Maggie Gallagher, Naomi Miller, Vesna Neskow, Samuel Preston, Ann Swidler, Barbara Dafoe Whitehead, and the interviewers and families who participated in the research.

For editorial help and guidance, we are grateful to Vesna Neskow and Deborah Strubel as well as to Jon Sisk and his colleagues at Rowman & Littlefield Publishers.

We also extend our thanks to New York University Press and to the

William J. and Dorothy K. O'Neill Foundation. The essay "Postmodern Family Law: Toward a New Model of Status" was adapted by permission of New York University Press from *Family Law and the Pursuit of Intimacy* by Milton C. Regan, Jr. (1993). Barbara Dafoe Whitehead's essay "The Decline of Marriage as the Social Basis of Childrearing" is published by permission of the William J. and Dorothy K. O'Neill Foundation and first appeared in their book *Family: The First Imperative* (1995).

The essay "Comparative and Historical Perspectives on Marriage, Divorce, and Family Life" by Arland Thornton was presented to both the Council on Families in America and the Utah Law Review Symposium (October 1993).

This book is part of a larger conference and publication series sponsored by the Institute for American Values on the topics of family well-being, family policy, and civil society. For a publication list or for more information, contact the Institute for American Values at 1841 Broadway, Suite 211, New York, New York 10023. Phone: (212) 246-3942. Fax: (212) 541-6665.

Introduction

David Popenoe

In March 1995 the Council on Families in America—a national, nonpartisan, interdisciplinary group of scholars and family experts whose purpose is to examine family and child well-being—issued its first major report. Entitled *Marriage in America: A Report to the Nation*, it received widespread media attention including segments on ABC's *DayOne* with Diane Sawyer and *All Things Considered* on National Public Radio, a feature article in *USA Today* and other major newspapers, coverage by many national newspaper columnists, and much attention from the nation's talk radio hosts. The report was the result of some two years of intensive investigation, including the commissioning of essays on marriage topics from leading experts around the nation. This book presents the full text of the report, plus a selection of those essays. They are a stirring reflection of the deep concerns about the state of marriage among the nation's marriage experts.

Marriage in America is in trouble. A culture that once treasured the institution of marriage has been steadily displaced by a culture of divorce and unwed parenthood. In the past several decades the divorce rate has doubled and the percentage of unwed births has quintupled. Trends such as these have created tragic hardships for children, generated poverty within families, and burdened us with insupportable social costs. At the same time, no one seems to be much happier.

The essays here, written by lawyers, theologians, social scientists, policy makers, and activists, go to the heart of the problem at a level of detail which the report could not develop. Most were the subject of intense deliberation by Council members at regular meetings in New York City and contain the seeds of the major ideas included in the final report. Many lay out clearly—and unequivocally—the depth of the problem we face. Others point us down the path of marital resurrection. Although the authors do not agree with one another on every issue, together they provide a remarkably penetrating statement of the state of marriage in America today.

Part One examines the issue of marriage decline. The lead article, by social historian Barbara Dafoe Whitehead, lays out the major lines of thinking about the issue that were used in the report. Whitehead points out that "the family lives of American children have been fundamentally restructured during the last decades of the twentieth century," with massive parental "disinvestment" and "a shift in the notions of parental obligations toward children." The empirical data to back up Whitehead's propositions about the decline of marriage are set forth in the article by sociologist Norval Glenn. He finds from the data that "an increasingly hedonistic form of marriage seems to be decreasingly able to facilitate the hedonistic strivings of those who participate in it."

In all revolutions, myths—beliefs that have no foundation in fact—are put forth to justify positions that are being advocated. So it is with the divorce revolution. One family myth making the rounds today is that marriage is good for men but bad for women. Australian family specialist Moira Eastman discusses this myth and others, examines their genesis, and reviews the empirical data that tell a different story. In the process she points out that the divorce revolution is found worldwide among the wealthier nations. Arland Thornton follows Eastman's comparative approach by looking at marriage and the family historically. Through an examination of five hundred years of the European experience, he suggests that "a major restructuring of the institution of marriage" has taken place in recent decades. In the final selection of this section, the social work scholar Janet Giele points out that while marriage and the family have clearly changed course in recent decades, not everyone is in agreement about what to do. She forcefully advocates a feminist ideological position which accepts growing family diversity and calls for a range of government programs to provide family support.

Part Two includes essays that look carefully at marriage in America today from the perspectives of religion, law, and the clinical world of the human service professional. In a review of the history of major lines of Christian thought, theological scholar Don Browning suggests that there are many aspects of Christian thinking that remain highly relevant to today's family issues, especially with reference to the growing absence of men from families—what he calls "the male problematic." By no means does Christianity merely provide an ideological apology for a traditional patriarchy, as some have argued. Legal scholar Milton Regan shows how American family law has changed over the years, in keeping with a changing culture, from an emphasis on "status" as the governing principle—bestowing impersonal rights and obligations on those who assume legal identities, such as spouse, parent, and child—to the far more individualistic principle of "contract," which views marriage as a place where the participants alone decide the terms of their rights and obligations. In this shift, he argues, society has not always been well served. He suggests ways that the concept of status can be brought back into contemporary family law in a fashion sensitive to modern marriage, so that law maintains a dynamic balance between both status and contract. Legal scholar Carl Schneider's essay follows, showing a variety of ways that family law could be changed to help reinstitutionalize marriage. He wisely points out, however, that the goal of reinstitutionalization cannot be accomplished through law alone—there must be widespread cultural change. The final essay, by sociologist Robert S. Weiss, examines one of the major problems of today's family scene bearing on children—how to continue parenting even though a marriage has broken up. To this end he makes specific policy recommendations, including a role for government.

The final group of essays, in Part Three, deals with the issue of rebuilding a marriage culture. Social analyst Maggie Gallagher in no uncertain terms tells us what our society can do to deal with marriage decline, which she states is the one social problem in America about which we have largely thrown up our hands. At the very least, she says, we should have the modest goal of a society "in which more marriages succeed than fail." My essay follows. It suggests that because going back to earlier marital forms is both impossible and undesirable, we need a new marital script for the roles that husband and wife in the modern family are expected to play. Such a script is outlined, based on the latest evidence from the social sciences. Finally, former Clinton domestic policy adviser William Galston outlines a challenging array of policies, covering economics, culture, and the government, that are needed if our marriage institution is ever to be recovered. He calls for a middle range of public policies, those which fall between the poles of the growing libertarian spirit in America and the often highly conservative reaction to it.

Each of these authors strongly agrees on one thing—that the time has come for our society to change course. The marriage report, which concludes the book, goes into detail about the steps which can be taken to bring this about. We must, it asserts, "reclaim the ideal of marital permanence and affirm marriage as the preeminent environment for childrear-

David Popenoe

ing." Noting that "we are all part of the problem, and therefore we must all be part of the solution," the report makes some fifty-eight specific recommendations to fifteen sectors of society. "No domestic challenge of our era," the report concludes, "is more important than this one."

PART ONE

The Decline of Marriage

CHAPTER 1

The Decline of Marriage as the Social Basis of Childrearing

Barbara Dafoe Whitehead

With each new report from the Census Bureau, we are reminded that American family life is changing. The continuing rise in the percentage of children born out of wedlock, the historically high levels of divorce, the high percentage of births to unwed teenage mothers, the decline in the age of sexual initiation, and the normalization of premarital sex all testify to the fundamental reorganization of family life and intimate relationships in recent decades.

The question of what these changes mean for the nation and the society provokes intense debate in both political and scholarly circles. This paper will not attempt to address, much less resolve, this debate. However, since our views of family change are inevitably influenced by our own disciplinary and personal perspectives, I do think it is useful to identify my own bias at the outset. I have a bias toward children's interests and well-being. A large body of popular and scholarly literature has chronicled and analyzed recent changes in family life but for the most part this literature has looked at these events from an adult perspective and especially from the perspective of the changing experience of American women.

While this approach is valid, it neglects the fact that adults' and children's experiences of these events are different. Even women's interests in family life are less closely identified with children's interests than in the past, as historian Carl Degler has observed. Thus, I will focus on children's experience and the impact on children of changes in family structure. With this objective in mind, I intend to point to a major discontinuity in American family life: the decline of marriage as the social basis for childrearing.

Marriage and Parenthood as Individualistic Pursuits

The family lives of American children have been fundamentally restructured during the last decades of the twentieth century. As the result of the escalating levels of unwed childbearing and historically high levels of divorce, a growing proportion of American children are likely to spend part or all of their childhood in single-parent families. Many will also be members of step-parent families. If current trends continue, it is estimated that as many as 60% of all children born in the 1980s are likely to have their families disrupted by divorce or nonmarriage.

Why did this restructuring occur? The reasons are varied and complex but many scholars cite a major ideational shift in Western societies as a primary cause. According to sociologist Alice S. Rossi, "Westerners are shifting from a concern for their children's futures to a self-orientation that gives priority to individuals' desires rather than to the needs of spouses and children."[1] This shift has profoundly altered the social and psychological bases for childbearing and childrearing in American society.

I want to call attention to two ways in which the change is manifested. First, marriage is declining as the central institution of family life. This does not mean that marriage itself has fallen into disfavor. Americans are a marrying people, and marriage is highly regarded as a means to achieving intimacy and personal happiness in relationships. Americans remain starry-eyed about the magical transformation wrought by marriage, even when it comes to the revolving door of celebrity marriage. We fervently hope that Elizabeth Taylor will find true happiness with a future ninth husband. But marriage is less important as the social basis of childrearing than it has ever been in the nation's history. Increasingly, marriage and parenthood are coming apart.

The second way that this ideational shift manifests itself is in the greater tendency to see marriage and parenthood as individual pursuits rather than socially defined roles. Getting married and having children are no longer requirements of adulthood nor responses to social norms. Increasingly, these important life events are dictated by individual goals and purposes. Psychologist Elizabeth Douvan observes that we used to judge an individual by the way he or she managed social roles; now we measure roles by the rewards they hold for the individual.[2]

Additionally, both marriage and parenthood are defined in expressive terms. One elects to be married or to become a parent because it is "what I want to do." This understanding is widely accepted: as one pastor told the *Los Angeles Times*, "it is everyone's choice to fulfill a dream. If a woman can't find Prince Charming and wants a baby and is ready, society should not dictate what is acceptable."[3]

The emphasis on the expressive side of parenthood is most dramatically evident in the small but growing "single mothers by choice" movement. One of the leading popular books on the subject, *Single Mothers By Choice*, advises women on how to avoid the social and legal entanglements of involving a father in the rearing of a child. Its author, Jane Mattes, warns: "You need to be aware that putting a father's name on the birth certificate opens up a hornet's nest of potentially serious legal complications."[4] But Mattes is not alone in seeing motherhood as an expression of selfhood. In one recent survey, a majority of Americans, including 70 percent of younger adult Americans, agree that women should have the right to bear a child out of wedlock without reproach.[5] Taken together, these two changes suggest a trend toward a "postmarriage" society, marked by the decline of marriage as a childrearing institution and the rise of a more voluntary system of family relationships with easily dissoluble ties and more contingent and limited commitments.

It is worth underscoring how rapidly all of this has taken place. A popular book written in the 1970s offered what seemed at the time to be a utopian vision of future family relationships:

> My granddaughter, at the moment unborn, may live well into her nineties, if not beyond, and be married at least twice, maybe three, perhaps four times. Her divorces will be no-fault divorces. It is also likely that she will be the complacent biologic mother of two or three children by various fathers and the affectionate social mother of another brood via her several husbands and their ex-wives.[6]

To a remarkable degree, this forecast proved accurate. In the early 1980s, the distinguished historian Lawrence Stone noted:

> The characteristics of the post-modern family are as follows: . . . sexual relations have been almost entirely separated from both the biological function of procreation and the legal institution of marriage. . . . Despite the high psychic and economic costs of divorce, marriage itself is now only a temporary arrangement. It is predicted that today one half of all marriages will end in divorce, so that we are moving into an era of serial polygamy.[7]

Because a postmarriage society is characterized by more fragile and impermanent relationships, it is also marked by greater churning and instability in family life. In the past, family instability was caused by high mortality and morbidity, but these causes are largely absent today. As social demographer Samuel Preston noted in his 1984 Presidential address to the Population Association of America: "It seems incredible that we have reached this level of instability when collectively we have better health, more teeth, better odor, and more orgasms."[8]

From an adult perspective, greater fragility and instability in familial relationships is not necessarily undesirable. More open-ended and contingent commitments may provide greater freedom and opportunity for adults to seek and perhaps find satisfying relationships. When marriage fails to offer emotional satisfactions, when it proves difficult, disappointing, or demeaning, it can be abandoned. Important, too, when marriages are easily dissoluble, there is greater opportunity for women to escape abusive and violent marriages than in the past. (Neverthless, there has been no decline in domestic violence with the rise in divorce. Some scholars suggest that this is because domestic violence grows out of sexual possessiveness and jealousy rather than out of the marital institution itself.)[9]

Moreover, the ability to shape and reshape family relationships endows individuals with a greater sense of possibility. When nothing is forever, anything can happen, if not today, then tomorrow or the next year. This engenders a sense of hope and optimism, even when the reality doesn't always measure up. The *Wall Street Journal* recently reported on a Department of Agriculture study that measured divorced mothers' perceptions of their postdivorce lives. The women's appraisals were remarkably sunny. Over 60 percent considered their career opportunities better after divorce, and 54 percent reported that their overall situation for caring for their children had improved. The researcher concluded that despite heavier work and childcare burdens, the women enjoyed greater freedom from spousal conflict and therefore had an improved outlook on life.[10]

However, though it offers advantages to adults, a more voluntary system of family relationships is problematic for children. Children have an important stake in a marriage. Marriage provides the basis of children's primary attachments and the foundation of children's social security. A large body of evidence suggests that children suffer emotionally and economically when these primary attachments are severely disrupted.[11] Consequently, in a society where adults increasingly engage in marriage and parenthood as individualistic and expressive pursuits, the basis of children's security is threatened. To be sure, parents' interests and children's interests in marriage have never been identical. But for reasons I will explore in this paper, their interests are now increasingly divergent and competing. Thus, the principal challenge of a postmarriage society may be stated as follows: how to reconcile the adult pursuit of individual happiness with children's needs for secure and stable family attachments.

Children's Dependence on Marriage

Why does marriage matter to children?

To answer that question, it is necessary to offer an overly broad and simplified, but I hope useful, historical observation. Two great structural changes in children's family lives have occurred in modern Western societies. The first occurred in northern Europe during the eighteenth century with the rise of what historians call the "modern nuclear family."

Historian Lawrence Stone describes the change as a shift from families organized around the kin group to families organized around the married couple. This shift involved a corresponding shift in the pattern of authority and deference from one characterized by a hierarchical distribution of power, the arranged marriage, and the fostering out of children to one based in a more egalitarian distribution of power, companionate marriage, and the child-centered family.

The new family structure contributed to higher levels of parental investment in children. With the decline of kin responsibility for children, the responsibility for the economic upkeep of children fell more directly on fathers while mothers began to assume responsibility of child nurture rather than handing the child over to the care of servants and wetnurses. As a result of declining mortality rates, moreover, there were greater incentives to invest in children. Thus, a more affectionate ideal of childrearing emerged during the eighteenth century.

But the restructuring of the family around the married couple had a second profound impact on children. It made children dependent on the permanence and stability of marital bonds. At the heart of the modern nuclear family was a radically new marital ideal. While marriages in the past had been dictated and regulated by the larger kin group as an "economic deal or a political alliance," the new marriage ideal was defined by individual choice and mutual regard. Thus the foundation of family life was rooted not in property or status but in affection.

In these new, more streamlined families, organized around the married couple, children's fortunes were closely tied to the quality and stability of spousal affection. Compared to the marriage arranged by the kin group and dominated by patriarchal power relationships, the companionate marriage offered many advantages for marital partners, especially for wives. However, bonds of mutual affection proved a fragile foundation for marriage. Therefore, at the same time that the new marital ideal fostered greater parental investment in children and a greater childcenteredness, it also contributed to a new source of vulnerability for children.

Because of the patterns of early immigration, the "modern nuclear family," defined by companionate marriage and child-centeredness, became the dominant family structure in the new American republic. The rise in the nineteenth century of a "separate spheres" domestic ideology linked women's identity and status to that of children, further increasing maternal investment in children.

The second historic restructuring of children's family lives began in the late 1960s with the rise in voluntary family disruptions. In 1974, divorce replaced death as the principal cause of family breakup. The same period saw a rise in unwed childbearing, from 5 percent in 1960 to close to 30 percent in 1990. Although the divorce rate leveled off in the mid-1980s, the percentage of births to unwed mothers continues to increase. From the child's perspective, it is hard to exaggerate how significant this restructuring has been. Indeed, the historical demographer Daniel Scott Smith notes that the period of most rapid change in the history of the Western household, at least since the Middle Ages, lies in the immediate past.[12]

Because of children's dependence on marital stability as the basis of parental investment and affection, the weakening of marriage has had harmful consequences for children. Yet, given that structural reality, there has been remarkably little attention devoted to the interests of children in marriage. Indeed, over the past two-and-a-half decades, the trend in both the popular advice and scholarly literature has been to focus on the adult interests in marriage. To cite a single example from the advice literature, consider the following: in *Quality Time: Easing Children Through Divorce*, Dr. Melvin Goldzband writes: "All the comments about the needs of children for intact families should not cause any divorcing parent to consider reconciliation for the sake of the children."[13]

Parental Disinvestment in Children

The decline of marriage often leads to parental, and especially paternal, disinvestment in children. Though the family is no longer economically self-sufficient, it remains the central social institution for transferring dollar resources between generations. Historically, the principal beneficiaries of these transfers have been children, and the most prominent group of donors have been adult men. In a postmarriage society, however, the family structure for male investment in children is weakened as is the incentive structure. Men who live apart from their children are less reliable providers than married fathers who share a residence with their children. Fathers who have never been married to their children's mothers are the least likely to provide regular income support to their children, partly because they have not been identified and paternal identification is the essential first step to securing child support and partly because they tend to be younger and poorer than divorced fathers.

Contributions of nonresidential fathers to the family household are dramatically less than the contributions of married fathers who live with their children. Nonresidential fathers (mainly divorced) who reliably meet child support obligations contribute an average of $3,000 a year to their children while married fathers contribute a much higher proportion of their earnings to the family's maintenance and care. (According to 1990 figures, the median male wage is $30,000; this figure may be taken as a rough proxy for the median paternal income available for investment in children.)[14]

The loss of paternal support is not offset by higher levels of maternal support. Most children live with their mothers and, despite improving wages, greater workforce participation, and better economic opportunities for women, single-mother households lack the earning capacity of the two-parent and, especially, dual-earner households. Median family income for married-couple families with at least once child under age eighteen was $41,260 in 1990 compared to a median income of $13,092 for single-mother families with at least one child.

Consider this gap in light of the very conservative estimates from the U. S. Department of Agriculture for a no-frills annual childrearing budget. According to USDA figures, a middle-income married couple with one three- to five-year-old child would spend a total of about $8,000 in direct annual expenditures.[15] Obviously, a single mother with a $13,000 income and one similarly aged child would have a hard time achieving even this modest level of expenditure, a level that would be expected to increase as the child got older.

Nor is the falling off of family investment in children offset by increasing public investment in children. Although overall public spending on children continues to rise, it has not increased fast enough to lift children out of poverty. European nations do a much better job than the United States in reducing child poverty through tax and transfer policies. In Western nations that treat children as generously as they do their older citizens, government benefits lift from half to three-quarters of poor children out of poverty.[16]

Nonetheless, reducing poverty among children is only a first step in securing the bases for economic well-being. Indeed, the decline in family investment in children could not have come at a worse time. A postindustrial society requires a "high-investment" childrearing strategy, because economic success depends on longer schooling and the acquisition of more sophisticated technical and conceptual skills than in the past. Thus, in addition to increased public spending on children, lavish expenditures of parental time and money are required to endow each child with the competencies for achieving economic independence. According to a study by Thomas Espenshade, a middle-income family raising a first child born in 1981 can expect to spend $150,000 per child to age eighteen assuming a low inflation level (5.2 percent per annum). Anticipated college costs, which are increasing at a level higher than 5 percent, obviously boost that projection, perhaps to as high as $310,000.[17]

Moreover, in America, the principal responsibility for postsecondary education rests with parents. Public spending on education drops dramatically after high school. Compared to a country like France where publicly supported university education is tuition-free for eligible students, the United States depends on families to bear the principal cost of preparing the next generation of American workers and citizens for life in a global economy.

Consider, too, that most states do not require child support after age eighteen. At the very moment when parental investment in children's education ideally should increase, legal requirements for child support end. The consequence is that many college-eligible students in disrupted families have a hard time realizing their educational goals.[18]

The economic disinvestment in children might be compared to the earlier family disinvestment in older Americans. In the 1940s, the sociologist Talcott Parsons argued that poverty among elderly Americans was due to a diminished sense of obligation for their suport within the conjugal family. Samuel Preston points out that it is not too farfetched to think that the family may be divesting itself of the economic upkeep of children largely as a result of widespread family disruption.[19]

However, there is an important difference between these two classes of dependents. The elderly have been the beneficiaries of public investment for roughly half a century. As the result of a generous tax-and-spend program, a large proportion of elderly have been lifted out of poverty. Indeed, the reduction of poverty among the elderly is one of the great social achievements of the twentieth century. During the same period that the elderly have improved their economic status, however, children have lost ground. In the mid-1970s, about 15 percent of young and old Americans were poor. In 1991, only 12.3 percent of elder Americans were poor, while 22 percent of children were poor.[20]

A second key difference between the elderly and children is that the elderly hold the franchise. Because they vote in large numbers and because their numbers continue to grow, the elderly possess great political power. Children, on the other hand, represent a shrinking proportion of the population and are not able to vote, much less organize politically. Thus, it is probably unrealistic to think that children can pursue the same route to improved economic well-being that has worked so well for older Americans.

With high levels of divorce, we see yet another pattern of family disinvestment in children. Not only is there evidence of diminished capacity for intergenerational transfer of resources but there is also a sectoral shift in investment—from the family sector to the professional service sector. This pattern is especially strong among middle- and upper-income families.

A large divorce industry made up of lawyers, investigative accountants; real estate appraisers and salespeople; pension specialists; therapists and psychologists; expert witnesses; and private collectors of child support has sprung up to harvest the fruits of family discord. However necessary their services, these professionals are the recipients of family income that might, in happier circumstances and earlier times, have been invested in children.

This pattern of parental disinvestment has been accompanied by a shift in notions of parental obligation to children. As parents are less able or less willing to invest large amounts of time and money in children, as parent-child relationships are forged across separate, often distant, households, there is a growing emphasis on the affective side of parental commitment. Today, more than in the past, notions of parental obligation place greater emphasis on expressive rather than instrumental considerations as the central requirement of family life. Above all else, what parents "owe" children is love, sympathy, and understanding. It is the emotional interior rather than the structural exterior of family life, the strength of affective bonds rather than the stability of marital bonds, the feeling rather than the doing, that counts.

A corollary to this is the emphasis on adult marital satisfaction as a key determinant of children's happiness. Today's conventional wisdom is that happy parents make for happy children. Conversely, parents who are unhappy in marriage will damage their children's prospects for a happy and secure family life. Leaving an unhappy marriage or refusing to marry a child's biological father because he is an unsuitable husband is commonly thought better for the child than a commitment to raise the child in an intact family.

This argument has some merit. High-conflict marriages are distressful and damaging to children. Indeed, children who live in households dominated by constant parental strife and violence often exhibit emotional disturbances long before the parents divorce.

Nonetheless, divorce does not reliably institute a new reign of family peace and harmony. The aftermath of divorce often brings intensified conflict, even violence, over postdivorce issues like custody, visitation, and child support. Nor are high-conflict marriages the only marriages that break up. Parents leave marriages for a much broader set of reasons. For children in stepfamilies particularly, the idea that parental happiness determines children's happiness is flawed. A parent who finds a new partner may be ecstatically happy, freed from the loneliness and economic hardship of solo parenting, while the children may be resentful or hostile to the new stepparent.

Marriage as a Childrearing Institution

As a result of these trends, we might characterize parent-child relationships in a postmarriage society as moving in the direction of "low investment, high affect." While no one would argue with the idea that strong affective bonds between parent and child are vital to child well-being, there is reason to believe that affections alone may not be enough to foster good outcomes for children. And there is the very real danger that a sentimental rhetoric of caring and sharing will eventually replace the daily donations of parental time, attention, and supervision that are the currency of parental love.

To paint so bleak a picture without offering a shred of hope is probably un-American. Therefore, I conclude this discussion with two suggestions that may, at the very least, slow this trend of childrearing outside of marriage.

The first is to turn away from an adult-centered focus on marriage toward a more child-centered focus that takes into account children's interests in parental marriage and recognizes the central importance of marriage as an institution for childrearing.

The second and more radical suggestion is to speak up in support of marriage. Over the past two and a half decades, marriage has been subjected to a withering critique. This critique was prompted by the best of intentions: to improve marriage by creating more egalitarian spousal relationships and by establishing a fairer division of responsibility for housework and childcare between spouses. However, this critique did not so much improve marriage as breed cynicism and despair about marriage as an institution.

As a human institution, marriage may be perfectible but it will never be perfect. Yet it serves some very essential human purposes: to bind fathers to their biological children; to foster high levels of parental responsibility and investment in children; and to regulate sex and childrearing.

As a society, we have developed a kind of amnesia about the purposes of marriage that extend beyond the self. In recent years, we have tended to view long-lasting marriage as a matter of accident, happenstance, and luck rather than as an achievement based on intention, effort, and struggle. Finally, we have—to belabor the point of this paper—rejected the notion that marriage exists not only to serve the needs of adults but also "for the sake of the children."

Quite possibly, it is too late to change the minds or behavior of the generation of adults who have participated in the divorce revolution. But there may be an opportunity—indeed, a responsibility—to try to reach the children of the divorce generation with a different message about marriage.

Notes

This essay was prepared for the Symposium on "Family: The First Imperative," held on October 21–23, 1994, in Cleveland and sponsored by the William J. and Dorothy K. O'Neill Foundation, Cleveland, Ohio. It was previously published in *Family: The First Imperative* (Cleveland, OH: William J. and Dorothy K. O'Neill Foundation, 1995).

1. Alice S. Rossi, "Parenthood in Transition: From Lineage to Child to Self-Orientation," in *Parenting Across the Life Span: Biosocial Dimensions*, ed. Jane B. Lancaster et al. (New York: Aldine de Gruyter, 1987), 38. See also, Carl Degler, *At Odds: Women and the Family in America from the Revolution to the Present* (New York: Oxford University Press, 1980), 458.

2. Elizabeth Douvan, "The Age of Narcissism: 1963–1982," *American Childhood: A Research Guide and Historical Handbook*, ed. Joseph M. Hawes and N. Ray Hiner (Westport, CT: Greenwood Press, 1985), 591.

3. "Single Parent Issue Touches Sensitive Nerve," *Los Angeles Times*, Thursday July 22, 1993, E1–2.

4. Jane Mattes, *Single Mothers By Choice: A Guidebook for Single Women Who Are Considering or Have Chosen Motherhood* (New York: Times Books, 1994), 112.

5. "Most Believe Dan Quayle Was Right: Kids Do Fare Best in Two-Parent Families," *In Focus*, Family Research Council, survey conducted in September 1993 among sample of 1,100 randomly-selected adults. Margin of error is plus or minus three percentage points.

6. Davidyne Mayleas, *Rewedded Bliss: Love, Alimony, Incest, Ex-Spouses, and Other Domestic Blessings* (New York: Basic Books, 1977), 3.

7. Lawrence Stone, "The Historical Origins of the Modern Family," O. Meredith Wilson Lecture, Department of History, University of Utah, May 11, 1981, 24–25.

8. Samuel Preston, "Children and the Elderly: Divergent Paths for America's Dependents," *Demography* 21, no. 4 (November 1984): 444.

9. See, for example, the interesting discussion by Martin Daly and Margo Wilson in *Homicide*, especially the chapter entitled "Till Death Do Us Part," 187–213, *passim*.

10. "Divorce Doesn't Damp Mothers' Lives," *Wall Street Journal*, Friday, August 12, 1994, p. B1.

11. See my summary of the research evidence in Barbara Dafoe Whitehead, "Dan Quayle Was Right," *Atlantic Monthly* 271, no. 4 (April 1993): 47–84.

12. Daniel Scott Smith, "The Curious History of Theorizing About the History of the Western Nuclear Family," *Social Science History* 17, no. 3 (Fall 1993): 325–353.

13. Melvin Goldzband, *Quality Time: Easing Children Through Divorce* (New York: McGraw Hill, 1985), 58.

14. U. S. Bureau of the Census, "Money Income of Households, Families and Persons in the United States: 1990," *Current Population Reports*, Consumer Income, Series P-60, No. 174 (Washington, DC: Government Printing Office, August 1991).

15. Family Economics Research Group, *Expenditures on a Child by Husband-Wife Families: 1990* (Hyattsville, MD: U.S. Department of Agriculture, January 1991), 7.

16. Sandra K. Danziger and Sheldon Danziger, "Child Poverty and Public Policy: Toward A Comprehensive Antipoverty Agenda," *Daedalus* 122, no. 1 (Winter 1993): 68.

17. Thomas Espenshade, *Investing In Children: New Estimates of Parental Expenditures* (Washington, DC: The Urban Institute Press, 1984), 5–6.

18. See especially, Judith S. Wallerstein and Shauna B. Corbin, "Father-Child Relationships After Divorce: Child Support and Educational Opportunity," *Family Law Quarterly* XX, no. 2 (Summer 1986): 109–125.

19. Preston, op. cit., 443. My discussion is based on Preston's excellent summary of the divergent paths of the elderly and children.

20. Danziger and Danziger, op. cit., 59–60.

CHAPTER 2

Values, Attitudes, and the State of American Marriage

Norval D. Glenn

This chapter deals with a paradox, namely, that marriage remains very important to adult Americans—probably as important as it has ever been—while the proportion of Americans married has declined and the proportion successfully married has declined even more. Most people say that having a good marriage is one of their most important goals in life, and no other variable is more predictive of the health, happiness, and general well-being of adults than whether or not they are in satisfactory marriages. The importance high school seniors say they place on marriage has increased in recent years, even though journalistic and social scientific observers of adults continue to see signs of a "retreat from marriage."[1]

This paradox can be resolved by assuming that the decline in the probability of marital success has resulted from forces external to values, attitudes, and feelings concerning marriage. For instance, if economic and demographic changes have erected new barriers to marital success, a continued high motivation to achieve that success is unlikely to be sufficient to prevent a decline in achievement. Indeed, most authorities on American marriage rely partly on such trends as the declining earnings of young men and the increasing financial independence of women to explain the decrease in the proportion of adults who are married.

Most of these same authorities also believe, however, that changes in values, attitudes, and norms have affected American marriage. Rarely do discussions of contemporary marriage fail to mention, for instance, that spouses now expect more from marriage than they once did and that the roles of husband and wife have been redefined. A few authors refer to a decline in commitment to marriage as an institution and similar cultural

15

and psychological changes that tend to weaken the institution and lower
the probability that individual marriages will succeed.

Critics of the latter view cite national survey data on the importance of
marriage to Americans as evidence that the alleged cultural undermining
of marriage has not occurred. However, having a good marriage could
remain a salient goal while the values and norms conducive to attainment
of that goal become weaker. People could want and expect more from
marriage while they become less willing to make the sacrifices and "investments" needed for marital success.

My purpose here is to consider whether or not such cultural changes
have recently occurred in American society—whether or not the resolution
of the paradox mentioned above is substantially within the realm of values
and attitudes. For evidence I turn to data from recent national surveys of
adults and adolescents, first, to review the trends in American marriage
that need to be explained and then, to assess the attitudes that may help
to explain them.

The State of American Marriage

The initial reaction of American family social scientists to the "divorce
boom" that began in the mid-1960s and continued through the 1970s
was generally positive. Most discussions of this trend emphasized that it
did not indicate a corresponding increase in the tendency for marriages
to go bad, since it reflected primarily, if not entirely, a decreased willingness of spouses to endure unsatisfactory marriages. And the latter change,
according to the prevailing view, indicated that people were coming to
place more, not less, importance on marriage.

If this view (which remained virtually unchallenged among family social scientists until I began reporting evidence inconsistent with it early in
the 1990s) had been correct, the average quality of intact marriages
would have increased steadily and rather sharply as the divorce rate
climbed and as persons in the older and less divorce-prone cohorts became a smaller percentage of the married population—a trend that continued after the divorce rate leveled off in the early 1980s. However, the
predicted increase in marital quality did not occur, as the 1973–93 data
for currently married persons in Figure 2.1 show.[2]

Rather, the proportion of married persons who reported that their marriages were "very happy" declined slightly—an indication that the probability of marital failure increased substantially. Furthermore, a downward
trend in the probability of marital success is clearly indicated by the de-

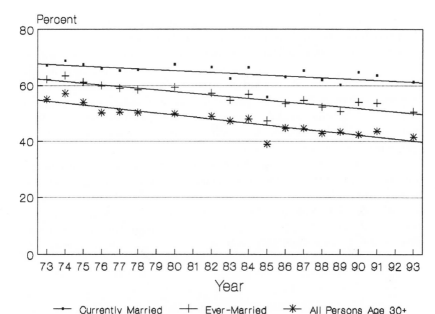

Figure 2.1. Percent of adults in each of three categories who were in "very happy" marriages, by year

clines from 1973 to 1993 in the proportions of ever-married persons, and of all persons age thirty and older, who were in marriages they reported to be "very happy" (Figure 2.1).[3]

One might think that the lowering of legal, moral, and social barriers to divorce would at least have diminished the proportion of adults in poor marriages, but the 1973–93 data in Figure 2.2 on the percent of all persons age eighteen and older who were in marriages they reported to be less than "very happy" (labeled "unhappily married") show virtual stability. The percent in "very happy" marriages (labeled "happily married") declined substantially while the percent unmarried (never-married, divorced, separated, or widowed) increased proportionately.

A major reason for concern about the decline in marital success is its effects on children, and the trends shown in Figure 2.3 suggest that those effects have been more than trivial. Virtually everyone agrees that the best situation for children, all else being equal, is for them to live with biological (or adoptive) parents who have a good marriage. There is no agreement on the relative badness of other situations—single-parent, stepfamily, and unhappily married parent situations all being considered

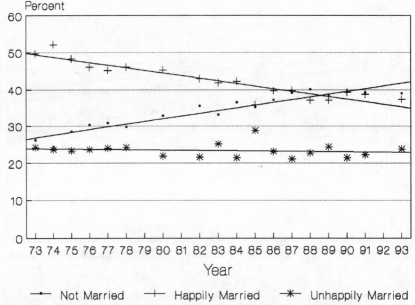

Figure 2.2. Percent of persons age eighteen and older in each of three marital situations, by year

less than ideal. The percent of persons under age eighteen living with a less-than-happily married parent remained about the same, the percent living with a happily married parent declined, and the percent living with a single parent increased. The negative changes were even greater than the data indicate, since some of the pre-adults living with happily married parents were in stepfamilies, which is less than ideal, and the percent in such situations is known to have increased.

The percent of persons who were in successful (that is, intact and happy) first marriages at any given number of years after they first married has declined substantially in recent years,[4] the proportion after ten years now being about one-third. When the tendency for some survey respondents to overreport the quality of their marriages is taken into account, along with the fact that some persons who report their marriages to be "very happy" have spouses who disagree, the estimate of the proportion of first marriages that are successful after ten years almost certainly should not exceed about 25 percent.

This evidence, though inconsistent with the sanguine views that have prevailed among family social scientists, is congruent with what most lay

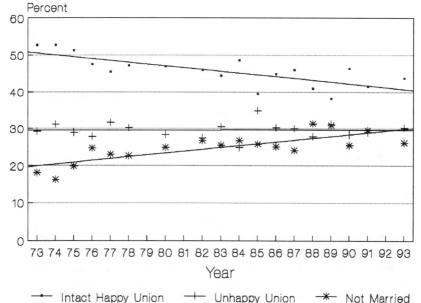

Figure 2.3. Percent of Persons under age eighteen whose parents were in each of three marital situations, by year

persons think has happened to American marriage. For instance, a majority of the respondents to the Virginia Slims American Women's Opinion Polls in 1974, 1979, 1985, and 1989 said they thought the institution of marriage was weaker than it was ten years earlier, although the percent was lower in 1989 (61) than in 1974 or 1979 (70).[5]

The Importance of Marriage

An observer exposed only to the data in the preceding section might be inclined to suspect that the "retreat from marriage" has been to a large degree psychological, that Americans are marrying less and succeeding less often at marriage because alternatives have become more attractive, relative to marriage, than they once were. Such a change could have occurred because persons perceive that marriage has become less effective in meeting their needs and desires, and/or because they perceive that alternatives to marriage have become more effective. One cannot be certain that no such psychological retreat from marriage has occurred, but survey data on attitudes toward marriage gathered over the past quarter of a century provide scant evidence for it.

Unfortunately, there are no strictly comparable data gathered at regular intervals over a period of years concerning the importance that American adults place on marriage. However, all of the relevant data from the past thirty or so years show that adults of all ages say that having a "happy marriage" is one of their most important life goals. Some of the most sophisticated evidence on this topic is from the Quality of American Life Study conducted in 1971 by researchers in the Institute for Social Research at the University of Michigan. Respondents were asked to rate twelve "life domains" (ranging from "an interesting job" and "a large bank account" to "having good friends" and "a happy marriage") on a five-point scale ranging from "extremely important" to "not at all important." The highest percentage of "extremely important" ratings (74) were given to "having a happy marriage," followed by "being in good health and in good physical condition" (70) and "having a good family life" (67). When the respondents were asked to pick the two most important of the twelve domains, "a happy marriage" was selected most frequently (by 55 percent of the respondents), followed by "a good family life" (36) and "being in good health and in good physical condition" (35).[6]

More recent studies have yielded similar findings. For instance, the Massachusetts Mutual American Family Values Study in 1989 asked 1,200 respondents, who were interviewed by phone, to rate twenty-nine "values" on a five-point scale ("one of the most important," "very important," "somewhat important," "not too important," and "not at all important"). Among the "values" that could reasonably be considered life goals, "having a happy marriage" ranked first, being indicated as "one of the most important" by 39 percent of the respondents and "one of the most important" or "very important" by 93 percent. In contrast, the percent giving the "one of the most important" rating to each of the individualistic and materialistic goals was much smaller, being 18 for "earning a good living," 16 for "being financially secure," 8 for "having nice things," and 6 for "being free from obligations so I can do whatever I want to."[7]

Each year since 1976, the Monitoring the Future Survey conducted by the Institute for Social Research at the University of Michigan has asked a sample of high school seniors to rate fourteen life goals on a four-point scale ranging from "extremely important" to "not important." In Table 2.1, I report the percent of the 1992 respondents who rated each of the goals "extremely important." "Having a good marriage and family life" ranked first, being given the highest rating by almost four-fifths of the students, although "being able to find steady work" was a close second.[8]

TABLE 2.1.
Percent of High School Seniors Who Said Certain Life Goals Were
"Extremely Important," 1992

Goal	%	Rank
Having a good marriage and family life	78	1
Being able to find steady work	77	2
Being successful in my line of work	66	3 (tie)
Being able to give my children better opportunities than I've had	66	3 (tie)
Having strong friendships	62	5
Finding purpose and meaning in my life	58	6
Having plenty of time for recreation and hobbies	30	7
Having lots of money	29	8
Making a contribution to society	22	9
Discovering new ways to experience things	21	10
Working to correct social and economic inequalities	15	11
Getting away from this area of the country	13	12 (tie)
Being a leader in my community	13	12 (tie)
Living close to parents and relatives	12	14

Source: Monitoring the Future Project, Institute for Social Research, University of Michigan. Data are from approximately 2,700 respondents.

The trend data from the annual Monitoring the Future Survey are generally inconsistent with the hypothesis that there has been a psychological retreat from marriage among young persons on the threshold of adulthood. For instance, the trend in the "extremely important" ratings given to "having a good marriage and family life" shown in Figure 2.4 was slightly upward for both males and females from 1976 to 1992. There were also slight upward trends in the percent who said they definitely would prefer to have a mate most of their lives and in the percent who said they most likely would choose to marry or who were already married (Figures 2.5 and 2.6). Of course, the period covered by these data began after most of the increase in divorce that started in the mid-1960s had already occurred, and there could have been attitudinal changes prior to 1976 opposite in direction from those shown in the figures. However, it seems unlikely that any such trends that were substantial in the 1960s and early 1970s would have completely ceased by the late 1970s.

The importance that people say they place on marriage does not necessarily mean, of course, that marriage continues to have important effects on their lives, but there is ample evidence that it does. As a whole, persons

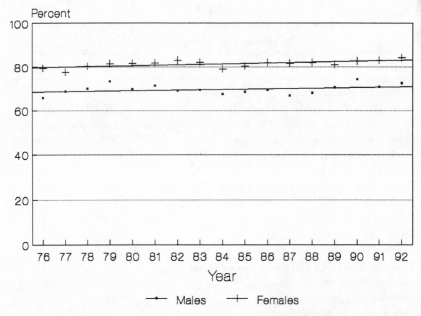

Figure 2.4. Percent of high school seniors who said having a good marriage and family life was extremely important, by sex and year

in satisfactory marriages are happier, healthier, more productive, and less inclined to engage in socially disruptive behavior than other adults, and at least among persons beyond the earliest stages of adulthood, there is no evidence of appreciable recent decline in these differences.[9] For instance, the data in Figure 2.7 on the reported personal happiness of persons age thirty-five or older who were unmarried, happily married, and unhappily married show virtual stability from 1973 through 1993.[10] The relationships indicated by these and similar data reflect to some degree the selection of happy, well-adjusted, and healthy persons into successful marriages, but most researchers who have studied them believe that they also result to a large extent from effects of marital situation on well-being and behavior.

Although the importance Americans say they place on marriage is consistent with the strength of the effects that marital situation seems to have on them, what survey respondents say about their attitudes and values concerning marriage should not necessarily be taken at face value. Many people may tend to give socially desirable responses or to respond in terms of what they think their values and attitudes should be rather than in terms of what they are—a topic to which I return below.

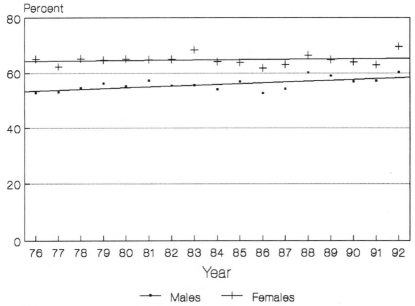

Figure 2.5. Percent of high school seniors who said they definitely would prefer to have a mate most of their lives, by sex and year

Some Evidence of Anti-marriage Influence

The evidence I have presented so far would seem to support the view that values and attitudes supportive of marriage are strong and that any "retreat from marriage" must have resulted largely from situational influences, such as changes in job opportunities and economic pressures. However, there is also evidence of attitudinal and value changes that are likely to have lessened the probability of marital success.

The trends in the attitudes of high school seniors shown in Figures 2.8, 2.9, and 2.10 can be considered anti-marriage, although the indicated changes are not large and their precise meaning is unclear. For instance, in view of the generally positive views of marriage expressed by the students in responses to other questions, it is not clear what one should make of the fact that a substantial and increasing proportion said they were inclined to question marriage as a way of life (Figure 2.8). The downward trend in the expectation of marital permanence shown in Figure 2.9 is more understandable and is not inconsistent with other trends, but the meaning of the decline in pro-marriage responses from females shown in

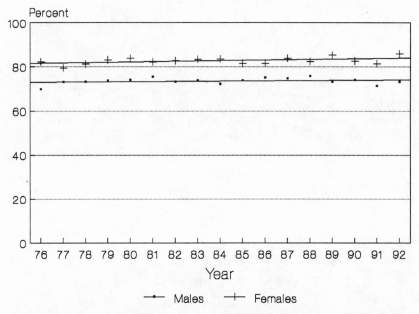

Figure 2.6. Percent of high school seniors who said they would most likely choose to marry or who were already married, by sex and year

Figure 2.10 is uncertain. It could reflect primarily a greater acceptance of being single for others, but not for oneself, or changes in views of nonmarital cohabitation rather than of solitary living.

The limited trend data on adults' attitudes toward marriage suggest changes likely to have weakened the institution. For instance, the Americans View Their Mental Health Surveys, conducted in 1957 and 1976, asked respondents how a person's life is changed by being married and classified the responses into positive, neutral, or negative. The positive responses declined from 43 to 30 percent from 1957 to 1976 and the negative ones increased from 23 to 28 percent.[11]

Probably the most important change in attitudes toward marriage has been a weakening of the ideal of marital permanence—a change that virtually all observers of American marriage agree has occurred even though there apparently are no national trend data on the topic. The best "hard" evidence on the topic is from the Study of American Families, a panel study that interviewed the same sample of mothers at four different dates. In 1962, 51 percent of the respondents said parents who do not get along should *not* stay together because there are children in the family, com-

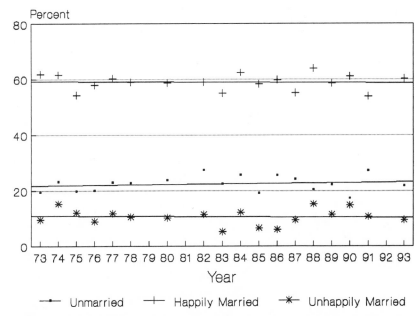

Figure 2.7. Percent of persons age thirty-five or older who said they were personally "very happy," by marital situation and year

pared with 80 percent in 1977 and 82 percent in 1980 and 1985.[12] Since there is no reason to think that the respondents' growing older would cause such a change, it almost certainly reflects a similar but probably larger change in the entire adult population.

Almost as important as changes in values and attitudes about marriage are changes in the strength of other values and goals, such as materialistic and achievement ones, that may detract from the pursuit of marital success. The best evidence on trends in such values is, again, for late adolescents and very young adults. Among the high school seniors who responded to the Monitoring the Future Surveys, the percent who said "having lots of money" was extremely important went from 15 in 1976 to 29 in 1992, and the percent rating "being successful in my line of work" extremely important went from 53 to 66. The Cooperative Institutional Research Program of the American Council on Education and UCLA found that only 40 percent of college freshmen in the early 1970s, compared with 70 percent in 1985, said "to be very well off financially" was a very important or essential life goal.[13] It is not known whether these changes were part of a longer-term trend or were merely a return to the

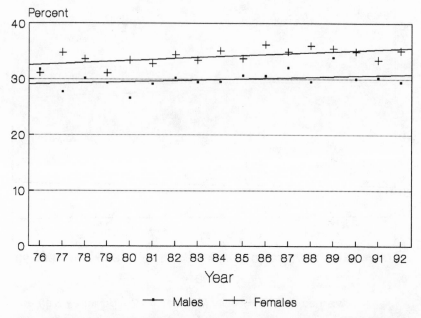

Figure 2.8. Percent of high school seniors who said they agreed or mostly agreed that "one sees so few good marriages that one questions it as a way of life," by sex and year

values that existed prior to an atypically anti-materialistic period in the late 1960s and early 1970s.

There are no comparable trend data for American adults, but there is evidence that many of these persons let values they say are less important interfere with their pursuit of marital success and other family values. The respondents to the 1989 Massachusetts Mutual American Family Values Study, who as a whole rated "having a happy marriage" their most important life goal and such goals as "having nice things" and "being financially secure" much lower, were asked to imagine that they were thirty-eight years old and were offered a new job in a field they liked, that the job would require more work hours and take them far away from their families more often, and that it would be more highly rewarded in certain ways than their present job. Just how the new job would be more highly rewarded differed among three versions of the question, each of which was asked of one-third of the sample (400 respondents). For two of the subsamples, the increment in reward included higher pay, but for the third subsample it was only greater prestige. The respondents were then asked how likely it would be that they would take the new job—very

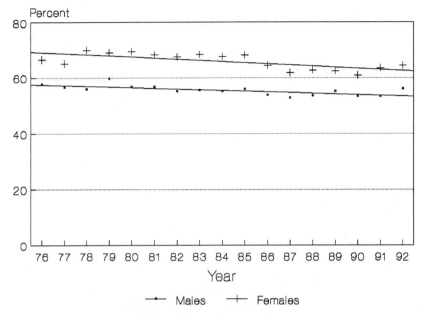

Figure 2.9. Percent of high school seniors who said it was very likely they would stay married to the same person for life if they got married, by sex and year

likely, somewhat likely, somewhat unlikely, or very unlikely. The responses are shown in Table 2.2.

In each of the three subsamples, around one-third or more of the respondents said it was very likely they would take the new job, and almost another third or more said it was somewhat likely they would do so. Not a single respondent said it was very unlikely that he or she would take the job. Belief that the spouse and other family members would benefit might help account for the willingness of the respondents to accept a job with higher pay, but prestige is primarily a personal reward rather than one readily shared with family members.

These data take on added meaning in light of the fact that the question about the new job came in the middle of the interview after many questions about family values and almost directly (with only one intervening question) after the following ones:

1. Do you think most people today put a higher value on family, or do most people put a higher value on material things?
2. Over the course of an average week, please tell me what percentage of your waking time you spend being with your family?

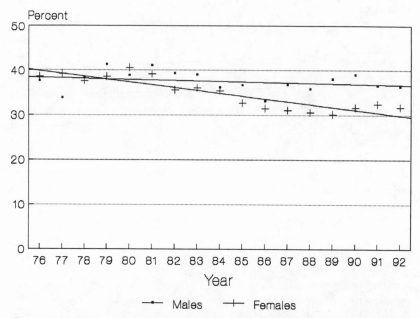

Figure 2.10. Percent of high school seniors who said they agreed or mostly agreed that most people will have fuller and happier lives if they choose legal marriage rather than staying single, or just living with someone, by sex and year

TABLE 2.2.

Responses (in Percent) of Three Adult National Subsamples to Questions About the Likelihood of Their Taking a More Highly Rewarded Job That Would Take Away Family Time, 1989

	Increment in Reward		
	more prestigious only	plus 15% more pay	plus 35% more pay
Very likely	38	34	32
Somewhat likely	27	33	37
Somewhat unlikely	36	34	31
Very unlikely	0	0	0
Total	101*	101*	100
(n)	(400)	(400)	(400)

*Percentages do not add to 100 because of rounding.
Source: The Massachusetts Mutual American Family Values Study conducted in June of 1989 by Mellman and Lazarus, Inc.

3. Would you say that you spend too much, about the right amount, or not enough time with your family?

It is well established that responses to survey questions can be influenced by the content of preceding questions, and in this case the expectation is that having responded to the earlier questions should have lowered the respondents' tendency to say "very likely" or "somewhat likely." This is especially the case in view of the fact that 85 percent said most people today put a higher value on material things, and 46 percent admitted they did not spend enough time with their families. Indeed, a "question order effect" is the only reasonable explanation for the "very likely" responses not being higher when greater pay was part of the increment in rewards associated with the new job than when the increment was only greater prestige. The earlier question about "material things" seems to have predisposed respondents not to choose greater pay over family time but apparently had less effect on their tendency to choose prestige.

These findings suggest that survey respondents are inclined to exaggerate the importance they place on marriage and the family and that many people will risk sacrificing marital success in pursuit of goals they say are less important.

Reasons for the Decline of Marriage

The survey data reviewed above provide only a very sketchy picture of what has happened to American marriage. Many of the questions that could have provided insight into changes in marriage-related values and attitudes have not been asked,[14] and structured survey questions are inherently limited in their ability to deal with the subtleties and complexities of cultural phenomena. Furthermore, since it is impossible to demonstrate conclusively just how the trends in marital success and in attitudes toward marriage are causally interrelated, the data are amenable to differing interpretations.

To me, however, the data, when considered in light of theory and along with other kinds of evidence, suggest one major conclusion: The very importance that people place on marriage as a source of gratification has contributed to the decline of marriage as an institution. Explanation is in order.

A conjugal family system, of which the United States has an extreme form, is centered around the marriage relationship, in contrast to a consanguine family system, in which "blood" relationships are the crucial ones. In a conjugal system, spouses choose one another instead of their marriages being arranged by others, and providing for the needs and desires of the spouses is considered a primary purpose, if not *the* main purpose, of marriage. Of course, marriage in any family system performs societal functions, such as providing much of the early care and socialization of children, but in conjugal systems marital success tends to be defined in hedonistic terms and from the perspective of the spouses. The successful marriage is one that provides happiness, satisfaction, and other positive feelings to the husband and wife.

The United States has always had a conjugal family system, and by the time social scientists began writing about American marriage early in this century, hedonistic and individualistic criteria of marital success already prevailed. However, at that time persons were encouraged to pursue marital success by choosing spouses wisely and working to maintain the marriage—not, except in extraordinary circumstances, by moving from one marriage to another. Furthermore, the happiness and satisfaction pursued and attained through marriage were to a large degree through such practical benefits as economic security, social standing, and the receipt of domestic services, and these benefits were more obviously enhanced by marital stability than the less tangible ones resulting from companionship and the pleasures of associating with the spouse. Only in the past few decades has the single-minded pursuit of marital happiness through the attraction and retention of an intrinsically desirable spouse received strong and virtually unqualified social encouragement.

The greater emphasis on having an intrinsically good marriage has been accompanied by a decline in the ideal of marital permanence. To many progressive thinkers, it has seemed reasonable that lowering the legal, moral, and social barriers to divorce would enhance the average quality of intact marriages and facilitate movement from poor marriages to better ones. Although the increase in divorce that began in the mid-1960s may have come about largely for other reasons, such as the decline in economic dependence of wives on husbands, professionals interested in improving marital quality, such as social scientists and therapists, provided a strong rationale, based on the goal of enhancing personal happiness, for a greater social acceptance and even encouragement of divorce.

According to Bernard Farber, the decline in the ideal of marital permanence has taken us substantially toward a condition he calls "permanent availability." By this he means that all adults, regardless of marital status, tend to remain on the marriage market. That is, married persons as well as unmarried ones tend to assess the marital desirability of members of the opposite sex they know and meet, whether those persons are married or not, and will consider moving from their current marriage to one they anticipate will be more satisfactory. If permanent availability were to become universal, few persons would remain married for life to their first spouse.[15]

The progressives who believed that lowering the barriers to divorce and moving toward permanent availability on the marriage market would necessarily enhance the quality of marriages and contribute to personal happiness ignored what the most astute social philosophers have always known, namely, that a completely unfettered pursuit of self-interest by individuals does not lead to the maximization of the well-being of the population as a whole.[16] They ignored the fact that the freedom of one spouse to leave the marriage at will is the other spouse's insecurity, and that without a reasonable degree of security, it is unlikely that a spouse will commit fully to the marriage and make the sacrifices and investments needed to make it succeed.[17]

Furthermore, marital discontent will almost certainly result when a person constantly compares his or her marriage to real or imagined alternatives to it. Persons are hardly aware of needs well served by their marriages but are acutely aware of those not very well served, and there always are some. Therefore, the grass will always tend to look greener on the other side of the marital fence; people will always tend to imagine they would be happier married to someone else or not married. It is also relevant that persons not intimately known often appear to be more desirable as prospective spouses than they really are. The person who has revealed all or most of his or her faults and weaknesses to a spouse is always at a disadvantage when competing with the well-cultivated public images of other men or women.

Although the weakening of the ideal of marital permanence is likely to be a crucial reason for the decline in marital success, I do not believe it is the only one. Increased expectations of marriage and a breakdown in consensus on the content of marital roles are almost certainly involved, and other cultural trends may have had an effect. For instance, if, as some social critics maintain, there has been a general increase in American society of a sense of entitlement—in what people believe they should receive from others—while there has been a decline of a sense of duty—of what people believe they should give to others—all institutions, including marriage, must have suffered.[18] A related change may have been an increased tendency for people to feel they can, and deserve, to have it all—including success at marriage, parenthood, and work—and a decreased recognition that a relentless pursuit of career goals and financial success is likely to interfere with attainment of marital and parental goals.

Situational influences, such as the decline in the earnings of young men, are also undeniably responsible for some of the changes in marriage, but it seems to me that the resolution of the paradox addressed by this chapter is largely in the realm of culture. As the purpose of marriage is coming to be defined more exclusively as the gratification of the married persons, and as marriage is becoming more nearly just a personal relationship, the nature of which is determined largely by the private negotiations of each married couple, the traditional institutional functions of marriage are being less well performed. The consequences of this change for children are now widely recognized, and those for adults, while less severe, also seem to be distinctly negative. An increasingly hedonistic form of marriage seems to be decreasingly able to facilitate the hedonistic strivings of those who participate in it.

Notes

1. E.g., Bryce Christensen, ed., *The Retreat from Marriage: Causes and Consequences* (Lanham, MD: University Press of America, 1990).

2. These and all other data from the General Social Surveys are weighted on the number of persons in the household age 18 and older because the sampling is representative of households and not adult individuals. Unweighted data do not accurately indicate the trends of interest here.

3. A false appearance of a decline in the probability of marital success could have been created by persons' becoming more willing to admit their marriages were not of the highest quality, but apparently no such change occurred. If the reports of marital happiness had become more nearly accurate, their correlation with other variables, such as reports of personal happiness, should have increased, and that did not happen.

The alternatives presented to the respondents by the marital happiness question are "very happy," "pretty happy," and "not too happy." There is evidence that most respondents who fail to give their marriages the highest rating have rather serious marital problems.

4. Norval D. Glenn, "The Recent Trend in Marital Success in the United States," *Journal of Marriage and the Family* 53 (1991): 261–70.

5. These data were provided by the Roper Public Opinion Research Center at the University of Connecticut.

6. Angus Campbell, Philip E. Converse, and Willard L. Rodger, *The Quality of American Life: Perceptions, Evaluations, and Satisfactions* (New York: Russell Sage Foundation, 1976), chap. 3.

7. The data were provided by the Roper Public Opinion Research Center at the University of Connecticut.

8. All data from the Monitoring the Future Surveys reported here are from an

18-volume set authored/compiled by Jerald G. Bachman, Lloyd D. Johnston, and Patrick M. O'Malley (order of names varies by year) entitled *Monitoring the Future: Questionnaire Responses from the Nation's High School Seniors [year]* (Ann Arbor, MI: Institute for Social Research, 1975 through 1992). The data for 1975 are not reported here, since changes in question order after 1975 make the 1975 data incomparable with the later data.

9. Walter Gove, "The Relationship Between Sex Roles, Marital Status, and Mental Illness," *Social Forces* 51 (1972): 34–44; James S. House, Karl R. Landis, and Debra Umberson, "Social Relationships and Health," *Science* 241 (1988): 540–45.

10. The differences did decline noticeably for very young adults due to an increase in the reported happiness of young never-married persons.

11. Joseph Veroff, Elizabeth Douvan, and Richard A. Kulka, *The Inner American: A Self-Portrait from 1957 to 1976* (New York: Basic Books, 1981), chap. 4.

12. Arland Thornton, "Changing Attitudes toward Family Issues in the United States," *Journal of Marriage and the Family* 51 (1989): 873–93.

13. Alexander W. Astin, Kenneth C. Green, and William S. Korn, *The American Freshman: Twenty Years of Trends* (Los Angeles: Higher Education Institute, 1987), 23.

14. My review here of the survey data is by no means comprehensive, but adding the missing evidence would not make the picture appreciably less sketchy.

15. Bernard Farber, "The Future of the American Family: A Dialectical Account," *Journal of Family Issues* 8 (1987): 431–33.

16. It is ironic that many persons who are adamant in their rejection of the notion of an "invisible hand" in the economic marketplace (that produces social benefits from the self-interested strivings of economic actors) believe that something akin to an invisible hand can be depended on to enhance general well-being in the realm of marriage and other family relations.

17. I do not claim that the lowering of barriers to divorce was not beneficial to a point. People need the freedom to leave abusive and extremely unsatisfactory marriages, but the barriers can be, and I believe in American society now are, too weak.

18. These critics include, but are not limited to, many of the leaders of the communitarian movement. See various issues of the journal *The Responsive Community*.

CHAPTER 3

Myths of Marriage and Family

Moira Eastman

Many myths are still held about marriage and family (myth is used in the sense of "having no foundation in fact" rather than in the anthropological and literary sense of being a profound truth couched in symbolic form). These myths are held not by the uneducated public but by policy makers, planners, academics, bureaucrats, and social welfare professionals. The aim of this essay is to draw attention to a number of these beliefs, to indicate that they are indeed myths (they have no foundation in fact), and to consider why these myths are so readily believed and so strenuously adhered to when strong evidence exists to indicate they are false.

The commonly accepted beliefs referred to are: that family (especially the nuclear family) is a recent historical invention; that the (traditional) family has almost disappeared—that the two-parent family is no longer the norm; that marriage is good for men and bad for women; that families are unsafe places; that no productive work takes place in the family home; and that family is essentially an issue only of and for the extreme Right. These beliefs culminate in another belief, that current trends to greater fragmentation in families cannot (and perhaps should not) be reversed.

Myths of Marriage and Family

Recently I asked a young woman if she had any plans to marry—I have known her and her family for many years, and she has been "going with" a man for some time. She replied, "Oh, *no! Definitely not!*" On further query she explained that she and her friends see no need of marriage. There is just no point in it. They find it works very well to live in shared households. She spoke of how at work, when you ask a married woman to be involved in some social or other activity she will say, "I'll have to ask my husband." She talked of the amount of violence in marriage and said, "Marriage is just not safe." She also spoke of how men dominate women, and this too was a reason why marriage has no appeal to her.

I was struck by the sharp disparity between the values of the generations. Her views would not be shared by her parents and aunts and uncles, nor her grandparents, nor her great-grandparents (many of whom I know or knew). On the other hand, many of her contemporaries agree entirely with her opinions. On my part, I disagreed with much of what she said and many of her assumptions, but found it surprisingly hard to put my disagreement into words. On further reflection it seemed to me that part of my difficulty was that her views compactly summarized a number of commonly held beliefs. Although there is strong evidence to disprove these beliefs, this evidence is rarely reported and the beliefs go unchallenged, especially in Australia. The vigorous recent debate on some of these issues in the United States has yet to occur in Australia, but even when some of these beliefs are addressed individually, these beliefs, as a "mind-set," prove remarkably resilient to challenging and contradictory evidence.

Myth 1: Family Is a Recent Invention

The idea of the family as a social unit separate from the rest of society just didn't exist in the fifteenth and sixteenth centuries.[1]

The book argues that the so-called traditional family was a quite recent creation, and that its fragmentation is obscured by new redefinitions of the family.[2]

The enduring image of the Australian family: the mother is obliging and has excellent cooking skills, and cheerily attends to her two sparkling children. Her husband, the bread-winner, comes home to their brick-veneer in the suburbs after a day at work. . . . The only problem is that the image fits less than a fifth of all families. The traditional nuclear family, long regarded as the cornerstone of Australian society, is splintering—so much so that social researchers predict a return to the defacto living popular before World War II. Whereas the notion of family was once solid, a kaleidoscope of family units now fractures and re-forms within generations. Sole parents, divorcees, house husbands, "blended families" of natural and step-children, gay families and a growing proportion of de facto relationships and deliberately childless couples all share the suburbs with the 2.2 children brigade.[3]

A friend told me of a conversation he had on the train the morning after the third extract above appeared in the paper. A fellow commuter and colleague referred approvingly to the article, especially the reference to the return to de facto living instead of marriage.

My friend replied, "That has to be wrong. I grew up in Coburg (a working-class Melbourne suburb). We kids were in and out of all the houses in the street playing with our friends. In not one of the houses was there a de facto marriage situation. In fact, in every house, in pride of place, was the wedding photo. It was the primary symbol of the house. We had many aunts and uncles (my parents came from large families on both sides, and they met regularly). There was not one case of a de facto marriage or a 'living-together' situation in our street, or among our relations, or in the church we attended, or among the members of the football club which provided another of the networks to which we belonged. I can't believe that defacto living was popular or common before World War II."[4]

His fellow commuter said, "You know, that's right. Which makes you wonder why we believe it, or want to believe it."

Why is belief in the ephemerality of family so readily conceded? Not because of the facts. In its least sophisticated form, belief that family is a recent historical invention is held of family in general. In its more sophisticated form, it is believed only of the nuclear family. Even with only a lay-person's knowledge of other times and other cultures gained through such documents as the Bible, the classical Greek and Latin writers, Shakespeare, and writers such as Chinua Achebe and Camara Laye, who describe life in pre-European African societies, something clearly recognizable as family is evident, though with different customs and rules to those governing family life either in Australia or the U.S. in the late twentieth century. Anthropologists agree that family (in a variety of forms) has been a part of every known society.[5]

One way the idea that family is a recent historical invention was able to get acceptance was through confusion of family in general with one narrowly defined version of family. This is the way Edmund Leach argues in the much quoted BBC "Reith Lecture of 1967."

Psychologists, doctors, schoolmasters and clergymen put over so much soppy propaganda about the virtue of a united family life that most of you probably have the idea that "the family," in our English sense is a universal institution, the very foundation of organised society. This isn't so. Human beings, at one time or another, have managed to invent all sorts of different styles of domestic living and we shall have to invent still more in the future.[6]

The fact that family has varied from time to time and place to place does not prove that family is a recent historical invention, or that it has not existed in all societies. The fact that different societies and cultures have different norms governing family life does not lead to the conclusion that the family norms of our own society are thereby somehow ridiculous or wrong and should (or could) be dispensed with. To realize that many social norms are conditional not absolute does not lead logically to the conclusion that they can be dispensed with without ill effects. In every functioning society, social life (including family life) is governed by certain norms which may, and do, change over time. Surely a major theme of anthropological studies is that no society can flourish or even survive without norms, values, and maybe even taboos. Yet Leach proceeds from his statement of the obvious, that the English family is not universal, to his famous statement that "far from being the basis of the good society, the family, with its narrow privacy and tawdry secrets is the source of all our discontents." If Leach had said that the English family of the 1960s is the source of all our discontents it would have been immediately obvious that he was making a claim that could not be substantiated, but it would still have been a more limited claim than that "the family is the source of all our discontents."[7]

Even marriage, formerly considered to be the foundation stone of family, now increasingly declared to be "just a piece of paper," is included in Arnold van Gennup's classic work on rites of passage as one of the universal rites of passage along with rites for birth, initiation, and death. A glance through *The Circle of Life*,[8] a recent coffee-table book based on Van Gennep's *Rites of Passage*,[9] with photos of marriage ceremonies in places as diverse as Autun (France), India, Tokyo, Monrovia (Liberia), Morocco (a Berber wedding), Morcillo (Spain), Herat (Afghanistan), and Schoffau (Germany) is sufficient to challenge the idea that family and marriage are recent inventions of late capitalist society.

In its more sophisticated form, belief in the novelty of the family is restricted to the nuclear family. But historians of the family dispute the notion that even the nuclear family is a recent invention. In northern Europe the two-generation household (which is usually what is meant by the term "nuclear family"[10]) extends at least as far back as the Middle Ages, probably earlier. Laslett's work in such books and essays as *The World We Have Lost, Household and Family in Past Time*, and "Family Life and Illicit Love in Earlier Generations"[11] showed that the nuclear family (that is, the two-generation family of parents or parent and children in a separate dwelling) has, for centuries past, been the norm in British society.

The idea that the nuclear or two-generation family is a relatively recent, impoverished form of family descended from a more culturally rich extended family (due to the destruction wrought by capitalism and industrialization) is not supported by Laslett's and Mitterauer's studies, at least as far as northwestern Europe is concerned. Some authors suggest that the two-generation family was essential to the creativity that generated the industrial revolution which occurred in the areas where the two-generation household predominated. Paradoxically, while the extended or stem family is often written of as more culturally rich ("nuclear family" is now often used as a derogatory term in comparison with the extended family), it is the form of family that is most oppressive of individual liberty and freedoms, and it is the restrictive aspect of current family life that is most unacceptable to its critics. Despite the fact that the nuclear family is often spoken of as a poor second best to the extended family, *in all countries*, when given a choice, people *prefer* the two-generation household, and they will accept a smaller house or dwelling rather than share a house or household with others.[12] In recent times no alternative to the family such as orphanages, boarding schools, institutions, communes, or kibbutzes has been able to satisfy as well the needs of adults for intimacy and belonging and for children for nurture.[13]

It is amazing that the newness of the family is so often proclaimed because two genuinely new social institutions do exist: the school (mass schooling is less than 200 years old) and the corporation. We do not find in the pre-industrial societies mentioned earlier any counterpart to the school or the corporation. (Passing university entrance exams, the business suit, and the office with corner windows do not appear in van Gennep's *Rites of Passage*.) James Coleman is one sociologist who has drawn attention to how recent the school and corporation are compared with the family.[14] In his book, *The Asymmetric Society*, he documents the rise of the corporation, a form of organization which exists legally as a "corporate person,"[15] and also outlines the immense competitive advantages that the corporation or corporate person has over "natural persons." Coleman believes that the work of society will increasingly be done in corporations, but he sounds a warning note. The power of corporations and their competitive advantage over the family group and "natural persons" is damaging to the ability of families to rear "natural persons" (a term he uses to distinguish between what we normally mean by person and the "corporate person"—the corporation's legal entity). Just one of the disadvantages Coleman notes of the asymmetry between the power of corporations and families is the strange pattern of our society which results in young people growing to an ever delayed adulthood in age-segregated institutions where they scarcely ever see their parents or other adults in their functional (work) roles: surely a flawed system of socialization.

Ivan Illich has been quoted as saying that whatever has a birthday can have a funeral. When applied to family this aphorism means that as family has arrived on the scene recently, its imminent demise is no great deal. This would be in marked contrast to the physical environment, for example, which does not "have a birthday" and cannot be allowed to be destroyed as our survival depends on its well-being. So an implication of the belief that the family is a recent arrival on the social scene is that it can disappear without serious damage or loss.

Yet, opposed to the belief in the recent invention of the family is strong evidence that family, and the ties of attachment and cooperation on which it relies, are the foundation of our development as a species and go deep into our link with earlier life-forms. Family plays a key role in transmitting culture, and the fact that the human baby is born so "young" and so helpless means that the intimacy and attachments of family life are necessary to allow optimum development of the infant's great capacities. The belief that the family "has a birthday" (was invented in recent memory) is based on no evidence and faulty arguments. Related to the belief in the recent invention of the family are the beliefs that the (traditional) family has virtually disappeared and that the two-parent family is now a minority and is certainly no longer the norm.

Myth 2: The (Traditional) Family Has Almost Disappeared

Myth 3: The Two-Parent Family Is No Longer the Norm

"Riveting . . . provides a final laying to rest of sociological shibboleths about the 'normal' nuclear family." Nancy J. Chodorow.[16]

According to Australian Bureau of Statistics figures in 1989, the traditional family—the bread-winner husband, homemaker wife and dependents—accounted for only 16.6 per cent of all families.[17]

American sociologists have abandoned the term family altogether in favor of "primary group."[18]

Recently I gave a workshop to the sales staff of an Australian publishing company on a new series of school texts on Family Life Education for Roman Catholic schools. The first question asked following an introductory video on the program was, "Why did they use a two-parent family in the video?" A little surprised (this *was* a Roman Catholic Family Life Education program), I asked if this was a problem, and staff replied that it was. Some schools think that all families are two-parent families, and this video would entrench this myth. Some schools would be put off by a two-parent family in the introductory video. I explained that a variety of family structures were presented in a positive way in the text but that the video used one family as a story-line or linking device to present a number of concepts about the program. (It was not an option, therefore, to present a whole lot of families in a fifteen-minute video.) I reminded them that over 80 percent of Australian children live in an intact family with both biological parents, so it was probably acceptable that the family shown was a two-parent one. The sales staff could not accept that 80 percent of Australian children live with two parents and were clearly uncomfortable about a family life education program leading with a two-parent family.

Almost a year before the above incident I had given a workshop at a national conference to celebrate *Rerum Novarum*, the Catholic Church's first social encyclical. The topic I was given was, "Families in the new society." I began with some data on changes in families over the century. I was later called into one of the working groups. They wanted to check one piece of data I had presented. It was, in fact, the graph that appears on page 42 of this chapter. They wanted to know where these figures had come from because they could not believe that anything like 82 percent of Australian children were living in an intact, two-parent family. I explained that the figures were Australian Bureau of Statistics (ABS) figures. The situation was quite uncomfortable because the group, which included school principals, parish priests, and directors of social welfare agencies, firmly believed that at least one third of children were living with only one parent or in stepfamilies and were convinced that my figures were wrong. The group contained very knowledgeable people with practical and professional experience in a range of sectors and not one appeared to be able to countenance the idea that over 80 percent of Australian children could still be living in an intact two-parent family.

As I was working on this article, an advertisement arrived from one of Australia's leading publishers of materials on parent education. The first sentence on a flyer for a book on parenting teenagers in the 1990s said, "Only 27% of teenagers in our society live with both parents." I telephoned the publishers concerned. The person who had prepared the advertisement, herself a specialist in parent education, explained that the figure had come from either ABS statistics or from the expert reviewer of the book. She called me back to say it was from the expert reviewer who was sure the figure was an ABS statistic and meant that only 27 percent of teenagers were living with both biological parents. She added that the expert reviewer considered "my" figure of over 80 percent of teenagers living with both biological parents quite unbelievable.[19] I could easily add to these anecdotes examples of intelligent, well-informed professionals in

the areas of social welfare, education, parent education, church, even researchers in sociology and psychology who are convinced that rates of
marriage break-up in Australia are much higher than they actually are.

The following graph, based on Australian Bureau of Statistics data,
shows that in 1986 over 81 percent of children were living in an intact
family situation with both biological parents still married to each other.[20]
This 1986 census data was the most recent data available at the time the
anecdotes described occurred. Unfortunately it remains the most recent
data as the 1991 census does not provide tables from which a comparable
graph can be drawn. However, there is evidence to suggest that the current situation is not markedly different. ABS data released in 1993 shows
that 3.9 percent of Australian children will have experienced the divorce
of their parents by the time they are five years old, 10.2 percent by the
time they are ten, and 16.5 percent by the time they are sixteen.[21]

These official statistics obviously totally contradict the belief so widely
held that at least one-third of Australian children live in one-parent families. How and why is there such confusion and misinformation about a
significant aspect of social life?

Several factors have contributed to this confusion. In the first place
there is a tendency for the definitions of "family," "traditional family,"
and "two-parent family" to slide imperceptibly into each other. When

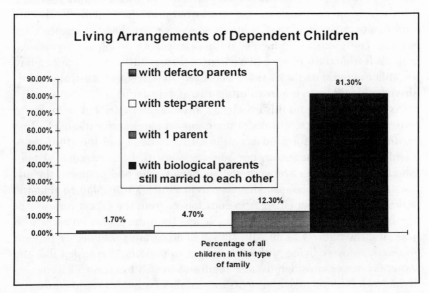

Figure 3.1. Living Arrangements of Dependent Children[22]

journalist Anne Crawford claims that "only 16.6 per cent of all families" are traditional families she is defining family, even "traditional family" very narrowly—"bread-winner husband, homemaker wife and dependents." Crawford's definition of "traditional family" excludes the families of widows and widowers, other single-parent families, families where mothers work in the paid labor force, where fathers work part-time or care for house and children, step-families, adoptive families, and so on. Yet in reality virtually everyone has friends and relations in all these family constellations and accepts them unquestioningly as "really family." Why has Anne Crawford chosen such a narrow definition? The impact of her article relies on showing that something that so many people consider to be important is, in reality, a vestige of a past way of life. Perhaps the writer chooses this unreal and narrow definition because she wishes to show that the "traditional" family has withered away.

Even if Crawford's 16.6 statistic is true—she cites no actual reference—it tends to be interpreted to mean that only 16.6 percent of families are two-parent families. Perhaps this is because for most people what distinguishes marriage from cohabitation and other forms of living together is commitment, a public declaration of intention to form a permanent union. If commitment (not whether or not the wife works in paid employment or the husband works full- or part-time) is what characterizes marriage to most people, and if many people still see marriage as the basis of family, this may be why they tend to interpret statistics such as Crawford's claim that only 16.6 percent of families are traditional families to mean that only 16.6 percent of families are two-parent families.

Adam Jamrozik criticizes the statistics that lead to the belief that the traditional family or the two-parent family has virtually disappeared on different grounds, that of including single persons as a type of family. To avoid further confusion it will help to remember that in what follows Jamrozik is referring to statistics on *various types of family* or family units such as families with or without dependent children, one-parent or two-parent families, families with or without other adults in the household, etc. His data show the proportion of each family type that is as a *percentage of all family types*. The ABS statistics in Figure 1 give the percentage of dependent children living in various family types. Jamrozik writes:

> Much confusion has been demonstrated by these perceptions and interpretations. For example, writing about changes in family structure, Edgar asserts that the "traditional," or "typical" nuclear family of two parents with dependent children accounted in 1981 for only 28.6 percent of all family units. However, in identifying various types of family units, Edgar includes single

individuals living alone as one type of family unit: 23.1 percent of all family units in 1981 were such "families." To count people living alone as a family clearly means stretching the definition of family too far!

Jamrozik goes on to compare family statistics for 1966 and 1986 finding some significant changes (the increase in single-parent families and in childless couples) but also considerable continuity.

> [T]he largest grouping in both years is the family of two parents with dependent children: 50.7 percent in 1966 and 44.6 percent in 1986. Single-parent families show a growth from 5.9 percent of all family units and 10.4 percent of families with dependent children in 1966, to 7.8 percent and 14.8 percent respectively in 1986. . . . Undoubtedly, the data indicate certain other trends, but the "traditional" or "typical" family, that is a couple with dependent children, remains the most prevalent family type.[23]

So including single persons as a family type is another way statistics showing the disappearance of the traditional family or the two-parent family are generated.

Confusing extremely narrow definitions of family with the two-parent family and counting single persons as families are two contributors to the generation of statistics which "prove" the disappearance of the family. A third way these apparently contradictory statistics are generated is by totally ignoring the life cycle. In the definition of "traditional family" given above[24] the assumption is that the only "traditional" family is one with dependent children. Yet one thing families in the 1990s share, not only with families in every other age and culture but, in fact, with all other forms of life, is a life cycle. What then could be more "traditional" than the life cycle? The phase of rearing young children is only one part of that life cycle. How then, can passing through the various stages of that life cycle—being single and childless, being a childless couple, being the parents of children over age seventeen who are living at home (parents of non-dependent children are routinely used in statistics to bolster the "non-traditional families" sector), being the parents of adult children who have left home, being a widow or widower, being grandparents—be counted as evidence of not being in a "traditional family"? It is ridiculous to define the family only in terms of one phase of that life cycle and conclude, on the basis of the fact that just under half of all households do not include dependent children that the traditional family has almost disappeared. What does need explaining is how such sloppy thinking is so routinely accepted, even by professional social scientists.

The above factors go some way to explaining why professionals in the fields of social welfare, education, the church, and the media tend to underestimate the percentage of two-parent families. But all this does not explain how "statistics" that completely reverse the proportions of one-parent and two-parent families in the community are so readily accepted, recycled, and believed. After all, the data are very clear and totally available. An explanation is needed of why some writers seem to wish to show that the percentage of traditional families has diminished almost to vanishing point and why people wish to believe it.

Of most concern is the fact that such "statistics" disguise, as an accomplished fact, trends in social life that are of the utmost importance for the well-being of individuals and society as a whole. By presenting the change as accomplished, research, debate, and critical thought on the impact and effect of the trends are silenced. The human responsibility to assess these trends, to choose the future with consciousness and will, and to work to bring about the chosen future is abdicated in favor of bowing down to the "gods" of the current trends.

Why is it so important to declare that the family (or the traditional family) is virtually extinct? Why is its death announced with a note of expectancy and even of triumph? Why is the belief in the extinction of the family so resistant to the strong evidence refuting it?

Myth 4: Marriage Is Good for Men and Bad for Women

Recent research also indicates that marriage offers more benefits to men. Married men on the whole enjoy better physical and psychological health than both unmarried men and married women.[25]

Psychologist and author Sonya Friedman said, "The truth of the matter is that the most emotionally disturbed women are those who are married and into traditional full-time, lifetime homemaker roles. Single women have always been happier than married women. Always. And there isn't a single study that has disproven that."[26]

This belief seems to be a subset of the belief that family is a (perhaps *the*) major barrier to women's aspirations. A common source given for the belief that marriage is good for men and bad for women is Jessie Bernard's *The Future of Marriage*, a sociological study of marriage that appeared in 1972. Bernard argues that while marriage confers health and happiness on men, it has the opposite effect on women. Marriage contributes to women's unhappiness and ill health. She lays the blame for this on the restrictions imposed on women by traditional marriage and writes, "[T]o be happy in a relationship which imposes so many impediments on her, as traditional marriage does, a woman must be slightly ill mentally."[27]

Psychiatrist Julian Hafner supports Bernard's basic thesis in his book *The End of Marriage*. The book received considerable media attention when it was published. He calls on data from the North American Epidemiological Catchment Area Study to support his claim that "twice as many women as men suffer from anxiety and depressive disorders."[28] On further investigation, Hafner reports that it is not women in general who have higher rates of anxiety and depression than men but *married women*, who report levels two to three times higher than single women. Further investigation again shows that it is only *married women who have no employment outside the home* who have raised rates of anxiety and depression. It is not marriage so much as exclusion from paid employment that is related to increased rates of mental illness in women. Yet the opening chapter in which this is reported is named "Modern marriage a health hazard for women." Why does Hafer give such a misleading title to the chapter? At the very least, one assumes it is a more acceptable or commercial title. Australian research supports this latter conclusion of Hafner's: married women who are not employed have higher rates of anxiety and depression, but employed married women have lower rates of symptoms of mental illness than do single women.

> It has been shown that married women experience higher rates of mental disorders than married men whereas single women experience rates similar or even lower than those of single men. Married individuals of both sexes experience better physical health than the unmarried. It would appear that being married as compared with being single is generally associated with better physical health for both men and women, but is not associated with better mental health for women unless they are gainfully employed.[29]

Bernard's claims that marriage makes women sick can be seen to be true if being married is equated with a full-time housewife role and permanent exclusion from paid work. It is understandable that she wrote from that assumption in 1972. But it is a long time since being married could be equated with exclusion from paid employment, though many women still take time out from paid employment while they have children under school age.

Australian data show that while never-married women have rates for mental illness virtually as low as married women, never-married men's rates are almost one-third as high as those of the separated, widowed, and divorced males. So on indicators of mental health, never-married men suffer more from not being married than never-married women. But in all other categories women show a higher level of benefit from marriage than men. Separated, widowed, and divorced men were 55 percent above the male average in rates of mental illness while the separated/widowed and divorced category of women had rates 67 percent above the women's average.[30]

This is despite the fact that married women who are not employed have particularly high rates of depression and anxiety, and many women caring for young children take time out from paid employment, and both groups are included in these overall statistics.

Despite Bernard's claims, research in a number of countries finds that being married is correlated with markedly better mental and physical health and higher levels of happiness than being never married, separated, widowed, or divorced and that this is true for both men *and women*.[32] W. R. Gove found that divorced men suffer five times the rate of mental illness and suicide of married men.[33] Michael Argyle and Monika Henderson comment on this data: "It can be seen that the divorced and separated in particular are more likely to be mentally ill, become in-patients, or commit suicide (which is linked to depression) than the married. They also suffer more from alcoholism. The effect is again greater for men and is less for the widowed."[34]

Higher rates of mental illness for never and no longer marrieds can be partly explained by the fact that those with problems of mental illness do not make particularly good spouses, and their mental illness can be the

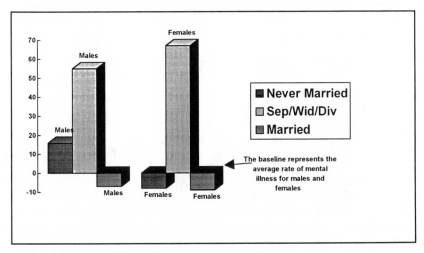

Figure 3.2. Rates of Mental Illness According to Marital Status[31]

reason they find themselves single or divorced. However, Argyle and Henderson report that this explains only a small part of the difference between the two groups. The major problem is depression often exacerbated by loneliness.

Although rates for mental illness and suicide among the widowed, divorced, and separated are much higher for men than for women, in Gove's study, divorced women still suffered over three times the suicide rate of married women and more than twice the amount of mental illness. The belief that marriage is good for men and bad for women is hard to defend as far as mental and emotional health is concerned and even harder to defend in relation to physical health.

The Australian National Health Strategy summarized its findings on the protective role of marriage as follows:

Both men and women who are married have much lower standardised death rates than those who are not. Compared with their married counterparts, never-married men have a death rate which is 124% higher and divorced/widowed men have a death rate which is 102% higher; never-married women have a death rate which is 91% higher and divorced/widowed women have a death rate which is 49% higher.[35]

There is no data to support the commonly made claim that marriage is good for men and bad for women. In some areas it could be said that marriage protects men even more than it protects women, but in other areas women show greater benefits from marriage than do men. For example, Dennis Ladbrook's study of the 1968–72 death rates of white Wis-

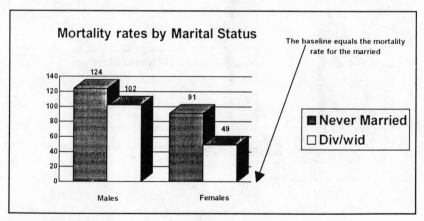

Figure 3.3 Mortality rates by marital status[37]

consin professionals found a reversal of the pattern of women living longer than men. Professional women in Wisconsin in that period were dying earlier than men. Substantially more professional women than men were not married, and this high percentage of never married, widowed, and divorced largely accounted for women dying earlier than men across the whole category of the technical and professional workforce.[37] Ladbrook's study is a challenge to the "marriage is good for men but bad for women" thesis. If virtually any other factor was shown to be causing women to die sooner than men (reversing the pattern of women living seven to nine years longer than men) one would expect a vigorous response comparable to concern about breast cancer.

The differences in mortality rates of the married and nonmarried vary with age, being much sharper in the younger age groups and tapering away after age 50. Yuanreng Hu and Noreen Goldman analyzed data in sixteen countries, two in North America, two in Asia, and the rest in Europe.

[W]idowed and divorced persons in their twenties and early thirties experience the highest mortality risks, risks that are sometimes 10 times as high as those for married persons of the same age. . . . The consistency of findings across a large number of countries suggests that similar processes are responsible for producing the higher death rates of unmarried persons in diverse social settings. Such results strengthen previous speculations about the importance of marriage in maintaining health and reducing the risk of dying and the increased stresses associated with both the single and the formerly married states. The next step is to obtain a better understanding of the ways in which marriage is beneficial to health and nonmarriage is hazardous. For example why is it that divorced men have especially high risks of dying relative to married men? Why have these risks been increasing over time, even though divorce has become more common?[38]

The myth that marriage is good for men but bad for women is constricting thought to such a degree that the questions Hu and Goldman raise cannot even be thought about, let alone be the focus of significant research funding.

Being married and living in a family is a strong protection of physical health. In view of the strength of this evidence, it is amazing that it is so widely believed that being married is good for men's health and bad for women's health (that men benefit from marriage but women suffer). It seems more accurate to say that both men and women benefit in terms of health, happiness, and life satisfaction from marriage. It seems that overall, in terms of health, men suffer even more than women from the lack of being in a marriage relationship. But there is some truth in the myth:

women do suffer more in one way. There seems to be no doubt that social
isolation undermines both mental and physical health, happiness, and
contentment. Those women who are permanently restricted to the housewife role frequently find themselves increasingly isolated both geographi-
cally and psychically from the world of work and from the mainstream of
life. Women who combine marriage, work in the marketplace (as distinguished from unpaid work at home), and children have the best health
statistics of any group. But marriage not only protects mental and physical health, it is also strongly associated with happiness and contentment.

Researchers at the Research School of Social Sciences at the Australian
National University (ANU) found marriage to be the single most important source of a satisfying life. While money does buy some happiness, the
ANU researchers found it to be a less important ingredient to a satisfying
life than being married. In fact, the researchers concluded that single people would need to increase their income by $50,000 (that is, to $70,000)
to have a level of satisfaction comparable to a married person on a *family*
income of $20,000.[39] Apparently marriage drastically reduces our need
and craving for material goods. It provides a high level of nonmaterial
contentment. Both men and women benefit from this increased happiness
and contentment due to marriage.

A more recent study that confirms the ANU findings found that men
and women are nearly equally satisfied with their family relationships.[40]
Fifty-eight percent of people under 50 were very satisfied, while overall
89 percent were satisfied with their family relationships.[41] Those over 50
were even more satisfied with 69 percent of them very satisfied and 95
percent either satisfied or very satisfied. The equality of satisfaction with
family challenges the notion that marriage is good for men and bad for
women. Those who espouse the "good for men, bad for women" position
seem often to be unaware of its elitist and patronizing elements. Between
58 and 89 percent of women are very satisfied or satisfied with their family relationships. But in Jessie Bernard's terms, this vast majority of Australian women must be mentally ill to be satisfied and married, or else
they are so stupid that they stay married even though it is bad for them.
To override women's self-definitions (very satisfied) and to impose another definition (unhappy, sick—especially when the data totally discount
this imposed definition) can hardly be a feminist position. It fits more the
category of elitist paternalism. It is surprising, in view of the fact that so
many Australians are married, that the myth that marriage is good for
men and bad for women is not more strongly challenged.

What is the effect of this belief? For a start, marriage is defined as an
essentially unjust and delinquent social arrangement. Anyone who at-

tempts to argue that research and other resources should be allocated to seeking ways to support and strengthen marriage is immediately assumed to be "really" trying to force women back into demeaning and violent relationships. Thus, debate is silenced on issues that are central to our well-being as individuals and communities.

Myth 5: Families Are Unsafe Places

The young woman I quoted in the beginning of this essay cited the fact that "marriages are unsafe" as a reason not to marry, and I have been told a number of times when leading workshops that "families are unsafe places." Earlier, a brief overview indicated the considerable evidence from many countries which showed that the health of the married is strongly protected compared with the never married, the widowed, and the divorced. Much of this evidence is based simply on legal marital status. Therefore people who are, in fact, going through the extremely stressful experience of separating are counted as married. (United Kingdom research indicates that this separation phase is the most stressful phase of all. Those who are separated, but not yet divorced, are at four times the risk of suicide as those who are divorced and at twenty times the risk of those who are married.[42]) And all the unhappy and stressful marriages are included in the married statistics.

But the young woman, of course, was not referring to general health risks. She was referring to violence in families. She was stating, as a fact, a belief that is widely held in social science, social policy, and welfare circles: the *majority* of families are sites of violence and sexual abuse. (Once, in a discussion of violence in families, I asked what those present [this was a government-funded center combining both practice, research, and policy on families] thought was the incidence of violence or abuse in families. They answered, "About 95 percent.") I do not deny these horrors exist and at a higher incidence than most people thought possible. But the statistics cited above on correlations between marital status and mental and physical health and happiness call the belief that violence and abuse are *typical* of marriage and family into question. If violence and abuse are present in a majority or a large minority of marriages and families, would not the rates of physical and mental health and of happiness and contentment of the married and those living in families be lower than for the never married, the widowed, and the divorced? But they are not. They are considerably higher. If the majority of families and marriages are sites of violence and abuse (and if the above statistics on correlations between marriage and health and happiness are sound), does this not lead to the preposterous conclusion that violence and abuse make people healthy and happy? How can the contradiction in these statistics be resolved?

Findings on the positive effect of being married on health and well-being have been found so often and from such well-respected research studies in many countries that they cannot be lightly dismissed. But cautions have been voiced about statistics on rates of violence in families. In its 1986 report on domestic violence, the Australian Law Reform Commission wrote, "It is extremely difficult to discover the extent of domestic violence in any community. In fact, it is probably impossible to obtain a reliable picture of domestic violence." Murray Straus, and others, from whose research the Australian domestic violence campaign drew its claims of the incidence of domestic violence found that, in a random sample of 2,000 United States citizens married or living with a partner, 16 percent had experienced an act of violence within the relationship during the previous 12 months.[43] When questioned about the lifetime of the relationship, this rose to 28 percent. This finding is the basis for the claim that "one in three wives is likely to be subjected to domestic violence" which received official sanction during the Australian "Domestic violence: Break the silence" campaign of the late 1980s. In an article titled "Rubbery figures," Ron Brunton criticized a statistic that was widely publicized in the campaign: "one in three wives is likely to be subjected to domestic violence." His criticism is based first on the fact that Straus's study collapsed into one category actions ranging from throwing something, whether or not it hit anyone, to use of guns or knives, without making clear distinctions about the level of violence. Second, it can be questioned on the basis that it assumes that U.S. data (data that showed very marked differences in violence levels in different groups) can be applied to Australia.[44] More seriously, in view of the way the data was used in the campaign, for acts of serious violence female to male violence outweighed the amount of male to female violence. But this was never mentioned.

Later research by Straus and Kersti Yllo investigated the hypothesis that cohabiting couples can be expected to have lower rates of violence than married couples.

> Since they are not legally bound to their relationship, they may be more likely to leave an unsatisfactory situation. If the marriage licence is, in effect, a covert hitting licence (that cohabitors do not have), cohabitors might be expected to view violence as less legitimate and also feel less bound to tolerate it.[45]

Yllo and Straus found that the reverse was in fact the case—"cohabitors are more violent than marrieds"—and suggested a different hypothesis: that violence is not caused by the marriage license but "may be a reflection of the intense conflict that occurs in all intimate relationships." Yllo and Straus's finding that cohabitors are more violent than marrieds was well-known when the government-funded domestic violence campaign was devised. Why did the advertisements say, "One in three *wives* is likely to be subjected to domestic violence"? Why not "partners" or some other term indicating that violence was not *only* a problem of marriage? Has it become unacceptable to report a finding that is less flattering to cohabiting couples than to married couples?

The above is not intended as a whitewash of the very real issue of violence in families and between married and cohabiting couples. There is no need to manufacture statistics on rates of domestic violence to argue the case that it is a horror that must be stopped. But if violence between married couples is being overestimated (especially in comparison with cohabiting couples), this is undermining marriage. And if marriage is actually a social and cultural institution that protects individuals in their mental and physical health, then its undermining will lead to higher rates of illness, violence, and abuse. People who lose confidence in marriage will become unwilling to make investments of the kind that make it possible to build a satisfying and stable marriage (and being happily married is a strong predictor of well-being). United States data show clearly that the percentage of intact happy marital unions has fallen steadily over the last two decades while the percentage of the not married has increased and the number of unhappy unions has stayed exactly the same. (The high divorce rate has not reduced, at all, the proportion of unhappy marriages.) Norval Glenn has commented on this trend.

> Among married people in the United States, quality of marriage is by far the strongest known predictor of overall happiness and life quality and is highly related to both physical and mental health. Happily married persons, as a whole, also fare better in almost all respects than do unmarried persons, and the former engage in far less antisocial and socially disruptive behavior. These relationships to some degree reflect selection of well-adjusted, happy, and healthy persons into successful marriages, but most researchers who have studied them believe that they also result to a large extent from the effects of marital situation on well-being and behavior.[46]

But marriage and family do not protect only from physical and mental ill health, from unhappiness and from violence. They protect also from poverty and from the risks of homelessness, juvenile crime, and sexual abuse.

Marriage and family protect against poverty. Family factors and poverty are closely linked and the influences flow both ways. It is well-known that poverty is a major cause of family break-up and that family violence increases when economic conditions worsen. But it is also true that family break-up is the major route into poverty and is the key factor in the increasing poverty of women and children. Sole-parent families are a major component of the poor.[47] In the United States, Daniel Moynihan has shown that the gains that should have been achieved by the War on Poverty were drastically undermined by increasing instability and fragmentation of families, especially of black families.[48]

There is also evidence that marriage and family can mediate (and significantly relieve) the effects of stress due to severe social upheaval. Glen Elder's study of the Great Depression found that the apparently small, fragile, private, and personal family group had the potential to ameliorate and even cancel out the negative outcomes to be expected in families and in individual lives from the Great Depression, one of the most powerful social upheavals of the century.[49] Jean McCaughey's research on homelessness found that in the face of overwhelming odds, some homeless families maintain good quality of family life. And this they value above all else as the one thing that enables them to survive their desperate situation.[50]

Family also protects against homelessness. The Australian Human Rights Commissioner, Brian Burdekin, has warned that one million young Australians are at risk of homelessness because of family breakdown and unemployment. (This in a total population of only 17 million.) Burdekin's 1989 inquiry into youth homelessness found that 25 percent of children living on the streets came from single parent homes. Another 45 percent of homeless children came from blended homes where the father or the mother had re-partnered.[51]

Another area in which marriage and family provides protection is against juvenile crime. Alan Tapper has argued that of eight possible causes of offending listed in the Select Committee of Youth Affairs discussion paper, the one that received the most peremptory exploration and discussion is family breakdown. Yet a 1992 study of serious juvenile offenders found that, on admission, three-fourths were not living with their father, one-half were not living with their mother and only one-fifth were living in a two-parent family (of these, fewer again were living with both biological parents). Also, while the other factors thought to be responsible for juvenile crime (such as unemployment, poverty, and child abuse) are almost certainly pertinent, they do not show the startling statistical correlation that Tapper has demonstrated between the dramatic rise of family breakdown in the early 1970s and equally dramatic rises in juvenile crime rates ten years later.[52] One would think that attempts to address the problem of juvenile crime would at least investigate its correlations with family dysfunction and family break-up, but this is avoided.

How can a social institution or group that so clearly protects its members against physical and mental illness, against depression, unhappiness, and discontent, and against homelessness, social upheaval, and juvenile crime get a reputation as being unsafe? Perhaps one reason is that it has become unacceptable to quote statistics showing the power of marriage and family to protect because it appears that in so doing one is attacking and demeaning those who are experiencing or have experienced marriage or family breakdown. Two English social scientists (one a sociologist who has specialized in the study of working-class culture) give a more challenging interpretation—that middle-class intellectuals have carried out an unrelenting assault on the key institution of working-class life, the family. They call this "the intellectual's new betrayal" because the role of the intellectual is to monitor and critique social changes. Norman Dennis and George Erdos accuse intellectuals of abandoning their role of critically analyzing changes in relation to family, with failing to tell the truth to the best of their ability and instead getting caught up with their own "good causes."[53]

And what is the effect of the belief that marriages and families are unsafe places? At the very least, it is to undermine confidence in marriage and the family and to undermine its claims for resources, for social status, and approval. It results in an unwillingness to invest in marriage—which, paradoxically, is likely to lead to an increase in the very pathologies attributed to marriage and family.

The next myth to which I wish to refer is difficult to name because it refers to the invisibility of the family and to a denial of the contributions made by families.

Myth 6: No Productive Work Takes Place in the Family Home

No country in the world includes in its national accounts the value of work in the home. For Australia, the value of that work has been calculated to be $140 billion per year. Duncan Ironmonger of Melbourne University writes:

> Collectively the household is a far larger industry than any other sector of the "market" economy. Australian households actually produce about three

times the output of Australia's entire manufacturing industry or ten times
the GDP of Australia's much publicised mining industry. . . . How can such
a vast amount of production be omitted from our National Accounts?[54]

While the value of work in the home continues to be ignored, that work
and the contribution of those who perform it is denied. They are declared
to be "not working," "unoccupied," "economically inactive" or "dependent." This denial results in economic and other decisions being made on
the basis of a radically incomplete picture of the economy. What difference would it make to take into account the value of the productive work
that is done in the home? In the first place, it would be immediately obvious that there is not one economy but two—a formal or market economy
and an informal or domestic economy. It would then be obvious that these
two economies are in competition, a competition that is totally denied
along with the denial of the domestic economy. The formal or market
economy is clearly advantaged in the competition for resources and status
by this denial of the domestic economy.

A case in point is the child-care industry. There are funded bodies to
argue the claims of the formal child-care industry, but how can the wishes
of the home child-care sector be heard? In Australia, until quite recently
government subsidies were provided only to those who "chose" the formal
child-care option, apparently on the basis that by entering the formal
economy, parents of very young children were doing productive work.
Those who cared for their children themselves were deemed to be "not
working" and not contributing to the economy and therefore not deserving of any subsidy to enable them to survive on one income and provide
the kind of child care they judged best for their child. A new policy announced in 1993, to take effect in July 1994, provided $61 a week for
two-income families to have their small children cared for by someone
else, yet only $30 a week for single-income families whose small children
are cared for by a parent. Despite the fact that 62 percent of parents of
children under five wish to provide full-time home care for their children,
only 47 percent are able to do so. But the views of this group seem not to
be adequately represented in research agendas.

Another area where the productive work that is done at home tends to
be denied is in the area of education. For over 30 years, educational research has been finding that differences in children's learning in school
are more related to differences in the families they come from than differences in the schools they attend.[55] The classic study that drew attention
to the links between family and education was the Equality of Opportunity Report of 1965. The Coleman Report, as it was often called after the

major researcher, James Coleman, was a massive investigation of 570,000 U.S. students, 60,000 teachers, and 4,000 schools. It set out to discover whether schools provided equality of educational opportunity. The major finding was that schools do not overcome educational disadvantage. "Differences between schools account for only a small fraction of the differences in pupil achievement." The study concluded that it is family background rather than school input that most strongly accounts for differences in pupil achievement. Despite the fact that many studies before, and since, that time have come to the same conclusion (including surprising findings on the "stunning" success of Indo-Chinese students in U.S. schools[56] being due "overwhelmingly" to the pivotal role of the family) there has been virtually no institutional, structural response to these findings.

A study by the Victorian Ministry of Education of reading achievement shows what a small amount of difference in reading achievement is explained by socioeconomic status compared with reading activity at home, attitudes toward reading, and attentiveness.[57] Home makes a very big contribution to attentiveness and attitudes toward reading.

Despite a mountain of such evidence, educational research has continued as if the findings of the Coleman Report were the reverse of what they actually were: as if children's learning in school were primarily related to school policies and programs—curriculum, books, buildings, teacher-training programs, and so on—and only very marginally affected by family factors. For example, the Report of the Committee of Review of New South Wales Schools (1989) is the only substantial Australian Educational policy document to acknowledge the extent of the family's impact on educational outcomes. If it were acknowledged in policy that families contribute at least as much as schools to children's learning achievements in schools, it would be obvious that a significant proportion of the educational budget should be allocated to researching and resourcing the family contribution. Parents should be partners in reality not just rhetoric, for example, by being allocated a share of the research budget so that they could initiate and supervise research into the issues that they consider of importance. Parents should be properly represented in educational structures with funded bodies that can keep the family contribution in the mind of the educational establishment. The U.S. Center for Families, Communities, Schools, and Children's Learning is an example of the kind of institution that could achieve this "keeping the family in mind." (However, the center referred to is an institute of professional educators and educational researchers. It does not have parents *as parents* on its staff or overseeing board—but if parents were *really* partners in the educational project such representation would be automatic.)

As differences in children's learning achievement in schools are more
related to differences in the families they come from than differences in
the schools they attend, it could be expected that some leading educational journals would be devoted to the family impact on education, yet it
is hard to think of a substantial educational journal that adopts such a
focus. Millions of dollars have been devoted to educational research since
the Coleman Report, but one would find it difficult to name any major
research or curriculum projects that focused on understanding further or
making use of the family impact on children's learning in school. As families account for more of the differences in children's learning achievements than schools, it could be expected that learning about this family
impact and learning how to work in partnership with it would be a key
focus of teacher training. Whenever I speak to groups of teachers or school
principals I always ask, "What were you taught about the impact of families on children's learning in school when you were training as a teacher?"
The answer is usually, "Nothing."

Myth 7: Family Is Essentially an Extreme Right Wing Issue

Some time ago in speaking to a Labor politician I said, "You know, it's
not true that the Right has captured the issue of family from the Left. The
Left has thrown it away."

I went on to describe anecdotal evidence that the myths outlined above,
and others, were influencing the advice given to government officials and
politicians on issues related to the family. "I believe you should be very
careful of the advice you are given in this area by bureaucrats and advisors," I said. He paused for a long while before he replied, very circum-
spectly, that he did not entirely disagree with what I was saying. "But,"
he said, "George Bush is on about families!"

Implicit in the Labor politician's comment is the assumption that family is an ultra-conservative political issue. Being "on about family" is unthinkable for a Labor politician. Surveys consistently find that family and
marriage are the aspects of life that are most valued by Australians.[58]
And there is considerable evidence that the family protects and promotes
physical and mental health and protects against poverty, youth homelessness, juvenile crime, and sexual abuse. Families contribute at least as
much to children's learning in school as the formal education system and
provide far more welfare than the government and nongovernment welfare systems combined. They are the major providers of child care. They
contribute enormously to people's happiness and contentment and are a
source of nonmaterial contentment, a most important consideration in

view of the impact of our material acquisitiveness on the ecology of the planet.

Would it not be more in touch with the facts, then, to adopt the position that the family is the people's most valued and valuable social and cultural institution? The question then becomes how can the political party that speaks for and defends the people not be in the forefront of those who speak for and defend families, and defend them especially in the unfair competition they face with bureaucracies, institutions, market, and media. The view that family is an essentially conservative issue needs to be critically examined, especially by the Left.

Myth 8: Current Family Trends Cannot (and Perhaps Should Not) Be Reversed

I argued in an earlier section that announcements of the death of the family are premature. But there is no doubt about continuing trends towards fragmentation of families. Often the view seems to be taken that these trends cannot be reversed and, hence, there is no point in evaluating their impact. Despite the fact that divorce is associated with increased rates of poverty, mental illness, suicide, physical illness, mortality, depression, drug abuse, cigarette smoking, homelessness, juvenile crime, and school failure, I have never seen it argued by any prestigious academic or social science institute that a reputable focus for research would be to study whether there are ways to reduce the rates of divorce or increase the rates of happiness and success in marriages and committed relationships. A recent study of premarriage education in Australia found that although over 80 percent of those attending such programs claimed to have learned valuable information to help them in their future marriage, and there was a significant increase in those who professed themselves willing to seek help if their relationship was in trouble, virtually none of the marriage educators received their training in a tertiary institute.[59] Marriage education is not on the agenda of any tertiary educational institution in Australia at the moment. No university in Australia has a chair in Family Studies.

In relation to the child-care debate, the value of work to the mother is often aired and research frequently cited to show that mothers benefit from being in the workforce. (Recent research showing that mothers of very young children who did not wish to be in the workforce but with their child had the highest rates of depression and distress of all women was dismissed with the comment that these mothers needed help to get over their guilt and depression at leaving their child.) But there is little attempt to discover why 62 percent of the parents of children under five wish for one of the parents to be a full-time caregiver. There is little serious attempt to evaluate whether the parents' desires may be based in sound knowledge. Their viewpoint is dismissed with comments to this effect: "There is just no choice. Now, both men and women need to work in the paid workforce to create a viable living standard." Or, "This is the way things are going: you can't turn the clock back."

The view that these trends are irreversible, that this is the way things are going and cannot be reversed is often presented as an enlightened, realistic, or even progressive one. But to hand our future over to the "gods" of statistical trends, market forces, and so on is to be more swayed by ignorance and ideology than were those earlier peoples who believed that illness and poverty were the will of God and there was no point in fighting against them. We do not passively accept rates of smoking, alcohol drinking, or traffic accidents as inevitable. There are many examples where social trends have been reversed once it has been understood that they are harmful. Perhaps one reason there has been so little attempt to turn around trends of fragmentation in families is because the above myths are commonly accepted. If the family was a brief historical aberration of the 1950s and most societies in history worked perfectly well without it, if the two-parent family is already an historical remnant, there is no point in considering reversing the trends. If marriage and family are inherently oppressive and unjust structures, if expressed concerns about family trends are "really" the bleatings of a few flat-earthers wishing to return to a mythical golden age of the past (arguments and data such as those above are routinely dismissed in this way) then current trends are a cause for celebration, not for reversal. If marriage is the major barrier to women's freedom and development, if marriage is good for men but bad for women, if rates of violence are much higher in marriage than among cohabiting couples, if families are unsafe places, then current trends of fragmentation of families may herald a flowering of freedom and growth in human capacity, and the trends should not be reversed. Unfortunately, current statistics being what they are, the latter situation does not seem to be the case.

What Difference Does It Make If These Myths Are Accepted?

I have mentioned some of the results of the acceptance of these myths throughout this essay. Acceptance of these myths will have an impact on research agenda, perhaps leading to neglect of certain areas. I have men-

tioned the striking failure to follow up findings of the impact of families
on schooling by significant research into how effective families achieve
their stunning success. The Daniel Moynihan story is just one example of
how research can be expected to neglect certain areas. For twenty years
there was a failure to research the links between family break-up and
poverty to which his work had drawn attention. In Australia, Alan Tapper
has shown that there is strong evidence to link family break-up with the
dramatic increases in juvenile crime in Western Australia. Yet this is a
factor that is given scant attention in research on juvenile crime.

There may be a failure to notice if resources are removed from families.
Again, Tapper has shown that this has, in fact, happened in a striking
way to families with children in Australia. Tapper compares the fortunes
of two typical couples, one born in 1920 and the other in 1950, and compares lifetime earnings, taxes, and benefits. He shows that the 1950s couple pay more in taxes and receive less in benefits than the 1920s couple.
The difference is large. "If we convert the total disparity between generations into today's dollars, it amounts to about half a million dollars per
average family."[60] Couples born in the 1950s will need to work full-time
about fifteen years more than the 1920s-born to enjoy comparable real
incomes. Despite the fact that Tapper has published his views in virtually
all the major newspapers and some journals of opinion, and the issues he
is addressing could not be called trivial, there has been virtually no response to his analysis. No one has challenged his data or analysis, but
there has been a total failure to engage in debate about the issues he
raises.

It has been suggested above that one effect of these myths is a silencing
of debate on issues of fundamental importance. If "defense of the family"
is the litmus test of extreme conservatism (and if 95 percent of U.S. social
scientists identify themselves as radical or liberal—with the Australian
situation likely to be similar[61]), this may explain the apparent reluctance
of intellectuals to engage in the issues Tapper raises.

Perhaps the major change to be hoped for from a reversal of these
myths is that some way would be found to develop a voice for families
so that the concerns of ordinary families could be more readily heard in
developing research agendas, policy affecting families, and funding priorities.

Why Are These Myths So Readily Accepted?

Why are the above myths so common, especially among members of professions that have access to more information than the average citizen?

The Bergers attribute this to the influence of the New Class.[62] Schumpeter first drew attention to this new class, who had come to be a new elite with considerable power, in terms of the bureaucracy within socialist societies. His analysis was later applied to the Knowledge Class within Western societies—the bureaucrats, intellectuals, and those with influence in the media—who were seen to have a power comparable to the New Class identified by Schumpeter. Their power stems from their influence and control of the powerful institutions that dominate public life. The Bergers write of the "imperialistic" drives of this class and their hostility to family issues.[63]

A closely related hypothesis is that the myths are readily believed because there is a conflict of interest between families and the major institutions that dominate the public sphere of life. Ironmonger's work alerts us to the fact that beside the market economy there is a domestic economy. It can be further claimed that these two economies are in competition (but because the existence of the domestic economy is denied, so too is the competition). Resources will be diverted to one or other economy. But the market economy has vast resources to lobby for its claims. Families are inevitably disadvantaged in this denied competition.

Another theorist whose work relates to the readiness to believe these myths is Jürgen Habermas. At least two of his major themes seem relevant to understanding the contradictions outlined above. One theme is that of the domination of technocratic rationality: one form of knowledge, that of empirical study of the material world with a view to predicting and controlling outcomes, has claimed to constitute the whole field of knowledge. One result is the belief that has overtaken mainstream social science since the time of Weber: social science must be value-free, and the only way the study of society can be "scientific" is that it emulate the objective, value-neutral approaches of the physical sciences. Habermas argues that instead of delivering us from irrationality and superstition as promised, this has, in fact, delivered us over to a more insidious irrationality, an irrationality that it is almost impossible even to perceive.

The second theme has been developed in Habermas's later writings. He has developed the notion of two competing structures within society, the system and the lifeworld. As usual in his work, the concept of the lifeworld is not straightforward. By it he seems to mean the social and cultural background to the community and, hence, to the individual. It is what lies implicitly behind all acts of communication. It is a reservoir of unconscious beliefs, of unshaken convictions, that people draw on in cooperating together. Another word for it is human community. It operates according to norms, to consensus formation, and to discourse. While Habermas is always loath to give a concrete example, family would seem to be a classic case.

The other major set of structures is the systems dimension, the structural elements which operate independently of this process of consensus formation. Among the examples Habermas gives of the systems dimension are money, power, and the market. Habermas believes that a successful society must hold system and lifeworld in a balance in which lifeworld will, in the last word, have priority. Habermas believes that in capitalist society there is always a threat of a reversal of the right relationship with money, power, and the market in which they gain the ascendancy and become the facts of life before which culture and consensus must bend. Michael Pusey's book *Economic Rationalism in Canberra*[64] analyzes how in Australia in the 1980s the traditional balance between the economy, the state, and society changed as the new dominance of the economy eroded the primacy of the political and social orders. In the second-to-last paragraph of his book, he writes of how society has become the "object" of the economy (a reversal of the right order of the economy being there to serve society):

> It is an aggressive reduction that pretends not to see that in the West in the space of little more than a generation, extended family, church, and local community neighbourhood have all been burnt up as fuel in the engine of economic "development". Yet economic rationalism assumes all social relations, social norms, and traditions, all culture and remembered inheritance, and all the institutions of education, of the family, of work, of political participation, and indeed the social formation of ordinary individual identity—that all this is malleable plastic that will obediently find expression merely as individual calculations of utility co-ordinated through the market.[65]

Habermas refers to this process of system dominating lifeworld as the system *colonizing* the lifeworld. When we consider what colonizing meant to the societies subjected to it, the diversion of their wealth and resources to the control of the invaders, the destruction of their culture, their myths, the rituals and patterns by which life was ordered, and the substitution of the rationality and mindset of the conquerors, it makes a striking parallel to the ways the norms, values, rituals, and the overlooked people on which so much of family life depends are subjugated to the technocratic, "value free," so-called rationality of the system dimension. The conversation with a young woman quoted at the start of this essay demonstrates concisely this colonization of one family. Perhaps one reason the above myths are so readily believed is because they fit so well with the technocratic, "value-free," supposed rationality of the system dimension.

A myth is a widely held belief or story that is taken for granted, that provides the assumptions out of which action arises. It has been defined as "a collective belief that is built up in response to the wishes of the group rather than an analysis of the basis of the wishes."[66] On that definition, it is not too extreme to call the beliefs outlined above myths. I have not attempted to specify how widely held these patterns of beliefs are. If they are as widely held as I believe, they will be recognizable to many. The evidence to contradict them is sufficient to support the claim that they are myths in the sense that they are not based on fact. Their wide acceptance in the media, bureaucracies, and policy sectors means that they have a powerful impact, and will become self-fulfilling.

Notes

1. "The Family—Some Facts" in *AWD Newsletter*, no. 5 (October 1989). This is the newsletter for Action for World Development, an ecumenical church movement of people for justice and peace.

2. Cover blurb for Michael Gilding, *The Making and Breaking of the Australian Family* (North Sydney: Allyn and Unwin, 1991).

3. Anne Crawford, "The Changing Face of Families," *The Sunday Age*, July 12, 1992, 12.

4. However, it is certainly true that de facto living was common in the early days of the colony.

5. Ronald Fletcher (1988) *The Shaking of the Foundations: Family and Society* (London and New York: Routledge, 1988). David W. Murray, "Poor Suffering Bastards: An Anthropologist Looks at Illegitimacy," *Policy Review* (Spring 1994).

6. Edmund Leach, *The Reith Lecture, The Listener*, "Ourselves and Others," vol. 78, no. 2018 (November 30, 1967): 693.

7. And yet that latter claim is the most often-quoted sentence on family issues (at least in English and Australian contexts) and is frequently quoted as evidence to support the view it expresses. See, for a recent example, Barbara Ehrenreich, "Oh, those family values," *Time* (July 18, 1994). Those who use it in that way are no doubt unaware that Leach offered no evidence at all to support this provocative sentence.

8. David Cohen, ed., *The Circle of Life: Rituals from the Human Family Album* (San Francisco: Harper, 1991).

9. Arnold Van Gennep, *Rites of Passage* (Chicago: University of Chicago Press, 1960).

10. *The Macquarie Dictionary* defines nuclear family as "1. the family as a unit of social organisation, comprising only parent and children where the children are the responsibility of the parents alone. 2. the stereotype of this unit, typically seen as husband, wife, and two children."

11. P. Laslett, *The World We Have Lost* (London: Methuen, 1965); *Household and Family in Past Time* (Cambridge: Cambridge University Press, 1972); and "The Myth of the Large Pre-industrial Family" in *The European Family*, ed. Michael Mitterauer and Reinhard Sieder (Oxford, England: Basil Blackwell, 1982).

12. Ronald Fletcher, *The Shaking of the Foundations*, 114–15. Current households in Western societies are virtually without exception "nuclear" in the sense of being two-generation. There is something strange about the frequency with which the form of family life which most people prefer is denigrated.

13. Jean Bethke Elshtain, *Public Man, Private Woman: Women in Social and Political Thought* (Oxford: Martin Robertson, 1981), 290–97, 322–35; Bruno Bettelheim, *The Children of the Dream* (London: Collier-MacMillan, 1969).

14. James Coleman, "Families and Schools," *Educational Researcher* (August–September 1987): 36. *The Asymmetric Society* (Syracuse, NY: Syracuse University Press, 1982).

15. The development of the corporation required the recognition by law of a "fictional person." The corporation is a "fictional person." It is legally owned by a set of shareholders but with a personality distinct from any one of them.

16. From the cover blurb for Judith Stacey, *Brave New Families* (New York: Basic Books, 1991).

17. Anne Crawford, "The Changing Face of Families," *The Sunday Age*, 1992, news 4.

18. Sarah Pinkney, "The Fight over the Family" (paper presented at the Australian International Year of the Family Conference, Adelaide, November 1994). Quoted in *The Age*, December 9, 1994, 22.

19. See the Australian Bureau of Statistics (ABS) information on page 13.

20. Source: ABS, Census of Population and Housing, 1986, Table VFI24. See also Gai Ochiltree, *Children in Stepfamilies* (Australia: Prentice Hall, 1990).

21. ABS Labour Force Status and Other Characteristics of Families, 1979, 1983, 1987, and 1992. Cat. no. 6224.0. See also *The Age*, October 27, 1993, 9, article on recent Australian Institute of Family Studies report.

22. Source: ABS, Census of Population and Housing, 1986. Table VF124.

23. Adam Jamrozik, *Class, Inequality and the State* (South Melbourne: Macmillan, 1991), 125–6.

24. "According to the Australian Bureau of Statistics figures in 1989, the traditional family—the bread-winner husband, homemaker wife and dependents—accounted for only 16.6 percent of families." ABS, 10.

25. Jane Sullivan, "For Better, for Worse," *The Age*, March 23, 1994, 15.

26. Quoted in Warren Bennis, *On Becoming a Leader* (London: Century Business, 1992; first published in U.S.A. by Addison-Wesley, 1989), 50.

27. Barbara Dafoe Whitehead, "The Experts' Story of Marriage," working paper no. 14, Institute of American Values, New York, August 1992.

28. Julian Hafner, *The End of Marriage: Why Monogamy Isn't Working* (London: Century, 1993), 5–7.

29. Lorraine Dennerstein, Jill Astbury and Carol Morse, *Psychosocial and Mental Health Aspects of Women's Health* (Melbourne: University of Melbourne, Key Centre for Women's Health in Society, Department of Public Health and Community Medicine, 1992), 30. The report was commissioned by the World Health Organization.

30. Sun-Hee Lee et al., *Health Differentials for Working Age Australians* (Canberra: Australian Institute of Health, 1987), 24–26. See also U.K. evidence in J. Dominian et al., *Marital Breakdown and the Health of the Nation* (London: One Plus One, November 1991).

31. Source: Sun-Hee Lee et al., *Health Differentials*, 24–26. ABS 1977/78 Australian Health Survey.

32. J. Lynch, *The Broken Heart: The Medical Consequences of Loneliness* (New York: Basic Books, 1977); L. Weitzman, *The Divorce Revolution* (New York: Free Press, 1985); L. F. Berkman, and S. L. Symes, "Social Networks, Host Resistance and Mortality: A Nine-Year Follow-up of Alameda County Residents," *American Journal of Epidemiology* 109, no. 2 (1979): 186–204; S. Coleman, "Life-Cycle and Loss—the Spiritual Vacuum of Heroin Addiction," *Family Process* 25 (1986): 5–23; T. Holmes and R. Rahe, "The Social Readjustment Rating Scale," *Journal of Psychosomatic Research* 11 (1967): 213–18; B. L. Bloom, S. J. Asher and S. W. White, "Marital Disruption as a Stressor: A review and Analysis," *Psychological Bulletin* 85 (1973): 867–94; C. Wallis, "Stress: Can We Cope?" *Time* (June 6, 1983): 64–70; Dennis Ladbrook, "Sex Differentials in Premature Death among Professionals," pt. 1, *Journal of the Australian Population Association* 7, no. 1 (1990): 1–26 and pt. 2 in *JAPA* 7, no. 2: 89–115; Yuanreng Hu and Noreen Goldman, "Mortality Differentials by Marital Status: An International Comparison," *Demography* 27, no. 2 (May 1990): 233–50; and J. Dominian et al., *Marital Breakdown and the Health of the Nation*, One Plus One, U.K., November 1991.

33. W. R. Gove, "The Relationship between Sex Roles, marital Status, and Mental Illness," *Social Forces* 51, (1979): 34–44.

34. Michael Argyle and Monika Henderson, *The Anatomy of Relationships* (London: Penguin, 1985), 17.

35. National Health Strategy Research Paper no. 1, "Enough to Make You Sick: How Income and Environment Affect Health." Available from Department Health, Housing and Community Services, (Box 9848, Canberra, ACT: GPO, 1992), 33. See also Sun-Hee Lee et al., *Health Differentials*. (Lee supports the findings.)

36. "Enough to Make You Sick," 33.

37. Ladbrook, "Sex Differentials," 1–26, 89–115.

38. Hu and Goldman, "Mortality Differentials," 246-47.

39. Jonathan Kelly and Mariah Evans, "Ingredients of the Good Life" in *Report* 2, no. 4 (1990), Research School of Social Sciences, Australian National University, Canberra, ACT.

40. Assirt/Financial Planning Foundation Survey report, "Australians and Their Money," from the Financial Planning Foundation, (February 1992).

41. The latter figure should be viewed with some caution. A variety of studies leads to the conclusion that those who claim to be "happy" in marriage rather than "very happy" often have quite serious problems.

42. Barraclough cited in J. Dominian et al., *Marital Breakdown*, 22.

43. Murray Straus et al., *Behind Closed Doors: Violence in the American Family* (New York: Anchor/Doubleday, 1980).

44. Ron Brunton, "Rubbery Figures," *The Independent Monthly* (May 1993): 22.

45. Kersti Yllo and Murray A. Straus, "Interpersonal Violence among Married and Cohabiting Couples," *Family Relations* 30 (1981): 340.

46. Norval D. Glenn, "The Re-evaluation of Family Change by American Social Scientists" (International Year of the Family Conference, Australian Catholic University, Melbourne, June 1994), 9.

47. Moira Eastman, *Family the Vital Factor* (Melbourne, Australia: Collins-Dove, 1989), 101–4, 141–58.

48. Daniel P. Moynihan, *Family and Nation* (San Diego: Harcourt, Brace, Jovanovich, 1986); Eastman, *Family the Vital Factor*.

49. G. H. Elder, Jr., *Children of the Great Depression: Social Change in Life Experience* (Chicago: University of Chicago Press, 1974); G. H. Elder and R. C. Rockwell, "Economic Depression and Post-war Opportunity: A Study of Life Patterns in Hell," in *Research in Community and Mental Health*, ed. R. A. Simmons (Greenwich, CT: JAI Press, 1978).

50. Jean McCaughey, *Where Now? Homeless Families in the 1990s*, background paper no. 8, Australian Institute of Family Studies, 1992.

51. Brian Burdekin, *Our Homeless Children: Report of the National Inquiry into Homeless Children* (Human Rights and Equal Opportunity Commission: Australian Government Publishing Service, 1989).

52. Alan Tapper, "State Welfare Policy and the Juvenile Crime Debate," in *Reform and Recovery: An Agenda for the New Western Australian Government*, ed. Mike Nahan and Tony Rutherford (Perth Institute of Public Affairs, 1993), 187–214. Tapper, "Juvenile Crime and Family Decline," *IPA Review* 46, no. 1 (1993): 46–48.

53. G. H. Elder, "Historical Change in Life Pattern and Personality," in *Life-span Development and Behavior*, vol. 2, ed. P. Baltes and O. Brim (New York: Academic Press, 1979); N. Dennis and G. Erdos, *Families without Fatherhood* (London: IEA Health and Welfare Unit, 1992); N. Dennis, *Rising Crime and the Dismembered Family: How Conformist Intellectuals Have Campaigned Against Common Sense* (London: IEA Health and Welfare Unit, 1993).

54. Duncan Ironmonger, "Australian Households: A $90 Billion Industry" (paper presented to the 1989 Summer School at the University of Melbourne: "Changes in the Household: Implications and Future Strategies"). See also "Household Industries," in *The Changing Structure of Australian Industry*, ed. K. Sawyer and J. Ross (Sydney: McGraw-Hill, 1994); "Why Measure and Value Unpaid Work?" (paper presented to the International Conference on the Measure-

ment and Valuation of Unpaid Work, Ottawa, Canada, April 28–30, 1993); "National Time Accounts and Accounts for the Household Economy," (paper presented to the fifteenth meeting of the International Association for Time Use Research, University of Amsterdam, Netherlands, June 15–18, 1993); and "The Value of Care and Nurture Provided by Unpaid Household Work," *Family Matters* (April 1994).

55. Eastman, *Family the Vital Factor*, chap. 8.

56. Nathan Caplan, Marcella H. Choy and John K. Whitmore, "Indochinese Refugee Families and Academic Achievement," *Scientific American* (February 1992).

57. Ken Rowe, "The Influence of Reading Activity at Home on Reading Achievement," *British Journal of Educational Psychology* 61, no. 1 (1991): 19–35.

58. "Attitudes to the Family," Saulwick Poll, *The Age*, March 1986; "Attitudes to Christmas and the Family," Saulwick Poll, *The Age*, December 5–6, 1990; Don Edgar, "Family Life as Important as Ever to Australians," *The Age*, December 22, 1990; "Australians Score Highly on Contentment Barometer," *The Age*, March 19, 1993, 6. This reports research by Assirt and the Financial Planning Advancement Foundation.

59. Michele Simons et al., *Love, Sex and Waterskiing: The Experience of Pre-Marriage Education in Australia* (The Catholic Society for Marriage Education, the Australian Association for Marriage Education in collaboration with the Centre for Human Resource Studies at the University of South Australia, 1992).

60. Alan Tapper, "Family Changes in a Transformed Welfare State: The View from Down Under," *The Family in America* 9, no. 1 (Rockford, IL: The Rockford Institute Center on the Family in America, January 1995), p. 3.

61. Most American social scientists consider themselves to be liberal or radical (more than 90 percent of the members of the American Sociological Association, according to a recent survey conducted by one of my students). See also Norval D. Glenn, "The Re-evaluation of Family Change," 4.

62. B. Berger and P. Berger, *War over the Family: Capturing the Middle Ground* (Harmondsworth, U.K.: Penguin, 1984).

63. Ibid.

64. Michael Pusey, *Economic Rationalism in Canberra: A Nation Building State Changes Its Mind* (Cambridge: Cambridge University Press, 1991).

65. Ibid., 241–42.

66. *The Macquarie Dictionary.*

CHAPTER 4

Comparative and Historical Perspectives on Marriage, Divorce, and Family Life

Arland Thornton

Five Hundred Years of European Discovery

It has now been five centuries since Europeans discovered the land they named America. The discovery of America by Christopher Columbus five hundred years ago capped one era of European exploration and discovery and opened up a second round of discovery, exploration, and conquest. For the next few centuries, Europeans were to circle the globe, making innumerable discoveries in Australia, Asia, Africa, America, and the islands of the seas.

While our history books primarily chronicle the discoveries and conquests of these European explorers in physical and geographical terms—by listing the various lands, rivers, and seas that they discovered—there were numerous social and cultural discoveries as well. For example, as they expanded their exploratory horizons, the Europeans found numerous groups, each with their own histories, cultures, and customs. In the subsequent five centuries, the centers of European population were inundated by the reports of numerous explorers, missionaries, travelers, colonial administrators, and scholars concerning the customs of the many peoples with whom they came into contact.

In the beginning of this chapter, I document some of the central findings of northwestern European scholars concerning marriage and family life around the globe. I also discuss some of the central conclusions which they derived from their discoveries.[1] As scholars from northwestern Europe began to assimilate, understand, and systematize the information they gleaned from societies around the world, several things became clear. First, they found that family ties and kinship relations were central social structures in all of the populations they encountered. Large fractions of the activities of individual human beings took place within family units. Individuals were born into families, socialized by family members, protected by kinsmen, and organized into economic production units along kinship lines.[2]

Second, these scholars discovered that the human species has been enormously innovative in creating a nearly infinite variety[3] of different family forms and structures.[4] The different forms of family life and marriage were so varied that it was difficult, if not impossible, to construct universally applicable definitions for such concepts as "family" and "marriage." While each culture had similar concepts, the differences were of such magnitude that the concepts and meanings could not easily be translated across cultures and languages. This problem still plagues social scientists today.[5]

Third, northwestern European scholars found that while the family structures of their own cultures shared much in common with those of many other peoples, a cluster of features made northwest Europe unique in many respects. Of central importance in this regard were the marriage, family, and household formation systems of northwestern Europe.[6] Unlike many other societies, households in several northwestern European countries were generally nuclear rather than extended. Instead of multiple generations of married couples living and working together in the same household and economic unit, households generally consisted of only one married couple and their children. Since marriage between northwestern Europeans generally involved the establishment of a separate household and economic unit, it could not usually be contracted until such units were available to the couple desirous of marriage. This marriage system was also characterized by relatively late marriage, with many women postponing marriage until their mid-20s, and many men not marrying until their late 20s. Furthermore, many men and women never married.[7] Yet, although many people never married, marriage was still preferred over remaining single because of the status, opportunity, and stability advantages associated with marriage.

Many of the countries of northwestern Europe also had a system of "lifecourse servanthood," in which a young man or woman would leave the parental home at a relatively young age—sometimes before reaching the teenage years—to live and work in the households of others.[8] This institution of servanthood was not limited to poor children living and working in wealthy households but involved a wide range of families as both receivers and senders of young people. As a result, large fractions of young people in northwestern Europe lived and worked away from their parental families during the young adult years before marriage, often for extended periods of time.[9]

Young people in northwestern Europe undoubtedly received extensive direction and supervision from their parents and other adults as they matured into adulthood. Nevertheless, when compared to their peers in numerous other societies, these young people also enjoyed a remarkable amount of latitude in their behavior and relationships.[10] In particular, northwestern European marriages, unlike those in many other settings, generally were not arranged by parents. Instead, spouses generally were chosen by young people through a courtship and selection system which they managed themselves. While economic, property, and status considerations were undoubtedly important components in this mate selection system, romance was also a central feature. Young people married for love as well as for money.

Sex, pregnancy, and childbearing before marriage were strongly discouraged in northwestern European societies.[11] However, these activities could not be controlled as effectively as they were in those societies where parents exercised strong parental control over children and where marriages were early and arranged. As a result, the courtship system of northwestern Europe resulted in numerous couples having sex before marriage, many brides being pregnant at marriage, and some children being born outside of wedlock.[12]

Northwestern European populations, like those in most other parts of the world, experienced a high rate of marital dissolution. Since divorce was relatively infrequent in the northwestern European past, however, these marital dissolutions were primarily the result of mortality due to the precarious health conditions of the time.[13] Nevertheless, the result was the creation of significant numbers of single-parent families. Even worse, some children experienced the death of both parents.

As I have documented in detail elsewhere, scholars of the eighteenth, nineteenth, and early twentieth centuries were unable to accept the enormous differences that they observed among societies as simply representing cross-cultural variations in family structure and form.[14] Instead, they interpreted the cross-cultural variation within an overarching framework of developmental and historical change.[15] Using a biological analogy, these scholars assumed that all societies experienced the same developmental or historical trajectory, with some societies developing at faster rates than others.[16] These scholars also assumed that their own societies were the most advanced and that other societies were situated at various lower positions on the developmental ladder.[17] Using this model of developmental change, these scholars believed they could describe the history of family change by comparing family structure and relationships in their own societies with those observed in other parts of the world.[18] They did so by assuming that the family forms they observed contemporaneously in other parts of the world had existed in northwestern Europe's past.[19]

Given this last assumption, these scholars concluded that northwestern Europe had once had the family structures and processes so prevalent in other parts of the world.[20] They believed that their own societies had once been characterized by extended family households, young and universal marriage, arranged marriage, a lack of romance in the courtship process, and strong parental control over children. Furthermore, these observers concluded that the key features of the northwestern European family and marriage systems—including nuclear family households, marriage at a relatively older age, many people never marrying, love marriages, and extensive autonomy in young adulthood—were the result of recent social and economic development.

It was only in the 1960s that scholars began to examine the records of the past to verify these historical conclusions. Unfortunately, for long periods of the historical past there were no survey research organizations that collected systematic data about courtship, marriage, romance, and family relationships. Consequently, the data we have to work with are scarce and subject to extensive error. Nevertheless, numerous historical studies now document that the basic and unique features of the northwestern European family system described above were *not* the result of recent historical change but instead had existed for centuries.[21] In fact, it now appears that these unique family and marriage characteristics have existed for at least as long as half a millennium—which is as far back as reliable systematic historical evidence goes.[22] As a result, the conclusions of earlier scholars about extended households, arranged marriage, the lack of affection, and young and universal marriage in the northwestern European past are now frequently referred to as myths.

Relevant Family Changes in Western Societies

The documentation of family change in Western societies since the European discovery of America is hampered greatly by shortcomings in the time series of available empirical data. Nevertheless, the available historical record does suggest that family change since the European discovery of America involves an interesting mixture of continuity and change.

One of the most important changes in Western societies during recent centuries has been the proliferation of social organizations and institutions that are not based upon kinship relations. With the creation and expansion of factories, schools, medical and public health organizations, police, commercialized leisure, the mass media, and other nonfamilial organizations, the lives of individuals increasingly have been conducted within, and organized by, nonfamilial institutions. While families, of course, continued to be important organizations for individuals, numerous other institutions began to organize and influence their lives as well.[23]

Of particular importance to this change was the separation of many of the activities of individuals from the family and home. With the rise of industrialization and paid employment, the work activities of men and unmarried women increasingly shifted away from the home to bureaucratic production institutions such as factories and offices.[24] As industrialization and paid employment shifted many of the productive activities of society from the home and farm to the factory and office, married women became increasingly segregated from activities that brought in money and instead concentrated their time and energies on caring for the home and their children. In the last several decades, however, there has been a return of married women to income-producing activities, but that activity now occurs primarily outside the home. With the separation of home and work in recent decades for both mothers and fathers, the combination of employment and parenting has become a particularly difficult concern for both individual families and the larger society.[25] The growth of school systems has also transferred children away from activities within the home to activities in the schools for many of their growing-up years.

The leaving-home process in Western societies continues to be complex, but the nature of that complexity has shifted in the past two centuries.[26] The shift of the workplace from the home to factories and offices terminated the institution of servanthood, where young people left their own families to work and live in the homes of others. Servanthood was replaced during the years of industrialization and urbanization by the practice of boarding and lodging. Young people would migrate from rural agricultural areas to cities to work in factories and offices and to live in factory-owned dormitories or in private rooming houses. More recently, as Western society has become almost completely urbanized, boarding and lodging has nearly disappeared, having been replaced by young people living in their own apartments or houses, either by themselves or with unrelated roommates.

The history of marriage in northwestern European countries reveals important swings in the timing and propensity of marriage but few long-term secular trends in these marital dimensions. Eighteenth-century England experienced an important increase in the propensity to marry, with both the age at marriage and the number of people never marrying declining sharply. These changes helped to initiate two centuries of population growth in that country.[27] Most countries of northwestern Europe as well as the European immigrant populations in North America and Australia also experienced an important marriage boom following World War II, with marriage rates increasing, age at marriage falling, and the fraction of the population never marrying declining.[28] During the 1970s and 1980s, marriage rates declined rapidly in most of these populations.[29] In the United States, the prevalence of marriage at the end of the 1980s was slightly lower than that observed at the beginning of the twentieth century.

However, the decline in marriage in the 1970s and 1980s was not due to abandonment of intimate coresidential male-female relationships. Nonmarital cohabitation was increasing sharply at exactly the same time that the prevalence of marriage was declining. In fact, unmarried cohabitation has increased so much in recent years that it has become a part of the life course for a large fraction of young people in many Western populations. Furthermore, the increase in cohabitation has been so pervasive that the fraction of young people who have never experienced a coresidential union—either marriage or cohabitation—is only slightly lower in the United States today than it was at the height of the post–World War II marriage boom.[30]

In some respects, the increase in unmarried cohabitation in this country is part of a larger increase in sexual relationships outside of marriage. Numerous studies have revealed a high and increasing rate of premarital sex among young unmarried Americans, with the great majority experiencing sexual relations before marriage.[31] One result of this rise in premarital sex has been the large increase in premarital pregnancy and childbearing among young unmarried women. In fact, this increase in out-of-wedlock childbearing has become so significant that more than one child in four is now born outside of marriage.[32] Additionally, the growing prevalence of premarital pregnancy has contributed to the increased number of abortions performed in Western societies.[33]

Of course, the increasing divorce rate has been one of the most important and well-publicized family trends in recent years. While divorce has been increasing in most Western countries, including the United States, for well over a century, the pace of that increase quickened sharply in the 1960s and 1970s. By the end of the 1970s, the upward expansion of divorce did come to an end. Nevertheless, it is now projected that more than one-half of all marriages in the United States will end in divorce.[34]

Less well appreciated than the rising divorce rate, however, is the equally dramatic decline in marital dissolutions produced by the death of a husband or wife—a phenomenon that has been occurring for long periods of Western history. In fact, the decline in human mortality has been so substantial that the overall rate of marital dissolution from both divorce and mortality in the United States is now only somewhat higher than it was a century ago.[35] Of course, with the switch of marital dissolution from mortality to divorce, the meaning of marital dissolution and remarriage in the lives of both children and adults has changed dramatically. People now must deal with the realities and difficulties associated with voluntary marital dissolution and adjust to blended and reconstituted families. In many instances, these blended families can be very complex and include multiple households involving both a divorced father and mother. Such complexities can be sources of both support and strain in the lives of parents and their children.

The changes in family behavior occurring in the United States after 1960 were accompanied by significant trends in attitudes, norms, and values. During the years following 1960, there were fundamental changes in views concerning marriage, divorce, childbearing, gender roles, premarital sex, cohabitation, abortion, and out-of-wedlock childbearing.[36] One important general phenomenon of this period was the relaxing of social prescriptions for family behavior and the expanding range of choices available to individuals. There was an important weakening of the normative pressure to get married, to stay married, to postpone sexual relations until marriage, to have children, to wait until marriage to have children, to *not* have an abortion, and to have a strict segregation of labor between men and women. It has thus become more acceptable in recent decades to go through life without marrying, to get a divorce, to have sexual relations before marriage, to cohabitate without being married, to bear children outside of marriage, to obtain an abortion, and for women to pursue careers outside the home. As a result, many important behaviors that were previously restricted by prevailing norms have become both relatively common and accepted by significant fractions of Americans.

These shifts in values and norms have also been institutionalized in the law. Whereas morality and the public regulation of intimate behavior were previously important components of legal philosophy, such matters now receive little emphasis. Instead, there is now a focus on the right of privacy and the non-involvement of the larger community in the private lives of individuals.[37] Examples of this legal trend are the universal adoption of no-fault divorce laws in America and the extension of the right of privacy to cover abortion (although the latter is now under serious attack).

These widespread changes in marital behavior, attitudes, values, norms, and laws suggest a major restructuring of the institution of marriage in Western societies in recent decades. The meaning of, rights in, and obligations associated with marriage may now be different from what they were in the past, and the future may hold additional changes. Marriage today is much less of a lifetime commitment than it was in previous decades. Also of crucial importance is the fact that the institution of marriage, as legitimated and regulated by the church and state, is much less of a regulator of human behavior than it was in the past. Legal marriage as sanctioned by religion, government, and the local community is less important today than in past decades as an institution for legitimizing sexual relations and co-residence. Furthermore, with the increase in out-of-wedlock childbearing and divorce, marriage has become substantially separated from parenthood and childrearing. With such changes, it seems likely that young people will now approach marriage with a significant amount of uncertainty and ambivalence about its centrality and meaning in their lives.

While it is difficult to underestimate the importance of the trends toward acceptance of previously prohibited behaviors, we should observe that these trends do not necessarily represent an endorsement of behaviors that were previously proscribed.[38] For example, the shift towards tolerance of sex among unmarried people, unmarried cohabitation, unmarried childbearing, abortion, never marrying, getting divorced, and remaining childless does not mean that there is now widespread endorsement of these same behaviors. That is, while these previously proscribed behaviors have become increasingly accepted, there is no evidence suggesting that they have become positive goals to be achieved. The vast majority of Americans continues to value family life, plans to marry and have children, and is optimistic about achieving success in marriage.

Increasing acceptance of these previously proscribed behaviors also should not be interpreted as a simple rejection of historical values and the adoption of a permissive approach to life. While attitudes about such things as remaining single, divorce, cohabitation, out-of-wedlock childbearing, and premarital sex were becoming more accepting, attitudes toward extramarital sex were becoming less tolerant.[39] This suggests that fidelity within relationships may have become more, rather than less, valued in recent years. Once a marital relationship is contracted, norms against intimate involvement outside of that relationship may now be stronger among young people than they were in previous decades. There is also recent evidence suggesting that the extent of marital infidelity is not particularly great.[40]

The increased emphasis in America on individual freedom and privacy, coupled with a decreased emphasis on conformity to a set of rules and standards concerning family life, has been accompanied by important value shifts in many other domains of American life, including religion, socialization values, civil liberties, and politics.[41] Childrearing values have changed over most of the past century, with Americans now placing less importance on children being obedient, conforming, and loyal to the church. The values of tolerance, autonomy, and thinking for yourself now receive substantially more support than in the past.[42]

There also have been substantial changes in religious values, practice, and authority in recent decades. These changes include declines in the authority of religious leaders and institutions, the value of the Bible as a guide to personal decisions, and confidence in religious answers to the problems of life.[43] Although church membership and attendance increased in the United States before 1960, there were declines after 1960 in membership in religious institutions, the number of people identifying with religion, the perceived importance of religion, the frequency of prayer, and attendance at religious services.[44] Parents also became more willing to permit their children to make their own religious decisions, and they have provided less religious training and less encouragement for their children to pray.[45] These changes have generally been more marked for Catholics than for Protestants.[46]

There is also evidence that the structure of religious experience has been changing. The pluralistic nature of American religion is now generally recognized, and Americans increasingly accept the authenticity of the beliefs and faith of other religions while at the same time believing less that their own religion and morals are necessarily applicable to others.[47] Furthermore, just as family and intimate behavior have been privatized, so has religion, with faith and morals being largely shifted from the community arena to the individual.[48] Consequently, religion today is less compulsory, more voluntaristic, and less condemning and punitive towards those who deviate from its religious teachings.[49] In fact, it now appears that a norm of tolerance has emerged to replace the norm of conformity regarding many dimensions of religious teaching. As a result, most religions now permit more freedom of individual choice and exhibit less intolerance and censorship of the behavior of those who do not follow the teachings of the church.

The expanding power of the norm of tolerance also extends to politics.

In the years following World War II, there were substantial increases in support of free speech for atheists, communists, and socialists. There have also been recent increases of independent thinking in politics, with political party identification declining.[50]

Some Implications for Public Policy Formulations

I noted at the beginning of this chapter that the age of European exploration revealed some central facts about the nature of human lifestyles around the world. One of the most important conclusions emanating from these explorations was the discovery of the universal importance of family institutions. Family and kinship relations historically have been central principles of social organization throughout the world. Kinship structures have been central features of virtually every society studied by several generations of explorers and scholars.

It is also true that one of the most important historical trends of the last two centuries in many societies, including our own, has been the dramatic differentiation of society, which has increased the number and importance of nonfamily institutions. Whereas our society in the past was primarily organized around kinship relations, today there are many nonfamilial units that organize people's time, determine their well-being, and exercise authority over them.

One of the most interesting and powerful accounts of the differentiation of society into many specialized nonfamilial units was provided a century ago by Emile Durkheim, a scholar still revered in sociology and anthropology today.[51] Durkheim went so far as to postulate a "law of contraction," in which the family would continuously decline in importance over time until it would finally disappear as a vital means of social organization.[52] This decline of the family theme has been echoed by others over the intervening years of the twentieth century.[53]

The only thing we can say for certain about Durkheim's prediction about the disappearance of families is that it is currently far from being fulfilled. Scholarly literature contains many studies showing the continuing importance of family units in organizing the activities and well-being of individual human beings.[54] In fact, family and kinship relationships continue to be so important to life in America that it is difficult to imagine social life without them. While humility requires us to be careful about dogmatic assertions about the future, it is difficult to imagine this fundamental fact about the centrality of family life changing in the foreseeable future. This suggests that family relationships will continue to be of central importance in shaping the well-being and activities of individuals and their social milieu well into the future.

The continuing importance of family relationships indicates that the nature of family life should be an important concern for people interested in the quality of contemporary and future well-being in the United States. While policy makers should not ignore the potential roles that government, business, schools, and other bureaucratic organizations can play in enriching the lives of individuals, they should not lose sight of the fact that families are important producers and distributors of the necessities and luxuries of life.

A key discovery of the age of exploration was the enormous diversity of family forms found around the world. The human species has been very innovative in creating a substantial number of marriage types and family forms to solve the basic problems of human existence. This fundamental fact has been recognized by scholars who have tried to create definitions of marriage and family that transcend specific cultural forms and arrangements. This definitional problem, as mentioned earlier, has been so profound and difficult to solve that it has seriously impeded comparative research across international boundaries.

The rapid social changes of the last two centuries in the United States and elsewhere have created similar problems of definition within our own cultural tradition. As marriage and family patterns have changed, it has become increasingly difficult to specify exactly what is meant by such universally-used words as *family* and *marriage*. This problem continuously plagues policymakers in their attempt to find solutions to perceived problems in marriage and family life.

As I have already indicated, the tremendous array of family diversity found around the world has both marveled and puzzled several generations of social scientists and has provided the raw material for some of the most complex and intricate accounts of historical change ever created by the human mind. Central to this entire scholarly endeavor was the simple and powerfully ethnocentric assumption that the family systems existing in northwestern Europe were in some way better and more advanced than those existing elsewhere around the world. With this assumption, scholars created a powerful account of the evolution of family types in human history. Included within this historical story was a picture of family life in the northwestern European past.

Despite its elegance in describing and explaining the history of contemporary northwestern European family life, this story of family evolution was eventually discredited because of one simple but fatal flaw: it did not fit the facts. The ethnocentric assumption of the superiority of one type of family over another turned out to be a faulty foundation for scientific and historical description and explanation.

This scientific critique brings me to a key observation about the current policy debate regarding the family: ethnocentric assumptions about the relative merit of various family types may be as deleterious to public policy discussions as to scientific discourse. While I recognize that by necessity the public policy debate brings into the picture many factors, including preferences and values which are appropriately excluded from scientific discourse, it is also true that ethnocentric assumptions about the relative merits of family organization may also damage the appropriateness of public policies.

My point here is *not* to say that all forms of human organization are equally beneficial. Rather, I want to say that the history of human experience has demonstrated that many forms of family organization work well, and that it is easy to make value judgments about the various forms of family life that are greatly influenced by upbringing or personal preference. We should, therefore, proceed very cautiously and carefully when making public statements about the relative merits of different kinds of personal and family arrangements. This, of course, is not a call for silence concerning our evaluations and values but an invitation for a strong awareness and appreciation of the range of acceptable alternatives created throughout the history of human experience.

There is also some hope that the historical and comparative record can provide useful insights into the criteria we might use in distinguishing among the various alternative approaches today. By looking broadly across the range of human experience, we may be more effective in identifying those features of family life that are effectively built into the systems of many cultures. This may enable us to move beyond the immediate contingencies of form and structure and identify the principles that would allow us to choose more effectively among alternatives.

While such an undertaking is clearly beyond both my current capabilities and the scope of this paper, there are some dimensions of family life that seem to be universal enough to merit serious consideration for this purpose. As previously noted, social organization throughout the world has been characterized by multiple kinsmen being organized into small communities called families where individual relatives intertwine their energy and resources to accomplish individual and group goals. These family members share energy, space, resources, and social organization to meet the numerous goals of life. Thus, the family has been the central primary unit that provides the resources and social support needed to navigate life. This means that family members are supposed to care about each other and be committed to shared interests. Of course, as in all communities, relationships within families are and always have been characterized by conflict as well as cooperation, by hate as well as love.

It is also useful to note that while family units have sometimes been as small as two individuals, families more typically have included additional members. In fact, most family systems have recognized substantial numbers of relatives and relationships. This suggests that many of the tasks of human existence can frequently be handled more effectively and pleasantly in families with multiple dyads than in those consisting of a single dyad. This observation may be relevant when considering family groups involving a single parent with children. While one-parent families may be able to handle the numerous tasks of life, multiple adults can probably take care of those tasks more efficiently and productively. This consideration, of course, should be only one of the factors taken into account as individuals and the larger society consider and contemplate such issues as marriage, out-of-wedlock childbearing, divorce, and single parenthood.[55]

Another feature of family life commonly found around the world is stability and permanence. Although the ways in which permanence has been achieved vary across cultural boundaries, the continuity of family units has been an important feature of virtually all family systems. For example, in Chinese society, the ancestral chain permanently linking together the living with their ancestors and their future unborn children provides an identification with a stable family unit that permeates Chinese life.[56] In a somewhat different way, the indissolubility of marriage in the Western world in the past gave the nuclear family unit a sense of stability.

Of course, the termination of a marriage by the death of a parent was particularly disruptive in Western societies. The rise in divorce in recent decades represents a new and in some ways more powerful form of family impermanence. The actual and perceived fragility of family life in the United States today undoubtedly has significant ramifications for the ways in which people conduct their lives. Accordingly, the issue of permanence and stability should be given clear prominence among the myriad of considerations that individuals and the larger society take into account when they consider issues of family formation and dissolution.

The final commonality I would like to draw from the cross-cultural and historical record is the significant extent to which family and marriage have been embedded within the sacred. Historically, the scope and meaning of marriage and family relationships have not been limited to the biological or social but have also extended to the cosmological. For example, the key feature of the Chinese cosmos was the ancestral chain that linked together ancestors with the living and the as yet unborn.[57] Marriage and childbearing thus took on eternal significance as key acts in the continuation of the ancestral chain. Similarly, in many Western societies, marriage was considered to be a sacrament undertaken with the blessing of deity and the church. This blending of the mundane with the sacred in the institutions of marriage and family undoubtedly gave marital and family relationships favored status in these communities. As such, these relationships could call forth loyalty and sacrifice unavailable to many nonfamilial relationships.

Unfortunately, I am unaware of any data indicating the extent to which family relationships today are intertwined with the sacred. The evidence discussed earlier about recent changes in religious orientation, however, suggests that the sacred underpinnings of family relationships today may be less extensive than in the past. This hypothesis, if correct, has ramifications for many dimensions of family life today.

Conclusion

It should be clear that I have not presented anything resembling a public policy agenda for marriage, family life, or personal relationships in the United States. Rather, I have tried to draw some principles and cautionary notes from international and historical family experience. If these observations and concerns make some small contribution to the continuing debate about the American family, I will judge my time in presenting them well spent.

Notes

This essay was presented at the Utah Law Review Symposium (University of Utah College of Law, October 15–16, 1993) and the Marriage Symposium of the Council on Families in America (Institute for American Values, New York, June 3–4, 1993).

1. In order to facilitate communication, I use the term *northwestern Europe* and its population and scholars to refer not only to the geographical area of northwestern Europe, but also to the migrant populations from northwestern Europe to North America, Australia, and New Zealand.

2. See generally Peter Laslett, *The World We Have Lost* (New York: Charles Scribner, 1965) for a discussion of English society before and after industrial revolution); Arland Thornton and Thomas E. Fricke, "Social Change and the Family: Comparative Perspectives from the West, China, and South Asia," *Socio-*

logical Forum 2 (1987): 746–79, for an examination of the effects of social and economic transformations upon the family.

3. Included within the many family and marriage forms of humanity are the following: cross-cousin marriages, polygyny, polyandry, bride service, bride price, matrilineality, patrilineality, extended households, nuclear households, arranged marriages, love matches, adoption, child fosterage, lifecourse servanthood, patrilocal residence, matrilocal residence, neolocal residence, child marriage, universal marriage, extensive celibacy, marriage alliances, exogenous marriage, and exogamous marriage.

4. For discussions of the diverse family and marriage structures from various societies, see Myron L. Cohen, *House United, House Divided* (New York: Columbia University Press, 1976), studying family organization in Yen-Liao, Taiwan; Thomas E. Fricke, *Himalayan Households: Tamang Demography and Domestic Processes* (Ann Arbor, MI: UMI Research Press, 1986), studying "the demography and household process of an agro-pastoral people of North Central Nepal"; Hildred Geertz, *The Javanese Family* (New York: The Free Press, 1961), examining kinship and socialization in Java, Indonesia; Nancy E. Levine, *The Dynamics of Polyandry* (Chicago: University of Chicago Press, 1988), discussing polyandry as practiced among Nyinba, Tibetan residents of northwestern Nepal; Alan MacFarlane, *Marriage and Love in England: Modes of Reproduction 1300–1840* (Oxford, England: Basil Blackwell, 1986), discussing the history of Malthusian family system and its effects on economic growth in England; Arthur P. Wolf and Chieh-Shan Huang, *Marriage and Adoption in China, 1845–1945* (Stanford, CA: Stanford University Press, 1980), studying marriage and adoption practices in northern Taiwan and concluding Chinese marriages and adoptions were complex reflections of various sources that shaped family organization; John Hajnal, "Two Kinds of Preindustrial Household Formation System," *Population and Development Review* 8 (1982): 449–94, contrasting preindustrial northwest European household formation systems with those of other populations; Hilary J. Page, "Childrearing versus Childbearing: Coresidence of Mother and Child in Sub-Saharan Africa," in *Reproduction and Social Organization in Sub-Saharan Africa*, ed. Ron J. Lesthaeghe (Berkeley, CA: University of California Press, 1989), 401–41, discussing the nature of family systems in Africa.

5. See E. Kathleen Gough, "The Nayars and the Definition of Marriage," *Journal of the Royal Anthropological Inst.* 89 (1959): 23–34, stating that anthropologists have had difficulty satisfactorily defining "marriage"; Sylvia J. Yanagisako, "Family and Household: The Analysis of Domestic Groups," *Annual Review of Anthropology* 8 (1979): 196–200, arguing against ability to reduce "family" to one universal definition.

6. MacFarlane, *Marriage and Love in England*, 35–48; John Hajnal, "European Marriage Patterns in Perspective," in *Population in History*, ed. D. V. Glass and D. E. C. Eversley (Chicago: Aldine, 1965), 101; Hajnal, "Two Kinds of Household Formation," 452–59. See generally Laslett, *The World We Have Lost*, arguing that marriage at young age was rare in nineteenth-century England.

7. In some societies, up to 20 percent of the adult population remained unmarried. See Hajnal, "European Marriage Patterns in Perspective," 101–04.

8. Ann Kussmaul, *Servants in Husbandry in Early Modern England* (Cambridge, England: Cambridge University Press, 1981), 3; Hajnal, "Two Kinds of Household Formation," 470–73.

9. Kussmaul, *Servants in Husbandry*, 3; Hajnal, "Two Kinds of Household Formation," 471.

10. See MacFarlane, *Marriage and Love in England*, 87–96; Alan MacFarlane, *The Origins of English Individualism: The Family, Property, and Social Transition* (Cambridge, England: Cambridge University Press, 1978), 197-98, arguing that romantic love basis for marriage has predominated in England since at least 1300; Thornton and Fricke, "Social Change and the Family," 753–55.

11. Edward Shorter, *The Making of the Modern Family* (New York: Basic Books, 1975), 51.

12. See Edward Shorter et al., "The Decline of Non-Marital Fertility in Europe, 1880–1940," *Population Studies* 25 (1971): 375, 376–78; Daniel S. Smith and Michael S. Hindus, "Premarital Pregnancy in America 1640–1971: An Overview and Interpretation," *Journal of Interdisciplinary History* 5 (1975): 537, 548.

13. Arland Thornton and Deborah Freedman, "The Changing American Family," *Population Bulletin* 38 (1983): 1, 10.

14. Arland Thornton, "Reading History Sideways: The Negative Effect of the Developmental Paradigm on Family and Demographic Research" (Ann Arbor: Institute for Social Research, University of Michigan, 1992).

15. Ibid., 21–33; see also Robert A. Nisbet, *Social Change and History* (New York: Oxford University Press, 1969), 166–88; Anthony D. Smith, *The Concept of Social Change* (London: Routledge and Kegan Paul, 1973), 26–28.

16. Nisbet, *Social Change and History*, 166–88; Smith, *The Concept of Social Change*, 26–28; Thornton, "Reading History Sideways," 21–33.

17. George W. Stocking Jr., *Victorian Anthropology* (New York: The Free Press, 1987), 235; Edward B. Tylor, *Primitive Culture* (London: John Murray, Albermarle Street, 1871), 23–24; Thornton, "Reading History Sideways," 25–31.

18. Edward A. Westermarck, *The History of Human Marriage* (London: Macmillan and Co., 1891), 1–2; Thornton, "Reading History Sideways," 25–31.

19. Westermarck, *The History of Human Marriage*, 1–2; Thornton, "Reading History Sideways," 25–31.

20. Tylor, *Primitive Culture*, 23–24; Westermarck, *The History of Human Marriage*, 1–2; Thornton, "Reading History Sideways," 25–31.

21. See William J. Goode, *The Family* (Englewood Cliffs, NJ: Prentice-Hall, 1964), 193–94; William J. Goode, *World Revolution and Family Patterns* (New York: The Free Press, 1963), 6–7; Laslett, *The World We Have Lost*, 90–91; Steven Ruggles, *Prolonged Connections: The Rise of the Extended Family in Nineteenth-Century England and America* (Madison, WI: University of Wisconsin Press, 1987), 3–4; Thornton, "Reading History Sideways," 1–7.

22. Laslett, *The World We Have Lost*, 3–4; Macfarlane, *Marriage and Love in England*, 35–48; Hajnal, "Two Kinds of Household Formation," 452–59.

23. Thornton and Fricke, "Social Change and the Family," 755–69.

24. Ibid., 758–62.

25. Kingsley Davis, "Wives and Work: The Sex Role Revolution and Its Consequences," *Population and Development Review* 10 (1984): 397, 413.

26. Frances K. Goldscheider and Julie DaVanzo, "Living Arrangements and the Transition to Adulthood," *Demography* 22 (1985): 545–63; Frances E. Kobrin, "The Fall in Household Size and the Rise of the Primary Individual in the United States," *Demography* 13 (1976): 127, 128, 134–36; John Modell and Tamara K. Hareven, "Urbanization and the Malleable Household: An Examination of Boarding and Lodging in American Families," *Journal of Marriage and the Family* 35 (1973): 467, 478.

27. E. A. Wrigley and R. S. Schofield, *The Population History of England 1541–1871: A Reconstruction* (Cambridge, MA: Harvard University Press, 1981), 174–75, 257–69.

28. Susan C. Watkins, "Regional Patterns of Nuptiality in Europe 1870–1960," *Population Studies* 35 (1981): 199–215.

29. Andrew J. Cherlin, *Marriage, Divorce, Remarriage* (Cambridge, MA: Harvard University Press, 1992), 2, 6–7, 67.

30. Ibid., 11–13; Larry L. Bumpass et al., "The Role of Cohabitation in Declining Rates of Marriage," *Journal of Marriage and the Family* 53 (1991): 913–18; Larry L. Bumpass and James A. Sweet, "National Estimates of Cohabitation," *Demography* 26 (1989): 615–21; Kathryn A. London, "Cohabitation, Marriage, Marital Dissolution, and Remarriage: United States, 1988," in *Advance Data from Vital and Health Statistics*, ed. National Center for Health Statistics, (1991), 1–4.

31. Shorter, *Making of Modern Family*, 79–85, 163–65; Jacqueline D. Forrest and Susheela Singh, "The Sexual and Reproductive Behavior of American Women, 1982–1988," *Family Planning Perspectives* 22 (1990): 206–09; Freya L. Sonenstein et al., "Levels of Sexual Activity Among Adolescent Males in the United States," *Family Planning Perspectives* 23 (1991): 162; Melvin Zelnik and John F. Kantner, "Sexual Activity, Contraceptive Use and Pregnancy Among Metropolitan-Area Teenagers: 1971–1979," *Family Planning Perspectives* 12 (1980): 230–33.

32. See National Center for Health Statistics, Public Health Service, *Monthly Vital Statistics Report 39, Advance Report of Final Natality Statistics, 1988*, no. 4 (Washington, DC: Department of Health and Human Services, 1990).

33. Forrest and Singh, "Sexual and Reproductive Behavior," 213; Zelnik and Kantner, "Sexual Activity, Contraceptive Use," 233–34.

34. Cherlin, *Marriage, Divorce, Remarriage*, 24; Larry L. Bumpass, "What's Happening to the Family? Interactions Between Demographic and Institutional Change," 1990 Presidential Address before the Population Association of America, in *Demography* 27 (1990): 483, 485.

35. Thornton and Freedman, "The Changing American Family," 7–8.

36. Arland Thornton, "Changing Attitudes Toward Family Issues in the United States," *Journal of Marriage and the Family* 51 (1989): 873, 887.

37. Carl E. Schneider, "Moral Discourse and the Transformation of American Family Law," *Michigan Law Review* 83 (1985): 1803, 1833–46.

38. Thornton, "Changing Attitudes Toward Family Issues," 887–91.

39. Ibid., 885–87.

40. Andrew M. Greeley et al., "Americans and Their Sexual Partners," *Sociology* (July–August 1990): 36–38; Tom W. Smith, "Adult Sexual Behavior in 1989: Number of Partners, Frequency of Intercourse and Risk of AIDS," *Family Planning Perspectives* 23, (1991): 102, 104.

41. Thornton, "Changing Attitudes Toward Family Issues," 887–91.

42. Duane F. Alwin, "Changes in Qualities Valued in Children in the United States, 1964–1984," *Social Science Research* 18 (1989): 195, 203–14; Duane F. Alwin, "From Obedience to Autonomy: Changes in Traits Desired in Children, 1924–1978," *Public Opinion Quarterly* 52 (1988): 33, 41–44; Duane F. Alwin, "Religion and Parental Childrearing Orientations: Evidence of a Catholic-Protestant Convergence," *American Journal of Sociology* 92 (1986): 412–13; Duane F. Alwin, "Trends in Parental Socialization Values: Detroit, 1958–1983," *American Journal of Sociology* 90 (1984): 359, 366–79.

43. Theodore Caplow et al., *All Faithful People* (Minneapolis, MN: University of Minnesota Press, 1983), 87–108, 147–49; Andrew M. Greeley et al., *Catholic Schools in a Declining Church* (Kansas City, MO: Sheed and Ward, 1976), 29–36; Andrew M. Greeley, *Religious Change in America* (Cambridge, MA: Harvard University Press, 1976), 16, 20, 57–66; Norval D. Glenn, "Social Trends in the United States," *Public Opinion Quarterly* 51 (1987): S109, S115–17; Michael Hout and Andrew M. Greeley, "The Center Doesn't Hold: Church Attendance in the United States, 1940–1984," *American Sociological Review* (1987): 325–37.

44. Greely, *Religious Change in America*, 37–40, 55–66; Glenn, "Social Trends in the U.S.," S115–17.

45. Duane F. Alwin, "Religion in Detroit, 1958–1988" (unpublished paper, Institute for Social Research, University of Michigan, Ann Arbor, 1988), 14.

46. Greely, *Religious Change in America*, 16–20, 57–66; Hout and Greeley, "The Center Doesn't Hold," 326–27.

47. Robert N. Bellah et al., *Habits of the Heart* (Berkeley, CA: University of California Press, 1985), 225–27; Caplow et al., *All Faithful People*, 98–99, 166–69; Wade C. Roof and William McKinney, *American Mainline Religion* (New Brunswick, NJ: Rutgers University Press, 1987), 40–45, 50–57, 244–49.

48. Roof and McKinney, *American Mainline Religion*, 40–57.

49. Ibid.

50. Clyde Z. Nunn et al., *Tolerance for Non-conformity* (San Francisco: Jossey-Bass, 1978), 69, 167–78; Glenn, "Social Trends in the U.S.," S112–15. See generally John Mueller, "Trends in Political Tolerance," *Public Opinion Quarterly* 52 (1988): 1, 12–17, discussing trends in tolerance of political groups.

51. Emile Durkheim, "The Conjugal Family," in *Emile Durkheim on Institutional Analysis*, trans. and ed. Mark Traugott (Chicago: University of Chicago Press, 1978), 229–39. See generally Emile Durkheim, *The Division of Labor in*

Society, trans. W. D. Halls (New York: The Free Press, 1984) explaining consequences of complex systems of division of labor on cohesion and solidarity of society.

52. Durkheim, "The Conjugal Family," 232–33.

53. See, e.g., Jan E. Dizard and Howard Gadlin, *The Minimal Family* (Amherst, MA: University of Massachusetts Press, 1990), 199–221, describing rise in public familialism; David Popenoe, *Disturbing the Nest: Family Change and Decline in Modern Societies* (Hawthorne, NY: Aldine De Gruyter, 1988), 43, 51–54, discussing decline of family within societies.

54. See, e.g., Ronald Fletcher, *The Family and Marriage in Britain*, 3d ed. (London: Penguin Books, 1973), 203–33, concluding that family is a central figure in a broad array of human activities; Donald J. Hernandez, *America's Children: Resources from Family, Government and the Economy* (New York: Russell Sage, 1993), 417–46, studying consequences to children's lives of changing family structures; Alice S. Rossi and Peter H. Rossi, *Of Human Bonding: Parent-Child Relations Across the Life Course* (Hawthorne, NY: Aldine De Gruyter, 1990), 455–58, exploring extent to which family ties remain a support system across the life course.

55. For a discussion of the effects of single parents on children, see Sara McLanahan and Gary Sandefur, *Growing Up with a Single Parent: What Hurts, What Helps* (Cambridge, MA: Harvard University Press, 1994).

56. See Arland Thornton and Hui-Sheng Lin, *Social Change and the Family in Taiwan* (Chicago: University of Chicago Press, 1994).

57. Ibid.

CHAPTER 5

Decline of the Family: Conservative, Liberal, and Feminist Views

Janet Z. Giele

In the 1990s the state of American families and children became a new and urgent topic. Everyone recognized that families had changed. Divorce rates had risen dramatically. More women were in the labor force. Evidence on rising teenage suicides, high rates of teen births, and disturbing levels of addiction and violence had put children at risk.

Conservatives have held that these problems can be traced to a culture of toleration and an expanding welfare state that undercut self-reliance and community standards. They focus on the family as a caregiving institution and try to restore its strengths by changing the culture of marriage and parenthood. Liberals center on the disappearance of manual jobs that throws less educated men out of work and undercuts their status in the family as well as rising hours of work among the middle class that makes stable two-parent families more difficult to maintain. Liberals argue that structural changes are needed outside the family in the public world of employment and schools.

The feminist vision combines both the reality of human interdependence in the family and individualism of the workplace. Feminists want to protect diverse family forms that allow realization of freedom and equality while at the same time nurturing the children of the next generation.

The Conservative Explanation: Selfishness and Moral Decline

The new family advocates turn their spotlight on the breakdown in the two-parent family, saying that rising divorce, illegitimacy, and father absence have put children at greater risk of school failure, unemployment, and antisocial behavior. The remedy is to restore religious faith and family commitment as well as to cut welfare payments to unwed mothers and mother-headed families.

Conservative Model

| Cultural and moral weakening | → | Family breakdown, divorce, family decline | → | Father absence, school failure, poverty, crime, drug use |

Cultural and Moral Weakening

To many conservatives, the modern secularization of religious practice and the decline of religious affiliation have undermined the norms of sexual abstinence before marriage and the prohibitions of adultery or divorce thereafter. Sanctions against illegitimacy or divorce have been made to seem narrow-minded and prejudiced. In addition, daytime television and the infamous example of Murphy Brown, a single mother having a child out of wedlock helped to obscure simple notions of right and wrong. Barbara Dafoe Whitehead's controversial article in the *Atlantic* entitled "Dan Quayle Was Right" is an example of this argument.[1]

Gradual changes in marriage law have also diminished the hold of tradition. Restrictions against waiting periods, race dissimilarity, and varying degrees of consanguinity were gradually disappearing all over the United States and Europe.[2] While Mary Ann Glendon viewed the change cautiously but relativistically—as a process that waxed and waned across the centuries—others have interpreted these changes as a movement from status to contract (i.e., from attention to the particular individual's characteristics to reliance on the impersonal considerations of the marketplace).[3] The resulting transformation lessened the family's distinctive capacity to serve as a bastion of private freedom against the leveling effect and impersonality of public bureaucracy.

Erosion of the Two-Parent Family

To conservatives, one of the most visible causes of family erosion was government welfare payments, which made fatherless families a viable option. In *Losing Ground*, Charles Murray used the rise in teenage illegitimate births as proof that government-sponsored welfare programs had actually contributed to the breakdown of marriage.[4] Statistics on rising divorce and mother-headed families appeared to provide ample proof that the two-parent family was under siege. The proportion of all households headed by married couples fell from 77 percent in 1950 to 61 percent in 1980 and 55 percent in 1993.[5] Rising cohabitation, divorce rates, and births out of wedlock all contributed to the trend. The rise in single-person households was also significant, from only 12 percent of all households in 1950 to 27 percent in 1980, a trend fed by rising affluence and the undoubling of living arrangements that occurred with the expansion of the housing supply after World War II.[6]

The growth of single-parent households, however, was the most worrisome to policymakers because of their strong links to child poverty. In 1988, 50 percent of all children were found in mother-only families compared with 20 percent in 1950. The parental situation of children in poverty changed accordingly. Of all poor children in 1959, 73 percent had two parents present and 20 percent had a mother only. By 1988, only 35 percent of children in poverty lived with two parents and 57 percent lived with a mother only. These developments were fed by rising rates of divorce and out-of-wedlock births. Between 1940 and 1990, the divorce rate rose from 8.8 to 21 per thousand married women. Out-of-wedlock births exploded from 5 percent in 1960 to 26 percent in 1990.[7]

To explain these changes, conservatives emphasize the breakdown of individual and cultural commitment to marriage and the loss of stigma for divorce and illegitimacy. They understand both trends to be the result of greater emphasis on short-term gratification and on adults' personal desires rather than on what is good for children. A young woman brings a child into the world without thinking about who will support it. A husband divorces his wife and forms another household, possibly with other children and leaves children of the earlier family behind without necessarily feeling obliged to be present in their upbringing or to provide them with financial support.

Negative Consequences for Children

To cultural conservatives there appears to be a strong connection between erosion of the two-parent family and the rise of health and social problems in children. Parental investment in children has declined—especially in the time available for supervision and companionship. Parents had roughly 10 fewer hours per week for their children in 1986 than in 1960, largely because more married women were employed (up from 24 percent in 1940 to 52 percent in 1983) and more mothers of young children (under age 6) were working (up from 12 percent in 1940 to 50 percent in 1983). By the late 1980s just over half of mothers of children under a year old were in the labor force for at least part of the year.[8] At the same time fathers were increasingly absent from the family because of desertion, divorce, or failure to marry. In 1980, 15 percent of white children, 50 percent of black children, and 27 percent of children of Hispanic origin had no father present. Today 36 percent of children are living apart from their biological fathers compared with only 17 percent in 1960.[9]

Without a parent to supervise children after school, keep them from watching television all day, or prevent them from playing in dangerous neighborhoods, many more children appear to be falling by the wayside, victims of drugs, obesity, violence, suicide, or failure in school. During the 1960s and 1970s the suicide rate for persons aged fifteen to nineteen more than doubled. The proportion of obese children between the ages of six and eleven rose from 18 to 27 percent. Average SAT scores fell, and 25 percent of all high school students failed to graduate.[10] In 1995 the Council on Families in America reported, "Recent surveys have found that children from broken homes, when they become teenagers have 2 to 3 times more behavioral and psychological problems than do children from intact homes."[11] Father absence is blamed by the fatherhood movement for the rise in violence among young males. David Blankenhorn and others reason that the lack of a positive and productive male role model has contributed to an uncertain masculine identity which then uses violence and aggression to prove itself. Every child deserves a father and "in a good society, men prove their masculinity not by killing other people, impregnating lots of women, or amassing large fortunes, but rather by being committed fathers and loving husbands."[12]

Psychologist David Elkind, in *The Hurried Child*, suggests that parents' work and time constraints have pushed down the developmental timetable to younger ages so that small children are being expected to take care of themselves and perform at levels which are robbing them of their childhood. The consequences are depression, discouragement, and a loss of joy at learning and growing into maturity.[13]

Reinvention of Marriage

According to the conservative analysis, the solution to a breakdown in family values is to revitalize and reinstitutionalize marriage. The culture should change to give higher priority to marriage and parenting. The legal code should favor marriage and encourage parental responsibility on the part of fathers as well as mothers. Government should cut back welfare programs which have supported alternative family forms.

The cultural approach to revitalizing marriage is to raise the overall priority given to family activities relative to work, material consumption, or leisure. Marriage is seen as the basic building block of civil society, which helps to hold together the fabric of volunteer activity and mutual support that underpins any democratic society.[14] Some advocates are unapologetically judgmental toward families who fall outside the two-parent mold. According to a 1995 *Newsweek* article on "The Return of Shame," David Blankenhorn believes "a stronger sense of shame about illegitimacy and divorce would do more than any tax cut or any new governmental program to maximize the life circumstances of children." But he also adds that the ultimate goal is "to move beyond stigmatizing only teenage mothers toward an understanding of the terrible message sent by all of us when we minimize the importance of fathers or contribute to the breakup of families."[15]

Another means to marriage and family revitalization is some form of taking a "pledge." Prevention programs for teenage pregnancy affirm the ideal of chastity before marriage. Athletes for Abstinence, an organization founded by a professional basketball player, preaches that young people should "save sex for marriage." A Baptist-led national program called True Love Waits has gathered an abstinence pledge from hundreds of thousands of teenagers since it was begun in the spring of 1993. More than 2,000 school districts now offer an abstinence-based sex education curriculum entitled "Sex Respect." Parents who are desperate about their children's sexual behavior are at last seeing ways that society can resist the continued sexualization of childhood.[16]

The new fatherhood movement encourages fathers to promise that they will spend more time with their children. The National Fatherhood Initiative argues that men's roles as fathers should not simply duplicate women's roles as mothers but should teach those essential qualities which are perhaps uniquely conveyed by fathers—the ability to take risks, contain emotions, and be decisive. In addition, fathers fulfill a time-honored role of providing for children as well as teaching them.[17]

Full-time mothers have likewise formed support groups to reassure themselves that not having a job and being at home full-time for their children is an honorable choice, although it is typically undervalued and perhaps even scorned by dual-earner couples and women with careers. A 1994 *Barron's* article claimed that young people in their twenties ("generation X") were turning away from the two-paycheck family and scaling down their consumption so that young mothers could stay at home. Al-

though Labor Department statistics show no such trend but only a flat-
tening of the upward rise of women's employment, a variety of poll data
does suggest that Americans would rather spend less time at work and
more time with their families.[18] Such groups as Mothers at Home (with
15,000 members) and Mothers' Home Business Network (with 6,000
members) are trying to create a sea change that reverses the priority given
to paid work outside the home relative to unpaid caregiving work inside
the family.[19]

Conservatives see government cutbacks as one of the major strategies
for strengthening marriage and restoring family values. In the words of
Lawrence Mead, we have "taxed Peter to pay Paula."[20] According to a
Wall Street Journal editorial, the "relinquishment of personal responsibility" among people who bring children into the world without any visible
means of support is at the root of educational, health, and emotional
problems of children from one-parent families, their higher accident and
mortality rates, and rising crime.[21]

The new congressional solution is to cut back on the benefits to young
men and women who "violate social convention by having children they
cannot support."[22] Sociologist Brigitte Berger notes that the increase in
children and women on welfare coincided with the explosion of federal
child welfare programs—family planning, prenatal and postnatal care,
child nutrition, child abuse prevention and treatment, child health and
guidance, day care, Head Start, and Aid to Families with Dependent Children (AFDC), Medicaid, and Food Stamps. The solution is to turn back
the debilitating culture of welfare dependency by decentralizing the power
of the federal government and restoring the role of intermediary community institutions such as the neighborhood and the church. The mechanism for change would be block grants to the states which would change
the welfare culture from the ground up.[23] Robert Rector of the American
Heritage Foundation explains that the states would use these funds for a
wide variety of alternative programs to discourage illegitimate births and
to care for children born out of wedlock, such as promoting adoption,
closely supervised group homes for unmarried mothers and their children,
and pregnancy prevention programs (except abortion).[24]

Government programs, however, are only one way to bring about cultural change. The Council on Families in America puts its hope in grass-
roots social movements to change the hearts and minds of religious and
civil leaders, employers, human service professionals, courts, and the
media and entertainment industry. The Council enunciates four ideals:
marital permanence, childbearing confined to marriage, every child's
right to have a father, and limitation of parents' total work time (60 hours
per week) to permit adequate time with their families.[25] To restore the

cultural ideal of the two-parent family, they would make all other types of family life less attractive and more difficult.

Economic Restructuring: Liberal Analysis of Family Change

Liberals agree that there are serious problems in America's social health and the condition of its children. But they pinpoint economic and structural changes that have placed new demands on the family without providing countervailing social supports. The economy has become ever more specialized with rapid technological change undercutting established occupations. More women have entered the labor force as their child-free years have increased due to a shorter childbearing period and longer lifespan. The family has lost economic functions to the urban workplace and socialization functions to the school. What is left is the intimate relationship between the marital couple, which, unbuffered by the traditional economic division of labor between men and women, is subject to even higher demands for emotional fulfillment and is thus more vulnerable to breakdown when it falls short of those demands.

Liberal Model

Changing economic structure	→	Changing family and gender roles	→	Diverse effects: poor v. productive children

The current family crisis thus stems from structural more than cultural change—changes in the economy, a paired-down nuclear family, and less parental time at home. Market forces have led to a new ethic of individual flexibility and autonomy. More dual-earner couples and single-parent families have broadened the variety of family forms. More single-parent families and more working mothers have decreased the time available for parenting. Loss of the father's income through separation and divorce has forced many women and children into poverty with inadequate health care, poor education, and inability to save for future economic needs. The solution that most liberals espouse is a government-sponsored safety net which will facilitate women's employment, mute the effects of poverty, and help women and children to become economically secure.

Recent Changes in the Labor Market

Liberals attribute the dramatic changes in the family to the intrusion of the money economy rather than cultural and moral decline. In a capitalist society individual behavior follows the market. Adam Smith's "invisible hand" brings together buyers and sellers who maximize their satisfaction through an exchange of resources in the marketplace. Jobs are now with an employer, not with the family business or family farm as in preindustrial times. The cash economy has, in the words of Robert Bellah, "invaded" the diffuse personal relationships of trust between family and community members and transformed them into specific impersonal transactions. In an agricultural economy husbands and wives and parents and children were bound together in relationships of exchange that served each others' mutual interests. But modern society erodes this social capital of organization, trust among individuals, and mutual obligation that enhances both productivity and parenting.[26]

The market has also eroded community by encouraging maximum mobility of goods and services. Cheaper labor in the South, lower fuel prices, and deeper tax breaks attracted first textile factories, then the shoe industry, and later automobile assembly plants which had begun in the North. Eventually, many of these jobs left the country. Loss of manufacturing jobs has had dramatic consequences for employment of young men without a college education and their capacity to support a family. In the 1970s, 68 percent of male high school graduates had a full-time, year-round job compared with only 51 percent in the 1980s. Many new jobs are located in clerical work, sales, or other service occupations traditionally associated with women. The upshot is a deteriorating employment picture for less well educated male workers at the same time that there are rising opportunities for women. Not surprisingly, ever more middle-income men and women combine forces to construct a two-paycheck family wage.[27]

Changing Family Forms

Whereas the farm economy dictated a two-parent family and several children as the most efficient work group, the market economy gives rise to a much wider variety of family forms. A woman on the frontier in the 1800s had few other options even if she were married to a drunken, violent, or improvident husband. In today's economy this woman may have enough education to get a clerical job that will support her and her children in a small apartment where the family will be able to use public schools and other public amenities.[28]

Despite its corrosive effect on family relations, the modern economy has also been a liberating force. Women could escape patriarchal domination; the young could seek their fortune without waiting for an inheritance from their elders—all a process that a century ago was aligned with a cultural shift that Fred Weinstein and Gerald Platt termed "the wish to be free."[29] Dramatic improvements took place in the status of women as they gained the right to higher education, entry into the professions, and the elective franchise.[30] Similarly, children were released from sometimes cruel and exploitive labor and became the object of deliberate parental investment and consumption.[31] Elders gained pensions for maintenance and care that made them economically independent of their adult children. All these developments could be understood as part of what William J. Goode has referred to as the "world revolution in family patterns" which resulted in liberation and equality of formerly oppressed groups.[32]

The current assessment of change in family forms is, however, mostly negative because of the consequences for children. More parental investment in work outside the family has meant less time for children. According to liberals, parents separate or divorce or have children outside of marriage because of the economic structure, not because they have become less moral or more selfish. Young women have children out of wedlock when the young men whom they might marry have few economic prospects and when the women themselves have little hope for their own education or employment.[33] Change in the family thus begins with jobs. Advocates of current government programs therefore challenge the conservatives' assertion that welfare caused the breakup of two-parent families by supporting mothers with dependent children. According to William Julius Wilson, it is partly the lack of manual labor jobs for the would-be male breadwinner in inner-city Chicago—the scarcity of "marriageable males"—which drives up the illegitimacy rate.[34]

Among educated women, it is well known that the opportunity costs of foregone income from staying home became so high during the 1950s and 1960s that ever increasing numbers of women deserted full-time homemaking to take paid employment.[35] In the 1990s several social scientists have further noted that Richard Easterlin's prediction that women would return to the home during the 1980s never happened. Instead women continued in the labor force because of irreversible normative changes surrounding women's equality and the need for women's income to finance children's expensive college education.[36] Moreover, in light of globalization of the economy and increasing job insecurity in the face of corporate downsizing, economists and sociologists are questioning Gary Becker's thesis that the lower waged worker in a household (typically the woman) will tend to become a full-time homemaker while the higher waged partner becomes the primary breadwinner. Data from Germany and the United States on the trend toward women's multiple roles suggests that uncertainty about the future has made women invest more strongly than ever in their own careers. They know that if they drop out for very long they will have difficulty reentering if they have to tide over the family when the main breadwinner loses his job.[37]

Consequences for Children

The ideal family in the liberal economic model, according to political philosopher Iris Young, is one which has sufficient income to support the parents and the children and "to foster in those children the emotional and intellectual capacities to acquire such well-paid, secure jobs themselves, and also sufficient to finance a retirement."[38] Dependent families do not have self-sufficient income but must rely on friends, relatives, charity, or the state to carry out their contribution to bringing up children and being good citizens.

Among liberals there is an emerging consensus that the current economic structure leads to two kinds of underinvestment in children that are implicated in their later dependency—material poverty, characteristic of the poor, and "time" poverty, characteristic of the middle class.

Thirty years ago Daniel Patrick Moynihan perceived that material poverty and job loss for a man put strain on the marriage, sometimes to the point that he would leave. His children also did less well in school.[39] Rand Conger, in his studies of Iowa families who lost their farms during the 1980s, found that economic hardship not only puts strain on the marriage but leads to harsh parenting practices and poorer outcomes for children.[40] Thus it appears possible that poverty may not just be the result of family separation, divorce, and ineffective childrearing practices; it may also be the *cause* of the irritability, quarrels, and violence which lead to marital breakdown. Material underinvestment in children is visible not just with the poor but in the changing ratio of per capita income of children and adults in U.S. society as a whole. As the proportion of households without children has doubled over the last century (from 30 to 65 percent, per capita income of children has fallen from 71 percent of adult income in 1870 to 63 percent in 1930 and 51 percent in 1983.[41]

The problem of "time" poverty used to be almost exclusively associated with mothers' employment. Numerous studies explored whether younger children did better if their mother was a full-time homemaker rather than employed outside the home but found no clear results.[42] Lately the lack of parental time for children has become much more acute because parents are working a total of twenty-one hours more per week than in 1970 and because there are more single-parent families. In 1965 the average child spent about thirty hours a week interacting with a parent, compared with seventeen hours in the 1980s.[43] Moreover, parents are less dependent on their children to provide support for them during old age, and children feel less obligated to do so. As skilled craftsmanship, the trades, and the family farms have disappeared, children's upbringing can no longer be easily or cheaply combined with what parents are already doing. So adults are no longer so invested in children's futures. The result is that where the social capital of group affiliations and mutual obligations is the lowest (in the form of continuity of neighborhoods, a two-parent family, or a parent's interest in higher education for her children), children are 20 percent more likely to drop out of high school.[44]

It is not that parents prefer their current feelings of being rushed, working too many hours, and having too little time with their families. Economist Juliet Schor reports that at least two-thirds of persons she surveyed about their desires for more family time versus more salary would take a cut in salary if it could mean more time with their families. Since this option is not realistically open to many, what parents appear to do is spend more money on their children as a substitute for spending more time with them.[45]

Fixing the Safety Net

Since liberals believe in a market economy with sufficient government regulation to assure justice and equality of opportunity, they support those measures which will eradicate the worst poverty and assure the healthy reproduction of the next generation.[46] What particularly worries them, however, is Charles Murray's observation that since 1970 the growth of government welfare programs has been associated with a *rise* in poverty among children. Payments to poor families with children, while not generous, have nevertheless enabled adults to be supported by attachment to their children.[47] Society is faced with a dilemma between addressing material poverty through further government subsidy and time poverty through policies on parental leave and working hours. It turns out that the United States is trying to do both.

Measures for addressing material poverty would stimulate various kinds of training and job opportunities. The Family Support Act of 1988 would move AFDC mothers off the welfare rolls by giving them job training and requiring them to join the labor force. Such action would bring their economic responsibility for supporting their children into line with their parental authority. A whole program of integrated supports for health insurance, job training, earned income tax credits for the working poor, child support by the noncustodial parent, and supported work is put forward by economist David Ellwood in *Poor Support*.[48] An opposite strategy is to consolidate authority over children with the state's economic responsibility for their care by encouraging group homes and adoption for children whose parents cannot support them economically.[49]

Means for addressing time poverty are evident in such legislative initiatives as the Family and Medical Leave Act of 1993. By encouraging employers to grant parental leave or other forms of flexible work time, government policy is recognizing the value of parents having more time with their children, but the beneficiaries of such change are largely middle-class families who can afford an unpaid parental leave.[50] Another tactic is to reform the tax law to discourage marital splitting. In a couple with two children in which the father earns $16,000 annually and the mother $9,000, joint tax filing gives them no special consideration. But if they file separately, each taking one child as a dependent, the woman will receive about $5,000 in Earned Income Tax Credit and an extra $2,000 in food stamps.[51] Changing the tax law to remove the incentives for splitting, establishing paternity of children born out of wedlock, and intensifying child support enforcement to recover economic support from fathers are all examples of state efforts to strengthen the kinship unit.

Interdependence: The Feminist Vision of Work and Caregiving

A feminist perspective has elements in common with both conservatives and liberals, a respect for the family as an institution (shared with the conservatives) and an appreciation of modernity (valued by the liberals). In addition, a feminist perspective grapples with the problem of women's traditionally subordinate status and how to improve it through both a "relational" and an "individualist" strategy while also sustaining family life and the healthy rearing of children.[52] At the same time feminists are skeptical of both conservative and liberal solutions. Traditionalists have so often relied on women as the exploited and underpaid caregivers in the family to enable men's activities in the public realm. Liberals are sometimes guilty of a "male" bias in focusing on the independent individual actor in the marketplace who does not realize that his so-called "independence" is possible only because he is actually *dependent* on all kinds of relationships that made possible his education and life in a stable social order.[53]

By articulating the value of caregiving along with the ideal of women's autonomy, feminists are in a position to examine modern capitalism critically for its effects on families and to offer alternative policies that place greater value on the quality of life and human relationships. They judge family strength not by their *form* (whether they have two-parents) but by their functioning (whether they promote human satisfaction and development) and whether both women and men are able to be family caregivers as well as productive workers. They attribute difficulties of children less to the absence of the two-parent family than to low-wage work of single mothers, inadequate child care, and inhospitable housing and neighborhoods.

Feminist Model

Lack of cooperation among community, family, and work	→	Families where adults are stressed and overburdened	→	Children lack sufficient care and attention from parents

Accordingly, feminists would work for reforms that build and maintain the social capital of volunteer groups, neighborhoods, and communities because a healthy civil society promotes the well-being of families and individuals as well as economic prosperity and a democratic state. They would also recognize greater role flexibility across the life cycle so that both men and women could engage in caregiving, and they would encourage education and employment among women as well as among men.

Disappearance of Community

From a feminist perspective, family values have become an issue because individualism has driven out the sense of collective responsibility in our national culture. American institutions and social policies have not properly implemented a concern for all citizens. Comparative research on family structure, teenage pregnancy, poverty, and child outcomes in other countries demonstrates that where support is generous to help *all* families and children, there are higher levels of health and general education and lower levels of violence and child deviance than in the United States.[54]

Liberal thinking and the focus on the free market have made it seem that citizens make their greatest contribution when they are self-sufficient, thereby keeping themselves off the public dole. But feminist theorist Iris Young argues that many of the activities that are basic to a healthy democratic society (such as cultural production, caretaking, political organizing, and charitable activities) will never be profitable in a private market. Yet many of the recipients of welfare and Social Security such as homemakers, single mothers, and retirees are doing important volunteer work caring for children and helping others in their communities. Thus the social worth of a person's contribution is not just in earning a paycheck that shows economic independence but also in making a social contribution. Such caretaking of other dependent citizens and of the body politic should be regarded as honorable, not inferior, and worthy of society's support and subsidy.[55]

In fact it appears that married women's rising labor force participation from 41 percent in 1970 to 58 percent in 1990 may have been associated with their withdrawal from unpaid work in the home and community.[56] Volunteer membership in everything from the PTA to bowling leagues declined by over 25 percent between 1969 and 1993. There is now considerable concern that the very basis that Alexis de Tocqueville thought necessary to democracy is under siege.[57] To reverse this trend, social observers suggest that it will be necessary to guard time for families and leisure that is currently being sucked into the maw of paid employment. What is needed is a reorientation of priorities to give greater value to unpaid family and community work by both men and women.

National policies should also be reoriented to give universal support to children at every economic level of society, but especially to poor children. In a comparison of countries in the Organization for Economic Cooperation and Development, the United States ranks at the top in average male wages but near the bottom in its provision for disposable income for children. In comparison with the $700 per month available to children in Norway, France, or the Netherlands in 1992, U.S. children of a single nonemployed mother received only sightly under $200.[58] The discrepancy is explained by very unequal distribution of U.S. income, with the top quintile, the "fortunate fifth," gaining 47 percent of the national income while the bottom fifth receives only 3.6 percent.[59] This sharp inequality is, in turn, explained by an ideology of individualism that justifies the disproportionate gains of the few for their innovation and productivity and the meager income of the poor for their low initiative or competence. Lack of access to jobs and the low pay accruing to many contingent service occupations simply worsen the picture.

Feminists are skeptical of explanations that ascribe higher productivity to the higher paid and more successful leading actors while ignoring the efforts and contribution of the supporting cast. They know that being an invisible helper is the situation of many women. This insight is congruent with new ideas about the importance of "social capital" to the health of a society that have been put forward recently by a number of social scientists.[60] Corporations cannot be solely responsible for maintaining the web of community, although they are already being asked to serve as extended family, neighborhood support group, and national health service.

Diversity of Family Forms

Those who are concerned for strengthening the civil society immediately turn to the changing nature of the family as being a key building block. Feminists worry that seemingly sensible efforts to reverse the trend of rising divorce and single parenthood will privilege the two-parent family to the detriment of women; they propose instead that family values be understood in a broader sense as valuing the family's unique capacity for giving emotional and material support rather than implying simply a two-parent form.

The debate between conservatives, liberals, and feminists on the issue of the two-parent family has been most starkly stated by sociologist Judith Stacey and political philosopher Iris Young.[61] They regard the requirement that all women stay in a marriage as an invitation to coercion and subordination and an assault on the principles of freedom and self-determination that are at the foundation of democracy. Moreover, as Christopher Jencks and Kathryn Edin conclude from their study of several hundred welfare families, the current welfare reform rhetoric that no couple should have a child unless they can support it, does not take into account the uncertainty of life in which people who start out married or with adequate income may not always remain so. In the face of the worldwide dethronement of the two-parent family (approximately one-quarter to one-third of all families around the globe are headed by women), marriage should not be seen as the cure for child poverty. Mothers should not be seen as less than full citizens if they are not married or not employed (in 1989 there were only 16 million males between the ages of 25 and 34 who made over $12,000 compared with 20 million females of the same age who either had a child or wanted one).[62] National family policy should instead begin with a value on women's autonomy and self-determination that includes the right to bear children. Mother-citizens are helping to reproduce the next generation for the whole society, and in that responsibility they deserve at least partial support.

From a feminist perspective the goal of the family is not only to bring up a healthy and productive new generation; families also provide the intimate and supportive group of kin or fictive kin that foster the health and well-being of every person—young or old, male or female, heterosexual, homosexual, or celibate. Recognition as "family" should therefore not be confined to the traditional two-parent unit connected by blood, marriage, or adoption, but should be extended to include kin of a divorced spouse (as Stacey documented in her study of Silicon Valley families), same-sex partnerships, congregate households of retired persons, group living arrangements, and so on.[63] Twenty years ago economist Nancy Barrett noted that such diversity in family and household form was already present. Among all U.S. households in 1976, no one of the six major types constituted more than 15–20 percent: couples with and without children under eighteen with the wife in the labor force (15.4 and 13.3 percent respectively); couples with or without children under 18 with the wife not in the labor force (19.1 and 17.1 percent); female- or male-headed households (14.4 percent); and single persons living alone (20.6 percent).[64]

Such diversity both describes and informs contemporary "family values" in the United States. Each family type is numerous enough to have a legitimacy of its own, yet no single form is the dominant one. As a result the larger value system has evolved to encompass beliefs and rules that legitimate each type on the spectrum. The regressive alternative is "fundamentalism" that treats the two-parent family with children as the only legitimate form, single-parent families as unworthy of support, and the nontraditional forms as illegitimate. In 1995 the general population appears to have accepted diversity of family forms as normal. A Harris poll of 1,502 women and 460 men found that only two percent of women and one percent of men defined family as "being about the traditional nuclear family." One out of ten women defined family values as loving, taking care of, and supporting each other, knowing right from wrong or having good values, and nine out of ten said society should value all types of families.[65] It appears most Americans believe that an Aunt Polly single-parent type of family for a Huck Finn that provides economic support, shelter, meals, a place to sleep and to withdraw is better than no family at all.

Amidst gradual acceptance of greater diversity in family form, the gender-role revolution is also loosening the sex-role expectations traditionally associated with breadwinning and homemaking. Feminists believe that men and women can each do both.[66] In addition, women in advanced industrial nations have by and large converged upon a new life pattern of multiple roles by which they combine work and family life. The negative outcome is an almost universal "double burden" for working women in which they spend eighty-four hours per week on paid and family work, married men spend seventy-two hours, and single persons without children spend fifty hours.[67] The positive consequence, however, appears to be improved physical and mental health for those women who, though stressed, combine work and family roles.[68] In addition, where a woman's husband helps her more with the housework, she is less likely to think of getting a divorce.[69]

The Precarious Situation of Children

The principal remedy that conservatives and liberals would apply to the problems of children is to restore the two-parent family by reducing out-of-wedlock births, increasing the presence of fathers, and encouraging couples who are having marital difficulties to avoid divorce for the sake of their children. Feminists, on the other hand, are skeptical that illegitimacy, father absence, or divorce are the principal culprits they are made out to be. Leon Eisenberg reports that *over half of all births in Sweden* and *one-quarter of births in France* are to unmarried women, but without the disastrous correlated effects observed in the United States. Arlene Skolnick and Stacey Rosencrantz cite longitudinal studies showing that most children recover from the immediate negative effects of divorce.[70]

How then, while supporting the principle that some fraction of women should be able to head families as single parents, do feminists analyze the problem of ill health, antisocial behavior, and poverty among children? Their answer focuses on the *lack of institutional supports* for the new type of dual-earner and single-parent families that are more prevalent today. Rather than attempt to force families back into the traditional mold, feminists note that divorce, lone-mother families, and women's employment are on the rise in every industrialized nation. But other countries have not seen the same devastating decline in child well-being, teen pregnancy, suicides and violent death, school failure, and a rising population of children in poverty. These other countries have four key elements of social and family policy which protect all children and their mothers: (1) work guarantees and other economic supports; (2) child care; (3) health care; and (4) housing subsidies. In the United States these benefits are scattered and uneven; those who can pay their way do so; only those who are poor or disabled receive AFDC for economic support, some help with child care, Medicaid for health care, and government-subsidized housing.

A first line of defense is to raise women's wages through raising the minimum wage, then provide them greater access to male-dominated occupations with higher wages. One-half of working women do not earn a wage adequate to support a family of four above the poverty line. Moreover, women in low-wage occupations are subject to frequent lay-offs and lack of benefits. Training to improve their human capital, provision of child care, and broadening of benefits would help raise women's capacity to support a family. Eisenberg reports that the Human Development Index of the United Nations (HDI), which ranks countries by such indicators as life expectancy, educational levels, and per capita income, places the United States fifth and Sweden sixth in the world. But when the HDI is recalculated to take into account equity of treatment of women, Sweden rises to first place and the United States falls to ninth. Therefore, one of the obvious places to begin raising children's status is to raise the economic status and earning power of their mothers.[71]

A second major benefit which is not assured to working mothers is child care. Among school-age children up to thirteen years of age, one-eighth lack any kind of after-school child care. Children come to the factories where their mothers work and wait on the lawn or in the lobby until their mothers are finished working. If a child is sick, some mothers risk losing a job if they stay home. Others are latchkey kids or in unknown circumstances, such as sleeping in their parents' cars or loitering on the streets. Although 60 percent of mothers of the 22 million preschool children are working, there are only 10 million child care places available, a shortfall of one to three million slots.[72] Lack of good quality care for her children not only distracts a mother, adds to her absences from work, and makes her less productive, it also exposes the child to a lack of attention and care that leads to violent and antisocial behavior and poor performance in school.

Lack of medical benefits is a third gaping hole for poor children and lone-parent families. Jencks and Edin analyze what happens to a Chicago-area working woman's income if she goes off welfare. Her total income in 1993 dollars on AFDC (with food stamps, unreported earnings, help from family and friends) adds up to $12,355, in addition to which she receives Medicaid and child care. At a $6 per hour full-time job, however, without AFDC, with less than half as much from food stamps, with an Earned Income Tax Credit, and help from relatives, her total income would add to $20,853. But she would have to pay for her own medical care, bringing her effective income down to $14,745 if she found free child care, and $9,801 if she had to pay for child care herself.[73]

Some housing subsidies or low-income housing are available to low-income families. But the neighborhoods and schools are frequently of poor quality and plagued by violence. To bring up children in a setting where they cannot safely play with others introduces important risk factors that cannot simply be attributed to divorce and single parenthood. Rather than being protected and being allowed to be innocent, children must learn to be competent at a very early age. The family, rather than being child-centered, must be adult-centered, not because parents are selfish or self-centered but because the institutions of the society have changed the context of family life.[74] These demands may be too much for children, and depression, violence, teen suicide, teen pregnancy, and school failure may result. But it would be myopic to think that simply restoring the two-parent family would be enough to solve all these problems.

Constructing Institutions for the Good Society

What is to be done? Rather than try to restore the two-parent family as the conservatives suggest or change the economy to provide more jobs as recommended by the liberals, the feminists focus on the need to revise and construct institutions to accommodate the new realities of work and family life. Such an undertaking requires, however, a broader interpretation of family values, a recognition that families benefit not only their members but the public interest, and fresh thinking about how to schedule work and family demands of everyday life as well as the entire life cycle of men and women.

The understanding of family values has to be extended in two ways. First, American values should be stretched to embrace all citizens, their children and families, whether they are poor, white or people of color, or living in a one-parent family. In 1977, Kenneth Keniston titled the report of the Carnegie Commission on Children *All Our Children*. Today many Americans still speak and act politically in ways suggesting that they *disown* other people's children as the next generation who will inherit the land and support the economy. Yet in the view of most feminists and other progressive reformers, all these children should be embraced for the long-term good of the nation.[75] By a commitment to "family values" feminists secondly intend to valorize the family as a distinctive intimate group of many forms that is needed by persons of all ages but especially children. To serve the needs of children and other dependent persons, the family must be given support and encouragement by the state to carry out its unique functions. Iris Young contends that marriage should not be used to reduce the ultimate need for the state to serve as a means to distribute needed supports to the families of those less fortunate.[76] Compare the example of the GI Bill of Rights after World War II, which provided educational benefits to those who had served their country in the military. Why should there not be a similar approach to the contribution that a parent makes in raising a healthy and productive youngster?[77]

At the community level families should be embraced by all the institutions of the civil society—schools, hospitals, churches, and employers—as the hidden but necessary complement to the bureaucratic and impersonal workings of these formal organizations. Schools rely on parents for the child's "school readiness." Hospitals send home patients who need considerable home care before becoming completely well. The work of the church is carried out and reinforced in the family; and when families fail, it is the unconditional love and intimacy of family that the church tries to replicate. Employers depend on families to give the rest, shelter, emotional support, and other maintenance of human capital that will motivate workers and make them productive. Increasingly, the professionals and managers in these formal organizations are realizing that they need to work more closely with parents and family members if they are to succeed.

Feminists would especially like to see the reintegration of work and family life that was torn apart at the time of the industrial revolution when productive work moved out of the home and into the factory. Several proposals appear repeatedly: parental leave (which now is possible through the Family and Medical Leave Act of 1993); flexible hours and part-time work shared by working parents but without loss of benefits and promotion opportunities; home-based work; child care for sick children and after-school supervision. Although some progress has been made, acceptance of these reforms has been very slow. Parental leave is still *unpaid*. The culture of the workplace discourages many persons from taking advantage of the more flexible options which do exist because they fear they will be seen as less serious and dedicated workers. In addition, most programs are aimed at mothers and at managers, although there is growing feeling that fathers and hourly workers should be included as well.[78]

Ultimately these trends may alter the shape of women's and men's life cycles. Increasingly, a new ideal for the life course is being held up as the model that society should work toward. Lotte Bailyn proposes reorganization of careers in which young couples trade off periods of intense work commitment with each other while they establish their families so that either or both can spend more time at home.[79] Right now both women and men feel they must work so intensely to establish their careers that they have too little time for their children.[80] For the poor and untrained, the problem is the opposite: childbearing and childrearing are far more satisfying and validating than a low-paying, dead-end job. The question is how to reorient educators or employers to factor in time with family as an important obligation to society (much as one would factor in military service, for example). Such institutional reorganization is necessary to give families and childrearing their proper place in the modern postindustrial society.

Conclusion

A review of the conservative, liberal, and feminist perspectives on the changing nature of the American family suggests that future policy should combine the distinctive contributions of all three. From the conservatives comes a critique of modernity that recognizes the important role of the family in maintaining child health and preventing child failure. Although their understanding of "family values" is too narrow, they deserve credit for raising the issue of family function and form to public debate. Liberals see clearly the overwhelming power of the economy to deny employment, make demands on parents as workers, and drive a wedge between employers' needs for competitiveness and families' needs for connection and community.

Surprising though it may seem, since feminists are often imagined to be "way out," the most comprehensive plan for restoring family to its rightful place is put forward by feminists who appreciate both the inherently premodern nature of the family and at the same time its inevitable interdependence with a fast-changing world economy. Feminists will not turn back to the past because they know that the traditional family was often a straightjacket for women. But they also know that family cannot be turned into a formal organization or have its functions performed by government or other public institutions that are incapable of giving needed succor to children, adults, and old people which only the family can give.

The feminist synthesis accepts both the inherent particularism and emotional nature of the family and the inevitable specialization and impersonality of the modern economy. Feminists are different from conservatives in accepting diversity of the family to respond to the needs of the modern economy. They are different from the liberals in recognizing that intimate nurturing relationships such as parenting cannot all be turned into a safety net of formal care. The most promising social policies for families and children take their direction from inclusive values that confirm the good life and the well-being of every individual as the ultimate goal of the nation. The policy challenge is to adjust the partnership between the family and its surrounding institutions so that together they combine the best of private initiative with public concern.

Notes

1. Barbara Dafoe Whitehead, "Dan Quayle Was Right," *Atlantic Monthly* (April 1993): 47. Her chapter in this volume on the "Story of Marriage" continues

the theme of an erosion of values under the guise of tolerance for cultural diversity.

2. Mary Ann Glendon, "Marriage and the State: The Withering Away of Marriage," *Virginia Law Review* 62 (May 1976): 663–729.

3. See chapters by Milton Regan and Carl Schneider in this volume.

4. Charles A. Murray, *Losing Ground: American Social Policy, 1950–1980* (New York: Basic Books, 1984). Critics point out that the rise in out-of-wedlock births continues, even though welfare payments have declined in size over the last several decades, thereby casting doubt on the perverse incentive theory of rising illegitimacy.

5. U.S. Bureau of the Census, *Statistical Abstract of the United States: 1994*, 114th ed. (Washington, DC: 1994), 59.

6. Suzanne M. Bianchi and Daphne Spain, *American Women in Transition* (New York: Russell Sage Foundation, 1986), 88.

7. Donald J. Hernandez, *America's Children: Resources from Family, Government, and the Economy* (New York: Russell Sage Foundation, 1993), 284, 70; Janet Zollinger Giele, "Woman's Role Change and Adaptation, 1920–1990," in *Women's Lives through Time: Educated American Women of the Twentieth Century*, ed. K. Hulbert and D. Schuster (San Francisco: Jossey-Bass, 1993), 40.

8. Victor Fuchs, "Are Americans Underinvesting in Children?" in *Rebuilding the Nest*, ed. David Blankenhorn, Stephen Bayme, and Jean Bethke Elshtain (Milwaukee: Family Service America, 1990), 66. Bianchi and Spain, *American Women in Transition*, 141, 201, 226. Janet Zollinger Giele, "Gender and Sex Roles," in *Handbook of Sociology*, ed. N. J. Smelser (Beverly Hills, CA: Sage Publications, 1988), 300.

9. Hernandez, *America's Children*, 130. Council on Families in America, *Marriage in America* (New York: Institute for American Values, 1995), 7.

10. Fuchs, "Are Americans Underinvesting in Children?" 61. Some would say, however, that the decline was due in part to a larger and more heterogeneous group taking the tests.

11. Council on Families in America, *Marriage in America*, 6. The report cites research by Nicholas Zill and Charlotte A. Schoenborn, "Developmental, Learning and Emotional Problems: Health of Our Nation's Children, United States, 1988." *Advance Data*, National Center for Health Statistics, Publication # 120, November 1990. See also, Sara McLanahan and Gary Sandefur, *Growing Up with a Single Parent* (Cambridge, MA: Harvard University Press, 1994).

12. Edward Gilbreath, "Manhood's Great Awakening," *Christianity Today* (February 6, 1995): 27.

13. David Elkind, *The Hurried Child: Growing Up Too Fast Too Soon* (Reading, MA: Addison-Wesley, 1981).

14. Jean Bethke Elshtain, *Democracy on Trial* (New York: Basic Books, 1995).

15. Jonathan Alter and Pat Wingert, "The Return of Shame," *Newsweek* (February 6, 1995): 25.

16. Tom McNichol, "The New Sex Vow: 'I won't' until 'I do'," *USA Weekend*,

March 25–27, 1994, 4 ff. Lee Smith, "The New Wave of Illegitimacy," *Fortune* (April 18, 1994): 81 ff.

17. Susan Chira, "War over Role of American Fathers," *New York Times*, June 19, 1994, 22.

18. Juliet Schor, "Consumerism and the Decline of Family and Community: Preliminary Statistics from a Survey on Time, Money and Values," Harvard Divinity School, Seminar on Families and Family Policy, April 4, 1995.

19. Karen S. Peterson, "In Balancing Act, Scale Tips toward Family," *USA Today*, January 25, 1995.

20. Lawrence Mead, "Taxing Peter to Pay Paula," *Wall Street Journal*, November 2, 1994.

21. Tom G. Palmer, "English Lessons: Britain Rethinks the Welfare State," *Wall Street Journal*, November 2, 1994.

22. Robert Pear, "G.O.P. Affirms Plan to Stop Money for Unwed Mothers," *New York Times*, January 21, 1995, 9.

23. Brigitte Berger, "Block Grants: Changing the Welfare Culture from the Ground Up," *Dialogue* (Boston: Pioneer Institute for Public Policy Research), no. 3, March 1995.

24. Robert Rector, "Welfare," *Issues '94: The Candidate's Briefing Book* (Washington, DC: American Heritage Foundation, 1994), chap. 13.

25. Council on Families in America, *Marriage in America*, 13–16.

26. Robert Bellah, "Invasion of the Money World," in *Rebuilding the Nest*, ed. David Blankenhorn, Steven Bayme, and Jean Bethke Elshtain (Milwaukee: Family Service America, 1990), 227–36. James Coleman, *Foundations of Social Theory* (Cambridge, MA: Harvard University Press, 1990).

27. Sylvia Nasar, "More Men in Prime of Life Spend Less Time Working," *New York Times*, December 1, 1994, A1.

28. John Scanzoni, *Power Politics in the American Marriage* (Englewood Cliffs, NJ: Prentice-Hall, 1972). Ruth A. Wallace and Alison Wolf, *Contemporary Sociological Theory* (Englewood Cliffs, NJ: Prentice-Hall, 1991), 176.

29. Fred Weinstein and Gerald M. Platt, *The Wish to Be Free: Society, Psyche, and Value Change* (Berkeley, CA: University of California Press, 1969).

30. Kingsley Davis, "Wives and Work: A Theory of the Sex-Role Revolution and Its Consequences," in *Feminism, Children, and the New Families*, ed. S. M. Dornbusch and M. H. Strober (New York: Guilford Press, 1988), 67–86. Janet Zollinger Giele, *Two Paths to Women's Equality: Temperance, Suffrage, and the Origins of American Feminism* (New York: Twayne Publishers, Macmillan, 1995).

31. Vivianna A. Zelizer, *Pricing the Priceless Child: The Changing Social Value of Children* (New York: Basic Books, 1985).

32. William J. Goode, *World Revolution in Family Patterns* (New York: The Free Press, 1963).

33. Constance Willard Williams, *Black Teenage Mothers: Pregnancy and Child Rearing from Their Perspective* (Lexington, MA: Lexington Books, 1990).

34. William Julius Wilson, *The Truly Disadvantaged: The Inner City, the Underclass, and Public Policy*, (Chicago: University of Chicago Press, 1987).

35. Jacob Mincer, "Labor-force Participation of Married Women: A Study of Labor Supply," in *Aspects of Labor Economics*, Report of the National Bureau of Economic Research (Princeton, NJ: Universities-National Bureau Committee of Economic Research, 1962). Glen G. Cain, *Married Women in the Labor Force: An Economic Analysis* (Chicago: University of Chicago Press, 1966).

36. Richard A. Easterlin, *Birth and Fortune: The Impact of Numbers on Personal Welfare* (New York: Basic Books, 1980). Valerie K. Oppenheimer, "Structural Sources of Economic Pressure for Wives to Work—Analytic Framework" *Journal of Family History* 4, no. 2 (1979): 177–97; and Valerie K. Oppenheimer, *Work and the Family: A Study in Social Demography* (New York: Academic Press, 1982).

37. Janet Z. Giele and Rainer Pischner, "The Emergence of Multiple Role Patterns Among Women: A Comparison of Germany and the United States," *Vierteljahrshefte zur Wirtschaftsforschung* (Applied Economics Quarterly) (Heft 1–2, 1994). Alice S. Rossi, "The Future in the Making," *American Journal of Orthopsychiatry* 63, no. 2 (1993): 166–76. Notburga Ott, *Intrafamily Bargaining and Household Decisions* (Berlin: Springer-Verlag, 1992).

38. Iris Young, "Mothers, Citizenship and Independence: A Critique of Pure Family Values," *Ethics* 105, no. 3 (1995): 535–56. Young critiques the liberal stance of William Galston, *Liberal Purposes* (New York: Cambridge University Press, 1991).

39. Lee Rainwater and William L. Yancey, *The Moynihan Report and the Politics of Controversy* (Cambridge, MA: MIT Press, 1967).

40. Glen H. Elder, Jr., *Children of the Great Depression* (Chicago: University of Chicago Press, 1974). Rand D. Conger, Xiao-Jia Ge, and Frederick O. Lorenz, "Economic Stress and Marital Relations," in *Families in Troubled Times: Adapting to Change in Rural America*, ed. R. D. Conger and G. H. Elder, Jr. (New York: Aldine de Gruyter, 1994), 187–203.

41. Coleman, *Foundations of Social Theory*, 590.

42. Elizabeth G. Menaghan and Toby L. Parcel, "Employed Mothers and Children's Home Environments," *Journal of Marriage and the Family* 53, no. 2 (1991): 417–31. Lois Hoffman, "The Effects on Children of Maternal and Paternal Employment," in *Families and Work*, ed. Naomi Gerstel and Harriet Engel Gross (Philadelphia: Temple University Press, 1987), 362–95.

43. Juliet Schor, *The Overworked American: The Unexpected Decline of Leisure* (New York: Basic Books, 1991). Robert Haveman and Barbara Wolfe, *Succeeding Generations: On the Effects of Investments in Children* (New York: Russell Sage Foundation, 1994), 239.

44. Coleman, *Foundations of Social Theory*, 596–97.

45. Schor, "Consumerism and Decline of Family."

46. Iris Young, "Mothers, Citizenship and Independence," puts Elshtain, Etzioni, Galston, and Whitehead in this category.

47. Coleman, *Foundations of Social Theory*, 597–609.

48. Sherry Wexler, "To Work and To Mother: A Comparison of the Family

Support Act and the Family and Medical Leave Act" (Ph.D. diss. draft, Brandeis University, 1995). David T. Ellwood, *Poor Support: Poverty in the American Family* (New York: Basic Books, 1988).

49. Coleman, *Foundations of Social Theory*, 300–21. Coleman, known for rational choice theory in sociology, put forward these theoretical possibilities in 1990, fully four years ahead of what in 1994 was voiced in the Republican Contract with America.

50. Wexler, "To Work and To Mother."

51. Robert Lerman, "Marketplace," National Public Radio, April 18, 1995.

52. Karen Offen, "Defining Feminism: A Comparative Historical Approach," *Signs* 14, no. 1 (1988): 119–51.

53. Young, "Mothers, Citizenship and Independence."

54. Robert N. Bellah et al., *Habits of the Heart* (Berkeley, CA: University of California Press, 1985), 250–71. Gosta Esping-Andersen, *The Three Worlds of Welfare Capitalism* (Princeton, NJ: Princeton University Press, 1990). Susan Pedersen, *Family, Dependence, and the Origins of the Welfare State: Britain and France, 1914–1945* (New York: Cambridge University Press, 1993).

55. Young, "Mothers, Citizenship and Independence."

56. Giele, "Woman's Role Change and Adaptation" presents these historical statistics.

57. Elshtain, *Democracy on Trial*; Robert N. Bellah et al., *The Good Society* (New York: Knopf, 1991), 210; Robert D. Putnam, "Bowling Alone: America's Declining Social Capital," *Journal of Democracy* 4, no. 1 (1995): 65–78.

58. Heather McCallum, "Mind the Gap" (paper presented to the Family and Children's Policy Center colloquium, Waltham, MA, Brandeis University, March 23, 1995). The sum was markedly better for children of employed single mothers, around $700 per mother in the United States. But this figure corresponded with over $1,000 in eleven other countries, with only Greece and Portugal lower than the U.S. Concerning the high U.S. rates of teen pregnancy, see Planned Parenthood advertisement, "Let's Get Serious About Ending Teen Childbearing," *New York Times*, April 4, 1995, A25.

59. Ruth Walker, "Secretary Reich and the Disintegrating Middle Class," *Christian Science Monitor*, November 2, 1994, 19.

60. For reference to "social capital," see Coleman, *Foundations of Social Theory*; Elshtain, *Democracy on Trial*; and Putnam, "Bowling Alone." For "emotional capital," see Arlie Russell Hochschild, *The Managed Heart: The Commercialization of Human Feeling* (Berkeley, CA: University of California Press, 1983). For "cultural capital," see work by Pierre Bourdieu and Jurgen Habermas.

61. Judith Stacey, "Dan Quayle's Revenge: The New Family Values Crusaders," *The Nation*, July 25/August 1, 1994, 119–22. Iris Marion Young, "Making Single Motherhood Normal," *Dissent* (winter 1994): 88–93.

62. Christopher Jencks and Kathryn Edin, "Do Poor Women Have a Right to Bear Children," *The American Prospect* (winter 1995): 43–52.

63. Stacey, "Dan Quayle's Revenge"; Arlene Skolnick and Stacey Rosencrantz, "The New Crusade for the Old Family," *The American Prospect* (summer 1994): 59–65.

64. Nancy Smith Barrett, "Data Needs for Evaluating the Labor Market Status of Women," in *Census Bureau Conference on Federal Statistical Needs Relating to Women*, ed. Barbara B. Reagan (U.S. Bureau of the Census, 1979) Current Population Reports, Special Studies, Series P-23, no. 83, pp. 10–19. These figures belie the familiar but misleading statement that "only 7 percent" of all American families are of the traditional nuclear type because "traditional" is defined so narrowly—as husband and wife with two children under 18 where the wife is not employed outside the home. For more recent figures and a similar argument for a more universal family ethic, see Christine Winquist Nord and Nicholas Zill, "American Households in Demographic Perspective," working paper no. 5, Institute for American Values, New York, 1991.

65. Tamar Levin, "Women Are Becoming Equal Providers," *New York Times*, May 11, 1995, A27.

66. Marianne A. Ferber and Julie A. Nelson, *Beyond Economic Man: Feminist Theory and Economics* (Chicago: University of Chicago Press, 1993).

67. Fran Sussner Rodgers and Charles Rodgers, "Business and the Facts of Family Life," *Harvard Business Review*, no. 6 (1989): 199–213, especially 206.

68. Ravenna Helson and S. Picano, "Is the Traditional Role Bad for Women?" *Journal of Personality and Social Psychology* 59 (1990): 311–20. Rosalind C. Barnett, "Home-to-Work Spillover Revisited: A Study of Full-Time Employed Women in Dual-Earner Couples," *Journal of Marriage and the Family* 56 (August 1994): 647–56.

69. Arlie Hochschild, "The Fractured Family," *The American Prospect* (summer 1991): 106–15.

70. Leon Eisenberg, "Is the Family Obsolete?" *The Key Reporter* 60, no. 3 (1995): 1–5. Arlene Skolnick and Stacey Rosencrantz, "The New Crusade for the Old Family," *The American Prospect* (summer 1994): 59–65.

71. Roberta M. Spalter-Roth, Heidi I. Hartmann, and Linda M. Andrews, "Mothers, Children, and Low-Wage Work: The Ability to Earn a Family Wage," in *Sociology and the Public Agenda*, ed. W. J. Wilson (Newbury Park, CA: Sage Publications, 1993), 316–38.

72. Louis Uchitelle, "Lacking Child Care, Parents Take Their Children to Work," *New York Times*, December 23, 1994, 1.

73. Jencks and Edin, "Do Poor Women Have a Right," 50.

74. David Elkind, *Ties That Stress: The New Family in Balance* (Boston: Harvard University Press, 1994).

75. It is frequently noted that the U.S. is a much more racially diverse nation than, say, Sweden, which has a concerted family and children's policy. Symptomatic of the potential for race and class division that impedes recognition of all children as the nation's children is the book by Richard J. Herrnstein and Charles A. Murray, *The Bell Curve: Intelligence and Class Structure in American Life* (New York: The Free Press, 1994).

76. Young, "Making Single Motherhood Normal," 93.

77. If the objection is that the wrong people will have children, as Herrnstein and Murray suggest in *The Bell Curve*, then the challenge is to find ways for poor women to make money or have some other more exciting career that will offset the rewards of having children, "such as becoming the bride of Christ or the head of a Fortune 500 corporation," to quote Jencks and Edin, "Do Poor Women Have a Right," 48.

78. Beth M. Miller, "Private Welfare: The Distributive Equity of Family Benefits in America" (Ph.D. thesis, Brandeis University, 1992). Sue Shellenbarger, "Family-Friendly Firms Often Leave Fathers Out of the Picture," *Wall Street Journal*, November 2, 1994. Richard T. Gill and T. Grandon Gill, *Of Families, Children, and a Parental Bill of Rights* (New York: Institute for American Values, 1993). For gathering information on these new work-family policies, I wish to acknowledge help of students in my 1994–95 Family Policy Seminar at Brandeis University, particularly Cathleen O'Brien, Deborah Gurewich, Alissa Starr, and Pamela Swain, as well as the insights of two Ph.D students, Mindy Fried and Sherry Wexler.

79. Lotte Bailyn, *Breaking the Mold: Women, Men and Time in the New Corporate World* (New York: The Free Press, 1994).

80. Penelope Leach, *Children First: What Our Society Must Do and Is Doing* (New York: Random House, 1994).

PART TWO

Religious, Legal, and Clinical Dimensions

CHAPTER 6

Biology, Ethics, and Narrative in Christian Family Theory

Don S. Browning

Narrative and Biology in Christian Thomism

Christianity has had enormous influence on the marriage and family theory of Western societies. This influence, however, is not well understood. Furthermore, it is widely believed in most intellectual quarters that this influence is over. It is difficult to believe that this prediction is entirely accurate, especially in view of the continuing high percentage of individuals who consider themselves generally Christian, especially in the United States. Furthermore, there has been extensive impact of Christian symbols and beliefs on wider aspects of our cultural understandings and institutions—especially the law. It is not widely understood that Christian understandings are complex and a product of several interacting lines of knowledge and judgment.

In this chapter, I will illustrate how biological, ethical, and narrative dimensions of moral thinking have become interwoven in certain formative texts shaping Christian marriage and family theory in Western societies. I also will venture a hypothesis about an overlooked basic feature of Christian family theory—that some of its classic formulations served to remedy what I will call the "male problematic." By the male problematic, I mean a central ambivalence in males about which of two evolutionarily successful ways of organizing their sexuality they will follow at any moment in history.

It will be useful to illustrate some contemporary manifestations of the

119

male problematic and then go backward in history to Thomas Aquinas, then to the Gospels, then Aristotle, and finally to the Epistle to the Ephesians. I make these moves to demonstrate how these ancient sources may have addressed this male ambivalence. I must warn the reader now that, although we will spend much time investigating the role of sacrificial love in overcoming the male problematic, I will hold that equal regard is the deeper meaning of Christian love.

Allow me to gradually build the meaning of the male problematic by beginning with the contemporary experience of families in technologically advanced societies. The most dramatic change in families throughout the industrial world is the retreat of biological fathers from families and children.[1] This trend is integrally related to another, that is, the move of mothers—with the help of increased reliance on the wage economy, the government, and various informal networks—toward increasingly raising their children without significant presence of a father.[2] One-half of all children under 18 today spend some time in a single-parent home, generally the mother's. One-third will spend as much as six years without an immediate father present.[3] The absence of fathers, plus their failure on average to pay adequate child support, has now been cited as a leading reason that one-fifth of all mothers and their children in our nation are poor.[4] Furthermore, children of absent fathers are now believed on average to do more poorly in school, become more involved in crime, and have poorer health.[5] The factor of the absent father seems to be an independent variable that functions, as well, across class and economic lines.

Various reasons have been advanced to explain the growing absence of fathers from children. The move of men in the eighteenth and nineteenth centuries out of the family farm and business into a wage economy separated the male spheres of public life from the private spheres of domesticity and child care.[6] This created the modern, industrial family—the family we mistakenly call the traditional family. When women in the twentieth century entered the wage economy, they became more economically independent from their husbands. With less economic dependency, both men and women resorted more frequently to divorce and nonmarriage.[7] Government programs are thought to have taken the place, for many poor women, of the husband's financial support, leading some commentators to speak of "state polygamy"—the marriage of millions of women to the state which, indeed, some poor women sometimes call "the man."[8]

The post-Enlightenment cultural drive toward individualism is often cited as the great engine fueling these trends. Respected commentators as diverse as Robert Bellah, Christopher Lasch, Ron Lesthaeghe, and David Popenoe see modern individualism as an important underlying motive behind these more proximate economic trends—trends which Western societies seem to have neither the desire nor capacity to reverse.[9]

Human Evolutionary Ecology and the Male Problematic

All these factors may be operating to produce this grand new issue facing postmodern families—the growing absence of fathers. Of course, there are powerful voices such as Judith Stacey, Judge Richard Posner, Stephanie Coontz (and more recently Iris Young) who believe that if the economic contributions of fathers can be replaced by higher incomes for mothers or better government supports, then father absence need be no major threat to the welfare of children.[10] But others disagree.[11] Human evolutionary ecology (sometimes called sociobiology, evolutionary psychology, or behavior biology) throws light on both the male problematic (the tendency of men to drift away from families) and why the father's contribution to children is more than material benefits alone, as important as these may be. Furthermore, the general knowledge about the conditions of male parental investment, I will argue, was known in the ancient world and provided the assumptive background beliefs to some of the key expressions of Christian family theory.

Human evolutionary ecology has developed, in recent years, powerful theories to explain the asymmetrical reproductive strategies of males and females and the conditions under which male parental investment emerges among homo sapiens. Three concepts from evolutionary ecology are important—the theories of inclusive fitness, kin altruism, and parental investment. The theory of inclusive fitness extends the official position in evolutionary theory that the individual is the basic unit of evolutionary retention and survival. This is still held to be true in the newer developments, but since the work of W. D. Hamilton in 1964, it is now thought that the individual includes the genes that he or she shares with close kin (50 percent with one's siblings and children, 25 percent with nephews, nieces, and grandchildren, 12.5 percent with first cousins, etc.).[12] Individuals, according to this perspective, do not just fight for their own survival; they also work for the survival and flourishing of their biological relatives. They do this because these genetically related individuals are literally extensions of themselves. This is the meaning of the concept of kin altruism or kin selection. It means that under some circumstances, individuals are willing to sacrifice their own inclusive fitness in direct proportion to the degree of genetic relatedness of the other and the degree of gain in the other's fitness in comparison to the loss of the one making the sacrifice.[13]

Finally, the concept of inclusive fitness has relevance for a theory of parental investment, which is in fact our main interest here. Parental investment is a concept developed by biologists Ronald Fisher and Robert Trivers. Trivers defines it as "any investment by the parent in an individual offspring that increases the offspring's chance of surviving (and hence reproductive success) at the cost of the parent's ability to invest in other offspring."[14] Evolutionary ecology is showing that both inclusive fitness and parental investment strategies are different for males and females of mammalian species. Females, because of their limited periods of child-bearing capacity and the energy required to carry infants to birth, put their investment in a relatively few offspring. The males of most mammalian species, on the other hand, follow a different strategy. They are inclined to mate with several different females, producing as many offspring as their life span permits, a potentially limitless number.[15] Males of almost all mammalian species, including most higher primates, make little or no parental investment in their offspring. The human male for much of his evolutionary history has been an exception.

According to evolutionary theorist Don Symons, by the time that hominids had left the forests and become hunter-gatherers in the open grasslands, males put behind the promiscuous pattern of inclusive fitness typical of their chimpanzee ancestors and became attached for the most part to a single female, formed a relatively egalitarian nuclear family, and helped care for their children.[16] Their primary contribution to their children was protein and protection, but studies of contemporary hunter-gathers such as the !Kung San suggest that these earliest fathers also may have cuddled their infants, fed them, played with them and later taught them various skills.[17]

Since these earliest hunter-gatherers, human males have, on the whole, joined females and followed what evolutionary theorists call the "K" rather than the "R" strategy of inclusive fitness. The K-strategy invests a large set of resources into raising only a few children to adulthood. This contrasts with the R-strategy, which procreates a large number of offspring (the case of fish and frogs), leaving it to luck as to whether a few survive.[18] The question is, how did this transition from what evolutionary theorists jokingly call the "cad" strategy to a "dad" strategy come about for the human male? How deeply grounded in male human nature is the so-called dad strategy? Is the cad strategy laying just below the surface of the male ego ready to manifest itself in actual social behavior?

Several factors worked together to bring the dad strategy into existence for males. First, there is the long period of dependency characteristic of the human infant and child in contrast to other mammalian infants; this condition puts more pressure on the mother to both feed and care for dependent children for many years. Infant dependency stimulated females to turn to males for assistance, protection, and food—particularly protein.

Second, conditions supporting paternal certainty began to emerge.[19] By parental certainty, I mean the recognition by a father that an infant is indeed his and not some other male's biological offspring. Although mammalian mothers are always certain that an infant is their biological offspring, males can only hold varying degrees of certainty about whether they are indeed the father. Trivers and others have argued that human males became parentally invested when they acquired the capacity to learn that a child was biologically theirs; they began to intuit that through their parental investment they were contributing to their own inclusive fitness by furthering the fitness of a child who carries their genes.[20] In those societies where paternal certainty is difficult to achieve because of high degrees of female sexual freedom, the mother's brother, who of course is also genetically related to the child, often becomes the surrogate father.[21]

Third, male parental investment also seems to be a part of a wider pattern of male helpfulness to a female in order to gain sex. In addition, males help with infants and children in return for help from females in their daily tasks. All this means that paternal investment is a part of reciprocal helpfulness between males and females. According to evolutionary ecologists, paternal certainty is a necessary, but not sufficient, condition for the development of paternal investment. Sexual exchange and reciprocal helpfulness also seem to be necessary.

An example of the interrelation of these conditions can be seen in Aka pygmies of central Africa, who show the highest level of male infant care in the world. Aka husbands and wives fish together. According to Barry Hewlett, a male takes care of children as a trade off for his wife's sexual favors and her help with the tasks of fishing.[22] From the standpoint of evolutionary theory, paternal investment is a result of paternal certainty, sexual exchange, and other forms of reciprocal altruism. The evolution of high levels of paternal investment in children among homo sapiens appears to be important for the flourishing of children, in spite of contemporary voices such as Stacey, Posner, Coontz, and others who play it down.[23] Others believe paternal investment was a key to the rise of civilization among homo sapiens and that its decline is one of our society's greatest threats.[24]

Biology and Narrative in Aquinas's Family Theory

It would seem a long distance from contemporary evolutionary ecology to the family theory of the great father of the Catholic Church, St. Thomas

Aquinas. The distance, however, is shorter than one might think. Aquinas's family theory depends, in part, on several crucial observations based on the comparative biology of his day—primarily the work of Aristotle—as well as on various refinements Aquinas found in the writings of his own teacher, Albertus Magnus.[25] In reading this great Catholic scholastic, we will begin to inhabit a world strangely close yet quite far from the powerful evolutionary ecological perspectives which we have just encountered.

Aquinas had his version of what I have called the male problematic. It was implicit in his theories of marriage and the family. The center of his theory of marriage was his belief that the symbol of Christ's union with the church described in Ephesians 5:20–33 was the foundation of marriage between baptized Christians. Paul Ricoeur's understanding of the relation of archeology and teleology in religious and artistic symbols gives a deeper understanding of the transformative meanings carried by that symbol of Christ's union with the church. Ricoeur, in *Freud and Philosophy* and other writings, argued that in order to interpret a symbol, one must understand the unconscious archeology that is brought to the symbol and, to some extent, transformed by it. A symbol, he argued, has a "mixed language" containing a primitive archeology based in natural inclinations plus a teleology pointing to a direction in which these inclinations are being called and, indeed, possibly transformed.[26] Ricoeur thought that the language of dreams, interpreted in part by the naturalism of Freud's theory of instinctual energies, might be a way of capturing this human archeology of desire.[27] In what follows, I will not use Freud, as did Ricoeur. I will use, instead, evolutionary ecology's theory of the asymmetrical patterns of inclusive fitness between males and females and determine what light it can throw on the archeology of human desire. The extent to which it is possible to find something like this same archeology of desire in Aquinas's theory of marriage and the family is surprising. It is important, however, to observe how this archeology of desire interacts with religious symbols and, at least to some extent, becomes altered by them.

Aquinas saw marriage as both a natural and a supernatural institution. As a natural institution, it is grounded in some deep inclinations—inclinations which must be refined by will, culture, and divine revelation if they are to become fully human. I will quote Aquinas rather heavily to convey the full flavor of his thought. In the "Supplement" to *Summa Theologica*, he writes that humans share with all animals an inclination to have offspring. Having asserted this, Aquinas introduces a very modern-sounding distinction.

Yet nature does not incline thereto in the same way in all animals; since there are animals whose offspring are able to seek food immediately after birth, or are sufficiently fed by their mother; and in these there is no tie between male and female; whereas in those whose offspring needs the support of both parents, although for a short time, there is a certain tie, as may be seen in certain birds. In man, however, since the child needs the parents' care for a long time, there is a very great tie between male and female, to which tie even the generic nature inclines.[28]

Aquinas, along with the modern evolutionary thinkers, believed that humans form families because of the long period of human infantile dependency. In the *Summa Contra Gentiles* he writes, "in those animals in which the female alone suffices for the rearing of the offspring, . . . the male and female do not remain together after coition."[29] The human female, he insists, is "far from sufficing alone for the rearing of children, since the needs of human life require many things that one person alone cannot provide."[30] For this reason, it is "in keeping with human nature that the man remain with the woman after coition, and not leave her at once, indulging in promiscuous intercourse. . . ."[31]

This last quote seems to suggest, as William James and Mary Midgley have argued so cogently in the twentieth century, that human beings (especially human males) are creatures of multiple impulses which sometimes conflict with one another.[32] Aquinas recognized that under certain conditions, males have inclinations to form families and assist females in raising children. But they also have other, possibly even more primal, inclinations toward promiscuity or something akin to what the evolutionary ecologists call the R-strategy of inclusive fitness. In the *Summa Contra Gentiles*, he writes that male animals desire "to indulge at will in the pleasure of copulation, even as in the pleasure of eating." For this reason, they fight with one another for access to females and they "resist another's intercourse with their consort."[33]

Aquinas, as do today's evolutionary theorists, recognized the role paternal certainty plays in forming monogamous relations between males and females. Aquinas held that human males have an instinct for paternal certainty. For modern evolutionists, however, paternal certainty is less an instinct and more a condition for paternal investment in their children. Nonetheless, let us hear his words: "Man naturally desires to be assured of his offspring: and this assurance would be altogether nullified in the case of promiscuous copulation. Therefore the union of one man with one woman comes from a natural instinct."[34]

Of course, even in the framework of Aquinas's own argument, this union cannot be seen as a result of any one instinct; rather, it is the result of a compromise and reorganization of a wide range of inclinations which permit and enhance multiple satisfactions pertaining to pleasure, child-rearing, safety, and inclusive fitness. Although Aquinas had no concept of inclusive fitness in the technical sense we use it today, he did hold some features of that idea. For instance, he taught that fathers care for their children as a way of enhancing their own immortality. With a distinctively masculine bias typical of his day, he wrote, "since the natural life which cannot be preserved in the person of an undying father, is preserved, by a kind of succession, in the person of the son, it is naturally befitting that the son succeed in things belonging to the father."[35] As Aristotle said before him in the *Politics* and evolutionary ecologists say today, Aquinas believed that, on the whole, parental investment (including paternal investment) follows parental certainty.

We already have heard the voice of the evolutionary ecologists. Let's consider Aristotle since he provides the intellectual background to Aquinas. In one place Aristotle wrote, "in common with other animals and with plants, mankind have a natural desire to leave behind them an image of themselves."[36] This sense that a child is a kind of copy of the parents, Aristotle believed to be, as a general rule, crucial for parental care and interest in their children. This is why he opposed Plato's thought experiment in *The Republic*; it proposed that civil harmony would be enhanced if the state raised the children and parents were ignorant about which children were theirs. Aristotle believed this would lead to the general neglect of all children. He wrote, "that which is common to the greatest number has the least care bestowed upon it."[37] Hence, for Aristotle, parental investment comes with parental recognition. He thought that in Plato's state, "love will be watery. . . . Of the two qualities which chiefly inspire regard and affection—that a thing is your own and that it is your only one—neither can exist in such a state as this."[38] Aquinas, it is clear, sided with Aristotle, not Plato, on this matter and incorporated the Aristotelian perspective into his Christian theory of the family.

Although Aquinas agreed with Aristotle that, as a general rule, parental recognition or certainty is a positive contribution to high levels of parental investment, he was close to contemporary evolutionary theorists in believing this certainty is much easier to achieve for females than males. Because females carry the infant and give birth to it, they know the child is theirs. Males never know with absolute certainty that a particular child is theirs, although there are some circumstances of procreation which provide higher degrees of certainty than others. Aquinas was in step, at least, with the general contours of evolutionary theorists when he wrote,

In every animal species where the father has a certain care for his offspring, the one male has but one female, as may be seen in birds, where both unite in feeding their young. On the other hand where the male animal has not the care of the offspring, we find indifferently union of one male with several females, or of one female with several males: such is the case with dogs, hens, and so forth.[39]

In short, Thomas believed—as human ecologists Martin Daly, Margo Wilson, Donald Symons, and Robert Trivers do today—that paternal investment in children, paternal certainty, and monogamy tend to go together. Contemporary evolutionary ecologists are clearer than Aquinas about how paternal certainty is supplemented by two other conditions, as we saw above, before paternal investment occurs (that is, sexual exchange and general reciprocal altruism between the couple). From the perspective of the modern discussion, however, Aquinas was playing in the right ball park and, for his time, batting rather well.

Ethics and Narrative in Aquinas's Family Theory

Aquinas's theory of marriage and family does not remain at the biological level, as important as it is. There are really three major dimensions to his argument, paralleling the first three of five dimensions of practical moral thinking I have outlined in several of my books and essays.[40] The biological discussion orders what modern moral philosophers call the premoral level of his argument; it clarifies several questions pertaining to the ordering of a variety of premoral, natural goods in light of the needs created by the long period of infantile dependency. A more properly moral argument based on appeals to freedom, dignity, and the status of persons emerges when Aquinas argues for the superiority of monogamy over polyandry and polygyny. Polyandry is immediately rejected because it does not provide paternal certainty; that is the major reason it has not been widely used as a family form in the history of the world. Polygyny itself, according to Aquinas, does provide a degree of paternal certainty and hence at least some modicum of paternal investment in children on the part of males. But Aquinas's major criticism of polygyny is now advanced as a moral rather than a strictly biological argument. Polygyny is rejected by Aquinas because it is simply an unjust institution.

Besides. Equality is a condition of friendship. Hence if a woman may not have several husbands, because this removes the certainty of offspring; were it lawful for a man to have several wives, the friendship of a wife for her husband would not be freely bestowed, but servile as it were. And this argu-

ment is confirmed by experience; since where men have several wives, the
wives are treated as servants.[41]

The point is that women, for Aquinas, are made in the image of God just
as are men. In this respect, they are equal to men. They are fit candidates
for friendship with their husbands. He writes, "if the wife has but one
husband, while the husband has several wives, the friendship will not be
equal on either side; and consequently it will be not a freely bestowed but
a servile friendship as it were."[42]

Aquinas concludes this part of his argument by quoting Genesis 2:24:
"*They shall be two in one flesh.*" This verse, of course, is repeated many
times throughout the New Testament.[43] Aquinas interprets it to mean that
husband and wife are to have a friendship of equality that binds them
together in their task of raising and educating their children. This friendship and mutual assistance, as the "Supplement" says, is for Aquinas the
second main task of matrimony in addition to the procreation and education of children.[44]

Of course, the equality that Aquinas has in mind is one of proportional-
ity rather than the egalitarianism that moderns associate with liberal, contractual models of business and marriage. That is an issue, however, to be
elaborated later in this chapter. The point is this: for Aquinas monogamy
brought into existence a new level of care and investment by the father
for his children, but it also created a new level of equality and friendship
between the wife and her husband.

The third level of his argument about matrimony and the family is what
I will call the narrative level. This is the level of supernatural grace and
sacrament, but it is also the level where the narrative of Christ's sacrificial
death on the cross is used as an analogy to the role of Christian fathers in
their families. Even here, the biological dimension of the argument still
shines through. It has to do with Aquinas's belief that the male-female tie
that infantile dependency calls into existence must last longer than a few
years—it must last for life. In fact, it must be indissoluble.[45]

Chapter 123 of the *Summa Contra Gentiles* is a key text on the indissolubility of marriage. It combines arguments based on several levels of debate—an analysis of human inclinations and natural law, a theory of
justice between the sexes, and a rendering of the narrative implications of
divine revelation. There are in humans, he believed, some natural, although unstable, inclinations toward indissoluble monogamy which
should inform and be consolidated by human law and then finally per-
fected by divine revelation.[46]

The argument is stated from the male point of view and for this reason is grating to the liberal sensibility. On the other hand, it is clearly stated as a way of overcoming what we have called the male problematic—the tendency of males to mate without parental investment. His arguments could be restated from the perspective of both parents, but there is value in first hearing Aquinas's own logic. There are several points. Three arguments have to do with paternal investment. First, fathers care for their children, the argument goes, as a way of extending their own lives. Therefore, fathers should give appropriate degrees of care to their children indefinitely as a way of extending and enriching those who are literally parts of themselves. Marriage should be indissoluble, he concludes, because it provides the context for this life-long investment.[47] Second, because of the long years of human childhood dependency, children need parental (including paternal) authority indefinitely. Third, if couples exchange partners, paternal certainty is obscured.[48] And when this happens, fathers may care less or not at all for their progeny.

Three additional arguments are distinctively moral in character. To dissolve a marriage is an affront to equity and fairness. Aquinas assumes that men have a tendency to dispose of older women and take as mates younger, more fertile females. He writes, "if a man after taking a wife in her youth, while she is yet fair and fruitful, can put her away when she has aged, he does her an injury, contrary to natural equity."[49] Second, in addition to procreation, marriage is for friendship and this friendship will be all the more stable if it is thought to be indissoluble.[50] Third (and most out of tune with the liberal modern mind), Aquinas thought women were necessarily financially dependent on men and, furthermore, "naturally subject" to the man's superior wisdom. Therefore, neither women nor men should be allowed to initiate divorce since this would, in the end, deprive women of the resources and guidance they need.[51]

None of Aquinas's reasons more strikingly points to the different situation of women in modern societies in contrast to their situation in all premodern societies. Women are far less economically dependent on men in modern societies. Furthermore, all that we know in the research on moral and cognitive development indicates that there are no significant differences between men and women in their deliberative capacities, at least not of a kind that necessitates male guidance. But the question remains: Do women need men to help raise children and do children need fathers to be strong? Aquinas could concede these two points about female economic dependency and mental inferiority and still have grounds for arguing that women do need men's participation in childrearing. The question being debated today is whether he is right and whether the reasons he advanced have backing.

Aquinas's final argument for the indissolubility of marriage makes a direct appeal to revelation and is the cornerstone of his understanding of marriage as a sacrament. It points to a paradigmatic narrative action which Christian men as husbands and fathers are charged to imitate in their relation to wives and children. Furthermore, it also shows how narrative about divine action was seen by Aquinas to supplement both natural human inclination and the positive law in regulating marriage. Both human law and divine revelation should be based on, yet remedy the defects of, natural inclination. Divine laws not only "express the instinct of nature, but they also supply the defect of natural instinct."[52] Divine law adds to human law "a kind of supernatural reason taken from the representation of the indissoluble union of Christ and the Church, which is union of one with one."[53]

The analogy between the indissoluble union of husband and wife and Christ and the church refers, of course, to Ephesians 5:32. Here Aquinas follows the Vulgate in rendering the original Greek *mysterion* with the Latin word *sacramentum* rather than the more accurate *mysterium*, which we translate as "mystery." During the Patristic period, neither *sacramentum* nor *mysterium* communicated the idea that marriage was a source of supernatural grace in the way that Aquinas now wants to assert.[54] In fact, this is what separates Augustine's three purposes of marriage set forth in "The Good of Marriage" from Aquinas's three purposes stated in Question 49 of the Supplement. Both say that marriage concerns 1) procreation and education of children, 2) mutual obligations in sexuality and other domestic affairs, and 3) *sacramentum*. But *sacramentum* meant to Augustine only permanence or indissolubility and not supernatural grace.[55] *Sacramentum* meant to Aquinas both indissolubility and supernatural grace.

Protestants, as is well known, returned to the idea that matrimony was primarily a natural, nonsacramental institution. That is, the act of marriage for them bestowed no special supernatural grace. Nor did the early Reformers see it as indissoluble, although there were strong constraints placed against divorce.[56] Of course, for Aquinas, matrimony was both natural (since it had been willed by God from the foundations of creation) and supernatural (when mutually consented to by baptized Christians, supernatural grace was infused into the marriage to overcome the weaknesses of the couple, especially the weakness of the male).[57]

There was another dimension of Aquinas's understanding of *sacramentum*. This aspect is far more dramatic and actional than the more mechanical idea of the infusion of a grace to overcome our concupiscence and moral inadequacies. It is still designed to help couples have a love adequate to the task of remaining in lasting marriages. This additional dimension invites imitation or participation in a model or archetypal pattern of divine action. It is closer to the true meaning of the Ephesians 5:20–33 passage which first stated the analogy between matrimony and Christ's relation to the church. This is the dimension of matrimony as sacrament that enacts the sacrificial love of Christ for the church. Aquinas is addressing this dimension when he writes, "Although Matrimony is not conformed to Christ's Passion as regards pain, it is as regards charity, whereby He suffered for the church who was to be united to Him as His spouse."[58]

This means, as the Ephesians passages instruct, that the husband is to imitate Christ both in his unbreakable commitment to the family but also in his capacity for sacrificial love or charity (*caritas* in the Latin and *agape* in the Greek). Hence, when Aquinas invokes the narrative of Christ's passion for the redemption of the church, he doubtless has several of the Ephesians passages in mind. In this New Testament letter we read these words:

> Husbands, love your wives, just as Christ loved the church and gave himself up for her. . . . In the same way, husbands should love their wives as they do their own bodies. He who loves his wife loves himself. For no one ever hates his own body, but he nourishes and tenderly cares for it, even as Christ does the church, because we are members of his body. For this reason a man will leave his father and mother and be joined to his wife, and the two will become one flesh. This is a great mystery, and I am applying it to Christ and the church. Each of you, however, should love his wife as himself, and a wife should respect her husband. (Eph. 5:25–33)

Aquinas's use of the Ephesians call to male sacrificial love and life-long endurance in families must be understood in the context of his archeology of male sexual ambivalence (his prescientific version of the two strategies), the vulnerability of wives (the possible decline of interest by males after the childbearing years), and the needs of highly dependent human infants and children (which require, Aquinas thought, an indefinite commitment).

There is little doubt that Aquinas retains, in a qualified way, some of the patriarchy present in the Ephesians passage. Husbands are the heads of their families as Christ is the head of the church (Eph. 5:23). Both are carriers of an ethic of "love paternalism." This is a qualified and chastened patriarchy that emphasizes responsibility, commitment, and care; but the power, nonetheless, is still in the hands of the husband, in spite of the respect he is to have for his wife and children. Aquinas has mitigated the oppressiveness of ancient patriarchies, but he has not left it altogether. Yet to fail to place the symbolic relation between the servanthood of Christ and the husband against the background of Aquinas's analysis of the male problematic is to fail to recognize the potential richness of his contribution, both in the history of Western thought and even for today.

Is it possible that Aquinas formulated a powerful religio-cultural symbol that served to reinforce unsteady male inclinations toward paternal investment and the monogamy generally associated with paternal investment? Is it possible, as Margaret Mead once observed, that without powerful cultural reasons for men to invest in their children and remain with the women who give them birth, human males have deep inclinations to follow another sexual strategy?[59] Before Aquinas introduced the concept of the indissolubility of marriage and his version of marriage as a supernatural sacrament, he advanced mostly naturalistic and moral arguments about why men should be dedicated to their children and their wives. His concept of matrimony as a sacrament, both in its capacity to infuse grace and its invitation to imitate the drama of Christ's sacrificial love, simply gives added cultural and religious reinforcement to what he has argued for on humanistic terms.

This reinforcement, however, is classically religious. It follows in considerable detail Mircea Eliade's widely respected phenomenology of the sacred. It makes matrimony a recapitulation of an act of divine beings in their creation of sacred space and time.[60] Aquinas may be wrong in believing that Ephesians 5:32 makes marriage a special conveyor of supernatural grace, but he certainly is not wrong in sensing that Ephesians makes marriage (especially the husband's role within it) a recapitulation of the cosmic drama of a divine being who creates from acts of *agape*, or self-sacrificial love, the marital bond between a man and a woman. Matrimony as a symbol of Christ's cosmic sacrificial union with the church is all the more striking when one understands it, following Ricoeur's dialectic between archeology and teleology, as the reinforcement of some, and the transformation of other, basic male inclinations. The symbol of Christ's steadfast and sacrificial love for the church becomes, as Ricoeur calls it, a "figure of the spirit" attracting inchoate male inclinations and shaping them into a new organization—an organization that is possibly even more satisfying for men than the older strategy, more productive for children, and more just to their wives.[61]

The modern papal encyclicals beginning with *Arcanum* in 1881 and ending with *Familiaris Consortio* in 1981 restated several times this understanding of marriage as a cosmic drama. "Casti Connubii" exemplifies this regularly repeated theme: "For matrimonial faith demands that husband and wife be joined in an especially holy and pure love, not as adulterers love each other, but as Christ loved the Church."[62] For men who actually believed that their marriages had this meaning and reality, it doubtless affected their behavior and self-understanding. Just how much and how deeply these powerful symbols affected men's actions and values, only good historical research, of the kind we do not presently have, can tell.

One can speculate, however, that these symbols may have set up two competing trends: one toward a reinforcement of a declining and defensive patriarchy but another toward a norm of male responsibility expressed in the care of their children and a respectful, lifelong commitment to their wives. The first possibility has been examined by a variety of hermeneutics of suspicion in recent decades; the second possibility has been largely ignored. More specifically, the particular archeology of human desire that Aquinas assumed and which was dialectically related to the symbol of Christ's love for the church has been mostly lost to history. It is certainly not retained in the papal encyclicals on marriage published in the twentieth century; there is no hint in these documents of Aquinas's view of the male problematic and its roots in natural male inclinations.

The gradual disappearance of such powerful, religio-cultural reinforcements for the roles of husbands and fathers as the symbol found in Christ's love for the church raises an important question. Will our modern, liberal, and contractual models of male-female relations (which increasingly do not include even the idea of formal marriage) address the male problematic with the same power as this older paradigm? Certainly no secular alternative to this older symbolic matrix comes immediately to mind. Furthermore, since both the forces of secularization and the ghost of patriarchy haunt the official teachings of the churches that still carry this symbolism, there seem to be few prospects for this symbol addressing once again the male problematic with the force that it may once have done.

The Male Problematic and Early Christianity

Is the dialectical relation between archeology and teleology in the symbol of Christ's love for the church something peculiar to Aquinas? Does it only reflect a formulation that he stumbled upon but which has no visibility elsewhere in Christian teachings?

Martin Luther, of course, was greatly influenced by his Catholic predecessors yet revolted against the medieval church on a variety of matters, especially issues pertaining to marriage and the family. It is widely known that he believed marriage was a worthier arena of Christian vocation than celibacy, that he rejected the sacramental view of marriage, that he emptied German monasteries and nunneries and encouraged marriage among Catholic religious, that he saw fatherhood (even the care of infants by men) as a divine vocation, and that he repudiated the medieval practice of secret marriage, seeing marriage instead as a public affair under the control of the state.[63] All of these steps were in tension with Catholic traditions.

But the formal outlines of his theory of marriage were very close to Aquinas's views. Luther did not correlate the disciplines of biology with scripture in the fashion of Aquinas. But he believed scripture alone (*sola scriptura*) supported his conclusions. He was more likely to quote the creation stories in Genesis and their restatement in the Gospels than he was Ephesians or the Pastoral Epistles. He quoted Genesis 1:27, "So God created man . . . male and female he created them." Males and females were not to "be alone" (Gen. 2:18) but become "one flesh" (Gen. 2:24) and "be fruitful" (Gen. 1:28). These were not commands of God, but they are "ordinances." They are stamped in creation and nature. Luther wrote:

> It is a nature and disposition just as innate as the organs involved in it. Therefore just as God does not command anyone to be a man or a woman but creates them the way they have to be, so he does not command them to multiply but creates them so that they have to multiply. And wherever men try to resist this, it remains irresistible nonetheless and goes its way through fornication, adultery, and secret sins, for his is a matter of nature and not of choice.[64]

Luther wrote that the mundane and distasteful things that mothers and fathers do for their children—rocking the baby, changing diapers, staying up all night—are "adorned with divine approval." Like Aquinas, Luther aims his theology of parental responsibility even more toward fathers than he does toward mothers. In the "Estate of Marriage," he offers a prayer of thanks for his paternal vocation:

> O God, because I am certain that thou hast created me as a man and hast from my body begotten his child, I also know for a certainty that it meets with thy perfect pleasure. I confess to thee that I am not worthy to rock the little babe or wash its diapers, or to be entrusted with the care of the child

and its mother. How is it that I, without any merit, have come to this distinction of being certain that I am serving thy creature and thy most precious will? O how gladly will I do so, though the duties should be even more significant and despised. Neither frost nor heat, neither drudgery nor labor, will distress or dissuade me, for I am certain that it is thus pleasing in thy sight.[65]

Such divine approval is hardly on the same plane as participation in the cosmic drama of Christ's love for the church, yet it does bestow divine weight to paternal investment. But Luther did invoke the Ephesians drama as well and is aware that it is especially addressed to men. In Luther, this drama is more of a sign of the meaning of marriage than a sacrament that bestows supernatural grace, even though he occasionally used the word "sacrament." In his "Order of Marriage for Common Pastors," he gives prominence at the beginning of the text to the analogy between Christ and the church and the servant relation of husband to the family (Eph. 5:25–29). He then concludes with a prayer that thanks God for creating man and woman, ordaining them for marriage, blessing their fruits, and typifying "therein the sacramental union of the dear Son, the Lord Jesus Christ, and the church, his bride."[66]

Luther has no clear analysis of the male problematic in the fashion of Aquinas, but the message seems very much the same. But it should be clear that in both Aquinas and Luther, this appeal to male responsibility was still formulated within the frameworks of a vigorous even though modified and mostly humane patriarchy. In his "Order of Marriage," Luther, using another side of Ephesians, can still instruct wives to submit "in everything" to their husbands (Eph. 5: 22–24). The issue is this: Are there resources within the Christian tradition that make it possible to retain the symbolism of male paternal and maternal investment but within a vision of marriage that sees it as more radically egalitarian? It is to this issue that I will turn in the remaining portions of this chapter.

The Greco-Roman Context of the Ephesians' View of Marriage

There is an unresolved tension in early Christianity between an ethic of equality and an ethic of male responsibility and servanthood. It is never satisfactorily resolved in the scriptures of the early church. This tension looks less extreme if we carefully place early Christian literature in its historical context and compare it to surrounding Greco-Roman views on family, marriage, and sexuality. Early Christian teachings look more egalitarian than almost any religious or philosophical movement contemporary to early Christianity. On the other hand, to be honest, Greco-Roman views were more complicated than we sometimes think and themselves were giving birth to new degrees of gender equality and male parental involvement.

Early Christianity spoke simultaneously of equality between the sexes (what I will later call an ethic of equal regard) and male "headship" or authority over the family. This is visible in the classic text from Ephesians 5:21–33; both elements can be found there. These two elements are reconcilable only if we remember two things: 1) that the husband as "head of the wife" is humbled and modeled after the sacrifice of Christ and 2) the equality of the wife even here contains some of the elements of "proportional" justice characteristic of the ancient world wherever Aristotle's philosophy influenced civic life. This happened almost everywhere in the Mediterranean world, including most of the urban centers of Israel and Asia Minor. The Christian sacrificial husband could possibly see his wife as ontologically equal before God yet requiring male guidance because of her supposedly inferior deliberative capacities—or at least according to Aristotle.[67]

Hence, early Christianity in comparison to surrounding contexts could have made higher demands on male servant responsibility and enhanced the equality of wives but still seem deficient from the perspective of our modern egalitarian views. But to leave it at that could be an error: there may be a realism about the male problematic in the early Christian view which is needed today. Furthermore, these remaining tensions in early Christianity may themselves be reconcilable when submitted to careful theological reflection. Achieving this coherence may be the task of theology, whether systematic or practical. I will take some tentative steps toward this reconciliation at the conclusion of this chapter.

A Discipleship of Equals

Early Christianity can best be thought of as a Jesus movement. It was, in its early years, a reform movement within Judaism consisting of a group of men and women who followed Jesus in his itinerant ministry of preaching and healing. Jesus' preaching announced that the Kingdom of God, long awaited in Judaism, was in fact already beginning to unfold in the midst of the Jewish community.

This movement had a complicated relation to families. On the one hand, Jesus is depicted as an enthusiastic wedding guest and one who blessed the marriage wine; on the other, the Jesus movement is portrayed as in conflict with the patriarchal family structure of the Jewish and Greco-Roman worlds. Note the famous words, "For I have come to set a

man against his father, and a daughter against her mother . . ."
(Matt.10:34–35; see also Matt. 10:21–23; Mark 13:12–13; Luke 21:12–
17). But these passages are not attacks on families by the Jesus movement;
they were instead reports of the divisions created in Christian families
when Christians were arrested and jailed by civil authorities.[68] Family
members, under such conditions, would literally disclaim each other, as
can be imagined. They are also criticisms of Jewish and Greco-Roman
family clans who functioned as patriarchal religiopolitical units inhibiting
their members from becoming a part of the Kingdom Jesus was proclaiming. Early Christianity clearly relativized the patriarchal tribe as a family
form, but it should not be thought that Jesus was against families as such.
The tradition does represent him as wanting families, and individuals
within them, to submit their lives to the rule of the Kingdom of God rather
than the tribal codes and cults which were the center of family clans
throughout the Mediterranean world at that time.

Jesus is also portrayed as objecting to the patriarchal patterns of unilateral divorce of Jewish wives by their husbands, a practice that meant the
ranks of the poor consisted primarily of women. Jesus is reported to have
said that Moses allowed husbands to divorce their wives "because of your
hardness of heart." But from the beginning of creation, " 'God made them
male and female.' 'For this reason a man shall leave his father and mother
and be joined to his wife, and the two shall become one.' So they are no
longer two but one. What therefore God has joined together, let not man
put asunder" (Mark 10:5–9). Elisabeth Schüssler Fiorenza gives a particularly egalitarian reading of this passage when she argues that Jesus is
claiming here that God did not create patriarchy, did not intend that
women be given into the power of men to continue their house and family
line, but intended instead "that it is the man who shall sever connections
with his own patriarchal family and 'the two shall become one *sarx*
(flesh).' "[69]

Fiorenza claims that the pre-Markan and pre-Q fragments of the Gospels depict the early Jesus movement as "a discipleship of equals" between men and women. As the Jesus movement became a missionary
movement to the Greco-Roman world, evidence of this equality can be
found in the prominence of women as leaders in the early house churches.
Some of these women were wealthy and hosted meetings of these early
Christian "clubs" in their homes. Some, like Prisca, were married but
achieved distinction independently of their husbands as founders of important churches throughout Asia Minor—a leadership role rare for
women in the Greco-Roman world (Rom. 16:3). These pre-Pauline house
churches were scenes of important rites which enacted liminal dramas of

radical equality, at least for that day. Galatians 3:28 is thought to refer to a widely practiced baptismal formula that announces the new status of those who "have clothed yourselves with Christ." "There is no longer Jew or Greek, there is no longer slave or free, there is no longer male and female; for all of you are one in Christ." This formula is thought to reveal how relations between husband and wife, master and slave, Greek and Jew were restructured in these house churches. These redefined relationships may have radiated outward into broader public life. All of these pairs were equal in the house church because they were thought to be made in the image of God (thus having equal status before God) and believed to equally belong to Christ.

Several scholars believe that these little religious clubs enacted rituals which had egalitarian consequences for gender relations in the actual families of early Christians. Stephen Barton says it most forcefully when he writes,

> It is most likely that the potential created by church-in-house for the extension of the social range of female activity, represented at the same time a potential for redefining the women's social world generally (which, *ipso facto*, included that of their men as well). I mean by this that the ways in which women perceived themselves and expressed themselves within the sacred time and sacred space of the gathering-for-church-in-the-house will have *carried over* into secular time and space, especially because sacred time and space were linked so closely with secular time and space by virtue of the fact that church time constituted a segment of household time and church space was identical with household space.[70]

Entire families often joined these clubs. Although the house churches themselves functioned as a "new family of God" into which all members were adopted, these associations were not ascetic and natural family relations were rarely renounced.[71] Paul, in fact, specifically prohibited Christians from seeking divorce, even from their non-Christian partners (1 Cor. 7:10–16). Family relations, however, may have received a new meaning through the acceptance of the baptismal formula as a model of more equal family relations. David Balch points out that although Paul's interest in equality between the sexes was less than the pre-Pauline church, he still made egalitarian remarks that were unique in antiquity. In 1 Cor. 7:4 he writes, "For the wife does not have authority over her own body, but the husband does; likewise the husband does not have authority over his own body, but the wife does." Balch says that the last half of this statement giving the wife authority over the husband's body was "astounding in Greco-Roman culture."[72] Furthermore, Paul agreed with most of antiquity that sexuality was somewhat dangerous and that for the sake of spiritual purity in the eschatological end-time, it was better to be abstinent (1 Cor. 7:1–7). Nonetheless, marriage was natural and need not be sinful. In fact, Paul spent much time, as Balch points out, explaining the mutual obligations of Christian spouses (1 Cor. 7:1–16).

The pre-Pauline baptismal formula unleashed different consequences depending on the location of the Christian community. For instance, in the Corinthian church, the new gender equality inspired some women to experiment with wearing their hair loose, keeping their heads bare, and participating in provocative forms of ecstatic behavior. Such behavior was troubling to the outside pagan world. Christians were seen as undermining the normative model of the Greco-Roman family—powerfully stated by Aristotle in his *Politics*—which gave clear authority to the father over slaves, wives, and children.[73]

Paul, in an effort to minimize this criticism, made a distinction between inner and outer freedom. In public roles, he advised Christians to retain their pre-Christian positions: slaves should remain slaves, Jews should remain circumcised, and wives should remain obedient to their husbands. This external bondage was of little importance, Paul counseled, in comparison to the deeper freedom and equality they enjoyed through their identification with Christ (1 Cor. 7:17–24). This advice, and Paul's attempt to deflect the criticism of the Greco-Roman world, suggests that Christians in the privacy of their house churches were experimenting with new freedoms and equalities that were affronts to the stability of the official order.

There was an impulse toward gender equality in the early Christian communities that had social consequences. Although this was true enough, it is best not to overstate these consequences or conceive of them in modern terms. In addition to the distinction between inner-ecclesial roles and outer-public roles, there was also the easy tendency to interpret the language of equality in terms of the widely influential Aristotelian concepts of proportional justice. In the *Nicomachean Ethics* Aristotle writes, "In all friendships between unequals, the love also should be proportional, i.e., the better should be more loved than he loves . . ."[74] This is the form that equality was to take between people that were not of the same status, such as parents and children and, indeed, husbands and wives. Husbands and wives throughout the Hellenistic world were thought to have different degrees of excellence because men were believed to have higher powers of deliberation than women. We saw remnants of this belief in Aquinas who taught that equity required that wives should not through divorce be deprived of the superior guidance of their husbands.

In early Christianity, in contrast to the pagan world, equality between the sexes could become still more complicated. On the one hand, males and females were both made in the image of God; and if the male and female were Christian, both of them were equal in their identification with Christ. On the other hand, after the early days of the Christian missionary movement, there was a gradual return of the language of male headship and the associated idea that wives required the guidance of husbands. Both Paul and the author of Ephesians said outright that the "husband is the head of the wife" (1 Cor. 11:4; Eph. 5:23). There was also, as we said above, the distinction between inner equality in one's relation to God and outer conformity to conventional public roles. This much can be said: early Christianity constituted an ambivalent challenge to the patriarchies—Jewish, Greek, and Roman—of the ancient world. It was a challenge that moved from the semi-private space of the house church to the public space of the *polis*. It was not the only challenge. For instance, certain Epicurean groups accepted women as equals, but they were also ascetic and, for this reason, did not directly challenge the public relation between family and *polis*.[75]

But early Christianity seems to have inadvertently challenged the Aristotelian model of the public father governing his private household made up of noncitizen slaves, wife, and children. Hence, in the early Christian era, transformative currents came from the domestic realm outward into the public. John Milbank says it well when he writes,

> Where neither women, slaves, nor children were citizens, then the relationship of *oikos* to *polis* was *external*, and mediated by the father. But where, on the other hand, women, slaves and children . . . are equally members of an *ecclesia*, then the relationship of every part of the *oikos* to the public realm is a much more direct one . . . Inversely the domestic . . . becomes 'political,' a matter of real significance for law, education, religion, and government (although this has only been spasmodically realized in Christian history).[76]

Even though only "spasmodically" realized, there still may be much to learn from the way these Christian domestically based associations indirectly influenced the wider public realm.

The Honor-Shame Codes and the Early Christian House Church

One issue remains. What was the meaning in the early church of the analogy between Christ's sacrifice for the church and the father's servant-hood to the family? Did this cosmic analogy found in Ephesians and elsewhere only serve to bolster male authority, or was it a genuine reversal of ancient, heroic models of male authority in families? There is evidence that the second interpretation is the more accurate. To understand how this might be true, we must examine more closely the logic of male authority that functioned firmly throughout the Mediterranean world during the Hellenistic period and remained largely intact into Roman Hellenism. Some scholars now believe that this was an honor-shame code based on heroic military virtues of dominance and submission—virtues which had their roots in a culture reflected in the poetry of Homer.

In such a culture, individuals were thought of in relation to their families and their family's reputation or honor. Honor is maintained through the praise of respected equals.[77] It is established in political life and in war through achieving dominance in situations of challenge and riposte. Such interaction is a distinctively male activity. If the person who is challenged fails to respond, he is dishonored; if he responds but loses in either conflict or public debate, he is still dishonored. Honor is gained through winning, dishonor or shame through losing.

Anthropologists call cultures dominated by honor-shame ethics "*agonistic* cultures."[78] Public life is thought to be conflictual at its core and private life under constant threat of being dishonored by intrusive agents outside the family. Hence, a male's private sphere—his wife, children, mother, sister, and slaves—are in constant threat of being insulted, molested, raped, seduced, and stolen. On the other hand, it adds to the honor of a man if he can penetrate the private space of another male outside his own family.

Men are shamed if their space is challenged and they lose. For women, on the other hand, shame is a positive thing; they are to "have shame" and resist losing their shame or being "shameless."[79] For a man to avoid shame and for a woman to keep her shame, men must protect, control, guide, and circumscribe the lives of their women so that their private space will not be dishonored. Such an ethic celebrates the virtues of active dominance for males and passive conformity for females. The virtue of male activeness, as opposed to passivity, seems also to have been part of the widespread, but controversial, practices of pederasty whereby young adult males would take boys for their lovers until their own marriages, at which time such relations often subsided.[80] The honor-shame code also legitimated a double standard for male sexual activity after marriage; males could with ease have access to female slaves, possibly young boys, or even their neighbor's wife if they were clever enough to go unchallenged. It was a sign of their agency—their dominance.

Although this characterization of family relations under the honor-shame code is generally true, recent research qualifies it in several respects. While most women in Hellenistic societies led circumscribed lives, they had surprising freedom and power within these limits.[81] It is also wrong to believe that because men enjoyed extensive control of the domestic sphere and provided household security through public conflict, there was no genuine love, affection, and friendship between husbands and wives, fathers and children.[82] In spite of these qualifications, honor-shame patterns generally held true in the Greco-Roman world and provided the contextual background to an alternative family ethic (and an alternative understanding of the relation of *oikos* to the *polis*) that emerged in early Christianity, albeit fragmentarily.

The pagan world had a different form of the "male problematic" than that experienced in modern societies. The male problematic in modern societies is only superficially one of domination in the Greco-Roman sense. If our earlier analysis is correct, it is more a matter of neglect, absence, and failure of responsibility. Cultural individualism and technical rationality in both the market and state bureaucracies may be the more proximate social causes of this male neglect and absence. Domination and violence are part of the male problematic in modern societies, but now more capriciously—more as a way of asserting power in a social context that gives them increasing freedom but declining institutionalized control. In the shadows of both cases, however, we can detect the archaic inheritance of the ambivalent male reproductive strategy. The honor-shame code may be a particular cultural elaboration of ancient male reproductive strategies; it was a way of controlling wives, assuring paternal certainty, but also exploring the advantages of the R-strategy. The modern form of the problematic is different; as men increasingly renounce their control of women, they also renounce their concern with paternal certainty and paternal investment. Modern men seem increasingly unable to live by an ethic of equal regard which renounces control but maintains high degrees of mutual respect with spouses and paternal investment in children.

Was early Christianity exploring still another strategy? It may have been. In addition to its real but unsteady attempt to create an ethic of equal regard between husband and wife, there is evidence that it attempted to fracture the honor-shame code that dominated male behavior in families in the Mediterranean world. I use the word "fracture" to communicate that at best the Christian revolution was uneven, setting up certain ambiguous trends that even today we are still trying to resolve.

The Epistle to the Ephesians, which influenced both Aquinas and Luther so decisively, will help us understand how early Christianity engaged the honor-shame culture. Written to a group of second-century urban Christians living in cities in the Lysus Valley, the author is attempting to save them from sinking back into the pagan existence of the surrounding culture. This pagan existence can be best understood as the continuing manifestation of the honor-shame code with its belief in conflict and dominance as a method for achieving peace and respect. For rhetorical purposes, the author borrows from the metaphors of the male culture he opposes. In contrast to the armor and weapons of the heroic culture he criticizes, the author tells his readers to "take up the whole armor of God . . . the belt of truth around your waist . . . the breastplate of righteousness. As shoes for your feet put on whatever will make you ready to proclaim the gospel of peace" (Eph. 6:13–15). The new male armor and the new male ethic is an ethic of peace. More specifically, it is an ethic "with all humility and gentleness, with patience, bearing with one another in love, making every effort to maintain the unity of the Spirit in the bond of peace" (Eph. 4:2–3). The opposing pagan ethic is an ethic of contest or "wrath" which follows the desires of the "flesh and senses" (Eph. 2:2–3). It is not just simple immorality that Ephesians opposes; it is a systematic male ethic which enshrined the virtues of courage, strength, dominance, and conflict as means for achieving domestic and civic order. Ephesians is in tension with the honor-shame code of the Greco-Roman world.

It is within this context that we must understand the way Ephesians addresses the male problematic by electing Christ's sacrificial relation to the church as a model for the husband's relation to his wife. It is, in effect, a reversal of the logic of the honor-shame ethic guiding male behavior in antiquity. Rather than being the agentive guarantor of domestic security through challenge and riposte in the public world and control over the private world, the husband is now admonished to imitate the peace of God and the self-giving love of Christ. It is against the heroic ethics of the Greco-Roman world that we should understand the words, "Husbands, love your wives, just as Christ loved the church and gave himself up for her" (Eph. 5:25). It is true that the model of male headship is retained in this passage, but the logic of the ancient heroic codes is at least fractured, if not overturned.

The struggle to state the grounds of gender equality between spouses typical of the pre-Pauline missionary movement is not totally absent in this passage. But its status is ambiguous. In 5:21 we read, "Be subject to one another out of reverence for Christ." Then we read admonitions for the wife to be subject to the husband. Shortly after this, the author tells husbands to love their wives like Christ loves the church. He adds, "Husbands should love their wives as they do their own bodies." This, now, seems to introduce the principle of neighbor love into the discussion of how husbands should love their wives. This principle, "You shall love your neighbor as yourself" is presented by Jesus in Matthew 22:39 (and also Mark 12:31 and Luke 10:27). It can be found in the Hebrew scriptures and is repeated several times in the Pauline and Pastoral Epistles.[83] It is thought by many theologians to be the center from which all New Testament ethics should be understood. It first was thought to apply primarily to the neighbor (even the stranger) but not necessarily to family members themselves. In this passage, a variation is used to show just what it means for husbands to love their wives like Christ loves the church; it means that "husbands should love their wives as they do their own bodies." The author continues,

> He who loves his wife loves himself. For no one ever hates his own body, but he nourishes and tenderly cares for it, just as Christ does for the church, because we are members of his body. "For this reason a man will leave his father and mother and be joined to his wife, and the two will become one flesh." This is a great mystery. . . . (Eph. 5:29–32)

In short, husbands were to fulfill their servant roles by treating their wives equally to their own bodies.

One should conclude, I believe, that this text can be interpreted as fracturing the honor-shame codes of male conduct in the ancient world. It tried to do so within the patriarchal language game of antiquity. It also attempted to reconcile its view of male servanthood with the more egalitarian moments of the early Christian movement, but it accomplished this synthesis in an unstable way. It left to posterity, however, a passage difficult to interpret and susceptible to being read in a variety of ways. There is little doubt that it has been used quite frequently to bolster the crudest forms of Western patriarchal family ethics. It is unlikely, however, that such use was its original intent.

It is also clear that Aquinas's use of Ephesians was in keeping, for the most part, with its original spirit, if not its exact intent. Both Aquinas and Ephesians address two different but overlapping versions of the male problematic. They may have supplied Western society with its most powerful statements as to why men should marry, stay married for a lifetime, treat their wives with respect, and serve the welfare of their children. As this powerful symbol of the marital relation declines in our culture, we must ask ourselves whether we will gradually sink back into a heroic ethic of dominance and submission or an even more archaic form of mammalian existence in which females raise children and males expansively sow their seeds with little or no paternal investment in their children?

If Aquinas and contemporary evolutionary ecology are correct, such a world is likely to be punctuated by intermittent fits of male jealously, heightened domestic violence (which is not always the same as marital violence), male isolation from families, and lower states of child well-being. We must ask ourselves at this moment, when it seems that the last vestiges of this religious view of the family is losing its grip on the modern imagination and slipping into the safekeeping of books on library shelves, is this the condition of families we can expect for the indefinite future?

Some Tentative Proposals

So far my argument has been primarily historical. I have not asked whether the views I have described are right or wrong, good or bad. I simply have tried to tell the story of Christian family theory from a fresh perspective—from the perspective of how it coped with the male problematic. But has this led to a one-sided picture? Is not this entire story too oriented to the male point of view or, at least, the male problematic? Furthermore, is sacrificial love the complete understanding of *agape*? If so, is it true that self-sacrifice is the final goal of the Christian life? Finally, if there is a male problematic, is there not also a female problematic, and what would Christian family theory say about this?

From the perspective of human evolutionary ecology, there is a female problematic as well but it is less well understood. If males have an inherited tendency to follow, under some conditions, the cad strategy of reproductive fitness, females, under some conditions, may have tendencies to raise children without paternal participation. This was, after all, the original mammalian condition—mothers raising children more or less on their own. Whereas fathers may have tendencies to drift away from their women and children, mothers may have tendencies, if other supports are in place, to drift away from fathers. For different reasons, mothers may need to value more the contributions of fathers and the importance of long-term (maybe lifelong) marital commitment, just as fathers may need to value more their wives and children.

Is the symbolism of Christ's marriage to the church a model of sacrificial love for wives and mothers as well as husbands and fathers? Could a sense of participating in the cosmic drama of Christ's relation to the church function as a counter to the primal female problematic just as it did the primal male problematic? Is Christianity, and probably other forms of religion as well, in tension with short-term evolutionarily adap-

tive strategies in the name of certain long-term, and ultimately more fruitful, strategies? Are there inner-theological grounds for asserting that as
the husband can represent Christ's sacrifice to the family, so can the wife?

But this raises a troubling point: most of contemporary theological feminism has resisted, for good reasons, models of Christian love that overem-
phasize the features of self-sacrifice. They have resisted identifying
Christian love too completely with the symbolism of the cross. Would
claiming that wives as well as husbands can enact the Christic drama
mean that women once again would be asked to play the role of sacrificial
worker, denying their own selfhood, their needs and potentials, and assuming the role of endless servant to the other members of the family?

There is little said in the Pauline writings, Ephesians, or Aquinas about
whether wives can be to the family as Christ was to the church. The problem in these texts was not principally the wife but rather the husband.
Especially was this true of Aquinas and to a lesser extent Ephesians,
which addressed an honor-shame culture where men by definition were
assigned power, agency, and control. Although women from wealthy families did divorce in Greek and Roman societies during Roman Hellenism,
on the whole, it was a male prerogative, as were the prerogatives of the
double sexual standard.

Although it is not elaborated, Paul does, however, imagine the possibility of wives being unto their husbands and children as Christ was to the
church. They too could enact the drama of *agapic* love of which Christ
was the supreme example. In his first letter to the Corinthians, Paul advises people facing marital issues to remain in their present state. The
unmarried should remain unmarried. The married should remain married. These recommendations were due to his eschatological expectations
that the end of this world and the beginning of a new creation were about
to occur. These instructions were not commandments from the Lord but
his personal opinion which he believed was "trustworthy." This held even
for Christians married to non-Christians; they should not divorce, and if
they separate, they should not remarry. He writes,

[I]f any believer has a wife who is an unbeliever, and she consents to live
with him, he should not divorce her. And if any women has a husband who
is an unbeliever, and he consents to live with her, she should not divorce
him. For the unbelieving husband is made holy through his wife, and the
unbelieving wife is made holy through her husband (1 Cor. 7:13–14).

What is remarkable about this passage is the idea that the wife can "make
holy" (some translations say "sanctify") the unbelieving husband. Does

this mean that the wife can be like Christ, who sanctifies and makes holy the church? If so, this suggests that Paul could imagine how women can mediate Christ's transforming and self-giving love to the family. Women too can participate in the Christic drama.

In light of this possibility, I offer three suggestions for the reconstruction of Christian family theory. This reconstruction, I would claim, is consistent with its genius and is little more than a systematic ordering, in light of contemporary conditions, of what is already there. Furthermore, I hope to order what is there as a general philosophy of marriage that might be attractive to people who do not consider themselves Christians. In short, I handle the Christian tradition as a classic of Western culture—a classic, like most classics, that may contain a deep wisdom of general significance beyond the confines of those confessional communities that call themselves Christian. Since Christian family theory has influenced many aspects of Western culture from law and imaginative literature to the visual arts, its deep truth should be of interest far beyond the confines of confessional Christian bodies.

My suggestions are as follows. First, both husbands and wives should take part in the drama of sacrificial or self-giving love needed to energize families for lifelong commitments. Second, sacrificial love is not the whole of love, even in the Christian tradition. Sacrificial love is an important moment within a wider context of love as equal regard. The appropriate relation of sacrificial love and love as equal regard can be stated in ways both consistent with the Christian tradition and philosophically adequate for a general theory of love within marriage. Third, to keep the proper balance between love as sacrificial and love as equal regard, it is useful to see love and marriage as life-cycle phenomena in which love takes slightly different forms depending on where a family is in its cycle. The brief words about these points which follow should be seen more as an agenda for further work than a finished theology or philosophy of marriage.

With regard to the first point, we have already seen that there are grounds within the Christian tradition for saying that both husbands and wives can perform the Christic drama. This means that both husbands and wives are called to moments of self-sacrifice, endurance, commitment, and forgiveness. For those who can step into the cosmic drama, as Christians are called to do, this may prove to be a great privilege and a source of strength. According to much of the Christian tradition, it endows the sacrificial moment with the power of the divine. Some theologians would argue that true and lasting self-sacrifice is not genuinely possible without participation in the divine power and vision. I will not settle that issue here. It seems possible, for the mind of some liberal Christians, to

conceive of degrees of sacrificial love as standing independently of participation in this divine drama. Whether or not this is possible, it seems clear,
however, that no long-term married relationship can survive without
some capacity for self-sacrifice, however justified. Needs of individual
family members never totally synchronize, never completely fit. No matter
what the degree of reciprocal altruism, something like this deeper capacity
to love without the assurance of immediate return seems required. Both
men and women, both husbands and wives, must have this capacity.

The male problematic may be particularly threatening to family commitment because it can, so easily, let slip the commitment to both wife
and child. But the female problematic, with its easier commitment to the
child but more ambiguous commitment to the husband, must also be acknowledged. Both parties must be inducted into a culture, religious or
nonreligious, that celebrates the capacity for self-giving love—the capacity to extend commitment beyond the immediacies of reciprocal altruism
as such. It is clear that in its classic expressions (Aquinas and Luther),
Christian family theory, as did much of the family theory of the ancient
world, reinforced most of the conditions for male marital and parental
commitment—paternal certainty, monogamy, sexual exchange, and reciprocal helpfulness. What it added to all these elements, in addition to
its blessing, was the understanding of love as *agape* and the drama of
Christ's love for the church as a paradigm for the love of parents for one
another and their children.

With regard to the second point, this much should be said now. Sacrificial love is an important element in Christian love as it is also for a love
adequate for the demands of marriage. But it is not the whole of love in
either context. It is more accurate to conceive of Christian love as a challenging requirement of equal regard of the kind expressed in the love
command—"You shall love your neighbor as yourself" (Matt. 22:39).
Christian ethicists have for generations studied the logic of this command.
It is now widely agreed that the love command does not, first of all, require a life of perpetual self-sacrifice, self-abnegation, or self-denial.
Neighbor love and its analogous Golden Rule ("so whatever you wish that
men would do to you, do so to them" Matt. 7:12) both mean something
else. The Catholic moral theologian Louis Janssens gives us an insightful
interpretation when he writes, "Love of neighbor is impartial. It is fundamentally an equal regard for every person, because it applies to each
neighbor qua human existent."[84] "Valuing the self as well as others remains a manifest obligation" of the principle of neighbor love, according
to Janssens.[85]

We saw a modified formulation of neighbor love in the midst of Ephesians 5:20–33. Remember verses 28–29: "Even so husbands should love their wives as their own bodies. He who loves his wife loves himself. For no man ever hates his own flesh, but nourishes and cherishes it, as Christ does the church, because we are members of his body." This remarkable passage demonstrates the close relation of the symbol of Christ's union with the church and neighbor love as models of Christian love in marriages. The husband loves his wife like his own body. According to the extension that we are developing, the wife too should love the husband like her own body.

Even in this passage, it is assumed that the husband has a natural inclination and right to cherish and nourish his own body. Even in this passage, considered to be the great passage in the Christian heritage that calls for sacrificial love in marriage, we have a full legitimation of the right of self-regard. Hence, self-regard is built into the principle of neighbor love; it is part of its logic to give equal regard to both the neighbor and the self *qua* existents—*qua* humans made in the image of God.

How then does the call for sacrificial love—for long-term endurance in marriage through hard times and even at some cost to the self—become a factor in marriage if we take this tradition seriously? Is there room for sacrifice within *agape* when it is first interpreted as equal regard? Janssens has a suggestive proposal. He holds that self-sacrifice is in fact not the ideal of the Christian life. Instead, love as mutuality and equal regard is the ideal, and sacrificial love, as important as it is, is derived from equal regard. For Janssens, self-sacrifice is "justified derivatively" from the other regard built into love as equal regard.[86] We sacrifice for the other, extend ourselves, and go the second mile not because self-sacrifice as such is the end of love, either within or outside of marriage. Rather, we do these things not as ends in themselves but to restore our relations with our spouses, and others, to the more ideal state of equal regard.

Christian realism holds that we live in a world of finitude and sin, and as long as this is true, perfect mutuality and equal regard will not prevail. There will always be degrees of imbalance, inequality, and injustice in relations, in and outside of marriage. Self-sacrifice is not in itself the goal of the Christian life. It is, rather, a transitional obligation designed to restore broken relations to mutuality once again. This self-sacrifice was first of all charged to the male in both Ephesians and Aquinas. But in both contexts, neighbor love as equal regard (with a genuine role for self-regard) is the larger context of meaning.

Because of the challenge, the strain, the near impossibility of this sacrificial moment, the Christian tradition has offered an additional resource—the belief that this sacrificial moment in marriage (with all of its attendant features of forgiveness, patience, and renewal) can participate in a deeper cosmic drama rooted in the divine life and manifest in Christ's love for the church. Husbands were first of all invited to participate in this drama, partially, I think, because of intuitions about the male problematic. It is a natural extension of beliefs implicit in the Christian story to offer this invitation to wives. For those who cannot accept this belief in this cosmic drama, either as reality or symbol, it is their task in our time to find other grounds for justifying the sacrificial moment within a wider concept of love as equal regard.

Third, I am aware that love as equal regard seems to leave behind the biological and developmental features borrowed from evolutionary ecology and found, in prescientific form, in Aquinas and Aristotle. But we have not completely left behind this world. The sacrificial moment required from both husband and wife is there precisely, according to this model, to temper both the male and the female problematic, as different as they are. Love as equal regard, with its sacrificial moment, may help order the asymmetries of our reproductive strategies. Evolutionary ecology helps us understand the archeology of desire that fuels male and female behavior and which our religio-cultural symbols, when they have functioned well, have served to transform and redirect.

But evolutionary ecology has more to offer our constructive reflections. It also tells us that humans have a life cycle. It tells us that our evolutionarily grounded potentialities, in interaction with our environments and cultures, develop and subside in phases. These phases are marked with various tasks, opportunities, and responsibilities which must be met if our intertwined life cycles are to be strong and healthy.

Equal regard, as a model of marital love, can be fine tuned when articulated within a theory of the marital life cycle. David Gutmann has shown us in *Reclaimed Powers* that throughout the world marriages entail an exchange of roles. He studied at depth Mayan, Navajo, and Druze societies and made observations about modern societies as well. In all of these he discovered that typically active and protective roles of husbands generally last only through the period of the "parental emergency" when mothers and infants are vulnerable and dependent.[87] As infants grow into maturity, women become more active, even agentive, and husbands relinquish their active and protective roles. Men become more contemplative, even religious. Women become, if social circumstances permit, more involved in work, community, and the wider family.

The human life cycle in families entails a reversal of roles, a kind of life-cycle process of taking turns. Potentialities that husbands or wives may sacrifice at one stage in life may be explored and reclaimed at another stage in life. Sacrifices, in the societies that Gutmann studied, were transitional. Equality was not so much something achieved moment by moment but over the life cycle as a whole.

What would this mean for a theory of marital love formed by Christian sensitivities? It would mean that husbands and wives should understand the rhythms of equal regard and self-sacrifice. Clearly, the principle of equal regard would be the pervasive guide to their attitudes and actions. But it may mean that for a moment, one or the other partner will carry a special role, delay the development of a talent or gift, take time out to give birth, ask for leave from work to give child care, with the trust that at later moments in the marital life cycle a deeper actual equality will be restored. Sacrifice is not an end in itself but is what is done to contribute to an even deeper equal regard.

Furthermore, equal regard, when given a life-cycle interpretation, is an important guide for raising children. Raising children takes extreme effort and some self-sacrifice. But it is important, even for the health of children, to realize that self-sacrifice cannot alone be the foundation of child care. Rather, self-sacrifice is what must be done to help children grow toward capacities for equal regard with others as well as their parents. Elements of equal regard must inform parental relations with their children from the beginning, and acts of sacrifice should be constantly moderated as children's capacities for mutuality develop. Even here, sacrificial love is essential but serves the deeper goal of love as equal regard.

These brief constructive notes must remain incomplete. They are designed to illustrate how this tradition might be reconstructed both for Christians and for those who indirectly might learn from it. There are many issues which must be left untouched. These are the big issues that have plagued public debate—abortion, contraception, divorce, homosexuality, the limits of reproductive technology, the claims of natural parents in adoption, etc. These important issues must be addressed if this theory can hold true.

As important as they are, these issues must not be allowed to wipe from consciousness this most basic discussion—the nature and meaning of marriage and the role that classic religious sources will play in informing this institution in the future. We may have tried for too long to address these sensational issues without fully developing our fundamental theories of marriage and family. I hope that these historical and constructive notes make a contribution to this deeper task.

Notes

1. For popular but reliable accounts of this phenomena, see Paul Taylor, "Life without Fathers," *Washington Post*, June 1992; Louis Sullivan, "Fatherless Families," *Television and Families* (summer 1992), 34–36.

2. Sara McLanahan and Karen Booth, "Mother-Only Families: Problems, Prospects, and Politics," *Journal of Marriage and the Family* 51, no. 3: 557–80.

3. Frank Furstenberg and Andrew Cherlin, *Divided Families* (Cambridge, MA: Harvard University Press, 1991).

4. Ibid.

5. Victor Fuchs and Diane M. Reklis, "America's Children: Economic Perspectives and Policy Options," *Science* 255 (Jan. 3, 1992): 42.

6. Jan E. Dizzard and Howard Gadlin, *The Minimal Family* (Amherst, MA: University of Massachusetts Press, 1991), 25–67.

7. Ibid., 125-39; Richard Posner, *Sex and Reason* (Cambridge, MA: Harvard University Press, 1991), 169–72.

8. Posner, *Sex and Reason*, 171.

9. Robert Bellah et al., *Habits of the Heart* (Berkeley, CA: University of California Press, 1985); Christopher Lasch, *Haven in a Heartless World* (New York: Basic Books, 1977); Ron Lesthaeghe, "A Century of Demographic and Cultural Change in Western Europe," *Population and Development Review* 9, no. 3 (September 1983): 411–35.

10. Judith Stacey, *Brave New Families* (New York: Basic Books, 1990), 268; Posner, *Sex and Reason*, 192; Stephanie Coontz, *The Way We Never Were* (New York: Basic Books, 1992), 277–85.

11. David Popenoe, *Disturbing the Nest* (New York: Aldine De Gruyter, 1988); Irwin Garfinkel and Sara McLanahan, *Single Mothers and Their Children* (Washington: Urban Institute, 1986); Barbara Dafoe Whitehead, "Dan Quayle was Right," *Atlantic Monthly* (April 1993): 47–84.

12. Pierre L. van den Berghe, *Human Family Systems* (New York: Elsevier, 1979), 14; W. D. Hamilton, "The Genetical Evolution of Social Behavior, pt. 2," *Journal of Theoretical Biology* 7 (1964): 17–52.

13. Hamilton, "Genetical Evolution," 17.

14. Martin Daly and Margo Wilson, *Sex, Evolution and Behavior* (Belmont, CA: Wadsworth Publishing Co., 1978), 56; Robert Trivers, "Parental Investment and Sexual Selection," in *Sexual Selection and the Descent of Man*, ed. Bernard G. Campbell (Chicago: Aldine De Gruyter, 1972), 139.

15. Van den Berghe, *Human Family Systems*, 20–21; Helen Fisher, *Anatomy of Love* (New York: W. W. Norton, 1992), 63.

16. Donald Symons, *The Evolution of Human Sexuality* (Oxford: Oxford University Press, 1979), 131–36.

17. Van den Berghe, *Human Family Systems*, 131–40; David Popenoe, "The Fatherhood Problem" (New Brunswick, NJ: Dean's Office, Rutgers University), 17–19 (the materials in this paper appear in revised form as Chapter 6 of David

Popenoe, *Life Without Father: Compelling New Evidence that Fatherhood and Marriage Are Indispensable for the Good of Children and Society*, forthcoming from The Free Press, 1996).

18. Daly and Wilson, *Sex, Evolution and Behavior*, 124–29; van den Berghe, *Human Family Systems*, 25–26.

19. Barry S. Hewlett, ed., *Father-Child Relations: Cultural and Biosocial Contexts* (New York: Aldine De Gruyter, 1992); Robert Trivers, *Social Evolution* (Menlo Park, CA: The Benjamin/Cummings Publishing Co., 1985), 203–38.

20. Trivers, "Parental Investment and Sexual Selection," 139–41.

21. Steven Gaulin and Alice Schlegel, "Paternal Confidence and Paternal Investment: A Cross Cultural Text of a Sociobiological Hypothesis," *Ethology and Sociobiology* 1, no. 4 (December 1980): 301–09.

22. Hewlett, *Father-Child Relations*, 21; Barry Hewlett, *Intimate Fathers* (Ann Arbor, MI: University of Michigan Press, 1991).

23. John R. Snarey, *How Fathers Care for the Next Generation* (Cambridge, MA: Harvard University Press, 1993), 311–60; Hewlett, *Intimate Fathers*, 151–66.

24. Popenoe, "The Fatherhood Problem," 38; James Q. Wilson, *The Moral Sense* (New York: The Free Press, 1993); see also James Q. Wilson, "The Family-Values Debate," *Commentary* (April 1993): 24–31.

25. James A. Weisheipl, ed., *Albertus Magnus and the Sciences* (Toronto: Pontifical Institute of Medieval Studies, 1980).

26. Paul Ricoeur, *Freud and Philosophy* (New Haven, CT: Yale University Press, 1971), 12–26.

27. Ibid., 419-58.

28. St. Thomas Aquinas, *Summa Theologica*, vol. 3, "Supplement," trans. Fathers of the English Dominican Province (New York: Benzinger Brothers, 1948), Q41, A1 (hereafter referred to as *ST*). I also want to express my thanks to Professor Stephen Pope of Boston College for his many excellent articles on the biological dimensions of Aquinas's thought and its analogues to modern biological theory. See particularly his article "The Order of Love and Recent Catholic Ethics," *Theological Studies* 52 (1991): 255–88. Although his unpublished essay titled "Sociobiology and Family: Toward a Thomistic Assessment and Appropriation" came into my hands after this chapter was complete, it was encouraging to see how closely our interpretation of Aquinas was converging, since he is the leading Aquinas scholar on these matters.

29. St. Thomas Aquinas, *Summa Contra Gentiles*, bk. 3, pt. 2, trans. The English Dominican Fathers (London: Burns, Oates and Washbourne, 1928), 112 (hereafter referred to as *SCG*).

30. Ibid.

31. Ibid.

32. William James, *The Principles of Psychology*, vol. 2 (New York: Dover Publications, 1951), 383-441; Mary Midgley, *Beast and Man* (Ithaca, NY: Cornell University Press, 1978).

33. Aquinas, *SCG*, 117.

34. Ibid., 118.

35. Ibid., 114.

36. Aristotle, "Politics," in *The Basic Works of Aristotle*, ed. Richard McKeon (New York: Random House, 1941), bk. 1, chap. 2.

37. Ibid., bk. 2, chap. 3.

38. Ibid., bk. 2, chap. 4.

39. Aquinas, *SCG*, 118.

40. Don Browning, *Religious Thought and the Modern* (Minneapolis, MN: Fortress Press, 187), 17.

41. Aquinas, *SCG*, 118.

42. Ibid., 119.

43. See also Matt. 19:5; Mark 10:7; 1 Cor. 6:16; 7:10–11; Eph. 5:31. All scripture quotations are taken from the Revised Standard Version, © 1982 by Thomas Nelson and Sons.

44. Aquinas, *ST*, Q41, A1.

45. Aquinas, *SCG*, 114.

46. Ibid., 115.

47. Ibid., 114.

48. Ibid., 115.

49. Ibid.

50. Ibid., 115–16.

51. Ibid., 115.

52. Ibid., 116.

53. Ibid.

54. Rudolf Schnackenburg, *Ephesians: A Commentary* (Edinburgh: T. and T. Clark, 1991), 255–56.

55. St. Augustine, "The Good of Marriage," *The Fathers of the Church*, vol. 15, ed. Roy Deferrari (New York: Fathers of the Church, Inc., 1955), 4.

56. Martin Luther, "The Estate of Marriage," in *Luther's Works*, vol. 45 (Philadelphia: Fortress Press, 1962), 30–35; Stephen Ozment, *Protestants: The Birth of a Revolution* (New York: Doubleday, 1992), 151–69.

57. Aquinas, *ST*, Q42, A2.

58. Ibid., Q42, A1.

59. Margaret Mead quoted in Popenoe, "The Fatherhood Problem."

60. Mircea Eliade, *The Sacred and the Profane* (New York: Harper and Row, 1961).

61. Ricoeur, *Freud and Philosophy*, 462–68.

62. "Casti Connubii: Encyclical of Pope Pius XI," in *The Papal Encyclicals*, ed. Claudia Carlen (Wilmington, NC: McGrath Pub. Co., 1981), par. 23.

63. Steven Ozment, *The Protestants* (New York: Doubleday, 1992). Furthermore, it must be noted that much of Catholic canon law on marriage was taken over by the Protestant Reformation, but now administered by the state more or less as civil law rather than by the church itself and its courts, as it had been

under Catholicism. See James A. Brundage, *Sex, Law, and Marriage in Christian Society in Medieval Europe* (Chicago: University of Chicago Press, 1989).

64. Luther, "The Estate of Marriage," 18.

65. Ibid., 39–40.

66. Luther, "Order of Marriage for Common Pastors," in *Luther's Works*, vol. 53 (Philadelphia: Fortress Press, 1965), 115.

67. Aristotle, "Politics," bk. 1, chaps. 12–13.

68. Elisabeth Schüssler Fiorenza, *In Memory of Her: A Feminist Theological Reconstruction of Christian Origins* (New York: Crossroad, 1987), 74.

69. Ibid., 143.

70. Stephen C. Barton, "Paul's Sense of Place: An Anthropological Approach to Community Formation in Corinth," *New Testament Studies* 32 (1986): 74.

71. Fiorenza, *In Memory of Her*, 214.

72. David Balch, "Theses about the Early Christian Family" (paper prepared for the annual seminar of the Religion, Culture, and Family project, located at the Divinity School of the University of Chicago and sponsored by the Division of Religion of the Lilly Endowment, Inc., 1993).

73. For the best discussion of the tensions of pre-Pauline and Pauline churches with the official household codes of the Aristotelian tradition, which dominated the urban life of Roman Hellenism, see David Balch, *Let Wives Be Submissive: The Domestic Code in I Peter* (Atlanta: Scholars Press, 1981); for the original statement of the household code outlining the respective obligations and rights of free Greek men over slaves, wives, and children, see Aristotle, *Politics*, bk. 1, chap. 12.

74. Aristotle, "Nicomachean Ethics," in *Basic Works of Aristotle* (New York: Random House, 1941), bk. 8, chap. 7.

75. Fiorenza, *In Memory of Her*, 75.

76. John Milbank, *Theology and Social Theory* (Oxford: B. Blackwell, 1990), 368.

77. Jerome H. Neyrey, *The Social World of Luke-Acts* (Peabody, MA: Henrickson Publishers, Inc., 1991), 32; for an application of the honor-shame concepts to classical Greece, see David Cohen, *Law, Sexuality and Society* (Cambridge: Cambridge University Press, 1991).

78. Cohen, *Law, Sexuality and Society*, 29.

79. Neyrey, *The Social World of Luke-Acts*, 41–44.

80. Eva Canterella, *Bisexuality in the Ancient World* (New Haven, CT: Yale University Press, 1992); for its controversial character of male bisexuality, see Cohen, *Law, Sexuality and Society*, 171–201.

81. Cohen, *Law, Sexuality and Society*, 133–69.

82. Richard Sallers, *Patriarchy, Property, and Death in the Roman Family* (Cambridge: Cambridge University Press, 1994).

83. See Rom. 13:2, Gal. 5:14, James 2:8. The analogous Golden Rule is found twice: Matt. 7:12, Luke 6:31.

84. Louis Janssens, "Norms and Priorities of a Love Ethic," *Louvain Studies* 6 (1977): 219.

85. Ibid., 220.
86. Ibid., 228.
87. David Gutmann, *Reclaimed Power: Toward a New Psychology of Men and Women in Later Life* (New York: Basic Books, 1987).

CHAPTER 7

Postmodern Family Law: Toward a New Model of Status

Milton C. Regan, Jr.

Many observers have attested to the crucial role that marriage tradition-ally has played in the nurture and care of children. They have spoken eloquently about the ways in which divorce can disrupt this role, placing children in both psychological and financial peril.[1] Efforts to strengthen marriage as a social institution therefore can be seen as an important vehicle for enhancing the welfare of children.

In this chapter, however, I want to focus on a different, less tangible, function of marriage. This is the way in which it has served as the model of an alternative to the calculating egoism of individualism. Over the last century and a half or so, marriage has been regarded as a cultural exem-plar of the relational self—the individual whose identity is bound up in part through relationship with others.[2] As such, it has been held up as the embodiment of altruism and commitment, a form of life in which a sense of responsibility arises not solely through choice but also through interde-pendence. What is particularly significant about marriage is that, unlike the relationship between parent and child, this sense of obligation arises between the ostensibly sovereign, fully-formed adult individuals exalted by liberal political theory. For this reason, marriage has had the potential to subvert the dominance of social contract theory's account of human relationships.

Appreciation of this function of marriage suggests that its potential de-mise may be problematic for reasons independent of its role in nurturing children. Because of the traditional centrality of marriage to our concep-

157

tion of family, we should at least contemplate the possibility that a weakened sense of marital obligation might in turn undermine the family more generally as a locus of relational identity. To be sure, an ethic of connection still has powerful resonance with respect to family relationships. In a recent survey by Massachusetts Mutual Insurance Company, for instance, people expressed intense devotion to the idea of family as a realm of unselfish commitment and unconditional acceptance. "Caring, loving, and nurturing" were the words most often used to describe the family.[3]

Yet the same survey suggests that actual experience may not always accord with this vision. Researchers report that many respondents do not believe that their families "provide emotional support, are close, or communicate well."[4] Furthermore, almost 60 percent of the respondents rated family life negatively.[5] This sense of a gap between the aspiration of solidarity and the experience of isolation is reinforced by indications that involvement in family life is more likely than a generation ago to be based on the extent to which it contributes to individual needs. Frank Furstenberg and Graham Spanier, for instance, report that those who regard remarriage after divorce as successful typically attribute success to the fact that their current spouse recognizes the way that they "really" are or helps them be the person that they "really" want to be.[6] Similarly, Philippe Ariès has suggested that the decision to have children increasingly is a product of the belief that parenthood will be a satisfying experience that will enhance self-development.[7]

This heightened emphasis on the family as a vehicle for the achievement of individual purposes places a premium on negotiation and interpersonal skills, tools that can be used to fashion family life according to mutually agreeable terms. Thus, as one observer notes, "whatever its 'commitment,' the current interpersonal relationship must include a commitment to continuing negotiation."[8] As a result, some suggest, the idea of family obligation as a conscious individual choice has become so influential that ongoing emotional support now is apt to be something that a family member earns, rather than something that she automatically receives.[9] Many children today deciding whether to take an aging parent into their home, for instance, are apt to base their decision on whether they have a warm personal relationship with the parent, rather than on a sense of duty arising from the fact of the parent-child relationship itself. These trends are complex, and most people live with multiple messages about the conduct of family life. Nonetheless, it is fair to say that individualistic tenets have gained more influence within the family in recent years.[10]

There have been indisputable benefits from this development. Most dramatically, women now are accorded more dignity as individuals in their own right, persons whose identities are not wholly defined by their service as wives or mothers. Individualism also has its costs, however. The modern family has taken on many of the characteristics of a voluntary association, in which self-interest plays a more prominent role in shaping a sense of obligation to others. As a result, commitment may become even more tenuous for residents of a postmodern world marked by fragmentation and discontinuity in intimate relationships. If we believe that individualism should not serve as the uncontested principle of family life, we need to explore how we might preserve an alternative vision that emphasizes the relational self. In ways that are complex, diffuse, and perhaps even counterintuitive, family law may serve as one vehicle for sustaining a cultural narrative that joins both intimacy and commitment. Its potential for doing so may depend on our ability to reconstruct a family law principle that has fallen into disfavor in recent decades: the model of status.

Individualism and Family Law

In family law, the recent shift in sensibilities about the family is reflected in what legal scholars call a movement from status to contract.[11] Until the last couple of decades, family law relied on status as its governing principle, bestowing impersonal rights and obligations on those who assumed legal identities such as spouse, parent, or child. Status fostered the understanding of the family as an institution, which "claim[ed] authority over the individual independently of the subjective meanings that [he or she] attach[ed] to any particular situation."[12] Particularly relevant for my purposes, the relationship of marriage was deemed to involve certain basic terms that the parties were legally powerless to alter by agreement.[13] Furthermore, spouses who wished to part had to prove to the satisfaction of the state that their marriage should end, since divorce marked the relinquishment of a status, not simply the end of a private agreement.[14] A regime of status thus expressed a substantive moral vision of what marriage should be like. As the Supreme Court expressed it in 1888:

> Marriage is more than a mere contract. The consent of the parties is of course essential to its existence, but when the contract to marry is executed by the marriage, a relation is created between the parties which they cannot change.[15]

By contrast, an emphasis on contract, which has become more prominent in recent years, sees marriage primarily as the domain of private ordering, an intimate setting in which people decide for themselves the terms of their relationships. One example of this trend is that the law now is far more willing than before to treat spouses as any other contracting parties. The Uniform Premarital Agreement Act, for instance, which has been adopted in almost twenty states, provides that spouses may contract with regard to economic matters and any other subject, "including their personal rights and obligations," as long as the agreement does not violate public policy or criminal law.[16] Most courts will enforce agreements that absolve one spouse from any postdivorce financial duty to the other, unless a spouse is left destitute by the agreement, a posture that allows contract to trump obligations that otherwise would be imposed by statute.[17] As one court said of the policy of deference to the terms of marital contracts, spouses "should be free to execute agreements as they see fit and whether they are 'fair' is not material to their validity."[18] No-fault divorce reflects a similar attitude of deference, proclaiming that the spouses themselves are the only legitimate judges of whether a marriage should continue. Indeed, the individualistic flavor of modern family law is underscored by the fact that in all but two states one spouse can obtain a divorce over the objection of the other.[19]

This commitment to private ordering over the obligations imposed by status tends to be qualified only by the Millian principle of preventing harm to others.[20] Thus, courts will examine more closely spousal agreements that affect child support and custody.[21] Furthermore, several states will take marital misconduct into account in making decisions about custody and property division at divorce, suggesting that the law is not completely agnostic about how the spouses have conducted their lives.[22]

Even in the latter instance, however, misconduct tends to be considered relevant only if it has dissipated assets or produced direct injury.[23] In sum, family law, like many other modern liberal institutions, professes to be neutral among visions of the good life, intervening only when necessary to prevent one individual from directly harming another.[24] The individualistic premises of this stance are reflected in the Supreme Court's well-known characterization of marriage in *Eisenstadt v. Baird*: "The marital couple is not an independent entity with a mind and heart of its own, but an association of two individuals each with a separate intellectual and emotional make-up."[25] Thus, to the extent that there has been a legal movement from status to contract, there has been an evolution of marriage from social institution to private association.[26]

Much of the impetus for this heightened emphasis on personal choice is, of course, aversion to the gender roles that were enforced by status in traditional family law. Dissatisfaction with these roles, however, itself can be seen as part of a movement stretching back at least as far as the Enlightenment. While shorthand descriptions are never wholly adequate, one way to characterize this movement is as the advance of modernity.[27] Under the inspiration of modernity, the individual sheds supposedly contingent attributes such as class, race, ethnicity, and gender, achieving respect as an individual in her own right. On this view, as Alasdair MacIntyre puts it, "I am what I choose to be. I can always, if I wish to, put in question what are taken to be the merely contingent social features of my existence."[28] Modernity thus posits a core self that is *acontextual*, defined in its essence not by any particular social context in which it may be located, but by its abstract capacity to choose among them. From this perspective, achieving selfhood demands the ability to discern and be guided by one's authentic inner voice in the face of social pressures to conform.

A powerful ethic in contemporary life is that this inner voice speaks through feeling and emotion. This ethic reflects what Charles Taylor has called the "expressivist turn,"[29] and what Robert Bellah and his colleagues have termed "expressive individualism."[30] On this view, we should privilege those attributes and intimate encounters that seem most spontaneous and free of the ostensibly distorting influence of social convention. In the modern world, "private" life is the domain in which we can cultivate these attributes and pursue these encounters on our own terms. Through intimate relations with others, we gain access to our deepest feelings in a process of mutual self-discovery. Not surprisingly, research indicates that intimacy has become a more highly valued experience over the last generation, with a greater premium on close relationships as a vehicle for personal growth.[31] As a result, the modern demand for privacy has come to encompass not only protection of secrets from disclosure, but the assertion of individual sovereignty over the conduct of intimate relationships.

The concept of status is in sharp conflict with modernist sensibilities. First, while modernism posits an acontextual self, status offers a relational one. The person constituted by legal status is the object of attention insofar as she is part of some network of relationships. Thus, being a father involves having a child, being a wife means having a husband, and being a landlord implies having a tenant. Status locates the individual within a particular context, and prescribes behavior based on the expectations that apply in that context.

Second, modernism involves, borrowing from Erving Goffman, what we might call "role distance."[32] This attitude is suspicious of, and even antagonistic toward, social roles, regarding them as artificial intrusions on genuine self-expression. By contrast, status reinforces the salience of social roles. It serves as the legal expression of the behavioral expectations that are associated with a given role. Third, the modern emphasis on self-realization through intimacy privileges spontaneous emotion as a window into the true inner self. Status, on the other hand, seems to demand the subordination of personal feelings to the performance of "externally" imposed obligations. Finally, modern intimacy purports to rest on freely chosen commitment and personal choice. Status, however, involves impersonal duties applicable to all status occupants, and treats individual preferences as largely irrelevant.

To modernist sensibility, then, status in family law represents a kind of forced intimacy, an effort to impose by fiat commitment that should flow from genuine emotion. In this view, the family is a vestige of premodern ascription, and contract represents a vehicle for eliminating perhaps the last obstacle to realizing the Enlightenment dream of individual emancipation. Once this occurs, the family will be seen as but one possible type of intimate relationship, one option among many, governed less by social norms and more by individual desires. Indeed, some family scholars already suggest that "the family" is of diminishing value as an analytical concept. John Scanzoni, for instance, argues that the family should be seen as a particular instance of the more general category of the "close relationship situation."[33]

In such a world, the family begins to lose its distinctive character, and our culture begins to lose a discourse in which to contest the premises of individualism. Some might argue that this cost is justified if we gain a society in which family life offers greater self-realization through more satisfying experiences of intimacy. Yet there is reason to question whether this would be the case. Insistence on the primacy of a domain supposedly governed by individual preference rather than social norms neglects the social foundations of both identity and intimacy. Ironically, the result may be a rootless individual with neither a stable sense of self nor a capacity for intimate commitment. We may gain a glimpse of this world in which the modernist quest for identity and intimacy negates itself by attending to what some have called the postmodern loss of self.

Postmodern Personal Life

With various metaphors and from different perspectives, several scholars suggest that we are entering an age in which the maintenance of a stable sense of identity is a precarious undertaking. Kenneth Gergen, for instance, argues that an exponential increase in exposure to others through modern communications technology has led to a self that is buffeted by multiple, often conflicting demands.[34] In the face of such incessant stimulation, an individual may feel that the "self" elicited at any given moment is difficult to reconcile with a "self" evoked at another instant. As a result, the notion of a core self that unifies experience over time may give way to the fragmentation of different "selves" that occupy discrete moments of interaction.[35] The metaphor for such experience might be Music Television (MTV), that rapid succession of disconnected images that many observers regard as the paradigm postmodern art form.[36]

Frederic Jameson is another observer who has explored the idea of the loss of the self, from a perspective that focuses on our changing experience of time.[37] Jameson suggests that contemporary society has begun to lose the capacity to retain a sense of its past by virtue of relentless changes that undermine historical traditions. As a result, contemporary experience often seems characterized by "the fragmentation of time into a series of perpetual presents."[38] Jameson uses the metaphor of schizophrenia to describe the type of personality that may emerge under such circumstances. The schizophrenic, says Jameson, is "given over to an undifferentiated vision of the world in the present," in which each moment is vivid and intense but is unconnected to any larger pattern of experience that unifies past, present, and future.[39] In this image, the stable self dissolves amid exposure to a succession of stimuli, each of which seems to have its own integrity and force.[40]

At first glance, this condition may seem the precise opposite of the acontextual self exalted by modernity. Instead of a core self defined apart from any context, the self seems nothing *but* the context that characterizes a given moment. If we look more closely, however, we can see that this immersion in context is possible only for a subject who sees no context as constitutive. The acontextual self is defined by her sovereignty, her ability to move among various situations without being defined by any. Ideally, therefore, she is fully open to the stimuli of each setting. Yet each context necessarily elicits distinct sensibilities, which can seem vivid in their insistence that these preferences, instead of others, should guide behavior. If no context is constitutive, there is no sense of identity capable of providing a trans-contextual perspective from which to weigh the claims of each moment of experience. Each moment, then, would seem to involve a different "self," no one of which has priority over the other. The result is a subject inundated by, and merged within, her surroundings. The radical disengagement of the acontextual self thus ultimately may be indistinguishable from the radical engagement of the fragmented self. The modernist quest for an unfettered core identity ironically seems to end in the dissolution of the self as a unified concept.

By contrast, if the self were seen as defined in part by relationships in particular contexts, that identity would serve as a perceptual filter in other situations. This sense of self would limit the radical openness to experience that threatens the sense of a unified identity. Jameson maintains that it is the absence of such a filter that distinguishes the schizophrenic from others. "Our own present," he says, "is always part of some larger set of projects which force us selectively to focus our perceptions."[41] These projects locate us within specific relationships with particular people, which enables us to evaluate critically, rather than simply receive passively, the stimuli to which we are subject. A man on a business trip, for instance, may regard his identity as husband as sufficiently important that he eschews opportunities for romantic involvement to which he otherwise might be attentive. A sense of being rooted in particularity therefore may be crucial in preserving the sense that one is a purposive agent, rather than an entity prey to the winds of each passing experience.

Fragmentation of identity in turn threatens the pursuit of intimacy. Intimate commitment rests on the notion that a person will feel bound by earlier promises because those promises were made by the same person who now is asked to fulfill them. If no overarching sense of identity unites a person at different times, then there seems no basis for holding a person to a commitment that another "self" may have made at an earlier time. The result may be the dominance of what Kenneth Gergen calls the "fractional relationship,"[42] a postmodern world in which intimacy consists of discrete moments of connection, with no more extensive promise of attachment beyond each experience.

In sum, once personal life comes to be seen as the domain of the acontextual self, the way is open for "pure" subjectivity to emerge as the only legitimate basis for intimate connection. The increasingly fragmented nature of that subjectivity, however, makes any connection fragile and tends to limit the influence of any given relationship. The ethereal subject seems to float from context to context, visiting all but at home in none. In short, she seems bereft of both identity and intimacy. The result may be a postmodern world in which there is no stable repository of meaning beyond an elusive self, nothing that seems worthy of the foreclosure of possibility that intimate commitment necessarily entails.

Status and Intimacy

The scenario that I have sketched is in direct conflict with our vision of the family as a source of enduring support. It therefore should lead to skepticism about the wisdom of categorically embracing contract as the governing principle in family law. If we desire family law to vindicate not the acontextual but the relational self, is there still a role that status might play in the contemporary world?

The Victorian Vision of Family

One way to approach this question is to examine the period when family law first emerged as a distinct field: the Victorian era. Much recent scholarship suggests that the Victorians regarded the family as a vehicle for confronting the disruptions of communal life wrought by modernization and the atomistic individualism that these disruptions seemed to threaten. As do we, Victorians saw the family as a haven of affection in an often hostile and increasingly egoistic world.[43] Indeed, it was during their time that this image gained widespread cultural acceptance. In contrast to the prevailing stereotype of the Victorian age, the result was a greater emphasis on marital companionship, affection, and sexuality.[44]

Yet this vision of the family as emotional haven had the potential to foster the radical individualism that Victorians feared because of its focus on personal emotion and its rhetoric of withdrawal from the larger social world. As Carl Degler has pointed out, for instance, the emergence of love as the basis for marriage "was the purest form of individualism; it subordinated all familial, social, or group considerations to personal preference."[45] The Victorians sought to temper this potential for atomism by promoting the family, rather than the individual, as the central unit of private life and by conceptualizing that family in terms of the performance of interdependent roles. Through identification with such roles, the individual ideally gained a sense of self that was at least partly rooted in communal notions of responsibility. Unlike romantic love, deemed to be a mysterious and uncontrollable force, "[r]ole duty was conceived as willable, therefore the individual could be held accountable both in his own mind and in a social sense."[46] In this way, a relational understanding of identity might be preserved in a period in which the acontextual self had begun to loom as a distinct possibility. The founding of family law upon the principle of status, thus, can be seen as part of an effort to temper the rise of an individualistic ethic that chafed at the idea of social constraint.

We need no reminder, of course, that the Victorian conception of family roles was based on gender, reflecting discredited assumptions about the respective destinies of men and women. As a result, we might say that the Victorians gave status a bad name. Certainly, much of the insistence on private ordering within the family in recent years is based on justified rejection of rigid gender roles that first emerged in the nineteenth century.

Many women have seen contract as an instrument of liberation in family law, a way of proclaiming an independent identity apart from family relationships. In this respect, greater deference to private choice in intimate matters has been beneficial and salutary.

But do we really want to affirm individualism completely by embracing contract as the governing principle of family law? Aren't we now more sensitive to the dangers of an acontextual self unencumbered by any family obligations not freely chosen? Shouldn't the postmodern prospect of fragmented identity and fleeting intimacy give us pause? Some feminists have suggested that the modernist vision is in fact a distinctly male one, which exalts separation over connection and independence over responsibility.[47] Certainly, women and children have borne the brunt of many recent family law reforms that emphasize autonomy and self-sufficiency instead of care and obligation.[48] Contract in family law thus may be a double-edged sword for women.

A New Model of Status

We may do better by attempting to preserve the vision of a relational self and of marriage and family as a distinct discourse of opposition to individualism. If we appreciate the extent to which the Victorians' use of status was animated by this objective, we may extract from their effort something of value even as we reject its gendered form. The challenge is to construct a new model of status, sensitive to our desire for greater equality within the family and to the diversity of contemporary family forms. This model would embrace the substantive values of commitment and responsibility within intimate relationships, rejecting the notion that family law should remain agnostic about family behavior absent a threat of direct harm.

Any attempt to construct a new model of status in family law must contend with the perception that status and intimacy are adversaries. Yet appreciation of the connection between identity and intimacy suggests that status may in fact enhance intimacy in ways in which a regime of pure contract cannot. First, status may protect the vulnerability and reliance that typically arise within intimate relationships. Second, status can contribute to a unified sense of self over time, the prerequisite for intimate commitment, because it offers a model of identity defined in terms of communal norms. Each of these ideas deserves closer attention.

We can begin our exploration of the use of status to respond to interdependence not with the family but with the market. Specifically, the demise of freedom of contract as the reigning principle in economic life indicates the perils of an uncritical embrace of private ordering. Even as the nineteenth and early twentieth centuries exalted status within the family, they proclaimed devotion to contract in the realm of the market.[49] Perhaps the best known expression of this tenet was the Supreme Court's decision in *Lochner v. New York* in 1905, which struck down a New York law limiting the working hours of bakers to ten hours a day.[50] Such a law, declared the Court, was "an illegal interference with the rights of individuals, both employers and employees, to make contracts regarding labor upon such terms as they may think best."[51] The vision of freedom of contract thus was of a free market of unfettered bargainers, who themselves determined the obligations to which they would be subject.

While this vision still has some resonance as part of "free market" rhetoric, its hold in the law has steadily declined throughout this century. Legal theorists have pointed out the inequality in bargaining power that characterizes many economic relationships,[52] and the Depression and New Deal provided direct and practical challenges to the paradigm of contract. The result has been what some scholars describe as a new regime of status in economic life, as regulation, rather than private negotiation, determines many of the terms on which parties deal in the market.[53] Thus, for instance, contracts between landlords and tenants, insurance companies and policyholders, and employers and employees all contain standard terms that the parties are not free to alter, in the interest of protecting the weaker party. In each case, one's status as landlord, insurer, or employer automatically gives rise to certain rights and obligations. In each case, the assumption is that relationships that are characterized by vulnerability and dependence should not be governed by a regime of unqualified private ordering.

Current claims for the primacy of freedom of contract in family life bear some resemblance to earlier arguments in favor of freedom of contract in commercial life. Proponents of a regime of private ordering in family matters implicitly posit a self that is prior to and independent of personal relationships, which interacts with others in a free market of personal choices. Just as contracting parties once were regarded as the only persons capable of evaluating the terms of their commercial agreement, so intimate partners now tend to be regarded as the only legitimate arbiters of the terms of their relationships. In each instance, the "public" sphere is deemed incapable of passing judgment on the fairness or desirability of "private" arrangements.[54]

Yet, just as protecting the vulnerable through the use of status can enhance freedom in commercial life, so acknowledging reliance through the use of status can promote intimacy in family life. If we reject the model of the acontextual self and instead are sensitive to the social foundations of identity, then we can recognize that intimate relationships give rise to a distinct type of vulnerability. Personal relationships are integral to our sense of who we are, and the family plays a particularly important role in the formation of identity. Marriage, for instance, is the occasion for the joint creation of a "nomos," a structure of meaning that serves as an important basis for making sense of the world.[55] This process involves mutual reliance and mutual dependence, for one's very sense of self is significantly intertwined in relationship with another.[56] Just as the use of status in regulating commercial life expresses social norms about the behavior of persons in interdependent economic relationships, so status in family law can proclaim certain expectations with respect to interdependent intimate relationships. Vulnerability, in other words, creates responsibility.

We know that many marriages end in divorce; feelings may change, devotion may wane, and other alternatives may come to seem more attractive. While contract seeks merely to effectuate whatever choices individuals may make, status can provide a buffer against the full force of changes in sentiment. It can provide some assurance that intimate commitment will not result in undue hardship if the other person has a change of heart. The imposition of a waiting period for obtaining a divorce, for instance, or the requirement that certain financial obligations continue after a marriage ends, signals that a spouse assumes responsibilities that cannot be abruptly disavowed. Status is a way of acknowledging that individuals do not pass in and out of intimate relationships untransformed but create a shared life that provides an important sense of meaning. Status thus can encourage intimacy by reducing, even if it can't eliminate, the risks that commitment necessarily involves.

Status as a Foundation for Self-Understanding

The postmodern vision of personal life, however, suggests that protection of reliance may be insufficient alone to promote intimacy because the fragmentation of the self may result in less emotional involvement in any given relationship. Status has the potential to address this problem because it offers the possibility of providing a social foundation for self-understanding that is more stable than the acontextual model. This understanding in turn can enhance the capacity for intimate commitment. One way to appreciate this is to focus on George Herbert Mead's theory of selfhood.[57]

Mead, who wrote in the early decades of this century, argued that self-consciousness, the sense of a self that is distinguishable from the random flow of sensory stimuli, requires a perception of oneself as a "me."[58] The "me" is the understanding of the self as a distinct object within the environment. Mead maintained that language and other social practices are essential to the emergence of the "me," because they involve a process in which we can see ourselves as others see us.[59] Through interaction with others, we can move "outside" ourself and grasp the self as an object in the world. In turn, this makes it possible to say that certain experience is *my* experience, attributable to a specific agent. Mead suggested that the "me" can be seen as the repository of communal expectations that orient the self within the world.[60]

By contrast, Mead argued, the "I" can be seen as pure subjectivity, an existential margin of freedom to reject a course of action in accordance with social norms.[61] Individual behavior can be seen as a dialectic between the "me" and the "I." The situated "me" presents to the "I" options that it may or may not accept; the response of the "I" in turn changes the social world that is the source of the expectations embodied in the "me." As Mead put it:

> We are individuals born into a certain nationality, located at a certain spot geographically, with such and such family relations, and such and such political relations. All of these represent a certain situation which constitutes the "me"; but this necessarily involves a continued action of the organism toward the "me" in the process within which that lies.[62]

The "me" and the "I" thus are dependent on one another. Without the "I," for instance, the "me" would be virtually an automaton; it is the "I" that represents the possibilities of the self that lie beyond the expectations of a particular situation. Even more important for my purposes here, the "I" needs the "me." The "me" enables the "I" to regard experience as *her* experience, as belonging to a self that spans the series of existential moments that the "I" confronts. In other words, the "me" makes possible "the establishment of a coherent and continuous identity."[63]

While Mead's analysis is not without its difficulties, the important point is that it allows us to see the modernist quest for the acontextual self as the search for a pure "I," unconstrained by the communal expectations encoded in the "me." From this perspective, the postmodern loss of the self is predictable. Without a "me," there is no object rooted in experience on which the "I" can reflect. Thus, there is no unified selfhood but an endless stream of experience from which the self is indistinguishable.

Mead's framework suggests that the identity created by legal status may offer one way of constituting a "me" that can serve as the basis for a coherent sense of self. This identity reflects social expectations that are presented to all status holders, evoking in them an understanding of themselves as the community sees them. It reflects the obligations that arise by virtue of the self's location in a web of particular relationships. Status offers an interpretive filter that rejects the notion that one should approach each situation fully open and receptive to all the stimuli that it may offer. The "me" associated with a given status will find some stimuli relevant and rewarding and others less so, in light of the commitments and expectations that arise through relationships with others.

One may, of course, occupy various statuses based on several relationships, none of which enters in any strong way into one's sense of self. For the last century and a half, however, family has served as the paradigm of relationships in American culture that are bound up with identity. As such, it has served as a model of what it means to have a relational sense of self. The legal identities of family members, and the rights and obligations associated with them, traditionally have served to create a "me" that most people believe *should* have influence across a variety of contexts. The "me" embodied in the status of spouse, for instance, may prompt two people to try to work through their marital difficulties rather than immediately conclude that the demands of the relationship are incompatible with the needs of an unfettered "I." Family law is one way in which culture reinforces the idea that the "me" reflected in the status of spouse or parent is one that should be treated as an important constituent of identity.

This promotion of a relatively stable identity enhances the prospect of attaining meaningful intimacy in two ways. First, it contributes to the ability to make commitments, since a promise made in one context can have force in a different one if it is seen as made by a self that is relatively constant in both. Second, this in turn inspires trust on the part of others, who will be more willing to make commitments if they believe that they will be reciprocated. The trust essential to intimacy thus does not, as modernism would have it, rest upon the union of two radically free wills who reveal their "true" selves apart from social context. Instead, as Niklas Luhmann observes, "freedom bound up with and moderated through the social order . . . is the source of the ability to learn trust."[64]

The impersonality of status therefore is not inherently antagonistic to intimacy. Indeed, status may promote intimacy more effectively than an unqualified regime of contract because it uses communal obligation to root the self in context, locating the individual within forms of life in which it can act meaningfully as an agent capable of making commitments and inspiring trust. The point is not that status, rather than contract, should be enthroned in family law, for we need to be sensitive to both the solitary and the social dimension of our being. Rather, it is that we may do best if we strive to sustain an equilibrium in which both status and contract play a role.

Status and Family Law

How might a new model of status, based on shared norms of responsibility, specifically inform contemporary family law? Consider two examples from current divorce law: the role of fault in divorce proceedings and the allocation of financial rights and responsibilities between divorcing spouses.

Fault

Under no-fault divorce, available now in all states, divorce is available without any allegation of marital misconduct. In addition, several states exclude consideration of fault altogether in property and custody determinations, and many that do take it into account tend to define fault quite narrowly.[65] The justification for eliminating or circumscribing consideration of fault is that it reduces acrimony in divorce proceedings and that we lack any consensual standards for evaluating the propriety of marital behavior.[66] Thus, the argument goes, the law should simply make it possible for spouses to go their separate ways, by allocating their assets and children, without passing judgment on their conduct. In other words, courts should make arrangements for the future rather than engage in moral evaluation of the past.

Studies indicate, however, that spouses tend to care very much about moral responsibility when they go through a divorce.[67] Persons typically regard marriage as a venture that implicates in fundamental ways concepts such as trust, fairness, sacrifice, loyalty, and care. Daily married life derives much of its meaning from shared assumptions about what it means to live a good life together. Our earliest moral lessons are learned within the family; it remains a powerful symbol of what we can legitimately expect from others and they from us. The creation of a new family through marriage is an effort consciously to construct a way of life that resembles, even if it does not replicate, our earliest experience of a shared moral order.

Divorce represents the loss of this structure of meaning. In some cases, that loss occurs despite the desire of one spouse that it not. At a minimum, there is often asymmetry in the rate at which each party comes to accept the dissolution. In any event, spouses going through divorce struggle to fashion an interpretation of events that can serve as the basis for constructing a new order of meaning that still draws on certain basic precepts of the old.[68] As a result, legal insistence on a sharp distinction between past and future may be misguided in the divorce context, since "examination of the past and planning for the future may well be part of the same exercise."[69] In sum, there is good reason to believe that many divorcing spouses do not regard divorce as merely a technical exercise designed to allocate assets and children.

The excision of fault from the divorce process thus may eliminate any outlet for divorcing spouses to express themselves on things that matter deeply to them. A wife who has provided nurture for her husband through difficult times, only to be abandoned for another woman as soon as his prospects improve, receives no legal recognition that her conduct has been honorable and that her feeling of betrayal is legitimate. It is not surprising, then, that research indicates that a good deal of bitterness still characterizes divorce actions despite the advent of no-fault divorce.[70] Despite the reduction in the opportunity for formal assertions of fault in the grounds for and consequences of divorce, disputes over property and custody are often battlegrounds on which spouses indirectly work through their feelings about the end of the marriage. We must ask whether the provision of an explicit mechanism for dealing with marital misconduct in certain instances might better channel and control these impulses. In sum, one danger of the banishment of fault from the divorce process is that "the people the law seeks to affect themselves think in moral terms. A law which tries to eliminate those terms from its language will both misunderstand the people it is regulating and be misunderstood by them."[71]

Few would argue that we should return to a system in which divorce is available only on fault grounds. The reasons that marriages end are complex, and the identification of one blameworthy and one innocent spouse seems unrealistic and misguided. We may do better if we conceptualize a fault determination not as the assignment of blame for the breakdown of a marriage but as the identification of behavior that violates certain basic norms of marriage. It seems reasonable to believe that, with all our diversity, there are certain minimum standards of marital conduct on which most people would agree. Spousal abuse, for instance, is something that the vast majority of people find reprehensible. Promiscuous sexual infidelity may be another. It is difficult to establish bright-line rules in this area. Nonetheless, it is likely that there is some consensus on what constitutes an egregious breach of marital trust.

This suggests, for instance, that fault grounds for divorce should be preserved as an option along with no-fault divorce.[72] We can be reasonably certain that most divorces will proceed on a no-fault basis, given the large number of uncontested divorces even under the fault-based system.[73] We should leave available, however, a divorce action based on fault when a spouse desires legal recognition that an egregious abuse of trust has occurred. This option provides a way of affirming that there are shared social norms that should guide spouses in their dealings with one another. It gives those who have been victimized by the breach of those norms a declaration of that fact and a vindication of their feelings of pain and betrayal. Permitting battered wives, for instance, an opportunity to recount their experience may lessen the prospect that women will blame themselves for the violent behavior of their husbands.[74] The language of fault in such instances is a far more sensitive expression of experience than dry no-fault language that depicts the reason for divorce as mere incompatibility.

In addition, fault should play some role in financial and custody determinations even in states that provide only no-fault divorce. Treating serious misconduct as irrelevant in these matters sends the message that those who abuse the marital relationship ought to share its fruits equally with those whom they have abused. The notion that only misconduct that results in specific circumscribed forms of "harm" should be taken into account ignores the fact that marital behavior necessarily occurs within a context of interdependence in which cause and effect cannot be easily isolated. Serious misconduct disrupts this web of relationships and those who are reliant on it. It constitutes harm to the family unit, not simply to discrete assets or particular children.

It seems fair to use financial awards to penalize those who are responsible for this disruption, because the end of the marriage often exposes a spouse to economic hardship that she would not have endured had the marriage continued. Most states, for instance, permit a divorcing spouse to bring a separate tort action for physical or emotional abuse.[75] If there is general agreement that a spouse who seriously misbehaves should suffer a financial penalty through a tort action, there is no reason to refuse to levy that penalty instead in the form of financial allocations at divorce. The law will not want to leave an offending spouse penniless because of misconduct, but the financial effect of the award on that spouse would necessarily be one of the factors that a court would take into account.

Similarly, it seems fair to take fault into account in a custody determination because the spouse's misconduct has made the child more vulnerable than if the marriage had continued. Furthermore, while the spouse's relationship with the child may be relevant in awarding custody, that relationship cannot be segregated from the larger pattern of irresponsibility that the spouse has exhibited toward the family as a unit. A parent ideally provides an example of moral integrity, a concept that necessarily draws on a unitary, rather than fragmentary, understanding of personality. One spouse's serious misconduct toward another must at least be taken into account in determining which parent can better provide this example.

Consideration of egregious fault in financial and custody determinations therefore would affirm the view that marital conduct can be evaluated according to shared norms of behavior. It would reject the view that relations between spouses are "private" matters on which society is incapable or unwilling to pass judgment. Instead, family law would assert that marital status necessarily involves the assumption of certain basic responsibilities toward one's spouse.

Financial Obligations at Divorce

In recent years, the predominant aim of the law concerning financial obligations at divorce has been to effect a "clean break" between the spouses.[76] This approach seeks to minimize the need for the parties to deal with each other after the divorce. The theory is that all assets are put into a pot, each party is awarded a share, and each then uses this stock of capital to start a new life unburdened by the claims of the past. Property division thus is favored as the means of meeting the spouses' financial needs while alimony tends to be disfavored, available only in exceptional circumstances.[77] This desire to achieve a "clean break" is reflected in the typical statement that marriage is an "economic partnership."[78] The image is of members of a voluntary association who withdraw their investment in order to move on to other ventures; the law's purpose is to help them do so efficiently.

As recent observers have noted, however, divorcing spouses typically have little property available for distribution. Future earning capacity is the most important asset of most married couples but it is one that each spouse takes with him after divorce. Access to postdivorce income thus appears to be crucial to the postdivorce welfare of women and children. This realization has prompted efforts to find a basis for imposing financial responsibility after divorce that is still consistent with the "clean break" approach.

One alternative has been to broaden the definition of marital property to include items such as professional degrees, advanced training, medical residencies, licenses, and professional practices and goodwill. The theory is that any enhancement of earning power that occurs during a marriage represents "human capital" that is the product of joint spousal efforts.[79] Each spouse therefore is entitled to a share of this capital. Since few couples have enough assets for this entitlement to be paid in full at divorce, the person in whom the investment has been made is liable for periodic payments to the other spouse of her share. This theory justifies postdivorce obligation as the payment of a return on the other spouse's investment.

The investment approach has met with mixed results. While some states have accepted the approach,[80] most balk at classifying income enhancements as property,[81] while others are selective in doing so.[82] Resistance is based on the speculative calculations necessary to value future earnings; the fact that enhancements do not possess many of the attributes conventionally associated with property, such as market value or alienability; and the belief that it is inequitable "to pay a spouse a share of intangible assets that could not be realized by sale or another method of liquidating value."[83]

Courts have been more comfortable with a second approach. This is to recognize a right to reimbursement for contributions made during the marriage by one spouse to enable the other to acquire human capital.[84] On this theory, one partner typically sacrifices enhancement of her own earning power, by assuming greater household and childrearing responsibility, in order to help her spouse increase his.[85] For the latter spouse to retain all the benefits of this sacrifice would be to permit unjust enrichment. Efforts have been made to refine this approach by specifying what kinds of sacrifices should be compensable under what circumstances.[86] Whether the payments are classified as a cash award in lieu of property[87] or as alimony,[88] they are based on a theory of postdivorce obligation as restitution.

The human capital theory that underlies both these approaches to postdivorce financial obligation is more sensitive than were initial reforms to the effect of marriage on the welfare of spouses after divorce. Its approach, however, still reflects a "clean break" philosophy that emphasizes voluntary rather than relational obligation. Entitlement to postdivorce assets is earned through the specific exchanges and sacrifices that a spouse makes during the marriage. Postdivorce obligation is based on voluntary acceptance by the other spouse of the benefits of such efforts. The objective is to make sure that no spouse gets something for which he has not paid full price. Human capital theory thus reconstructs the marriage according to an exchange model of the relationship, which focuses on the implicit costs and benefits of each spousal interaction.[89] Beyond providing compensation for the benefits bestowed by one's partner, a spouse has no obligations that extend beyond the marriage. The emphasis is on paying one's bills and getting on with a new life.

Basic economic justice between spouses is important, and the law should vindicate the principle that spousal sacrifice should be recognized. Human capital theory also is useful in drawing attention to the value of women's nonmarket contributions to marriage. Its limitation of obligation to a strict accounting model, however, has some serious drawbacks. For instance, a husband whose earning capacity has been enhanced by his wife's economic sacrifice would seem to have a plausible argument that she has been compensated for her efforts if the couple has been able to enjoy a higher standard of living as a result.[90] Such an outcome would seem to undermine the theory's utility as a basis for taking career sacrifice into account, but it is also consistent with the underlying logic of this approach.

Second, the theory is not fully responsive to the character of marriage as a shared life. For instance, what of a spouse who became ill or disabled during the marriage and who thus represented a net economic drain on the household? Does she owe compensation at divorce to her husband for his sacrifices that preserved her earning potential? What of a single mother who works two jobs for many years, then marries a man sufficiently wealthy that she can finally afford to go to college? If the couple divorces, does she owe her husband at least tuition and expenses for her college years, if not a portion of her future salary?

In each instance, the logic of human capital theory would demand that the wife compensate her husband. Yet I suspect that a good number of people would be unwilling to impose this burden on her. Indeed, many would argue that she is entitled to some postdivorce support from him. The reason for this difference is a consideration that human capital theory regards as irrelevant: need. The belief that need can be a source of obligation is based on the idea of marriage as a commitment of two people to care for one another. Marriage is a proclamation that one need not battle alone the vicissitudes that life can bring but can rely on a partner to share the burdens of living in what sometimes seems a capricious and indifferent universe. Spouses agree in essence to pool their risks in face of an uncertain future.

Seen in this way, marriage ideally involves the cultivation of a relational identity that infuses costs and benefits with an intersubjective character. Individual acts take on meaning only against a background of shared commitment; to analyze them apart from this context fails to capture their full significance. Spouses generally have access to marital resources without regard to a strict accounting based on individual merit.[91] The longer they are married, "the more their human capital should be seen as intertwined rather than affixed to the individual spouse in whose body it resides."[92] Over time, then, occurs a process in which daily actions are made with reference to a collective welfare that powerfully informs the calculation of individual utility. Put differently, the boundaries of both identity and self-interest are not sharply demarcated by the individual body.

Human capital theory is reasonable in assuming that, despite this communal experience, spouses still expect some rough equivalence of individual costs and benefits. They expect this equivalence, however, within the context of an ongoing marriage. Specifically, a spouse anticipates that she and her partner will enjoy a roughly comparable standard of living. If we want to vindicate the development of a relational sense of self in marriage and still do justice between the parties, then it seems appropriate not to try to reconstruct spouses' past behavior but to compare their postdivorce financial condition. In this formulation, we might think of need as the gap between the higher- and lower-income spouse's standard of living. The difference in earning potential between the spouses arose within a community that de-emphasized such individual comparisons. The lower-income spouse relied on the continuation of this community in ordering her life, and the higher-income spouse achieved greater earning potential because of this reliance. This interdependence gives rise to a responsibility that the higher-income spouse cannot abruptly disavow at divorce.

How strong was this interdependence? We cannot measure it precisely, but time is a good indication of its likely intensity. The longer the marriage, the more the spouses have arranged their lives around its existence, even if their relative satisfaction with the relationship has varied. This suggests that the duration of the marriage should be a crucial, if not the primary, consideration in financial arrangements made at divorce. Specifically, we might aim at equalizing the postdivorce standard of living between the spouses for a certain period, based in some way on the length of time that the parties were married.[93] This approach might replace calculations based on human capital theory or might be used in conjunction with them to justify allocations that exceed what that theory would provide.[94] The important point is to affirm a theory of postdivorce obligation that is based on the responsibilities that inherently arise within marriage—responsibilities that may continue for some time after it ends.

We should be wary about letting the "clean break" philosophy dominate discourse about property and alimony. Not only does that philosophy have limitations in the context of relations between spouses, its influence may attenuate a sense of postdivorce obligation toward children as well. As Elizabeth Scott notes, in every matter except child support, "modern divorce law encourages parties to put the marriage behind them. Many fathers apparently adopt the general norm and fail to preserve their parental role and responsibility."[95] An approach sensitive to the cultivation of relational identity can help strengthen the sense of both marriage and parenthood as a communal experience that does not leave the individuals within it untransformed.

Conclusion

It is important to keep in mind that family law's most important contributions may be indirect. It is unlikely that many people directly take account of the law in deciding how to behave in family settings. On this "regulative" view of law, family law seems pretty insignificant.[96] Yet, paradoxically, few other legal subjects seem to evoke as much interest and passion. This suggests that the regulative aspect of family law does not exhaust its significance. More important may be its constitutive function—its role as an element in creating and sustaining cultural narratives about ourselves and our intimate relationships with others.[97] Spouses have been among the most important characters in those narratives. Traditionally, they have followed a cultural script for marriage that has encouraged the cultivation of a relational identity. A new model of status offers a way of affirming that this script should continue, even as another competing story begins to beckon.

Notes

Adapted from Milton C. Regan, Jr., *Family Law and the Pursuit of Intimacy* (New York: New York University Press, 1993).

1. See, e.g., Judith S. Wallerstein and Sandra Blakeslee, *Second Chances: Men, Women and Children a Decade After Divorce* (New York: Ticknor & Fields, 1989); James A. Holdnack, "The Long-Term Effects of Parental Divorce on Family Relationships and the Effects on Adult Children's Self-Concept," in *Divorce and the Next Generation: Effects on Young Adults' Patterns of Intimacy and Expectations for Marriage*, ed. Craig A. Everett (New York: Haworth Press, 1992), 137.

2. Women traditionally have been socialized particularly vigorously according

to this ethic, but marriage nonetheless has been seen as a way to induce a less solitary and more communal orientation in men as well.

3. Mellman and Lazarus, Inc., *Massachusetts Mutual American Family Values Study* (Springfield, MA: Massachusetts Mutual Life Insurance Co., June 1989), 14.

4. Ibid.

5. Ibid.

6. Frank Furstenberg and Graham Spanier, *Recycling the Family* (Beverly Hills, CA: Sage Publications, 1984), 74.

7. Philippe Aries, "Two Successive Motivations for the Declining Birthrate in the West," *Population and Development Review* 6 (1980): 645, 650.

8. Harold Rausch, "Orientations to the Close Relationship," in *Close Relationships: Perspectives on the Meaning of Intimacy*, ed. George Levinger and Harold Rausch (Amherst, MA: University of Massachusetts Press, 1977), 163, 182. Similarly, John Scanzoni and his colleagues suggest that the basic tenet of the modern intimate relationship, including marriage, is that "[e]verything is negotiable except the principle that everything is negotiable." John Scanzoni et al., *The Sexual Bond: Rethinking Families and Close Relationships* (Newbury Park, CA: Sage Publications, 1989), 78.

9. Joseph Veroff, Elizabeth Douvan and Ronald Kulka, *The Inner American* (New York: Basic Books, 1981), 19; Bernard Farber, "The Future of the American Family: A Dialectical Account," *Journal of Family Issues* 8 (1987): 431–32.

10. See David Popenoe, *Disturbing the Nest: Family Change and Decline in Modern Societies* (Hawthorne, NY: Aldine De Gruyter, 1988); William Goode, "Individual Investments in Family Relationships Over the Coming Decades," *The de Tocqueville Review* 6 (1984): 1.

11. This terminology first gained influence in the work of Henry Maine in the mid-nineteenth century. See Henry Maine, *Ancient Law*, 2d ed. (New York: Charles Scribner, 1864), 168–70. Maine argued that the progress of civilization was marked by the diminishing role of the family as a source of legal identity, as the individual emerged in civil society as the locus of legal capacity. Within the family itself, however, status continued to order relationships for perhaps as long as a century after Maine's observations.

12. Peter Berger and Thomas Luckmann, *The Social Construction of Reality* (Garden City, NY: Anchor Books, 1967), 62. On the character and significance of social institutions, see ibid. at 47–92; Robert Bellah et al., *The Good Society* (New York: Alfred A. Knopf, 1991), 3-18.

13. See, e.g., James Schouler, *A Treatise on the Law of the Domestic Relations* (Boston: Little, Brown & Co., 1870), 262; *Graham v. Graham*, 33 F. Supp. 936 (E.D. MI 940).

14. See Joel Bishop, *2 New Commentaries on Marriage, Divorce, and Separation* (Chicago: T. H. Flood & Co., 1891), 217, 219; Schouler, *A Treatise*, 291.

15. *Maynard v. Hill*, 125 U.S. 190, 211 (1888).

16. Uniform Premarital Agreement Act (UPAA), sections 3(a)(1)–(6) (West Supp. 1991).

17. See, e.g., *Matlock v. Matlock*, 576 P.2d 629 (KS 1978); *Newman v. Newman*, 653 P.2d 728 (CO 1982) (*en banc*); *Osborne v. Osborne*, 428 N.E.2d 810 (MA 1981); Remarriage of Burgess, 485 N.E.2d 504 (IL 3d Dist. 1985).

18. *Chiles v. Chiles*, 779 S.W.2d 127, 129 (Dist. Ct. App. TX 1989). As Elizabeth Scott has observed, "the current trend is toward more routine judicial enforcement" of marital contracts. Elizabeth Scott, "Rational Decisionmaking About Marriage and Divorce," *Virginia Law Review* 76 (1990): 9, 80.

19. New York and Mississippi are the only two states that require mutual consent for no-fault divorce.

20. See John Stuart Mill, *On Liberty*, ed. Elizabeth Rapaport (Indianapolis, IN: Hackett Publishing Co., 1978), 73–91.

21. See, e.g., Uniform Marriage and Divorce Act (UMDA), section 306(b) (West Supp. 1991); UPAA section 3(b).

22. See Doris Freed and Timothy Walker, "Family Law in the Fifty States: An Overview," *Family Law Quarterly* 21 (1988): 417, 451–52, 472.

23. See *Mosbarger v. Mosbarger*, 547 So.2d 188 (Dist. Ct. App. FL 1989); *Smith v. Smith*, 331 S.E.2d 682 (NC 1985).

24. On the difficulties of this position, see Milton C. Regan, Jr., "Market Discourse and Moral Neutrality in Divorce Law," *Utah Law Review* 605 (1994); Milton C. Regan, Jr., "Reason, Tradition, and Family Law: A Comment on Social Constructionism," 79 *Virginia Law Review* 79 (1993): 1515.

25. 405 U.S. 438, 453 (1972).

26. An early suggestion of this trend is found in Ernest W. Burgess and Harvey J. Locke, *The Family: From Institution to Companionship* (New York: American Book Co., 1945). David Gauthier suggests that the movement toward contract has been prominent in social life generally: "Institutions and practices which derive their rationale from noncontractarian considerations are being discarded or rejected." D. Gauthier, "The Social Contract as Ideology," in *Moral Dealing: Contract, Ethics, and Reason* (Ithaca, NY: Cornell University Press, 1990), 350.

27. For discussions of the concept of modernity, see Marshall Berman, *All That Is Solid Melts Into Air: The Experience of Modernity* (New York: Simon & Schuster, 1982); Anthony Giddens, *Modernity and Self-Identity* (Stanford, CA: Stanford University Press, 1991); Anthony Giddens, *Consequences of Modernity* (Stanford, CA: Stanford University Press, 1990); Ross Poole, *Morality and Modernity* (New York: Routledge, 1991); Charles Taylor, *The Ethics of Authenticity* (Cambridge, MA: Harvard University Press, 1992); Charles Taylor, *Sources of the Self: The Making of the Modern Identity* (Cambridge, MA: Harvard University Press, 1989).

28. Alasdair MacIntyre, *After Virtue*, 2d. ed. (Notre Dame, IN: University of Notre Dame Press, 1984), 220.

29. Taylor, *Sources of the Self*, 368.

30. Robert Bellah et al., *Habits of the Heart: Individualism and Commitment in American Life* (Berkeley, CA: University of California Press, 1985), 333–34.

31. See, e.g., Veroff, Douvan, and Kulka, *The Inner American*, 8; Daniel Yan-

kelovich, *New Rules: Searching for Self-Fulfillment in a World Turned Upside Down* (New York: Random House, 1981), 251. For an analysis of the increasingly powerful aspiration to intimacy, see Richard Sennett, *The Fall of Public Man* (1977).

32. See Erving Goffman, "Role Distance," in *Encounters: Two Studies in the Sociology of Interaction* (Indianapolis, IN: Bobbs-Merrill, 1961), 85.

33. John Scanzoni, "Families in the 1980s: Time to Refocus Our Thinking," *Journal of Family Issues* 8 (1987): 394, 407 (emphasis omitted).

34. Kenneth Gergen, *The Saturated Self: Dilemmas of Identity in Contemporary Life* (New York: Basic Books, 1991).

35. Ibid., 73–74.

36. See E. Ann Kaplan, *Rocking Around the Clock: Music Television, Postmodernism, and Popular Culture* (New York: Methuen, 1987); Lawrence Grossberg, "MTV: Swinging on the (Postmodern) Star," in *Cultural Politics in Contemporary America*, ed. Ian Angus and Sut Jhally (New York: Routledge, 1989), 254.

37. See, e.g., Frederic Jameson, "Postmodernism and Consumer Society," in *The Anti-Aesthetic: Essays on Postmodern Culture*, ed. Hal Foster (Port Townsend, WA: Bay Press, 1983), 111.

38. Ibid., 125.

39. Ibid., 119–20.

40. For other similar observations, see Jean-Francois Lyotard, *The Postmodern Condition* (Minneapolis, MN: University of Minnesota Press, 1984); Jean Beaudrillard, "The Ecstacy of Communication," in *The Anti-Aesthetic*, ed. Foster, 126.

41. Jameson, "Postmodernism and Consumer Society," 119.

42. Gergen, *The Saturated Self*, 178.

43. For an insightful exploration of both the persistence and ambiguity of this conception, see Christopher Lasch, *Haven in a Heartless World: The Family Besieged* (New York: Basic Books, 1977).

44. See Carl Degler, *At Odds: Women and the Family in America From the Revolution to the Present* (New York: Oxford University Press, 1980); Peter Gay, *The Tender Passion* (New York: Oxford University Press, 1986); Peter Gay, *Education of the Senses* (New York: Oxford University Press, 1984); Karen Lystra, *Searching the Heart* (New York: Oxford University Press, 1989); Clelia Mosher, *The Mosher Survey: Sexual Attitudes of 45 Victorian Women*, ed. J. MaHood and K. Wenburg (New York: Arno Press, 1980).

45. Degler, *At Odds*, 14. See also Lystra, *Searching the Heart*, 226.

46. Lystra, *Searching the Heart*, 225–26.

47. See Jean Bethke Elshtain, *Public Man, Private Woman* (Princeton, NJ: Princeton University Press, 1981); Carol Gilligan, *In a Different Voice* (Princeton, NJ: Princeton University Press, 1982); Jean Baker Miller, *Toward a New Psychology of Women* (Boston: Beacon Press, 1976); Nel Noddings, *Caring* (Berkeley, CA: University of California Press, 1974); Sara Ruddick, *Maternal Thinking* (Boston: Beacon Press, 1989).

48. See Barbara Baker, *Family Equity at Issue*, monograph conducted by the

Alaska Women's Commission (1987); Lisa J. Brett et al., *Women and Children Beware*, monograph prepared for the Connecticut Women's Education and Legal Fund, the Women's Research Institute/Hartford College for Women, and the Permanent Commission on the Status of Women (1990); Gloria J. Sterin et al., *Divorce Awards and Outcomes*, monograph prepared by the Federation for Community Planning at the request of and in conjunction with the Cleveland, Ohio Women's Counsel (1981); Lenore J. Weitzman, *The Divorce Revolution* (New York: Free Press, 1985); Marsha Garrison, "Good Intentions Gone Awry: How New York's Equitable Distribution Law Affected Divorce Outcomes," *Brooklyn Law Review* 57 (1991): 619; James B. McLindon, "Separate But Unequal: The Economic Disaster of Divorce for Women and Children," *Family Law Quarterly* 21 (1987): 351. For a discussion of the gender implications of recent family law reforms, see Milton C. Regan, Jr., "Divorce Reform and the Legacy of Gender," *Michigan Law Review* 90 (1992): 1453 (review essay).

49. See generally Lawrence Friedman, *Contract Law in America* (Madison, WI: University of Wisconsin Press, 1965); Morton Horwitz, *The Transformation of American Law 1780–1860* (Cambridge, MA: Harvard University Press, 1977), 160–210; J. Willard Hurst, *Law and the Conditions of Freedom in the Nineteenth-Century United States* (Madison, WI: University of Wisconsin Press, 1956).

50. 198 U.S. 45 (1905).

51. Ibid., 61.

52. See, e.g., Morris Cohen, "The Basis of Contract," *Harvard Law Review* 46 (1933): 553; Morris Cohen, "Property as Sovereignty," *Cornell Law Quarterly* 13 (1927): 8; Robert Hale, "Bargaining, Duress, and Economic Liberty," *Columbia Law Review* 43 (1943): 603.

53. See, e.g., Cunningham, "The New Implied and Statutory Warranties of Habitability in Residential Leases: From Contract to Status," *Urban Law Annual* 16 (1979): 3.

54. One proponent of marital contracts (Marjorie Schultz, "Contractual Ordering of Marriage: A New Model for State Policy," *California Law Review* 70 [1982]: 204, 258), for instance, argues that contractual ordering of marriage reflects a preference for "private ordering over the intrusion of outside norms as the basis for choices about life-styles."

55. See Peter Berger and Hansfried Kellner, "Marriage and the Construction of Reality," *Diogenes* 46 (1964): 1.

56. See Susan Kraus Whitbourne and Joyce B. Ebmeyer, *Identity and Intimacy in Marriage* (New York: Springer-Verlag, 1990), 127.

57. My focus here is on George Herbert Mead, *Mind, Self, and Society* (Chicago: University of Chicago Press, 1934).

58. Ibid., 138. Mead actually first uses the term "me" on page 173, but the discussion prior to this clearly relates to this concept.

59. Ibid., 139.

60. Ibid., 196.

61. Ibid., 177.

62. Ibid., 182.

63. Berger and Luckmann, *Social Construction of Reality*, 133.

64. Niklas Luhmann, *Trust and Power* (New York: J. Wiley, 1979), 41.

65. See UMDA section 306(b) (West Supp. 1991); UPAA section 3(b) and accompanying texts.

66. See, e.g., Ira Ellman, "The Theory of Alimony," *California Law Review* 77 (1989): 1, 13.

67. See Erlanger, Chambliss, and Melli, "Participation and Flexibility in Informal Processes: Cautions from the Divorce Context," *Law and Social Review* 21 (1987): 585; Ingleby, "Matrimonial Breakdown and the Legal Process: The Limitations of No-Fault Divorce," *Law and Policy* 11 (1989): 1.

68. See generally Catherine Kohler Riessman, *Divorce Talk* (New Brunswick, NJ: Rutgers University Press, 1990).

69. Ingleby, "Matrimonial Breakdown," 14.

70. See Paul Bohannon, "Matrimonial Lawyers and the Divorce Industry," in *Tax, Financial and Estate Planning Developments in Family Law*, 1981 ed., ed. J. DuCanto (Chicago: Schiller and DuCanto, Ltd., 1981), 127; Erlanger, Chambliss, and Melli, "Participation and Flexibility," 591; Frank, Berman, and Mazur-Hart, "No Fault Divorce and the Divorce Rate: The Nebraska Experience—An Interrupted Time Series Analysis and Commentary," *Nebraska Law Review* 58 (1978): 1, 50–52; Ingleby, "Matrimonial Breakdown," 12–14.

71. Carl E. Schneider, "Rethinking Alimony: Marital Decisions and Moral Discourse," *Brigham Young University Law Review* (1991): 197, 243.

72. The majority of states currently make available both fault and no-fault options.

73. See Lynn Wardle, "No-Fault Divorce and the Divorce Conundrum," *Brigham Young University Law Review* (1991): 79, 103.

74. See Naomi Cahn, "Civil Images of Battered Women: The Impact of Domestic Violence on Child Custody Decisions," *Vanderbilt Law Review* 44 (1991): 1041; Martha Minow, "Words and the Door to the Land of Change: Law, Language, and Family Violence," *Vanderbilt Law Review* 43 (1990): 1665.

75. See, e.g., *Stuart v. Stuart*, 421 N.W.2d 505 (WI 1988).

76. See Herma Hill Kay, "An Appraisal of California's No-Fault Divorce Law," *California Law Review* 75 (1987): 291, 313.

77. See, e.g., UMDA section 308.

78. *Price v. Price*, 503 N.E.2d 684, 687 (NY 1986).

79. See Combs, "The Human Capital Concept as a Basis for Property Settlement at Divorce," *Journal of Divorce* 2 (1979): 329; Joan Krauskopf, "Recompense for Financing Spouse's Education: Legal Protection for the Marital Investor in Human Capital," *Kansas Law Review* 28 (1980): 379.

80. The only state high court that has adopted this theory is New York. See *O'Brien v. O'Brien*, 489 N.E.2d 712 (NY 1985) (medical license is marital property). One appeals court in Michigan has done so as well, *Woodworth v. Woodworth*, 337 N.W.2d 332 (MI Ct. App. 1983) (law degree is marital property), while

another has rejected the argument, *Krause v. Krause*, 441 N.W.2d 66 (MI Ct. App. 1989) (dental degree is not marital property).

81. See, e.g. *Stevens v. Stevens*, 492 N.E.2d 131 (OH 1986); *Holbrook v. Holbrook*, 309 N.W.2d 343 (WI Ct. App. 1981).

82. In Maryland, for instance, the professional goodwill of a solo dental practice is treated as marital property, see *Hollander v. Hollander*, *Family Law Reporter* 18 (1991): 1029, (BNA) (MD Ct. Spec. App. 1991), while the professional goodwill of a solo law practice is not, see *Prahinski v. Prahinski*, 582 A.2d 784 (MD Ct. Spec. App. 1990).

83. *Holbrook v. Holbrook*, 309 N.W.2d at 355 (footnote omitted).

84. See, e.g., *Haugen v. Haugen*, 343 N.W.2d 796 (WI 1984); *DeLaRosa v. DeLaRosa*, 309 N.W.2d 755 (MN 1981).

85. See generally Allen Parkman, *No-Fault Divorce: What Went Wrong?* (Boulder, CO: Westview, 1992).

86. See, e.g., Ellman, *The Theory of Alimony*, 53–73.

87. See, e.g., *Hubbard v. Hubbard*, 603 P.2d 747 (OK 1979).

88. See, e.g., *Mahoney v. Mahoney*, 453 A.2d 527 (NJ 1982).

89. For examples of the application of social exchange theory to the family, see Ivan Nye, ed., *Family Relationships: Rewards and Costs* (Beverly Hills, CA: Sage Publications, 1982); Ronald M. Sabatelli, "Exploring Relationship Satisfaction: A Social Exchange Perspective on the Interdependence Between Theory, Research and Practice," *Family Relations* 37 (1988): 217.

90. See Stephen D. Sugarman, "Dividing Financial Interests at Divorce," in *Divorce Reform at the Crossroads*, ed. Stephen D. Sugarman and Herma Hill Kay (New Haven, CT: Yale University Press, 1990), 130, 158–59.

91. See Deborah Rhode and Martha Minow, "Reforming the Questions, Questioning the Reforms: Feminist Perspectives on Divorce Law," in *Divorce Reform at the Crossroads*, ed. Sugarman and Kay, 191, 193.

92. Sugarman, "Dividing Financial Interests," 159.

93. See Jana Singer, "Divorce Reform and Gender Justice," *North Carolina Law Review* 67 (1989): 1103; Sugarman, "Dividing Financial Interests," 159–60.

94. In some cases, human capital theory might be used to justify a larger financial claim than my equal living standard approach would provide. For instance, one spouse may have made significant sacrifices of earning potential during the course of a relatively brief marriage.

95. Scott, "Rational Decisionmaking About Marriage," 36.

96. A classic expression of the regulative view is by Justice Oliver Wendell Holmes:

> If you want to know the law and nothing else, you must look at it as a bad man, who cares only for the material consequences which such knowledge enables him to predict, not as a good one, who finds his reasons for conduct whether inside the law or outside of it, in the vaguer sanctions of conscience.

Oliver Wendell Holmes, Jr., "The Path of the Law," in *Collected Legal Papers* (New York: Harcourt, Brace & Co., 1920), 171.

97. For diverse versions of this approach, see Mary Ann Glendon, *Abortion and Divorce in Western Law* (Cambridge, MA: Harvard University Press, 1989); Clifford Geertz, "Fact and Law in Comparative Perspective," in *Local Knowledge* (New York: Basic Books, 1983), 167; Melton and Saks, "The Law as an Instrument of Socialization and Social Structure," in *The Law as a Behavioral Instrument*, ed. G. Melton (Lincoln, NE: University of Nebraska Press, 1986), 235; James Boyd White, *Justice as Translation* (Chicago: University of Chicago Press, 1990); James Boyd White, *Heracles' Bow: Essays on the Rhetoric and Poetics of the Law* (Madison, WI: University of Wisconsin Press, 1985); James Boyd White, *When Words Lose Their Meaning* (Chicago: University of Chicago Press, 1984); Katharine Bartlett, "Re-Expressing Parenthood," *Yale Law Journal* 98 (1988): 293; Carl E. Schneider, "State-Interest Analysis in Fourteenth Amendment 'Privacy' Law," *Law and Contemporary Problems* 51 (1988): 79; Carol Weisbrod, "On the Expressive Functions of Family Law," *University of California Davis Law Review* 22 (1989): 991.

CHAPTER 8

The Law and the Stability of Marriage: The Family as a Social Institution

Carl E. Schneider

[T]he true beginning is rather with the direct but unreflective education of our loves and hates, our pleasures and pains, gained only in practice, through habituation and by means of praise and blame, reward and punishment. Anyone concerned with influencing conduct must be concerned with those in-between powers of the soul, themselves irrational (in the sense of nonreasoning) but fully amenable to reason (in the sense of being formed, to begin with, in accordance with the reasons of one's parents, teachers, and laws, and being open to further refinement through the exercise of one's own powers of deliberation and discernment).

> —Leon Kass
> *Practicing Ethics: Where's the Action?*

Legislation ought in all cases to be graduated to the existing level of morals in the time and country in which it is employed. You cannot punish anything which public opinion, as expressed in the common practice of society, does not strenuously and unequivocally condemn. . . . Law cannot be better than the nation in which it exists, though it may and can protect an acknowledged moral standard, and may gradually be increased in strictness as the standard rises.

> —James Fitzjames Stephen
> *Liberty, Equality, Fraternity*

Samuel Johnson once wrote, "It is so far from being natural for a man and woman to live in a state of marriage that we find all the motives which they have for remaining in that connection, and the restraints which civilized society imposes to prevent separation, are hardly sufficient to keep them together." In this chapter I shall pursue Dr. Johnson's provocative suggestion by asking what restraints (if any) society might impose through law on couples to join them in marriage in the first place and to keep them in it after they have married.

But why might society wish to do so? For the purposes of this chapter, I am instructed to make a crucial, if controversial, assumption. I am required to assume that, in general, it is best for spouses to make an enduring marriage and for their children to be brought up by both of their parents in a stable home.[1] Like most worthwhile assumptions about social life, this one may be wrong. No doubt there will always be individual cases where the spouses and their children alike will benefit if the marriage ends. Nevertheless, it seems to me a plausible and useful social generalization that couples will be happiest where they can develop a relationship on whose permanence both can depend and build and that children will prosper most where they can rely securely on the attention of two committed caretakers.

My assignment imposes a (not unwelcome) limitation. I will not survey the entire range of governmental policies that might enhance marital stability. Rather, I will limit this essay to those rules that fall within the field of "family law." I will leave to people more expert than I those family policies that fall within the category of social welfare programs. Obviously, this limitation is not born out of any belief that those programs cannot contribute significantly to marital stability (or, even failing that, to the happiness of families and the children in them). Quite the contrary. For example, single-parent families may be relatively common in some communities because in them young men cannot easily find the jobs they need to make marriage seem reasonable. And divorce rates seem to fall as income rises. If these observations are correct, programs to alleviate poverty might well do more to promote marriage and marital stability than the more direct ministrations of family law.[2]

In sum, then, I will ask how family law can promote the marital stability that we hope will lead to happier couples and happier children. I will argue that family law tries to serve that goal by some direct means. But I will contend that it tries to do so more broadly by indirect means—by laboring to shape and support the social institution of the family. In recent decades, that social institution appears to have weakened, perhaps so much so that the family is beginning to be deinstitutionalized. And in that period, family law has, if anything, contributed to this trend. This raises the question whether the trend can be reversed. To answer that question, I will systematically survey family law's repertoire of rules. I will then canvass some of the limits of those tools. I will close by concluding that those limits are substantial, but that it does not follow either that there is no useful work to be done or that the law must do it all.

The Family as a Social Institution

At least in America, almost everyone wants to marry. Almost everyone does marry. Almost everyone expects his or her marriage to last a lifetime. Almost everyone hopes to be a faithful and affectionate spouse. Almost everyone hopes to be a dedicated and generous parent. Almost everyone looks forward to the satisfactions of a lifelong commitment to a spouse and of rearing children to successful adulthood. But despite their rewards, marriage and parenthood can be perplexingly, painfully difficult. People almost always disappoint their own hopes for themselves and their family, as well as the hopes of other people for them. People try to make their marriages and their ties to their children stronger and better through a host of personal devices. They remind themselves, for example, of the ideals they brought into their relationships. They calculate the long-term benefits of overcoming short-term family disappointments. They talk with their families about means of improvement. They undertake therapy terminable and interminable.

However, people are not left to struggle toward their ambitions for their family life alone. Nor is society's not-insubstantial interest in those relationships entirely left to the private strivings of family members. Marriage and parenthood are social institutions. A social institution is "a pattern of expected action of individuals or groups enforced by social sanctions, both positive and negative."[3] Such institutions critically shape the lives of individuals and crucially form the mold of society, for, as James Fitzjames Stephen wrote, "The life of the great mass of men, to a great extent the life of all men, is like a watercourse guided this way or that by a system of dams, sluices, weirs, and embankments. . . . [I]t is by these works, that is to say, by their various customs and institutions—that men's lives are regulated."[4]

Marriage and parenthood as social institutions offer the hope of nurturing families by offering models of human relations. These models serve several crucial functions. First, they relieve each of us of the burden of having to reinvent afresh the forms of family life. As Alfred North Whitehead memorably put the point, "It is a profoundly erroneous truism, repeated by all copybooks and by eminent people when they are making speeches, that we should cultivate the habit of thinking of what we are doing. The precise opposite is the case. Civilization advances by extending the number of important operations which we can perform without thinking about them."[5] Institutions embody society's experience with human relationships and provide a "background of habitualized activity [that] opens up a foreground for deliberation and innovation."[6]

Social institutions, then, first, preserve the teachings of history and permit us to conserve our energies for decisive moments. Second, they help us coordinate our lives with other people's. To live in society, we must anticipate what our fellows will want and do. Social institutions and the norms they embody help us count on, cope with, and cooperate with strangers, friends, and relatives. That help is specially important in families, for in their close, complex, and continuing relationships, reliance and trust are imperative. Some of that reliance and trust comes from our faith in the love and steadfastness of our families. But faith may be more comfortably sustained and reciprocating love more easily offered where personal feelings are reinforced and expectations are coordinated by social institutions.

Third, finally, social institutions are vital not just because they provide *some* forms for family life; they also embody specific norms that are thought to serve desirable social ends. In the American institution of the family, members are conventionally expected to be affectionate, considerate, and fair, to be animated by mutual concern, to sacrifice for each other, and to sustain these commitments all their lives. These ideals compose a kind of social prescription for enduring family relationships which family members may benefit by following. They also form the basis for the social sanctions, positive and negative, which can help sustain people in stable family life when other incentives temporarily fail.

In sum, social institutions offer patterns of behavior that channel people into family life, that sustain them in their efforts to live up to the obligations they undertake, and that help hold them to the commitments they make. Of course, as the legal scholar Karl Llewellyn warned, too much can be "thought and written as if we had a pattern of ways that ma[k]e up marriage."[7] Of course, as Llewellyn knew, " 'The' norm is none too uniform."[8] But as he also knew, "major features are observed, are 'recognized,' are made the measure of the 'right.' Right in such matters is most powerfully felt: these are compacted patterns, backed by unreasoning tradition, built around interests that lie deep and close."[9]

To be sure, the usefulness of any social institution will critically depend on the wisdom of the norms it embodies. No social institution will embody only the most desirable norms. No one would suggest that all the norms of the contemporary social institution of the family are optimal. Nor should anyone deny that those norms, like any social norms, like any social tool, can be and are twisted and abused. But whether those norms are wholly ultimately desirable is an issue my assignment requires me to postpone to another time. For now, it must suffice to observe that the family's status as a social institution is at least a potential source of its power to do good.

I have been describing what sociologists call the "ideal type" of social institutions generally and of the institution of the family particularly. Of course, few institutions have ever entirely had the kind of effect I have been describing. And this is desirable, for the limits and even weaknesses of social institutions allow people the room to adjust themselves to social patterns that are a useful part of freedom. The question we need to ask today, however, is whether there is some reason to believe that, in recent decades, the American family has begun to be deinstitutionalized.

In particular, the models of family life and the norms the institution of the family has proffered have been widely challenged. I am not, it should be clear, suggesting that *any* change in an institution must weaken it. Many recent developments in family life have been simply the kind of evolution that is quite normal in the history of any social institution and which need not diminish the family's ability to serve the ends of a social institution. For instance, common understandings about gender roles within the family have shifted seismically. But that shift is not only compatible with the institutional role of the family; it might well be demanded by it. Yet while some institutional changes will not alter the patterns that make an institution distinctive and the sanctions that make it effective, others will. And this may be happening to the institution of the family.

For example, the rate of divorce, always loftier in America than elsewhere, has risen to momentous heights. It has become remarkably common for parents to have children out of wedlock and for children not to live with both their parents. The line between families and other relationships continues to blur, as a growing range of social relationships has been assimilated to the family. And the institution is decreasingly able to impose special obligations on its members.[10]

Another measure of the changes we seem to be experiencing is that the deinstitutionalization of the family has been explicitly defended. Thus it is increasingly felt that the nature of marriage and parenthood ought not be determined by social pressure. Some proponents of this view argue that family behavior is solely a matter of individual preference and should thus be left to the private choice of the people involved. Other proponents of it argue that family behavior is most properly shaped (if it is to be shaped at all) by the social subgroup to which a family belongs, and that more broadly based social institutions threaten the diversity a pluralist society should value. Some people feel that for social institutions to embody normative views is for them wrongly to "punish" people of differing opinions. Deinstitutionalization is even celebrated, on the grounds that all forms of family life should be encouraged and treated equally. For instance, there are express efforts to give nonmarital institutions the same dignity as marriage. And Justice Brennan recently cited a string of cases he believed indicated that "we have declined to respect a State's notion, as manifested in its allocation of privileges and burdens, of what the family should be."[11]

It would be quite wrong to say that deinstitutionalization is at all complete or that it must become so. Even though deinstitutionalization may be noticeably advanced in many elite sectors of American society, it is less so in much of the rest of the country. But it would also be wrong to say that deinstitutionalization is not underway. And if what I said earlier about the family as a social institution is correct, this development threatens to decrease the stability of couples and thus the well-being of children.

The Law and the Deinstitutionalization of the Family

What is the role of law in the deinstitutionalization of the family? In some ways, it is ultimately tangential. "The family" is a social institution, predominantly created, shaped, and sustained by social forces and not primarily by law. Nevertheless, the law may well have confirmed and promoted the social forces that have eroded the family's institutional strength. For example, a number of legal developments seem to have lessened the extent to which the law encourages specially binding familial commitments. Most conspicuous among these is the rise of no-fault divorce, which essentially makes available divorce on demand (even if the demand is only met after time, trouble, and trauma). Antenuptial agreements were until recently limited in an attempt to deter couples from planning for and easing their way into divorce; today the range of those agreements is steadily expanding. A variety of "functional equivalents" of marriage have been given some kind of legal recognition, recognition which has eroded the special status of marriage. The law has been more reluctant to blur the relationship between parent and child,[12] but the proliferation of divorce has produced legions of fathers who no longer see their children and stop supporting them.

Perhaps as notable as specific legal reforms have been changes in the attitudes and languages of the law. Consider one example. Perhaps even more than other institutions, the family as a social institution can be crucially defined in moral terms. Historically, the law's discourse about the family was critically, though never exclusively, a moral discourse. In the last two or three decades, however, we have seen such a diminution in moral discourse as to amount to a transformation of American family law. By this, I do not mean that the law's decisions have necessarily been less moral or that the law's direction cannot be plausibly explained in moral terms. But the law has been less willing to discuss the issues before it in specifically moral terms, and it has been more anxious to transfer moral decisions from the law to the people the law once regulated. The law is thus less likely to reason and talk in moral terms.[13]

Two examples of this trend may suffice. The law used to say that marriage vows so committed the couple to a life together that they could only separate if one spouse violated his or her most basic moral obligations to the other. Thus divorce was available only on "fault" grounds, grounds which the law defined in general and discussed in moral terms case by case. With the advent of "no-fault" divorce, the law has implicitly concluded that, if a divorce should have some moral basis, that basis must be articulated and analyzed by one of the spouses, and not by the law.[14] In other words, the moral decision has been transferred away from the law and to the spouses (or rather, to whichever spouse seeks the divorce).

Another modal example of the trend toward diminished moral discourse is the recent constitutional reform of the law of abortion. The traditional American law held that abortion raised moral and social issues the state had the authority to address. In *Roe v. Wade*,[15] the Supreme Court concluded that, even if abortion does raise moral issues, they may only be considered by the pregnant woman. But *Roe* was significant for another reason: Despite the issue's indelibly moral aspects, the Court's opinion repeatedly professed to avoid any moral discussion and to rest on quite nonmoral bases.

Replacing moral discourse have been languages which, however apt they may be for resolving social and psychological issues, have been quite unsuited to providing the normative basis social institutions require. Let us briefly examine two of the more prominent substitutes for moral discourse. The first is rights thinking. The long-standing American tendency to conceive social and political issues in terms of rights has recently been invoked by a strong-minded Supreme Court to provide a vocabulary for thinking about familial problems which is adamantly nonmoral. After all, the very function of a right is to transfer a moral decision from the state to the individual involved.

A second leading substitute for moral discourse has been the language of medicine, or, more accurately, of psychology. Whatever the intention of Sigmund Freud, and whatever the subtlety and complexity of its more sophisticated variants, that language is in its now-prevalent version persistently relativist and remissive.[16]

These two substitutes for moral discourse (like a number of their fellows) have something in common. Both are apt vehicles for expressing a view of family relations that stresses the predominance of the interests of the individual member of the family and the centrality of each member's autonomy from the structures and strictures of the family and society alike. As the constitutional scholar Laurence Tribe writes, "[T]he stereotypical 'family unit' that is so much a part of our constitutional rhetoric is becoming decreasingly central to our constitutional reality. Such 'exercises of familial rights and responsibilities' as remain prove to be *individual* power. . . ."[17] Both languages, then, have helped corrode the moral and social basis for the family as a legal and social institution.

Law and the Reinstitutionalization of the Family

I have suggested that one basic way of promoting marital stability is to recruit the strengths of the family as a social institution. But I have also argued that that institution has been weakened by legal as well as social forces. Having furthered the deinstitutionalization of the family, can the law foster its reinstitutionalization? Or can't we go home again? In the complex world in which we live, these questions are ultimately unanswerable. But in trying to approximate answers to them, it will be useful to examine the full range of family law reforms that might promote marital stability and help reinstitutionalize the family. Thus, I will make my survey more complete than critical, including in it proposals that may be politically infeasible, ultimately impractical, socially expensive, or normatively even undesirable. While I will comment on a few of these drawbacks while presenting my list of possibilities, I will reserve most of my doubts for the next section of this chapter.

Confining Family Life to Marriage

If law is to increase the odds that children will be reared in the homes of two parents committed to staying together at least during their children's minority, it probably must try to induce people who contemplate having children to marry. Traditionally, the law has sought exactly that goal. But the law's tools have long been woefully blunt, and the law has relied for its effectiveness more on social pressure than legal coercion. Historically, though, fornication and "open and notorious cohabitation" (to say nothing of adultery) have been crimes. And historically the law has made it disadvantageous to have children out of wedlock by depriving illegitimate children of some of the legal prerogatives of legitimate children (for example, the right to inherit the property of a parent who dies without a will). Today, criminal sanctions for fornication and cohabitation have largely fallen into disrepute and desuetude, and the Supreme Court has held that many of the law's distinctions between legitimate and illegitimate children are unconstitutional (just as many legislatures have found those distinctions morally untenable).

In addition to trying to persuade people to marry before becoming parents, the law historically sought to prevent unmarried parents from escaping their responsibilities to their children. Bastardy proceedings, for instance, were intended to identify the fathers of illegitimate children and assign them responsibility for supporting their children. Today, the desire to accomplish those ends has if anything heightened, and a number of social welfare programs have sought to do so, if only to protect the fisc. Indeed, this is probably the area in which the most progress has been made in recent years toward enlivening some sense of parental duty.

One way the law may be hastening the deinstitutionalization of marriage is its growing (though hardly enthusiastic) willingness to permit and even promote what are sometimes called "functional equivalents" of marriage. A number of courts and legislators have reasoned that if a grouping of people serves the functions that legally recognized families serve, then that grouping ought to be treated as a family. *Marvin v. Marvin*[18] is a celebrated example of this approach. There, the California Supreme Court invited unmarried couples who were living together to enter into contracts organizing their relations and, where they failed to do so, to invoke a broad set of equitable doctrines in settling their economic disputes when they separated.[19] *Marvin*, then, can be understood as putting unmarried cohabitants in something like (if not something better than) the position of married couples.[20] Similarly, a number of cities have adopted "domestic partnership" ordinances or administrative regulations which give lovers some of the benefits of spouses.[21]

How might the "functional equivalence" approach exacerbate the deinstitutionalization of the family? The strength of the family as a social institution has depended in part on a sense that family obligations are special and perpetual, that they are not "to be entered into unadvisedly or lightly; but reverently, discreetly, advisedly, soberly." The functional-equivalence approach seems to equate relationships which will often lack these special qualities (indeed, which will sometimes have been chosen exactly to avoid them) with relationships which do have them.

A similar, and similarly incomplete, recent change in the law is its increasing willingness to allow married couples to organize the terms of their marriage and of their divorce by legally binding contracts. In some ways, this trend might mean little, since couples have always had considerable freedom to arrange their affairs in whatever patterns they informally agreed upon. In other ways, however, this trend could further deinstitutionalization. For instance, as it becomes more common to plan for divorce even before marriage begins (which is exactly the function of most present antenuptial contracts), divorce can come to seem normal and expected. And if it becomes common for spouses to make their agreements about their relations legally binding, marriage as a social institution will lose some of its power to shape marital expectations and behavior, and the differences between marriage and its alternatives will be further blurred.

What change in the law would slow these pressures toward the deinstitutionalization of the family? More than one answer to that question is possible. But a logical conclusion is that the law should become more skeptical of functional-equivalence approaches and the contractualization of marriage. In other words, the reform proposal I have been investigating is simply to stop pursuing some courses that seem to have contributed to the family's deinstitutionalization.

Restricting Entry to Marriage

We continue our survey of the ways family law might try to promote marital stability and stem the deinstitutionalization of the family by asking how people who are unsuited to marriage might be deterred from attempting it. Historically, the law has most significantly tried to discourage primarily one such category of people from marrying—the very young. Statistics about divorce suggest a basis for this attempt: teenage marriages are particularly prone to fail. A consensus of states now prohibits marriage before the age of eighteen, unless the minors have the consent of their parents. Since eighteen is generally the age of majority, it may be difficult to raise the age of marriage beyond that point.

There is also some evidence that couples who have known each other for a relatively short time (perhaps less than a year) are likelier to divorce than those whose courtships have been longer. It might be inferred from this evidence that the law should try to deter couples from marrying unless they can show that they have been acquainted for a prolonged period. Less dramatically, the law might extend the period between the time a couple apply for a license and the time they may marry. Such an extension might deter a few people from marrying hurriedly, and it might say something about the desirability of prudently considered marriages.

Finally, marriages may fail because couples do not understand themselves, their partners, or the dynamics of marriage. It might follow from this hypothesis that people should be allowed to marry only after having some kind of training or counseling. Anecdotal information about the success of the counseling some churches provide their communicants suggests that some participants find such efforts rewarding. Of course, even if this information is accurate and representative, one might doubt that a universally required, compulsory program administered by heaven-knows-what sort of counselors would achieve similar success.[22]

Promoting Family Stability by Encouraging Marital Happiness

In principle, it should be possible to increase familial stability by enhancing the degree of satisfaction husbands and wives find in their marriages. This tactic seems doubly attractive, for not only should happy spouses be less likely to divorce than unhappy ones, but their marital happiness should make their household a better place to raise children. Does family law have any means of increasing marital happiness?

Historically, family law has most directly pursued that ambitious goal by the rather modest step of making it illegal for spouses to assault each other. For a variety of reasons, that prohibition has never been vigorously enforced. Recent years have, however, seen experiments—whose success is debated—to increase the energy and effectiveness of government's response to spouse abuse. These experiments include programs to protect abused spouses, to encourage them to prosecute their attackers, and even to take the decision whether to prosecute away from the abused spouse. It has also been suggested that the abused spouse ought to have a civil remedy (that is, a suit for damages) against the abuser on divorce. One cause and consequence of these and other efforts may have been a cultural change—a strengthening of the norm of beneficence that has long been an element of the family as a social institution. In any event, an attraction of enhanced efforts to combat spousal violence is that, despite some significant disagreements about methods, there is more prospect of a political consensus about spousal assaults than about many other problems of family law.

Family law has also pursued family peace—if not family harmony—by attacking the abuse and neglect of children. The law's techniques have included programs to deliver services to abusive or neglectful parents that might reduce their propensity to harm their children and increase their ability to help them, providing therapy for abusive parents, removing children from unsuitable homes, and prosecuting abusive parents. As with programs against spouse abuse, political consensus is relatively easy to find as to the goal, but quite elusive as to methods.

The financial relations between the spouses are a frequent source of marital distress. In principle, therefore, the law ought to be able to increase marital satisfaction and stability by ensuring that those relations are just. You will not be surprised to learn that this is easier said than done. While a couple remains married, the legal principle has roughly been that their finances are their business. True, the laws of the different states impose various minimal obligations of spousal support. And those laws make other essentially precatory announcements, such as stating that in community property jurisdictions husbands and wives are comanagers of their common property. But these statutes have had relatively slight effect, and generally the law has not been bold (or rash) enough to try to adjudicate economic disputes during marriage.[23]

The law has, however, played a much larger role in supervising the spouses' economic affairs when they divorce. In this area, there have recently been several trends. First, there has been a movement away from lifelong alimony and toward alimony only for a "rehabilitative" period during which the recipient is supposed to learn to support herself. Second, states have moved toward the "equitable distribution" of property. At its purest, this means that all the property of both spouses is put into a pot and then distributed in whatever way the judge thinks "fairest" (instead of being divided according to one of the more mechanical traditional principles). Third, the law has increasingly sought to recognize all the possible ways a spouse can contribute economically to a marriage. Thus courts are called on to recognize the economic benefits of housework and childrearing and to treat as divisible assets such forms of wealth as professional degrees, the goodwill of businesses, and pensions.

All these changes are commonly justified on the grounds that they are fair. But can they or any other changes in the law of alimony and marital property bolster marital stability? In principle, these reforms might assure spouses that, when they make a contribution to their marriage at a sacrifice to themselves, their contribution will be returned to them if the marriage should end. This ought to make it safer for spouses to invest in their marriages, thereby strengthening them. On the other hand, it is not clear that spouses in fact know about or respond to such incentives. And in terms of marital stability, these incentives cut both ways, since they can make divorce economically easier. Just which effect these incentives have is an empirical question as to which there is little compelling evidence.

Making Divorce More Difficult

The most direct and historically the most common way to try to increase marital stability is to restrict divorce. In the last few decades, however, that battle has essentially been abandoned. Over that time, every state has instituted some form of no-fault divorce. In general, that has meant that divorce is available on demand, although ending a marriage may take a long time and exact much misery. No-fault divorce was adopted relatively easily, partly because influential participants in the debate felt that courts could not assess fault accurately, that the process of fault-based divorce was harshly painful, that perjury had become too central an element in many divorces, and that couples ought to be free to decide for themselves whether to stay married.[24]

In recent years, doubt and regret about the no-fault reform have grown. While the factors that precipitated that reform remain potent, a long-standing sense of dismay at the high American divorce rate (which is higher than in virtually any Western country) has recently been intensified by an increasingly detectable sense that the law says the wrong things about divorce.[25] What, then, are the law's choices? How might the law of divorce be rewritten to increase marital stability and to resist the deinstitutionalization of the family?

Most obviously, we might reinstitute fault-based divorce. Doing so would narrow the grounds of divorce. If these grounds were taken seriously (and courts administering fault-based divorce did not always do so),[26] some couples would presumably be deterred from seeking a divorce in the first place and some would be denied the divorce they had sought. Further, a persuasive statement of the grounds for divorce might help strengthen the institutional norms of marriage, particularly the principle that marriage is for life. Less dramatically (but more plausibly), one might follow the example of a number of American jurisdictions and allow divorce on no-fault grounds but take marital fault into account in awarding alimony and dividing marital property.

Perhaps the most intriguing proposal for reforming divorce law—and a proposal particularly palatable to modern sensibilities—has been made by Elizabeth S. Scott.[27] She suggests that "for many persons, marriage (and remaining married) represent 'rational' decisions that take into account long-term interests, and divorce results from choices that reflect short-term preferences." However, "[w]ithdrawal, boredom, pursuit of other relationships, immersion in career, and conflict over finances, children, and other family may all weaken the resolve to sustain a lasting relationship and may ultimately lead to marital breakdown." She proposes that, recognizing this possibility, couples should make "precommitments" intended "to reinforce the objective of a stable, lasting marriage."

Precommitment strategies might work in three ways. First, they may directly make divorce less appealing, either by penalizing it or by making the process unattractive. Second, by making a marriage harder to leave and thus convincing a couple that they should make the best of their marriage, precommitment strategies may improve the quality of marriages. Third, by making marriages harder to leave, they may encourage people to think more carefully about entering them in the first place.

Scott observes that precommitment strategies either could be made available to all spouses who wished to use them or could be made mandatory. Voluntary precommitment strategies would be legally implemented by enforcing contracts in which those strategies were used. Such contracts might call for economic sanctions for divorce. These could include "provisions for a stipulated level of child or spousal support, a designated division of property, or a direct fine, to benefit the children or the spouse who wants to continue in the marriage." These contracts might also require "an extensive period of delay [at least two years] before final divorce."

Scott also sees attractions in a mandatory scheme of precommitment strategies. For one thing, "[l]egislatively announced precommitments presumably reflect a socially defined consensus about appropriate barriers to divorce under different circumstances." For another thing, legislatures are not in love, and thus might write more realistic rules than an enamored couple. "Finally, legislative precommitments express societal aspirations for marriage and family through mechanisms that may influence behavior and attitudes more effectively than a permissive policy." Among the "precommitment" devices a legislature might invoke are "mandatory rules creating premarital and predivorce waiting periods, rigorous support obligations and enforcement, required mediation or counseling, and family property trusts."

The device of imposing waiting periods on anyone seeking a divorce deserves special notice. It has long been a technique for deterring people from divorcing and for expressing social disapproval of divorce without wholly preventing divorces where they are most urgently wanted. Waiting periods are in fact already in place in a number of states, and some European jurisdictions require waits as long as several years.

Since the effect of divorce on children is a preeminent social concern, it might make sense to concentrate on dissuading parents of children from divorcing. Scott, for instance, would make precommitment strategies mandatory in divorces involving minor children. She suggests imposing on parents of minors substantial [perhaps two-year] mandatory delay periods to promote more thoughtful divorce decisions and to make divorce less attractive. . . . Parents could be bound to more substantial support obligations than currently and to property distribution schemes that are beneficial to children. Counseling, mediation, and mental health evaluation of the children might be required before divorce is permitted.

A particularly far-reaching version of the precommitment strategy might be called the "marriage commitment fund." Whenever a couple married, they would be required to place in a marriage commitment fund an amount equivalent to, say, 10 percent of their combined income. Thereafter, they would be required to contribute monthly to their fund an amount ranging from, say, one to three percent of their pre-tax income. Those in the poorest third of the population would contribute one percent; those in the middle third, two percent; and those in the wealthiest third, three percent. Contributions to the fund would be from pre-tax income. The fund would remain the property of the couple as long as the couple remained married. Should the couple reach retirement without divorcing, the fund would be converted to an annuity which the couple would receive until both died or until they divorced.

Should the couple divorce without having had children, or should they divorce when all their children had reached the age of majority, their fund would escheat to the state marriage commitment fund. Should a couple divorce after retirement and after annuity payments had begun, the annuity would cease and the capital amount of their fund would similarly escheat.

Should the couple divorce with children under the age of majority, their fund would be placed in trust for the benefit of their minor children. In addition, the couple would be able to borrow from the state fund in order to help cushion their children from the economic consequences of their parents' divorce. The amount the parents needed to borrow would be set in the following way. The divorce court would determine the amount necessary to cushion the children from the economic effects of divorce. The court would then calculate the amount each parent was able to contribute to the support of their children. The custodial parent's noncash economic contributions would be taken into account in this calculation. The couple would be responsible for borrowing the difference between those two amounts in proportion to their ability to repay the loan. When the children reached the age of majority, the parents would be responsible for repaying the loan.

The marriage commitment fund program has two rationales—deterring divorce and diminishing the injuries divorce does to children. The program deters divorce in two ways. First, it provides an incentive for staying married. Couples who stayed married all their lives would receive the full benefit of the contributions they had made to their fund. For them, the fund would be a kind of tax-advantaged forced-savings plan. Second, the program provides a disincentive to divorce. Couples who divorced would most commonly lose all that they had contributed to the fund. The program would benefit the children of divorce by making available to children whatever money had accumulated in the fund and to parents a source from which child support could be borrowed. The practical obligation to take such a loan would additionally help deter parents from divorce, but it might be independently justifiable on the ground that it does nothing more than oblige parents to keep the commitments they implicitly undertook by having children.[28]

A less dramatic and novel way of reforming divorce law would build on the current law's nominal structure. Many laws now make divorce available where there has been an "irretrievable breakdown" of the marriage. In practice, however, this standard is essentially ignored in favor of divorce on demand. Revitalizing that standard might require spouses contemplating divorce to consider more directly whether their marriage had ended and might allow courts to, in effect, send some divorce petitions back for reconsideration.

The proposals for changing divorce law that I have described have an important element in common: they recruit the law's powers to speak in words and symbols to make a statement about the social institution of the family. Mary Ann Glendon has suggested that those "expressive" powers be more deliberately and fully used. She proposes that America follow the example of European countries, which temper the effect of no-fault divorce rules by deploying those powers.[29] She describes the modal European statute as "hedging in" no-fault grounds by "provisions granting courts the power to deny a unilateral nonfault divorce altogether if legal dissolution of the marriage would involve exceptional unfairness or hardship for a nonconsenting spouse who has committed no marital offense." Generally, these clauses are not used to prevent a divorce, and Glendon suggests that they may not be easy to justify theoretically. However, she believes they are important because (in conjunction with waiting periods) they have "officially maintained the idea of marriage as an enduring relationship involving reciprocal rights and obligations."

Protecting Children from the Effects of Divorce

Another series of proposals for promoting family stability—or at least its simulacrum—centers on protecting children from the effects of divorce. These proposals essentially seek to preserve for children as many of the benefits of family stability as are compatible with a parental divorce. Some of these proposals might also have the subsidiary effect of making divorce less attractive.

There is some reason to think that children suffer where their divorced parents are hostile to each other. And it is sometimes believed that the process of getting a divorce in an adversary legal system exacerbates the spouses' hostility. This has led to suggestions that more divorces should be mediated. Indeed, a few states either allow judges to refer disputes to mediators or even require that custody disputes be mediated before judicial proceedings can be obtained.[30]

While people disagree about divorce's psychological effects on children, there is widespread agreement that divorce's economic effects on them are severe, if only because two households cannot live as cheaply as one. Recently, reforms have begun to be instituted to ameliorate the economic situation of children of divorce. Those reforms fall into two categories.

First, some reforms are designed to increase the amount the law requires noncustodial parents to pay for the support of their children. For instance, the federal government has recently required states to write guidelines for judges to use in setting child-support payments. One argument for the guidelines has been that judges have set support awards in inconsistent ways. But many people also believe that judges have tended to set awards too low. Glendon has further proposed that where parents of minor children divorce, their property should not be divided between them in the now-standard ways. Rather she suggests a "children-first" principle which states that "the fact of having children impresses a lien upon all of the parents' income and property to the extent necessary to provide for the children's decent subsistence at least until those children reach the age of majority."[31]

The second kind of child-support reform asks how to collect whatever support awards a court makes. As a class, noncustodial parents have long paid only a fraction of what they owe. In the last two decades, the federal and state governments have instituted a variety of programs for making collection easier. These include establishing devices for coordinating enforcement of support orders among states, creating a "parent locator" service, developing agencies to help custodial parents collect support payments, arranging income-withholding and lien mechanisms, intercepting tax refunds, mandating reviews of the adequacy of support awards, and so on. More dramatically, a few jurisdictions have used jail and the threat of it with marked effect.[32]

Even the most effective enforcement procedures, however, cannot reach noncustodial parents who simply do not have the money to pay. And is it desirable to compel a parent to support his children by a first marriage if doing so means he cannot support his children by a second one? A remarkable attempt to address these two problems was a Wisconsin statute which prohibited noncustodial parents under a support order from marrying without submitting proof of their ability to support both their present and future children. The Supreme Court found that this statute violated the constitutional right to marry,[33] but the present Court might not reach the same conclusion about a better-drafted version of that law.

A second means of trying to protect children from the effects of their parents' divorce seeks to maintain the stability of the child's parental ties even though the family's stability as a whole has been disrupted. This approach looks to the law's rules governing child custody and rights of visitation. One version of it suggests that children's sense of stability is best maintained after divorce by awarding custody to the "primary caretaker" or the "psychological parent." This version's proponents argue that it is crucial for the child to stay with the parent with whom the child has the closest emotional ties. A conflicting version of this approach favors a presumption in favor of "joint custody." In its purest form, this means that the child lives alternately with each parent. This version's proponents argue that it is crucial for the child to maintain the closest possible relations with both parents. They also hope that establishing the joint-custody principle might encourage *both* parents—fathers as well as mothers—to be deeply involved in the day-to-day care of their children during, as well as after, the marriage.[34]

In principle, the law has long endorsed the principle that the children of divorce should stay close to both parents, and it has sought to accomplish that end by awarding the noncustodial parent the right to visit his children. In practice, these awards have often proved fruitless: many noncustodial parents find that (for many reasons) they gradually become estranged from their children. Two direct approaches to this problem may be imagined. First, one could penalize people who do not exercise their visitation privileges by devices like taking those privileges away or by increasing the amount of child support they owe. Second, since sometimes custodial parents thwart visitation, one could penalize such interferences.[35]

Changing the Languages of Family Law

I said earlier that one force contributing to the family's deinstitutionalization was the law's increasing preference for speaking in "languages" that are more congenial to an atomized than a social view of family members. If this argument is correct, deinstitutionalization might at least be slowed by using such languages less. This might be done in three ways.

First, family law could try to move away from the atomizing language of rights to a more encompassing language of relationships, responsibilities, and contexts. In some ways, this could be done relatively easily. Much of the language of rights in family law is spoken because in recent years the Supreme Court has interpreted the Constitution's Due Process Clause as creating a right to "privacy." This interpretation is controversial both as a reading of the Constitution and as an extension of judicial power, and at least some members of the Court apparently wish to reconsider it at least partially. And even if the privacy right should be retained, it need not be read in the unsubtle way the Court has sometimes seemed to prefer. There is room for courts to honor the values expressed in rights talk while acknowledging the limitations of those values and appreciating the values that compete with them.[36]

A second way family law could protect its vocabulary is to be skeptical of its tendency to encourage people to organize their relationships through contracts. The language of contract has two disadvantages. First, it lets people set the terms of their relationships in ways that may damage the social goal of strengthening the family institutionally. Second (and perhaps more consequentially), when people are led to organize their lives with contracts, they are encouraged (even if not required) to bargain to maximize their own advantage and to enforce the rights they have won. A famous study of the use of contracts in commercial settings found that business people often avoid thinking in contractual terms because those terms interfere with the sense of trust and mutual accommodation necessary to good business relations.[37] How much more, then, must contracts be inimical to the harmonious entity we want the family to be?

Family law might alter its languages in a third way—by being more willing to use the language of morals and less anxious to substitute for it alternatives like the languages of medicine, psychiatry, and economics. Family relations are, among other things, ultimately moral. Unless the moral aspects of those relations are taken into account, the law will be poorly equipped to understand what people are doing in family relations. And the strength of the family as a social institution lies in central part in the moral obligations family members assume toward each other. For the law to ignore those obligations is for it to weaken that institution.

The Inefficacy of Family Law

I have been surveying a range of family-law reforms that might enhance marital stability and inhibit the family's deinstitutionalization. However,

I have generally ignored the problems with those reforms. Here, then, I
will try to summarize them. They are, in fact, the problems of all of family
law.

To begin with, American family law faces a special problem. The states,
not the federal government, are primarily responsible for writing family
law. This means that any national effort to reform family law takes on a
large political burden. It also means that one state's goals can be thwarted
by another state's policies. For many years, for instance, New York's efforts to maintain a narrow standard for divorce were eroded because
many of its citizens went to states like Nevada, which had a broader standard.

The federal structure of American government is not the least of the
political problems the proposals I have listed would face. In many states,
some of those proposals are just not in the political cards, since they would
repel too many influential points of view. Some others of them might not
provoke political distaste, but neither would they find a political constitu-
ency. In addition, some of the proposals—like the suggestions about functional equivalents of the family and the languages of family law—are both
diffuse and primarily within the control of a judiciary not readily reached
by political means.

But the problems the proposals I have surveyed confront go much
deeper than the political. More basically, family law is highly interstitial.
That is, there are only a few points in most people's lives when family law
directly touches them. Indeed, most of the standards the law sets for families are actually enforced only if a couple divorces. And even then a couple
which can agree on the terms of their divorce can usually escape judicial
scrutiny, for most courts are far too busy to pay close attention to uncontested suits.

Family law is interstitial partly because we think families ought to be
as free as possible to organize their own affairs. Indeed, many people believe that the strength of the family as a social institution comes partly
from its autonomy from governmental supervision. But family law is also
interstitial because it must be. And it must be because of a classic dilemma
of family law—the enforcement problem. The enforcement problem per-
vades all of law. The law can call spirits from the vasty deep, but they
often do not come when called for. More frequently than lawyers like to
think, people do not know what the law is, do not care to find out, do not
obey it, do not suffer consequences from disobedience, and do not plan to
comply even if they do suffer consequences.

But perhaps nowhere is the enforcement problem as severe as in family
law. As James Fitzjames Stephen wrote, "To try to regulate the internal
affairs of a family, the relations of love or friendship, or many other things

of the same sort, by law or by the coercion of public opinion, is like trying to pull an eyelash out of a man's eye with a pair of tongs. They may put out the eye, but they will never get hold of the eyelash."[38] As he explained, "A law which enters into a direct contest with a fierce impetuous passion, which the person who feels it does not admit to be bad, and which is not directly injurious to others, will generally do more harm than good; and this is perhaps the principal reason why it is impossible to legislate directly against unchastity, unless it takes forms which every one regards as monstrous and horrible."

Indeed, the enforcement problem has multiple sources. First, despite the valiant efforts of several social sciences, we know painfully little about how families behave and about how to make them behave well. Second, we often disagree about how we want families to behave. Third, the privacy in which family life occurs (and which we are properly reluctant to violate) can prevent us from discovering misconduct within families. Fourth, even where information about misconduct can be had, remedies for misconduct are often either ineffective or as likely to injure the innocent as punish the guilty.

Consider the example of spouse abuse. In many ways, it is the easiest case for intervention in a family, exactly because it is "directly injurious to others." But its prevention is hampered by all the factors that contribute to the enforcement problem. Research about the causes and cures of spouse abuse has been sadly inadequate. Despite our detestation of abuse, we disagree about which levels of abuse are so serious as to justify governmental intervention. It is widely thought that much abuse occurs which the law never discovers. And there are questions about remedies for abuse: It is not wholly clear which modes of punishment are most effective in curing the abuser and deterring other abusers. And the more severe the punishment, the likelier it is indirectly to injure the spouse and the couple's children. In short, even in the easiest case—spouse abuse—family law's enforcement problems are marked.[39]

The difficulties of reforming the family through law become yet clearer when we remember that we are trying to reconstruct a social institution. That can only be done if the institution commands powerful social support. That support cannot be created solely by the law, although the law can help shape and sustain it. That social support may be hard to come by today, for the deinstitutionalization of the family has many causes, and many of them run deep. Further, many of those causes are not easily reached by the law. Yet without adequate social support, legal attempts to reinstitutionalize the family will be merely coercive.

Finally, all the reforms I canvassed will exact costs, including costs in human freedom and happiness. All social institutions necessarily impose costs, because social institutions are, in part, sets of rules. Like all rules, they are based on generalizations about people and how they behave. Like all generalizations, social institutions will not fit everyone precisely well. Where institutions do not fit, they can cause unhappiness. Further, social institutions exact costs because, like all rules, they are enforced through coercion—directly or indirectly, weakly or strongly. And coercion always imposes costs in freedom. As George Eliot rightly remarked, "There's no rule so wise but what it's a pity for somebody or other."

I have been arguing that family law is a dull chisel for reshaping family life. It may well be that the whole toolbox of public policy offers few implements well-suited to that purpose. Thus, for example, a number of scholars are "skeptical about economic policy as a means to reverse unfavorable family structure developments" and believe that government policy has not had and could not have "direct, important effects on family structure: marriage, fertility, divorce, and separation."[40] Indeed, there is a school of thought that holds that, far from strengthening families, social welfare programs have inadvertently created incentives which have weakened families.

Finally, we must acknowledge how little we actually know about how to make families better. Some of the proposals I have surveyed have an *a priori* appeal. But we simply have little sound basis for knowing whether they would work. Worse, we cannot even be confident that we could establish whether they had worked even after they had been implemented.

Conclusion

I have asked how and whether family law can improve the stability of American families and thus, it is to be hoped, the happiness of both spouses and their children. I have argued that one central means of serving those goals is to reinstitutionalize the family. I have offered a brief survey of ways family law might try to do so. In the preceding section, I suggested that in crucial ways the list is thin and unsatisfying, that all the proposals are in a useful sense speculative, that some of them probably would not work, that some of them would be too costly, and that some of them are politically impossible. These are gloomy suggestions, but I do not believe they demonstrate that trying to promote marital stability and to reverse the deinstitutionalization of the family need be futile.

It is true that these efforts must rest on inadequate information and on speculations about the social effects of legal doctrine. But this must be true of any social enterprise of great pith and moment. These efforts would constitute an experiment, but all life is an experiment.

It is true that these efforts will exact both economic and social costs. But there is no way to avoid exacting costs. Abolishing social institutions imposes costs just as certainly as sustaining them does. Social institutions serve all the functions I described at the beginning of this chapter, so that when they are weakened, we are deprived of something of value. The tendency of our age is to be richly sensitive to the dangers institutions pose. But, as Alan Wolfe reminds us, "We are not born free and corrupted by our institutions. If anything, . . . we are born as selfish egoists, and only our institutions and practices save us from ourselves."[41]

Nor should the likely costs in human freedom be exaggerated. All social institutions exact their cost in freedom. But a world without social institutions—if such a world is imaginable—would exact its own large costs in freedom. Furthermore, the point is not to maximize freedom, but to optimize it, to find the best mix of freedom and the other undoubted goods that compete with it. Finally, the inefficacy of family law imposes its own constraints on any excessive attempt to constrict human freedom. Exactly because family law is interstitial, most of the proposals I have surveyed would leave families with a good deal of freedom.

It is true that the reinstitutionalization of the family runs against many of the trends of our time. And it is true that this makes it harder to attract the political and social support any such development would require. But it is wrong to overestimate the extent of the social change we have undergone or to think that the trend of society must be unidirectional. As Richard Randall writes, "History provides almost as many examples of retreats from permissiveness as of abandoned proscriptions."[42] And it is wrong to conclude that we must accept every change that has occurred, however damaging it may turn out to be.

Finally, it is true that family law can only act interstitially and that reinstitutionalization is, if anything, more a social than a legal enterprise. But this need not counsel against attempting reforms. Rather, it can teach a proper modesty: we should not expect any single reform to bear the full weight of reinstitutionalization. The law supports institutions by surrounding them with helpful rules and attitudes where the opportunity presents itself. The rest must be accomplished through all the standard processes of social change. Yet it is not necessarily bad news that law is not the only way of pursuing social change. Other methods of doing so exist, they are well known, and they are open to those who would use them. Indeed, one of those methods is exactly the activity of proposing and propounding legal reform. Even if the reform of family law falls short of its immediate goals, exploring that reform can itself help accomplish the goal of strengthening the social institution of the family.

But I must close this chapter with the same caution that I hope has characterized all of it. Promoting marital stability and reinstitutionalizing the family may well be desirable goals. But that does not mean that they are achievable. Human nature invariably disappoints. Human institutions inevitably fail. In human affairs, to muddle through is to succeed.

Notes

I wish to thank Arland Thornton for his helpful comments on an earlier draft of this paper.

1. And further to assume that "not divorced" is a rough surrogate for "stable."

2. On the other hand, during this century American families have become both much wealthier and much likelier to divorce. And toward the end of this chapter I will note that doubts about the efficacy of economic and social policy to achieve such goals are not uncommon. Indeed, the argument has recently and vigorously been made that such policies have actively defeated their own purposes. See, for example, Charles Murray, *Losing Ground: American Social Policy, 1950–1980* (New York: Basic Books, 1984).

3. Robert N. Bellah et al., *The Good Society* (New York: Knopf, 1991), 10.

4. James Fitzjames Stephen, *Liberty, Equality, Fraternity* (1873; reprint, New York: H. Holt & Co., 1991), 63–64.

5. Alfred North Whitehead, *An Introduction to Mathematics* (New York: H. Holt & Co., 1911), 61. As Peter Berger writes, "Today, it is not so much that individuals become convinced of their capacity and right to choose new ways of life, but rather that tradition is weakened to the point where they *must* choose between alternatives whether they wish it or not. . . . [O]ne of the most archaic functions of society is to take away from individuals the burden of choice." Peter Berger, "Toward a Critique of Modernity," in *Facing Up to Modernity*, ed. Peter Berger (New York: Basic Books, 1977), 77 (emphasis in the original).

6. Peter L. Berger and Thomas Luckmann, *The Social Construction of Reality: A Treatise in the Sociology of Knowledge* (Garden City, NY: Doubleday, 1966), 53.

7. Karl N. Llewellyn, "Behind the Law of Divorce: Pt. 1," *Columbia Law Review* 32 (1932): 1281, 1285.

8. Ibid., 1286.

9. Ibid. For a more complete and nuanced description of the family as a social institution and of the law's relation to that institution, see Carl E. Schneider, "The Channelling Function in Family Law," *Hofstra Law Review* 20 (1992): 495.

10. For a fuller description of these developments, see chap. 13, pt. 1.E, of Carl

E. Schneider and Margaret F. Brinig, *An Invitation to Family Law* (St. Paul, MN: West, 1996).

11. *Michael H. v. Gerald D.*, 109 S.Ct. 2333, 2353 (1989) (dissent).

12. Although the "functional equivalence" argument has found expression as to that relationship too.

13. This development is described in some detail in Carl E. Schneider, "Moral Discourse and the Transformation of American Family Law," *Michigan Law Review* 83 (1985): 1803.

14. My discussions with students in family-law classes suggest that the law here mirrors the attitudes of at least one part of American culture. I regularly ask students whether people in a series of hypothetical situations are morally entitled to seek a divorce. The predominant answer I hear is that the question is incomprehensible and irrelevant. I analyze that reaction at length in Carl E. Schneider, "Marriage, Morals, and the Law: No-Fault Divorce and Moral Discourse," *Utah Law Review* 1994 (1994): 503.

15. 410 U.S. 113 (1973).

16. As the mordant social critic Philip Rieff writes, "evil and immorality are disappearing . . . mainly because our culture is changing its definition of human perfection. No longer the Saint, but the instinctual Everyman, twisting his neck uncomfortably inside the starched collar of culture, is the communal ideal, to whom men offer tacit prayers for deliverance from their inherited renunciations." Philip Rieff, *The Triumph of the Therapeutic: Uses of Faith After Freud* (New York: Harper & Row, 1966), 21. For an analysis of the languages of family law, see Schneider, "Moral Discourse," 1803.

17. Laurence Tribe, *American Constitutional Law* (Mineola, NY: Foundation Press, 1978), 1416–17 (footnotes omitted).

18. 557 P.2d 106 (1976).

19. Interestingly, it appears that, after an initial flurry, that invitation has not been widely accepted.

20. *Marvin* also illustrates the complexity of many of the problems I am discussing. For instance, I will suggest that that case has contributed to the family's deinstitutionalization. But *Marvin* may not have enhanced the freedom of unmarried couples. On the contrary, it has been argued that it reduces that freedom by bringing such couples within the law's purview. And, for instance, while generally the "dejuridification" of the family has contributed to its deinstitutionalization, *Marvin* expands the juridification of intimate relations. Furthermore, rather than weakening marriage, *Marvin* might lead to its strengthening by creating a legal category for people who do not wish to make the special commitments marriage entails and by thus deterring from marriage couples who are unsuited for it.

21. The case of *Borough of Glassboro v. Vallorosi*, 568 A.2d 888 (NJ Sup. Ct. 1990) shows how far the "functional equivalence" principle can be taken. Glassboro's zoning ordinance said that only "families" could occupy homes in residential districts. The ordinance defined a family as " 'one or more persons occupying a dwelling unit as a single non-profit housekeeping unit, who are living

together as a stable and permanent living unit, being a traditional family unit or the function equivalency [sic] thereof.' " Ibid., 889. Each of ten college students signed a four-month lease on a house in a residential district. The New Jersey Supreme Court upheld the trial court's conclusion that the students were a family: "The students ate together, shared household chores, and paid expenses from a common fund." (The court acknowledged that two years after the lease had been first signed, the main renter withdrew from school and the students stopped using the house.)

22. The restrictions I have been discussing could also be combined. For instance, young couples or couples whose acquaintance was short could be allowed to marry only on completing a course of counseling.

23. However, it seems likely that governmental action that has helped open the job market to women and the large-scale entry of married women into that market have significantly affected the economic relations of husbands and wives.

24. For a critical review of the arguments advanced in favor of no-fault divorce and a stimulating argument that the reform has not met its aims, see Lynn D. Wardle, "No-Fault Divorce and the Divorce Conundrum," *Brigham Young Univ. Law Review* 1991 (1991): 79.

25. See, e.g., Mary Ann Glendon, *Abortion and Divorce in Western Law: American Failures, European Challenges* (Cambridge, MA: Harvard University Press, 1987), 105.

26. For example, they knowingly countenanced perjured testimony and radically expanded the grounds of "cruelty."

27. Elizabeth S. Scott, "Rational Decisionmaking About Marriage and Divorce," *Virginia Law Review* 76 (1990): 9.

28. One way that people could evade the requirement would be divorcing in a foreign state. Thus a state might choose to have parents contract with each other and the state to accept the terms of the marriage-commitment-fund program wherever they might divorce.

29. Glendon, *Abortion and Divorce in Western Law*, 63–111. 30. Those less sanguine about mediation essentially make three arguments. First, they suggest that the research on mediation is weak. Second, they conclude that mediation cannot "produce settlement in a sizeable proportion of cases, has not been notably effective in altering dysfunctional patterns of family relating, and is still of uncertain value as a tool for helping children." Kenneth Kressel, *The Process of Divorce: How Professionals and Couples Negotiate Settlements* (New York: Basic Books, 1985), 200. Third, they fear that mediation provides inadequate means of protecting the weaker party and of assuring the fairness of the settlements that are reached.

31. Mary Ann Glendon, "Family Law Reform in the 1980s," *Louisiana Law Review* 44 (1984): 1553, 1559. Glendon suggests that this principle "would not alter the outcomes of cases so much as it would sanction and encourage what most judges are already trying to do. . . ."

32. For an illuminating description of those jurisdictions, as well as a thoughtful (if dated) discussion of the child-support problem generally, see David L. Chambers, *Making Fathers Pay* (Chicago: University of Chicago Press, 1979).

33. *Zablocki v. Redhail*, 434 U.S. 374 (1978).

34. If so Solomonic a solution is available, why is it not obviously preferable? The impediments to joint custody include the fact that many parents do not wish to have custody of their children and that many parents divorce exactly because they cannot agree about important decisions like how to rear their children. In the states that have tried to encourage parents to share custody, it appears that many parents have wound up with hardly more than the conventional arrangements under a more fashionable name.

35. "Although most observers, ourselves included, have believed that continued contact [with the noncustodial parent] makes a difference in children's adjustment, the evidence in support of that assertion is mixed at best." Frank F. Furstenberg, Jr., and Andrew J. Cherlin, *Divided Families: What Happens to Children When Parents Part* (Cambridge, MA: Harvard University Press, 1991), 107.

36. For criticisms of rights discourse in family law and proposals for less extreme versions of that discourse, see Mary Ann Glendon, *Rights Talk* (New York: The Free Press, 1991); Carl E. Schneider, "Rights Discourse and Neonatal Euthanasia," *California Law Review* 76 (1988): 151; Carl E. Schneider, "State-Interest Analysis in Fourteenth Amendment 'Privacy' Law: An Essay on the Constitutionalization of Social Issues," *Law and Contemporary Problems* 51 (1988): 79.

37. The study is Stewart Macaulay, "Non-contractual Relations in Business: A Preliminary Study," *American Sociological Review* 28 (1963): 55.

38. These striking observations and many others equally arresting are to be found in Stephen, *Liberty, Equality, Fraternity*.

39. Similarly, the most ambitious study of divorce law concluded that historically that law has not significantly affected marital stability. See Max Rheinstein, *Marriage Stability, Divorce, and the Law* (Chicago: University of Chicago Press, 1972).

40. Mary Jo Bane and Paul A. Jargowsky, "The Links Between Government Policy and Family Structure: What Matters and What Doesn't," in *The Changing American Family and Public Policy*, ed. Andrew J. Cherlin (Washington, DC: Urban Institute Press, 1988), 245. Similarly skeptical "that marriage bonds can be strengthened substantially by public policy" are Furstenberg and Cherlin, *Divided Families*, 105. For broader and fuller expressions of pessimistic views, see Gilbert Y. Steiner, *The Futility of Family Policy* (Washington, DC: The Brookings Institution, 1981), and Nathan Glazer, *The Limits of Social Policy* (Cambridge, MA: Harvard University Press, 1988).

41. Alan Wolfe, *Whose Keeper? Social Science and Moral Obligation* (Berkeley, CA: University of California Press, 1989), 258–59.

42. Richard S. Randall, *Freedom and Taboo: Pornography and the Politics of a Self Divided* (Berkeley, CA: University of California Press, 1989), 137.

CHAPTER 9

Parenting from Separate Households

Robert S. Weiss

The prospect that a child's two parents will live apart from each other is now more likely than was the case a generation ago. With increasing frequency married parents separate. Also with increasing frequency, children are born to unmarried couples who lived together, if at all, only temporarily. Furthermore, it seems to be more likely than was formerly the case that both parents, despite living in separate households, will remain involved as parents with their children. Although fathers in past years were probably no less emotionally invested in their children, changes in our beliefs about the need of children for access to both parents and about the ability of fathers as well as mothers to care for children have made it easier for today's separated fathers to seek to share child care with their children's mothers. Belief that it is desirable for both of a child's parents to retain parental relationships with the child is expressed in current court decisions as much as it is expressed elsewhere in our society. Judges tend now to agree that, unless one of the parents is severely disturbed or the two parents are hopelessly antagonistic, having the two parents remain active in a child's life is desirable for the child.

However, couples who embark on two-household parenting are likely to encounter problems in managing their relationships with each other and with their children stemming simply from their having separate households. Some of the problems have to do with managing the coordination necessary for a parental partnership while living separately, some have to do with each parent being affected by the other's life decisions without being able to influence those decisions, and some, like recurrent experiences of loss, are inescapable concomitants of intermittent child

215

care. All these problems are likely to confront parents in different households, whether the parents get along reasonably well or not.

Still other problems are associated with acting as a single parent or a
remarried parent when the other parent is no longer in the picture. There
is extensive literature dealing with these problems and I will not do more
than note, here, that they exist. My concern in this chapter is with the
problems associated with arrangements in which parents alternate in their
custody of their children, whether their arrangement is understood as custody to the one parent, reasonable visitation to the other, or as joint custody.[1]

Problems of Partnership

One of the ways parents who live together are helpful to each other is by
modifying each other's judgment. As an example, a married respondent
in a study of occupationally successful men relied on his wife to modify
his reaction to a son's misdemeanor:

> Occasions when I might be going a little bit overboard in one direction, I
> may blurt out something like, "All right, the bike goes in the garage! You
> were told not to ride it in the street and now it stays there for a week!" Then
> some time later Myra will say, "Do you think a week is right?" And we'll
> decide maybe two days or four days or whatever. We'll say to the kid, "We've
> talked about this," and one of us will say, "maybe a week is a little bit too
> much punishment. For this time it is two days. But if it happens again, it will
> be a week."[2]

Given an effective and trusted parental alliance, each parent can anticipate that the other parent will act to modify a mistaken or unconsidered
way of treating the children. A trusted partnership makes it possible for
parents to search together for the most sensible resolution of the dilemmas
of child-raising, not least by each parent offering alternatives to the other's initial proposals.

Some married and cohabiting parent couples never establish an effective and trusted alliance. But even those who do are likely to find the
alliance difficult to maintain should they move to separate households. As
parents in different households, they are less likely to make joint decisions; indeed, each is more likely to hear of a problem with a child after
the problem has been responded to than when the response is being considered. In consequence, each parent's awareness that the other parent

may have a different view is more likely to lead to anticipatory defensiveness than to better parenting.

One couple had maintained a fairly effective partnership during their marriage but found it more difficult to do so after their separation. The father, although a devoted parent, had at times blown up at his kids. His concern was not so much working with his ex-wife on modifying his behavior as fear that his ex-wife would condemn him.

> There have been a few times in the past where I lost control, and I was worried about those. I think a couple of times I had even told my ex that I kind of lost control. It was better to just let her know about it in case they say something about it. Then she'll know what it was all about.

> On a lower scale it is just getting kind of low grade pissed off and being kind of crabby and wondering if they're going to go back and say, "Oh, Dad was in a real bad mood; he wasn't any fun at all." You always wonder about that.

A difficult issue for many parents, whether or not partnered, is how to deal with a child's entering situations in which there is risk of failure and emotional or physical injury. Often, although not always, mothers give more weight to safety, security, and immediate well-being, fathers more weight to the child's need to develop self-confidence and social skills.[3] Thus, in children's adolescence, fathers may take the lead in supporting the children's movement toward independence, while mothers remain aware of the children's continued need for support and nurturance.

When parents live together, this complementarity of concern is likely to result in representation of both ways of reacting to a child's encounter with challenge. How this can occur may be suggested by a vignette reported by a father in a reasonably well-functioning marriage.

> The respondent's four-year-old son had been unable to tie his shoes. The boy's mother said that the boy's fingers were not yet developed enough for him to guide the shoe laces. The respondent said that on hearing this he had exploded with, "I won't have him grow up unable to do anything!" (The respondent did not know the source of his fear that his son would be incompetent as an adult and was surprised to hear himself voice it.) The respondent then constructed a lace-tying practice board by stapling half laces to a flat piece of wood. The respondent's son quickly learned to tie his laces, although the respondent was uncertain whether it was the practice board that made the difference or the boy's recognition of the respondent's determination that the boy master the task.

It may be surmised that in this instance the child profited from his parents' different concerns. In addition to learning to tie his laces, the boy almost surely learned that while his father insisted that he develop socially important competencies, his mother's love was his, no matter what.

Although fathers seem generally to represent the importance of competence and mothers to represent the foolishness of risk, what is important in a well-functioning parental partnership is not so much which parent represents which position as having two parents who together recognize that children need both challenge and security. To be sure, parental complementarity of concern can give rise to genuine conflict. Rather than father and mother finding a resolution of the different principles, they may remain in disagreement. The father may subordinate his views to those of the mother in the belief that the mother is the parent more responsible and more knowledgeable in the area of child care. Or the father may think the mother wrong but, rather than attempt to modify her approach, become silently critical. Or the father may insist on his views, so that the mother is made to feel helpless and beleaguered. Sometimes parents living separately say they are pleased to be able to parent as they think best, without the burden of a partner whose views are in conflict with theirs.

Often, however, when parents live together their decisions in child care incorporate the concerns of both. When parents live apart, their different views are more likely to give rise to different household cultures. Eleanor Maccoby and Robert Mnookin report this issue:

> Some parents talked about the confusion their children experienced when the two households differed in their standards. For example, one father in a dual-residence family [the children lived sometimes with the mother, sometimes with the father] said that he allows his five-year-old son to play on a skateboard while the mother considers this dangerous and does not allow it.[4]

It is unlikely that the father here was unaware of the need for caution or that the mother had no interest in promoting the child's exploration of his abilities. But each parent had to come to a decision alone regarding which principle should govern the particular issue. Each parent might, indeed, try to compensate for the other parent's emphases, the father by encouraging the child to be adventuresome despite the mother's restrictions, the mother by cautioning the child to be careful when in the father's home. Each might, in consequence, exaggerate the importance of caution or enterprise. But neither could affect the culture of the other home.

Issues of Alliance

It is damaging to the parental partnership, when parents live together, if either parent forms an alliance with a child from which the other parent is excluded. Children will, of course, talk more about some issues to one parent than to the other, and parents can respect children's confidences without disrupting the parental partnership. However, it would be most harmful to a parental partnership if one of the parents developed an alliance with a child that took precedence over that parent's alliance with the other parent. Under such circumstances the excluded parent, in dealing with the child, would be without the other parent's backing and in any conflict with the child would have to act alone against the alliance of the child and the other parent.

Parents living apart, just as parents living together, may be aware of the importance of a trustworthy parental alliance. Parents living apart often say they discourage any effort by the child to play one of them against the other: to say to the father, for example, that mother allows a late bedtime and to the mother that father allows it. And they sometimes recognize the distortion of the parent-child relationship produced by one parent attempting to establish an alliance with a child by indulgence of the child. Nevertheless, parenting from different households encourages each parent to make common cause with the child.

Because each parent's household includes, part of the time, the child and never the other parent, parent and child, rather than the two parents, develop a sense of mutuality based on being fellow members of a household. It is the parent and child who have to work out together how chores will be done, how the day will be spent, and how to function cooperatively. It is the parent and child who sit across from each other at dinner and talk about the day. The single-parent household, by its structure, fosters a parent-child alliance from which the other parent is excluded.

Other factors may also play a role in fostering an alliance between a parent and child when parents are separated. Each parent may be impeded in maintaining an alliance with the other parent by the antagonisms associated with the separation. Because the two parents are likely to have different policies in child-raising, each may distrust the other as a parent. Antagonisms may also have been produced by conflicts associated with child care, especially by conflicts over visiting times or support payments.

Paradoxically, one result of the weakness of parental alliances with each other can be that each parent may worry about losing the child to the other parent. A child who becomes sufficiently resentful of a parent's rules or behavior can always withdraw into his or her relationship with the other parent. It is not at all rare for adolescent children who have mainly lived with one parent through their early years to decide to live with the other, partly because this is their last chance to base themselves in the noncustodial parent's home, but partly to escape things they don't like in what had been their custodial parent's home.

Another paradoxical consequence of each parent establishing an alliance with the child from which the other parent is excluded is that each parent may find that a significant part of the child's life is inaccessible. Indeed, each parent may collude in making it so, by accepting that the child would rather not talk about the child's experience in the other parent's household. Older children, especially, seem regularly resistant to being "put in the middle" by being asked by one parent to talk about the other. The result is that the alliance of a separated parent and his or her child, despite its likely strength, has important gaps.

Persisting Linkage

It is unusual for a separated parent to take the other parent's situation into consideration when planning his or her own future. Most custodial parents will not decline an otherwise attractive job opportunity only because accepting it would require relocation and so make visiting difficult for the other parent. And very few separated parents take into account how the other parent might get along with a boyfriend or girlfriend before establishing a new partnership. And yet, because separated parents are linked through their children, what each parent does affects the other parent's life. If a custodial parent decides to relocate to another part of the country, the noncustodial parent must adapt to seeing the child less often and paying for airline fares if the child is to be seen at all. Similarly, a noncustodial parent's new marriage will mean that the custodial parent must adapt to the child bringing home stories of a stepparent. Nor are these the only ways in which parents' lives are linked. A change in a parent's financial situation can change that parent's willingness to pay part of a camp bill or bill for private school. A parent's sudden emergency can mean that the other parent is called on to look after the child. A parent's religious conversion can impose on the other parent constant concern over what may be happening to the child.

Commitments to a new partner can produce troubling difficulties in coordination with the other parent. The parent with the new partner must now juggle obligations, often with awareness that the other parent questions the legitimacy of the obligations to the new partner. One father said:

> She's got a boyfriend. I've got a girlfriend. And we want to spend some time with our respective people, and sometimes it runs at odds with some of the other things. Because I think we're both a little uneasy and sensitive to the fact that probably it annoys the other a little bit, those things don't get conveyed as much. It's easier to say I have a golf game Sunday morning and I'm going to be tied up until one o'clock than saying I want to go out with my girlfriend Sunday evening at seven and I want you to be back so I can [bring over the kids and] leave. I think that's hard.

A parent's new partner inevitably has great importance for the other parent. The other parent may worry about being displaced in the children's lives and affections by the new figure. The other parent may want to communicate with the new figure regarding a child's activities or needs. Certainly the other parent will be concerned about the new figure's influence on the child and treatment of the child. And yet the other parent will have had no voice at all in the choice of the new figure.

Issues of Parental Attachment

The very investment that each parent has in his or her child can make for difficulties in the parents' relationships with each other and introduce problems into the other parent's relationships with a child. This comes about because parental investment can lead each parent to experience loss on relinquishing the child to the other parent, and to be ready to respond as a rescuer should he or she believe the child is equally distressed by the separation.

There are, of course, many sources of parents' investments in their children. One source almost certainly is biological, a parental attachment not easily modified by experience. Recognizing the strength and resilience of this parental attachment makes more understandable the persistence in conflict of parents who have come to distrust each other.

Parental attachment can develop only gradually, but seems often to develop suddenly, all at once: it was not there before, but then it is fully there. Pamela Daniels and Kathy Weingarten, referring to parental attachment among men, report: "Time and time again in our interviews, men singled out a particular moment that generated . . . the click of fatherhood."[5] The same sudden onset has been reported in connection with maternal investment, in the form of the sudden awareness of emotional linkage when an expectant mother experiences movement or a newly delivered mother holds her newborn.[6] That there can be such sudden onset suggests that what has been triggered is a deep-seated emotional system rather than the kind of liking that can wax or wane with experience. Among parents who have had caretaking responsibilities for a child, and who accept the child as theirs, parental attachment is so much the rule that it seems almost invariable.

The system of parental attachment seems to function in ways that make sense if the child were understood by the parent as an aspect of the parent's self. So parental attachment is displayed by pride when children do well, as though an aspect of the self is in this way validated, and, most vividly, by alarm reactions and an urgent need to act to protect the child should a child seem endangered.

Parental attachment proves to be not only strongly motivating but also tenacious; Lehman, Wortman, and Williams, on the basis of interviews with the parents of children who had been killed in auto accidents, report that years after the event almost all of the parents remain grief-stricken, their inability to have come to their children's rescue still the central fact of their lives.[7] A study of parents whose children were abducted by the children's other parent reports that worry about the children's well-being dominates the lives of almost all of these parents and does not diminish, no matter how much time has passed.[8]

Parents react to a belief that their child is in danger in the other parent's home in just the way they would react to any threat to the child. A custodial parent who does not trust the noncustodial parent (because, for example, the custodial parent believes the noncustodial parent is alcoholic and will drink and drive) is likely to be anxious when the child is with the noncustodial parent. Indeed, custodial parents are able to tolerate visitation outside their homes only if they can believe that the child is safe with the other parent. Parents find it reassuring to remind themselves (if they can) that the other parent is a good parent and loves the child. But for the parent who does not trust a child's other parent, a court order requiring that the child sometimes be with the other parent is a sentence to intense anxiety, frustration, feelings of helplessness and self-condemnation.

All the foregoing material regarding the difficulties of parents living separately is illustrated, I believe, by the case that follows. My discussion of the case is based on interviews I conducted with both the custodial mother and the noncustodial father. The case illustrates the way in which the attachment feelings of each parent for a child can complicate the functioning of parents living separately. The case also illustrates the ease with which mutual distrust develops in the absence of a parental alliance, and the way in which the parents' lives nevertheless are linked through their child. In addition the case suggests the way in which each of the two households maintained by a separated couple can develop a distinct household culture, different from the culture in the other household.

An Exemplary Case

The parents in this example were among parents living apart who had never been married to each other. The mother, whom I shall call Ms. Davies, had only a brief relationship with her daughter's father, Mr. Martin, before becoming pregnant by him. Because Ms. Davies was no longer seeing Mr. Martin when she discovered that she was pregnant, she did not inform him of the pregnancy. Nor did Mr. Martin learn that he was a father until his daughter was almost two years old. At that time unemployment forced Ms. Davies to apply for welfare assistance, and the Welfare Department would accept her application only if she first sought child support from Mr. Martin.

Ms. Davies said that Mr. Martin's initial reaction, on learning that he was a father, was outraged denial that the child was his. Only after blood tests demonstrated his paternity beyond doubt did Mr. Martin accept responsibility for the child. But then, in a turnabout that Ms. Davies found perplexing, Mr. Martin insisted on visiting the child. Ms. Davies permitted this only reluctantly. For almost two years she had raised the child alone. By what right did Mr. Martin, a stranger to her daughter, suddenly introduce himself into the child's life?

Nevertheless, Mr. Martin visited her daughter several times in Ms. Davies's home. Then Mr. Martin, who was now married, asked Ms. Davies for her permission to take her daughter, now not quite three, for visits in his home. Ms. Davies refused. Mr. Martin went to court and won. The little girl began spending Sunday afternoons from one to five o'clock in Mr. Martin's home. Mr. Martin complained to Ms. Davies that his time with her daughter was too short, given that the first and last hour of his visit was consumed by traveling between Ms. Davies home and his. When Ms. Davies refused to permit Mr. Martin to keep her daughter longer, Mr. Martin returned to court to have his visiting time extended to 7:30 in the evening. Again, he won.

After a few months, to Ms. Davies' total consternation, Mr. Martin unaccountably returned yet again to court, now to contest Ms. Davies' custody. He did this despite not having known of the child's existence for the first two years of the child's life, and having fought to avoid being designated as the child's father. Ms. Davies's only explanation was that Mr. Martin was so angered by having to pay child support that he had decided to contest her custody to get back at her. However, Ms. Davies's lawyer and Mr. Martin's lawyer agreed that Mr. Martin would drop his suit for custody in exchange for Ms. Davies's agreeing to Mr. Martin having their daughter with him each summer for 10 days. Ms. Davies's perceptions of Mr. Martin as a parent now underwent change; she became reconciled to Mr. Martin as a fellow parent and accepted that he was a good parent who loved their daughter.

Mr. Martin corroborated Ms. Davies's outline of events. His relationship with Ms. Davies had lasted no more than a month. He had had a number of girlfriends at that time in his life, none of whom, until he met the woman he married, he had felt to be especially important. His marriage was only three months old when he received the letter from the Department of Welfare telling him that he was in arrears in child support and threatening him with jail.

Mr. Martin said that his reaction to the letter from the Department of Welfare still seemed to him a reasonable one. Of course he would contest an effort to make him responsible for a pregnancy and birth of which he had been unaware, brought by a woman he had nearly forgotten. And so he retained an attorney who arranged for a blood test. The test found that Mr. Martin was almost surely the child's father and a second test confirmed the first. Mr. Martin wanted his lawyer to demand further tests. Mr. Martin's lawyer said that he would if Mr. Martin insisted but that the results would almost surely be the same. With something of a wrench, Mr. Martin acknowledged to himself that he was the child's father.

I asked Mr. Martin what had gone through his mind when he finally accepted that the child was his. He said, "Well, she was a part of me. And I wanted to see my daughter, and proceed from there." Here was the click of attachment—even though Mr. Martin had not yet seen his daughter.

When Mr. Martin discovered that Ms. Davies did not want him to see his daughter, he had his lawyer petition the court for visitation rights. (Mr. Martin's income, augmented by his wife's, could barely cover legal fees. No matter.) Mr. Martin's determination to see his daughter, which was so perplexing to Ms. Davies, seemed to him entirely natural. This was his child, from whom it was intolerable that he be separated.

Mr. Martin's lawyer obtained a court order for two-hour Sunday visits in Ms. Davies's home. Mr. Martin said that he and his daughter, in his phrase, "bonded immediately." After two months of Sunday visits in Ms. Davies's home, Mr. Martin asked Ms. Davies if he could take his daughter to his home for their visits. Ms. Davies' reply was, as Mr. Martin reported it, not so long as she lived. So Mr. Martin had his lawyer return to court. The court ordered that Mr. Martin be permitted to have his daughter visit him in his home every other Sunday for a few hours. A further appeal to the court made possible overnight visits every other weekend in addition to the Sunday visits. An effort to obtain custody was dropped in exchange for a vacation interval once a year.

Mr. Martin's wife said that their marriage had nearly ended during the months that followed the appearance of the letter demanding support payments. It had been hard for her to accept that her husband had already fathered a child. But now, she said, she fully accepted her husband's determination to be an active father and, more than this, admired his investment in his daughter's well-being. She described the relationship of her husband and his daughter in this way:

> When I see them, it is just pure love and affection between the two of them. It's just the looks on both of their faces, it's just pure admiration. It's wonderful to see them together. . . . I mean, they're always together. She follows him like a little puppy dog. You know, Daddy's little girl. And she is.

This quotation, while intended as a description of a child's affection, could also be interpreted as a description of an anxious attachment, in which the child needs the reassurance of having the parent always in sight. But there seems no question of the emotional importance of father and daughter for each other.

My interview with Mr. Martin and his wife occurred the evening Mr. Martin's daughter had returned to her mother's home after the first vacation visit of 10 days. Mr. Martin said his daughter hadn't wanted to leave his home to return to her mother's home and he hadn't wanted her to go. He was especially unhappy because Ms. Davies intended soon to move to the West Coast to join a boyfriend she planned to marry. Mr. Martin said he did not want his daughter raised by the boyfriend. He suspected that when the boyfriend had lived with the mother, before the boyfriend moved to the West Coast, the boyfriend had abused his daughter. It was this belief that had led him to attempt to obtain custody. His lawyer had told him he had little chance of success, and so he had agreed to drop the effort. When he learned that Ms. Davies planned to relocate, Mr. Martin had sought an injunction against her moving their child out of the court's jurisdiction. He had gained a temporary injunction, but then had lost his effort to make the injunction permanent. Now Mr. Martin was afraid that Ms. Davies would not honor the commitment she had made to the judge to send the child back East—at Mr. Martin's expense—for the 10-day vacations she had earlier agreed to. Mr. Martin was despairing at the thought that he might not see his daughter again for years.

This story displays, among other things, how strongly motivating is parental attachment. Mr. Martin's desire to be the father he thought his daughter needed was strong enough to cause him to risk a marriage important to him, and to spend, on lawyer's fees, money he could not afford. And the mother's equally compelling investment in the child caused her to fight every effort the father made to establish times in which the mother would be replaced as the parent with responsibility for the child's care and control. Each parent's behavior displayed the resilience of parental investment; each parent was determined to be the child's caretaker, and each pursued this end despite frustration in the courts and financial and emotional cost.

Also exemplified in this case is how easily antagonism can develop between parents whose parental partnership is, to begin with, flawed or, as in this case, absent. Mr. Martin and Ms. Davies did not begin their relationship as fellow parents with antagonism produced in the course of ending a marriage. Nor was there intense antagonism between the two when Mr. Martin reacted with anger and upset on being notified of his paternity although Ms. Davies was irritated that Mr. Martin would seek to escape responsibility. Intense conflict between the parents occurred only when Mr. Martin sought to establish and maintain a relationship with his child. Then Ms. Davies' desire to protect her own relationship to the child led her to attempt to limit and control Mr. Martin's relationship. There followed the court contests in which Mr. Martin sought successfully to escape Ms. Davies's supervision of his relationship with the child and to enlarge the interval in which he could be with the child. Finally, Mr. Martin's belief that the child would be better cared for in his home than in the home Ms. Davies planned to make with her boyfriend, together with his desire to maintain his relationship with the child, made him sue to take custody of the child away from Ms. Davies. All these actions both expressed antagonism between the parents and produced further antagonism.

The parental antagonism, together with the physical separation of the parents, made planning for the child's well-being awkward. Because the parents disliked talking with each other, neither parent shared with the other information regarding the child's experience in that parent's home. Nevertheless, despite the narrowness of communication between the households, each parent was forced to adapt to the other parent's circumstances: Ms. Davies to Mr. Martin's marriage, which made Mr. Martin's wife a stepparent to Ms. Davies's daughter, and Mr. Martin to Ms. Davies's planned move to join a boyfriend.

Perhaps most distressing of all these troubling aspects of parenting in different households was, for each parent, witnessing the child's discomforts and confusions and feeling helpless to remedy them. Each parent repeatedly witnessed the child's distress because of an impending separation and each was helpless to prevent the separation. Mr. Martin reported to us his daughter's unwillingness to leave his home to return to her mother's home. Ms. Davies reported to us that her child was now often upset, whereas before Mr. Martin appeared on the scene the child had been easygoing and generally happy. Furthermore, each parent, like the child, experienced repeated intervals in which the child was inaccessible. Thus, because of the separation of their households, together with the alternation of custody, each parent saw the child distressed and experienced personal distress.

The story also demonstrates how much persistent effort can be required of a legally noncustodial parent if that parent is to maintain a parental relationship despite the opposition of the custodial parent. When parents cohabit, parental relationships are part of the life of the family. But when parents are in different households, the noncustodial parent can no longer take for granted an ongoing relationship with the children.

Some Recommendations

1. We need programs that support parents staying together and working together as parents. There are any number of ways in which it is better for children if parents remain cooperative co-residential partners. When parents share their residence, their children can have a sense of continuous access to each parent; they need not separate from one in order to be with the other. When parents live apart, children are apt to feel that they can have access to one parent or the other, but never both at once. Furthermore, as this chapter has argued, co-residential parents who can work together cooperatively can much more easily and more effectively meet the needs of their children.

A great many programs have been developed for enhancing the satisfactoriness of marriages and reducing the likelihood of marital dissolution. Some are designed for young people, preparing them for later marital commitment; some are designed for people already married and support their commitment to their marital partnership; some focus on marriage enhancement; some support effective parental partnerships through the teaching of parental skills; some support effective partnerships through bettering partnership communication; some are remedial, aimed at keeping together partners who are unable by themselves to make their partnerships satisfactory. All these programs have proponents who believe them to be effective. We need some process for choosing which among them should be supported, and we then need to move to make as available as possible those programs most deserving support.

2. We also need programs that provide conceptual models for parents who have become heads of separate households. Separated parent couples have little preparation for the challenges they will confront. Educational programs can help them. Such programs should use what have been shown to be effective teaching devices in other settings, including not only lecture material but also dramatic productions (such as videotapes) and opportunities for discussion, even role-playing. Topics reviewed should include ways in which separated parents can establish shared policies for the children, ways in which the parents can each facilitate the other's caring for the children, and devices for managing the conflicts between the parents that are almost inevitable when parents live apart.

Parents who live in different households are likely to have only limited understandings of each other's experience. It might help to foster cooperativeness between such parents if each could learn the other's perspective and problems. This might also mitigate the sense of personal misuse that separated parents sometimes develop: the sense that the other parent has all the benefits of the separated parent arrangement and none of its problems.

3. Parents should recognize that change is always disruptive. Parents who are contemplating major changes in their lives should consider the extent to which they are requiring adaptation in their children that may exceed the children's capacities. Changes that might be considered severe would, of course, include ending a co-residential parental partnership. Among parents already living in different households, major changes would include both a change of residence through which the children become more distant from the noncustodial parent, and the entrance into the children's home of a parent's new partner. Change is not necessarily to be avoided; the parent's own well-being must be considered, and sometimes change is useful for children as well. But change is generally disruptive in the short term at least, and attention should always be given to its effects on a parent's relationships with the other parent and with the children.

4. We need to make it easy for parents living apart to consult, as necessary, a supportive professional who has continuing responsibility for the family. All parents, but particularly parents living apart, are likely to find it useful to have access to a professional who can act as a friend of the

family, to whom the parents can take issues that baffle them or about which they cannot agree. Very occasionally separated parents who have enough of a feeling of partnership now bring uncertainties, dilemmas, and conflicts to therapists or pediatricians or members of the clergy. Worth exploring would be institutionalizing this sort of resource. People trained both in the mental health field and in child development might be available to parents in separate households in the same way pediatricians are, setting appointments as there are specific issues to be dealt with. It could then be the prerogative of either parent to propose that a problem in parenting be taken to the professional working with their family, and the responsibility of the other parent to agree.

Retired mental health professionals might serve as friends of the family through at least some of the children's growing-up years. Such professionals would expect to be called on from time to time until the children were grown. The institutionalization of the practice would be a way these retired professionals could continue to contribute to the society. And couples attempting to manage parenting from separate households could recognize that even though the enterprise is one fraught with difficulties, the society values their efforts enough to provide them with help.[9]

Notes

This chapter is based in part on my experience co-leading groups for parents living separately who are embroiled in quarrels over visitation or custody. My partner in leading these groups was JoAnne Steeves. Other members of the research project of which these groups were a part were Amy Koel, Barbara Hauser, Susan Clark, Mary Coffey, Marla Desatnik, John Drabik, Michael Melzner, Sherry Moss, Leah Sherman, and Rob Straus. The project was funded by a grant from Health and Human Services, Office of Child Support Enhancement, Project No. 91-4-CAMA-006. In addition I have profited from membership in a research group exploring the problems of separated parents. Other members of this group are Dr. Koel, Mrs. Clark, Mr. Drabik, Stephanie Howard, David Jacobson, and Joan Liem. I want to thank Dr. Koel and Mrs. Clark for their help with this chapter.

1. Single-parent problems can be severe. While single parents generally manage the tasks of child care with some effectiveness, they ordinarily find that such tasks leave them little spare time and energy. In consequence, they are more vulnerable than are parents living jointly to finding that additional demands—as might result from a child's illness—bring about emotional depletion and feelings of being overwhelmed by unshared chores and responsibilities. Single parents are especially vulnerable if they work full-time, have small children, have more than one child, and can call on no other adult to help them with child care. I have

described the problems of the single parent in *Going It Alone: The Family Life and Social Situation of the Single Parent* (New York: Basic Books, 1979). Problems associated with remarriage have been described by several authors, including Jamie Kelem Keshet, *Love and Power in the Stepfamily* (New York: McGraw-Hill, 1987), and Anne Bernstein, *Yours, Mine, and Ours: How Families Change When Remarried Parents Have a Child Together* (New York: Scribner's, 1989).

2. Robert S. Weiss, *Staying the Course: The Emotional and Social Lives of Men Who Do Well at Work* (New York: The Free Press, 1990), 152.

3. This may, perhaps, be more true with boys than girls. Fathers tend to be less confident as parents of daughters. See, for further discussion, *Staying the Course*, 174–76.

4. Eleanor E. Maccoby and Robert H. Mnookin, *Dividing the Child: Social and Legal Dilemmas of Custody* (Cambridge, MA: Harvard University Press, 1992), 225.

5. Pamela Daniels and Kathy Weingarten, *Sooner or Later: The Timing of Parenting in Adult Lives* (New York: W. W. Norton and Company, 1982), 150–51.

6. Marshall Klaus and John B. Kennel, *Maternal-Infant Bonding: The Impact of Early Separation on Family Development* (St. Louis: Moby, 1977).

7. D. R. Lehman, C. B. Wortman, and A. F. Williams, "Long-Term Effects of Losing a Spouse or Child in a Motor Vehicle Crash," *Journal of Personality and Social Psychology* 52, no. 1 (1987): 218–31.

8. Geoffrey L. Greif and Rebecca L. Heggar, *When Parents Kidnap: The Families Behind the Headlines* (New York: The Free Press, 1993).

9. This model has been described in lectures by Dr. Gerald Caplan.

PART THREE

Rebuilding a Marriage Culture

CHAPTER 10

Re-creating Marriage

Maggie Gallagher

Optimism is America's birthright.

There is no enemy too tough to beat, no age-old problem Americans do not insist on trying to cure, rather than endure. Slavery, prostitution, and drunkenness were the nineteenth century's crusades; poverty, prejudice, domestic violence, and inequality are among the twentieth century's crusades. Total victory often eludes reformers. Still, Americans have an impressive record of refusing to bow to historical inevitabilities. There is no social problem Americans dare not attack. No problem, that is, except one: about marriage, and marriage alone, we despair.

The collapse of marriage can best be captured in two simple statistics. Today, according to demographers, up to 65 percent of new marriages will fail. Meanwhile, almost one-third of all American children are born out of wedlock. Add to that the fact that divorce creates its own momentum—children of divorce are both more likely to divorce themselves and more likely to have illegitimate births than are children of intact marriages—and it becomes increasingly difficult to deny that we are facing an unprecedented crisis in marriage.

Nonetheless, the overwhelming consensus among experts, even those disturbed about the decline of marriage, is that there is nothing we can do about it. As Arlene Skolnick writes in *Embattled Paradise: The American Family in an Age of Uncertainty*, "[T]here is no way of going back to where we were before."[1] David Ellwood concludes his study of single parents and poverty on a similar fatalistic note: "[T]he changes in the structure of the family are probably the result of some sizeable and largely unstoppable changes in social and economic patterns."[2] Even Judith Wallerstein, whose groundbreaking fifteen-year study of children of divorce

233

broke the taboo against recognizing divorce's ill effects, opposes changes in divorce laws as counterproductive for kids. A February 27, 1995, *Time* magazine cover story, dramatically titled "For Better, for Worse: The growing movement to strengthen marriage and prevent divorce," could find no bolder proposal to combat the collapse of marriage than more counseling and mandatory waiting periods for marriage licenses.

The proposed reforms amount to less of a crusade than a white flag of surrender. For the first time in American history, a whole generation of children appears likely to be worse off than their parents. Yet even in our minds we dare go no further than timidly considering how to take the edge off children's worst deprivations: Democratic policy wonks ponder what government policies can keep kids just the right side of the poverty line, while their GOP counterparts merely add the proviso, at the least cost to the taxpayers.

What accounts for this anomalous, this un-American passivity in the face of catastrophe? There is a strong new consensus on the damaging effects divorce has on children, and the role family breakdown plays in social problems from crime to poverty, child abuse, infant mortality, homelessness, drug abuse, and declining education. So, after thirty years of the divorce revolution, why has no serious political effort been made—or even proposed—to restore marriage?

One reason for our current pessimism about marriage is surely our former optimism about divorce. The divorce revolution was in itself originally something of a crusade. Divorce promised women in particular an escape from age-old problems: domestic abuse, unequal sex roles, boredom, and unhappiness. And for many adults, let us be frank, the dreams of the divorce culture were realized. Like all wars, the divorce revolution has its winners and losers, and in America everybody prefers to dwell on the winners.

For a while, experts viewed remarriage as the solution to the crisis of divorce. This optimism was battered by two discoveries. First, remarriages turned out to be even more unstable than first marriages. Second, researchers discovered to their surprise that in psychological terms, children in stepfamilies do no better, on average, than children in single-parent homes.[3] While remarriage does raise household income, the money may not be as available to children: stepparents and noncustodial parents are both, for example, far less willing to lay out cash for college than parents in intact marriages.[4] It is not the "two-parent family" so much as the intact family, that holds substantial advantages for children.

Despite the growing body of evidence against divorce, it is not hard to find experts who dissent. Some, such as Frank Furstenberg, Jr., and Andrew Cherlin, acknowledge that divorce has some negative effects, but argue that these are mild. Many children of divorce are doing just fine, they point out, accurately enough.

But these experts tend to underestimate the effects of the divorce culture for two reasons. The first is methodological. As social scientists they are committed to an intellectual process of analytically separating what in the real world are inevitably intertwined. Thus many researchers spend considerable energy and ingenuity in teasing out, say, what percentage of the damage divorce causes is due to lower income and what percentage is due to "the divorce itself."

But controlling for income actually understates the true consequences of divorce. In the real world, less money is one of the most consistent by-products of the collapse of marriage. Manipulating government subsidies and child support payments may keep more kids above an arbitrary poverty line. But there is no social program on the horizon which can give back to divorced couples the economies of marriage, nor can the law compel the kind of enormous sacrifices—from working overtime, to taking a second job, to mortgaging the house to pay for college—that married fathers routinely make for their children, but which divorced fathers seldom do. The collapse of marriage leaves everyone poorer. For children, the decline is partly fueled by the inexorable law that two households cannot live as cheaply as one, but it is fueled too by the equally inexorable reality that over time mothers and fathers who are not married develop conflicting economic interests and competing family obligations.

Secondly, these experts often focus on the wrong question. If the question is, "Will my particular children survive my particular divorce?," the answer is quite likely to be, with some caveats, "Probably." Almost all children find their parents' divorce painful and traumatic. Most, however, do not go on to become juvenile delinquents or high school dropouts as a result.

But to judge the true effects of the divorce revolution we need to ask a different question as well: what happens when a whole society—or a large subsection thereof—adopts a risky pattern of childrearing? A 10 or 20 percent chance your child will suffer long-lasting damage may seem to a harassed parent a risk worth running. But a society which, in each generation, progressively loses an extra 10 or 20 percent of its children to drugs, crime, suicide, ignorance, or mere idleness and despair, is a society defined not, as America's has always been, by upward progress but by slow decline. If we fail to restore marriage, our children will find it small comfort to live in an America in which each generation is only "moderately" worse off than the last.

Collectively and institutionally, the divorce culture exerts a relentless downward pressure on the ability of families to transmit values, aspirations, and opportunities to the next generation. After divorce, families become weaker, parents less able to protect their young or to pass on their own status and values to their children. One study that attempted to assess the effects of divorce on social mobility concluded that family disruption "substantially increases men's odds of ending up in the lowest occupational stratum." Divorce also weakens the resemblance between parents' economic status and that of their adult children. Married families are far more successful at passing on educational and occupational advantages. The culture of divorce, by contrast, has produced a new "inability of families to pass on advantages to their children."[5]

Daughters who divorce require far more financial aid from their aging parents than their married sisters.[6] In turn, they are able to give less social and financial support to their own adult children.[7] Divorce thus creates a crisis that to meet requires drawing upon the collected capital of the generations, a transfer of resources from both children and grandparents to meet the urgent needs of the current generation of adults.

A second group of experts, such as psychologist Arlene Skolnick and sociologists Stephanie Coontz and Judith Stacey, are even more optimistic: they maintain that it is not divorce *per se* but dysfunctional families that damage kids. The divorce revolution, by encouraging bad marriages to dissolve, is actually a blessing to kids in disguise. "The belief that married couple families are superior is probably the most pervasive prejudice about family life in the Western World," maintains Judith Stacey, a sociologist at the University of California at Davis and author of the book *Brave New Families*. "Research indicates that high conflict marriages harm children more than do low-conflict divorces. . . . In short the research scale tips toward those who stress the quality of family relationships over their form."[8]

This is the most powerful argument the divorce culture can muster on its behalf. For the moment when divorce culture displaced the old marriage ideal was not when the mere number of divorces passed a certain threshold, but when Americans began to view divorce as better—*morally* better—than remaining in a less than satisfying marriage. That divorce is better for the whole family than continuing a "bad" marriage is now a truism. But is it true?

There is no doubt that conflict is very damaging to kids. But behind this argument are several key, unexamined assumptions: especially that marriage *causes* conflict and that divorce can be counted on to relieve it. In the social science literature, conflict between parents is called "marital conflict." This is a label that implies its own solution: to put an end to marital conflict, you only have to put an end to the marriage. But of course, what really bothers children is not that two spouses are fighting, but that their own parents are fighting. If it is not marital conflict *per se* but parental conflict that hurts kids, then divorce is not necessarily the solution and may even be part of the problem.

The optimists, in short, like to compare angry marriages to low-conflict divorces on the magical assumption that a piece of paper called a divorce will put an end to parental fighting. But all the evidence suggests that, to the contrary, low-conflict divorces are usually the product of friendly marriages. Constance Ahrons, for example, recently published *The Good Divorce*, a study of middle-class divorced couples drawn at random from one Wisconsin county. She is remarkably optimistic about the prospects for friendly divorce. But in her sample, just 12 percent of divorced couples enjoyed such ideal divorces, and almost all these "perfect pals" were the product of remarkably amiable marriages. Most said their spouse had been their "best friend" and they remained friends after the divorce. (Five years later, however, one-third of even these perfect pals' relationships had degenerated into angry infighting; conflict usually arose around the time one or the other remarried.)[9] For most couples the ideal divorce is no more likely than the ideal marriage. Even five years after the divorce, about half of all divorced couples in Ahrons' sample were still locked in bitter, angry conflict.

As a group, kids of low-conflict divorced parents will look better off than the children in angry marriages or angry divorces. They will not, however, fare as well as children whose parents remain in low-conflict marriages. Dr. Rex Forehand, for example, compared the school performance of kids in four categories: low-conflict divorced, low-conflict intact, high-conflict divorced, high-conflict intact families. Kids from low-conflict divorced families did better than children in high-conflict marriages but not as well as children in low-conflict intact families. Meanwhile, the kids who did the worst of all, considerably worse than children in high-conflict marriages, were children in high-conflict divorced families. "Divorce may be a plausible option if it leads to less parental fighting," Forehand noted, "but it is a horrendous option if it does not. High conflict in conjunction with divorce was significantly more detrimental to the functioning of adolescents."[10]

There is, so far as I have been able to uncover, little reliable data on what proportion of divorces is precipitated by intense, sustained conflict that damages kids and what proportion of divorces occurs in what might be called (from the child's point of view) good-enough marriages. Cer-

tainly many women, married or not, remain locked in brutal relationships, while many divorces appear motivated less by violent infighting
than personal dissatisfaction.

Moreover, divorce, rather than signaling the end of parental conflict,
often merely raises the ante. Divorce is, after all, usually experienced by
the spouse who is left as a distinctly unfriendly act. It provokes angry
exchanges, bitter feelings, and even uncharacteristic acts of violence between parents. In Judith Wallersteins's study *Second Chances*, over half
the children of divorce witnessed physical violence between their parents,
whereas before the divorce most had never experienced violence in the
home.

The happy divorce myth that dominates our culture goes something
like this. Many married folk are very unhappy. They fight a lot, which
hurts the kids. Divorce gives adults a new shot at marital happiness. Children get a relief from conflict and a better model of adult love.

The hard truth is this: more divorce has not led to less parental conflict,
to happier marriages, or to more children living with happily married
parents.

As University of Texas sociologist Norval Glenn was the first to point
out, if divorce were merely replacing bad marriages with happier ones,
then existing marriages ought to be becoming markedly more happy, as
unhappy marriages dissolve at ever-increasing rates. Instead, he was troubled to find the opposite has occurred: data on marital happiness show
that marriages are becoming *both* much less stable and somewhat less
happy. Since 1973, the proportion of American adults who are unhappily
married has not changed at all, while the number who enjoy a happy
marriage has dropped by 20 percent. Meanwhile, the proportion of kids
living with unhappily married parents has also not changed, while the
number living in what all experts agree is the ideal situation—a happily
married family—also dropped sharply.[11]

Who are the winners in the collapse of marriage? The greatest drop in
happiness has occurred among married women in their childbearing
years. Meanwhile, the happiness rates of single men have more than tripled. It appears we are redesigning our social institutions to benefit the
least productive and most dangerous segment of the population, single
men, at the direct expense of married women.

The divorce culture appears to be competing with and gradually dis-
placing the older marriage culture, to the detriment of married persons'
happiness and children's well-being. The good marriage is slipping ever
further out of our grasp. Meanwhile, the ideal divorce remains even more
elusive. A good divorce is an ideal which—experience has painfully

taught—is certainly no easier to achieve than the good enough marriage while the returns to children and to society are far less.

To re-create marriage, we must step back from the angry couples and look at the system of incentives we have created over the past two generations which has made marriage a visibly less happy and less productive option.

Over the past 30 years, America has been systematically privatizing the responsibilities of marriages while just as systematically extending the rights of marriage to the unmarried and at the same time transferring the costs of nonmarriage to the general public.

So the law now aggressively forbids private individuals from distinguishing between married and unmarried couples, for the purpose of housing or credit or zoning or foster care or adoption, for example, while at the same time the government extends many of the privileges of marriage to the unmarried through new devices such as domestic partnership laws. Courts have actually held distinctions based on marital status to be a violation of equal protection. In the eyes of the law, marriage is increasingly reduced to a mere body count. Landlords, for example, may freely choose to limit the number of people living on their property; they may choose to rent only to an individual or to two individuals or to four. What they are no longer legally permitted to do is notice that there is any difference between a spouse and a sex partner, or for that matter between a family and a frat house.

In economic terms, public policy now systematically discriminates against the married, taxing married families at unprecedented rates to provide a wide array of benefits available only to single mothers or to families of such low-incomes that even working-class married couples do not qualify.

This pronounced public policy tilt against marriage was not always the case. Until the late 1960s, for example, New York City public housing projects gave a preference to low-income married couples. But along with federal money came federal strings: Washington insisted that public housing dismantle this preference for the married poor. The result was not only an erosion in the quality of life at housing projects but a dismantling of important supports for marriage in the working class. It is a measure of how far marriage has fallen from official favor that the Giuliani administration recently braved a controversy to bring back preferences—but only for "working" families, not necessarily for married families. (Meanwhile, in New York City public schools, children are taught that it is a violation of civil rights to "discriminate" on the basis of marital status.)

In recent decades, the economic basis of marriage has been allowed to erode, particularly in the question of tax policy. Federal tax relief has been targeted at taxpayers in general and at low-income families, disproportionally headed by single mothers. Meanwhile, the tax burden has shifted heavily onto married couples with children. Thanks to inflation, the dependent exemption, which in 1948 shielded three-quarters of the average family's income from federal taxes, now protects less than one-quarter. To restore the protection that has been lost to inflation, the dependent exemption would have to be more than tripled, from about $2,500 to close to $8,000 a year.

A second economic problem afflicting marriage, the ongoing decline in male wages, has been exacerbated by a huge rise in payroll taxes that took place in the 1980s. As Larry Kudlow has pointed out, between 1985 and 1994, thanks to a leap in payroll taxes, a man earning $50,000 a year (a little more than the average, married-family income), saw his after-tax purchasing power drop "a whopping 24 percent."[12] For low-income families, the recently enacted earned income tax credit helps offset payroll tax increases. But the majority of married families make over $40,000 a year, less than 20 percent make under $25,000 a year. (By contrast, the majority of single moms make less than $15,000 a year.) Policies like the earned income tax credit thus protect most single mothers but relatively few married couple families.

The theory behind the generous protections for the average family built into the 1950s tax code is simple: among the competing public interests of the nation, the needs of children ought to come first. Families must be allowed to keep all the income they reasonably need to raise children, before making other contributions to the national welfare. By allowing the dependent exemption to erode, we have implicitly transformed children (and the marriages that protect them) from public contributions into private consumption items.

The evidence that economic stress destabilizes marriage is plentiful; poverty, male unemployment, and declining male wages are all strongly associated with increased divorce rates (as well as with the failure to marry). As a culture, we shy away from this knowledge. Money has replaced sex as the great unmentionable in love. Nonetheless, as a recent Census Bureau study shows, money remains a far more reliable predictor of marital success than passion. The general rule is this: the less money, the less stable the marriage. Low-income couples are twice as likely to divorce as the average couple.

There is one exception which proves the rule: couples in which both spouses work full-time are very unlikely to be poor (over three times less likely than one-income married couples according to 1989 census data) yet they are also much more prone to divorce.[13]

Some like to argue that the relative instability of these marriages is actually a secret sign of strength: women with full-time jobs feel more *able* to leave unsatisfactory marriages. For those concerned about good enough marriage, this is a depressing argument; it implies that a 50 percent divorce rate is not too high but far too low. Sixty percent of married mothers currently either do not work or work part-time and (under this thesis) are presumably staying, far too often, in bad marriages. What we know of research about marital happiness does not particularly support this contention. It is far more likely that the greater instability of two-career marriages reflects not women's choices but the tremendous economic pressures on the family today, pressures certainly exacerbated, if not caused, by the punitive tax treatment of married families.

As the economic underpinnings of marriage continue to erode, more and more women have been forced into the workplace full-time—particularly mothers of very young children, many of whom would prefer to devote more time to the family and less time to the corporation. Since at least the late 1980s, polls have shown that a majority of working mothers would prefer to work part-time or not at all. The consequences of this new economic pressure for women's well-being are enormous. Not only are these women's marriages less stable but they are less successful. Research shows that the two groups of women most likely to suffer from depression are women at home with children who prefer to be in the workforce and women in the workforce who long to be home with their children.[14] Today, unlike thirty years ago, it is the latter which is the larger and most rapidly growing group.

Probably the most straightforward way to raise family income and stabilize marriage without discriminating either for or against working mothers is to restore the value of the dependent exemption to $8,000 per dependent. Such a policy would relieve the economic distress of many married families (who have been increasingly taxed as if they had the discretionary income of childless singles), provide more money for day care for those women who choose to work (and which would, unlike day-care tax credit, improve the lot of families in which both parents work shifts to care for their kids), and allow many other women to withdraw from the labor force, perhaps temporarily or part-time. To counter the anti-marriage bias of welfare policy, Congress should use the tax code to create a special marriage bonus, targeted at low-income married couples with young children, a particularly vulnerable group of the population.

Re-creating marriage requires that we change our ingrained economic assumptions that only the poorest require support and that married couples constitute an inexhaustible deep pocket government can tap for other purposes without undermining marriage in the process. At the same time, more progress entails the equally difficult reexamination of our beliefs about the relation between law and marriage.

The legal transformation of marriage from a key public institution to a private consumption item is a remarkable story. In a single generation marriage has been demoted from a covenant to a contract to a mere private wish, in which "caveat emptor" is the prevailing legal rule. It is surely an irony of history that at the same moment the law has increasingly rejected the age-old notion that employees are terminable "at will," it has embraced the idea that marriages should be so at the will of one party. We now live in a society where it is legally easier and less risky to dump a wife than to fire an employee.

They called it "no-fault divorce," but the term is something of a misnomer. Under the guise of merely making a technical adjustment to the legal mechanics of divorce, the legal profession radically transformed the legal and moral basis of marriage, creating a new beast more properly termed not "no-fault" but *unilateral divorce*. Today, while it still takes two to marry, it takes only one person to divorce, at any time and for any reason.

Society chooses to protect those relations it deems most important. An anthropologist from Mars (to borrow a phrase from Oliver Sacks), surveying our legal system and our cultural mores, would surely conclude that "consumer" and "employee" are our most valued and irreplaceable roles, around which society builds (for better or worse) increasing legal and social protections, while relations such as "husband," "wife," and (to a lesser extent) "mother," "father" are considered bit players which can be safely left to the workings of chance and the unregulated sexual marketplace.

This is often portrayed as an increase in individual choice or freedom. But the legal changes that constitute the divorce revolution are more accurately described as *a shift in power*: from the married to the unmarried in general, from the spouse who wants to stay married to the spouse who wants to leave, and from the person who wants to commit to the person who wants the right to revoke his or her commitments.

Try this thought experiment: what would happen if courts treated property and business contracts as we now treat the marriage contract? What if American law refused to enforce business contracts, and indeed systematically favored the party who wished to withdraw, on the grounds that "fault" was messy and irrelevant and exposed judges and attorneys to unpleasant acrimony? What if property were viewed, as marriage increasingly is, as a strictly private matter in which, when disputes arose, thieves and owners would have to work things out among themselves, because, after all, you cannot legislate morality?

If the corporation were required to operate on the same legal principles that animate our marriage laws, the economy would surely collapse. It is not surprising then that, under the same regimen, marriage also is on the verge of doing so.

If the purpose of our legal system is to create pleasant working conditions for lawyers, then no-fault has been a rousing success. No-fault divorce was passed, not in response to growing public pressure (in 1966, the last poll before the no-fault revolution, only 13 percent of the population considered divorce laws "too strict"), but in response to the technical discomfort of the legal profession. Every survey of family court judges and divorce lawyers reveals the legal profession remains immensely satisfied that the no-fault revolution achieved its goals: eliminating "hypocrisy," raising the social status of divorce lawyers, and reducing acrimony around divorce—or at least the amount of acrimony to which judges and lawyers are exposed. An Iowa evaluation concluded, for example, that according to "a satisfied majority of both judges and attorneys" no-fault resulted in "a more honest and civilized approach void of fraud, perjury and abuse." A poll of Nebraska judges found that two-thirds agreed no-fault had lessened animosity between divorcing parties. Judges acknowledged it had also introduced unilateral divorce, but they seemed unconcerned by the prospect.[15]

Quietly, behind the scenes, with little public scrutiny, in state after state, legal insiders "reformed" marriage out of existence. As difficult as it sounds to believe, the historical record is fairly clear. In the early 1970s, marriage was radically transformed—indeed, the traditional marriage commitment was virtually outlawed—in a way which has endangered millions of women and children largely in order to make lawyers' jobs more comfortable.

The chorus of approval for no-fault was aided by an initial flood of studies which nearly unanimously concluded that changes in the law had little effect on the divorce rate. But evaluating the effect of the law on divorce rates is not simple. Not only do state statutes vary, but different states changed some aspects of divorce law but not others. Some states merely added no-fault to other grounds for divorce. Others abolished fault altogether. Still others cut waiting periods.

There is no reason to assume (as many of the earlier studies did) that all the changes lumped under the no-fault rubric had the same effect on divorce rates. Moreover, many other states were suddenly labeled no-fault merely by being included in the catalog of no-fault jurisdictions assembled for a 1974 listing in the influential journal *Family Law Quarterly*.[16] Many early studies used this listing as definitive evidence of when states

adopted no-fault divorce, whereas in fact in many cases the change had
been introduced earlier, before the no-fault terminology became popular.
In other cases, states officially passed "no-fault" laws only after judges'
interpretations of the law had already effectively eased divorce, making it
more difficult yet to assess the effect of legal change on divorce rates.

Two more recent and sophisticated studies, one by Thomas B. Marvell
and another by Martin Zelder, however, have independently concluded
that some of the changes in divorce law did increase the divorce rate—and
by as much 20 and 25 percent.[17]

Which legal changes appeared to have the most effect? Apparently
changes in timing, such as cutting waiting periods, have the most impact.
When divorce is made quick, easy, as well as nonjudgmental, more marriages fail. Such has also been the experience in Canada, as one researcher
noted: "After falling for several years [the divorce rate] rose to an all-time
high following passage of the Divorce Act of 1985, which allows divorce
after one year's separation, regardless of the cause."[18]

The bad marriage and the good enough marriage are not always fixed,
easily discernable things. Many, if not most, marriages fall on hard times,
go through bleak periods, or endure angry interludes. Marriage, like old
age, is not for sissies. But when the law encourages the urge to flee, more
marriages suddenly "irretrievably break down." As one man put it, "I
believe I got a divorce too quickly and too easily. Our state has a no-fault
divorce law, so we were able to end a seven-year marriage in less than
four months. Now I really wish we had worked harder to save it."[19]

Simple decency requires that the law retreat from relentlessly favoring
the spouse who leaves and place some minimal power back into the hands
of the spouse who is being left. Imposing a five- to seven-year waiting
period for contested no-fault divorces (as many European jurisdictions
did) would serve the ends of both justice and prudence: raising the number of marriages that ultimately succeed while, at the very least, ensuring
that those who want a quick and easy divorce will have to negotiate with
their marriage partner in order to get it.

Some legal avenue should also be opened for those of us who wish, in
marrying, to make an even more enduring commitment. At a minimum,
the law should support permanent marriage by giving people the option
of making one. Prenuptial agreements are currently used to protect the
wealthier spouse in the event of a divorce. If the law can facilitate individuals' desires to limit their marital liability, should it not also, at the very
least, accommodate those who, out of love, longing, religion, or ideals,
seek to extend it? A prenuptial covenant, permitting divorce only for serious cause, or even, if the couple wished, prohibiting it altogether should
be a legally enforceable option.

Some people of course, may not wish to accept even the minimal restrictions implied by waiting periods. They cherish the right to leave a relationship for any reason at any time, in pursuit of their own happiness. They believe, quite sincerely that the law cannot bind love. As bestselling spiritual guru Marianne Williamson put it, "an escape clause is actually the deepest form of commitment: "I love you so much that I can release you to be where you need to be.""[20] So be it. But the freedom to flee and the freedom to commit are opposite and contradictory freedoms—to grant the first is to abolish the second. Those for whom love means the right to leave do not need a legal institution of marriage; those of us who wish, on the contrary, to bind ourselves in the name of love, do.

Re-creating marriage will be neither economically cheap nor politically easy. We may never return to the low divorce rates of the last century. But surely it is possible, as a step, to adopt this simple goal: to create a society in which more marriages succeed than fail and in which each year more children (rather than fewer) are born into the relative safety of marriage.

Such change will happen only when married families begin to view themselves (as senior citizens do) as a coherent interest group or when society as a whole rediscovers the central importance of marriage.

It is so much easier to seek solace in the comforting cliches underwriting the divorce cult: that marriages today are happier and more loving, that women are freer and better off now that marriage is failing, that our children will be happier if only we are "happy." (Funny how that never works in reverse—no one looks at the child and believes, "I'll be happy if only *she* is happy.") Above all, we cling to the comforting myth that "nothing can be done" about the collapse of marriage. Despair comforts because it relieves us of the hard necessity of taking responsibility for the world we have created for ourselves and our children.

For centuries, romantics imagined that heroic acts of love could only take place outside marriage bonds. Today we have learned, through the painful process of social experimentation, that it is not cohabitation but marriage that is daring, not free love but the vow. With the abolition of marriage, that last possibility for heroism has been taken from us.

Notes

1. Arlene Skolnick, *Embattled Paradise: The American Family in an Age of Uncertainty* (New York: Basic Books, 1991), 18.

2. D. T. Ellwood, *Poor Support: Poverty and the American Family* (New York: Basic Books, 1988), 46.

3. For a summary of research see, for example, Frank F. Furstenberg and Andrew J. Cherlin, *Divided Families: What Happens to Children When Parents Part* (Cambridge, MA: Harvard University Press, 1991), 99–90.

4. Barbara Grissis, "Effects of Parental Divorce on Children's Financial Support for College," *Journal of Divorce and Remarriage* 22 (1994): 155 ff., n. 1, 2.

5. Timothy J. Biblarz and Adrian E. Raftery, "The Effects of Family Disruption on Social Mobility," *American Sociological Review* 58 (1993): 97–109.

6. Glenna Spitze, "Adult Children's Divorce and Intergenerational Relationships," *Journal of Marriage and the Family* (May 1994): 279 ff.

7. Lynn White, "The Effects of Parental Divorce and Remarriage on Parental Support for Adult Children," *Journal of Family Issues* (June 1992): 234 ff.; Grissis, "Effects of Parental Divorce on Financial Support," 155 ff., n. 1, 2.

8. Judith Stacey, "The New Family Values Crusaders," *The Nation*, August 1, 1994, 119–20.

9. Constance Ahrons, *The Good Divorce: Keeping Your Family Together When Your Marriage Comes Apart* (New York: HarperCollins, 1994), 52–59.

10. "Parental Fighting Hurts Even After Divorce," *Washington Post*, November 12, 1986.

11. Norval D. Glenn, "The Re-Evaluation of Family Change by American Social Scientists" (speech prepared for the Committee for the International Year of the Family, Catholic Archdiocese of Melbourne, Australia, 1994; condensed versions presented at the Australian Catholic University, Canberra, June 7, 1994, and at the Australian Catholic University, Melbourne, June 14, 1994).

12. Lawrence Kudlow, "Middle-Class Tax Hike," *National Review*, June 13, 1994, 25.

13. "Poverty Termed a Divorce Factor," *New York Times*, January 15, 1993.

14. See, for example, Catherine E. Ross, John Mirowsky, and Joan Hubers, "Dividing Work, Sharing Work and In-between: Marriage Patterns and Depression," *American Sociological Review* 48 (1983): 809–23.

15. Herbert Jacob, *The Silent Revolution: The Transformation of Divorce Law in the United States* (Chicago: University of Chicago Press, 1988), 154–55.

16. Ibid., 81 ff.

17. Thomas B. Marvell, "Divorce Rates and the Fault Requirement," *Law and Society Review* 23 (1989): 554–67; Martin Zelder, "The Economic Analysis of the Effect of No-Fault Divorce Law on the Divorce Rate," *Harvard Journal of Law and Public Policy* 16, no. 1 (1992): 241 ff.

18. See Gertrude Schaffner Goldberg, "Canada: Bordering on the Feminization of Poverty" in *The Feminization of Poverty: Only in America?*, ed. Gertrude Schaffner Goldberg and Eleanor Kremens (New York: Greenwood Press, 1991), 77.

19. Rev. William Rabior and Vicki Wells Bedard, *Catholics Experiencing Divorce: Grieving, Healing and Learning to Live Again* (Ligouri, MO: Ligouri Publications, 1991), 10.

20. Marianne Williamson, *A Return to Love* (New York: Harper Perennial, 1993), 166.

CHAPTER 11

Modern Marriage: Revising the Cultural Script

David Popenoe

Of all the parts in the cultural scripts of modern societies, few have become more vague and uncertain than those concerning marriage and marital gender roles. Should we even bother to marry? And if and when we do marry and have children, who should do what—within the home and outside of it? Throughout history the answers to both of these questions have been relatively clear. Marriage is one of the few universal social institutions found in every known culture. And in most historical cultures the scripts for marital gender roles have been unambiguously formulated; indeed, in the world's remaining premodern societies the prescription of marital gender roles is a principal cultural focal point.

In the industrialized nations today, marriage is becoming deinstitutionalized. Growing numbers of people are cohabiting outside of marriage. The assigned roles for husband and wife are endlessly negotiated, especially with regard to the allocation of work and child care responsibilities. You work now, I'll work later—no, let's both work. I'll take care of the kids while you work—no, let's both take care of the kids. One may call it the growth of personal freedom and self-fulfillment, and for many women it has been just that. But such endless negotiation is no way to run a family—or a culture. The whole point of a cultural script, or in sociological terms an institutionalized set of social norms, is to provide people in common situations with social expectations for behavior that are geared to maintaining long-term societal well-being and promoting generational continuity.

Is there not some way out of this predicament? With full realization that I am climbing out on a long limb, I believe that a new set of role

expectations for marriage and marital gender roles can be established
which is adapted to the new conditions of modern life and which, in a
balanced and fair manner, maximizes the life experiences of men, women,
and children, helps to maintain social order, and represents a "best fit"
with biosocial reality. The purpose of this chapter is to review the sociocultural and biological bases for a new set of marital norms and to put
forth for discussion some tenets toward establishing these norms.

An Assumption and Some Alternatives

If the family trends of recent decades are extended into the future, the
result will be not only growing uncertainty within marriage but the gradual elimination of marriage in favor of casual liaisons oriented to adult
expressiveness and self-fulfillment. The problem with this scenario is that
children will be harmed, adults will probably be no happier, and the social order could collapse. For this chapter, therefore, I hold the assumption that marriage is a good and socially necessary institution worthy of
being preserved in some form, and that the alternative of "letting things
go on as they are" should be rejected.

In considering what marriage path modern societies should take instead, several broad alternatives have been widely discussed. We could try
to restore the traditional nuclear family of bread-winning husband and
full-time housewife that flourished in the 1950s (a time when marriage
rates were at an all-time high). This alternative, I suggest, is neither possible nor desirable. We could encourage married women to shift to the traditional marital role of men, centered on a full-time career and involving
a high level of detachment from the home, leaving the children to be
raised by someone else. This would mean, however, that large numbers of
children would face the highly undesirable prospect of being raised in
institutional day care. Or we could encourage married men to shift to the
so-called "new man" role in which, based on the ideal of social androgyny, men and women in marriage fully share both outside work and child
care on an exactly fifty-fifty basis. There are a variety of problems with
this solution, which I will discuss.

In place of these alternatives, what is needed is a marriage pattern and
set of marital gender-role expectations that will feel "comfortable" yet be
reasonably fair and equitable to both men and women, that stands the
best chance of generating an enduring marriage, and that will benefit children. (Of these factors, the generation of a lasting marriage is often overlooked, yet it is wisely said that the very best thing parents can give their

children is a strong marriage.) Obviously, this is a tall order, and there are some basically conflicting needs that must be reconciled—those of men, of women, of children, and of society as a whole.

Setting the Scene: Today's Confusion over Marital Roles

For about 150 years, from the early eighteenth century to the 1960s, what we now call the traditional nuclear family was the prevailing family ideal in American culture. The main distinguishing characteristics of this family form were a legally and culturally dominant breadwinning husband and an economically dependent full-time housewife; both parents were devoted to raising their children, but the wife played the role of primary nurturer and teacher.[1] Marital gender-role expectations were unequivocally clear.

At least in its distribution across the American population, this family form had its apogee in the 1950s. More adults were able to live up to these family expectations in "the '50s" than at any other period of our history. Part of the reason is demographic. For women born between the periods of 1830 to 1920, maternal and child mortality rates steadily declined and marriage rates increased.[2] A high point was reached in America by the mid-twentieth century in the percentage of women who married, bore children who survived, and had husbands who lived jointly with them until at least the age of fifty.[3] This was a time when death rates had dropped sharply, leaving many fewer widows, and divorce rates had not reached their current high levels. Another reason is economic. The 1950s in America was an era of unparalleled affluence and economic growth, enabling many families to live comfortably on the income of a single wage earner.

Then, with the coming of age of the baby boom generation in the 1960s, traditional family expectations began to falter. Associated with this faltering was what many today see as "family decline," not just a shift to some different family form but a manifest weakening of the family as an institution—especially as regards the care of children.[4] Today, even though many Americans would probably still claim the traditional nuclear family as their family ideal, a sizable segment of the younger generation—especially the college educated—has largely rejected it.

Much confusion over family expectations and marital gender roles now exists. To the degree that they think about such things, young people coming into adulthood today are highly uncertain about the kind of marital gender roles they want, although almost everyone plans to marry eventually and nearly 90 percent are likely to do so if current age-specific rates continue.[5] Many men still tend to prefer the traditional family form, yet a growing number would also like their wives to work in order to bring in a second income. At the same time, most men believe that childrearing is fundamentally a woman's responsibility. Many women plan to work after they are married and have children, often believing that they will have to in order to make ends meet. And many college-educated women desire to have full-blown work careers combined with marriage. Among women, both ordinary workers and careerists are uncertain about how they will mesh work goals with family responsibilities and child care.

Some women (and a few men), especially those influenced by left-feminist thinking, hold to a new ideal of coequal and fully-shared breadwinning and parenting, what can be called social androgyny. Believing that primary authority for child care should rest with women, however, this is an arrangement that few men seem prepared to accept. Some women and men intend to rely heavily on day care to raise children, thus lessening the direct child-care responsibilities of both parents (for single parents, of course, this is sometimes a necessity). In general, women expect their husbands to play a larger role than earlier generations of fathers did in the home and with children. And, although resistance among men is seemingly widespread, the evidence points to a growing, albeit still modest, equalization of gender roles in this respect.[6]

Before children arrive, marital gender roles across all segments of society now tend to be relatively similar to one another, or "egalitarian." Typically, both partners work outside the home, and both share in the domestic responsibilities. Cooking, for example, can be done by either sex. Moreover, with ever-increasing median ages at first marriage and at the birth of the first child, such marital role similarity takes up an ever-longer portion of each person's life, especially if one includes the stage of premarital cohabitation that precedes more than half of all formal marriages today. Indeed, males and females living together with similar roles and no children has become a formative period of young adulthood, a far cry from the days when women (especially) lived with their parents until they married, and then had children soon thereafter.

If people today never moved beyond this stage of life, the present chapter would not have to be written. With the coming of children, however, the situation of marital-role similarity suddenly changes. Far from bringing joy to the new parents, an abundance of scholarly studies has shown that the least happy time in the life course of recently married couples is when they have young children.[7] A major reason is that the division of labor within the household abruptly shifts, and gender-role expectations become uncertain; it is no longer clear who should do what. Marital gender-role expectations not only become ambiguous, but they typically revert to their traditional family form—with wife at home taking care of the children and husband becoming the sole breadwinner—to a degree far beyond anything anticipated by either party.

The marital-role stresses that arise from this sudden change can be enormous, especially after the couple have settled in with their new infant. Frequently, the wife becomes resentful and the husband becomes angry. The wife becomes resentful because she has had to leave her job while her husband is still occupationally progressing and because her husband doesn't help out enough. Often, in addition, she herself has had little preparation for the trials and tribulations that come with infant care. Also, she suddenly finds herself economically dependent (and perhaps guilty about not contributing financially), vulnerable, and stuck at home doing a job that has low status in our society. The husband, meanwhile, is angry because of his sudden new responsibilities and loss of freedom and because he has diminished sexual access to his wife and no longer receives as much of her attention. The baby has become the important figure in the home and the new focus of the wife's affections. While having young children (especially sons) slightly retards the chances of divorce, the animosities set up during this period are often long lasting and can lead to eventual breakup.[8] The animosities negatively impact not only the marriage, of course, but also the children.

Probably the most common piece of advice now offered to young people at this stage of life is that "every situation is different," and they will simply have to work things out for themselves—find what is best for them. But this is not "cultural advice"; it is an unthoughtful reaction in an over-optioned society. It does forcefully raise the question, however: If not the marital roles of the traditional nuclear family, then what? The traditional roles were at least clear cut: the wife's job in life was childrearing, and the husband's was to provide economically for the mother-child unit.

The Traditional Nuclear Family: Why We Cannot Return

While some are tempted to think that a return to the era of the traditional nuclear family would provide a solution to this set of problems, there are powerful reasons why this is neither desirable nor possible. To understand these reasons, we must consider why the traditional nuclear family fell into decline in the first place. Although most readers are probably well aware of the causes for this decline, they are worth a moment's reflection.

Social change of the past few centuries has affected women's roles much more than men's. Throughout history, the role of married men has principally been that of provider and protector of the mother-child unit. And, in virtually every known human society, the main role of married women has been that of child nurturer. Unlike today, however, married women almost never undertook the childrearing task all by themselves. Many others were around to help, especially older children, parents, and other close relatives. Most mothers were involved as well in what was the equivalent in preindustrial times of today's paid labor force where "productive work" took place, the typical work being home-generated agricultural production.

It was not until economic conditions permitted, mainly after the industrial revolution, that women left the labor force and became full-time mothers.[9] Although most American women in the last century were in the labor market sometime during their lives, the pattern was typically this: They finished school at fourteen or fifteen and only worked until they got married in their early twenties. They then soon had children, and for the rest of their lives (shorter than today) they played the role of mother of at-home children. At the turn of the twentieth century, less than 10 percent of married women were gainfully employed, and the chances were that a woman would die before her last child left home.[10]

But by the late 1940s, the Bureau of Labor Statistics listed nearly half of all American women as "essentially idle." They did not have children under eighteen, did not work in the labor force, and were not aged or infirm, a combination leading to the proverbial "bored housewife."[11] In what represents a major historical shift, only about one-third of the adult life of the average married women today will be spent as the mother of at-home children. This is because of later ages at first marriage and birth of the first child, average family sizes of less than two children, and a much longer life span. Thus, even if one were to assume that a woman's main purpose in life was to be a mother, that role today clearly would no longer take up more than a fraction of her adult years. Moreover, because of the high divorce rate, a woman may well spend one-half to two-thirds of her adulthood not only without children but also without a husband to care for and to rely on economically, forcing her to rely on her own resources.

With such a steep reduction in the portion of women's lives that is taken up by marriage and childrearing, is it any wonder that women have been looking more to their own careers as separate individuals, and attaching less importance to their domestic roles? Under the new social circumstances, the demographers Kingsley Davis and Pietronella van den Oever have noted, "for best results [women] must choose an occupation early in order to get the necessary training, and they must enter employment while young and remain employed consistently in order to build up experience, seniority, reputation, and whatever other cumulative benefit comes from occupational commitment."[12]

The Downside

"Once under way," Davis and van den Oever continue,

the system of change exhibits a dynamic of its own. Insofar as demographic trends lead women to downgrade marriage and stress employment, they also lead them to reduce not only their dependence on their husbands but also their service to them. Men, in turn, are induced to reconsider the costs and benefits of marriage. They sense that, at older ages, men are increasingly scarce compared with women, that they do not have to marry to enjoy female company, and that if they do marry, their role as father and family head has somehow been eroded. Not surprisingly, the divorce rate rises to unprecedented levels, making marriage less secure and therefore less valuable for both sexes. Marriage undergoes attrition in two ways: it is postponed or not undertaken at all, and when it is undertaken, it is increasingly brittle.[13]

The available evidence suggests that, for durable demographic and economic reasons, this scenario of "family decline" has largely come to pass and it has been accompanied by some devastating personal and social consequences.[14] First, more families have broken up, fatherlessness has rapidly increased, and parents have had less time to spend with their children. Such family instability has undoubtedly been an important factor in the decline of child well-being in recent years, as indicated by numerous statistics.[15] Second, women have not entirely been well served. There is substantial evidence that almost all women deeply want not just a job or a career or financial independence, but also to be a mother and to have a strong and hopefully lasting relationship with a man.[16] And while women's financial independence has improved, their family relationships have deteriorated.[17] Third, and least widely discussed, there have been important negative repercussions for men. Despite the great importance for cultures to direct men into family roles (men gain tremendously in health and happiness from marriage and fatherhood, and single men are a universal social problem), any "new men" have probably been more than offset by men who have largely abandoned family life.

In all, society has suffered. Such trends are surely a major component in the view of most adult Americans today that, in many ways, "things are not as good as they were when I was growing up."

The Nuclear Family: Elements to Be Maintained

If the era of the traditional nuclear family must be recognized as a thing of the past, and if we should not continue in the direction we are headed, then what? Rather than the alternatives of institutional day care or androgynous gender roles in marriage, a strong case can be made for the maintenance of relatively traditional marital gender roles—*but only at the stage of marriage when children are young.* This case is based on the requirements of optimal child development, on the biological differences between men and women, and on what is ultimately personally fulfilling for men and women and what they "really want" out of marriage.

Childrearing Requirements

No one has spoken more eloquently about the requirements for optimum child development than Urie Bronfenbrenner. He recently summarized the main findings of the "scientific revolution" that has occurred in the study of human development. Two of his findings bear special attention:[18]

1. In order to develop—intellectually, emotionally, socially, and morally—a child requires participation in progressively more complex reciprocal activity, on a regular basis over an extended period in the child's life, with one or more persons with whom the child develops a strong, mutual, irrational attachment and who is committed to the child's well-being and development, preferably for life.

2. The establishment and maintenance of patterns of progressively more complex interaction and emotional attachment between caregiver and child depend in substantial degree on the availability and involvement of another adult, a third party, who assists, encourages, spells off, gives status to, and expresses admiration and affection for the person caring for and engaging in joint activity with the child.

Here we have not just the "main findings of the scientific revolution," but a statement of a relatively traditional division of labor in marriages between husbands and wives. Note that as they stand the statements are gender neutral, but we shall turn to that issue below.

The key element in proposition number one is the "irrational attachment" of the child with at least one caretaker. Empirical support for this proposition has grown enormously in recent years, mostly stemming from the many psychological studies that have upheld "attachment theory"—the theory that infants have a biosocial necessity to have a strong, enduring socioemotional attachment to a caretaker, especially during the first year of life. This is what pioneering attachment theorist John Bowlby has called starting life with "a secure base."[19] Empirical studies have shown that failure to become attached, to have a secure base, can have devastating consequences for the child, and that patterns of attachment developed in infancy and childhood largely stay with the individual in adulthood, affecting one's relationships and sense of well-being.[20]

The work on attachment theory has been paralleled by research showing some negative effects of placing infants in group care. While still controversial, a widely discussed finding is that extensive (more than twenty hours per week) nonparental care initiated during the first year of life is likely to cause attachment problems (insecurity, aggression, and noncompliance) in children.[21] Some recent evidence suggests that negative consequences may also occur from nonparental care during the second year of life.[22] None of this research is conclusive; social science research seldom is. But it certainly supports what almost every grandmother would have told us from the outset—that there is considerable risk during the first few years of life in the reduction of infant-parent contacts and in nonparental childrearing.

After the child reaches age three, on the other hand, there is little or no evidence that limited, high quality day care has any ill effects on children.[23] Indeed, American children have long gone to "nursery school" at ages three and four, and group care at these ages is common in most other industrialized nations, including Japan.[24]

Why is close contact with a parent so important in the first few years of life? Because parents are typically motivated, like no one else, to provide warm and supportive care for their children. The task of parenting could be, and occasionally is, successfully accomplished by a nonrelated caretaker, such as a full-time nanny. But attachment is much less likely in group settings, where there is normally a high caretaker-child ratio and also a very high turnover of staff members.

But why should the primary parent of young children ordinarily be a mother and not a father? There is now a substantial body of evidence that fathers can do the job "if they are well-trained and strongly motivated."[25] Some scholars have turned this research into the message that "daddies make good mommies, too," holding that the two roles might really be interchangeable.[26] Yet it is much harder to train and motivate men than women for child care. Most dads do not want to be moms, and they do not feel comfortable being moms. And, in my opinion, neither children nor society in general benefits from such androgyny. To understand why the sexes are not interchangeable with one another in child care, it is necessary to review the biological differences between them.

Biological Differences Between the Sexes

No society in the world has ever been known to exist in which men were the primary caretakers of young children, and the reason for this certainly has much to do with the biological nature of males and females. Unfortunately, any discussion of biologically influenced sex differences has in recent years been fraught with peril. As historian Carl Degler has noted, the idea of a biological rootedness to human nature was almost universally accepted at the turn of the twentieth century, only to all but vanish from social thought as the century wore on, mainly due to the vigorous (and reasonably successful) battle against sexism (and racism).[27] Understandably, this knowledge blackout on the discussion of sex differences was associated with the need to challenge centuries-old stereotypes about the capacities of women, and to overcome strong resistances to a more forceful and equal role for women in economic and public life. The result was, however, that about the only sex differences that everyone within the academic community has been willing to accept over the past few decades are that women menstruate and are capable of becoming pregnant, giving birth, and lactating and that men are on average taller and muscularly stronger. But, when they have been discussed at all, the behavioral implications of even these differences are left vague.

Today, the full recognition of biological influences on human behavior is returning, albeit very slowly. Although the idea is still foreign, even inimical, to most social scientists, in probably no other area has the idea of biological roots to human nature become more widely discussed than in the field of sex and gender. A cover story in *Time* on "Sizing Up the Sexes" began, "Scientists are discovering that gender differences have as much to do with the biology of the brain as with the way we are raised."[28]

Having been trained as a sociologist, I have long been partial to sociocultural explanations. But I must say, quite apart from the scientific evidence, that after a lifetime of experiences which consisted, in part, of growing up in a family of four boys and fathering a family of two girls, I would be utterly amazed if someone were to prove that biology is unimportant in gender differences. The "natural and comfortable" way that most males think, feel, and act seems to me fundamentally different from the way most women think, feel, and act, and I have encountered these differences across the world's societies. (I probably need add that I don't believe one way is better than the other; indeed, I find the symmetry and complementarity remarkable, even astonishing.)

It is not that biology is "determinant" of human behavior; that is a poorly chosen word. All human behavior represents a combination of biological and sociocultural forces, and it makes little sense, as sociologist Alice Rossi has stressed, to view them "as separate domains contesting for election as primary causes."[29] Also, the case can certainly be made, in the promotion of female equality, for a culture's not accentuating the biological differences that do exist. (Cultures differ radically in this respect; consider the difference in gender roles between Arab cultures and Nordic cultures.) Yet in my judgment a stronger case should be presented at this time, one of declining family stability and personal well-being, for a more frank acknowledgement of the very real differences between men and women. More acknowledgement by both sexes of the differences between them in sexual motives, cognitive styles, and communication patterns, for example, would probably make for stronger marriages,[30] and recognition that the roles of father and mother are not interchangeable would probably make for better parenting.

Differences between men and women have universally been found with respect to four behavioral/psychological traits: aggression and general activity level, cognitive skills, sensory sensitivity, and sexual and reproductive behavior.[31] That differences are universally found does not unequivocally mean they are heavily influenced by biology, but it seems to me that the implication is stronger than for most other scientific findings about human affairs. Moreover, a large body of evidence points to the fact that many universally found differences are rooted in a distinct "wiring" of male and female brains, and in a pronounced hormonal variation between the sexes.[32]

What some call the greatest behavioral difference is in aggression. From birth onward, boys tend to be more aggressive and, in general, to have a higher physical activity level than girls. To a large degree, this accounts for the male dominance that universally has been prevalent in human societies.[33] Differences in male and female cognitive skills are less well known and perhaps not as large as aggressive behavior, but they are now widely confirmed by empirical studies. From early adolescence onward, males tend to have greater visual-spatial and mathematical ability than females, and females tend to have greater verbal ability than males. (Spatial ability refers to being able to mentally picture physical objects in terms of their shape, position, geography, and proportion.) Also, there is a female superiority in being more sensitive to all sensory stimuli. Females typically receive a wider array of sensory information, are able to communicate it better, and place a primacy on personal relationships within which such information is communicated.

In brief, while male strengths rest with "things and theorems," female strengths rest with personal relationships. Even shortly after birth, girls are more interested than boys in people and faces, whereas boys "just seem as happy with an object dangled in front of them."[34] That these differences become accentuated at adolescence strongly suggests the role of hormones, specifically testosterone in men and estrogen in women. The role of hormones gains further support from the fact that the behavioral differences decline at older age levels, when hormonal levels are dropping. It is also worth noting that males are the best and the worst with respect to several of these traits. Males, for example, disproportionately make up math geniuses, but also math dysfunctionals.

Not all of these behavioral differences, however, could be expected to have a direct effect on family behavior. Most important for family behavior are differences that stem from the dissimilar role of males and females in sexual activity and the reproductive process. The differential "sexual strategies" of men and women have long been commented on; in popular terminology, they roughly boil down to the fact that women give sex to get love, and men give love to get sex. The world over, sex is something that women have that men want, rather than vice versa, while relationships and intimacy are the special province of women.

Probably the most compelling explanation for male-female differences in sexuality and sexual strategies comes from the field of evolutionary psychology. It goes something like this:[35] In evolutionary terms, the goal of each individual's life is to perpetuate one's genes through reproduction and maximize the survival of all those with the same genes. In the mammalian world, the primary reproductive function is for males to inseminate and for females to harbor the growing fetus. Since sperm is common and eggs are rare (both being the prime genetic carriers), a different sexual or reproductive strategy is most adaptive for males and females, with males having more incentive to spread their sperm more widely among many females, and females having a strong incentive to bind males to themselves for the long-term care of their offspring.

Thus males universally are the more sexually driven and promiscuous while females are universally the more relationship oriented, setting up a continuing tension between the sexes. One psychologist found, for example, that the strongest predictor of sexual dissatisfaction for American males was "sexual withholding by the wife," and for females was "sexual aggressiveness by the husband."[36] And, according to the plausible explanation of evolutionary psychologists, men tend to be far more upset by their mate's sexual infidelity than vice versa because a man can never be certain that a child born by his mate is really his, while women tend to be much more upset by the loss of their mate's emotional fidelity, which threatens long-term commitment and support.

Male promiscuity *à la* the tom cat is not characteristic of humankind, however.[37] Wide variation in male sexual strategies can be found, ranging from the relatively promiscuous and low-paternal-investment "cad" approach, in which sperm is widely distributed with the hope that more offspring will survive to reproduce, to the "dad" approach, in which a high paternal investment is made in a limited number of offspring.[38] But in every society the biological fathers of children are identified if possible, and required to hold some responsibility for their children's upbringing. In fact, compared to other species, human beings are noted for a relatively high paternal investment because human children have a long period of dependency and require extensive cultural training to survive, and because the character of human female sexuality (loss of estrus) encourages men to stay around.

Culture, of course, has a major say in which sexual strategies are institutionalized, and in all industrialized societies a very high paternal-investment strategy is the culturally expected one for males. Monogamy is strongly encouraged in these societies (although "serial monogamy" has become the norm in many nations, especially the United States), polygamy is outlawed, and male promiscuity is somewhat contained. Because it promotes high paternal investment, monogamy is well suited to modern social conditions.

Whatever the sexual strategies, our underlying biological nature dictates that every society faces the problem of how to keep men in the reproductive pair-bond. Especially for males, sex is rather ill-designed for lasting marriages. Margaret Mead is once purported to have said that there is no society in the world where men will stay married for very long unless culturally required to do so. This is not to suggest that marriage isn't "good" for men, only that their inherited biological propensities push them in another direction.

Biologically, male attachment to the mother-child pair is said to be largely through the sexual relationship with the mother.[39] Many anthropologists have noted that motherhood is a biological necessity while fatherhood is mainly a cultural invention. Because it is not so biologically based as the mother's, a father's attachment to the children must be culturally fostered. Cross-cultural comparisons have shown that men are most likely to take active care of their children "if they are sure they are the fathers, if they are not needed as warriors and hunters, if mothers contribute to food resources, and if male parenting is encouraged by women."[40] Fortunately, these conditions largely prevail in modern societies. But bear in mind that it is not male care of infants that is at issue here. Universally, men have almost never been highly involved in child care at the early stages of life.[41]

Sex Differences and Modern Family Behavior

What is the relevance for modern marriage and family behavior of all this biological and anthropological information? There is much evidence suggesting that men make a significant contribution to child development, especially in the case of sons, and that the absence of a male presence typically poses a handicap for the child.[42] Indeed, men's assistance to women in childrearing may be more important now than ever before because mothers have become so isolated from their traditional support systems. Even more than in the past, it is crucial to maintain cultural measures that induce men to take an active interest in their families.[43] It should be recognized, however, that the parenting of young infants is not a "natural" activity for males, and to perform well they require much training and experience plus encouragement from their wives.

All this said, there appear to be some dangers in moving too far in the direction of androgynous marital gender roles. Especially in American circumstances one hates to say anything that could possibly be used to feed stereotypes and to deter men from providing more help at home, yet it is important to point out that fully androgynous roles in marriage may not be best for child development, and they may not be the kind of personal relationships that men and women really want.

Regarding child development, a large body of evidence suggests that, while females may not have a "maternal instinct," hormonal changes occur after childbirth that strongly motivate women (but not men) to care for their new-born children.[44] These hormonal changes are linked, in part, to the woman's capacity to breast-feed. Also, a number of the female sex differences noted above are directly related to this stage of the reproductive process. "In caring for a nonverbal, fragile infant," it has been noted, "women have a head start in reading an infant's facial expressions, smoothness of body motions, ease in handling a tiny creature with tactile gentleness, and soothing through a high, soft, rhythmic use of the voice."[45] Such evidence provides a strong case for women, rather than men, being the primary caretakers of infants.

Men seem better able to perform the parental role after children reach the age of 18 months, by which age children are more verbal and men don't have to rely so much on a wide range of senses.[46] Yet even at that age many studies have shown that men interact with children in a different way than women, suggesting that the father's mode of parenting is not interchangeable with that of the mother's; for example, men emphasize "play" more than "caretaking," and their play is more likely to involve a "rough-and-tumble" approach.[47] Moreover, there is evidence to support the value of reasonably sex-typed parenting in which mothers are "responsive" and fathers are "firm"; one research review determined that "children of sex-typed parents are somewhat more competent than children of androgynous parents."[48] As social psychologist Willard W. Hartup has concluded, "The importance of fathers, then, may be in the degree to which their interactions with their children do not duplicate the mother's and in the degree to which they support maternal caregiving rather than replicate it."[49]

Less widely discussed, but probably no less important, is the effect of androgyny on the marriage relationship. The most common idea cited in this connection is that many men, being of a more independent spirit, will simply avoid marrying and having children if they are going to be asked to give up their independence and over-engage in "unnatural" nurturing and caretaking roles. And it is not as if they have few alternatives. Under the old system the marital exchange of sex for love was largely operative; if a man wanted regular sex (other than with prostitutes) he had to marry. Today, with permissive sexual standards and the availability of a huge pool of single and divorced women (to say nothing of married women), men obviously have abundant opportunities for sex outside of permanent attachments, much less those attachments which involve extensive child care responsibilities.[50] Such a sociocultural reality may help to explain men's current delay of marriage, and the growing complaint of women that "men will not commit."

Nevertheless, most men eventually do marry and have children, and when they do they receive enormous personal benefits. My real concern, therefore, is not with men's delay of marriage (it is largely to the good) but rather with what happens to the marriage after it takes place. If it is the case that the best thing parents can do for their children is to stay together and have a good marriage, one serious problem with the "new man" alternative, in which dad tries to become mom, is that there is some evidence that marriages which follow this alternative are not very happy and have a high likelihood of divorce, especially those marriages in which a "role-reversal" has taken place.[51] This is a most significant consequence that is seldom discussed by "new man" proponents.

Why should marriages in which the husband is doing "just what he thought his wife always wanted" have a high breakup rate? The answer concerns the fundamental nature of modern marriages. Marriages today are based on two basic principles: companionship, by which husbands and wives are expected to be each other's close friends, and romantic love based on sexual attraction, by which husbands and wives are expected to be each other's exclusive sexual partners.[52] The joining of these two different principles is not without problems. For a good companion, you want someone who is as much like yourself as possible. But for a sexual partner, people tend to be attracted to the differences in the other. Therein lies a continuing tension that must be resolved if the modern marriages are to endure—the partners must be similar enough to remain best friends, but different enough so that sexual attraction is maintained.

The basis of sexual and emotional attraction between men and women is based not on sameness but on differences.[53] If we closely examine the marital roles of childrearing couples who have been able to stay together and remain interested in each other for a long period of time (an important area for new research), I doubt that we will find such couples relentlessly pursuing the ideal of social androgyny.

Seven Tenets for Establishing New Marital Norms

What I propose as a remedy for society's confusion over marital gender-role expectations, in conclusion, is a pattern of late marriage followed, in the early childrearing years, by what one could call a "modified traditional nuclear family." The main elements of this pattern can be summarized as follows. (I recognize, of course, that this pattern—being a set of normative expectations—is not something to which everyone can or should conform.)

1. Girls, as well as boys, should be trained according to their abilities for a socially useful paid job or career. It is important for women to be able to achieve the economic, social, and psychic rewards of the workplace that have long been reserved for men. It is important for society that everyone be well educated, and that they make an important work contribution over the course of their lives.

2. Young people should grow up with the expectation that they will

marry, only once and for a lifetime, and that they will have children. Reproduction is a fundamental purpose of life, and marriage is instrumental to its success. Today, close to 90 percent of Americans actually marry and about the same percentage of American women have children; although these figures have been dropping, the social expectation in these respects is currently quite well realized. Lifetime monogamy is not so well realized, however, with the divorce rate now standing at over 50 percent.

3. Young adults should be encouraged to marry later in life than is common now, with an average age at time of marriage in the late twenties or early thirties (the average ages currently are twenty-six for men and twenty-four for women). Even later might be better for men, but at older ages than this for women who want children, the "biological clock" becomes a growing problem.[54]

From society's viewpoint, the most important reasons why people should be encouraged to marry relatively late in life is that they are more mature, they know better what they want in a mate, they are more established in their jobs or careers, and the men have begun to "settle down" sexually (partly due to a biological diminution of their sex drive). Age at marriage has proven to be the single most important predictor of eventual divorce, with the highest divorce rates found among those who marry in their teenage years.[55] But we must also recognize that both women and men want to have time, when they are young, to enjoy the many opportunities for personal expression and fulfillment that modern, affluent societies are able to provide.

We should anticipate that many of these years of young adulthood will be spent in nonmarital cohabitation, an arrangement that often makes more sense than the alternatives to it, especially living alone or continuing to live with one's family of origin. I am not implying, much less advocating, sexual promiscuity here, but rather serious, caring relationships which may involve cohabitation.

4. From the perspective of promoting eventual family life, however, the downside to late age of marriage is that people live for about a decade or more in a non-family, "singles" environment which reinforces their personal drive for expressive individualism and conceivably reduces their impulse toward carrying out eventual family obligations, thus making the transition to marriage and childrearing more difficult.[56] To help overcome the anti-family impact of these years, young unmarried adults should be encouraged to save a substantial portion of their income for a "family fund" with an eye toward offsetting the temporary loss of the wife's income after marriage and childbirth.

5. Once children are born, wives should be encouraged to leave the

labor market and become substantially full-time mothers for a period of at least a year to eighteen months per child. The reason for this is that mother-reared infants appear to have distinct advantages over those reared apart from their mothers. It is desirable for children to have full-time parenting up to at least age three, but after eighteen months—partly because children by then are more verbal—it is appropriate for fathers to become the primary caretakers, and some men may wish to avail themselves of the opportunity. At age three, there is no evidence that children in quality group care suffer any disadvantages (in fact, for most children there are significant advantages). Once children reach that age, therefore, the average mother could resume working part-time until the children are at least of school age, and preferably in their early to middle teen years, at which point she could resume work full-time. Alternatively, when the children reach the age of three the father could stay home part-time, and the mother could resume work full-time.

For women, this proposal is essentially the strategy known as "sequencing."[57] The main difficulty with it, as sociologist Phyllis Moen has noted, "is that child-nurturing years are also the career-nurturing years. What is lost in either case cannot be 'made up' at a later time."[58] Yet I would argue that it is possible to "make up" for career loss, but impossible to make up for child-nurturing loss. To make it economically more possible for a family with young children to live on a single income, we should institute (in addition to the "family fund") what virtually every other industrialized society already has in place—parental leave and child allowance programs. And, to help compensate women for any job or career setbacks due to their time out of the labor force, we should consider the development of "veterans benefits" type programs that provide mothers with financial subsidies and job priorities when they return to the paid work force. In general, women must be made to feel that caring for young children is important work, respected by the working community.

6. According to this proposal, the mother and not the father ordinarily would be the primary caretaker of infants. This is because of fundamental biological differences between the sexes that assume great importance in childrearing, as discussed above. The father should be an active supporter of the mother-child bond during this period, however, as well as auxiliary homemaker and care provider. Fathers should expect to spend far more time in domestic pursuits than their own fathers did. Their work should include not only the male's traditional care of the house as a physical structure and of the yard and car, but in many cases cooking, cleaning, and child care, the exact distribution of such activities depending on the individual skills and talents of the partners. And, as noted above, after

children reach age eighteen months it may be desirable for the father and not the mother to become the primary caretaker. This means that places of employment must make allowances for substantial flex-time and part-time job absence for fathers as well as for mothers.

7. It should be noted that there is some balancing out of domestic and paid-work roles between men and women over the course of life. Under current socioeconomic conditions husbands, being older, retire sooner than their wives. Also, in later life some role switching occurs, presumably caused in part by hormonal changes, in which women become more work-oriented and men become more domestic.[59] Given current male-female differences in longevity, of course, the average woman can expect to spend an estimated seven years of her later life as a widow.

Concluding Remarks

Later marriage, together with smaller families, earlier retirement, and a longer life in a society of affluence, provide both men and women in modern societies an historically unprecedented degree of freedom to pursue personal endeavors. Yet what David Gutmann has called the "parental imperative"[60] is also a necessary and important part of life, and during the parental years expressive freedom for adults must be curtailed in the interest of social values, especially the welfare of children.

Male bread winning and female childrearing have been the pattern of social life throughout history, albeit not always in quite so extreme a form as found in modern societies over the past century and a half. Except perhaps for adult pair-bonds in which no young children are involved, where much social experimentation is possible, it is foolhardy to think that the nuclear family can or should be entirely scrapped. When children become a part of the equation, fundamental biological and social constraints come into play—such as the importance of mothers to young children—and central elements of the nuclear family are dismissed at society's peril. Rather than strive for androgyny and be continuously frustrated and unsettled by our lack of achievement of it, we would do much better to more readily acknowledge, accommodate, and appreciate the very different needs, sexual interests, values, and goals of each sex. And rather than the unisex pursuit of "freedom with a male bias," we should be doing more to foster a culture in which the traditional female values of relationship and caring are given a higher priority and respect.

In a much modified form, then, traditional marital gender roles are necessary if the good of society—and of individuals—are to be advanced.

But the period of time in which these gender roles still apply has become a relatively short phase of life, and not adult life in its entirety as once was the case. This leaves individuals abundant time for the pursuit of self-fulfillment through social roles of their own choosing.

Notes

1. Steven Mintz and Susan Kellogg, *Domestic Revolutions: A Social History of American Family Life* (New York: The Free Press, 1988); Carl N. Degler, *At Odds: Women and the Family in America from the Revolution to the Present* (New York: Oxford University Press, 1980).

2. Paul C. Glick, "The Family Life Cycle and Social Change," *Family Relations* 38, no. 2 (1989): 123–29.

3. Sandra L. Hofferth, "Updating Children's Life Course," *Journal of Marriage and the Family* 47, no. 1 (1985): 93–115.

4. David Popenoe, "American Family Decline: 1960–1990; A Review and Appraisal," *Journal of Marriage and the Family* 55, no. 3 (1993), 527–55.

5. Larry L. Bumpass, "What's Happening to the Family? Interactions Between Demographic and Institutional Change," *Demography* 27, no. 4 (1990): 483–98.

6. Phyllis Bronstein and Carolyn Pape Cowan, *Fatherhood Today: Men's Changing Role in the Family* (New York: John Wiley, 1988).

7. Carolyn Pape Cowan and Philip A. Cowan, *When Partners Become Parents: The Big Life Change for Couples* (New York: Basic Books, 1992).

8. There has been a steep decline in the degree to which children retard divorce. See Linda Waite and Lee A. Lillard, "Children and Marital Disruption," *American Journal of Sociology* 96, no. 4 (1991): 930–53; Tim B. Heaton, "Marital Stability Throughout the Child-Rearing Years," *Demography* 27, no. 1 (1990): 55–63.

9. Louise A. Tilly and Joan W. Scott, *Women, Work and Family* (New York: Holt, Rinehart and Winston, 1978).

10. Kingsley Davis and Pietronella van den Oever, "Demographic Foundations of New Sex Roles," *Population and Development Review* 8, no. 3 (1982): 495–511.

11. Reported in "American Woman's Dilemma," *Life* 22, no. 24 (June 16, 1947): 101–16.

12. Davis and van den Oever, "Demographic Foundation," 508.

13. Ibid.

14. David Popenoe, *Disturbing the Nest: Family Change and Decline in Modern Societies* (New York: Aldine de Gruyter, 1988).

15. Deborah A. Dawson, "Family Structure and Children's Health and Well-Being: Data from the 1988 National Health Interview Survey on Child Health," *Journal of Marriage and the Family* 53 (August 1991): 573–84.

16. Sylvia Ann Hewlett, *A Lesser Life: The Myth of Women's Liberation in America* (New York: William Morrow, 1985).

17. Norval D. Glenn, "The Recent Trend in Marital Success in the United States," *Journal of Marriage and the Family* 53 (May 1991): 261–70.

18. Urie Bronfenbrenner, "Discovering What Families Do," in *Rebuilding the Nest*, ed. David Blankenhorn, Steven Bayme, and Jean Bethke Elshtain (Milwaukee: Family Service America, 1990), 27–38.

19. John Bowlby, *Attachment and Loss*, 3 vols. (New York: Basic Books, 1969–77).

20. Cindy Hazan and Phillip R. Shaver "Love and Work: An Attachment-Theoretical Perspective," *Journal of Personality and Social Psychology* 59, no. 2 (1990): 270–80; Mary D. Salter Ainsworth, "Attachments Beyond Infancy," *American Psychologist*, (April 1989): 709–16; Robert S. Weiss, "The Attachment Bond in Childhood and Adulthood," in *Attachment Across the Life Cycle*, ed. Colin Murray Parkes, Joan Stevenson-Hinde, and Peter Maris (London: Tavistock/Routledge, 1991), chap. 4; Carol E. Franz, David C. McClelland, and Joel Weinberger, "Childhood Antecedents of Conventional Social Accomplishment in Midlife Adults: A 36-Year Prospective Study," *Journal of Personality and Social Psychology* 60, no. 4 (1991): 586–95.

21. Jay Belsky, "Infant Day Care and Socioemotional Development: The United States," *Journal of Child Psychology and Psychiatry* 29, no. 4 (1988): 397–407; Jay Belsky, "The 'Effects' of Infant Day Care Reconsidered," *Early Childhood Research Quarterly* 3 (1988): 235–72.

22. Deborah Vandell and Mary Corasaniti, "Child Care and the Family: Complex Contributors to Child Development," in *Child Care and Maternal Employment: A Social Ecological Approach*, ed. K. McCartney (San Francisco: Jossey-Bass, 1990); Jay Belsky and David Eggebeen, "Early and Extensive Maternal Employment and Young Children's Socioemotional Development: Children of the National Longitudinal Survey of Youth," *Journal of Marriage and the Family* 53, no. 4 (1991): 1083–110.

23. Edward F. Zigler and Mary E. Lang, *Child Care Choices* (New York: The Free Press, 1991).

24. Patricia P. Olmstead and David P. Weikart, *How Nations Serve Young Children: Profiles of Child Care and Education in 14 Countries* (Ypsilanti, MI: High/Scope, 1989); Sheila B. Kamerman and Alfred J. Kahn, eds., *Family Policy: Government and Families in Fourteen Countries* (New York: Columbia University Press, 1978).

25. Kyle D. Pruett, *The Nurturing Father* (New York: Warner Books, 1987); Michael Lamb, ed., *The Father's Role: Cross-Cultural Perspectives* (Hillsdale, NJ: Lawrence Erlbaum, 1987); Robert A. Lewis and Marvin B. Sussman, eds., *Men's Changing Roles in the Family* (New York: Haworth, 1986).

26. C. Flake-Hobson, B. E. Robinson, and P. Sheen, *Child Development and Relationships* (Reading, MA: Addison Wesley, 1983).

27. Carl N. Degler, *In Search of Human Nature* (New York: Oxford University Press, 1991).

28. *Time*, January 20, 1992: 42.

29. Alice Rossi, "Parenthood in Transition: From Lineage to Child to Self-Orientation," in *Parenting Across the Life Span: Biosocial Dimensions*, ed. Jane B. Lancaster et al. (New York: Aldine de Gruyter, 1987), 31–81, quote from 64.

30. Apparently many Americans agree, causing such books as Deborah Tannen's *You Just Don't Understand: Women and Men in Conversation* (New York: Ballentine Books, 1990) to have been for over two years on the *New York Times* bestseller list.

31. Eleanor E. Maccoby and Carol N. Jacklin, *The Psychology of Sex Differences* (Palo Alto, CA: Stanford University Press, 1974); J. Archer and B. Lloyd, *Sex and Gender* (New York: Cambridge University Press, 1985).

32. For an up-to-date review, see Anne Moir and David Jessel, *Brain Sex* (New York: Lyle Stuart, 1991). An interesting discussion of how male-female differences also may stem from a "male wound," the fact that the growing boy but not the girl must differentiate himself psychologically from his mother, is contained in *The Way Men Think: Intellect, Intimacy, and the Erotic Imagination* by Liam Hudson and Bernadine Jacot (New Haven, CT: Yale University Press, 1991).

33. Steven Goldberg, *The Inevitability of Patriarchy* (New York: William Morrow, 1973).

34. Moir and Jessel, *Brain Sex*, 17.

35. Martin Daly and Margo Wilson, *Sex, Evolution, and Behavior*, 2d ed. (Belmont, CA: Wadsworth, 1983); D. Symons, *The Evolution of Human Sexuality* (New York: Oxford University Press, 1979).

36. David M. Buss, "Conflict Between the Sexes," *Journal of Personality and Social Psychology* 56 (May 1989), cited in Degler, *In Search of Human Nature*, 305.

37. Mary Maxwell Katz and Melvin J. Konner, "The Role of the Father: An Anthropological Perspective," in *The Role of the Father in Child Development*, 2d ed., ed. Michael E. Lamb (New York: Wiley-Interscience, 1981), 155–85.

38. Patricia Draper and Henry Harpending, "Father Absence and Reproductive Strategy: An Evolutionary Perspective," *Journal of Anthropological Research* 38, no. 3 (1982): 255–73.

39. D. B. Lynn, *The Father: His Role in Child Development* (Monterey, CA: Brooks/Cole, 1974). This proposition is not unchallenged however, with some scholars even positing a "fathering instinct." Also, males clearly have the "capacity" to become strongly attached to their infants and children.

40. M. M. West and M. L. Konner, "The Role of the Father: An Anthropological Perspective," in *The Role of the Father in Child Development*, 1st ed., ed. Michael E. Lamb (New York: Wiley-Interscience, 1976), 185–218, cited in Rossi, "Parenthood in Transition," 67–68.

41. The ideas in this section are further explored in David Popenoe, *Life Without Father: Compelling New Evidence that Fatherhood and Marriage Are Indispensable for the Good of Children and Society* (New York: Free Press, 1996), ch. 6.

42. Lynn, *The Father*; Irwin Garfinkel and Sara S. McLanahan, *Single Mothers and Their Children: A New American Dilemma* (Washington, DC: Urban Institute, 1986); Michael E. Lamb and David Oppenheim, "Fatherhood and Father-Child Relationships: Five Years of Research," in *Fathers and Their Families*, ed. Stanley H. Cath, Alan Gurwitt, and Linda Gunsberg (Hillsdale, NJ: The Analytic Press, 1989), chap. 1.

43. There is also strong evidence that children are important for the full maturation of men as adults. See Michael E. Lamb, Joseph H. Pleck, and James A. Levine, "The Effects of Paternal Involvement on Fathers and Mothers," in *Men's Changing Roles in the Family*, ed. Robert A. Lewis and Marvin B. Sussman (New York: Haworth, 1986), chap. 6.

44. Alice S. Rossi, "Gender and Parenthood," in *Gender and the Life Course*, ed. Alice S. Rossi (New York: Aldine de Gruyter, 1985), 161–91.

45. Rossi, "Parenthood in Transition," 69.

46. Ibid., 57–61.

47. M. W. Yogman, "Development of the Father-Infant Relationship," in *Theory and Research in Behavioral Pediatrics*, vol. 1, ed. H. E. Fitzgerald, B. M. Lester, and M. W. Yogman (New York: Plenum Press, 1982), 221–80; J. L. Roopnarine and N. S. Mounts, "Mother-Child and Father-Child Play," *Early Child Development Care* 20 (1985): 157–69.

48. Diana Baumrind, "Are Androgynous Individuals More Effective Persons and Parents?" *Child Development* 53 (1982): 44–75. In another study of adolescent outcomes, it was found that the most effective parenting was that which was both highly demanding and highly responsive, a difficult task for either a man or a woman to combine. Diana Baumrind, "The Influence of Parenting Style on Adolescent Competence and Substance Use," *Journal of Early Adolescence* 11, no. 1 [1991]: 56–95). See also Frances K. Grossman, William S. Pollack, and Ellen Golding, "Fathers and Children: Predicting the Quality and Quantity of Fathering," *Developmental Psychology* 24, no. 1 (1988): 82–92.

49. Willard W. Hartup, "Social Relationships and Their Developmental Significance," *American Psychologist*, February 1989: 120–26, quote from 122.

50. Maggie Gallagher, *Enemies of Eros* (Chicago: Bonus Books, 1989).

51. Graeme Russell, *The Changing Role of Fathers?* (New York: University of Queensland Press, 1983); Philip Blumstein and Pepper Schwartz, *American Couples* (New York: Pocket Books, 1983). Despite their hopes, Russell found that shared-caregiving couples had marriages of "significantly lower quality" than traditional couples, and Blumstein and Schwartz concluded "that when roles are reversed, with men doing housework and women taking over as provider, couples become dreadfully unhappy" (324). An additional problem is that when a divorce comes to a shared-caregiving couple, it is much more likely for a child-custody battle to ensue, since the man wishes to keep the children as much as the woman does.

52. This is an underlying theme in the recent (and brilliant) book of Richard A. Posner, *Sex and Reason* (Cambridge, MA: Harvard University Press, 1992).

53. Ellen Piel Cook, *Psychological Androgyny* (New York: Pergamon, 1985).

54. The late age of marriage is one of the many ways in which this marriage pattern differs significantly from that of the '50s; in 1957, the average woman who married was still a teenager!

55. Teresa Castro Martin and Larry L. Bumpass, "Recent Trends in Marital Disruption," *Demography* 26, no. 1 (1989): 37–51.

56. Alice S. Rossi, "Life Span Theories and Women's Lives," *Signs: Journal of Women in Culture and Society* 6 (1980): 4–32; Linda J. Waite, Frances K. Goldscheider, and Christina Witsberger, "Nonfamily Living and the Erosion of Traditional Family Orientations among Young Adults," *American Sociological Review* 51, no. 4 (1986): 541–54.

57. Arlene Rossen Cardozo, *Sequencing* (New York: Collier Books, 1986); Felice N. Schwartz, *Breaking with Tradition: Women, Management, and the New Facts of Life* (New York: Warner, 1992).

58. Phyllis Moen, *Women's Two Roles: A Contemporary Dilemma* (New York: Auburn House, 1992), 133.

59. David Gutmann, *Reclaimed Powers: Toward a New Psychology of Men and Women in Later Life* (New York: Basic Books, 1987).

60. David Gutmann, "Men, Women, and the Parental Imperative," *Commentary* 56, no. 5 (1973): 59–64.

CHAPTER 12

The Reinstitutionalization of Marriage: Political Theory and Public Policy

William A. Galston

For the purposes of this chapter I shall assume, as common ground, the thesis of what David Blankenhorn and others have called the deinstitutionalization of marriage in contemporary America. Statistics on such matters as divorce, births out of wedlock, single-parent families, and runaway fathers speak for themselves.[1] Nor can I break much new ground on the role of the family in a liberal democracy; splendid recent articles by Mary Ann Glendon and Jean Bethke Elshtain have already said nearly everything that needs saying on that subject.[2] Still, to fix ideas and clear our heads, it may be well to begin by sketching some key points.

It is frequently assumed (though perhaps less frequently than a generation ago) that America's Founders set in motion a regime that could survive and prosper through the interaction of institutions artfully balancing power against power and ambition against ambition. This assumption is not wholly unfounded, of course. It was James Madison who famously declared that the new constitution embodied "a policy of supplying by opposite and rival interests, the defect of better motives." But it was the same Madison who declared in *Federalist* number 55:

> As there is a degree of depravity in mankind which requires a certain degree of circumspection and distrust, so there are other qualities in human nature which justify a certain portion of esteem and confidence. Republican government presupposes the existence of these qualities in a higher degree than any other form.

The thesis that self-government rests in some measure on virtue is not the palpable absurdity that liberal democracy requires an impeccably virtuous citizenry, what Immanuel Kant called a "nation of angels." Nor is it incompatible with the mechanical-institutional interpretation of liberalism, for clearly the artful arrangement of what Madison called "auxiliary precautions" can go some distance toward compensating for the defect of motives. Nor, finally, does this thesis maintain that the liberal democratic polity should be understood as a tutelary community centrally dedicated to the inculcation of individual virtue or excellence. The claim is more modest: the functioning of liberal democracies is affected in important ways by the character of its citizens and leaders, and at some point the attenuation of individual virtue will create pathologies with which liberal political contrivances, however technically perfect their design, simply cannot cope.[3]

Civic Functions of the Two-Parent Family

Civic Character and Competence

In the extended quotation reproduced above, Madison speaks of "human nature." But he was under no illusion that the balance between depravity and estimable qualities that we actually observe in individuals is just given by nature. While we are endowed with certain capacities for virtue, we become virtuous only under certain circumstances—through appropriate upbringing, education, and experience. What is most striking about our constitution—a point Glendon stresses—is its failure to provide for, or even to mention, these formative forces. Our national political institutions presuppose the existence of certain kinds of individuals but do nothing to produce them.

There are, I think, three linked explanations for this odd hiatus. The first is that Madison and others saw American society—families, communities, and daily life—as fundamentally healthy, as productive of adequately virtuous citizens, and they assumed (or at least hoped) that these institutions would remain healthy of their own accord. Second, the federal, as opposed to purely national, design of our new political institutions was meant to leave nearly all social questions to states and local communities. Third, the rise of liberal democracy, in contradistinction to classical republicanism, meant an emerging (though constantly contested) demarcation between the public and private realms. The formation of character, including public character, was left to institutions such as families and religious communities, which were to be significantly free from public direction.

This is a long way of making a short point: in the American liberal democratic order, as opposed to totalitarian or even classical republican regimes, semi-autonomous families play a key role in the formation of citizens. It follows directly that if families become less capable of performing that role, the well-being of the entire community is jeopardized. There is evidence that the deinstitutionalization of marriage is yielding just that result. Showing how requires another brief theoretical digression.

There can be no single definition of civic virtue suitable for all times and places. As has been clear since Aristotle's classic analysis in the *Politics*, each form of government is linked to a corresponding set of public virtues. Liberal democracy is no exception; we can discern a distinctive canon of virtues that are prized by, and help sustain, liberal democratic polities.

Among these liberal virtues is what I have called "independence"—the disposition to care for, and take responsibility for, oneself and to avoid becoming needlessly dependent on others. Human beings are not born independent, nor do they attain independence through biological maturation alone. A growing body of evidence suggests that in a liberal democracy, the family is the critical arena in which independence is fostered. For example, after correcting for other variables such as educational attainment, the children of long-term welfare-dependent single parents are far more likely to become similarly dependent themselves.

Equally suggestive is the evidence concerning the difficulties that many young unwed mothers experience in raising their sons. The absence of fathers as models and co-disciplinarians contributes to the low self-esteem, anger, violence, and peer-bonding through gang lawlessness characteristic of many fatherless boys. The erosion of the two-parent family structure thus threatens to generate a growing subset of the population that cannot discharge the basic responsibilities of citizenship in a liberal democracy.

Attachment to the Community

A key function of strong families in liberal democracies is the encouragement of civic character and competence in young people. A second, closely related function is the linking of the young to the broader community. More than two centuries ago Edmund Burke suggested that the seeds of public concern are sown in the sense of connection we feel to our family and kin. A half century after the founding, Tocqueville's observations led him to conclude that America's families helped mute self-centered egoism and link individuals to their political institutions. Recent sociological studies confirm a strong correlation between family solidarity and the sense of obligation to a wider community and society.

In this connection, among others, the decline of stable marriages is a worrisome sign for our polity. Various studies suggest, for example, that children of divorced parents experience greater than average difficulty in making commitments and forging bonds of trust with others. Taken in conjunction with the Burke/Tocqueville thesis, these observations generate the prediction that in the aggregate, today's young people would feel a lower sense of connection to the political community than did those of previous generations. A recent Times Mirror study is consistent with this prediction. As Glendon summarizes its principal finding, the current group "knows less, cares less, [and] votes less" than young people at any time during the past half century.[4]

Economic Well-Being

A third key function of American families is economic. To a greater extent today than even a generation ago, two parents are needed to give children even modest levels of material security and opportunity. Conversely, the erosion of the stable two-parent family is the single most important cause of rising levels of children in poverty. The poverty rate among female-headed families was nearly 45 percent in 1988, compared to just over 7 percent for married-couple families. The poverty rate among single-parent families with children under five years old was even worse—57 percent. As David Ellwood shows, 73 percent of children from one-parent families will experience poverty at some point during their childhood, versus 20 percent for children from two-parent families; 22 percent of children from one-parent families will experience persistent poverty (seven years or more), versus only 2 percent from two-parent families.[5]

According to a recent study, child poverty rates today would be one-third lower if family structure had not changed so dramatically since 1960. Fifty-one percent of the increase in child poverty observed during the 1980s is attributable to changes in family structure during that period; changes in black family structure during the 1980s accounted for fully 65 percent of the increase in black children living below the poverty line.[6] Another study notes that the percentage of children living in households without an adult male has nearly tripled since 1960. The median income per child in 1988 for households with an adult male present was

$7,640; for households without an adult male, only $2,397. If the proportion of children without an adult male had remained at 1960 levels, average income per child would have been 9 percent higher in 1988 than the level actually recorded.[7]

These data suggest that the best anti-poverty program for America's children is a stable, intact family. And this conclusion holds for families with very modest levels of educational attainment. For married high school graduates with children, the 1987 poverty rate was 9 percent, versus more than 47 percent for families headed by female high school graduates. Even married high school dropouts with children fared better: their poverty rate was 25 percent, versus more than 81 percent for families headed by female high school dropouts.

Family structure differences between whites and African Americans (Table 12.1) are responsible for a large, and increasing, share of racial economic disparities. These structural divergences, already notable a generation ago when Daniel Patrick Moynihan published his controversial report, have continued to widen.

The gap in child poverty rates between black and white married couples has shrunk dramatically over the past thirty years while the corresponding gap among female-headed families has barely budged. During this period, the poverty gap between black married couples and black female-headed households has more than doubled and now stands at an astounding 50 percentage points (Table 12.2). Overall, conclude sociologists Frank Furstenberg and Andrew Cherlin, differences in family structure go "a long way toward accounting for the enormous racial disparity in poverty rates. Within family types, black families are still poorer than white families; but the racial gap in poverty shrinks considerably when the marital status of the household head is taken into account."[8]

I want to underscore the significance of these findings. It is sometimes argued that as economic opportunities for women have improved during

TABLE 12.1
Family Structure: Key Indicators, 1988

	Black	White
Married-couple families as % of all households	51	83
Female-headed family households (%)	43	9
Children not living with two parents	61	21
Children born to unmarried mothers	60	15
Children in poverty	44	15

TABLE 12.2
Child Poverty and Family Structure

	1960	1970	1980	1988
Children in poverty (white, %)	20.2	11.1	11.1	15.4
Children in poverty (black, %)	66.2	44.1	37.1	45.6
Children in poverty (married-couple families, %)	21.9	10.4	9.1	10.1
white	17.6	8.0	7.3	9.0
black	61.2	31.8	18.1	17.0
Children in poverty (female-headed families, %)	66.7	51.5	46.2	54.1
white	58.2	42.3	36.2	45.8
black	84.8	66.9	59.1	67.6

the past generation, the economic rationale for the two-parent family has eroded. The truth is just the reverse: economically, the two-parent family is more rather than less necessary because more and more families need two incomes to maintain even a marginally middle-class existence. Not only do husbands need wives more, but wives need husbands more. The thesis that increased workplace opportunities for women make it more possible for mothers with minor children to go it alone is supported neither by common sense nor by social scientific evidence.

The Two-Parent Family: Sources of Decline

There is more to be said on all these subjects, but I hope I have said enough to establish the thesis that the two-parent family performs a number of vital functions within the American polity and that its weakening over the past generation is an occasion for well-founded alarm. It is tempting to move directly from description of degeneration to prescriptions for renewal. I believe, however, that it is important to linger over an intermediate step—namely, diagnosis of the underlying disease. I shall examine three different hypotheses—economic, political, and cultural—as to the causes of family decline. As we shall see, each contains a measure of truth and each points toward a portion of the public response that is most likely to be effective.

Economic Sources of Family Decline

One popular version of the economic hypothesis runs roughly as follows. In recent decades, the economic prospects of many young males have declined while those of most women have improved. This has generated three sets of effects, each in its way at odds with stable marriages. Many young men are seen as less desirable mates; many young women have come to believe that they can achieve economic independence on their own; and two-earner families produce a shortage of family time and a conflict over gender roles, both of which increase the odds of separation and divorce.

These claims are broadly consistent with recent empirical analyses. For example, Frank Levy and Richard Michel have shown that between the early 1970s and late 1980s, the mean annual earnings of young high-school-educated men working full-time declined by 16 percent. Among those with less than a high school education, the decline was almost twice as steep. Levy suggests that coupled with declining unionization, increased international competition since 1973 reduced the availability of low-skill, high-wage jobs (especially in the manufacturing sector) and forced many poorly educated younger men to accept lower paying jobs in the service sector. For women, on the other hand, wages increased across the board, regardless of age and education, between the early 1970s and late 1980s.[9]

As male earnings declined, young men became less able to sustain their families at a middle-class standard as sole breadwinners. In 1973, median annual earnings for young high-school-educated men amounted to about 90 percent of median family income. By 1986, their earnings were only 72 percent of median family income. Meanwhile, women became increasingly able to translate their skills into income. Taken together, these facts go a long way toward explaining the surge of women, especially younger women, into the work force during the past two decades. The economic explanation gains further support from poll data, in which the majority of women cite economic need rather than psychological fulfillment as their prime motive for working full-time outside the home.

As women work in far greater numbers, and for much longer hours, outside the home, the contribution of men on average to homemaking and childrearing has increased only modestly. (There is, however, some evidence that behavior is changing more among upper-middle-class men than elsewhere.) The interaction of these two trends goes a long way toward explaining the dramatic drop in the amount of time that parents spend, on average, with their children. It may also help account for the belief of many women, squeezed between increased work outside the home and undiminished responsibilities at home, that marriage is an even less desirable bargain than it used to be.

The time squeeze seems most plausible as a partial explanation of increased separation and divorce, especially in the middle class. By contrast, diminished wage and employment prospects seem to fit best with the reduced propensity of many young people to get married in the first place. In *The Truly Disadvantaged*, William Julius Wilson offered an influential application of this thesis: reduced black marriage rates reflect dramatically higher rates of black male unemployment and plunging wages, which reduced the male marriageable pool (under the assumption that to be marriageable a man needs to earn something approaching a living wage).

Recent research offers modest, though hardly total, support for this hypothesis. For example, Robert Mare and Christopher Winship find that changes in employment rates among young black males account for about 20 percent of the decline in their marriage rates since 1960. With regard to the other 80 percent of the variance, they speculate that the various family disruptions of the past three decades may be self-reinforcing.[10] Though Wilson continues to defend the validity of his thesis for the hardest-hit central cities of the Northeast and Midwest, he is now willing to say that "the decline in marriage among inner-city blacks is not simply a function of the proportion of jobless men. . . . it is reasonable to consider [as well] the effects of weaker social strictures against out-of-wedlock births."[11]

The economic changes under discussion are also contributing to the decline of what social theorists call "civil society"—the network of neighborhood, community, religious, and voluntary associations that stand between the family and state institutions. As observers ever since Tocqueville have noted, civil society plays an especially important role in the United States as a counterweight both to our strongly individualistic ethos and to the (relative) weakness of our public sector. In particular, nuclear families have been sustained and strengthened by the efforts of local associations. It seems plausible to conjecture that the fraying of the fabric of civil society would exert added pressure on families already experiencing a double squeeze on income and time.

There is considerable, though not absolutely conclusive, evidence that American civil society has weakened in recent decades. Increased mobility (on the part of both young people impelled by economic necessity and the elderly liberated by economic sufficiency) has reduced the number of extended families living in the same or nearby communities. Economically induced differences among family schedules have interrupted what Barbara Dafoe Whitehead calls the "common rhythms" of neighborhood life, making it more difficult for parents to connect with each other, build friendships, and support each other as parents. The reduction in family time is exerting pressure on organizations that depend heavily on volunteers. What Robert Reich has called the "secession of the successful"—the growing tendency among upper-middle-class families of all races to leave economically mixed urban neighborhoods for more homogenous enclaves—has removed important assets of leadership from many communities. Conversely, as William Julius Wilson has argued, the isolation of very poor neighborhoods from other communities and the concentration of social problems found within them serve as powerful counterweights to broader societal norms of marriage and parenting.

In short, families breathe the air generated by a broader social environment. When that environment deteriorates, in part because of the economic stresses discussed in this section, an increase in the social equivalent of respiratory diseases is all but inevitable, especially among the most stressed and fragile families.

Politics: Programmatic Sources of Family Decline

Many conservatives (and some independent policy analysts) argue that the perverse incentives generated by government programs have helped undermine marriage and stable families. In particular, they allege, poorly designed welfare programs hurt children by diminishing the propensity of their parents to marry and work and by undermining the pride and independence so essential to a healthy childrearing environment.

The latest round of this long-running debate was sparked by the publication of Charles Murray's *Losing Ground* in 1984. His critics were quick to point out that while teen pregnancy and illegitimacy rates were rising through much of the 1970s and 1980s and marriage rates among the poor fell, cash payments to welfare recipients were actually diminishing in real terms. Moreover, comparisons among states with dramatically different levels of welfare support failed to sustain the thesis that high payment levels were correlated with undesirable outcomes. Murray responded that differences among states were less significant than the increased availability of welfare throughout the United States, that declines in Aid to Families with Dependent Children (AFDC) and other cash payments were more than offset by increases in in-kind assistance, and that the diminishing welfare stigma and rising utilization rates had created a new climate of overall incentives and effects.

By the mid-1980s, this exchange of volleys had resulted in an analytical standoff. Since then, however, additional evidence has helped crystallize a rough consensus. In an authoritative study of single mothers and their children, Irwin Garfinkel and Sara McLanahan estimate that rising government benefits were responsible for a 9 to 14 percent increase in the prevalence of single motherhood from 1960 to 1975—that is, between one-tenth and one-seventh of the 100 percent increase actually observed during that period. They go on to argue that this factor could account for as much as 30 percent of the growth within the bottom part of the income distribution.[12] And in a recently published comprehensive survey of literature on the incentive effects of the welfare system, Robert Moffit concludes that there is "unequivocal evidence" of undesirable consequences for work and family structure, particularly for female-headed families, although these effects explain only a modest fraction of overall trends during the past two decades.[13]

Cultural Sources of Family Decline

That significant cultural change has occurred in America during the past two decades is not open to serious doubt.[14] In a recent paper, Daniel Yankelovich has sought to catalog and explain some of the key shifts. Less value is now placed on what one owes others as a matter of moral obligation; on sacrifice as a moral good; on social conformity, respectability, and observing the rules; and on correctness and restraint in matters of physical pleasure and sexuality. Conversely, more value is now accorded to individualism, self-expression, self-realization, pluralism, and personal choice, as opposed to ascribed status and social roles.[15]

As Yankelovich and others have documented, these broad value shifts are translated into specific changes in attitudes toward children and families. Compared to forty years ago, Americans today are much more accepting of (inter alia) sex before marriage, birth out of wedlock, and divorce. Far more Americans value marriage primarily as a means to personal happiness; far fewer say that parents in an unhappy marriage should stay together for the sake of the children. Not surprisingly, the conflict (frequently unacknowledged) between, on the one hand, self-actualization and career advancement and, on the other, responsibilities and commitments to spouses and children appears to have intensified.

While conjectures abound, establishing cause-and-effect relations in cultural matters is notoriously difficult. Yankelovich argues that rising levels of affluence lead to demands for increased personal choice and to rising impatience with traditional bonds. William Julius Wilson suggests that cultural change is largely the consequence of economic change, that (for example) attitudes toward work are affected by changes in the availability and quality of jobs. Isabel Sawhill has proposed a multi-causal account with public policy, interest-group advocacy, demography, and behavior (and its perceived consequences) as some of the key variables.

Although these and other analysts are inclined to understand cultural change as at least partly induced by noncultural forces, most of them are inclined to ascribe at least relative autonomy to culture: once set in motion, cultural transformation takes on a life of its own and becomes an independent source of further changes. So, for example, attitudes toward divorce and premarital sex may have shifted initially in response to socioeconomic factors—such as increased affluence, mobility, and employment opportunities—that induced significant changes in individual behavior. In turn, however, a more permissive cultural atmosphere added impetus to these behavioral shifts.

Putting my political theorist's hat back on for a moment, and building on the previously cited works of Glendon and Elshtain, I would like to propose an additional hypothesis that gives even more weight to culture as an independent variable. The American Revolution and constitutional founding set in motion a new political order based to an unprecedented, steadily increasing (and for some of the Founders themselves, unexpected) extent on individual rights, personal choice, and democratic/egalitarian social relations.[16] These principles stood in tension not only with patterns of social deference and hierarchy but also with patterns of commitment and authority within the family. Along with many of his contemporaries, Tocqueville believed that maintaining differentiation among these spheres was not only possible but also desirable. The family would be somewhat democratized, to be sure, but the natural bonds of affection would form a bulwark against excessive voluntarism and individualism in intimate relations. Unfortunately, the proponents of this harmonizing view underestimated the power of what I have called "regime effects"— that is, the tendency of fundamental political principles to structure and dominate other spheres of existence.

That this tendency exists does not mean that it is wholly inevitable. Think of a society based on liberal democratic public principles as a rapidly flowing river. A few vessels may be strong enough to head upstream. Most, however, will be carried along by the current. But they can still choose where in the river to sail and where along the shore to moor. The mistake is to think of the liberal public order either as a placid lake or as an irresistible undertow.

It is in this light, I believe, that we must understand the contemporary arguments for social differentiation offered by theorists such as Michael Walzer. It is correct to assert that liberal polities offer more scope for diversity, including social spheres as well as individual lives, than any others. But it is mistaken to suggest that all spheres are created equal, that there is no hierarchy of authority and influence among them. On the contrary, I want to suggest that what has happened to the American family in the past two generations is in important respects a consequence of the unfolding logic of authoritative, deeply American moral-political principles and that efforts to renew the family must sail against this powerful current.

That does not mean, however, that nothing can be done or that cultural change is linear and unidirectional. (Indeed, this is where the partial dependence of culture on other variables may turn out to be an advantage.) In the first place, to the extent that heightened individualism is indeed an "affluence effect," economic hard times that interrupt the expectation of ever-rising prosperity should induce at least a partial return to traditionalism in matters of personal and family conduct as well as economic behavior such as increased savings and investment (as opposed to consumption and debt). Indeed, Yankelovich suggests that just such a shift is now underway and that the result is likely to be a new if uneasy synthesis of traditional (or communitarian) and progressive (or individualistic) values.

Second, individuals are capable of what I call "social learning": the consequences of certain patterns of belief and conduct may turn out to be different from (and worse than) early expectations. For example, optimistic predictions about the impact of less restrictive norms and laws of divorce have run up against the reality of economic privation and psychological distress for many custodial parents and their children. From this standpoint, it is hardly surprising that a wide-ranging reconsideration of divorce, including not only lawyers, legal scholars, and policy analysts but also family therapists, is now well underway. Nor is it surprising that after three decades of unprecedented increases, the divorce rate appears to have stabilized a bit below its peak of the early 1980s.

What Can We Do?

People get and stay married for all sorts of reasons, many of which are rather hard to recapture in retrospect. But setting aside transient lust and enduring affection, neither of which is much affected by public policy, two considerations should command our attention as we ask what can be done to reinstitutionalize marriage. Individuals get and stay married because they think it is in their interest to do so and/or because they believe that it is the morally correct thing to do. Social changes that either reduce benefits or weaken cultural sanctions will, *ceteris paribus*, weaken the institution of marriage. As we have seen, both these sorts of changes have occurred during the past generation. This suggests the right line of attack: in the most general terms, public policy can bolster marriage by increasing the practical advantages it offers and by reinforcing its moral standing.

Before outlining a public policy agenda that would move us in that direction, I want to distinguish between practically effective and morally appropriate policy changes. As we consider meaningful reform, we must be very careful not to betray the very important moral progress we have made as a society during the past generation toward greater liberty and equality. From this standpoint, some strategies for reinstitutionalizing marriage would clearly be unacceptable, even if they might work. For example, discriminatory barriers to the presence of women in the work force might well force more women to stay married to male workers, but such a proposal should not be entertained. Similarly, even if more restrictive divorce laws might keep some marriages together, I take it that there is little support for restoring the legal *status quo ante* of the 1950s, with its excessively narrow grounds for divorce and incentives for systematic manipulation and misrepresentation. Pro-marriage policies for the 1990s must strive for a synthesis of the good we have gained and lost in the past forty years, not for a simple restoration of any previous era. With these considerations firmly in mind, let me briefly sketch some elements of a pro-marriage policy agenda. I shall take as my guide the analytical structure of the previous section of this chapter—the sorting of sources of marital decline into broad categories of economy, polity, and culture. My intention is not to offer legislative-style proposals in all their endless detail but rather to put forward a handful of broad ideas as a basis for discussion.

The Economic Agenda

A principal aim of a pro-marriage economic agenda must be to improve the employment prospects, and hence marriageability, of young males. One step in that direction would be a crash program to raise high school graduation rates through systematic persuasion combined with a mix of positive and negative incentives. In this connection, Isabel Sawhill has proposed what she calls "Do the Right Thing" vouchers that turn into substantial cash grants for at-risk teens who finish high school. Arkansas already makes getting a first driver's license contingent on staying in school.

Another step toward improving employment prospects for young males is a better system of links between education and the workplace. Fully one-half of all our students go no farther than high school but we do almost nothing to help prepare them for, and make the transition to, the world of work. European countries have well-organized, workplace-based apprenticeship programs for such students; the German model is widely considered exemplary. We should move to replace our antiquated vocational education with a new approach that helps students acquire the skills and habits they really need and introduces them to potential employers. (This approach would also address what Wilson and many other sociologists have identified as a major obstacle to employment for the ghetto poor—namely, lack of participation in a social network of friends and relatives that connects them to future employers and alerts them to job opportunities.) The Clinton administration's School-to-Work Opportunities Act, enacted in 1994, represents an important step in this direction.

A third step is to make work pay by ensuring that no family headed by a full-time worker or the equivalent falls below the poverty line. The most effective way to do this is to expand the current Earned Income Tax Credit (EITC) and adjust it to reflect family size more adequately. A recent study suggests that for a relatively modest increment above current outlays, this approach would lift one million full-time working poor families out of poverty, including one out of five poor children in America.[17] In addition, young male workers would become more attractive as potential husbands, and the current gap between the full welfare-benefits package and minimum-wage jobs would be eliminated. Here again, the expansion of the EITC included in the Clinton administration's 1993 five-year budget plan represents an important advance.

Two other steps would ease strains on marriage by reducing the current tension between family and work. First, the federal government should stop taxing away the money parents need to raise young children. For example, the real value of the personal exemption has been allowed to erode by nearly three-quarters since the late 1940s. One sensible approach would be to raise it to between $6,000 and $7,500 for young children of lower and middle-income families. An alternative would be a tax credit of (say) $1,000 per child, made refundable so that families too poor to enter the income tax rolls would be able to benefit. The additional funds could help the parents of young children reduce the number of hours they must work outside the home, relieving some of the pressure on family time or, alternatively, to improve the quality of child care and other opportunities for children available through the market.

Second, business, labor, and government should enter into a new partnership to make the workplace more hospitable to workers with young children. Elements needed include these things: family leave policies that make it easier for parents to stay home with infants; more on-site child care; flextime and compressed-week arrangements; and increased opportunities for home-based employment. While the former Bush administration's preference for voluntary corporate programs in these areas was understandable, the evidence suggests that firmer government direction may be needed to accelerate the development of pro-marriage and family policies in the private sector. The Family and Medical Leave Act signed into law by President Clinton in 1993 is a good first step.

The Political Agenda: Public Programs and Laws

As I noted earlier, recent research indicates that most welfare programs tilt against marriage and families. A number of states are experimenting with new policies that might help redress the balance. For example, a New Jersey proposal would allow the continuation of AFDC benefits to children if the natural parents marry and live together in the home, as long as their income does not exceed state eligibility standards. A Wisconsin proposal would eliminate the requirement that one member of a low-income couple have a work history to be eligible for AFDC and it would provide larger grants for married parents. A more radical proposal, not yet enacted and implemented by any state, would provide a large one-time bonus to any woman who marries, leaves the AFDC rolls, and stays off for an extended period. A still more radical proposal, initially offered by David Ellwood and endorsed in its broad outlines by President Clinton, would eliminate welfare as an open-ended option, replacing it with a package of shorter-term assistance, job training, earned income supplements, medical care, and child support assurance. Reform legislation is currently trapped in a triangular tug-of-war involving the Clinton administration, congressional Republicans, and a bipartisan coalition of governors. Pending federal welfare reform, the extension of waivers to the states for policy experimentation is desirable and should be continued.

Another key area is divorce law reform. Reasonable changes could help reduce the frequency of divorce and would almost certainly make life better for custodial parents and their minor children.

To reduce the overall rate of divorce, I suggest a two-tier system. For couples without dependent children, current law can be left in place. For couples with dependent children, we should eliminate unilateral no-fault—where one party can readily obtain a divorce without the other's consent—and return to an updated fault system, with the alternative of a five-year waiting period. And even in cases involving minor children where both parties consent, there should be suitable braking mechanisms: a mandatory pause of at least a year for reflection, counseling, and mediation.

Not only should divorce for married couples with minor children be slowed; support awards should be raised and placed on a different basis. Mary Ann Glendon has argued that a new "children first" principle should govern our spousal support and marital property law:

> [T]he judge's main task would be to piece together, from property and income and in-kind personal care, the best possible package to meet the needs of children and their physical custodian. Until the welfare of the children had been adequately secured in this way, there would be no question of, or debate about, "marital property." All property, no matter how or when acquired, would be subject to the duty to provide for the children.[18]

During the past generation, the presumption in favor of awarding mothers custody of their children has been replaced in many cases by the presumption of equal claims. As I noted earlier, this "reform" has in fact worsened the postdivorce economic status of custodial mothers and their children: because women tend to view custody as a paramount issue, they often compromise on economic matters to avoid the custody battle made possible by the new, supposedly fairer and more egalitarian, legal framework. In this regard, scholars from various points on the ideological spectrum are converging on what is called a "primary caretaker standard": judges should be instructed to award custody of young children to the parent who has performed a substantial majority of direct caregiving tasks. With this issue off the table, negotiated economic arrangements are likely, on average, to be much better for children.

But even when child support awards are adequate, all too often they go unpaid. The law must give renewed sanction to the moral proposition that the responsibility of biological parents for their children does not cease simply because of divorce, separation, or for that matter, out-of-wedlock birth. We should create a far more uniform and straightforward method of child support.

Two major steps are needed. First, all absent parents would be expected to contribute a percentage of their income, which would vary with the number of children they father (or bear). Second, payments would be collected by employers, just like payroll taxes, and remitted to the federal government, which would then send the money directly to custodial parents every month. All absent or noncustodial parents would be included, not just child-support delinquents. Failure to pay would be an offense comparable to tax evasion. And major credit agencies could be enlisted in a nationwide effort to tell noncustodial parents that if they don't help support their children, they won't get credit themselves.

Taken together, these steps—the children first principle, the primary caretaker standard, and tougher child support enforcement—would improve the financial position of minor children and their custodial parents. But they are also pro-marriage. The reason is straightforward: under current arrangements, many men have strong financial incentives to walk away from marriages or not to enter them in the first place. They believe, with considerable justification, that their support obligations are optional and easily evaded and that leaving their children, or failing to acknowledge paternity, will leave them economically better off. By throwing society's weight on the side of significant long-term responsibilities, divorce law reform would both send a new set of moral signals to men and reduce their incentives to abandon marriages and minor children.

The Cultural Agenda

I turn, finally, to three measures that might help shift the cultural center of gravity towards marriage and stable, intact families.

In a recent article, Senator Moynihan draws an interesting parallel between family policy today and economic policy after World War II. The Employment Act of 1946 did little more than create the Council of Economic Advisors, yet it had a far greater impact than any jobs bill. The reason, Moynihan notes, is that the Act declared a national policy and marked the acceptance of a previously disputed social responsibility. Similarly, Moynihan suggests, it would be a significant step forward "for a national family policy to declare that the American government sought to promote the stability and well-being of the American family; that the social programs of the federal government would be formulated and administered with this object in mind; and finally, that the President, or some person designated by him, would report to the Congress on the condition of the American family."[19] While Moynihan does not identify a specific agency, it would seem appropriate for the Commissioner for Children, Youth and Families located within the Department of Health and Human Services to take the lead in such an endeavor. If you believe, as I do, that public speeches and deeds are influential moral expressions, then this kind of declaratory policy could carry great weight.

A second proposal concerns efforts to change beliefs among young people. I am struck by the apparent success of school-based campaigns against smoking that combine factual information, personal testimony, and sophisticated use of media. Is it not time for a comparably intense campaign against teen pregnancy and out-of-wedlock birth and in favor of marriage? Such a program could bring together government, academia, and the private sector, and it could enlist the talents of sports and entertainment figures as well as media experts. This national campaign could underscore the long-term adverse consequences of short-sighted behavior for teens themselves and for their children, drive home the personal effort and moral responsibility that parenthood entails, and reinforce the practical and emotional benefits of stable marriages. President Clinton called for just such a national campaign in his 1995 State of the Union address; in his 1996 address, he was able to announce the formation of a national leadership coalition to catalyze this campaign.

No doubt objections would be raised and fears expressed; it would be necessary to craft the message in close cooperation with parents, religious groups, and civil libertarians. Still, there seems little to lose in testing the efficacy of persuasion through the community's moral voice as an alternative to laissez-faire and partial replacement for public incentives or coercion.

My final proposal concerns television, without which no discussion of contemporary culture would be complete. Today, nearly every household has a television set, and the average child spends as much time watching television as with parents, and twice as much time as in school. While much research on the impact of television yields murky results, it is fairly well established that educational programming accelerates early learning and that televised violence exacerbates aggressive behavior. In 1991 prime time, the three major networks depicted 10,218 sexual incidents—93 percent of them outside of marriage.

It is difficult to believe that the accumulated impact of such stimuli on marriage and families is insignificant. Average citizens certainly do not think so. In a 1991 survey, for example, only 2 percent of respondents thought that television *should* have the greatest influence on children's values, but fully 56 percent believe that it *does* in fact have the greatest influence—more than parents, teachers, and religious leaders combined. In Barbara Dafoe Whitehead's community-level research, television emerges in the eyes of parents as a prime vehicle for intensifying hard-to-control consumer and sexual desires among children.

As Isabel Sawhill has recently observed, the 1980s witnessed a general effort to deregulate the broadcast industry as anti-government conservatives seized control of the Federal Communication Commission. In 1984, for example, virtually all restrictions on advertising and guidelines for children's programming were eliminated. More recently, however, the pendulum has begun to swing back. In 1990, Congress enacted the Children's Television Education Act, which "establishes the principle that the broadcast industry has a social responsibility in this area, limits the amount of advertising during children's programs, allows broadcasters to cooperate in limiting violence, and establishes a National Endowment for Children's Television."[20] And in February 1996, President Clinton signed a landmark telecommunications reform bill that mandates the inclusion (in new televisions) of the "V-chip" that will allow parents to screen out programs they judge excessively violent or explicitly sexual.

My suggestion is simple: building these important pieces of legislation, we should enter into a broader national discussion concerning the responsibilities of publicly licensed media in a free society. The dangers of excessive concentrations of government power cannot be ignored. But it is equally dangerous (and false) to argue that no alternative lies between moral laissez-faire and tyrannical censorship. For more than 60 years we have accepted the proposition that the allocation and conduct of licensed media present issues affecting the general public interest, not just the rights of individuals. It is time to apply this principle to the new problems of family disintegration, for which the media cannot escape their share of responsibility, and craft new regulations appropriate to changed circumstances.

Notes

1. David Blankenhorn, "American Family Dilemmas," in *Rebuilding the Nest: A New Commitment to the American Family*, ed. David Blankenhorn, Steven Bayme, and Jean Bethke Elshtain (Milwaukee, WI: Family Service America, 1990).

2. Mary Ann Glendon, "Virtue, Families, and Citizenship," in *The Meaning of the Family in a Free Society*, ed. W. Lawson Taitte (Dallas: The University of Texas at Dallas, 1991); Elshtain, "The Family and Civic Life," in *Rebuilding the Nest*, ed. Blankenhorn, Bayme, and Elshtain.

3. For a more extended discussion of these and related points, see William A. Galston, *Liberal Purposes: Goods, Virtues, and Diversity in the Liberal State* (Cambridge: Cambridge University Press, 1991), chap. 10.

4. Glendon, "Virtues, Families, and Citizenship," 67.

5. David Ellwood, *Poor Support* (New York: Basic Books, 1988), chaps. 4 and 5.

6. David J. Eggebeen and Daniel T. Lichter, "Race, Family Structure and Changing Poverty among American Children," *American Sociological Review* 56 (December 1991): 801–17.

7. Victor R. Fuchs and Diane M. Reklis, "America's Children: Economic Perspectives and Policy Options," *Science* 255 (January 3, 1992): 41–46.

8. Frank Furstenberg and Andrew Cherlin, *Divided Families: What Happens*

to *Children When Parents Part* (Cambridge, MA: Harvard University Press, 1991), 127 n. 1.

9. Frank Levy and Richard Michel, *The Economic Future of American Families: Income and Wealth Trends* (Washington, DC: Urban Institute, 1991).

10. Robert Mare and Christopher Winship, "Socioeconomic Change and the Decline of Marriage for Blacks and Whites," in *The Urban Underclass*, ed. Christopher Jencks and Paul E. Peterson (Washington, DC: The Brookings Institution, 1991).

11. William Julius Wilson, "Public Policy Research and the Truly Disadvantaged," in Jencks and Peterson, *The Urban Underclass*, 468.

12. Irwin Garfinkel and Sara McLanahan, *Single Mothers and Their Children: A New American Dilemma* (Washington, DC: Urban Institute Press, 1986), 62–63.

13. Robert Moffit, "Incentive Effects of the U.S. Welfare System: A Review," *Journal of Economic Literature* 30, no. 1 (March 1992): 56–57.

14. Cross-national studies reveal similar (though somewhat less intense) trends in most advanced industrial countries during the past 30 years.

15. Daniel Yankelovich, "The Affluence Effect" (paper prepared for the Brookings Institution Seminar Series on Values and Public Policy, Washington, DC, September 19, 1991).

16. For a stunning account of all this, see Gordon Wood, *The Radicalism of the American Revolution* (New York: Random House, 1992).

17. Robert J. Shapiro, "An American Working Wage: Ending Poverty in Poor Families" (Washington, DC: Progressive Policy Institute Report No. 3, 1990).

18. Mary Ann Glendon, *Abortion and Divorce in Western Law* (Cambridge, MA: Harvard University Press, 1987), 95.

19. Daniel Patrick Moynihan, "Family and Nation Revisited," *Social Thought* 16, no. 2 (1990): 52.

20. Isabel Sawhill, "Young Children and their Families," in ed. Henry J. Aaron and Charles L. Schultz, *Setting Domestic Priorities: What Can Government Do?* (Washington, DC: The Brookings Institution, 1992), 163.

PART FOUR

Marriage in America: A Report to the Nation

CHAPTER 13

Marriage in America: A Report to the Nation

The Council on Families in America

The Failed Revolution

America's divorce revolution has failed.

The evidence of failure is overwhelming. The divorce revolution—by which we mean the steady displacement of a marriage culture by a culture of divorce and unwed parenthood—has created terrible hardships for children. It has generated poverty within families. It has burdened us with unsupportable social costs. It has failed to deliver on its promise of greater adult happiness and better relationships between men and women.

We do not offer this assessment lightly. We recognize that these failures have been unanticipated and unintended. The divorce revolution set out to achieve some worthy social goals: to foster greater equality between men and women; to improve the family lives of women; and to expand individual happiness and choice. We recognize the enduring importance of these social goals.

Yet the divorce revolution has not brought us closer to these goals but has cast us at greater distance from them. Relationships between men and women are not getting better; by many measures, they are getting worse. They are becoming more difficult, fragile, and unhappy. Too many women are experiencing chronic economic insecurity. Too many men are isolated and estranged from their children. Too many people are lonely and unconnected. Too many children are angry, sad, and neglected.

We believe it is time to change course. The promises of the divorce revolution proved empty, its consequences devastating for both adults and children. It is time to shift the focus of national attention from divorce to

293

marriage. It is time to rebuild a family culture based on enduring marital relationships.

Changing the Subject to Marriage

We are scholars and analysts who make up the Council on Families in America—a volunteer, nonpartisan, interdisciplinary group of citizens from across the human sciences and across the political spectrum. We are a diverse group, reflecting a wide range of opinions about politics, philosophy, and public policy.*

What brings us together is our concern for children. This concern leads us to focus on the state of marriage and family life in America. Over the past two years we have commissioned and reviewed scholarly papers, conducted and monitored research, closely followed the national debate, and deliberated together.

We esteem tolerance and privacy as basic values. In a free society, people should be permitted to live in social arrangements over which they have a measure of choice and control. But we also point to this central fact: today there is widespread and growing evidence of failure in rearing children. Accordingly, it is vitally important to uphold those institutions and values which are most likely to meet children's needs and safeguard their interests.

The truth is that every child needs and deserves the love and provision of a mother and a father. The loving two-married-parent family is the best environment for children—the place where children gain the identity, discipline, and moral education that are essential for their full individual development. And, as the institution which most effectively teaches the civic virtues of honesty, loyalty, trust, self-sacrifice, personal responsibility, and respect for others, the family is an irreplaceable foundation for long-term social efficacy and responsibility.

The weight of evidence points to a most disturbing reality. Child well-being is deteriorating. Almost all of the key indicators point toward this conclusion: rates of delinquency and crime (including an alarming juvenile homicide rate), drug and alcohol abuse, suicide, depression, the growing number of children in poverty, and others. Some experts have suggested that the current generation of children and youth is the first in our nation's history to be less well-off—psychologically, socially, economically, and morally—than their parents were at the same age.

Many factors have contributed to the deteriorating well-being of chil-

---

*The opinions in this report are those of the Council members as individuals and not necessarily of the organizations with which they are affiliated.

dren. But what ranks as the most fundamental factor of all, in our judgment, is *the weakening of marriage as an institution*.

Marriage is under assault in our society. It is an institution in decline and even disrepute. The eminent demographer Kingsley Davis has said, "at no time in history, with the possible exception of Imperial Rome, has the institution of marriage been more problematic than it is today."[1]

With each passing year, an ever smaller percentage of the nation's citizens are married and an ever larger percentage of the nation's children live in households that do not consist of two married parents. This steady break-up of the married, mother-father childrearing unit is the principle cause of declining child well-being in our society.**

Moreover, with each passing year, more and more American children are growing up with little or no direct experience of married life. Many are growing up with little or no confidence that they could be, or even want to be, in a satisfying, enduring marital relationship. Increasingly, the cultural messages the children receive are either indifferent or hostile to marriage. Indeed, it does not seem at all far-fetched to say that we as a society are simply failing to teach the next generation about the meaning, purposes, and responsibilities of marriage. If this trend continues, it will constitute nothing less than an act of cultural suicide.

The core message of this report is basic and blunt. To reverse the current deterioration of child and societal well-being in the United States, we must strengthen the institution of marriage. We realize that strengthening marriage cannot be our only goal. But we insist that it must become our most important goal. For unless we reverse the decline of marriage, no other achievements—no tax cut, no new government program, no new idea—will be powerful enough to reverse the trend of declining child well-being.

We are not suggesting a return to the marriage forms of earlier eras. We endorse a marriage form which puts children first and is based on a full sense of mutuality and equal regard between husband and wife. We call for the nation to commit itself to this overriding goal: *To increase the proportion of children who grow up with their two married parents and decrease the proportion of children who do not.*

Many Americans will agree with this goal; some will not. But even those who do not agree, we trust, will acknowledge that our current national debate has been curiously silent on the subject of marriage. Who, today, is still promoting marriage? Who is even talking about it? In place of

---

**We recognize that some single parents, against difficult odds, are successfully raising their children and they deserve our support. And some married couples are failing at the task.

a national debate about what has happened to marriage there has been silence—stone-cold silence.

We increasingly accept as normal widespread reports of teenage pregnancies, absent fathers, neglected and abused children, child poverty, delinquent and violent teenagers. The nation is willing to debate each of these topics. But where is the debate about the common denominator that lies behind them all—the decline of marriage? The issue has hardly emerged on our public agenda. It is time to end this remarkable national silence on what is surely one of the most important issues of our time.

A primary purpose of this report, then, is to urge our society to switch the topic. Our society's current topic might be termed managing family decline, or ameliorating some of the worst consequences of a divorce culture. This discussion—in which many of us have participated and will continue to participate—is still necessary but no longer sufficient. It is time to raise the stakes, raise our standards, and begin a new discussion. The new discussion will be less about symptoms and problems than about causes and solutions. The new discussion we propose might be termed recreating a marriage culture.

The Decline of Child Well-Being

The deterioration of child well-being over the past three decades is one of our most tragic domestic trends. Moreover, when one stops to think about it, the trend in many ways should be quite surprising. No one could have predicted it 30 years ago. Today we are much richer than ever before and richer than any society in world history. Since 1960, the Gross Domestic Product has nearly tripled and the average income of Americans has doubled (in inflation-adjusted dollars). This prosperity has directly benefited children. Between 1964 and 1979 the income supporting the average preschool-age child in America increased (in inflation-adjusted dollars) by 42 percent.[2]

These per-child economic gains stem from several factors. Americans are having fewer children and they are having them later in life, when incomes are higher. In addition, many more mothers have entered the labor force. Not only do children have more money available to them,*** but they also have had more adults available who could, at least theoretically, care for them. The proportion of adults to children has jumped from

---

***We are aware that, underneath this broad economic trend, many blue-collar workers, beginning in the early 1970s, have experienced wage stagnation and even wage decline. In addition, we are aware of the declining economic prospects facing poorly educated young men, especially minority men.

fewer than two adults for every child in 1960 to a current ratio of three to one.[3]

Consider also these additional changes. Over the past three decades, the health of the nation improved, at least as measured by the key rates of infant mortality and longevity; money spent on education increased dramatically, with total expenditures on public elementary and secondary school education more than doubling in inflation-adjusted dollars; a new emphasis on children's rights emerged; informed psychological advice about childrearing was nationally promulgated as never before; and we witnessed the rise of the "new father," the man who is more directly involved with housework and the care of children.

Nevertheless, child well-being has not improved. It has gotten worse—much worse. A nonpartisan commission of prominent political, medical, education, and business leaders issued a report in 1990 on the health and well-being of American teenagers. They concluded: "never before has one generation of American teen-agers been less healthy, less cared for, or less prepared for life than their parents were at the same age."[4] The bipartisan National Commission on Children, chaired by Senator John D. Rockefeller IV, concluded in 1991 that "substantial evidence suggests that the quality of life for many of America's children has declined."[5]

What is the evidence for declining child well-being? Here are some examples.

- Juvenile violent crime has increased sixfold, from 16,000 arrests in 1960 to 96,000 in 1992, a period in which the total number of juveniles in the population remained relatively stable.
- Reports of child neglect and abuse have quintupled since 1976, when data were first collected. Confirmed reports of child neglect and abuse have also increased significantly.
- The psychological pathology of children and youth has taken a drastic turn for the worse. Eating disorders and rates of unipolar depression have soared among adolescent girls. Teen suicide has tripled. Alcohol and drug abuse among teenagers, although leveling off in recent years, continues at a very high rate.
- SAT scores have declined nearly eighty points, and most of the decline cannot be accounted for by the increasing academic diversity of students taking the test.
- Poverty has shifted from the elderly to the young. Since 1970, the percent of children who are poor has increased from 15 percent to 22 percent. Today, 38 percent of the nation's poor are children.

Is it merely a coincidence that child well-being declined sharply during a period of time in which marriage also declined? We think not. The rate of child poverty, for example, is five times higher for children living with single mothers than for children in intact families.[6] As Senator Daniel Patrick Moynihan has noted, poverty has historically derived from unemployment and low wages; today it derives from family structure.[7]

Recent surveys have found that children from broken homes, when they become teenagers, have two to three times more behavioral and psychological problems than do children from intact homes.[8] Of juveniles and young adults serving in long-term correctional facilities, 70 percent did not live with both parents while growing up.[9] Broken-home backgrounds contribute to as many as three in four teen suicides and four in five psychiatric admissions.[10]

The fragmentation of family structure extends far beyond the bounds of race, class, and ethnicity, but it can be seen most dramatically within the African American community.[11] Today, 68 percent of all black births are to unmarried mothers. Two-thirds of all black children are not living with two parents. And consider these economic consequences: only 15 percent of black children living with their married parents are in poverty, compared to 57 percent of those living with their mother only.[12]

The evidence continues to mount, and it points to one striking conclusion: the weakening of marriage has had devastating consequences for the well-being of children. To be sure, television, the movies, and popular music contribute to declining child well-being. So do poor teaching, the loss of skilled jobs, inefficient government bureaucracies, meager or demeaning welfare programs, and the availability of guns and drugs. But by far the most important causal factor is the remarkable collapse of marriage, leading to growing family instability and decreasing parental investment in children.

The Decline of Marriage

Not so long ago, America was probably the most marrying society in the world. The effects of that era can still be seen in the older generation. In 1990, 95 percent of women and 94 percent of men ages forty-five to fifty-four either were or had been married.[13]

Today, marriage is an institution in decay. Despite the fact that in recent years the number of marriages has been at record highs because of large population cohorts at the most marriageable ages, the marriage rate has been steadily declining. More people are postponing marriage to older ages, and more people are foregoing marriage altogether. The marriage rate for unmarried women ages fifteen to forty-four began to plummet around 1975 and by 1988 reached an all-time low of 91.0 per 1,000.[14]

In two decades, from 1970 to 1990, the percentage of married adults decreased from 72 percent to 62 percent. Demographers expect the marriage rate to drop still further in the future.

In addition, consider the dramatic and unprecedented current explosion of out-of-wedlock childbearing. The percent of nonmarital births stood at a fairly insignificant 5.3 percent in 1960; today the number is over 30 percent. Nearly one third of all American children are now born to unmarried parents. Most of those children will live through their childhoods in single-parent, mother-headed households.

A decline in the marriage rate might be good news if it meant that fewer couples would have to endure bad marriages and painful divorces. But this has not happened. While the marriage rate has declined, the divorce rate has climbed to a historically high level—and stayed there. In raw terms, the divorce rate has merely doubled over the past three decades. Yet the probabilities that a marriage will end in divorce have skyrocketed.

Only 14 percent of white women who married in the early 1940s eventually divorced, whereas almost half of white women who married in the late 1960s and early 1970s have already been divorced. For African American women, the figures are 18 percent and nearly 60 percent. For the average American, the probability that a marriage taking place today will end in divorce or permanent separation is calculated to be a staggering 60 percent.[15]

Again, children are heavily affected. Slightly more than half of divorcing couples in 1988 had children under the age of 18. The odds that a child today will witness the divorce of his or her parents are twice as great as a generation ago. Today, about half of all children in the United States are likely to experience a parental divorce before they leave home. What's more, a sizable percentage of children who now go through one divorce can expect to go through a second and even third divorce, as many of their parents' remarriages also end in divorce.[16] Quite simply, having children is no longer a strong deterrent to divorce.

Marital instability and nonmarriage have thus become dominant characteristics of our era. Consider these facts. In 1960, only 9 percent of all children lived in single-parent families; today, the percentage has increased to 27 percent.[17] More than one third (36 percent) of children today are living apart from their biological fathers, an increase from 17 percent in 1960.[18] Unlike in times past, when the paternal death rate was high, almost all of those fathers are living.

If both childhood experiences and adult risks of marital disruption are taken into account, only a minority of children born today are likely both to grow up in an intact family and also, as adults, to form and maintain an intact family. In part because children from broken homes are less

likely to form stable marriages of their own, the future for marital stability
in America does not look bright.[19]

Moreover, apart from the trends of divorce and nonmarriage, a growing
body of evidence suggests that the quality of married life in America has
also taken a turn for the worse. Here is one reason why: in a high-divorce
society, not only are more unhappy marriages likely to end in divorce, but
in addition, more marriages are likely to become unhappy. For in a society
where divorce has become a common and even normative experience,
people quite reasonably tend to hedge their bets regarding the durability
and even desirability of marriage. We become less willing to invest ourselves fully—our time, resources, dreams, and ultimate commitments—in
the institution of marriage. One result is a measurable rise in marital unhappiness.[20]

A Values Shift

The great majority of Americans still say that they believe in marriage as
a personal life goal. And they want their own marriage to last a lifetime.
But their actual behavior, as this report shows, diverges sharply from
these stated beliefs.

In our view, marriage has declined primarily because we no longer
value the institution as highly as we once did. Our culture has become
increasingly skeptical of marriage and of other institutions as well that
are thought to restrict or confine adult behavior. In their place, we now
put a much higher value on individualism, choice, and unrestricted personal liberty.

As a result, marriage has been losing its social purpose. Instead of serving as our primary institutional expression of commitment and obligation
to others, especially children, marriage has increasingly been reduced to
a vehicle—and a fragile vehicle at that—for the emotional fulfillment of
adult partners. "Till death us do part" has been replaced by "as long as
I am happy." Marriage is now less an institution that one belongs to and
more an idea that we insist on bending to our own, quite individualistic,
purposes. Fewer than 50 percent of Americans today include "being married" as part of their definition of family values.[21]

Daniel Yankelovich has summarized the cultural changes of recent decades, drawing heavily on survey research data:[22]

> The quest for greater individual choice clashed directly with the obligations
> and social norms that held families and communities together in earlier
> years. People came to feel that questions of how to live and with whom to
> live were a matter of individual choice not to be governed by restrictive

norms. As a nation, we came to experience the bonds of marriage, family, children, job, community, and country as constraints that were no longer necessary. Commitments were loosened.

Emotional fulfillment is an important and worthy goal. But it should not be the sole purpose of marriage when children are involved. If marriage is to remain a viable social institution, the self-fulfillment of parents as individuals cannot take precedence over their obligations to children.

A Culture of Divorce

Our nation has largely shifted from a culture of marriage to a culture of divorce. Once we were a nation in which a strong marriage was seen as the best route to achieving the American dream. We have now become a nation in which divorce is commonly seen as the path to personal liberation.

Marriage has come to be regarded as the problem and not the solution. Marriage, so we are told, is restrictive, confining, oppressive, and unliberating. The solution, many of us have come to believe, is the unencumbered life, the life without binding commitments, the life of new beginnings—a life that can often be achieved through divorce. In the recent past, divorce was limited to those marriages which had irreparably broken down, often because one spouse was seriously pathological or incompetent. Today, divorce may occur simply because one partner is unhappy or because a better partner has been located. And given the high rate of divorce, more and more possible partners are continually entering the market.

Divorces that involve children used to be in the category of the shameful, even the unthinkable. Today, children are only a minor inhibitor of divorce, although slightly more so when the children are male rather than female.[23] As one measure of the acceptance of divorce involving children, the proportion of persons who *disagree* with the statement, "when there are children in the family, parents should stay together even if they don't get along," has jumped from 51 percent in 1962 to a remarkable 82 percent as of 1985.[24]

Many experts argue that, because nothing can be done about it, we should simply accept the culture of divorce and adjust our other institutions accordingly. Some lawyers instruct people to prepare for the possibility of divorce as part of their preparation for marriage—by drafting, for example, a prenuptial agreement (which states the terms of any later divorce). Marriage therapists, adopting a stance of neutrality and an emphasis on self-actualization, often turn the focus of marriage therapy toward the goal of a "good divorce."

Family court judges often seem more interested in promoting "divorce counseling" than in promoting marriage counseling. We routinely expect stars of the entertainment industry to go through divorces and we rarely learn of their stable, long-term marriages. Policymakers in government, unpersuaded that anything can or even should be done to reverse the basic trend, settle for half-measures aimed at damage control. Instead of fatherhood, child support. Instead of marriage, divorce reform. Instead of parenthood, group homes.

The trend toward a divorce culture is also clearly evident in academic research and writing. Much of the scholarly discourse on family issues conducted over the past three decades has contained a strong anti-marriage bias. Many textbooks written for use in schools and colleges openly propagandize against any privileged cultural status for marriage and quite often even against marriage itself.

We are deeply disturbed by this new culture of divorce. While we certainly recognize that, in individual cases, divorce can sometimes be the least bad solution for a highly troubled marriage, our nation's increasingly casual acceptance of divorce as a normative experience for millions of parents and children should be a cause for profound alarm, not resignation, passivity, and excuse-making.

A Culture of Nonmarriage

We are even more disturbed about another culture that is replacing the culture of marriage—what can be called a culture of nonmarriage. What we mean by the culture of nonmarriage is the growing acceptance of unmarried parents and of having children out of wedlock.

Many Americans may frown on unmarried parenthood in our urban ghettos, where the number of unmarried teen parents has been growing by leaps and bounds. Yet toward the growing phenomenon of unmarried parenthood within the middle class, most Americans, especially younger adults, now refrain from judgement and simply look the other way. Many Americans, in fact, have come virtually to celebrate "single mothers by choice" despite the fact that the vast majority of single mothers live under considerable economic pressure and emotional strain and say, when they are asked, that they would prefer to be a part of a two-parent household.

The explosion of never-married motherhood in our society means that fathers are increasingly viewed as superfluous, unnecessary, and irrelevant. Remarkably, unwed parenthood has now reached virtual parity with divorce as a generator of fatherless homes in the United States.[25]

This growing belief that fathers are superfluous should be a major social concern for our society. First, fathers are vitally important to the task of childrearing. Certainly, we have never met the child who did not say that she or he wanted to be raised by both a father and a mother. And children know whereof they speak. The importance of fathers to childrearing is strongly supported by social science research.[26]

Second, it is extremely important to the larger society that men remain involved in family life. For men, married fatherhood is a civilizing force of no mean proportions. Conversely, having a large number of men disconnected from the patterns and satisfactions of family life—and thus much more prone to unhappiness, deviance, and crime—has always, and properly, been one of society's worst fears. In too many of our nation's communities today, this fear is becoming a reality.

The Meaning of Marriage

The enormous importance of marriage for civilized society is perhaps best understood by looking comparatively at human civilizations throughout history. Why is marriage our most universal social institution, found prominently in virtually every known society? Much of the answer lies in the irreplaceable role that marriage plays in childrearing and in generational continuity.

Simply defined, marriage is a relationship within which a community socially approves and encourages sexual intercourse and the birth of children. It is society's way of signalling to would-be parents that their long-term relationship together is socially important—a public concern, not simply a private affair. Kingsley Davis again:

> The genius of [marriage] is that, through it, the society normally holds the biological parents responsible for each other and for their offspring. By identifying children with their parents, and by penalizing people who do not have stable relationships, the social system powerfully motivates individuals to settle into a sexual union and take care of the ensuing offspring.[27]

More broadly, marriage has evolved in Western societies as a complex institution containing at least five dimensions: natural, religious, economic, social, and legal.

- First, marriage has long been viewed as a *natural* institution, meeting and guiding the primary human inclinations toward sexual expression, reproduction, and emotional intimacy. The English political philosopher John Locke describes marriage as humankind's "first Society."[28]
- Second, marriage is a *sacramental* institution, typically built on sacred promises and overseen by religious communities. In most cultures, powerful religious symbols and rites have sought to idealize and sanction the marital relationship.
- Third, marriage is an *economic* institution, constituting a primary unit of economic consumption, exchange, and production.
- Fourth, marriage is a *social* institution, nurturing and socializing children and regulating the behavior of both husbands and wives. It typically links together two extended families, thus widening the network of support, resources, and obligations available to help children and other vulnerable family members. From this perspective, marriage as an institution can be seen as a seedbed of civic virtue—perhaps society's most important contrivance for protecting child well-being, turning children into good citizens, and fostering good behavior among adults. Primarily for this reason, marriage is widely viewed in human societies as a "social good" worthy of strong support.
- Finally, due to the importance of each of these dimensions, marriage is also a *legal* institution, protected and regulated by a body of law that governs entry into the institution, exit from it, and expectations of behavior within it, including an enumeration of the rights and duties that flow from the status of being married.

One reason that marriage is ubiquitous is that, as a natural institution, it is partially rooted in human biology. The love attachments of marriage are more than just social constructs. Unlike most animals, human males and females have a predisposition to have some emotional affinity for each other beyond the sexual act and to establish "pair bonds."[29] Accordingly, there exists an "affective attachment" between men and women that causes us to be infatuated with each other, to feel a sense of well-being when we are together with a loved one, and to feel jealous when others attempt to intrude into our relationship. In evolutionary terms, children whose parents cooperate to nurture them to maturity are more likely to survive and reproduce and thus pass along their genes to posterity.

Yet the institution of marriage was designed less for the accommodation of adults in love than for the proper functioning of society, especially regarding the care of children. Indeed, marriage as an institution is historically based on a fundamental realization—that all affective ties between men and women, no matter how biologically based they may be, are notoriously fragile and breakable. Because of this fact, an important aspect of marriage, in both its legal and religious contexts, are the vows of fidelity and permanence that are almost always a part of the wedding ceremony. In large measure, these promises are designed to bind males to long-term commitment in order to foster the social institution of fatherhood.

It is important to add that divorce has also been a common and widespread institution in human societies. In the strict terms of our biological evolution, human beings may not be perfectly suited to monogamous relationships.[30] These values are human accomplishments, not biological givens. Yet in most traditional societies, children of divorce are quickly absorbed into surrounding kinship groups. Those groups are largely absent in modern societies, where families have been reduced to a bare nucleus. Also, the very high level of divorce found in modern societies is not only a historical rarity, but it has commonly been associated with overall social breakdown.

Until quite recently, the concept of illegitimacy has also been virtually ubiquitous. The concept is based on a universal cultural disapproval of casual sexual unions that create a child without married parents and especially a father responsible for it. As the famous anthropologist Bronislaw Malinowski wrote:

> In all human societies the father is regarded by tradition as indispensable. . . . No child should be brought into the world without a man—and one man at that—assuming the role of sociological father, that is, guardian and protector, the male link between the child and the rest of the community.[31]

Dropping the concept of illegitimacy in recent decades is a social and legal change that was well intentioned. Illegitimate children, through no fault of their own, have been highly stigmatized throughout history, and that stigma today has been greatly reduced. But the deeper message of this change is that marriage itself—and thus fatherhood itself—is no longer considered to be essential. And this means, tragically, that many children will suffer and that many men will become estranged from family life, at great social cost.

The Alternatives We Face

By insisting that today's negative trends for children cannot be reversed without strengthening marriage, we realize that many people will regard us as nostalgic and as hopelessly unrealistic. It is now a common view, especially among family scholars and other opinion leaders, that indeed it would be nice if everyone had a strong marriage, but that will never happen. The forces of modernism run against marital permanence; a free society cannot legislate matters of the heart; and in any event, expressive individualism and self-fulfillment are the regnant values of our age that have liberated millions of adults.

The tide simply cannot be turned, our critics will contend. They might remind us: "Where there is no solution, there is no problem." What we must do, they will insist, is ride with the tide, make the best of it, and design entirely new family solutions for a weak-marriage, high-divorce culture.

The tide against marriage does seem strong, and neither we nor anyone else can accurately predict the future. But nevertheless, and paradoxical though it may sound, we wish to assert that we, not our critics, are the realists. We are the ones, we submit, taking a tough-minded look at social realities. Our proposal is to arrest the downward spiral for children by reinvigorating marriage. This proposal stands a reasonable chance of reversing the current deterioration of child well-being in our society. The laissez-faire acceptance of the decline of marriage is premature and unwarranted. No consistent, widespread effort has been undertaken to try to reverse this trend. Until such an effort is made, it is irresponsible to say that nothing can be done.

The parental relationship is unique in human affairs. In most social relationships, the reciprocity of benefits is carefully monitored, since any imbalance is regarded as exploitative. But in the parental relationship, as has often been pointed out, "the flow of benefits is prolongedly, cumulatively, and ungrudgingly unbalanced."[32]

Who is willing to make this kind of massive, unbalanced investment in children? Evolutionary biologists tell us that, without question, pair-bonded biological parents are by far the most willing and the most highly motivated to the task. Who are the alternatives? Stepparents and other substitute parents? Peer groups? People especially hired for the task? Public and private childrearing organizations? Orphanages? If parents, especially biological fathers, are increasingly failing at the task of rearing our children, can we really expect these others to rear children successfully?

Let us look closely at the current family policy debate in America. Suppose that all the programs that family-policy advocates now dream of were, in some miraculous way, passed by Congress and signed into law by the President. Suppose that we had full funding for Head Start and for a wide range of family service and preservation programs; extensive parental-leave policies and other work-family policies; larger child tax credits; adoption reform; health care for all children; mandatory paternity identification; and every "deadbeat dad" in the country brought to his knees and made to pay child support.

Surely many of these changes would help. Indeed, we jointly endorse several of these policy ideas, and even more of these proposals are supported by many of the Council members whose names appear below. But by themselves, these policy reforms would do little—indeed, most of them would do almost nothing—to reinstitutionalize marriage and promote marital commitment. And if, for example, the growth of nonmarital births continues to increase at its current rate of 3 or 4 percent each year, could we really expect any or even all of these programs to reverse the current trend?

We do not underestimate the importance of government programs. But total social spending by all levels of government (in constant 1990 dollars) has risen from $143.73 billion to $787.0 billion over the past three decades—more than a fivefold increase.[33] Total inflation-adjusted spending on welfare has increased 630 percent.[34] Clearly, almost no amount of public investment in children could possibly offset the private disinvestment that has accompanied the decline of marriage.

There is no realistic alternative to the one we propose. We must, as a nation, reassess and change our basic cultural values. The values of marriage and marital permanence must be brought again to center stage.

Recommendations

There are some hopeful signs of change. Among marriage and family therapists, for example, we see a modest but potentially important shift toward what one best-selling author-therapist calls "divorce-busting," or asking, as a first obligation of good therapy, "Can this marriage be saved?" In our political discourse, both liberals and conservatives—both former Vice President Dan Quayle and President Bill Clinton—now largely agree that family fragmentation is a major growing threat to our society. There are also some small but hopeful signs that younger Americans are attaching, or at least would like to attach, greater importance than their elders did to the ideals of family life and committed marriage.

So perhaps the tide is already beginning to turn. Perhaps we will have, during the last years of this century, an important and long-overdue public debate in the United States about the possibility of reversing the trend of family fragmentation and reinstitutionalizing marriage.

To encourage this debate, we offer the following goals and recommendations. We offer these with the hope that the coming generation of parents will be able to make better choices than their own parents did. It may be unreasonable to expect a widespread change of heart about marriage among today's adults. We adults have made our decisions; we are all implicated in the current trends. But we remain optimistic about the desire and ability of young Americans to achieve strong and healthy family relationships.

Our message to young Americans is simple and challenging: As a foundation for family life and raising children, marriage is better than its fast-growing alternatives. It is our society's most important institution for bringing up children, for fostering high parental investment in children, and for helping men and women find a common life of mutual affection, care, and sexual intimacy. In your parents' generation, marriage got weaker. The challenge for your generation is to make marriage stronger.

Making marriage stronger will require a fundamental shift in cultural values and in public policy. Toward that end, we propose four broad goals:

1. Reclaim the ideal of marital permanence and affirm marriage as the preeminent environment for childrearing.
2. Decide unequivocally that out-of-wedlock childbearing is wrong, that our divorce rate is far too high, and that every child deserves a father.
3. Resolve in the next generation to increase the proportion of children who grow up with their two married parents and decrease the proportion who do not.
4. Resolve in the next generation to increase the time that parents spend raising their children. For married couples with children at home, aim for an overall commitment to paid employment that does not exceed sixty hours per week.

As possible strategies for achieving these goals, we offer the following recommendations. No one sector of society is responsible for the decline of marriage. We are all part of the problem, and therefore we all must be part of the solution. The strategies and recommendations we offer are thus addressed to all major sectors of society.

To religious leaders and organizations:

- Reclaim moral ground from the culture of divorce and nonmarriage. Retrieve and reinterpret inherited marriage symbols and rites. Recover the viewpoint that sees marriage as an institution of covenantal permanence, as the proper context for raising children, and as a relationship of mutual sharing and comfort between husband and wife.
- Avoid the mistake of equating marriage with concepts such as "committed relationships" which have no institutional embodiment. Restate theologically how the sacramental and covenantal components of marriage are related to its natural, economic, social, and legal components.
- Establish new educational and pastoral programs in seminaries and in congregations designed to promote commitment to marriage, prepare young people for the parental vocation, and uphold the ideal of marital permanence.
- In each local congregation, strive systematically to improve marital satisfaction and to lower rates of divorce and nonmarital childbearing. Establish and strengthen premarital counseling and marital enrichment programs. Strive to establish, in your congregation, a culture of marriage and support for marriage. Encourage young people in the congregation to honor, and learn from, older people who model excellence in marriage.
- Reach out, within the congregation and in the surrounding community, to the children of divorce and nonmarriage, offering them care and concrete assistance, while demonstrating by example the value of the marital commitment.
- Create a national Interfaith Council on Marriage devoted to defending and strengthening marriage in America.

To civic leaders and community organizers:

- Form grass-roots social movements designed to protect marriage and family life, not unlike movements today that seek to protect the natural environment.
- Create community-based organizations—from Fathers Clubs to MAD DADS to Boys and Girls Clubs—that model and promote married fatherhood and male responsibility.
- Disseminate information—for example, in schools, religious organizations, libraries, health clinics, and local media—about the personal and social value of marriage.
- Especially in urban America, develop economic strategies aimed at providing more job opportunities for young males, especially poorly

educated minority males, since jobless young men are less likely to marry and are less desirable as marriage partners.

- Strive to develop neighborhoods which are stable and supportive of family life. The ecology of safe, child-supportive, and marriage-friendly neighborhoods needs to be protected at least as much as does the ecology of natural environments.

To employers:

- Create personnel policies and work environments that respect and favor the marital commitment.
- Reduce the practice, currently quite common in many large corporations, of continually uprooting and relocating married couples with children.
- Create personnel policies and work environments that permit parents to spend more time with their children, thus helping to reduce the marital stress that accompanies childrearing. Examples include: job protections and other benefits, such as pay and health coverage, for parents wishing to take short-term (up to six months) parental leaves; job preferences and other benefits, such as graduated re-entry, for parents wishing to take longer-term (up to five years) parental leaves; and opportunities for job-sharing, compressed work weeks, career breaks, and working at home.

To social work, health care, and other human service professionals:

- Within the limits of good clinical practice, promote a culture of family formation and treat individuals as much as possible in the context of families.
- Within the limits of good clinical practice, discourage unwed child-bearing and assume that marriage is optimal for childrearing.
- Examine the ways in which current policies and models of service delivery either explicitly or implicitly undermine marriage formation and marriage stability.
- Reassess professional training and continuing education curricula, seeking to increase professional knowledge of the benefits and responsibilities of marriage, the predictable stages and crisis points in marriage, and the most effective support and treatment programs available to married couples.

To marriage counselors, family therapists, and family life educators:

- Begin with a bias in favor of marriage. Stress the needs of the marriage at least as much as the needs of the client.
- Help couples identify the likely pressure points in a marriage, such as the birth of the first child, and guide them toward the steps that can help their marriage to thrive.

To pregnancy health care providers and counselors:

- Tell young people unequivocally that every child deserves to grow up with two married parents.
- For every pregnancy, insist upon paternal identification—not simply for the purpose of child support payments, but for the purposes of fatherhood and, whenever possible, marriage. Establish community outreach programs to involve fathers in caring for their children and the mothers of their children, knowing that the reason to strengthen the paternal role is to foster marriage, not to foster substitutes for marriage.
- Encourage unmarried teenage mothers to give up their children for adoption by married couples.

To family law attorneys and judges:

- Strive to find ways to minimize unnecessary conflict in family disputes. As Abraham Lincoln once said, "Be peacemakers among neighbors whenever you can."
- Reassess current trends in family law, in such areas as child custody, adoption, and divorce, with an eye toward promoting marital and childrearing stability.

To children's advocates:

- Link advocacy for children to advocacy for marriage. While advocating better programs for children, also insist that no children's program, however well-funded and well-designed, can or ought to substitute for a stably married two-parent home.
- Organize grass-roots consumer boycotts of corporations whose advertisements or entertainment products (such as movies, music, or television shows) celebrate sexual violence and degrade the marital relationship.

To teachers, principals, and leaders in education:

- Eliminate the implicit and frequently explicit anti-marriage bias currently prevalent in many school curricula.
- Develop better procedures whereby parents can be informed about, and have some input into, what teachers are teaching children about marriage, procreation, and family life.
- Promote education for successful marriage as a regular part of school curricula. Include understanding of the historical roots of marriage, its desirability as an environment for childrearing, and its psychological, moral, legal, and economic requirements.

To foundation executives and philanthropic leaders:

- For every grant or charitable gift aimed at ameliorating the harmful impact of family fragmentation on children and on society, offer another aimed at strengthening marriage.
- Encourage objective research on marriage—what it is, how it works, and how it can be made to work better. (We have yet to find the word "marriage" in any leading foundation index.)

To family scholars:

- Re-write educational textbooks and family life education curricula so that marriage-with-children is portrayed as a desirable social good rather than as just one of many equally viable lifestyle alternatives.
- In educational textbooks and in other scholarly work, treat marriage as a basic societal institution with many dimensions—natural, legal, moral-religious, economic, and social—rather than examining marriage only, or mainly, from a psychological or therapeutic perspective.
- Undertake rigorous new research into the structure and experience of marriage—what makes it work, what makes it vulnerable, how it can be strengthened.[35]

To print and broadcast media journalists and editors:

- Encourage journalism on marriage and family life as a professional speciality and as a track for advancement.
- Examine the successes of marriage at least as often as its pathologies.

- Guard against widely circulated statistics which distort the realities of the marital institution and of family life.
- For editors of popular magazines aimed at teenage girls and teenage boys, realize that many teenagers are intensely interested in thinking about the kind of person they might marry, and that they would enjoy and benefit from good articles about marriage.
- Spend more time talking to ordinary families about family life today.

To entertainment industry writers, producers, and executives:

- Don't glamorize unwed motherhood, marital infidelity, alternative lifestyles, and sexual promiscuity. Imagine depicting divorce and unwed childbearing as frequently and as approvingly as you currently depict smoking and littering.
- Examine the ramifications of what happens every day on almost all daytime television talk shows regarding issues of sexuality and marriage. Do these sensationalistic stories accurately reflect the consequences of the behavior being described?
- Regarding a great deal of "gangsta" rap and other music for young people that celebrates sexual violence and is steeped in a predatory view of the male-female relationship, reconsider the popularization of these products. Balance commercial success with a sense of responsibility to the wider community of which you are a part.

To local, state, and federal legislators:

- Reconsider state marriage laws that lean toward "no-fault" divorce. Consider revisions that would emphasize the social importance of marriage, especially when children are involved, and that would shift the support of the law toward the marital partner trying to save the marriage.
- Formulate "vision statements" that publicly establish the goal of strengthening the married, two-parent home and decreasing the number of children born to unmarried parents.
- Revise the federal tax code to eliminate the "marriage penalty" and to provide more favorable treatment for married couples with children. Ideas with merit include:
  a. Increase the value of the personal income tax exemption by a factor of three or four, restoring the value lost to inflation during the years 1960–1990; and in addition, permit parents to claim a larger exemption for years in which a child is born or adopted.

b. Create a new, universal $1,000 per child refundable tax credit (as recommended by the National Commission on Children) as a partial substitute for means-tested programs that tend to disfavor married-couple families with children.

- Create new educational credits or vouchers, to be used for high school, vocational, college, graduate, or post-graduate education, available to parents who leave the paid labor force for a period of time to care for their young children.

- Replace the current welfare system with new anti-poverty approaches in which unwed motherhood is discouraged and in which marriage and the family are empowered rather than denigrated. Ideas with merit include:

  a. Mandatory identification of fathers prior to the receipt of benefits, linked to pro-marriage incentives, such as favorable tax and housing treatment;

  b. Encouragement toward the placement in adoptive, married-couple homes of babies born to unmarried teenage mothers;

  c. The substitution of a universal, refundable child-tax credit, or child allowance, for existing means-tested benefits;

  d. The creation of a bias in favor of marriages-with-children in the allocation of subsidized housing loans and public housing; and

  e. As a partial replacement for the existing system, the creation of a poverty tax credit, through which taxpayers could directly allocate a portion of their tax payments to one or more non-profit, community-based organizations devoted to reducing child poverty and strengthening families.

- Fundamentally reassess the current state-federal child support enforcement program, seeking whenever possible to foster not simply more child support but also more marriage and more fatherhood. Expecting child support payments in the absence of committed fatherhood is an elusive—and probably ultimately futile—goal.

- Create and disseminate for public discussion an annual measurement of our nation's marital health—an index of family strength based on such statistics as the following: percent of adults married, percent of first marriages intact, percent of births to married parents, percent of children living with their natural married parents, and percent of children living with two married parents.

To the general public:

- All of us need to consider ways in which we as individuals, on a daily basis, can demonstrate support for the marriages in which we are involved, as spouse, parent, child, or other relative.

Conclusion

We offer these ideas to the American public and especially to society's leaders who have the capacity and responsibility to strengthen marriage for a new generation of Americans. These recommendations are preliminary and imperfect and are certainly not the last word on the subject. Indeed, we hope this report will constitute the first round—an opening statement—in what we believe will be a new national debate about how to strengthen the essential institutions of marriage and the family. In our view, no domestic challenge of our era is more important than this one.

Notes

1. Kingsley Davis, "The Meaning and Significance of Marriage in Contemporary Society," in Kingsley Davis (ed.), *Contemporary Marriage* (New York: Russell Sage Foundation, 1985), 21.

2. Diane J. Macunovich and Richard J. Easterlin, "How Parents Have Coped: The Effect of Life Cycle Demographic Decisions on the Economic Status of Pre-School Age Children, 1964–87," *Population and Development Review* 16, no. 2 (June 1990): 301–25.

3. Victor R. Fuchs and Diane M. Reklis, "America's Children: Economic Perspectives and Policy Options," *Science* 255 (1992): 41–46.

4. The National Commission on the Role of the School and Community in Improving Adolescent Health, *Code Blue: Uniting For Healthier Youth* (Alexandria, VA: National Association of State Boards of Education, 1990).

5. National Commission on Children, *Beyond Rhetoric: A New American Agenda for Children and Families* (Washington, DC: 1991), 37.

6. U.S. Bureau of the Census, *Statistical Abstract of the United States: 1992* (Washington, DC: U.S. Government Printing Office), Table 719.

7. Daniel P. Moynihan, "Toward a Post-Industrial Social Policy," *The Public Interest* 96 (Summer 1989).

8. Nicholas Zill and Charlotte A. Schoenborn, "Developmental, Learning, and Emotional Problems: Health of Our Nation's Children, United States, 1988," *Advance Data*, National Center for Health Statistics, Publication #120, November 1990. Sara McLanahan and Gary Sandefur, *Growing Up with a Single Parent* (Cambridge, MA: Harvard University Press, 1994).

9. Bureau of Justice Statistics, *Survey of Youth in Custody, 1987* (Washington, DC: U.S. Department of Justice, 1988), 1.

10. Cited by Jean Bethke Elshtain in "Family Matters: The Plight of America's Children," *Christian Century*, July 14–21, 1993, 710.

11. William Julius Wilson, *The Truly Disadvantaged: The Inner City, the Underclass, and Public Policy* (Chicago: University of Chicago Press, 1987).

12. U.S. Bureau of the Census, "Poverty in the United States, 1992," Series P-60, No. 185 (Washington, DC: U.S. Government Printing Office, September 1993).

13. Dennis A. Ahlburg and Carol J. De Vita, "New Realities of the American Family," *Population Bulletin* 47, no. 2 (August 1992):12.

14. Ibid., 12.

15. Larry L. Bumpass, "What's Happening to the Family? Interactions Between Demographic and Institutional Change," *Demography* 27 (1990): 483–98; T. C. Martin and Larry L. Bumpass, "Recent Trends in Marital Disruption," *Demography* 26 (1989): 37–51.

16. Ahlburg, Op. cit., 16.

17. Donald J. Hernandez, *America's Children* (New York: Russell Sage Foundation, 1993), Table 31, 65; Arlene F. Saluter, *Marital Status and Living Arrangements: March 1993*, U.S. Bureau of the Census, Current Population Reports, Series P20–478 (Washington, DC: U.S. Government Printing Office, 1994), Table F, xi.

18. Calculation by Institute for American Values, New York.

19. Sara McLanahan & Larry L. Bumpass, "Intergenerational Consequences of Family Disruption," *American Journal of Sociology* 94 (1988): 130–52.

20. Research by Norval D. Glenn has shown that the probability that a marriage will be successful, in terms of being both intact and satisfactory to the spouses, at any given number of years after its beginning has declined substantially in recent years. See Norval D. Glenn, "The Family Values of Americans," Council on Families in America, Working Paper No. 7 (New York: Institute for American Values, 1991); and Norval D. Glenn, "The Re-Evaluation of Family Change by American Social Scientists," symposium paper (Melbourne, Australia: Committee for the International Year of the Family, Catholic Archdiocese of Melbourne, 1994).

21. Mellman and Lazarus polling firm for Massachusetts Mutual, June 1989, cited in Daniel Yankelovich, "How Changes in the Economy Are Reshaping American Values," in Henry J. Aaron, Thomas E. Mann, and Timothy Taylor (eds.), *Values and Public Policy* (Washington, DC: The Brookings Institution, 1994), 37.

22. Yankelovich, Ibid., 20.

23. L. Waite and L. A. Lillard, "Children and Marital Disruption," *American Journal of Sociology* 96 (1991): 930–953; T. B. Heaton, "Marital Stability Throughout the Child-Rearing Years," *Demography* 27 (1990): 55–63; S. P. Morgan, D. Lye, and G. Condran, "Sons, Daughters, and the Risk of Marital Disruption," *American Journal of Sociology* 94 (1988): 110–29.

24. Arland Thornton, "Changing Attitudes Toward Family Issues in the United States," *Journal of Marriage and the Family* 51 (1989): 873–93.

25. David Blankenhorn, *Fatherless America: Confronting Our Most Urgent Social Problem* (New York: Basic Books, 1995), 132.

26. See, for example, Henry B. Biller, *Fathers and Families: Paternal Factors in Child Development* (Westport, CT: Auburn House, 1993).

27. Kingsley Davis, Op. cit., 7–8.

28. John Locke, *Two Treatises on Government* (Cambridge, U.K.: Cambridge University Press, 1965; first published 1698), 319.

29. C. Owen Lovejoy, "The Origin of Man," *Science* 211, no. 4480 (1981): 341–50.

30. See, for example, Martin Daly and Margo Wilson, *Sex, Evolution and Behavior*, 2nd ed. (Belmont, CA: Wadsworth, 1983); and Helen E. Fisher, *Anatomy of Love* (New York: W. W. Norton, 1992).

31. Quoted in Daniel Patrick Moynihan, *Family and Nation* (San Diego, CA: Harcourt Brace, 1986), 169–70.

32. Martin Daly and Margo Wilson, *Homicide* (New York: Aldine de Gruyter, 1988), 83.

33. William J. Bennett, *The Index of Leading Cultural Indicators* (New York: Touchstone, 1994), i.

34. Ibid., i.

35. See, for example, Judith S. Wallerstein and Sandra Blakeslee, *The Good Marriage: How and Why Love Lasts* (New York: Houghton Mifflin, 1995).

The Council on Families in America

Co-Chairs:

Jean Bethke Elshtain, Laura Spelman Rockefeller Professor of Social and Political Ethics, Divinity School of the University of Chicago

David Popenoe, professor of Sociology and associate dean of the Faculty of Arts and Sciences, Rutgers University

Members:

Steven Bayme, director, William Petschek National Jewish Family Center, American Jewish Committee

Don S. Browning, Alexander Campbell Professor of Religious Ethics and the Social Sciences, Divinity School of the University of Chicago; director, Religion, Culture, and Family Project, sponsored by the Lilly Endowment, Inc., Allan C. Carlson, president, The Rockford Institute

William A. Galston, professor of Public Affairs, University of Maryland; director, Institute for Philosophy and Public Policy, University of Maryland; formerly deputy assistant to the president for domestic policy, White House Domestic Policy Council of President Bill Clinton (January 1993 to May 1995)

Mary Ann Glendon, Learned Hand Professor of Law, Harvard University Law School

Norval D. Glenn, Ashbel Smith Professor of Sociology and Stiles Professor in American Studies, University of Texas at Austin

James A. Hefner, president, Tennessee State University at Nashville

Sylvia Ann Hewlett, president, National Parenting Association

Leon R. Kass, Addie Clark Harding Professor in the College and the Committee on Social Thought, University of Chicago

Ray Marshall, Audre and Bernard Rapoport Centennial Chair in Economics and Public Affairs, LBJ School of Public Affairs, University of Texas; former United States Secretary of Labor

Judith Martin, novelist; author of the "Miss Manners" syndicated column and books

Martin E. Marty, Fairfax M. Cone Distinguished Service Professor of the History of Modern Christianity, Divinity School of the University of Chicago

Theodora Ooms, director, Family Impact Seminar

William Raspberry, nationally syndicated columnist for the *Washington Post*

Gloria G. Rodriguez, founder, president and C.E.O. of *AVANCE* in San Antonio, Texas

Judith Wallerstein, founder and director, Center for the Family in Transition, Corte Madera, California

Project Director:

David Blankenhorn, president, Institute for American Values

Project Associate Director:

Barbara Dafoe Whitehead, writer and social analyst

Index

Contributors

David Blankenhorn is president of the Institute for American Values. He is the author of *Fatherless America: Confronting Our Most Urgent Social Problem* and the chief editor of *Rebuilding the Nest: A New Commitment to the American Family*. He serves as Chairman of the National Fatherhood Initiative.

Don S. Browning is the Alexander Campbell Professor of Religious Ethics and the Social Sciences at the Divinity School of the University of Chicago and the director of the Religion, Culture, and Family Project sponsored by the Lilly Endowment, Inc. He is the author most recently of *Religious Thought and the Modern Psychologies* and *A Fundamental Practical Theology*.

Moira Eastman lectures at Australian Catholic University. Consultant to government and non-government organizations on the development and evaluation of family-focused programs, she has written and spoken widely on issues affecting families both in Australia and worldwide. Her books include *Family, the Vital Factor: The Key to Society's Survival* and *We're OK: Secrets of Happy Families*.

Jean Bethke Elshtain is the Laura Spelman Rockefeller Professor of Social and Political Ethics at the Divinity School of the University of Chicago and the author of numerous books and essays on women, politics, and the family. She was a Guggenheim Fellow in 1991–1992. Her books include *Public Man, Private Woman*, *Women and War*, and *Democracy on Trial*. Professor Elshtain serves as co-chair of the Council on Families in America.

Maggie Gallagher, a syndicated columnist, is Senior Research Associate at the Institute for American Values. She is the author of *Enemies of Eros:*

How the Sexual Revolution Is Killing Family, Marriage and Sex and *The Abolition of Marriage.*

William A. Galston is professor in the School of Public Affairs at the University of Maryland and Director of the University's Institute for Philosophy and Public Policy. From January 1993 to May 1995 he served as deputy assistant to the president for domestic policy on the White House Domestic Policy Council of President Bill Clinton. Professor Galston is the author of six books and numerous articles on American politics, public policy, political theory, and family issues in the United States, most recently *Liberal Purposes* and *Virtue.*

Janet Zollinger Giele is professor and director of the Family and Children's Policy Center at the Heller Graduate School of Social Welfare, Brandeis University. Her work centers around the changing lives of women and the growth of family policy. She is author most recently of *Two Paths to Women's Equality: Temperance, Suffrage, and the Origins of Modern Feminism.*

Norval D. Glenn is the Ashbel Smith Professor of Sociology and Stiles Professor in American Studies at the University of Texas at Austin. The former editor of the *Journal of Family Issues*, he is a widely published and nationally recognized scholar in the areas of marriage, family life, social stratification, and methods of survey data analysis.

David Popenoe is professor of sociology and associate dean of the Faculty of Arts and Sciences at Rutgers University. His widely acclaimed book on the family is *Disturbing the Nest: Family Change and Decline in Modern Societies.* He is author most recently of *Life Without Father: Compelling New Evidence that Fatherhood and Marriage Are Indispensable for the Good of Children and Society.* He serves as co-chair of the Council on Families in America.

Milton C. Regan, Jr. is professor of law, Georgetown University Law Center. He is the author of *Family Law and the Pursuit of Intimacy* and several articles on family law and social theory.

Carl E. Schneider is professor of law at the University of Michigan Law School, Ann Arbor. He has written extensively in the areas of family, medical, and constitutional law and is the author (with Margaret F. Brinig) of *An Invitation to Family Law.*

Arland Thornton is professor of sociology at the University of Michigan Department of Sociology, Institute for Social Research and Population

Studies Center. His research focuses on trends, causes, and consequences of marriage, cohabitation, divorce, gender roles, adolescent sexuality, and intergenerational relationships in the United States, Taiwan, and Nepal.

Robert S. Weiss is director of the Work and Family Research Unit at the University of Massachusetts in Boston. His books include *Marital Separation* and *Staying the Course: The Emotional Life and Social Situation of Men Successful in Their Work.*

Barbara Dafoe Whitehead writes frequently on issues of family and child well-being for *The Atlantic Monthly* and other publications. She is presently working on a book on divorce in America.

DATE DUE

APR 0 8 2002			
JUN 2 0 2002			
AUG 1 1 2002			
NOV 2 4 2007			

Stand and Deliver

Stand and Deliver

A History of Pinch-Hitting

PAUL VOTANO

McFarland & Company, Inc., Publishers
Jefferson, North Carolina, and London

LIBRARY OF CONGRESS CATALOGUING-IN-PUBLICATION DATA

Votano, Paul, 1929–
    Stand and deliver: a history of pinch-hitting / Paul Votano.
      p. cm.
    Includes bibliographical references and index.

    ISBN 0-7864-1588-6 (softcover : 50# alkaline paper) ∞

    1. Pinch hitting (Baseball)— United States— History.
    2. Baseball players— United States.   I. Title.
    GV869.V68 2003
    796.357'26 — dc21

                         2003007864

British Library cataloguing data are available

Cover photograph: Cy Williams, Courtesy Baseball Hall of Fame
Library, Cooperstown, NY.

Manufactured in the United States of America

*McFarland & Company, Inc., Publishers
  Box 611, Jefferson, North Carolina 28640
   www.mcfarlandpub.com*

Lovingly, to
Paul, Donna, Greg, Theresa and Tommy

Contents

Introduction

Some of the most successful pinch-hitters in history have actually loathed the role. Readers will find evidence of this as they continue reading.

Few baseball fans pay much attention to substitute batters, particularly since the rate of failure is so high. Consequently, those who come off the bench — often in critical situations — evoke very little respect on the whole. When they succeed, they are instant heroes. But their success, like all fame, is fleeting and soon forgotten.

Consider the fact that of the more than 250 players inducted into the Hall of Fame, only four — Joe Cronin, Johnny Mize, Enos Slaughter and Red Schoendienst — were effective pinch hitters. And even this quartet is best known for their accomplishments as everyday players and for the strength of their offensive numbers. It is worth noting that their performances as pinch-hitters, while significant, occurred primarily in the twilight of their careers.

That being said, when the names of people like Smoky Burgess, Jerry Lynch and Manny Mota come to mind, baseball historians and avid followers of the game all agree that these men's contributions were vital to the success of their teams. Clubs that have been fortunate enough to have reliable, consistent emergency batsmen on their rosters were indeed blessed.

Pinch-hitting is not for the faint of heart. Think about how difficult it must be for a player to spend the major portion of a game on the bench, come into a game cold and be called upon to provide a crucial at-bat.

More often than not, the leading or tying run is either on base or represented by the pinch-hitter himself as he coolly struts up to the plate. To

1

the opposition, he may symbolize the final out of the ballgame. Is that a pressure cooker situation or what?

What kind of player does it take to produce as a pinch-hitter? How does a player prepare for his one and only turn at bat while playing the waiting game in the dugout?

Some of the greatest hitters of all time were ineffective pinch-hitters. Ty Cobb, for instance, with a lifetime batting average of .367, hit only .247 in the pinch. Babe Ruth and Ted Williams batted .200 and .271 respectively as substitute batters. Conversely, some of the better hitters over the years have been pitchers: Red Ruffing, Don Newcombe and Red Lucas were all capable batsmen in the clutch.

Perhaps former manager Ralph Houk said it best: "Some of the game's greatest haven't been able to handle it. Yet men with .220 batting averages have been murder when sent up off the bench. I'll tell you this much: It's one of the toughest pressure jobs in baseball because most of the time it means the ballgame."[1]

The pinch-hitter's role compares favorably to that of a relief pitcher, particularly that of a closer. Both men usually come into a contest late, oftentimes with the game on the line. And like the pinch-hitter, the reliever doesn't get as much credit for the outcome of the game as he probably should. As a group, relievers earn less respect than their teammates. I learned this first-hand when doing research for an earlier book I wrote on the history of relief pitching called *Late and Close*.

In fact, a review of the lists of the 100 greatest players of the twentieth century compiled from the votes of writers, players, managers and fans shows that only three relievers—Hoyt Wilhelm, Rollie Fingers and Dennis Eckersley—consistently made most of the lists. Yet even that outstanding trio, among the greatest relievers ever, placed only in the nineties on most of those lists. Ask any of their teammates how far they would have gotten without those bullpen aces.

The same holds true for pinch-hitters—and so this book examines in considerable detail the scores of accomplishments and strengths of these heretofore unsung heroes. Also explored herein are little known facts about this extraordinary group of baseball players. With this book, perhaps pinch-hitters will at last receive the recognition they so richly deserve.

1

The Makeup of an Effective Pinch-Hitter

There probably has never been a player in a major league uniform who relished the idea of becoming a pinch-hitter. From the time that substitute batters first came into being in the 1890s, youngsters who dreamed of becoming big leaguers usually fantasized about being an everyday position player and getting at least three or four at-bats a game. Riding the pine until called upon late in a ball game to deliver a key hit has to be the furthest thought from the minds of would-be major leaguers. However, conditions beyond a player's control may arise that can typecast him forever as a part-timer.

Sometimes players reach the big leagues with a reputation. For example, some are not perceived to be good enough to earn a regular spot in a club's daily lineup. These situations might develop because scouts have branded them as less-than-adequate fielders. On the other hand, their bats may be considered sufficient to keep them at the major league level, but only as occasional backups to starters or as pinch-hitters.

One of baseball's most successful pinch-hitters early on was outfielder Eddie Murphy, who logged eleven years in the majors with the Philadelphia Athletics, Chicago White Sox and Pittsburgh Pirates. Murphy was one of the few who actually enjoyed being called upon as an emergency batsman. "A good pinch-hitter needs to have the same qualifications as a good all-round batter, with a little something extra thrown in," he was once quoted as saying.[1] "That something extra I would call coolness under fire, or if you prefer, ability to rise to the occasion. There are some men who never do themselves justice in a crisis. They seem to get flustered and go all to pieces. There are others who react to an emergency and do even better than common. They are the men who are natural pinch-hitters.

"I consider that my experience as a lead-off man has helped my batting in the pinch. A lead-off man is supposed to look them over, to make a pitcher work and not to bite at bad balls. To be perfectly fair, I must admit that luck plays an important part in pinch-hitting to an even greater degree than it does in ordinary batting. For the pinch-hitter faces the pitcher only once and his trial is quickly over. The thing which I most object to in pinch-hitting isn't the tense situation with men on bases and important results at stake. It is rather that I am called upon to act pretty much under manager's orders. It is difficult enough to hit safely under any circumstances. To do so under orders is still more of a task."[2]

Gavvy Cravath, a renowned slugger of his day and a teammate of Murphy's from 1912 to 1915 with the Philadelphia Phillies, was reluctant to give pinch-hitters too much acclaim. "A good pinch-hitter is a valuable man to have on a ball club and can win a lot of games provided he is lucky enough to come through with a hit," he once said.[3] "But I do not wish to give the pinch-hitter more credit than is coming to him. Perhaps the man he displaced in the lineup would have done equally well. For all that, I rather like to pinch-hit."[4]

George "Possum" Whitted, a utility player with five different National League teams including the 1914 "Miracle" Braves, believed that average players were often selected to pinch-hit for significant reasons. He put it this way: "The manager would prefer a mediocre player on his team, a man who is always trying and improving himself, always working for the club, to a batter of much larger natural gifts who was lazy or indifferent or dissipated and who wasn't living up to the full possibilities which were in him."[5]

A lot of successful pinch-hitters have actually despised the job. While they accepted the fact that it kept many of them in the majors, they remained unhappy with the role. One of the best of all time, Jerry Lynch, who played for the Cincinnati Reds and Pittsburgh Pirates, was very vocal about his hostility to the task.

Lynch was once quoted as saying that he was only up once per game while "the fellow playing regularly can strike out in the first inning, pop out in the fourth, single or double in a run or two in the sixth, he's judged to have a good day. With us there's no second chance."[6] Still, he followed the progress of the game intensely with a "how-does-this-figure-to-affect-me" concern.[7]

John Vander Wal, who made the New York Yankees his sixth major league team in 2002, will at first tell everyone listening that he hates pinch-hitting. "I guess I really don't hate it," he will also say, amending his knee-jerk statement. "But it's a job in which you get one shot in a game. A lot of times, you have runners in scoring position and the majority of times, you're going to fail.

"I feel it's the toughest part of baseball but it's kept me in the game for a long time," he says. "It's tough mentally. You look at the starting players, they're getting four at-bats a game. You're pinch-hitting, not playing and you may get four at-bats a week. That's a big difference, man. I mean, a big difference trying to feel comfortable at the plate."[8] And this from a man who owns the major league single-season record with 28 pinch-hits, set during the strike-shortened 1995 season as a member of the Colorado Rockies.

Bob Hale, one of those reputed good-hit, no-field players, who spent several seasons in the mid–1950s and early '60s pinch-hitting for the Baltimore Orioles, Cleveland Indians and Yankees, was deeply concerned about the one-at-bat-per-game syndrome. "As a pinch-hitter you only get one crack and you should at least wait for your ball," said Hale, a batter famous for leaving the dugout swinging.[9] "A pinch-hitter has his ups and downs just like anyone, only he doesn't get a chance to come back as soon. The hardest thing is conditioning yourself mentally — you have to take the sweet and the sour. I hate to strike out and I seldom do. I just hit the ball where it's pitched."[10]

It is said that Vic Wertz's palms began to sweat around the fifth inning of a ball game. Lee Walls would sit on the bench imagining himself already at bat. Although he was rarely called on to pinch-hit, Mickey Mantle was openly critical of the assignment. "I don't like to pinch-hit. I never did."[11] (Mantle only batted .236 — 25-for-106 — off the bench, but he had seven pinch-hit home runs.) Richie Ashburn, who also pinch-hit only occasionally, agreed. "You can have it. I no more get off the bench than I'm two strikes behind."[12]

Harry Lee "Peanuts" Lowrey of the Chicago Cubs also hated pinch-hitting when he first assumed that role. Later he came to approach it with devotion and self-assurance. Lowrey was the type of player who believed he would always get a hit, at least until he didn't.

"I knew just how hard my job was, which was plenty," Lowrey said. "I was supposed to get a hit; the pitcher was supposed to get me out. One of us was bound to win."[13]

Lowrey had a plan. "What I do when I get up there depends on how they're playing me and if we have a man on third," he once told a reporter.

"If we need a fly ball, I swing for a long one but if the infield's pulled in I try to drop one over their heads."[14]

Davey Lopes, a former manager of the Milwaukee Brewers, is one person who appreciated the difficulties involved in pinch-hitting. "Most regular players can't do it," he said. "You don't appreciate it until you're put into those situations. If you have a guy who doesn't seem to be affected by it, you like to have him on your team.

"You can't be productive if you don't accept the role. If you fight it, you're not going to be able to do it. If you're trying to get the attention of the manager and the coaching staff and you have a negative attitude about what they're asking you to do, you're going to get their attention but it's not going to be the way you want. From our standpoint, it's difficult to pull guys into other situations if they aren't having success in the first place."[15]

On the other hand, Johnny Mize, Mantle's teammate on the Yankees during the 1949 to 1953 world championship years, really enjoyed being a pinch-hitter. He believed that it was easier than batting regularly. Mize felt that a pinch-hitter usually got better pitches to hit than a starter. "The pitchers were in a jam by the time I got in there," he said. "The pressure was on them, not me. They couldn't fool around. They had to throw strikes."[16]

Yankees teammate Hank Bauer thought Mize was the best pinch-hitter of all time. "Mize was the ideal pinch-hitter because of his temperament," Bauer said. "He never got excited. He had an abnormal ability to stay calm and to respond to pressure. A single or a homer was all the same to Big John, who took them as they came."[17]

John Blanchard, who once shared catching duties on the Yankees with Yogi Berra and Elston Howard, was not entirely content as a pinch-hitter. "I say nobody has it tougher anywhere," he said. "I pray all the way to the plate, and then hope like the devil I connect."[18]

Veteran players who stay in the game long after they have stopped being regulars have to adjust to their new role. Dave Philley, another formidable emergency batsman, was one. "It took me a couple of years to adjust to pinch-hitting. The toughest thing is learning to sit on the bench. Everyone wants to play. It's a natural thing. But I learned to sit. No one knows the pitchers like the pinch-hitters. We watch 'em like hawks."[19]

Philley also believed that substitute batting is an acquired capability. "I don't know about other guys," he told reporter Bill Madden, "but pinch-hitting was something I had to learn."[20]

Philley, who claimed he had the ability to bear down and relax at the same time, also said: "When I went over to the National League, I kept a log on all their pitchers. I'd sit on the bench and take notes as to what pitches they threw for strikes and what pitches they went to in jams. I also took the attitude that I had the upper hand as a pinch-hitter. Even though I might be coming up there cold, the pitcher was probably in some sort of trouble if they were sending up a pinch-hitter. "Another thing I did was stay in shape. I always marveled at Smoky Burgess, who did nothing but pinch-hit at the end. I liked to play once or twice a week to stay sharp.

"I also learned something from Ted Williams—fingertip pushups. Did fifteen a day for the last ten years of my career and never felt like my bat was getting heavy."[21]

Former Boston Red Sox manager, Pinky Higgins wanted Philley and his other pinch-hitters to come off the bench swinging. Most pinch-hitters share this view. "You've got only one chance," Blanchard said. "So you can't take the time to be giving the pitches the once-over-lightly."[22]

Manny Mota of the Los Angeles Dodgers, whose all-time career record of 150 pinch-hits stood for 20 years until broken by Lenny Harris of the New York Mets in 2001, had a nine-step program that he used to prepare for his average of one time at bat every five days.

(1) Get to the park early and hit; an infrequent hitter needs a lot of batting practice to stay sharp.

(2) Go to the bullpen once the game begins and take additional batting practice, using the machine and the cage.

(3) Return to the bench by the third inning to start studying the pitcher.

(4) Study the target the catcher gives the pitcher and the way the infielders are positioned.

(5) Keep a book in your head on the bullpen pitchers; they are the ones you will be facing most often.

(6) If the possibility starts to develop that you might be called to hit by the seventh inning, go into the clubhouse and practice swinging and get your legs loose.

(7) Think about making contact and not swinging hard.

(8) Think positively; the pitcher doesn't know you may be stale.

(9) Study umpires' habits; for instance, some will give the hitter the low pitch, others will give it to the pitcher.[23]

Mota teamed with another effective veteran pinch-hitter, Vic Davalillo, from 1977 to 1980, to form one of the most potent pinch-hitting tandems ever. First baseman Steve Garvey, who played with them at the time, said of the Dodgers' Dynamic Duo: "They know the game in their own way. They know exactly what the pitcher is throwing. They know

Manny Mota once hit safely 10 or more times in six consecutive seasons as a pinch-hitter. (Courtesy of the National Baseball Hall of Fame Library, Cooperstown, New York.)

who is in the other bullpen and what he will throw when he gets to the mound."[24]

Dave Hansen of the present-day Dodgers has benefited from Mota's experience because the latter is now a coach with the club. "I don't think pinch-hitting has changed at all," says Hansen. "As far as the mental part of it and the preparation, it's exactly the same. When Manny played, and when I play now, you better put the bat on the ball. You better have your best swing at that particular moment because you don't know when you will get the next at-bat."[25]

Hansen agrees with Mota that pinch-hitters have to know the plate umpire's strike zone. "He may be calling a low strike or a high one," says Hansen. "You also have to know what a pitcher is getting over. What if he's not getting the breaking ball over? OK, put it aside. You have the little things to take into account. You have to look at pitch one until the end of the game. You might be the last at-bat ... So you are on pins and needles the whole night. Once you learn to handle that, then you are able to relax a little.

"We're not trying to hit the ball out," continues Hansen. "All you can control is how you hit that ball. All you can do is see the ball, hit it as hard as you can and know with confidence that you are going to put your best swing on the ball. I try to put the ball up the middle. Sometimes it goes out.

"Manny has kept me level-headed. It's been a heck of a ride. At first I wasn't experienced enough to handle the pinch-hitting role mentally. We are at a point now where Manny can say just a few words to me: 'Slow this down or see the ball.' I've been the luckiest guy in this role. It's not fun. It's not easy, but after all these years, I enjoy it."[26]

Many pinch-hitters quiz their teammates on what the pitcher is throwing most, and go to bat set for it. Still, Smoky Burgess and Vic Wertz, when pinch-hitting, would compulsively go for the first pitch; the pitchers knew it too and fed them low. Undeterred, Burgess said: "You're either going to hit it or not — simple."[27]

Outfielder Del Unser, who was an everyday player for years, also had to become accustomed to his new role as a part-time player and emergency batsman. "Can't be picky when you're pinch-hitting," he said. "Like when you're working a pitcher to see what he's got. You take your shot at him when you get it."[28]

Pinch-hitters can be categorized. There are the slap hitters who can be counted on to make contact and spray the ball around. They can also usually be called upon to advance the runners with a well-placed bunt.

Then there are the power hitters who are needed to supply the long ball, be it a home run, a long fly to bring home a base runner from third or to rocket a drive in the gap to clear the bases. So not only is the pinch-hitter a specialist summoned at a crucial time, but one who may be expected to provide a particular type of hit.

Pinch-hitters are also valuable if they are fast enough to reduce the chances of a potential double play, or if the scheduled hitter is especially inept against a particular side-armer, for example. They are also employed most often when they hit the opposite way from the opposing pitcher, such as a left-handed batter vs. a right-handed pitcher and vice versa. Switch hitters such as Philley and Red Schoendienst were especially valuable because of their flexibility.

Gene Freese, a journeyman infielder during the 1950s, became an explosive, long ball pinch-hitter late in his baseball life. In fact, after belting only seven home runs with two teams in 1958, he smacked five as a substitute batter in 1959 alone.

"The element of surprise has a lot to do with it," Freese said at the time. "No one expects a batter to come off the bench cold and pile into that first pitch. Even a guy like Lew Burdette figures he can get the edge on a hitter by throwing across a quick strike and then going to work on him. But I hit three of my first pinch-homers on the first pitch. They were good pitches, as good as or better than I'm likely to get later, so why shouldn't I swing?"[29]

Paul Richards, who managed successfully in the majors for many years, thought that choosing the right man as a substitute batter was serious business. "Most managers try to type the available pinch-hitters on their clubs," he once wrote in *Sports Illustrated*. "For example, one fellow may be better leading off, while another may be better equipped to hit a fly ball with a runner on third and less than two out. Still another available player might be more desirable in moving a runner from second to third with no outs."[30]

Richards was adamant about a manager knowing who his best hitter off the bench might be and to have him ready for emergencies. "That hitter should be a fellow who can be counted upon to deliver a game-winning hit. Of course, he should not be used too early in the game, or even, say, as a lead-off man in the eighth inning when the club is three runs behind. A base hit could be wasted that might still win the game in the ninth inning. A good hitter who may be used late in the game to pinch-hit should never be used as a pinch-runner."[31]

Richards contended that even in those rare circumstances when a manager is fortunate enough to have a pinch-hitter available to whom it does not matter who the pitcher is, he must still be careful, for instance, not to send up a fastball hitter against a pitcher with an outstanding change-up and vice versa.

"On the Chicago White Sox for several years, outfielder Eddie Stewart became the hitter we picked to move a man from second to third base with no men out," Richards noted. "Nine out of 10 times, even if he failed to get a hit, his action would move the man from second to third and put him in good scoring position with one out."[32]

When Leo Durocher managed the New York Giants, he would always use Bill Rigney to pinch-hit to loft a fly ball to the outfield with a runner on third and less than two out. The St. Louis Cardinals' Johnny Hopp became a specialist at batting with runners on the corners and less than two out. "His speed of foot made it virtually impossible to double him on a ground ball," declared Richards. "Often he would merely slap the ball on the ground far enough away from the pitcher to allow the runner to score and, of course, the opposition would have no chance to complete a vital double play."[33]

Another former manager, Bob Scheffing, put the value of an effective pinch-hitter this way: "What I want in a pinch is someone who can start a rally or keep one going. I plain don't care if they walk, hit or get hit, as long as they get on base."[34]

The score of the game affects the mood of the pinch-hitter. "Who cares what happens when you're six runs behind?" Richie Ashburn once asked rhetorically.[35] Putting the pressure on can help pinch-hitters accomplish great things. To Jerry Lynch a tight game was everything: "Give me the ninth inning with a man on, two outs and my team down one run, man, I lap that up."[36]

Ed Kranepool, who was Joe Torre's first choice off the bench when he managed the New York Mets, listed the disadvantages of pinch-hitting this way: "Number one, when you come to bat, your team is usually losing. Number two, it means the opposing pitcher is having a good day. Number three, it's usually the toughest time of the game to hit, often your team's only opportunity to score, or its last chance."[37]

Formerly the team's regular first baseman, Kranepool would rather have continued to play every day but he accepted his role because his manager thought it was the best use for the veteran on a team of young players. Like Dave Philley, Kranepool also thought that playing occasionally to stay sharp was essential for a pinch-hitter. Nevertheless, even that was not always possible.

"You have to prepare yourself mentally to pinch-hit," Kranepool once told Phil Pepe of the *New York Daily News*.[38] "You just have to accept what you're going to do and do it in a positive manner. You've got to be aggressive at bat. If the situation calls for a base hit, you have to get a base hit. I know the manager is not sending me up there to get a walk, so I go up swinging at the first strike I see.

"I start getting ready about the fifth inning. I'll take a bat and go into the clubhouse and take some swings. Then, in the seventh, I'll do some stretching exercises. A lot of people think when they see you coming to bat in the ninth, it's the first time you've held a bat all game. That's not true. I do everything I can to loosen up and be ready when Joe (Torre) calls on me. I don't want to let myself be surprised."[39]

Kranepool usually wasn't surprised. He watched the game aware of the situation and he knew, as the crowd did, when it was time to grab a bat and go up and hit.

Like most veteran pinch-hitters, experience and patience played a significant role in Kranepool's success, a player who got his first pinch-hit as a 19-year-old, his second year in the big leagues. As the club's primary pinch-hitter at the age of 33, Kranepool declared: "It's an interesting thing about pinch-hitting. It can extend your career if you're good at it. But it can shorten your career, too, if you're not."[40]

The Arizona Diamondbacks' David Dellucci is not one to divulge his secrets. "A lot of the success I can attribute to my makeup and how I take it on the inside," he has said. "You're at a disadvantage, you're the under-dog when you pinch-hit. You come in not necessarily warmed up 100 per-cent. You're usually facing a guy that throws 99 miles an hour with an unbelievable slider. I want to be that guy that overcomes those odds. I want to be in the game when the game's on the line. I want to be at the plate when the winning run is on second, or I'm the winning run at the plate. I want to be the guy that basically has the game in his hands. So I'm not afraid of going out there in that situation."[41]

Like so many successful pinch-hitters, Dellucci has his own method of preparation: "In the fifth inning, I go to the clubhouse and start swing-ing the bat. We have TV in every room and I'm always watching the start-ing pitcher. It's like I have to be my own manager in that I usually know who they're bringing in to pitch at certain points in the game and who I may face and what he may throw in any situation. You have to be ready physically and very strong mentally to succeed. Most important is an awful lot of luck. The bad thing about pinch-hitting is if you don't get the job done, you may not have an opportunity to go into a game for three or four days. I can't take that at-bat and carry it around for the next three days."[42]

Jose Morales, who made 445 official appearances as a pinch-hitter during a 12-year career in the 1970s and early 1980s, claimed he never felt the pressure of his one at-bat in any given game. "I've done it so often and for such a long time, I don't consider it a pressure job," he told an inter-viewer back in 1978.[43]

"I've always had success at coming off the bench to hit but I really don't know why," Morales claimed at the time. "I think you've got to love to hit, and I do. And I believe you must always be ready, and I always am. For instance, when you pinch-hit, you may only see one fastball. Well, when it comes, you better be ready to hit it. You can't let that pitch get past you."[44]

 Morales felt that he could not be seriously concerned if the pitcher he was to face was the opposing team's best reliever. "I can't think that way," he declared. "If you go to the plate thinking the pitcher is that good, there is no way you're going to get a hit. You have to have a positive attitude. So I bat thinking I'm going to get a hit every time. No one can bat 1.000. But I try. Then, if the pitcher does get me out, I have to admit he was the better man that time. But he doesn't destroy my confidence. I still feel I'll get home the next time."[45]

2

1876–1899:
The Pinch-Hitting Pioneers

Prior to 1891, the rules of organized baseball permitted substitute batters to be inserted into games only under emergency conditions, notably for injuries. Baseball historian Al Kermisch, in an article titled *From a Researchers' Notebook*, wrote that while no trace can be found in any box score, the first emergency batsman ever may have surfaced as far back as the first month of the National League's maiden season in 1876.

Kermisch's piece, which appeared in 1990 in the *Baseball Research Journal*, indicated that in a game played at St. Louis on Saturday, May 13, 1876, the Cincinnati Reds were beaten, 11-0, on a two-hitter by the home team's George Washington Bradley. The author claimed that in the first inning, Cincinnati's catcher, Dave Pearson, hurt his hand. Pearson was shifted over to shortstop while Amos Booth moved over from shortstop to third base and Will Foley went from third base to catcher.

"In the second inning," Kermisch wrote, "it was determined that Pearson could not continue and after a delay of ten minutes, Bobby Clack (strictly a bench player) was sent up to bat for Pearson and struck out."[1]

Others may have appeared as substitute batters between 1876 and the inception of the new rule in the 1892 season, but baseball reporting in those days was quite limited. Consequently, it was rather common for substitutes to be left out of box scores. In fact, the National League never credited either a pinch-hitter or pinch-runner with a game played until 1912. On the other hand, the American League recognized these players beginning with games played in 1907.

14

Substitutions in baseball were first legalized before the start of the 1889 season. Each team was permitted to designate one player to replace a starter at the beginning of an inning. Most managers selected pitchers for this type of substitution and, consequently, these players would pinch-hit and then stay in the game to pitch. In 1890, the rule was changed to allow two designees to be named and inserted into a team's lineup at any point in the game. In the following year, teams were allowed to include substitute batters in their lineups for other than emergency situations.

At first managers were reluctant to use pinch-hitters. It took nearly two decades before the practice became more extensive. The problem was that during the 1890s many teams only had three pitchers on their rosters and, at most, only one or two substitute position players.

Another distinguished baseball historian, the late L. Robert Davids, founder and former president of the Society for American Baseball Research (SABR), identified several instances of emergency batsmen being used in 1891, the year before the rules change officially took effect. Seven pinch-hitters were employed in both the National League and the rival American Association in 1891 and not one of them could deliver a base hit. According to the *Baseball Encyclopedia* a pitcher, "Happy Jack" Stivetts of the St. Louis Braves, batted twice as a pinch-hitter that season without success.

Among the handful of players used as emergency batsmen in 1891 was Boston's Bobby Lowe, a right-handed hitting utility player from Pittsburgh. The 5' 10", 150-pounder was a rookie in 1891 and on May 1, his first time in a major league uniform, he was inserted as a substitute batter. Lowe proceeded to pop out to short in the eighth inning against Monte Ward's Brooklyn Bridegrooms. He then stayed in to pitch in the ninth and surrendered two runs in a game that had long since been decided as the Bridegrooms ultimately prevailed, 13-6.

Lowe, who went on to play in 1,824 games in the big leagues during an 18-year career, never pitched in the majors again. He hit .273 for his career, including only one hit in nine pinch-hit at-bats for a .111 mark. Lowe died in Detroit on December 8, 1951 at the age of 83.

For many years, most baseball historians were convinced that John Joseph "Dirty Jack" Doyle of the old Cleveland Spiders was the first substitute batter to ever get a base hit. SABR, however, has since revealed that two pinch-hits actually preceded Doyle's feat in 1892.

The first one took place on April 28, 1892. Visiting Philadelphia trailed Chicago, 4-2, in the ninth inning with one out. Philadelphia manager Harry Wright called on a journeyman infielder, switch-hitting Charles Thomas "Princeton Charlie" Reilly, to bat for the pitcher, Wilfred "Kid"

Tom Daly was the first major leaguer to hit a home run in a pinch-hitting role. (Courtesy of the National Baseball Hall of Fame Library, Cooperstown, New York.)

Carsey. After getting — as the *Chicago Tribune* described it — "a nasty rap on the fingers from a pitched ball,"[2] the 5' 11", 190-pound Reilly promptly drilled a single off Chicago's "Wild Bill" Hutchison. However, the game ended two outs later with no further damage inflicted and Reilly still on base.

The *Tribune* attached no particular significance to the event to the point of misidentifying Reilly as "Kelly" in the box score. The paper explained, "As he played no position in the game, he is given none in the (box) score."[3] The *Philadelphia Inquirer* failed to even mention the New Brunswick, New Jersey native's hit or even put his name in the box score.

Reilly pinch-hit officially only twice more during the 1892 season and managed one more base hit in those appearances. In his remaining four seasons in the major leagues, he was never called upon to pinch-hit again. A career .250 hitter, Reilly passed away in Los Angeles on December 16, 1937, at the age of 82.

A more dramatic pinch-hit was produced a couple of weeks later on May 14 when the Brooklyn ball club — known as "Ward's Wonders" after manager John M. Ward — was playing on the road in Boston with over 6,000 fans in attendance. The *Boston Journal* reported: "Boston could do nothing in the ninth. Ward meant business in his turn at bat and instead of sending Collins [the left fielder] to bat, he substituted Tom Daly. Hardly had the spectators recognized the newcomer when he lifted one of [right-hander John] Clarkson's slow balls over the left field fence and the game was tied at 6-6."[4]

The Collins referred to in the game was Hub Collins, who was ill and replaced at bat in the ninth. The switch-hitting Daly's home run — he hit it left-handed off the first pitch he saw — sent the game into extra innings. It did not change the eventual result, however, an 8-7 victory for Boston. Brooklyn had gone ahead by scoring a run in the top half of the tenth, but Boston came back with two more in the bottom of the inning to win. An ironic twist to this first pinch-hit home run ever was the fact that Collins, the man for whom the Brooklyn-born Daly had hit, had typhoid fever. He never played in another game and died a week later.

Daly, originally a catcher, was thought to be a good receiver but lacked an adequate arm so Chicago dealt him to Washington in 1889. He moved to the infield when Brooklyn acquired him the following year. He was the club's regular second baseman for most of his 12 years in Brooklyn. Daly went to the Chicago White Sox in 1902 and moved on to Cincinnati in the middle of 1903. After his dramatic home run in 1892, he was called upon to be an emergency batsman only once more and failed to hit safely. A lifetime .278 hitter, Daly died in Brooklyn on October 29, 1939, at the age of 73.

Although SABR's information about the Reilly and Daly hits contradicts the long-held notion that Jack Doyle was the first player to get a hit as a substitute batter because Doyle's debut as a pinch-hitter on June 7, 1892, came some six weeks after Reilly and Daly had pinch-hit successfully. The colorful Doyle, a native of Killorglin, Ireland, was a member of the Cleveland Spiders when player-manager Pat Tebeau summoned him to bat for pitcher George Davies. It was the ninth inning of a game at long-departed Eastern Park in Brooklyn. Until that point, William Franklin "Bond Hilly Billy" Hart, a right-hander, had shut out the Spiders. Hart retired Jimmy McAleer to begin the inning, but catcher Jack O'Connor rapped a single. Doyle, the backup catcher, was sent up to bat for Davies.

According to the legendary sportswriter, Arthur Mann, the right-handed hitting Doyle, a 5' 9", 155-pounder, "hiked up his pants, spat on his hands, dug his toes into the dirt and passed up the first pitch. Then he whacked a clean single into right center advancing O'Connor to third. Hart eventually forced in a run with a pass to Jake Virtue with the bases full, but won the game, 2-1."[5]

Doyle believed he merited the distinction of being called the game's first pinch-hitter. He died thinking he should have been acknowledged as such. *The Sporting News* continued to advance the myth after his death at the age of 89 on New Year's Eve of 1958. In its obituary, the paper said that Doyle held the "historic distinction" of being organized baseball's first emergency hitter, citing the former player himself.[6]

"It happened in Brooklyn," the paper quoted Doyle as saying, "and I hit a single which won the game."[7] As indicated above, while his hit started a rally of sorts, Brooklyn wound up beating Cleveland, 2-1.

Doyle, who managed the New York club for part of the 1895 season, was among the 11,606 spectators who saw the Giants lose their last game at the Polo Grounds on September 29, 1957. The Pirates, behind Bob Friend, beat the Giants, 9-1. Johnny Antonelli took the loss that day.

Right-handed pitcher Michael Francis "Smiling Mickey" Welch of the New York Giants was another claiming to be the "first." Welch, a Brooklyn native, who won 311 games during a 13-year career, including 44 alone in 1885, was said to have been sent up to hit for starting pitcher Hank O'Day in a game played on August 10, 1889. Several books bear this out, but Welch had actually replaced O'Day on the pitching mound after the latter was scored on five times in the fifth inning. So Welch was actually the substitute "pitcher," not the substitute "batter" in New York's 9-6 victory.

There is no denying that Welch was an accomplished batsman. He hit safely 492 times, never hitting below .200 during his first eight years in the big leagues. Overall, he batted .224 for his career and, according to official record books, he was never credited with an at-bat as a pinch-hitter. He was elected to the Hall of Fame in 1973. Welch was 82 when he died in Nashua, New Hampshire, on July 30, 1941.

Despite the fact that three pinch-swingers delivered base hits in the first six weeks of the 1892 season, the use of emergency batsmen was at a premium for the balance of the year. Only four additional substitute batters were sent into games that season following Reilly, Daly and Doyle.

One of the major reasons why pinch-hitters saw limited action had to do with the game's reduction of players midway through the year. Rosters were cut from 15 to 13 players per team and most clubs elected to go with pitchers as extras rather than position players. Pitchers who could double as outfielders were most readily sought after for obvious reasons.

As rosters began to increase in subsequent years, so too did the popularity of pinch-hitters. When a substitute batter performed his task successfully, it made the manager look extremely good. And just as designated hitters in today's game have helped extend the careers of some aging ballplayers, so too did the new rule on emergency batsmen add years to some careers.

The first player to record two pinch-hits in one season was Camden, New Jersey's William J. "Kid" Gleason in 1894. Although he was primarily a pitcher, the 5' 7", 158-pounder acquired his nickname in part for his size, but mostly for his enthusiasm. When the distance from the mound to home plate was lengthened in 1894, Gleason's effectiveness as a pitcher decreased. He adapted. The Baltimore club's regular second baseman broke his collarbone that season, and Gleason took over the position. As a substitute batter, Gleason went 3-for-10. Overall, he batted .261 during his 22-year playing career. As a member of the Giants in 1900, Gleason and his infield teammates Jack Doyle and George Davis pulled off the first triple play of the twentieth century at the Polo Grounds on September 14. He was later credited by some as the first manager to order his pitchers to issue intentional passes to strong opposing hitters.

Gleason had the ill fortune of managing the White Sox of 1919, now remembered as the infamous "Black Sox." Chicago fell further and further in the standings in subsequent years as Commissioner Kenesaw M. Landis banished most of Gleason's best players. His heart broken by the players selling out their team in the series, Gleason continued to direct the club until 1923, but never managed again after that. He was a coach for the Phillies when he died in Philadelphia on January 2, 1933, at the age of 66.

Another pitcher, Boston's Jack Stivetts, mentioned earlier in this chapter, became the second player after Tom Daly to blast a home run as a pinch-hitter. He did it on June 28, 1894, when he was sent up in the ninth inning to hit for future Hall of Fame pitcher Charles Augustus "Kid" Nichols. Boston trailed St. Louis, 10-7, when the right-handed hitting Stivetts hit his home run with two on to tie the game. Stivetts then went in to pitch. Boston eventually won the game, 11-10.

Stivetts smacked two more home runs as an emergency batsman before ending his career with Cleveland in 1899. At 6' 2" and 185 pounds, he also may have been the first player to hit a triple as a substitute batter when he legged one out on August 15, 1895. Stivetts, the product of the anthracite coal fields of Ashland, Pennsylvania, batted .297 during his 11-year career, which included 35 home runs in 1,991 career at-bats. Three times he connected for homers twice in a game. As a pinch-swinger, he delivered 10 hits in 38 at-bats for a .263 mark. Stivetts passed away in his home town on April 18, 1930, at the age of 62.

The leading pinch-hitter in the National League in 1895 was Washington right-handed pitcher, Win Mercer. The ace of the staff, he produced two hits in his five pinch-hitting at-bats that season for a .400 average. The 5' 7" inch, 140-pound native of Chester, West Virginia, played the infield or the outfield when not pitching. Although he hit .285 for his nine-year career, he produced only two other hits in 22 at-bats as a pinch-swinger for a career mark of .182. He was only 28 when he checked into the Occidental Hotel in San Francisco on January 12, 1903, and killed himself by inhaling poison gas. In a suicide note, he cautioned against the perils of loose women and uncontrolled gambling. Mercer had been appointed player-manager for Detroit the previous winter.

As L. Robert Davids stated in this article, *The Pinch Hitters*, "Catchers also made an early contribution to pinch-hitting. Since they were so vulnerable to injury in those days, it was always necessary to have a substitute backstop available. One or the other then could be used as an emergency batsman. Jack Clements, best known as the left-handed catcher of the Phillies, hit baseball's third pinch–home run on May 5, 1896. However, he did poorly off the bench after that, collecting only one hit in 12 at-bats in 1898. Duke Farrell of New York and Washington had much better success, going 4-for-10, 8-for-14 and 5-for-10 in 1896-97-98, winding up with a solid 23-for-59 (.389) career mark."[8]

Clements was that rarity of rarities—a left-handed throwing catcher who played in the majors for 17 years, mostly in his home town of Philadelphia. He was not only the first lefty to catch over 1,000 games, but he was also the first to wear a chest protector. At 5' 8½" and 204 pounds, he was described as a "wide-shouldered grim-lipped man with the stature of a growing oak."[9]

Clements was said to have handled his catching job with finesse without demonstrating any sign of awkwardness. Right-handed batters had to learn to duck when a runner broke for second as Clements just fired away. A lifetime .286 batter, Clements went just 2-for-28 as an emergency batsman for an almost invisible .071 average. He passed away in his home town of Philadelphia on May 23, 1941, at the age of 76.

The switch-hitting Charles Andrew "Duke" Farrell, a 6' 2", 180-pound semi-pro from Oakdale, Massachusetts, had broken in as a prodigy of Cap Anson when the latter's White Stockings were barnstorming through New England. During an 18-year big league career, he hit .275 overall while his 23 base hits in 59 official pinch-hitting appearances produced a mighty .390 mark. Following his retirement, he worked as a scout for the Braves until his death in Boston on February 15, 1925, at the age of 58.

3

1900–1909: Pinch-Hitting
Begins Developing in Earnest

Beginning in 1900, the National League began to take note of the major statistics compiled by pinch-hitters, including times at bat, base hits and average. Boston's Shad Barry led the circuit in pinch-hitting appearances that year with 14. However, Mike Donlin of the St. Louis Cardinals set the pace in base hits and average with his 4-for-10 earning a .400 batting average.

Barry, a native of Newburgh, New York, was a player who filled in at almost every position except pitcher and catcher for seven different teams in a decade-long career. During World War I, he was in charge of all baseball programs for the American Expeditionary Forces. The right-handed hitter batted .267 for his lifetime in the majors but was only able to produce four hits in 32 pinch-hit at-bats for a smallish .125 mark. Barry passed away in Los Angeles on November 27, 1936, at the age of 58.

Donlin, a left-handed hitting outfielder from Peoria, Illinois, went on to become one of the Giants' most popular players after going to New York in 1904. A .300 hitter for 10 of his 12 seasons in the big leagues, he once left the game for a time to try his hand at a vaudeville and movie career. A career .333 hitter, his 15-for-79 as a pinch-swinger was only good for a .190 average. Donlin was 57 at his death in Hollywood on September 24, 1933.

Pitchers were used frequently as substitute batters after the turn of the century. Among the earliest and best were Win Mercer of the Senators, Mike O'Neill of the Cardinals, Jesse Tannehill of the Pirates, George Mullin of the Tigers, Frank Kitson of the Reds and Al Orth of the Phillies.

22

The Braves' Bill Dinneen, a right-handed pitcher who batted left-handed, paced the NL in pinch-hit at-bats with 11 in 1901. On July 17, 1901, two Boston Braves pitchers were sent up to pinch-hit: future Hall of Famer Kid Nichols and Bill Dinneen. Nichols slammed a triple while Dinneen's single brought him in to score. Duke Farrell, chronicled earlier as one of the great pinch-hitters of the nineteenth century, of Brooklyn and St. Louis' Pop Schriver tied for the league lead in pinch-hits with three apiece in 1901. However, Farrell's came in only four at-bats (.750 batting average) while Schriver's were attained in nine appearances (.333 batting average).

Dinneen, a 6' 1", 190-pounder from Syracuse, New York, won 20 games four times during his 12 years in the majors. When his playing days ended in 1909, he went straight from pitching in the American League into umpiring in that league. He remained an umpire for the next 29 years, including 45 World Series games. Dinneen passed away in his home town of Syracuse on January 13, 1955, at the age of 78.

The right-handed hitting Schriver, a 5' 10", 185-pounder from Brooklyn, was a catcher–first baseman and, like Farrell, a Cap Anson prodigy. Anson insisted that Schriver could catch a ball dropped 500 feet from the top of the Washington Monument and on August 25, 1894, Schriver proved it. He caught a ball dropped by Chicago pitcher Clark Griffith, a feat later duplicated by Washington's Gabby Street in 1908. Schriver batted .264 lifetime, but only .235 as a pinch-swinger (8-for-34). He died in Brooklyn on December 27, 1932, at the age of 67.

Over in the American League in 1901, Nixey Callahan of Chicago had the most pinch-hit at-bats with 10 but Ossie Schreckengost of Boston tied Callahan for the lead with three pinch-hits. Since Schreckengost's came in nine at-bats while Callahan had one extra at-bat, he edged out Callahan in the average category, .333 to .300.

A two-time 20-game winner who also played the outfield and infield, Callahan was a crowd-pleaser who could run, hit and field. The 5' 10½", 180-pound right-hander from Fitchburg, Massachusetts, served as player-manager for the White Sox for two years. He stayed on as an outfielder although he stopped pitching after he was dismissed as the team's manager in 1904. For his 13 years in the majors, he batted .273 overall while his 12 hits in 48 pinch-hit at-bats earned him a .250 BA. He was 60 when he died in Boston on October 4, 1934.

A highly-rated defensive catcher, the right-handed hitting Schreckengost was born in New Bethlehem, Pennsylvania. He and future Hall of Fame pitcher Rube Waddell of Connie Mack's early Philadelphia Athletics formed one of the most formidable batteries in the game at the time. Schreckengost never wore shin guards and also developed the one-handed style of catching adopted over a half century later by receivers like Hall of Famer Johnny Bench. A .271 hitter for his 11 years in the major leagues, Schreckengost managed nine hits in 45 at-bats off the bench for a .200 BA. He was only 39 when he died in Philadelphia on July 9, 1914.

In 1902, Brooklyn's Frank Kitson, came up with three base hits in seven appearances to lead the NL in pinch-hitting average with .429. The Cardinals' Mike O'Neill led the National League in pinch-hit at-bats with 12 in 1902 but could only muster one hit, albeit an historic one.

O'Neill, who had played as Mike Joyce a year earlier, delivered the first ever pinch-hit grand slam home run in Boston on June 3, 1902. A left-handed hitter, the 5' 11", 185-pound O'Neill hit his home run — of the inside-the-park variety — off Boston Beaneaters right-hander Togie Pittinger. The historic home run scored his brother Jack, a rookie catcher who doubled as his batterymate when Mike pitched.

A catcher, Pat Moral of Boston, crushed the second grand slam home run as an emergency hitter two months later. It would be eight years before the next one was to be hit by Beals Becker of the Giants.

Mike and Jack O'Neill were the eldest of four brothers who played in the major leagues. They were born in Galway, Ireland, while their younger siblings, Jim and Steve, were natives of Minooka, Pennsylvania. Steve, one of the best-liked men in the game during his many years in baseball, later managed the Indians, Tigers, Red Sox and Phillies. In fact, he led Detroit to a world championship over the Cubs in 1945.

Kitson was a left-handed pitcher who batted right-handed, who hailed from Hopkins, Michigan. A 22-game winner for Baltimore in 1899, he won 19 games for Brooklyn in both 1901 and 1902 before jumping to the American League in 1903. As a hitter, the 5' 11", 165-pounder batted .239 overall for his 10-year big league career while his seven hits in 24 appearances off the bench produced an even better .292 mark. Kitson died in Allegan, Michigan on April 14, 1930, at the age of 58.

Nixey Callahan's 12 at-bats led all AL pinch-hitters in 1902 while Harry Gleason of the Red Sox with three league-leading hits in eight at-bats registered the best average at .375. Gleason, a diminutive 5' 6", 150-pounder from Camden, New Jersey, only played in the big leagues for five years. The brother of 22-year veteran player Kid Gleason, Harry was primarily a third baseman who also played some outfield and was tried at other infield spots. He was only a regular in his final year in the majors with the Browns in 1905. Gleason only hit .218 for his career while his three hits in 13 at-bats as an emergency batsman was only slightly better at .231. He died in his home town of Camden on October 21, 1963, at the age of 88.

Red Dooin of the Phillies tied for the NL's lead in pinch-hit at-bats with nine in 1903. Dooin's three hits merited him a .333 average, but the Cardinals' Jack Dunleavy's 4-for-9 mark off the bench produced a better .444 mark. However, the Giants' Frank Bowerman beat them both by going 3-for-4 for a league-leading .750 BA.

Dooin, a 5' 9½", 165-pounder from Cincinnati, was an outstanding defensive catcher and supposedly the first player to don papier-mâché shin guards under his stockings. He was once offered a bribe to throw a series against the Giants, but he dutifully reported the incident. Dooin later became a player-manager for the Phillies. In his 15-year career, he only batted .240 overall, but his pinch-hitting average of .262 was even better with 17 hits in 65 at-bats. Dooin was 72 when he died in Rochester, New York, on May 12, 1952.

Dunleavy, 5' 6", 167-pounder from Harrison, New Jersey, had an abbreviated three-year stint in the big leagues. A left-handed hitting outfielder who also pitched on occasion, he was a .241 lifetime batter. Despite the pinch-hitting success of his rookie year, he never had another pinch-hitting appearance.

Bowerman was a 6' 2", 190-pound right-handed hitting catcher from Romeo, Michigan. The capable backstop was the first to catch the young Christy Mathewson in the major leagues. He also played 132 games at first base during his 15-year career. His lifetime average of .251 as an emergency batter (14-for-59) was better than his .237 career BA. Bowerman died in his hometown of Romeo on November 30, 1948, at the age of 79.

Rookies Jake Stahl of the Red Sox and Danny Hoffman of the Athletics tied for the AL in pinch-hit at-bats, base hits and average in 1903. Stahl and Hoffman went 5-for-11 apiece for a mighty .455 average.

The college-educated, independently wealthy Stahl simply played the game for the love of it. The 6' 2", 195-pounder from Elkhart, Illinois, had an older brother, Chick, who played for both Boston teams during a 10-year career. Jake started out as a catcher but was switched to first base by Washington in his second season in the big leagues. He later managed the Senators in 1905 and 1906 and even won a world title for the Red Sox in 1912. An overall .260 hitter during his nine playing years, he produced six hits in 22 pinch-hitting chores for a better .273 mark. He was 43 years old when he died in Los Angeles on September 18, 1922.

Hoffman, a 5' 9", 175-pound left-handed hitting outfielder from Canaan, Connecticut, was considered a top prospect by the Athletics until Boston's Jesse Tannehill hit him in the eye with a pitch that blurred his vision. As a result, he could not stand in against left-handed pitching, which curtailed his potential considerably. Blessed with good speed, he led the AL in stolen bases in 1905 with 46 and accumulated 185 steals for his nine-year career. Overall, Hoffman hit .256 while his 5-for-17 produced a healthy .294 mark in the pinch. He died in his home state of Connecticut in March of 1922 at the age of 42.

The first pinch-hitter ever to come to bat in a World Series was the aforementioned Duke Farrell of the Boston Pilgrims (later Red Sox). He batted twice in the very first Series played in 1903, and though he was hitless in two at-bats, he did manage to deliver a run batted in. In those early days, the Series was decided on a best-of-nine basis and Farrell's Pilgrims beat the Pittsburgh Pirates in eight games.

In the first year of the 154-game schedule in 1904, Frank Roth of the Phillies led NL pinch-hitters in all categories. Roth, a Chicago product and the older brother of Braggo Roth, made 12 appearances off the bench and collected four hits for a .333 average. A backup catcher for his entire six-year career, Roth had no power whatsoever, delivering but one homer in 783 big league at-bats. He hit .250 for his career. His 11 hits in 46 pinch-hitting attempts was lower at .239. He was 76 at the time of his death in Burlington, Wisconsin, on March 27, 1955.

The American League pace-setters in 1904 were Duke Farrell of the Red Sox and Deacon McGuire, now with the Highlanders (later Yankees) after 20 years with eight other clubs in both leagues. Farrell appeared in a pinch-hitting role 11 times to lead the league while McGuire was a perfect 2-for-2. Six other players in the league also had two hits but considerably more at-bats than McGuire.

One of the seven AL players connecting for two pinch-hits to tie for the league lead deserves additional mention: Red Sox pitcher Jesse Tannehill the Dayton, Kentucky native won 197 games in a 15-year career. A switch-hitter who threw left-handed, the 5' 8", 150-pounder won 20 games or more six times, including a no-hitter against the White Sox on August 17, 1904. His brother, Lee, cooperated by going 0-for-3 for Chicago that day.

A .256 lifetime batter, Jesse Tannehill was used often late in his career as an outfielder (87 games) and as a pinch-hitter (57 career pinch-hit at-bats). His 11 hits off the bench only produced a .196 average, but he was always a threat as almost 25 percent of his safeties went for extra bases. Tannehill died in his Kentucky hometown on September 22, 1956, at the age of 72.

Otto Krueger, a right-handed hitting utility infielder for the Phillies, led the NL in pinch-hit at-bats in 1905 with 16. Sammy Strang of the Giants at 8-for-14 was far and away tops in the league in both hits and average at .556.

The Chicago-born Krueger was a right-handed swinger who played every position in the infield except first base. The 5' 7", 165-pounder also appeared in the outfield on occasion during his seven-year career. A career .251 batter, he was not very successful as a pinch-hitter going only 5-for-31 for a miserly .161 BA. Krueger died in St. Louis on February 20, 1961, at the age of 84.

Strang, who was born Samuel Strang Nicklin in Chattanooga, Tennessee, played just about everywhere in the infield and outfield during his 10-year career. When he came to the Giants in 1905, he became the club's first option off the bench. It is said that since he thrived on coming through in the pinch he inspired use of the term "pinch-hitter." Strang batted .269 overall for his career while his 15 base hits in 46 times up as a pinch-swinger earned him a solid .326 average. Strang was 55 when he died in his home town of Chattanooga on April 13, 1932.

Over in the AL in 1905, Ike Van Zandt of the St. Louis Browns established a new major league record with 18 pinch-hit at-bats. He also tied Ed McFarland of the White Sox for the league lead in base hits with four. McFarland's average however, was double Van Zandt's at .444 because he had half as many at-bats.

Van Zandt was a Brooklyn native who started out as a pitcher but was switched to the outfield after only two games on the hill. He was never a regular appearing in only 100 games during his brief three-year stint in the majors. Van Zandt hit .224 overall while his four hits in 18 at-bats in his final season gave him a nearly similar average of .222. He died in Nashua, New Hampshire, on September 14, 1908, at the still-young age of 31.

The Cleveland-born McFarland was a reserve catcher for most of his 14-year career. At 5 feet 10 inches and 180 pounds, the right-handed batter was a defensive standout. After seven seasons in the National League, he jumped to the AL's Chicago entry where he shared responsibilities with Billy Sullivan. McFarland had a lifetime BA of .275 while his 11 hits in 38 times off the bench earned him a commendable .290 mark. He died in his home town of Cleveland on November 28, 1959, at the age of 85.

Substitute batters in the 1906 NL season were headed by Johnny Lush of the Phillies, who came to bat 14 times in a pinch-hitting role, and player-manager Fred Clarke of the Pirates whose five hits in seven at-bats gave him an untouchable .714 average.

Lush, who was born in Williamsport, Pennsylvania, was a youngster of 18 when he broke into the majors as an outfielder-first baseman with the Phillies in 1904. He was also the youngest player in the big leagues at the start of the twentieth century. Lush became a pitcher late in 1905, and in 1906 he won 18 games, including a no-hitter against Brooklyn at the tender age of 21. Left-handed all the way, the 5' 9½", 165-pounder had only one other winning season thereafter in his seven-year career. Overall, he hit for a .254 average and his 10 hits in 55 pinch-hit appearances only merited a .182 mark. Lush was 61 when he died in Beverly Hills, California, on November 18, 1946.

Clarke, who spent a distinguished 21 seasons in the big leagues as a player and manager, was a product of Winterset, Iowa. A left-handed hitting outfielder, he was one of the game's toughest competitors. He was only 25 with just three years behind him in the big leagues when he took over as manager of the Louisville franchise in 1897. When the club was merged with the Pirates, he led Pittsburgh to three straight NL pennants and an appearance in the first-ever World Series in 1903, won by the Boston Pilgrims (later Red Sox). In 1909, his Pirates beat the Tigers for the world championship.

When the 5' 10½" Clarke retired after the 1915 season, he ranked among the all-time leaders in batting average, runs scored, hits, triples and stolen bases. He was also Pittsburgh's most successful manager in both victories (1,422) and winning percentage (.592). He was elected to the Hall of Fame in 1945. His lifetime batting average was .315 and his 16 base hits in 41 swings as a pinch-hitter was an exceptional .390. Clarke died in Winfield, Kansas, on August 14, 1960, at the age of 81.

Over in the AL in 1906, Joe Yeager of the New York Highlanders tied Ike Van Zandt's record of 18 pinch-hit at-bats set the previous season. Washington's Howard Wakefield had the most hits with nine and the best average at .562.

Yeager, a Philadelphia product, started out as a pitcher in Brooklyn in 1898 but was turned into an infielder following his trade to Detroit in 1901. The 6-foot, 190-pound right-handed hitter was basically a utility player for the Highlanders. Yeager has been credited by some historians with having originated the squeeze play. During his 10-year career he batted .252 while his seven hits in 33 pinch-hit at-bats were only good for a .212 mark. He was 67 when he died in Cincinnati on June 5, 1940.

Wakefield, of Bucyrus, Ohio, had been dealt to Washington from Cleveland for the 1906 campaign. At 6-feet and 205 pounds, the right-handed hitting backup catcher only played in the majors for three years. Wakefield returned to Cleveland for his final season in 1907. He was only 23 at the time. He was the father of the noted bonus baby of the early 1940s, Dick Wakefield of the Detroit Tigers. For his abbreviated stay in the big leagues, Howard Wakefield batted .249 but his 11 base hits in 32 times up off the bench were good for a substantial .344 BA. He died in Chicago on April 16, 1941, at the age of 57.

"No one ever pinch hits for Cobb," the Georgia Peach once told Athletics owner-manager Connie Mack for whom he played later in his career, but actually he was pinch-hit for three times in the same season.

"Wabash George" Mullin, a fast-balling right-hander for the Tigers won 228 games during a 14-year stint in the majors, but he was called to pinch-hit for Cobb in Detroit on September 18, 1906 (Cobb's second year in the big leagues). Originally, it was reported that the Tigers were six runs behind the Red Sox as the ninth inning began. Cobb, who made the last out in the bottom of the eighth, headed for the clubhouse for an end-of-game shower, thinking he would never have to come up to bat again. However, the Tigers scored four runs in the bottom of the ninth and loaded the bases with Cobb due up. When manager Hughey Jennings was told that Cobb was showering, he summoned Mullin to pinch-hit.

That story was amended because it was William Armour and not Jennings who was Detroit's manager at the time. And the *Detroit Free Press* reported that the Tigers had lost, 7-2, and no such rally was in the works. In fact, the paper more or less indicated that Cobb was lifted because he was slumping. The newspaper report read: "In the ninth Armour derricked Cobb and Mullin, who subbed, hit center field with a triple. It was a run, (Fred) Payne coming right along with his third safe drive of the day."

In reality, Cobb had been pinch-hit for earlier that year. The date was April 24, 1906, in St. Louis. Armour sent Sam Crawford—normally a starter either in the outfield or first base—to bat for the left-handed hitting Georgia Peach against right-hander Barney Pelty. The Tigers still lost, 2-0.

He was actually lifted a third time by Armour in 1906 on May 30 for rookie Fred Payne, a lifetime .214 hitter during his six years in the majors. Payne, who was a backup catcher-outfielder and never a starter, singled. Cobb had fanned three times in a row before Armour sent Payne up to hit for him. It would be another 15 years before Cobb was again to be replaced by an emergency batsman. By then, Cobb was manager of the Tigers.

Another new NL record for pinch-hit at-bats was set in 1907 by Sammy Strang of the Giants and a rookie, Fred Osborn of the Phillies, with 19 apiece. Osborn's seven hits stood alone as the most that season and resulted in a league-leading .368 mark. Strang, on the other hand, was only able to deliver four hits in his at-bats for a .211 average.

Osborn, a left-handed hitting outfielder from Nevada, Ohio, only played in the majors for three years. The 5' 9", 174-pounder did not pinch-hit again until the 1909 campaign, his last in the big leagues. The year before he been installed as a regular in the in the outfield and played in 152 games. He finished up his short stay in the big leagues with a .251

overall average while his eight hits in 25 pinch-hit at-bats worked out to a well-above-average .320 BA. He was 70 when he died in Upper Sandusky, Ohio, on September 2, 1954.

The American League, meanwhile, began to recognize both pinch-hitters and pinch-runners with games played in 1907. The National League did not recognize such appearances until five years later. The AL's Charles "Piano Legs" Hickman was establishing a new major league record for pinch-hit at-bats with 22 that season. A second-year player, John Hoey of the Red Sox, registered the most hits with eight, and also had the best average at .444.

Hickman, a 5' 9", 185-pounder who started out as a pitcher but was quickly converted into utility infielder-outfielder, was born in Taylortown, Pennsylvania. The right-handed hitter's claim to fame was that he was the first player to lead a league in base hits while playing for two different teams. Earlier, in 1902, he had banged out 194 safeties for both Boston and Cleveland to accomplish the feat.

Hickman also carved out another niche for himself in baseball history on June 30, 1902 by combining with Nap Lajoie and Bill Bradley of the Indians to become the first trio to hit consecutive home runs in the twentieth century. Hickman finished up his 12-year career in the majors with a solid .301 BA but his 10 hits in 49 pinch-hit at-bats only garnered him a .204 average. He died at 58 in Morgantown, West Virginia, on April 19, 1934.

Hoey, who came from Watertown, Massachusetts, was a left-handed hitting outfielder who was unable to earn a regular spot for himself during his short three-year stay in the major leagues. He batted but .232 in 500 at-bats overall, but his nine hits in 20 career pinch-hitting spots brought him an excellent .450 average off the bench. Hoey was 66 when he died in Waterbury, Connecticut, on November 14, 1947.

Red Sox manager Deacon McGuire inserted himself as a pinch-hitter against Detroit in Beantown on July 27, 1907. The 43-year-old skipper blasted a home run to tie the game at 2-2, only the second pinch-hit four-bagger to be hit in the AL up until then. McGuire's homer also made him the oldest player in baseball history ever to hit a pinch-hit home run. The first one had occurred in Chicago on June 25, 1906, by Detroit infielder Herman A. "Germany" Schaeffer.

The NL pace-setters in 1908 were Ernie Courtney of the Phillies with 17 pinch-hit at-bats while Ed Phelps of the Pirates led with seven hits and a .583 average.

Courtney, of Des Moines, Iowa, was a 5' 10" left-handed hitting infielder. Supposedly, he had the largest hands in professional baseball at the time. He was a regular for only in 1905, when he started at third base for the Phillies and drove in 77 runs. The remainder of his six-year career was spent coming off the bench. Overall, Courtney hit .245 while his five hits in 29 pinch-hit appearances resulted in just a .172 BA. He died in Buffalo, New York on February 29, 1920, at the age of 45.

An Albany, New York native, Phelps spent his entire 11-year career in the National League playing for Pittsburgh, Cincinnati, St. Louis and Brooklyn. As a rookie in 1903, he was the Pirates' regular catcher in the first modern World Series. The 5' 10", 185-pounder was a much better player defensively than offensively. He batted .251 for his career and his 19 hits in 84 appearances as an emergency batsman earned him a .226 mark. He died in East Greenbush, New York, on January 31, 1942, at the age of 62.

It was not until 1908 that a pinch-hitter was able to record as many as 41 at-bats in a single season. That's as many times as the left-handed hitting rookie Dode Criss of the St. Louis Browns was called upon to pinch-hit. A 23-year-old right-handed pitcher who found home plate somewhat illusive, he hit successfully 12 times in those 41 at-bats as a substitute batter for an outstanding .341 average. Another rookie, Cliff "Gavvy" Cravath of the Red Sox, had the better average though by virtue of his six hits in only 14 at-bats for a .429 BA.

Criss, out of Sherman, Mississippi, is generally considered to be the game's first true professional pinch-hitter. He put together some 35 hits in 147 at-bats for a .239 average, which represented nearly half of his lifetime 304 total times at bat. From 1908 to 1911, the left-handed hitter led the league in both pinch-hit at-bats and base hits each season in his brief four-year major league career. As L. Robert Davids pointed out in his article, *The Pinch Hitters*, "the regular use of Criss as a substitute batter opened the doors for several other 'have bat, will travel' types." Dode Criss died at age 70 in his home town of Sherman, Mississippi, on September 8, 1955.

Cravath, a product of Escondido, California, went on to actually become the home run king of the deadball era. He set the twentieth-century record of 24 in 1915, which stood until Babe Ruth broke it with 29 in 1919. A tobacco-chewing, highly combative type player, the 5' 10½", 186-pound outfielder played mostly in the National League with the Phillies after being traded there from the Red Sox in 1912. He led the NL in homers in six of the nine years he played in Philadelphia. He later managed the team for a year-and-a-half in the 1919 and 1920 seasons but was considered to be too easy-going and was eventually let go.

The top pinch-hitter for average in the NL in 1909 was Chief Meyers, a rookie catcher with the Giants, whose eight hits in 24 at-bats merited a

.333 average. A Cahuilla Indian from Riverside, California, the 5' 11", 194-pounder was educated at Dartmouth and was later employed by the Department of the Interior as an Indian supervisor. He disdained the nickname, Chief—his given name was John—which was applied to almost every Native American athlete in those days. A right-handed batter, he hit a steady .290 during his nine-year career which featured appearances in three World Series for the Giants and one for Brooklyn. As a pinch-hitter, he collected 16 hits in 68 times up for a .235 mark. He died at 90 in San Bernardino, California on July 25, 1971.

When it comes to a player that in all probability could be considered the first true career pinch-hitter, certainly in the National League, it would have to be Robert Hamilton "Ham" Hyatt of County, North Carolina. He broke in with Pittsburgh in 1909 as a backup first baseman and sometime outfielder. In his rookie year, Hyatt slugged three triples as a substitute batter, a record that held up for 61 years until tied by the Cardinals' Vic Davallilo in 1970. Despite hitting only .243 as a pinch-swinger with nine hits in 37 at-bats, five of those hits went for extra bases.

During his seven years in the majors, the 6' 1", 185-pound Hyatt hit a total of five pinch-hit triples, another milestone that lasted until Gates Brown of the Detroit Tigers arrived on the scene over a half century later. A left-handed hitter, Hyatt also hammered out four pinch-hit homers in 1913 for yet another record until surpassed in 1932 by the Dodgers' Johnny Frederick.

Two physical problems hampered Hyatt during his major league career: a lack of speed compounded by a tendency to gain weight. The Pirates outfielders and their regular first-sacker, Bill Abstein, could all outrun him, thereby relegating Hyatt to the role of the club's first emergency batsman off the bench.

Fred Clarke, Hyatt's manager in Pittsburgh, was one of the first to employ the use of pinch-hitters as soon as he noticed the elasticity of the balls in use in 1909. The ball patented for use at the time was the "cork center" and started a new generation of hitting and record-making. Averages escalated—Ty Cobb went from .324 to .377 while Eddie Collins jumped from .273 to .346. Clarke took note and installed Hyatt as his main man off the bench.

While Honus Wagner was the Pirates' power hitter and won his seventh batting title in 1909, Hyatt's success as a pinch-hitter was crucial in Pittsburgh beating out the three-time champion Cubs for the NL pennant that season. Hyatt batted almost .400 as an emergency batter in 40 games. In fact, his season was so spectacular that the league's president, John Heydler, noted it in the annual averages.

What made Hyatt's contributions even more amazing was the fact that when Clarke tried to use him as a regular, he failed to produce and no one knew why. Yet when sent up in clutch situations, more often than not with the game on the line, Hyatt rose to the occasion. He left the majors after the 1918 season at the age of 34 while a member of the Yankees, becoming the first pinch-hitter to accumulate over 50 pinch-hits.

Dode Criss continued to set the pace in the AL in 1909 with 24 pinch-hit at-bats, down from his record of 41 a year earlier. Charlie Hemphill of the Yankees tied Criss with 24 appearances off the bench but it was his teammate, Al Orth, a pitcher with five hits in 13 times up, who led the league in average at .385.

Hemphill, also known as "Eagle Eye," put in 11 years in the big leagues and he even had a brief fling as manager of the Yankees when Hal Chase was ill. A 5' 9", 160-pound outfielder from Greenville, Michigan, he had a younger brother, Frank, who played briefly with the White Sox and Senators. A left-handed hitter, Hemphill batted .271 for his career, which included 11 hits in 49 at-bats in the pinch for a .225 average. He died in Detroit on June 22, 1953, at the age of 76.

Orth, a 6-foot, 200-pounder from Tipton, Indiana, amazingly won 202 games without the benefit of a curve ball. What he did expertly was change speeds off his fastball. As a hitter, he ranks seventh among pitchers all-time with 389 hits and a .273 BA. A left-handed hitter who threw right-handed, he occasionally played the outfield and was called upon to pinch-hit 78 times during his 15 years in the big leagues. His 17 hits off the bench earned him a .218 average. Orth was 76 when he died in Lynchburg, Virginia, on October 8, 1948.

The first pitcher to pinch-hit in a World Series was the aforementioned George Mullin of the Detroit Tigers in 1909. A 29-game winner that season, he was victorious in two of the three games the Tigers won in losing a seven-game set to the Pirates. The right-handed hitting Mullin flied out in the ninth inning of Game Five. He also went hitless in one other pinch-hitting appearance in the series. For his 14-year career, he batted .263 overall while his 20 hits in 101 pinch-hit at-bats during the regular season only gave him a somewhat ordinary .198 mark. Mullin died in Wabash, Indiana on January 7, 1944, at the age of 63.

4

1910-1919:
Moose McCormick,
the Best Yet Off the Bench

The use of pinch-hitters began to gain popularity beginning in 1910. Though successful at his new-found craft earlier in his career, Ham Hyatt had what for him was an off-year. He only hit safely six times in 31 times at bat for a lowly .193 average as a substitute batsman for the Pittsburgh Pirates that season.

Cincinnati manager Clark Griffith often employed fleet-footed out-fielder, Ward "Windy" Miller, as an emergency batter. In 1910 the 5' 11", 177-pounder from Mt. Carroll, Illinois, became the first National Leaguer to be called on as many as 40 times as a pinch-hitter in one year, registering 11 hits en route for a respectable .275 BA.

Al Burch, a chunky utility outfielder with Brooklyn that same season, went 7-for-18 to lead the NL in pinch-hitting average at .380. A 5' 8½", 160-pound left-handed batter, he played in the majors for six years and attained an overall .254 average while his eight hits in 33 pinch-hitting appearances topped off at .243. Burch, who was born in Albany, New York, was only 42 when he passed away in Brooklyn on October 5, 1926.

In the American League in 1910, it was Dode Criss, a pitcher with 44 at-bats as a pinch-hitter, also who led his circuit. He later became the first player to make over 100 appearances as an emergency batsman throughout his career. Like his National League counterpart Hyatt, Criss was the type of player who could produce timely hits as a pinch-hitter, but was ineffective as a regular. His club, the St. Louis Browns, felt that Criss probably lost as many games with his pitching as he won with his pinch-hitting.

Earl Gardner, a second baseman from Sparta, Illinois, had the AL's best pinch-hitting average in 1910 with a .286 mark off four hits in 14 at-bats. The 5' 11", 160-pound right-handed hitter hit .263 overall for his career but only 32 of his 249 hits were for extra bases. He was only called upon as an emergency batsman only one more time in his brief five-year career. Those four hits in 15 total at-bats earned him a .267 BA in the pinch. He died in his home town of Sparta on March 2, 1943, at the age of 59.

The NL was led in pinch-hit at-bats in 1911 by Beals Becker, a left-handed hitting outfielder with the Giants, who was called upon 26 times as a substitute batter that season. Troubled by southpaws, the El Dorado, Kansas native hit safely just three times for a poor .115 average. One of those hits, though, was an inside-the-park home run with the bases loaded against Brooklyn on September 10 in a 17-8 slugfest at the Polo Grounds won by the Giants. It was only the second pinch-hit grand slam ever recorded in baseball history; Mike O'Neill hit the first in 1902.

Becker reputedly played better on the road than at home because he was offended by the razzing of Giants' fans who felt he did not come through enough for them. For his eight-year career, including appearances in the 1911 and 1912 World Series for the Giants and the 1915 series with the Phillies, he batted .276 overall. Becker was hitless in three pinch-hit attempts in the 1912 series. The 18 hits he collected in 100 appearances off the bench only gained him a .180 BA. He passed away at 57 in Huntington Park, California, on August 16, 1943.

Patsy Flaherty, a left-handed pitcher and sometime outfielder for the Braves, was tops in the NL in pinch-hits and average in 1911 with 6-for-17 and a .353 mark. The 5' 8", 165-pounder, who was born in Mansfield, Pennsylvania, played for seven different clubs during his nine years in the big leagues. A .197 lifetime hitter overall, nonetheless his eight base hits in 28 official pinch-hit at-bats were good for a .286 BA. Flaherty was 91 when he died in Alexandria, Louisiana, on January 23, 1968.

Ham Hyatt's lack of speed and power frustrated the Pirates, who farmed him out to Kansas City in 1911. He returned to the team the following year and went 6-for-27 in the pinch for a .222 BA. Pittsburgh finished second, 10 games behind the pennant-winning Giants that year then managed by innovative John McGraw.

McGraw, who was experimenting with using certain pitchers like Otis "Doc" Crandall not only as a right-handed starter but in relief of his other moundsmen, also began to see the merits of pinch-hitters in certain game situations. In fact, he used the righty-swinging Crandall in both capacities in 1910. Not only did the 5' 10½", 180-pound Wadena, Indiana native reward his manager with a 7-1 relief record, a 10-3 mark as a starter, and a .342 BA as a substitute batter as well. For his 10-year career, Crandall batted a solid .285 overall while his 22 hits in 96 pinch-hit at-bats earned him a .230 average. He passed away in Bell, California, on August 17, 1951, at the age of 63.

McGraw really found what he was looking for in Harry Elwood "Moose" McCormick, a lanky college-educated outfielder whose fielding left much to be desired. In 1912 — the year the NL finally recognized pinch-hitters and pinch-runners in its official game statistics — the Philadelphia-born McCormick proved to be just what the doctor ordered. He led the National League with 11 hits in 30 pinch-hitting appearances to ring up a scintillating .367 average. Hall of Famer-to-be Roger Bresnahan had the best pinch-hitting average that season with .500 by dint of his seven base hits in 14 appearances.

Bresnahan, a rough-and-tumble player from Toledo, Ohio, was one of the greatest catchers in the history of the game. A stocky 5' 9", 200-pounder who batted from the right side, he hit .279 for his 17-year career with 20 hits in 63 times off the bench to produce an enviable .333 average. Elected to the Hall of Fame in 1945, the innovative Bresnahan experimented with batting helmets as far back as 1905, and later devised the use of shin guards for catchers. He died in his home town of Toledo on December 4, 1944, at the age of 65.

McGraw used to order the team's trainer to massage Moose McCormick's legs just before sending him up to pinch-hit. The process added a certain mystique factor to the left-handed hitter's role. The fans clamored for him.

The 5' 11", 180-pound McCormick played on two pennant-winning ball clubs in New York. His pinch-hitting successes in both the 1912 and 1913 World Series — he was 2-for-6 with a sacrifice fly and run batted in — helped foster acceptance for the continued use of emergency batsmen in the big leagues.

On April 28, 1913, McCormick was called on to get a hit twice during one at-bat. Initially he had driven in the winning run but celebrated umpire Bill Klem said that his back was turned and he was unable to see what happened. McCormick returned to the batter's box to try his luck again. This time, however, he ended the game by hitting into a double play.

McCormick and his manager did not see eye-to-eye on more than one occasion. There was the time when McGraw sent up his ace pinch-

The innovative John McGraw was one of the first managers to see the merits of employing substitute batters in certain game situations. (Courtesy of National Baseball Hall of Fame Library, Cooperstown, N.Y.)

Moose McCormick's success created a popularity for the increased use of emergency batsmen in the big leagues. (Courtesy of National Baseball Hall of Fame Library, Cooperstown, N.Y.)

hitter and specifically ordered him to bunt, but Moose swung away and tripled to win the game. McGraw was not impressed and fined McCormick anyway.

Another time, when Moose was in the on-deck circle waiting to hit, a runner on second base headed home on a teammate's base hit. The throw from the opposing outfielder went wide and headed straight for McCormick. Moose swung at it and hit it out of the park. The umpires were not amused though and called the runner out for interference. The rally was cut short then and there because of McCormick's hijinks. McGraw was, understandably, furious. "I just couldn't lay off it," McCormick declared. "It was right down my alley."[1]

McCormick was a major participant for the Giants in one of the most controversial games ever played. It took place against the Cubs on September 23, 1908 at the Polo Grounds in New York. With the score tied at 1-1 in the bottom of the ninth, McCormick was on third base representing the winning run. Fred Merkle, a 19-year old rookie, was on first base. Al Bridwell singled to score McCormick but it didn't count because Merkle did not touch second and just kept on running to the clubhouse in center field. The game had to be replayed and New York lost the game and the pennant. The play was forever known as "Merkle's Boner."

During his relatively short five-year career in the majors, McCormick batted .275 overall and recorded an exceptional .301 BA with 28 hits in 93 pinch-hitting attempts. Moose McCormick, under John McGraw's astute leadership, had brought new-found credibility to the art of pinch-hitting.

Nicknamed "Moose" because of his huge eight-foot stride, he would ink-stamp a little moosehead under his autograph. When he wasn't playing baseball, he was employed as an engineer in the steel industry. He also coached baseball at his alma mater, Bucknell, and later at the United Stated States Military Academy. McCormick died in Lewisburg, Pennsylvania, on July 9, 1962, at the age of 81.

Ted Easterly, like Jack Clements before him, was a left-handed catcher for both Cleveland and Chicago in the American League in 1912. He set the mark for pinch-hits in that circuit with 13 that season, a record that held up for 19 years. And he did it in only 30 at-bats for an extraordinary .433 average that gave him the crown in all three pinch-hitting departments that year.

During an interview, Easterly, who hailed from Lincoln, Nebraska, once said: "If I can go to the plate once a day and make a hit when needed, I am satisfied that I am earning my pay."[2] Easterly was considered by some historians at the time to have set the standard for the art and technique of pinch-hitting in the major leagues.

The World Series of 1912 produced a glorious moment for one Olaf "Swede" Henriksen who played in only 125 games in the outfield for the Red Sox during an otherwise uneventful seven-year career. With the series against the Giants tied at three games apiece, the Danish-born Henriksen was sent up to hit against the legendary Christy Mathewson. With two down and two on in the bottom of the seventh, the Giants led 1-0. The 5' 7½", 158-pounder swung and missed at the first pitch and then took a strike, putting himself into an 0-2 hole against the future Hall of Famer. Henriksen caught hold of the third pitch and lined a double down the line to score the tying run.

The run held up until the top of the tenth when the Giants tallied once more. But in the bottom half of the inning, Fred Snodgrass dropped a fly ball and Fred Merkle watched Tris Speaker's foul pop fall untouched to keep the inning alive. The Red Sox tied before winning it on a sacrifice fly by Larry Gardner. Had Henriksen not clubbed his game-tying two-bagger in the seventh, in his only at-bat of the Series, there may never have been any tenth-inning magic at Fenway Park.

Substitute batters did not have longevity in organized baseball at this point in the game's history. The ones who did have an impact made the most of their relatively abbreviated careers, though. One was Roy Oscar "Doc" Miller, a Chatham, Ontario, Canada native, who played on four different teams from 1910 to 1914. In his initial two years in the majors— he played one game with the Cubs before being sent to the Braves— he did almost no pinch-hitting at all. A regular outfielder in Boston, he came to bat once as an emergency batsman and failed to hit in 1910. The 5' 10½", 170-pounder turned his career around the following year when he lost the league batting title to Honus Wagner by a single point. Wagner had 104 fewer at-bats than Miller.

Two years later, Miller was no longer a regular and found himself with the Phillies. He established new season pinch-hitting records in 1913 with 20 hits and 56 at-bats for an amazing .357 BA. Miller's single-season pinch-hitting records lasted 19 years, just as long as Hyatt's four pinch-hit home runs in 1913 lasted. In 1932, the Giants' Sam Leslie's 22 pinch-hits broke Miller's mark and the Dodgers' Johnny Fredericks surpassed Hyatt's home run record with six.

Miller's five-year career was punctuated by a fine .295 BA overall while his 39 hits in 120 official pinch-hit attempts were good enough for a .309 mark. He died in Jersey City, on July 13, 1938, at the age of 55.

Ward "Windy" Miller was not related to Doc Miller, but they shared the common ability to hit in a pinch. Windy led all NL emergency batsmen in average in 1913 with an incomparable .615, thanks to his eight safeties in 13 times up. A left-handed hitting outfielder who had the most pinch-hit at-bats and base hits in the NL three years earlier, Windy Miller was in the majors for eight years. His overall lifetime BA was .278, but his 36 hits in 110 times up as a substitute batter produced an exceptional .327 mark. He passed away at 74 in Dixon, Illinois, on September 4, 1958.

In 1913 in the American League, Ted Easterly repeated as the player with the most pinch-hit at-bats but Jack Lelivelt, who split his season between the Yankees and Senators, had the most pinch-hits with 12. The colorful Germany Schaefer of Washington set the pace that year by coming off the bench 21 times and hitting successfully 11 times for a sensational .524 average.

A player who had next to no power and seldom hit for average, Schaefer was able to stay in the majors for 13 seasons because of his versatility in the field at a number of positions. Schaeffer once rattled an opposing pitcher by stealing second base and then coming back to first base, only to steal second again. He and teammate Nick Altrock were two of the most comical characters in the game at the time. The pair later formed a vaudeville act with Charley O'Leary of the Tigers that turned out to be the inspiration for the MGM movie musical, "Take Me Out to the Ballgame," starring Gene Kelly and Frank Sinatra.

Although he only batted .257 for his career, Schaefer was a .273 hitter in the pinch with 24 hits in 88 at-bats. His friend, John McGraw, made him a Giants' scout after his playing days ended. While on a scouting trip to Canada, the 42-year-old Schaefer had a massive heart attack and died aboard a train near Saranac Lake, New York, on May 16, 1919.

Lelivelt, a lumbering 5' 11", 175-pound outfielder from Chicago, went on from the majors to become an outstanding minor league manager for 21 seasons. During that span his teams won three Pacific Coast League titles. As a big leaguer, he hit .310 overall as a part-timer in six seasons while his 25 hits in 83 pinch-hit at-bats matched his lifetime average exactly. He was 55 when he died in Seattle on January 20, 1941.

Although he never led his league — the AL — in any individual single season category as a pinch-hitter, the aptly named Pinch Thomas was excellent off the bench from 1913 to 1918. In those six seasons—five with the Red Sox and another with the Indians— the left-handed hitting catcher from Camp Point, Illinois, batted a resounding .417 with 13 hits in 31 at-bats. Those were his final hits off the bench. For the remaining three years in his 10-season career, he was hitless in 16 consecutive pinch-hit at-bats. Thomas appeared in three World Series—in 1915 and 1916 with the Red Sox, and in 1920 with the Indians. Overall the 5' 9½", 175-pounder hit a mere .237 with but two home runs in 1,025 appearances. However, his 13

In all probability, Ham Hyatt should be judged as baseball's first true career pinch-hitter. (Courtesy of National Baseball Hall of Fame Library, Cooperstown, N.Y.)

safeties in 47 pinch-hit at-bats earned him a much better .277 BA. Thomas passed away in Modesto, California, on Christmas Eve in 1954 at the age of 64.

Meanwhile Ham Hyatt continued to do what he did best in Pittsburgh. Upon his return to the Pirates from the minor leagues in 1913, he banged out four home runs off the bench. Gavvy Cravath, an outfielder for the Phillies, hit two pinch-hit homers as well that year, the second one coming off the immortal Christy Mathewson on July 4. That season the National League alone accounted for 11 home runs by emergency batsmen.

Hyatt set still another new major league record for pinch-hit at-bats in 1914 in the NL by being called upon officially 58 times off the bench, exceeding Doc Miller's record of 56 set just the year before. Hyatt also produced 14 hits to lead the senior circuit but Josh Devore, who split his season between the Pirates and Braves, had the best average at .444 by virtue of 11 hits in 25 at-bats.

Devore, a left-handed hitting outfielder from Murray City, Ohio, was a superb bunter and baserunner who also drew more than his share of walks. The 5' 6", 160-pounder's splendid catch of a fly ball hit to deep right center in Game Three of the 1912 series saved a 2-1 victory for the Giants behind Rube Marquard. Devore was a .277 batter overall during his seven-year career, which included appearances in the 1911 and 1912 Series with the Giants, and in the 1914 Fall Classic with the "Miracle Braves," who went from last to first after July. As a pinch-hitter, he was 14-for-49 for a pretty fair .256 mark. He passed away in Chillicothe, Ohio, on October 6, 1954, at the age of 66.

Wally Rehg, a right-handed hitting reserve outfielder for the Red Sox, had the AL's most pinch-hit at-bats (36) in 1914. He also tied with the Browns' Ernie Walker, another backup outfielder, for the most base hits off the bench with 10. However, Walker's came in 29 at-bats for a .345 mark to lead the league, while Rehg's total in 36 at-bats only rated him a .261 BA.

Rehg, a 5' 8", 160-pound speedster was never able to earn a starting spot, particularly after having to sit out the entire 1916 season with a bad knee. He spent the last three years of his seven-year career with the Braves and Reds. Overall, Rehg hit .250 while his 12 hits in 47 pinch-hit attempts were slightly better at .255. He died in Burbank, California, on April 5, 1946, at the age of 57.

The left-handed hitting Walker — the older brother of future Brooklyn favorite Dixie Walker — played only three years in the big leagues. The 6-foot, 165-pounder from Blossburg, Alabama appeared in just 128 games for the St. Louis Browns and hit .256 for his 254 official times up. However, as a pinch-swinger, he collected 15 hits in 48 attempts for a nifty .316 average. Walker was 74 when he passed away in Pell City, Alabama, on April 1, 1965.

While Robert Frank "Braggo" Roth never led the American League in either pinch-hit at-bats, hits or average, he was one of the best substitute batters of the decade. He played with six different AL teams during his eight-year career, earning the additional nickname of "The Globetrotter." His seven home runs in 1915 were enough to lead the league while playing for both the White Sox and the Indians. For his career, he registered 15 base hits in 45 pinch-hit at-bats for an excellent .333 average. His overall BA was a better-than-average .284. Roth finished up his career in 1921 as a member of the Yankees. He died in Chicago on September 11, 1936, at the age of 44.

The Pirates were racked with dissent and finished seventh in the National League in 1914. The team's president, Barney Dreyfuss, was so confounded by the club's performance that he put 11 players, including five starters, on waivers in late July. Ham Hyatt was not one of them. He went on to record 14 hits in 58 pinch-hit at-bats to lead both leagues in each category that year. Among his hits was a two-run homer off Jim Lavender in Chicago on April 26 that rallied his club to victory. He also tripled with two on against Boston's George Davis in the eighth inning on July 22, to chalk up his fifth career three-bagger as an emergency batsman.

Unfortunately for Hyatt, he could not hit as well when inserted as a starter, recording only three hits in 21 times at bat. Since his overall average that year was a weak .215, the worst of his big league life, he drew his release from the Pirates on February 28, 1915. The Cardinals quickly signed him and used him as their regular first baseman and he hit a respectable .268 in 106 games. As a pinch-hitter he only mustered three hits in 14 at bats for a slight .214 mark.

After a couple of years in the minors with Chattanooga, Hyatt's friend and former teammate, Miller Huggins, replaced "Wild Bill" Donovan as manager of the Yankees and brought Hyatt to New York in 1918. As a utility player, he hit .229 in 53 games and was only 4-for-21 as a substitute batter for an even lower .190 BA. He drifted back into the minors the following year and played for another five years in the bushes before hanging up his spikes. Throughout his major league career, Ham Hyatt was credited with 57 pinch-hits in 240 at bats for a .239 BA.

"Dashing Dan" Costello, a left-handed hitting outfielder for the Pirates, led the NL with 46 pinch-hit at-bats and 14 base hits in 1915 for a solid .304 mark. However, it was Red Murray, who played for both the

Giants and Cubs that year, who had the best pinch-hit average at .471 coming via eight base hits in 17 at-bats.

The 6' ½", 185-pound Costello, a product of Jessup, Pennsylvania, played in the big leagues for four years. He only batted .243 overall without a single home run but his 20 base hits in 67 pinch-hit at-bats earned him a solid .299 BA. He passed away in Pittsburgh on March 26, 1936, at the age of 44.

The 5' 10½", 190-pound Murray, who was born in Arnot, Pennsylvania, once led the NL with seven homers in 1909. He also finished second in stolen bases three years running from 1908 to 1910. Some credited him with the greatest catch in Forbes Field history during the 1912 season. As a member of the visiting Giants, Murray made a leaping, fingertip catch while playing behind the great Christy Mathewson. In his last several years in the majors, Murray was relegated to the bench and employed primarily as a pinch-hitter and backup outfielder. For his 11-year career, Murray batted .270 and his 15 hits in 64 pinch-hit at-bats produced a .234 average. He died in Sayre, Pennsylvania, at the age of 74, on December 4, 1958.

Marty Kavanagh, who started out in the big leagues as the regular second baseman of the Detroit Tigers in 1914, eventually lost his job the following year to Ralph Young, a recent acquisition from the Yankees. Nevertheless, the 6-foot, 187-pound Kavanagh, out of Harrison, New Jersey, remained with the club as a valuable utility player who could do just about everything but pitch and catch. In 1915, he led the AL in the pinch, going 10-for-20 for a .500 average. In 1916, he was sent up to the plate 46 times as a substitute batter for both the Tigers and Indians but was only able to punch out seven base hits for a rather undistinguished .152 BA. One of those hits, however, was a pinch-hit grand slam. It happened on September 24, 1916, and was the deciding blow as the Indians defeated the Red Sox, 5–3. It was reported that the ball rolled down the third base line and through an opening in the left field fence. Although Kavanagh came to bat 121 other times that season, that was his only homer all year. In 1,033 official plate appearances in the majors, he hit only a total of 10 home runs.

After spending all of 1917 in Cleveland, Kavanagh played for three teams in 1918 — the Indians, Cardinals and Tigers — in what proved to be his fifth and final year in the majors. Apart from his overall .249 average, he produced 18 hits in 85 career pinch-hitting appearances for an unspectacular .212 BA. Kavanagh passed away in Eloise, Michigan, on July 28, 1960, at the age of 69.

Of the nine hits that the Yankees' Ray Caldwell delivered when he led the AL with 33 pinch-hit at-bats in 1915, two were home runs hit on consecutive days: June 10 and 11. The feat was not duplicated until Joe Cronin of the Red Sox did it in 1943. The 6' 2", 190-pound Caldwell actually hit another homer on the following day, June 12, but not as a pinch-hitter since he was the starting pitcher that day. The Croydon, Pennsylvania product only hit eight home runs in his entire 12-year, 582-at-bat career, yet three of them came on successive days.

Traded to the Indians late in the 1919 campaign, Caldwell was struck by lightning in his Cleveland pitching debut on August 24. He recovered to get the last out of the game, a 2-1 win over Philadelphia. Two weeks later, on September 10, he no-hit his former teammates, 3-0, at the Polo Grounds in New York. Caldwell batted .248 overall for his career while his 36 hits in 154 pinch-hit at-bats produced a modest .233 BA. He died at 79 in Salamanca, New York, on August 17, 1967.

Utility infielder Art Butler of the Cardinals was in the last of his six big league seasons when he led the NL in pinch-hit at-bats with 54 in 1916. He also corralled the most base hits (13) but his teammate, catcher Frank Snyder, had the best average at .362 with five hits in just 13 times at the plate.

The right-handed hitting Butler was a native of Fall River, Massachusetts, and had roomed with the legendary Honus Wagner when he played for the Pirates earlier in his career. On June 5, 1915, the 5' 9", 160-pounder lined a single off Philadelphia's Grover Cleveland Alexander with two out in the ninth inning to break up a no-hit bid by the future Hall of Famer. For his stay in the majors, he batted .241, the same average he compiled as a pinch-batter with 20 hits in 83 at-bats. When Butler died in his home town of Fall River on October 7, 1984, the 96-year-old Butler had been the oldest living major leaguer at the time.

Snyder was in the big leagues for 16 seasons that included four consecutive World Series appearances with the Giants from 1921 through 1924. Although he went hitless in two Series appearances as a substitute batter he did bat .333 or better as a regular in the 1921 and 1922 Fall Classics. He was a superb regular season pinch-hitter over his career, accumulating 32 base hits in 86 official at-bats for a marvelous .372 BA. Overall, the 6' 2", 185-pounder from San Antonio, Texas, batted .265. Snyder passed away in his home town on January 5, 1962, at the age of 68.

Sam Crawford of the Tigers, at the tail end of a brilliant career, banged out eight hits in 15 at-bats for an unreachable .533 average in 1916. The left-handed hitting outfielder from Wahoo, Nebraska, nicknamed "Wahoo Sam," was renowned for hitting the most triples in history, 312, during his 19-year Hall of Fame career. Crawford's total held up to be 15 more than his teammate, Ty Cobb, whom he despised. The 6-foot, 190-pounder has the distinction of being the first player in history to have led the majors in home runs in both leagues—with 16 for Cincinnati in 1901 and seven for Detroit in 1908. Crawford had the most inside-the-park home runs in one year, collecting 12 in his league-leading home run season of 1901 with the Reds. All told, he had 50 for his career; 47 other homers cleared the fence. Elected to the Hall of Fame in 1957, Crawford's lifetime overall BA was a steady .309. As a pinch-hitter, he connected for 18 base hits in 64 at-bats for a better-than-average .281 mark. He was 88 years old when he died in Hollywood, California, on June 15, 1968.

Del "Sheriff" Gainer, a backup first baseman/outfielder with the Tigers and Red Sox, played for 10 years in the major leagues. The 6-foot, 180-pound native of Montrose, West Virginia had the thrill of a lifetime with a fourteenth inning pinch-hit single that won the longest game in World Series history for Boston over Brooklyn, 2-1, on October 9, 1916. The victory marked the first post-season pitching win for a southpaw named Babe Ruth, who went the distance. The Red Sox went on to defeat the Dodgers in five games.

Gainer, who hit from the right side, was one of four players sent up to pinch-hit for Babe Ruth during his career as a pitcher. The first one was a pretty good hitter in his own right, Duffy Lewis, a lifetime .284 batter.

On Ruth's first day in the majors, July 11, 1914, he started a game against Cleveland in Fenway Park. He had just been purchased from Baltimore and was tabbed a "can't miss" pitching prospect.

At the end of six innings, the Bambino had held the Indians to five scattered singles and the Red Sox clung to a 3-1 lead. In the seventh, though, the visitors put together three singles and a sacrifice to tally two more runs and tie the score. Lewis, who helped form one of the greatest outfields in baseball history with Harry Hooper and Tris Speaker, was injured and out of the starting lineup, but in the bottom of the seventh, manager Bill Carrigan sent Lewis to bat for Ruth. Lewis singled in Steve Yerkes with the run that eventually helped to win the game, 4-3. Dutch Leonard relieved Ruth and struck out four of the six Indian batters he faced to gave the Babe his first major league pitching win.

In a 1962 interview, Lewis, a San Francisco native, recalled the game. "I was out with a bad ankle," he said. "The Babe could hit the long ball but he struck out a lot of the time. Our manager, Bill Carrigan, asked me if I could hit. I told him I thought I could and, as it turned out, I did."[3]

Besides Gainer and Lewis, the other two players who were called on to pinch-hit for Babe Ruth were Forrest "Hick" Cady, a reserve backstop, on April 24, 1915, and Olaf "Swede" Henriksen on July 7, 1916. The 6' 2", 179-pound Cady, out of Bishop Hill, Illinois, and Gainer failed to get hits while Henriksen, a sometime outfielder, drew a walk. Once Ruth became a full-time outfielder, it would be 10 years before anyone would hit for him again.

In 1917, the year of the United States' entrance into World War I, Reds catcher Tommy Clarke led the NL with seven pinch-hits and 27 emergency at-bats. Harry Wolter, an outfielder for the Cubs, had the league's best average at .438 coming off seven hits in 16 times up.

In 1917, Clarke was in the next-to-last year of his 10 seasons in the big leagues. (He played only one game in 1918 before he was gone.) He went on to become a coach for the Giants for many years under John McGraw and later Bill Terry. As a teenager, the New York City native played for George M. Cohan's semi-pro team, the "Yankee Doodle Dandies." The 5' 11", 175-pound Clarke batted .265 for his career, including 26 hits in 110 pinch-hit at-bats for a .236 BA. He died in Corona, New York, on August 14, 1945, at the age of 57.

Over in the AL, catcher Bill Rumler of the Browns registered 71 pinch-hit at-bats in 1917, the highest number of at-bats for an emergency batsmen in one season. Rumler, a 6-foot, 190-pounder out of Milford, Nebraska, hit successfully 16 times that year for only a .225 BA. His club, a seventh-place finisher in 1917, used no less than 14 different pinch-hitters—a record at the time—averaging at least one St. Louis pinch-hit at-bat a game in the 154-game schedule.

In three seasons in the big leagues, Rumler only came to bat only 131 times, 99 as a pinch-hitter alone. He was gone from the game at the age of 26 after the 1917 season. For his abbreviated career, Rumler hit .251 overall while his 24-for-99 as a pinch-swinger was good for a .242 average. He passed away in Lincoln, Nebraska, on May 26, 1966, at the age of 75.

In 1918, Mike Fitzgerald, a left-handed hitting outfielder for the Phillies, who had not played in the majors in seven years, led the NL in all three major pinch-hit categories: pinch-hit at-bats, 30; base hits, eight; and average, .267. Fitzgerald's only other big league season had been as a 21-year-old in 1911 when he was a member of the Yankees for 16 games. The native of San Mateo, California hit .288 in but 82 games while his nine hits in 37 at-bats as a substitute batter earned him a moderate .243 average. He died in San Mateo on January 17, 1945, at the age of 54.

The AL pace-setter in pinch-hit at-bats in 1918 was a familiar name, Ham Hyatt, who only batted 21 times as an emergency batsman, a far cry from Bill Rumler's 71 of a year earlier. Hyatt, then with the Yankees and in the final year of his seven-year career, only produced four hits for a .190 mark.

Left-handed hitting Jack Graney had seven pinch-hits and a .389

average to lead the AL in those two categories in 1918. A 5' 9", 180-pounder from St. Thomas, Ontario, who had started out as a southpaw pitcher for the Indians in 1908, Graney played the rest of his 14-year career with the Tribe in the outfield. When his career ended, he became the first former-big leaguer to enter the radio broadcast booth and became one of the most popular announcers the Indians ever had. Overall, he hit .250 in 4,705 at-bats, but his 29 base hits in 92 pinch-hit attempts earned him a terrific .315 average.

Outfielder Joe Schultz, Sr. of the Cardinals, also known as "Germany," went 8-for-31 in 1919 to lead the NL in both categories. Schultz was destined for more excellent seasons as a substitute batter in the 1920s. The league's best pinch-hitting average was turned in by teammate Verne Clemons, whose 5-for-10 pinch-hitting gave him a gaudy .500 BA.

Clemons, widely respected for his handling of pitchers, went on to become a semi-regular for St. Louis. Clemons, who hailed from — of all places — Clemons, Iowa, played in the big leagues for seven seasons, compiling a .286 BA overall. As a pinch-swinger, he came to bat 54 times and produced 15 hits for an equally steady .280 mark. He was 66 when he died in Bay Pines, Florida, on May 5, 1959.

Ray Demmitt, an outfielder for the Browns and in the last season of a seven-year career in 1919, was the AL leader in pinch-hit at-bats with 27. "Honest Eddie" Murphy, an outfielder with the White Sox, had the most hits — eight — and the best BA at .381.

Demmitt, a 5' 8½", 170-pounder from Illiopolis, Illinois was a graduate of the University of Illinois. As a member of the New York Highlanders on June 29, 1909, Demmitt, not known as a home run hitter, hit the second homer ever against young fireballer off Walter Johnson.

While with the Browns, Demmitt had the only hit off Frank Smith of the White Sox on April 14, 1910. The left-handed hitting Demmitt was a lifetime .257 hitter. His seven hits in 39 pinch-hit at-bats merited a feeble .179 mark. Demmitt passed away in Glen Ellyn, Illinois, on February 19, 1956, at the age of 72.

An interesting footnote to the 1919 season was that "Honest Eddie" Murphy, a Hancock, New York native, was a member of the infamous Black Sox that year. The 5' 9", 155-pound left-handed hitter, who at one time had been a regular outfielder with both the Athletics and White Sox, had no role in the infamous 1919 World Series fix, thus earning the nickname, "Honest Eddie." He pinch-hit twice in the Series without registering a hit. For his career, Murphy batted a solid .287 and his 43 hits in 145 pinch-hit at-bats earned him a substantial .297 BA. He died in Dunmore, Pennsylvania on February 21, 1969, at the age of 77.

5

1920-1929:
Cy Williams Starts
Setting Home Run Records

By the time the "Roaring Twenties" arrived, home run records everywhere were falling; pinch-hitters were no exception. The first player to establish a new mark was the home run king of the time — the so-called deadball era — Gavvy Cravath. The right-handed power-hitter was a rough-and-tumble outfielder for the Phillies, who had cups of coffee earlier in his career with the Red Sox, White Sox and Senators in the American League. After a couple of years in the minors he was given another shot at the big time with the Phillies in 1912 at the age of 31.

Gavvy led the National League in home runs five times as a regular outfielder and was tied for a sixth crown before Babe Ruth gave up pitching and aimed for the fences full time. Cravath was aided greatly by the smallish dimensions of his home park, Baker Bowl, regarded at the time as the easiest place in the majors in which to hit a home run. When Cravath led the NL in home runs in 1914, all 19 homers came at Baker Bowl. Five seasons later when he led the league once again with only eight round-trippers, every one was deposited over Baker Bowl fences.

The crusty Cravath gave up his full-time outfielding position in 1919 when he was named the Phillies' player-manager and limited himself mainly to pinch-hitting. On April 20, 1920, he inserted himself into a scoreless game against the Giants and smashed a three-run homer that won the game. The blast was not only the last one he ever hit in the big leagues but also represented his sixth all-time as a pinch-hitter, setting a new record for emergency batsmen. It would endure for less than eight years before his Phillies' teammate, Cy Williams, broke it.

Cravath, who also led the league in pinch-hits with 12 in 1920, retired from the game right after that season to become a justice of the peace in Laguna, California. The man who was called "Cactus" as a player because of his rugged personality lost his new job because — of all things — he was deemed too easygoing, a charge also leveled against him as a manager.

Reserve outfielder Fred Nicholson of the Pirates led the NL in 1920 in at-bats as a pinch-hitter with 38 and his 12 pinch-hits tied Cravath. Clarence Mitchell of the Dodgers, the league's only left-handed legal spitball pitcher, had the best pinch-hit average at .333 coming off the bench to collect six hits in 18 times up.

Nicholson, who was born in Honey Grove, Texas, never made it as a regular in the majors during his five-year stay although he batted a solid .311 overall. The right-handed hitter, who stood 5 feet 10½ inches tall and weighed 173 pounds, was the property of 11 different clubs in eight leagues over a 10-year period. His 21 hits in 80 pinch-hitting appearances amounted to a .247 BA. A World War I veteran, Nicholson was 77 when he died in Kilgore, Texas, on January 23, 1972.

The left-handed hitting Mitchell, who came from Franklin, Nebraska, was in the big leagues for 18 years with six teams. When the spitball was banned in 1920, several pitchers, including Mitchell, were allowed to continue to use the slippery pitch. He is remembered for slamming the line drive that Cleveland's Bill Wambsganss caught to start an unassisted triple play in Game Five of the 1920 World Series. Two innings later, he hit into a double play to account for five outs in two swings of the bat. Mitchell's lifetime average was .252; the 31 base hits in 145 pinch-hit at-bats spawned a .214 average. He passed away in Grand Island, Nebraska, on November 6, 1963, at the age of 72.

The 1920 AL leader in pinch-hit at-bats and base hits was Sammy Hale, a rookie third baseman for the Tigers, who came up 52 times and produced 17 hits for a very healthy .327 mark. However, "Honest Eddie" Murphy of the White Sox had the best average for substitute batters, a robust .394 coming off 13 hits in 33 at-bats.

Hale failed to last through the 1921 season in Detroit and wound up with Portland of the Pacific Coast League in 1922. The Athletics purchased his contract and he remained in Philadelphia from 1923 to 1929. A Glen Rose, Texas product, the 5' 8½", 160-pounder was a right-handed batter who batted a spiffy .302 for his 10-year major league career. As a pinch-

Cy Williams's 11 career pinch-hit home runs was a record that stood for 31 years. (Courtesy of National Baseball Hall of Fame Library, Cooperstown, N.Y.)

hitter, he was 36-for-134 and recorded a decent .268 average. Hale passed away in Wheeler, Texas, at the age of 77 on September 6, 1974.

Babe Twombly, a backup outfielder for the Cubs, had 38 pinch-hit at-bats and 15 hits to lead the NL in both categories in 1921. Joe Schultz, Sr. of the Cardinals registered the best average that season with .333 by virtue of his six hits in 18 at-bats off the bench.

Twombly, whose brother, George, had played in the big leagues for five years, had an even shorter major league career. A left-handed hitting 5' 10", 160-pounder from Jamaica Plain, Massachusetts, Babe Twombly hit .304 in his brief time in Chicago. However, only 14 of his 109 base hits went for extra bases. As a pinch-swinger, he batted an equally proficient .314 with 19 base hits in 60 plate appearances. He was just 25 when he departed the majors after the 1921 campaign. Twombly died in San Clemente, California, on November 23, 1974, at the age of 78.

Fred "Cy" Williams, who like Doc Crandall before him hailed from Wadena, Indiana, broke in with the Cubs in 1912. The former Notre Dame architectural student was an excellent collegiate sprinter and hurdler. He also played football there with the immortal Knute Rockne. After six mediocre seasons in Chicago, he was traded to the Phillies for whom he played 13 years and established himself as one of the top slugging outfielders in the game. In his first 14 years in the big leagues, Williams played for a different manager every season.

A left-handed power hitter, Williams led the National League in home runs four times, including 41 in 1923 and 30 in 1927. Like Gavvy Cravath, he was also aided by the short outfield porches in Philadelphia's Baker Bowl. Williams was a dead pull hitter who prompted the first ever "Williams Shift," used later by Indians manager Lou Boudreau against another Williams, Boston's illustrious Ted.

In one game against the Dodgers, Williams opted to cross up the shift by slapping the ball to left field, but he hit it solidly and scorched a drive down the line. Although he could have easily had an inside-the-park home run, he began to laugh hysterically while circling the bases. He laughed so hard that by the time he reached third base, he was forced to pull up with a triple.

The gawky 6' 2", 180-pound Cy Williams was a tremendous pinch-hitter and always a threat for the long ball. He broke former teammate Gavvy Cravath's record with his seventh pinch-hit homer on April 16, 1928, off a knuckleball served up by the youthful and then-svelte Freddie Fitzsimmons. (The left-hander's girth later in his career led to his being called "Fat Freddie.")

Williams hit three pinch-hit home runs altogether in 1928 and two more the following season. He closed out his 19-year big league career with a record 11 pinch-hit home runs. His home run record endured for 31 years before falling. His final season in the majors saw him do little more than pinch-hit, but he did it extremely well, batting .500 (8-for-16) to pace the league.

One of the better pinch-hitters in the early 1920s was the Canadian-born outfielder, 5' 9", 180-pound Jack Graney, who played his entire 14-year career with the Cleveland Indians. The converted pitcher usually hit lead-off for the Tribe because of his speed. A fine outfielder and smart base runner, the left-handed hitter once went through a five-year stretch delivering 16 base hits in 48 at-bats as a pinch-hitter for a impressive .444 BA.

At one time, Graney held the record for the number of games played in the big leagues by a Canadian (1,402) until it was broken in 1989 by Houston's Terry Puhl, who played in 1,531. Graney had the distinction of being the first player in the majors to bat against pitcher Babe Ruth in his debut on July 11, 1914. He was also the first player to bat wearing a number on his uniform on June 26, 1916, but the number sewn on his sleeve was so small it was hardly noticeable.

In 1921 and 1922, the leading pinch-hitter in the National League was utility infielder-outfielder Joe Schultz, Sr. of the Cardinals. The right-handed hitting Schultz, a 5' 11½", 172-pound Pittsburgh native, was 6-for-18 for .333 in 1921 and 8-for-22 for .363 in 1922. Because of his versatility, he was able to remain in the majors for parts of 11 seasons without ever securing a regular job. Later he coached with the Cardinals and the Pirates. Schultz became a scout for Pittsburgh and even signed his own son, Joe, Jr., to a big league contract. He died in Columbia, South Carolina, at the age of 47, on April 13, 1941.

The Tigers' Chick Shorten, a left-handed hitting outfielder from Scranton, Pennsylvania, had nine hits in 37 pinch-hit at-bats to lead the AL in both categories in 1921. The 6-foot, 175-pound left-handed batter never played regularly in the big leagues during his eight-year career. Nevertheless, he prolonged his time in the game by over a half century when he became a scout for the Indians. He hit .275 lifetime overall and his 38-for-154 as a substitute batter gave him a .247 mark off the bench. He was 73 years old when he passed away in his hometown of Scranton on October 23, 1965.

The Reds' Rube Bressler, a right-handed hitting outfielder from Coder, Pennsylvania, had 13 pinch-hits and 43 pinch-hit at-bats to set the pace in the NL in 1922. Although he began his major league career as a pitcher for the Athletics, he was converted into an outfielder in Cincinnati. Like Ty Cobb, he gripped the bat with both hands apart. A slap hitter, he batted .301 lifetime while the 45 hits in 145 pinch-hit at-bats produced a .239 BA in his 19-year career. Although he was on two pennant winners— the 1914 A's and the 1919 Reds— he never appeared in a World Series game. Bressler died in Mount Washington, Ohio, on November 7, 1966, at the age of 72.

A rookie utility infielder-outfielder for the Tigers, Danny Clark was the AL's leading pinch-hitter in at-bats in 1922 with 36. His eight hits produced a minuscule .222 BA. Meanwhile, the immortal Tris Speaker of the Indians, in the sixteenth year of an illustrious 22 year-career, had nine hits to lead the league in that department. His 17 at-bats also allowed him to earn the AL's best pinch-hitting average at an unsurpassed .529.

Clark's brief career spanned but three years in different cities and years: with the Detroit Tigers (1922), with the Boston Red Sox (1924) and with the St. Louis Cardinals (1927). The Meridian, Mississippi native was a left-handed batter standing 5 feet 9 inches tall and weighing 167 pounds. For his short stay in the big leagues, he hit .277 overall while his 21 base hits in 86 pinch-hit attempts merited him a .244 BA. He passed away in his hometown of Meridian on May 23, 1937, at the age of 43.

Speaker, a Hall of Famer in his first year of eligibility in 1937, rarely pinch-hit but when he did he almost matched his lifetime .344 average. The left-handed hitter's 20 base hits in 60 times up as an emergency batter earned him a hefty .333 mark. A 5' 11½", 193-pounder from Hubbard, Texas, "The Grey Eagle" was one of the greatest hitters and center fielders in history. Speaker was player-manager of the Indians from 1919 to 1926 and led his club to a world title in 1920 against the Dodgers. He died at 70 on December 8, 1958, in Lake Whitney, Texas.

Earl Smith had the most pinch-hit at-bats in the NL in 1923 with 35 but his six hits only merited him a paltry .172 average while playing for the Giants and Braves. The following year, with Boston and Pittsburgh, he led the league with 10 pinch-hits and a .476 average. A backup catcher, he hailed from Hot Springs, Arkansas and stayed in the majors for 12 years. Smith appeared in five World Series: two each with the Giants and Pirates and one with the Cardinals. Nicknamed "Oil," courtesy of newspaper columnist Westbrook Pegler, Smith was a belligerent sort who defied not only Giants manager John McGraw's signs, but his hotel bed checks as well.

In 1927 while a member of NL champion Pirates, Smith was suspended for one month after breaking the jaw of Braves manager Dave Bancroft for no apparent reason. For his career, he batted a consistent .303 and amassed 41 hits in 129 pinch-hit at-bats for an equally noteworthy .318 BA. He was not as fortunate in his World Series pinch-hit attempts going

0-for-5. Smith died in Little Rock, Arkansas, at the age of 66, on June 8, 1963.

Another top pinch-hitter of the decade was a left-handed pitcher, Jack Bentley of the Giants, a former Washington Senator. In 1923, his first year in New York, the Olney, Maryland product went 10-for-20 to lead the National League in pinch-hits. The following season the 5' 11½", 200-pounder not only beat Walter Johnson in Game Five of the World Series but also hit a home run off the "Big Train." Two games later, though, he lost to Johnson in relief on a bad-hop single in the twelfth by Earl McNeely for Washington's lone world championship.

In 1925, Bentley and Cotton Tierney led the league in pinch-hit at-bats with 28. Bentley also led the NL in base hits as a substitute batter that year with nine. For his career, he was 25-for-83 as a pinch-hitter, good enough for a .301 mark and 10 points above his fine .291 overall average. Bentley had weight problems late in his nine-year career, which ended in 1927 at the age of 32. He passed away in his hometown of Olney on October 24,1969, at the age of 74.

Amos Strunk of the White Sox, nearing the end of a productive 17-year big league career, led the AL in 1923 with 39 pinch-hit at-bats and 12 base hits for a smart .308 mark. The Yankees' Elmer Smith had the best average by far (.524) with 11 base hits in 21 appearances.

Born in Philadelphia, the 5' 11½", 175-pound Strunk played the outfield regularly for much of his career. Excellent defensively, he led the AL in fielding percentage five times. He batted left-handed with limited power but was a contact hitter who struck out only occasionally. Strunk was in four World Series with the Athletics and another with the Red Sox. A lifetime .283 hitter, he was 33-for-118 as a substitute batter for an efficient .263 BA. He lived to the ripe old age of 89 when he died in Linnerch, Pennsylvania, on July 22, 1979.

Elmer Smith's only year in New York was 1923, the year Yankee Stadium opened. A left-handed hitter, the Sandusky, Ohio native stood 5 feet 10 inches and weighed 165 pounds. The outfielder's claim to fame had come earlier in his career when he hit a grand slam home run for the Indians off Brooklyn's Burleigh Grimes in the 1920 World Series, the first slam in Series history. For his 10 years in the majors, Smith hit .276 overall while his 39 hits in 123 pinch-hit at-bats was even better at .317. He passed away in Columbia, Kentucky, on August 3, 1984, at 91.

Future Hall of Famer Bill Terry of the Giants had the most at-bats off the bench in the NL in 1924 with 38. The 6' 1", 200-pound Terry, also known as "Memphis Bill," played his entire 14-year career in New York and succeeded the great John McGraw as manager, serving in the role from

1932 to 1941. He is the last National Leaguer to hit .400, batting .401 in 1930. A career .341 batter, the left-handed hitting Terry was the best fielding first baseman of his era. Born in Atlanta, he appeared in three World Series, including two as manager.

Never a favorite of the writers in New York for his blunt demeanor and unwillingness to cater to them, Terry had to wait 18 years before his election to the Hall of Fame in 1954. However, he was not bitter and was a regular participant in the annual ceremonies in Cooperstown following his induction.

Terry was almost as good a pinch-hitter as he was a regular. His 34 hits in 113 times off the bench add up to a consistent .301 mark. Terry was 92 at the time of his death in Jacksonville, Florida, on January 9, 1989.

The top pinch-hitter in the American League in 1924 was a right-handed pitcher for the Indians, George "The Bull" Uhle, a 6-foot, 190-pounder from Cleveland, who also won 200 games in a 17-year career. He hit safely 11 times in 26 at-bats to post a .404 BA. Overall that season, he hit .308. He ranks third as a substitute batter among pitchers all-time with 44 base hits in 169 at-bats for a .261 mark. For his lifetime, Uhle batted a productive .288. He died in Lakewood, Ohio on February 26, 1985 at the age of 86.

Red Sox rookie first baseman Phil Todt topped the AL in pinch-hit at-bats in 1924 with 30 but only delivered four hits for an almost invisible .133 average. Born in St. Louis, the 6-foot, 170-pounder hit from the left side and was the club's regular first sacker from 1925 to 1930. The Red Sox finished last every year during his tenure.

He was only able to hit 52 home runs during his seven years in Fenway Park due to its deep center field and right-field fences. Overall, Todt hit .258 while his 7-for-47 as a pinch-swinger earned him a rather timid .150 average. He passed away in his home town of St. Louis on November 15, 1973, at the age of 72.

A switch-hitting catcher for the Braves, Frank Gibson, had the NL's best pinch-hitting average in 1925 with .467 coming off seven hits in 16 at-bats. The Omaha product spent 21 years in professional baseball but only eight of them in the majors. One year he held out with the Braves, not for money but for more work. A lifetime .274 hitter, he batted only .230 as a pinch-swinger with 29 hits in 117 official at-bats. He was 70 when he passed away in Austin, Texas, on April 27, 1961.

Santa Monica, California's Tex Vache, a reserve outfielder for the Red Sox, led the AL in pinch-hit at-bats in 1925 with 49. He only hit successfully 10 times for a tiny .205 BA. A 30-year-old, 6' 1", 190-pound rookie, he only played in the majors for this one season, even though he batted

.313 overall in 110 games and 25 of his 79 base hits went for extra bases. Vache died in Los Angeles on June 11, 1953, at the age of 57.

The Athletics' Walter French, who had been an All-American half-back at West Point, had the most base hits off the bench in the AL in 1925 with 13. The Browns' Herschel Bennett's 9-for-16 gave him a league-leading .562 BA. French left the academy in 1922 to try his hand at professional football with the Rochester Jefferson before switching to baseball a year later. Born in Moorestown, New Jersey, the left-handed hitter was a 5' 7½", 155-pounder who was a substitute outfielder, pinch-hitter and pinch-runner for his entire six-season career. In 1925, he played pro football for the Pottsville Maroons as well as in Philadelphia with the Athletics–he scored five touchdowns on the gridiron, but hit no home runs on the diamond that year. A .303 lifetime batter, his 28 hits in 113 pinch-hit appearances merited him a .fair 247 average. He passed away in Alameda, California, on April 3, 1978, at the age of 78.

Rookie switch-hitter Johnny Neun, a backup first baseman for the Tigers out of Baltimore, had the AL's most pinch-hit at-bats with 42 in 1926 and tied with Herschel Bennett, a reserve outfielder for the Browns, for honors with 12 hits. Bennett topped Neun in average with .462, since his base hits came in only 26 at-bats.

Never a starter, the 5' 10½", 175-pound Neun was a quick, slick-fielding player who once pulled off a rare unassisted triple play against the Indians on May 31, 1927. Following his playing days, he became a long-time coach for the Yankees under Joe McCarthy and interim manager for them in 1946. He also managed the Reds in 1947 and 1948. As a player, he batted .289 for his six-year career and his 41 hits in 160 pinch-hit at-bats gave him a fairly good .247 BA. Neun died in his home town of Baltimore on March 28, 1990, at the age of 89.

Bennett, a farmer's son from Elwood, Missouri, was hitting .330 until he broke his arm in 1924. The injury cost him not only the rest of the season but also a starting position in 1925. Additional physical damage later in his five-year career occurred when he crashed into a wall in Philadelphia, further curtailing his progress. After his playing days ended, he became the State of Missouri's Commissioner of Revenue. Bennett died in Springfield, Missouri, on September 9, 1964, at the age of 67.

One of those rare occasions when a pinch-hitter was sent up to bat for Babe Ruth took place in 1925. On August 9 of that year, in the eighth inning of a game played against the White Sox in Yankee Stadium, the veteran Bobby Veach was announced as Ruth's substitute batter. Then a reserve outfielder who had been acquired earlier that season from the Red Sox, the left-handed hitter from St. Charles, Louisiana drilled a single. He later went out to play center field while Earle Combs moved over from center to right in a game ultimately won by Chicago, 4-3.

Two somewhat conflicting newspaper reports were issued regarding this event. In one, the action was described as follows: "Babe Ruth was replaced in the eighth inning by Bob Veach, who was announced as pinch-hitter for the home-run king. Ruth had not been feeling well and was willing to retire."[1]

In the other, the *Chicago Tribune* couldn't resist reporting it this way: "The fans were treated to the unusual spectacle of His Royal Highness being yanked for a pinch-hitter."[2]

Just a week before this game, the 5' 11", 160-pound Veach pinch-hit for the "Iron Horse," Lou Gehrig. Veach had a creditable 14-year career in the big leagues, mostly with the Tigers with Ty Cobb acting as his batting tutor. He could later tell his grandchildren that he batted for Hall of Famers, Babe Ruth and Lou Gehrig, in the space of one week.

Gehrig was actually pinch-hit for on another occasion in 1925, this time by right-handed hitting reserve outfielder Ben Paschal, a 5' 11", 185-pounder out of Enterprise, Alabama. It happened during a game between the Yankees and the Indians at Yankee Stadium on August 2. Cleveland had taken a one-run lead into the eighth inning with a left-hander, Walter Miller, on the hill for the Tribe.

Manager Miller Huggins, playing the percentages, sent Paschal up to bat for the left-handed Gehrig, but the strategy backfired as Paschal was retired and the Yankees went on to lose, 3-2. At the time Gehrig was only in his first full year as the Yankees first baseman and was not quite the big-time slugger he eventually wound up to be on his way to Cooperstown.

On September 19, 1925, Bobby Veach — then with the Senators, his third club affiliation that season — put himself in the record books when he was sent up to pinch-hit in the ninth inning of a second game of a doubleheader in Washington. Ted Lyons of the White Sox had held the home club hitless for 8⅔ innings. The game was totally out of reach as the visitors held a 17-0 lead. Veach asked manager Bucky Harris what he wanted him to do. "You're going up there to hit, aren't you?" Harris responded.[3] Veach smacked a single to right to break up the no-hitter, the closest Hall of Famer Lyons ever came to pitching a no-hit, no-run game.

Alameda, California's Walter "Dutch" Ruether, whose career spanned the years of 1917 to 1927, is the only pitcher to pinch-hit for three different teams in the World Series. He accomplished this distinction by being called upon once each by the Reds in 1919 and the Senators in 1925 as well as twice by the Yankees in 1926. Unfortunately Ruether, who had gained a reputation as a troublemaker, was unable to come up with a base hit in those four at-bats. He compiled 34 hits in 145 pinch-hit at-bats during the 11 regular seasons in which he played, attaining a .234 mark as an emergency batsman. For his career, he posted a somewhat better average of .258. As a pinch-hitter among pitchers, he ranks fifth on the all-time list. Ruether passed away in Phoenix on May 16, 1970, at the age of 76.

Chick Tolson, a backup first sacker for the Cubs, paced the National League in pinch-hit at-bats with 40 and in base hits with 14 in 1926. The right-handed hitting Washington, D.C. native played in the big leagues for five years but only came to the plate 275 times. Slow enough to be nicknamed "Slug," the 6-foot, 185-pounder's only at-bat in a World Series game took place in 1929 when the Cubs lost to the Athletics in five games. He struck out.

Walter "Cuckoo" Christenson, a 27-year-old rookie for the Reds, had the NL's best pinch-hitting average in 1926 with .389 coming off a 7-for-18 season. A left-handed hitting San Francisco native, he only played in the big leagues for one more season, although the 5' 6½", 156-pounder hit .315 for his abbreviated career. As a pinch-hitter, he collected only five additional at-bats to register a .304 BA. He was 84 when he passed away in Menlo Park, California, on December 20, 1984.

Chick Tolson was succeeded as the season at-bat leader off the bench in the National League in 1927 by a future Hall of Famer, 18-year-old Mel Ott of the Giants. Ott, from Gretna, Louisiana, was sent up to the dish on 46 occasions. Teammate and future manager Bill Terry called the left-handed hitter the most natural batter he had ever seen. The 5' 9", 170-pounder was not hugely successful as he delivered but 11 pinch-hits for a .235 BA, but "Master Melvin" did hit the first of his 511 career home runs that year.

Meridian, Mississippi's Danny Clark of the Cardinals, a left-handed hitter standing 5 feet 9 inches tall and weighing 167 pounds, had the most pinch-hit base hits in the NL that year with 12 in 40 times up to post a .300 mark. Still another left-handed batter, Jack Fournier of the Boston Braves, a native of Au Sable, Michigan, and a 6-footer weighing 195 pounds, had the league's best batting average in the pinch at .421 (8-for-19).

No less a pitcher than Walter "Big Train" Johnson had this to say about Fournier: "I don't believe I ever pitched to a player who took more liberties with my stuff. No matter how I worked on him he seemed to have no trouble solving my offerings. Fournier was the original tough baby for me."[4] When his 15-year career was over, Fournier had a fine lifetime average of .313 overall and a better-than-average pinch-hitting mark of .266 via 29 hits in 109 at-bats. He died in Tacoma, Washington, on September 5, 1973, at the age of 80.

Over in the American League, Eddie Collins of the Athletics, back in Philadelphia after a dozen years in Chicago with the White Sox, set the pace for pinch-hitters in 1927. The 5' 9", 175-pound left-handed hitter, a peerless second baseman nearing the end of a storied career, produced 12 hits in 34 pinch-hit at-bats for an enviable .357 average. In a quarter of a century in the big leagues, the Millerton, New York native recorded a solid .333 mark overall while his 27 base hits in 104 pinch-hitting attempts earned him a decent .267 BA. Inducted into the Hall of Fame in 1939, Collins died in Boston on March 25, 1951, at the age of 63.

Veteran catcher Wally Schang of the Browns had a better average than Collins off the bench in 1927that season with seven hits in only 18 at-bats for .389. A 5' 10", 180-pound switch-hitter from South Wales, New York, he was in the major leagues for 19 seasons, including appearances in six World Series for the Athletics, Red Sox and Yankees. Overall Schang batted .284 but his 30 base hits in 145 pinch-hit at-bats only merited him a somewhat scrawny .207 average. He died in St. Louis on March 6, 1965, at the age of 75.

Also in 1927, the aforementioned Ben Paschal of the Yankees, who had batted for Ruth and Gehrig in the same week in 1927, had the honor of batting for Ruth once again. On April 12 when the Yankees beat the Athletics, 8-3, on opening day, the "Bambino" informed manager Miller Huggins that he was ill in the sixth inning and asked out. Paschal hit for him and singled. In three previous times at bat in the game against A's ace Lefty Grove, Ruth had been retired and fanned twice. It was the first game of Ruth's historic 60 homer season. For his eight-year career, Paschal hit a nifty .309 overall but his 29 pinch-hits in 128 appearances were only good for a dwarfish .227 average. He passed away at 79 in Charlotte on November 10, 1974.

A journeyman first baseman-outfielder, Joe "Moon" Harris, out of Coulters, Pennsylvania, was sent up to pinch-hit a National League-high 42 times in 1928 for both the Dodgers and Pirates. He produced nine hits that season, also tied for the lead, for a .214 mark. The 5' 9", 170-pound right-handed hitter spent parts of 10 seasons with six different teams in both leagues. A lifetime .317 batter overall, he collected only 25 base hits in 121 pinch-hit at-bats for a rather poor .168 average. He was 68 when he died in Renton, Pennsylvania, on December 10, 1959.

The best pinch-hitter in the league that year in both hits and average was part-time outfielder Jack Smith of the Boston Braves. He produced those hits in 25 appearances to register an admirable .360 BA. The 5' 8", 165-pound left-handed hitting Smith spent 15 years in the majors, mostly with the Cardinals. For his career, Smith hit a very respectable .287 overall while his 29 hits in 113 pinch-hitting attempts produced an adequate .256 mark. The Chicago native was 76 when he died in Westchester, Illinois, on May 2, 1972.

Guy Sturdy of the Browns led the AL in pinch-hit at-bats with 44 and in hits with 10, a .227 mark. Sturdy had just one non-pinch-hitting at-bat that year, and 22 for his brief two-year career. Overall, he batted .288 while his 10-for-44 off the bench represented the entire career output. He died in Marshall, Texas, on May 4, 1965, at the age of 65.

Backup journeyman catchers Bennie Tate of the Senators and Pinky Hargarve of the Tigers tied for the league's best pinch-hitting BA with 9-for-25 for .360. Both the left-handed hitting Tate, a 5' 8", 165-pounder out of Whitwell, Tennessee, and Hargarve, a 5' 8½", 180-pound switch-hitter from New Haven, Indiana, spent parts of 10 seasons in the majors with a number of different clubs in both leagues. Tate hit .279 for his career but his pinch-hitting average was a marvelous .358 off 29 hits in 81 at-bats. He died in West Frankfort, Illinois on October 27, 1973 at the age of 71.

Hargarve batted .278 overall for his career but his 14 hits in 96 at-bats off the bench were well below his lifetime average at an inferior .146 mark. He passed away in Fort, Wayne, Indiana on October 3, 1942. at the age of 46.

Two of the best pinch-hitters ever had their initial impacts upon the game in 1929. Charles "Red" Lucas was a right-handed pitcher unable to produce a major league fastball, so the Cincinnati Reds tried to make him an infielder. Though the Columbia, Tennessee product had 151 victories, it was his hitting from the left side that kept him around for 15 years. In 1929, he led the National League in pinch-hits with 13 but it was just the beginning of his exploits as a substitute batter.

Rookie Pat Crawford of the Giants, a 5' 11", 170-pound utility infielder who swung left-handed, had the most at-bats for a pinch-hitter in the NL that year with 44. What set the Society Hill, North Carolina native apart from other pinch-hitters—with the exception of the Braves' Les Bell—was what happened May 26, 1929. Each hit grand slam home runs for their respective teams in the same game, the only time in history that players from different teams pinch-hit home runs with the bases loaded in the same game.

Crawford played in the big leagues for just four seasons registering a .280 BA overall while his 33 base hits in 139 pinch-hit at-bats earned him a .237 BA. Bell, a veteran third baseman from Harrisburg, Pennsylvania who swung right-handed, also played for the Cardinals and Cubs during his nine-year career. He was used as a pinch-hitter on only 21 occasions and was only able to produce but three base hits (.143). Overall, though, he batted a solid .290.

Ervin Brame, a right-handed pitcher for the Pirates who batted left-handed, was far and away the league's best in average for pinch-swingers in 1929. The 6' 2", 190-pounder was 10-for-21 for a splendid .476 BA. The Big Rock, Tennessee native also had a relatively short career in the big leagues—five seasons—all in Pittsburgh. Nevertheless, he won 16 and 17 games in 1929 and 1930, respectively.

Brame batted .306 with 121 hits in 396 times at bat. As a pinch-swinger, he recorded 25 hits in 70 at-bats for an even better .357 mark. He was only 31 when he left major league baseball after the 1932 campaign. He was just 48 when he passed away in Hopkinsville, Kentucky in 1949.

Another pinch-hitter who made his mark in the American League in 1929 was Bob "Fatty" Fothergill of the Tigers. The right-handed hitting Massillon, Ohio product was constantly teased by teammates and opponents alike because of his girth. The 5' 10½" reserve outfielder weighed in at 230-pounds.

He not only looked like a football player but actually was one during several off-seasons until he felt it might jeopardize his baseball career. His Catholic teammates also took pleasure in kidding him about his last name by referring to him as "Father Gill."

Other stories abounded about Fothergill like the time he supposedly bit an umpire after a called third strike while on a fasting program. On several other occasions he was reported to have shattered outfield fences while chasing fly balls. Leo Durocher once muttered sarcastically that it was illegal to have two men in the batter's box at the same time.

Fothergill was a line drive hitter who led the American League in pinch-hits with 19 in 1929 as well as at-bats with 53 for a marvelous .359 average. Like Red Lucas, this was only the beginning of a superior pinch-hitting career for both men in major league baseball.

6

1930-1939:
Red Lucas, Johnny Frederick
and Bing Miller Excel

While pinch-hitting as a general rule did not continue to spiral upward in the 1930s, a special group of players made their presence felt in this ten-year period. Red Lucas, for example, a right-handed pitcher for the second division Reds, picked up right where he left off in the preceding decade. He led the National League in pinch-hit at-bats and hits in 1930 (14-for-39, .359), 1931 (15-for-60, .250) and 1937 (9-for-37, .243). In fact, in the five seasons from 1929 to 1933, Lucas averaged no less than 13 pinch-hits a year.

Two of the pitcher's three career home runs demonstrate his reliability in a pinch.

In the second game of a doubleheader at the Polo Grounds in New York City on September 20, 1930, Lucas was inserted into the game in the top half of the ninth inning with two on and the home-standing Giants ahead, 3-1. He got hold of a fastball from Freddie Fitzsimmons and deposited it into the upper deck in left field. The homer gave the Reds a 4-3 lead, however, the Giants rallied in the bottom half of the inning to score twice and pull the game out.

The other home run Lucas hit as an emergency batsman came on May 27, 1933, against the Dodgers in Crosley Field in Cincinnati. It was another three-run shot, this one in the sixth inning off Ray Benge, but this time the Reds were victorious, 4-3.

Also known as "The Nashville Narcissus," Red Lucas was far ahead of his time when it came to pinch-hitting. It took another generation before anyone could match his production. He remains today the only pitcher on a relatively short list of pinch-hitters who have compiled more than 60 hits during their careers. A .261 hitter overall, Lucas named "Wild Bill" Hallahan, a left-handed pitcher who spent most of his big league career with the Cardinals, as the toughest pitcher for him to hit against.

Upon his retirement from the majors after the 1938 season, the left-handed hitting, right-handed pitching Lucas had 114 hits in 437 at-bats as a substitute batter for a better-than-most .261 BA. His hit record as a pinch-hitter held up for some 30 years. Even today he ranks among the top 10 pinch-hitters of all time in both at-bats and base hits. After leaving the big leagues, he continued to pitch, coach and pinch-hit for the Montreal Royals of the International League, then a AAA Brooklyn Dodger farm club. Lucas died in Nashville on July 9, 1986, at the age of 84.

Another pitcher who struck fear into opposing pitchers whenever he came to bat during this era was Wes Ferrell, a right-hander who not only won 193 games but batted .280 for his 15-year career. Ferrell, the brother of Hall of Fame catcher Rick Ferrell, was born in Greensboro, North Carolina. He broke in with Cleveland in 1927 and played there until 1934 when he was traded to the Red Sox. It was with the Tribe that Wes Ferrell set the all-time record for home runs in a single season by a pitcher with nine in 1931. His 38 round-trippers overall are also unsurpassed by any other pitcher in history.

Ferrell also played for the Senators, Yankees, Dodgers and Braves before hanging up his spikes following the 1941 campaign. As a pinch-hitter he was sent up to the dish on 139 occasions and came away with 31 hits for a .223 mark. Wes Ferrell passed away in Sarasota, Florida, on December 9, 1976, at the age of 68.

Fatty Fothergill, who split his 1930 season between the Tigers and the White Sox, still managed to tie for the most number of pinch-hit at-bats that year in the American League with 34. Bibb Falk, an outfielder for the Indians, tied Fothergill in that category but collected the most base hits in the AL that season with 13. Of all the players who posted more than 200 at-bats in their careers as pinch-hitters, only Fothergill averaged .300 with 76 hits in 253 appearances at the plate. Ironically in 1933, Fatty Fothergill, then with the Red Sox and in his final season in the big leagues, was pinch-hit for himself by none other than Red Lucas.

Two .500 hitters, Cy Williams of the Phillies with 8-for-16 in the NL and the AL's Jimmy Reese of the Yankees with 10-for-20, paced their respective leagues in pinch-hitting averages in 1930. The 5' 11½", 165-pound

Reese, who was born James Herman Soloman, was a Los Angeles native
and Babe Ruth's roommate while with the New York club. He was traded
to the Cardinals in 1932, in only his third and final year in the big leagues.
He later became a long-time coach for the California Angels, where he was
well-known for his dexterity with the fungo bat. The Angels later retired
his uniform number.

Although Lucas led the NL in pinch-hit at bats and hits in 1931, Ethan
Allen, a 6' 1", 180-pound outfielder for the Giants, who was born in Cincinnati, had the league's best BA with eight base hits in 14 at-bats for an
unreachable .571 mark, his best ever as a substitute batter.

The American League leader in pinch-hit at-bats that season was
a reserve outfielder for the Red Sox named "Long Tom" Winsett. The
McKenzie, Tennessee native had a checkered seven-year career playing for
three different clubs in both leagues. The 6' 2", 190-pound left-handed hitter was a .237 hitter for his major league career. He accumulated 19 hits
in 71 pinch-hit at-bats for an OK .247 BA. Winsett was 77 years old when
he died in Memphis on July 20, 1987. Teammates Bibb "Jockey" Falk and
Smead "Smudge" Jolley of the White Sox deadlocked for the AL lead in
pinch-hits with 14 in 1931.

Falk, a 6-foot, 175-pound left-handed hitting outfielder from Austin,
Texas, had an enviable .326 mark as a pinch-hitter in the final season of a
distinguished 12-year-career in the big leagues. He averaged .314 overall,
and his 36 base hits in 114 pinch-hit at-bats also earned him an equally
proficient .316 BA.

A versatile athlete, Falk was undefeated for three years as a southpaw
pitcher for the University of Texas. He was also an All-Conference tackle
in football for the Longhorns. Falk, who never spent a day in the minor
leagues, took over as the leftfielder for the banished "Shoeless" Joe Jackson in Chicago after the Black Sox gambling scandal. He played there for
nine productive seasons. From 1940 to 1967 (except for three years in the
Air Force during World War II), he served as his alma mater's baseball
coach and won no less than 20 Southwest Conference championships and
two NCAA titles. The University of Texas ballpark was named in honor
of its witty, sharp-tongued coach. A lifelong bachelor, Falk passed away in
1988 at the age of 89.

Jolley, an outfielder out of Wesson, Arkansas, had the league's best
pinch-hitting average in 1931 as his 14 hits came in 30 at-bats for a terrific
.467 BA. A fine hitter, who won six batting titles in the minors, he could
not overcome his horrendous fielding deficiencies. He averaged .305 overall in his brief four-year career while his 20-for-52 as a pinch-hitter earned
him a superb .385 mark. The left-handed 6' 3½", 210-pounder left the

major leagues as a member of the Red Sox in 1932 at the age of 30. Jolley was 89 years of age when he passed away in Alameda, California, on November 17, 1991.

The year of 1932 turned out to be a breakout year for pinch-hitting at-bats as Sam Leslie, a left-handed hitting backup first baseman to Bill Terry of the Giants, was sent up to the plate 72 times as a substitute batter, eclipsing Bill Rumler's 15-year-old record of 71. Leslie, who was born in Moss Point, Florida, also had the most pinch-hits in the NL that year with 22, although outfielder Dave Barbee of the Pirates had a better average at .421 (8-for-19). Leslie's .306 mark, accomplished in nearly four times as many at-bats as Barbee, was a marvelous feat.

The 6-foot, 192-pound Leslie was a terrific hitter but was unable to field his position very well. A writer once said of him: "He could hit if you woke him at two in the afternoon but couldn't field if you played him at two in the afternoon." He was traded to the rival Dodgers where he played regularly for four years until he was reacquired by the Giants after the 1935 campaign. His pinch-hitting prowess helped the New York club win National League pennants in both 1936 and 1937. He was 2-for-4 as a substitute batter in World Series play. Leslie accumulated a total of 59 career pinch-hits in 216 at-bats for a noteworthy .273 BA, to go along with his even better lifetime .304 average. Leslie passed away in Pascagoula, Florida, on January 21, 1979, at the age of 73.

A brand-new single-season home run record for pinch-hitters was set in 1932 by outfielder Johnny Frederick of the Dodgers. In a game played on August 14 against the hated crosstown Giants, the Denver native was called upon to pinch-hit in the ninth inning against vaunted screwballer Carl Hubbell. The left-handed hitting Frederick belted a home run off the future Hall of Fame southpaw to tie the game at 1-1. It was the fourth of six pinch-hit homers he collected that year to set a new major league mark. A sidebar to the game, which the Giants wound up winning in the tenth, was that it enabled 49-year-old John Quinn to become the oldest pitcher ever credited with a victory.

Frederick's sixth pinch-hit homer of the year took place on September 10, 1932. It was a dramatic ninth inning two-run blast that beat spitballer Burleigh Grimes and the Cubs, 4-3. The old record of three pinch-hit homers in a season was originally established by the Pirates' Ham Hyatt in 1913 and was subsequently tied by Cy Williams of the Phillies in 1928 and Pat Crawford of the Giants a year later. Frederick's record lasted until the year 2000 when another Dodger, Dave Hansen, would hit seven to set yet another single season home run mark.

Frederick's overall pinch-hit production in 1932 (9-for-29, .310) was

Sam Leslie's 72 official at-bats as a pinch-swinger in 1932 set still another new major league record that season. (Courtesy of National Baseball Hall of Fame Library, Cooperstown, N.Y.)

unique because eight of those nine hits were for extra bases. These included the six homers and two doubles. Those 29 total bases in 29 at-bats gave him a remarkable slugging mark of 1.000. Frederick's 19 hits in 62 career pinch-hit at-bats was good for a .307 mark, a shade below his lifetime overall average of .308. Frederick, who did not reach the majors until the age of 27 in 1929, only played for six years in the big leagues, all of them in Brooklyn. He was 32 when he played in his last game. Frederick died in Tigard, Oregon, in 1977 at the age of 75.

In 1932, the American League leader in pinch-hit at-bats with 43 and base hits with 14 was outfielder Dave "Sheriff" Harris of the Senators. Never a regular, the Summerfield, North Carolina native none-

Johnny Frederick established the new single season home run mark for substitute batters with six in 1932. (Courtesy of National Baseball Hall of Fame Library, Cooperstown, N.Y.)

theless carved out an enviable .310 career average as a pinch-swinger with 40 base hits in 129 appearances, well above his .281 lifetime average.

On August 5, 1932, the right-handed hitting Harris was called upon by then-manager Walter Johnson to hit for pitcher Bobby Burke. The opposing hurler, Tommy Bridges of the Tigers, was working on a 13-0 perfect game with one out remaining in the game. When the 5' 11", 195-pounder's name was announced as a pinch-hitter, the home crowd of 7,000 let out a chorus of boos. Sheriff blooped Bridges's first pitch over second base to spoil the right-hander's bid for perfection. The next batter, Sam Rice, grounded out for the final out and Bridges was left with a one-hit shutout.

Hall of Famer Johnson expressed his regrets later for the loss of a perfect game but said he would not want to get one himself if he did not earn it. Said Harris: "I'm getting paid to hit and he's getting paid to pitch. He never gave me any breaks at the plate. Why should I give him any?"

Harris had gained his nickname Sheriff because he was once deputized to bring in a character who had stolen a mule. His roommate in Washington was the intellectual Moe Berg, who later became a spy for the United States. One day, Harris complained to Berg that he wasn't feeling well. Berg looked at his roommate's tongue and told him that he was just having a loss of intestinal fortitude. The following day, Harris told the press that he had shaken off the case of intestinal fortitude he had experienced the day before. Harris passed away in Atlanta on September 8, 1973, at the age of 73.

The years 1933 and 1934 were not terribly eventful for pinch-hitters in either league. Left-handed hitting Harry McCurdy, a slow-footed backup catcher for the Phillies in 1933, led the National League in pinch-hit at-bats with 52 and hits with 15 for a reliable .299 average.

That season was the best ever as a substitute batter for McCurdy. The 6' 2", 170-pounder out of Stevens Point, Wisconsin played in the majors for 10 seasons with the Cardinals, White Sox, Phillies and Reds. Overall he batted .282 while his pinch-hitting numbers— 37 hits in 158 times at bat — only gained him a .238 mark. He was 35 following his last season in the big leagues in 1934. He died in Houston on July 12, 1972 at the age of 72.

Reserve outfielder Joe Mowry of the Braves had a better pinch-hit average than McCurdy in 1933 with seven hits in 20 at-bats for a coveted .350 average. The switch-hitting 6-foot, 198-pounder from St. Louis, repeated as the best in pinch-hit batting average two years later when he was 10-for-30 for an even .300. Mowry only played in the major leagues for three years, leaving after the 1935 campaign at the age of 27. For his career, he only hit.239 while his 17 hits in 53 pinch-hitting at-bats earned him a far superior .321 BA. He passed away in his home town of St. Louis on February 9, 1994, at the age of 85.

Over in the American League in 1933, veteran outfielder Bing Miller, then with the Athletics, began to make his mark as a premiere pinch-hitter batting from the right side. The 6-foot, 185-pound Vinton, Iowa product was tied with left-handed hitting Earl Webb for the most pinch-hit at-bats that year with 30. Webb divided his season — his last in the majors— with two teams: the Tigers and White Sox. The slow-footed 6' 1", 185-pound outfielder, from Bon Air, Tennessee played for five different clubs in both leagues during his seven-year career. In 1931, he established the major league record for doubles with 67 as a member of the Red Sox, three years before the "Green Monster" was erected in Fenway Park's left field. Webb batted .306 for his career and his 21 hits in 81 pinch-hitting attempts left him with a fairly good .259 mark. He was 35 when he left the big leagues after the 1933 season. Webb died in Jamestown, Tennessee, on May 23, 1965, at the age of 66.

A left-handed hitting outfielder from Red Oak, Georgia, Jo-Jo White, had the most pinch-hits in the American League in 1933. He collected 10 hits in 26 at-bats for a wondrous .384 average. The 5' 11", 165-pound White was a teammate of Webb's on the Tigers. He was gone from the majors after 1938 but returned as a member of the Philadelphia Athletics during World War II. Though his lifetime BA was only .256, he batted a remarkably good .298 as pinch-hitter with 42 base hits in 141 at-bats.

White was involved in a curious event in 1960 while a coach for the Cleveland Indians. General Manger Frank "Trader" Lane swapped his manager, Joe Gordon, to the Tigers for their manager at the time, Jimmy Dykes. Without a skipper for one game, the Indians had Jo-Jo White run the team and he won his only game as a big league manager. White's son, Mike, played in the majors for Houston as a utility infielder from 1963-5. Jo-Jo White died at the age of 77 in Tacoma, Washington on October 9, 1986.

Meanwhile, High Point, North Carolina's Cliff Bolton of the Senators, a backup catcher, recorded the best pinch-hitting average in the AL in 1933 with 9-out-of-22 for a .409 BA. The 5' 9", 160-pound left-handed hitter was in the big leagues for seven years, only once playing in more than 100 games. In 1935, Bolton played in 110 games and had his best year ever offensively, batting .304. However, his size and lack of power prevented him from becoming anything more than a bench player. Overall for his career, the North Carolina farm boy batted .291 and registered an excellent .316 as a pinch-hitter with 21-for-66. Bolton died in Lexington, North Carolina, on April 21, 1979, at the age of 72.

In 1934, Bing Miller emerged as the best pinch-hitter around as he again had the most at-bats in the AL with 33 as well as the league's most hits with 10 for a .303 mark. He repeated in both categories in 1935 as a member of the Red Sox when he was sent up to pinch-hit 43 times and delivered a league-high 13 hits for a league-best .302 BA.

Miller was a contact hitter who eschewed taking a third called strike. He averaged .312 overall for his 16-year major league career and his pinch-hit numbers added up to 46 hits in 175 at-bats for a fine .263 average. He passed away in Philadelphia on May 7, 1966, at the age of 71.

The National League in 1934 saw the Cardinals' Pat Crawford set the pace in pinch-hit at-bats with 43 and in hits with 11 for .256. The Giants' Harry "The Horse" Danning had the NL's best pinch-hit average with 8-out-of-16 for .500. When he first began to play the game, the Los Angeles native passed himself off as a Mexican while playing in a semi-pro

league in and around the city. He got his nickname from the famous
Damon Runyon fictional character when he was starting his 10-year major
league career in New York. The 6' 1", 190-pounder never returned to the
big leagues after World War II developing an arthritic right knee while
serving in the military. A lifetime .285 hitter with fairly good power, Danning was inconsistent as a pinch-hitter, only going 19-for-85 during his
career for a mere .223 BA.

Another catcher, Ernie "The Schnoze" Lombardi of the Reds, led the
NL in pinch-hit at-bats in 1935 with 36. The .306 lifetime right-handed
hitter, who used an interlocking grip, only produced eight hits along the
way that season for a .222 average. Known for carrying the league's heav-
iest bat, his hitting was punctuated by powerful line smashes. Lombardi's
career mark as a pinch-hitter resulted in 66 hits in 281 for a .231 BA. The
painfully slow 6' 3", 230-pound Oakland product played for 17 years in
the big leagues. His ultimate election to the Hall of Fame by the Veterans
Committee in 1985 occurred eight years after his death.

Although Bing Miller was the leader in pinch-hit at-bats and base
hits in the AL in 1935, future Hall of Fame pitcher Red Ruffing of the Yankees, had the best average at .444 with his 8-for-18 subbing. The 6' 1½",
205-pound Ruffing, a Granville, Illinois native who played in the big
leagues for 22 years, won 273 regular season games as well as posting a
7-2 mark in seven World Series with the Yankees. He had 58 hits in 228
at-bats as a pinch-hitter for a .255 mark that places him second all-time
among pitchers.

Ruffing was sometimes inserted by manager Joe McCarthy in either
the seventh or eighth places in the batting order instead of the traditional
ninth spot for pitchers.

Among pitchers with over 500 at-bats throughout their careers,
Ruffing ranks tenth with his .269 lifetime BA. He is third in home runs
with 36 among pitchers. Right-handed all the way, Ruffing batted over
.300 eight times and his 40-for-110 for an outstanding .364 in 1930, which
included 6-for-17 as a pinch-hitter, is ranked second only to Walter Johnson's unreachable .433 in 1925. Elected to the Hall of Fame in 1967, Ruffing
passed away in Mayfield Heights, Ohio, on February 17, 1986, at the age
of 81.

In 1936, Sid "Pudge" Gautreaux, a right-handed hitting rookie backup
catcher for the Dodgers, led the National League in both pinch-hit at-bats
with 55, and base hits with 16 for an admirable .291 BA. The right-handed
hitting Schriever, Louisiana native spent only two years in the majors,
leaving after the 1937 season at the age of 25. For his short stay in the
majors, Gautreaux batted .247 overall while his 17-for-65 was good for

a respectable .262 mark. He died at 77 on April 19, 1980, in Morgan City, Louisiana.

The NL leader in pinch-hitting average in 1936 was reserve rookie outfielder Jimmy Ripple of the Giants who was 9-out-of-19 for an excellent .474 BA. The left-handed hitting Ripple split time with the Dodgers and the Giants in 1939 and led the NL in pinch-hit at-bats with 38. The 5' 10", 170-pound Export, Pennsylvania product played just seven years in the majors, but still managed to appear in three World Series, two with the Giants (1936 and 1937) and one with the Reds (1940). Ripple hit .282 for his career overall, just an eyelash below his fine pinch-hitting average of .284 coming via 25 hits in 88 at-bats. Ripple died in Greensburg, Pennsylvania on July 16, 1959 at the age of 49.

Another pinch-hitter of note in the American League during this decade was a left-handed pitcher, Alfred "Chubby" Dean. He had the league's best pinch-hitting average in 1936 at .382 with 13-for-34 as a rookie for the Athletics. The 5' 11", 181-pound Mt. Airy, North Carolina native repeated the honor in 1939 with Philadelphia when he was 10-out-of-26 for a tremendous .385 BA.

A graduate of Duke who was coached in college by former pitcher Jack Coombs, Chubby Dean was both a starting pitcher and reliever with control problems during his eight-year stay in the majors. Fortunately, he could hit and was often used as a pinch-hitter for both the A's and the Indians. Like Harry Danning, he never returned to the big leagues after serving in the military during World War II. His career average was .274 while as a pinch-hitter he batted .256 via 49 hits in 191 at-bats. He was only 54 when he died in Riverside, New Jersey, on December 21, 1970.

The player who led the AL in pinch-hit at-bats and hits that season was Ed Coleman, a reserve outfielder for the Browns. A left-handed hitter from Canby, Oregon who threw right-handed, he came to bat 62 times and pounded out 20 hits for a wonderful .323 average. The 6' 2", 200-pounder broke in with the Athletics in 1932 and was hitting .342 in the first month of the season when he broke his ankle. He was never able to crack the starting lineup again and left the big leagues after the 1936 campaign. Coleman batted .285 for his career overall and his 33 hits in 113 pinch-hit at-bats earned him a .292 mark. He passed away in Oregon City on August 5, 1964, at the age of 63.

In 1937, Les Scarsella of the Reds tied Red Lucas with the most base hits for a pinch-hitter that season in the National League with nine. Scarsella, a left-handed hitting 5' 11", 185-pound first baseman only played for five years in the big leagues leaving after the 1940 season at 27 years of age. He played for a number of years thereafter in the Pacific Coast League where he won several batting titles. Scarsella left the big leagues with a .284 career mark overall. As a pinch-hitter, his 12-for-46 earned him a fairly dependable .261 average. He died in San Francisco on December 17, 1958, at the age of 45.

Johnny Moore, a left-handed hitting outfielder for the Phillies from Waterville, Connecticut, had the NL's best pinch-hitting average in 1937 at .350 (7-of-20). At 5' 10½" and 175 pounds, he played in the majors for 10 years and compiled a consistent .283 pinch-hitting BA with 26 hits in 92 official appearances. For his career, he posted an even better lifetime batting average of .307 overall. Moore was 89 when he died in Bradenton, Florida, on April 4, 1991.

In the American League, Lynn "Line Drive" Nelson, a right-handed pitcher with the Athletics who batted from the left side, had the most at-bats in the pinch in 1937 with 38. He was tied in base hits at nine with future Hall of Fame outfielder Goose Goslin of the Tigers and outfielder Larry Rosenthal of the White Sox, both also left-handed hitters. A native of Sheldon, North Dakota, the 5' 11½", 170-pound Nelson also wrestled professionally and was known as the "Masked Marvel." He was a better hitter — and wrestler — than pitcher. In fact, he got his nickname from the batters who seemed to enjoy facing him and lacing liners off his deliveries. For his career he was only 33-42 with a 5.25 ERA, mostly as a reliever. As a hitter, though, he batted .281 overall but his 21 hits in 89 pinch-hitting attempts resulted in a .237 average. Nelson passed away in Kansas City, Missouri on February 15, 1955, at the age of 49.

Ethan Allen of the Browns had the best pinch-hitting average (.348) in the American League in 1937. He was 8-for-23. The 6' 1", 180-pound right-handed hitting outfielder was one of the few of his era who had never played in the minors. Later in life, he served as the motion picture director for the National League. He also became a successful college baseball coach, wrote several books on baseball playing techniques and developed a revolutionary table top baseball game for kids. Allen died on September 15, 1993, in Brookings, Oregon, at the age of 89.

Goslin, nearing the end of an illustrious career, had 22 hits in 75 at-bats as an emergency batsman for a nifty .293 average during his 18 years in the big time. Overall, the Salem, New Jersey-born Goslin batted .316 and was elected to the Hall of Fame in 1968.

He played in every World Series game in Senators history, including a .344 average in Washington's 1924 triumph. While a member of the Tigers in the 1935 World Series against the Cubs, Goslin was involved in a heated argument with the legendary umpire, Bill Klem. As it turned out, Goslin was instrumental in getting Klem fined for the incident. It marked the first time in history that an umpire had ever been fined for an altercation with a player. Goslin passed away in Bridgeton, New Jersey, on May 15, 1971, at the age of 70.

Rosenthal, who was born in St. Paul, Minnesota, played in the big leagues for eight years only as a reserve for four different teams in the American League. He batted .263 overall while his 31 hits in 139 pinch-hit at-bats produced a .222 BA. Rosenthal was 81 when he died on March 4, 1992, in Woodbury, Minnesota.

The much-traveled infielder-outfielder Stan "Frenchy" Bordagaray of the Cardinals tied with rookie Harl Maggert of the Braves for the National League lead in pinch-hit at-bats with 43 in 1938, but Bordagaray had the league's most hits (20) and the best average. In fact, the Costlings, California product's .465 BA is the best ever in the big leagues for substitute batters with over 40 at-bats or more in a single season.

Bordagaray was a gifted player who drove managers crazy at times because of his erratic play and habits. He often ran when he wanted to, failed to slide when he should have and would ignore signs from time to time as well. Bordagaray also displayed moustaches and sideburns when no other players dared do so in the conservative 1930s. The fun-loving Bordagaray appeared in two World Series— with Cincinnati in 1939 and the Yankees in 1941— but had no official at-bats.

Once fined and suspended for spitting in the eye of an umpire, Bordagaray opined: "Maybe I did wrong. But the penalty was a little more than I expectorated."[1] He posted a .283 overall batting average, but his pinch-hitting prowess was an even more potent .314 coming off 54 base hits in 173 at-bats.

Maggert, a Los Angeles native whose father played for the Pirates in 1907 and the Athletics in 1912, only played for one year in the big leagues. The right-handed hitting 5' 8", 155-pound outfielder-third baseman, recorded but 89 at-bats in his one and only season, 43 of which came as a substitute batter. Overall he hit .281 for the season, but 10 pinch-hits only earned him a .232 BA as an emergency batsman. He died in Citrus Heights, California, on July 10, 1986, at the age of 72.

The American League in 1938 also saw one man, Taffy Wright, dominate all three pinch-hitting categories. A left-handed hitting rookie outfielder for the Senators, the 5' 10", 180-pound Wright, out of Tabor City, North Carolina, led his league in at-bats with 39, in hits with 13 and in average at .333. A lifetime .311 hitter, Wright possessed only average fielding skills which, when combined with his four years out for World War II military service, limited his career in the big leagues to just nine years. As a pinch-hitter, he came to bat 115 times and produced 32 hits for a better-than-most .278 BA. Wright passed away in Orlando, Florida, on October 22, 1981, at the age of 80.

A left-handed hitting first baseman-outfielder, Lou Finney, who was traded from the Athletics to the Red Sox early in 1939, led the AL that year in pinch-hit at-bats with 40 and in hits with 13 for a terrific .325 BA. The 6-foot, 180-pounder, who came from Buffalo, Alabama, played for 15 years in the big time, always as a reserve. Connie Mack had hoped that Finney could replace Al Simmons in the Philadelphia outfield, but he was never able to deliver the goods to the owner-manager's satisfaction. Finney had an overall average of .287, including 41 hits in 159 pinch-hit at-bats, good for a moderate .258 career mark. His lack of power — only 31 homers in 4,631 at-bats — prevented him from becoming a starting outfielder or first baseman. After his retirement, he and his brother Hal, who had been a reserve catcher for the Pirates, ran a feed store in their native Alabama. Lou Finney died in Lafayette, Alabama, on April 22, 1966, at the age of 55.

Chubby Dean had the best average in the AL in 1939 with 10 hits in 26 at-bats for a top-notch .385 mark. In the NL, Jimmy Ripple, who spent the season with both the Giants and Dodgers, led in at-bats with 38. Future Hall of Fame outfielder, Chuck Klein, led the league in both pinch-hits and average that season with 11-out-of-26 for an excellent .423 BA.

The 6-foot, 185-pound Klein, a native of Indianapolis, was traded back to the Phillies from the Reds that year and was approaching the end of a fine career in which hit .320 overall during 17 years, including the Triple Crown in 1934. He was another of those Phillies who profited from Baker Bowl's 280-foot short right-field porch.

In actuality, the left-handed hitting Klein was not a very good pinch-hitter as he ranks among history's lowest in average for players with more than 85 career pinch-hit appearances. He was just 28-out-of-137 for a .204 BA. After his pinch-hitting banner year in 1939, he had one of the lowest single-season pinch-hitting averages ever for a future Hall of Famer — only 2-for-18 and a minuscule .111 average in 1940. Too old for military service in World War II, he played on a part-time basis for the Phillies until his retirement after the 1944 season. He passed away at the relatively young age of 53 in 1958 in his home town of Indianapolis. Chuck Klein was inducted into the Hall of Fame in 1980.

7

1940-1949: None Better Than a Couple of Joes Named Cronin and Schultz

Pinch-hitting was on a downward slide in the 1940s. No one got more than 52 at-bats in the entire decade — a far cry from Sam Leslie's record of 72 in 1932, and even Red Lucas's 60 the year before that. Part of that was due to the manpower shortage during World War II. Regulars were had to find and many subs were pressed into regular duty with the club, or the country. Nevertheless, there were a handful of effective substitute batters who were called upon to deliver in the clutch.

Among the best was first baseman Johnny McCarthy, a Chicago native who broke in with the Dodgers in 1934. Left-handed all the way, the 6' 1½", 185-pound McCarthy had hoped to pitch in the big leagues but was never given any glove to work with other than a first sacker's mitt. Traded to the Giants in 1936, he became the club's regular first baseman in 1937 when manager Bill Terry retired as a player. McCarthy started all five games in the 1937 World Series, which was won by the Yankees. Unable to deliver the long ball consistently, he played on a part-time basis the following year. He eventually lost his job to power-hitting Zeke Bonura, acquired from the Senators for the 1939 season.

McCarthy never played regularly again in the majors but carved out a respectable 11-year career for himself as a fairly reliable pinch-hitter for both the Giants and the Braves. In 1940, he led the National League with 43 appearances and 11 hits for a decent .256 BA. He repeated as the NL leader in both categories eight years later when he was 13-for-45 for an even better .288 average. He left the game following the 1948 season. Overall he averaged .277 and as a pinch-hitter he hit safely 37 times in 144 at-bats for a fairly good .257 BA. He died at 63 in Mundelein, Illinois, on September 13. 1973.

In 1940, third baseman Odell "Bad News" Hale, in the twilight of a productive career with the Indians, was a now a full-time right-handed pinch-hitter. The 5' 10", 175-pounder led the American League in pinch-hit at-bats that season with 40. His eight base-hits only earned him a .200 average.

Five years earlier, Hale was involved in one of the most unusual triple plays in baseball history in a game against the Red Sox. Joe Cronin smacked a liner that hit Tribe third baseman Hale on the head. The ball deflected to shortstop Bill Knickerbocker on the fly and was subsequently relayed to second and on to first for a triple play to end the game.

Traded to the Red Sox and also to the Giants in the following year, Hale, a Hosston, Louisiana product, never returned to the big leagues after World War II. For his 10-year career, he batted .299 overall; his 23-for-100 as a pinch-swinger was not as impressive. Hale passed away in El Dorado, Arkansas, at 71 on June 9, 1980.

Strikeout-prone Chet Laabs of the Browns, an outfielder who had been traded over from the Tigers early in 1939 in a nine-player deal, set the pace for pinch-hitters in the AL in 1940 with 14-for-35 earning him a significant .400 average. The 5' 8", 175-pound Milwaukee native became a regular for the club in the following year. A right-handed hitter power-hitter, he smacked 27 home runs for the lowly St. Louis franchise in 1942. Laabs also played on the only pennant winner the Browns ever had, albeit as a loser in six games in the 1944 World Series to the crosstown rival Cardinals. During his career, Laabs posted an adequate .261 BA as a pinch-hitter with 30 base hits in 115 at-bats. Oddly enough, his lifetime batting average was the exact same. He died in Warren, Michigan, on January 26, 1983, at the age of 70.

Ken O'Dea, a reserve catcher for the Giants, was the National League's leader in pinch-hit at-bats in 1941 with 42. His nine hits were only good for a .214 BA. The left-handed hitter from Lima, New York spent his entire career as a backup to three great catchers: Gabby Hartnett of the Cubs, Harry Danning of the Giants, and Walker Cooper of the Cardinals. O'Dea was an outstanding emergency batsman in five different World Series going 6-for-13 for a marvelous .462 BA, including a since-tied record three hits in one series as a pinch swinger. O'Dea batted .255 overall for his dozen years in the majors, but his 36-for-184 was only good for a .196 BA off the bench. He died in his home town of Lima on December 17, 1985, at the age of 72.

Three players in the NL deadlocked for the most hits by substitute batters in 1941 with 10 apiece: teammates Ed "Bud" Stewart and Debs Garms of the Pirates and Lew Riggs of the Dodgers. Stewart's safeties came in 23 at-bats for a resounding .435 mark; Riggs' did it in 29 at-bats for an excellent .356 mark; and Garms's came via 31 pinch-hit at-bats which merited him a fine .323 BA as well.

Riggs, a left-handed hitter from Mebane, North Carolina, had been the regular third baseman for the Reds for four seasons until injuries limited his playing time in 1939 and 1940. Although a good glove man, he was not considered a reliable hitter. Consequently, he lost his job to Billy Werber in 1939 and the Reds made it all the way to the World Series. Expendable in Cincinnati, the 6-foot, 175-pound Riggs was traded to the Dodgers where he became Manager Leo Durocher's first man off the bench in both 1941 and 1942.

Stewart, a 5' 11", 160-pound rookie outfielder in 1941, claimed that because Pirates manager Frankie Frisch was constantly on his back, his efficiency fell off in 1942 the next year. His six hits in 28 pinch-hit at-bats in 1942 were good for a meek .214 average. Following his two years in Pittsburgh and three years out for military service, it took the left-handed hitter a total of six more years to get back to the big time in 1948. He reached the majors again with the Yankees, who then traded him to the Senators that same year after only six games. He later played with the White Sox and led the AL in pinch-hits with nine in 1951. Overall, he hit .268, but .242 as a substitute batter with 49 hits in 202 at-bats.

Garms, a Bangs, Texas native, was a slightly built left-handed batter who rarely hit the long ball. He led the NL in batting in 1940 with a .355 mark but he had only come to bat 358 times officially. His claim to fame was that he connected with the first base hit off Johnny "Double No-Hit" Vander Meer of the Reds to end the southpaw's string of 21⅓ hitless innings. Garms batted .293 for his 12-year career while his 54 base hits in 198 pinch-hit at-bats earned him a fine .272 BA. He died in Glen Ross, Texas, on December 16, 1984, at the age of 76.

In the American League, one man, Dee Miles of Connie Mack's Athletics, set the pace in 1941 with the most pinch-hit at-bats (45) the most hits (15) and the best average (.333). The left-handed hitting reserve outfielder from Kellerman, Alabama, had been a pitcher in the Cardinals' chain early in his professional career. He played for seven seasons as a part-timer with the Senators and Red Sox as well as the A's. A line drive hitter whose fielding left something to be desired, he was never able to catch on as a regular. His 43 hits in 165 at-bats as an emergency batsman produced a .261 mark. Overall, he turned in a proficient .280 BA. He died in Birmingham, Alabama, on November 2, 1976, at the age of 67.

The 6' 1", 180-pound Glen "Rip" Russell of the Cubs, who had been the team's regular first baseman as a rookie in 1939, was now relegated to pinch-hitting almost exclusively in 1942, mainly due to injuries. He led the National League with 31 times at-bat as a pinch-hitter in 1942. However, he only delivered five hits for a rather lean .161 BA.

The Los Angeles-born Russell was displaced by Phil Cavaretta in 1940 and was traded to the Red Sox after the war. As a right-handed pinch-hitter in the losing 1946 World Series against the Cardinals, he distinguished himself with a perfect 2-for-2 and a run scored. He left the majors for good after the 1947 season at the age of 32. Russell batted only .245 overall during his short five-year career and his 13 hits in 67 pinch-hitting at-bats delivered a .194 average. He died in Los Alamitos, California, on September 26, 1976, at the age of 61.

"Diminutive Dominick" Dallessandro, a stocky left-handed hitting outfielder for the Cubs out of Reading, Pennsylvania, tied Lew Riggs for the NL lead in pinch-hits with nine in 1942.

The 5' 6", 168-pound Dallessandro, who began his career with the Red Sox in 1937, battled his way back to the majors in 1940 with the Cubs. He played the rest of his eight-year major league career with them and became a valuable role player. His 52 hits in 192 pinch-hit at-bats earned him a respectable .271 average as a pinch-swinger, an exact duplicate of his .271 overall mark. Dim Dom left the big leagues after the 1947 season at the age of 34. He died in Indianapolis on April 29, 1988, at the age of 75.

The tall, lithe Riggs was a good glove man with the Reds but not reliable enough with the bat as an everyday player. However, his 9-for-21 as an emergency batsman in 1942 led the NL in average at .429. He played only one season for the Dodgers after the war, leaving the game at the age of 36 following the 1946 season. His 32 hits in 106 pinch-hit at-bats produced a very fine .302 lifetime BA in the pinch, much better than his .262 overall career mark. Riggs died in Durham, North Carolina, on August 12, 1975, at the age of 65.

None other than future Hall of Fame second baseman Charlie Gehringer of the Tigers paced the American League in 1942 with 11 pinch-hits and 39 pinch-hit at-bats for a .257 BA. The left-handed hitting Michigan native was in the final year of his illustrious 19-year career and only played three games in the field. The 5' 11", 180-pound Gehringer retired from baseball after the 1942 season at the age of 39. A lifetime .320 hitter, his 23 hits in 91 pinch-hit at-bats merited a .253 BA. He was inducted into the Hall of Fame in 1949. Gehringer died in Bloomfield Hills, Michigan, on January 21, 1993, at the age of 89.

The leader in average in the AL in 1942 was Gehringer's teammate and utility infielder-outfielder Don Ross, who connected for eight hits in 22 at-bats and a heady .363 average. The 6' 1", 185-pound California-born Ross played in the majors for seven years with two other clubs, the Indians and the Dodgers. A career .262 batter, he proved to be a more-than-adequate pinch-hitter by delivering 23 base hits in 85 attempts for a .271 BA. Although he lacked power, Ross was a contact hitter and rarely struck out. He left the majors after the 1946 season at age of 32. He was 81 years old when he passed away in Arcadia, California, on April 14, 1996.

Another Hall of Famer, Stan "The Man" Musial of the Cardinals, played his first full year in the majors in 1942. The left-handed hitting outfielder-first baseman from Donora, Pennsylvania, vividly recalls being lifted for a pinch-hitter that year on a number of occasions. He platooned in the outfield with Coaker Triplett and says that it happened to him frequently. As his career in the big leagues progressed, the 6-foot, 175-pound Musial was himself called upon to pinch-hit on 126 occasions, delivering 35 hits for a .278 BA, well short of his .331 overall average during 22 years in the big leagues, all with the Cardinals. Musial made it to the Hall of Fame in 1969.

A pitcher, and a good one at that, 6' 4½", 210-pound Lynwood "Schoolboy" Rowe had the most at-bats for a pinch-hitter in the National League in 1943 with 49 while also recording the most hits with 15 and a very efficient .306 BA. A right-hander all the way, Rowe, out of Waco, Texas, had a sensational nine years with the Tigers, beginning in 1933. He was waived over to the Phillies from the Dodgers after the 1942 season. When he pinch-hit for Johnny Sain in the 1947 All-Star game at Wrigley Field in Chicago, he became the first player ever to appear in that game representing both leagues. His 28 hits in 101 pinch-hit at-bats gave Rowe a very respectable .271 average as a substitute batter, slightly better than his .263 overall average. He retired following the 1949 season at the age of 39 after 15 years in the big time. Rowe died in El Dorado, Arkansas, on January 8, 1961, at the age of 50.

Rip Radcliff, an outfielder-first baseman for the Tigers, wound up his 10-year journey in the majors by leading the American League in pinch-hit at-bats in 1943 with 44. He produced 11 hits for a fair .250 average. The Kiowa, Oklahoma left-handed hitter, played his first six years in with the Chicago White Sox, and later played for both the Browns and the Tigers. The 5' 10", 170-pounder never played another major league game after 1943, retiring at the age of 37. Although his overall BA was .311, as a pinch-

hitter he only hit .201 with but 24 hits in 119 at-bats. He passed away in Enid, Oklahoma, on May 23, 1962, at the age of 56.

The pinch-hitting league leader in both hits and average in 1943 was none other than future Hall of Famer Joe Cronin. The San Francisco-bred Cronin was the player-manager of the Red Sox at the time. As a pinch-swinger in 1943, the right-handed hitter was 18-for-42. More importantly, the 5' 11½", 180 pounder set a major league record by hitting five home runs as a pinch-hitter, including two on consecutive days which had not been done since the Yankees' Ray Caldwell accomplished it in 1915.

Two of Cronin's homers were three-run shots, one in each game of a doubleheader against the Browns on June 17. He had hit a three-run pinch-hit home run two days earlier against the A's, accounting for three round-trippers all told in his last four at-bats. His 25 RBI represented still another single season record for pinch-hitters, tied later by Jerry Lynch and Rusty Staub. As a pinch-hitter, Joe Cronin batted .288 with 30 hits in 104 at-bats during his 20-year career in the majors. Overall he hit .301.

Only three games into the 1945 season, Cronin broke his leg ending his playing days at the age of 39. He was elected to the Hall of Fame in 1956 and became the American League president in 1959. He presided over the league's first expansion, to 10 teams in 1960, and then to 12 clubs in 1969. Cronin died in Osterville, Massachusetts, on September 7, 1984, at the age of 77.

Al Rubeling, a right-handed hitting utility infielder-outfielder for Pirates, had the most pinch-hit at-bats for a National Leaguer in 1944 with 41, his fourth and final year in the big leagues. However, he only hit safely nine times for a rather poor .219 average. His career average of .249 was somewhat better than his .233 mark as a pinch-hitter (10-for-43). The 6-foot, 185-pound Baltimore native was only 31 when he made his last appearance in the majors. Rubeling died in his hometown of Baltimore on January 28, 1988, at the age of 74.

There was a tie in the National League in 1944 for the most pinch-hits (12) between future Hall of Fame outfielder Paul "Big Poison" Waner, who spent time that season with both the Dodgers and the Yankees, and Lou "The Mad Russian" Novikoff, a rather eccentric outfielder for the Cubs.

Novikoff, a 5' 10", 185-pounder from Glendale, Arizona, came up to the majors as a reputed "phenom" after winning four minor league batting

Opposite: Hall of Famer Joe Cronin's 25 RBIs in 1943 was a new season mark for pinch-hitters. (Courtesy of National Baseball Hall of Fame Library, Cooperstown, N.Y.)

crowns and earning *The Sporting News'* Minor League Player of the Year award in 1939. However, his press clippings failed to match his play in the big leagues and he was gone after the 1946 season at the age of 31. An atrocious fielder who was afraid to touch Wrigley Field's ivy-covered walls, he turned into a fine pinch-hitter. His 29 hits in 84 attempts garnered him an excellent .345 BA. Overall, he batted an above-average .282. An excellent softball player, he was inducted into that game's Hall of Fame. Novikoff played softball at one time with former heavyweight boxing contender, Lou Nova. He participated in softball until he was 53 years old. He died a year later in South Gate, California, on September 30, 1970.

The league's best average for a pinch-swinger in 1944 was generated by Paul Waner's younger brother, Lloyd. "Little Poison," another future Hall of Fame outfielder, had a .389 mark off seven hits in 18 at-bats for both the Dodgers and the Pirates.

The Waner brothers hailed from Harrah, Oklahoma and both hit left-handed, although Paul was a lefty thrower while Lloyd was a right-hander. The 5' 8½", 153-pound Paul Waner ranks atop the list of Hall of Fame pinch-hitters with his 10-for-21 in 1943 and a superb .476 average. Overall, he batted .333 in 20 years, the first 15 in Pittsburgh. Known for his persistent partying, Paul Waner had the sharpest bloodshot eyes in the game. He became an excellent hitting coach after his playing days ended but shunned managing because he disdained discipline. He was inducted into the Hall of Fame in 1952, and died in Sarasota, Florida, on August 29, 1965, at the age of 62.

Little brother, Lloyd, at 5' 9" and 150 pounds, had 39 hits in 134 career at-bats as an emergency batsman for a well above average of .291. An accomplished center fielder without a great arm, Lloyd still led the NL in assists in four different years. He was aided by spacious Forbes Field and his excellent speed which he used to run balls down. He batted .316 over an 18-year career that spanned 1,992 games, all but 189 of them in a Pittsburgh uniform. Lloyd passed away in Oklahoma City on July 23, 1982, at the age of 76.

In the American League in 1944, Racine, Wisconsin's Jimmy Grant, a left-handed hitting utility infielder with the Indians, had the most pinch-hit at-bats with 32, the lowest league-leading total since 1933. He had only five hits for a feeble .160 BA. Grant, at 5' 8" and 166 pounds, only remained in the big leagues for three years, leaving after the 1944 season at the age of 26. His 5.03 ERA in 36 career games hastened his exit. Although he had a .246 career average, his seven hits in 52 appearances as a pinch-swinger resulted in a decidedly underachieving .133 average. He died in Rochester, Minnesota, on July 8, 1970, at the age of 51.

Bill LeFebvre, a left-handed pitcher for the Senators from Natick, Rhode Island, led the AL in pinch-hits in 1944 with 10. Another short-timer — he only played for four years in the big leagues — the 5' 11½", 180-pounder had 12 hits in 32 pinch-hit at-bats in his brief career for a nifty .375 BA. Overall, he hit .276 with nearly half of his at-bats coming as a substitute batter. He was 29 at the time he left the majors in 1944.

A Canadian-born left-handed slugger, Jeff Heath of the Indians, was the AL's leading pinch-hitter in 1944 with 9-out-of-22 for an excellent .409 mark. Heath, a 5' 11½", 200-pounder, was a starter for the Tribe for most of his 10 years with the club. However, injuries curtailed his potential and, although he hit 194 homers and compiled a .293 lifetime BA, his numbers could have been greater had it not been for his injuries. As a pinch-hitter his career figures added up to .244: 20 hits in 82 at-bats. He finished up in the big leagues in 1949 after having also played briefly for the Senators, Browns and Red Sox. He left the majors after the 1949 season at the age of 34. He passed away in Seattle in 1975 at the age of 60.

Rene Monteagudo, a left-handed hitting outfielder from Havana, Cuba, who had failed earlier trials as a pitcher for the Senators, led the National League in all pinch-hitting departments for the Phillies in 1945. In what was his last season in the majors, the 5' 7", 165-pounder, also relieved in 14 games and batted .301 overall that year. He had the most at-bats — 52 — which represented the highest number by an NL pinch-hitter in a dozen years. He also tallied 18 hits and a .346 average to lead in those categories as well. For his career, he batted .289 overall and his 19 hits in 53 pinch-hit at-bats mark him as one of the best pinch-hitters with over 50 appearances with a .358 average. He retired to Hialeah, Florida where he died in 1973 at the age of 57.

Jimmie Foxx, one of the greatest home run hitters of all time, came off the bench and hit one out for the Phillies in a game played on May 18, 1945. Coupled with a pinch-hit four-bagger he had rapped out for the Athletics back on September 21, 1931, it constituted the first time that a player had ever pinch-hit a home run for teams in both leagues. It would be another 18 years before it was to be duplicated by Roy Sievers, also of the Phillies. Making the most of the final season of his 20-year career, "Double X" even pitched nine times as a part-time for the Phils. Foxx was 59 when he died in Miami, Florida, on July 21, 1967.

Joe Schultz, Jr., a right-handed hitting catcher used somewhat sparingly by the Browns, had the most at-bats (35), the most hits (11) as well as the best average (.315) in the AL in 1945. It is said that Schultz pinch-hit in a regular league game for Houston in the Texas League at the age of 13. He was the batboy at the time and his dad, Joe Schultz, Sr., a former top pinch-hitter himself, was the manager. According to the game report, Schultz, Jr. hit a single, stole second and third and scored a run.

Norman "Babe" Young, who had been the Giants' regular first baseman before going away to war, came back after serving in the Coast Guard. Despite having driven in over 100 runs in both 1940 and 1941, Young was without a starting spot on the team's roster. The Giants had acquired big Johnny Mize from the Cardinals and awarded him the first base job. Young, an Astoria, New York native and a graduate of Fordham University, became manager Mel Ott's first man off the bench in 1946 and led the National League in pinch-hit at-bats with 32. However, the 6' 2½", 185-pounder was only able to hit safely five times for a rather soft .156 BA.

All in all, Young only produced 17 hits in 97 pinch-hitting attempts throughout his major league career for a less-than-adequate .176 average, markedly below his lifetime .273 BA. He was traded to Cincinnati in 1947, and from the Reds to the Cardinals in 1948. Although invited to training camp with the Yankees in 1949, Young injured his leg and retired at 34, shortly before the season began. He died on Christmas Day of 1983 in Everett, Massachusetts, at the age of 67.

Overland, Missouri's Bob Scheffing, a backup catcher for the Cubs had the most pinch-hits and the best pinch-hitting average in the NL in 1946 with his 7-for-19 for a highly efficient .368 BA. Scheffing, a 6' 2", 180-pound right-handed batter, played in the big leagues for eight seasons, mostly with the Cubs, and later on with the Reds and Cardinals. An excellent defensive catcher, his 33 hits in 124 pinch-hitting appearances were good for an average of .267, just about the same as his overall career mark of .263. Scheffing went on to manage both the Cubs and the Tigers in the late '50s and early '60s, and served as the Mets' general manager from 1970 to 1975. He died in Phoenix, Arizona, on October 26,1985, at the age of 72.

Left-handed hitting outfielder Chuck Workman of the Braves and the Pirates, and switch-hitting infielder Jim Brown, also of the Cardinals, tied Scheffing for the most pinch-hits in 1946 with seven each. For Workman, out of Leeton, Missouri, and a two-time minor league home run king in the Indians chain, and Brown, a native of Jamesville, North Carolina, 1946 represented their final season in the major leagues.

The 6-foot, 175-pound Workman, who hit 25 homers as the regular third baseman for the Braves in 1945, like many other war-time ballplayers, was replaced by a returning veteran, in this case Nanny Fernandez. Workman's career average as a pinch-hitter was only .216 via just 11 hits in 51 at-bats. Following his major league career, he continued playing baseball in the minors. He established the Southern Association home run mark with 52 in 1948 while playing for Nashville, and hit 42 more dingers with Minneapolis of the American Association a year later. Workman was just 38 when he passed away in Kansas City, Missouri, on January 3, 1953.

The switch-hitting Brown, a product of the Cardinals farm system, had at one time been that team's lead-off batter. He rarely walked. In 1939 and 1942, he led the NL in at-bats with 645 and 606 respectively. He also hit .300 to pace his club in their World Series victory over the Yankees in 1942. Brown hit .279 lifetime and did very well on a limited basis as a pinch-swinger with his 12-for-39 gaining him a .309 BA during his eight seasons in the big leagues. He died in Bath, North Carolina, on December 29, 1977, at the age of 67.

While slugging Giants' outfielder-third baseman Sid Gordon only came to bat five times as a pinch-hitter in 1946, one of those at-bats resulted in a Hall of Famer benching himself. The Giants had lost the opener of a Labor Day doubleheader in Boston to Mort Cooper and the Braves, 6-2. Trailing in the seventh inning of the nightcap, 3-0, Mort's brother, Walker, smacked a three-run homer off right-hander Ed Wright to tie the game.

After a pair of singles and a double error followed Cooper's blast to bring in another run and leave two runners on base, southpaw Ernie White was sent in to relieve Wright. Player-manager Mel Ott, also a lefty, took himself out of the game and inserted the right-handed Gordon to pinch-hit for him. The Brooklyn-born Gordon promptly singled home Willard Marshall to extend the rally as the Giants plated a total of eight runs in the inning and an eventual 8-3 victory.

Gordon, who later played for the Braves and hit a total of 208 home runs, was not a very good pinch-hitter throughout his 13-year career. In fact, he only produced nine base hits in 67 pinch-hit appearances for an extremely weak .138 BA. Overall he batted a very respectable .283. Gordon died at 58 in New York City on June 17, 1975, right after playing in a softball game.

George "Bingo" Binks (born Binkowski in Chicago) got a chance to become a starting outfielder for the Senators during World War II at the advanced age of 30. A bench player for them in 1946, he led the American League in pinch-hit at-bats with 35 that season. He had only seven hits for a poor .200 BA. The speedy 6-foot, 175-pound left-handed batter was traded to the Athletics the following year, and later to the Browns in 1948 where he finished up his five-year career in the big leagues. He only hit safely 13 times in 61 career pinch-hit at-bats for a rather measly .216 average, as opposed to his .253 overall mark.

But Joe Schultz, Jr., who continued to make his mark as arguably the best pinch-hitter in the game at the time, had the most hits in the AL (ten) and the best average (.435) in his 23 at-bats. Schultz, who was mentioned prominently by Jim Bouton in *Ball Four* when he managed the expansion Seattle Pilots in 1969, played in the majors for nine years. He compiled a creditable .270 BA as a pinch-hitter with 43 hits in 160 attempts, even better than his .259 lifetime average. He only hit one homer in his entire career and it came as a member of the Browns in 1947.

Charlie Gilbert of the Phillies became another player who led his league in pinch-hits and retired from baseball in the following year. Gilbert came from a major league family, all out of New Orleans. His father, Larry, was an outfielder with the last-to-first "Miracle Braves" of 1914 and again in 1915. His younger brother, Harold "Tookie" Gilbert, one of the game's original "bonus babies," played some first base for the Giants in 1950 and 1953. The left-handed hitting Charlie Gilbert set the pace in the National League in 1947 with 40 pinch-hit at-bats but it was Frank "Buck" McCormick of the Phillies and the Braves who led the league with 13 hits. Ron "The Round Man" Northey, who was traded from the Phillies to the Cardinals early that year, had a league-best BA with 11-for-25 for .444.

Charlie Gilbert, a left-handed hitting outfielder .with little power broke in with Brooklyn in 1940. The 5' 9", 165-pounder never had a full-time job with any of the clubs he played for, including the Cubs and Phillies. After six seasons in the majors, not including time out for military service, he left the majors for good in 1947 at the age of 28. His lifetime pinch-hitting records were abysmal: 14 hits in 115 at-bats for an almost invisible .122 BA, nearly half his .229 overall average. He died in his home town of New Orleans on August 13, 1983, at the age of 64.

The right-handed hitting McCormick, who came from New York City, came up to the Reds in 1934 and was their starting first sacker from 1938 to 1945, which included the 1939 and 1940 World Series against the Yankees and Tigers, respectively. The 6' 4", 205-pound right-handed hitter was traded to Philadelphia in 1946 and later to the Braves where he played in the 1948 World Series against the Indians. McCormick quit the game following that Series loss to Cleveland at the age of 37. Although he rarely pinch-hit, when he did his numbers were more than adequate: 21-out-of-77 for a .273 mark, but lower than his fine .299 overall lifetime BA.

A notorious first-ball hitter, the seven-time NL All-Star said: "I learned early that pitchers tried to sneak a good one by you to get ahead in the count. I didn't let it go by."[1] After the 1948 season, McCormick went back to the Reds and became a minor league manager, scout, coach and broadcaster. He died in Manhasset, New York, on November 21, 1982, at the age of 71.

Northey, out of Mahanoy City, Pennsylvania, was a slugging starting outfielder for the Phillies when he came up in 1942. He was traded away to the Cardinals in 1947 and subsequently drifted on to the Cubs, White Sox and back to the Phillies, where he completed his 12-year career in 1957. Northey pinch-hit on 214 occasions, producing 59 hits for an efficient .275 BA, just one point lower than his overall lifetime average of .276. He hit nine pinch-hit home runs over the course of his career, three with the bases loaded. The grand slams were a record until Willie McCovey of the Giants tied it in 1975.

Unlike Frank McCormick, Northey shied away from the first pitch. He decided he would never swing at it reasoning that it would always be the pitch that was working best for the pitcher on that day. He actually kept tabs on it and for two months at one stretch he felt that 80 percent of the time, the first pitch thrown to him wasn't a strike anyhow. Also by watching that first pitch, Northey believed he could study the speed and break of the ball. He felt he would see that pitch again and when it came toward him, the pressure was at its highest peak.

The year of 1947 will forever be remembered in baseball history due to the pinch-hitting feat of one Harry "Cookie" Lavagetto of the Dodgers in Game Four of the World Series against the Yankees. The right-handed hitting Oakland, California native had been a dependable albeit unspectacular third baseman for the Brooklyn club since his acquisition from Pittsburgh after the 1936 campaign. Floyd "Bill" Bevens of the Yankees, a right-handed pitcher, was on the mound at Ebbets Field and despite giving up 11 walks, seemingly was on his way to pitching the first-ever no hitter in World Series history.

With two out and two on via walks in the bottom of the ninth and the Dodgers trailing, 2-1, The 6-foot, 170-pound Lavagetto was sent up to hit against Bevens. With the count at 1-1, Cookie lined an outside pitch for a double off the right field wall, where he seldom hit, to score both runs and give the Dodgers the victory, 3-2. It was the only hit in seven at-bats that Lavagetto had in the Series. Ironically, both he and Bevens never played in the major leagues again after 1947. Neither did Al Gionfriddo who scored the tying run after being sent in to run for Carl Furillo. Gionfriddo's remarkable catch of Joe DiMaggio's 415-foot drive in Game Six led to a seventh game, which the Yankees won.

The truth be told, Lavagetto was not a very good pinch-hitter during his regular season career. He only compiled 12 hits in 77 at-bats for a lowly .156 lifetime average, or over 100 points less than his .269 mark overall. His hit off Bevens was Lavagetto's only career World Series pinch-hit.

Not to be overlooked in that series was Game Three, a wild one at

Ebbets Field also won by the Dodgers, 9-8. In it future Hall of Famer Yogi Berra, in his first full season with the Yankees, cracked the first pinch-hit home ever hit in a World Series with a seventh inning blast off right-hander Ralph Branca, a 21-game winner that season. The squat 5' 7½", 185-pound St. Louis native was called upon to pinch-hit officially 178 times in his 19-year career and came up with 44 base hits for a .246 average, well below his overall lifetime mark of .285. He was inducted into the Hall of Fame in 1972.

Joe Schultz, Jr. of the Browns led the American League with 38 pinch-hit at-bats in 1947, Bobby Brown of the Yankees and Roger "Doc" Cramer of the Tigers had the most hits with nine.

Brown, a weak fielding, left-handed hitting third baseman from Seattle, led the league with a pinch-hitting average of .333 coming off nine hits in 27 at-bats. The 6' 2", 190-pound Brown smacked a tying double as a pinch-swinger in Game Seven of the 1947 World Series. His regular season pinch-hitting appearances were not that successful. He only produced 25 hits in 102 at-bats for a .245 average and well below his .279 career BA. Brown studied to become a surgeon while playing for eight years in the majors. He eventually was named president of the American League in 1980, a position he held until 1990.

The 6' 2", 185-pound Cramer, who was a major league ballplayer for 20 years, most often as a starting outfielder, played for Connie Mack's Athletics for seven seasons before moving on to the Red Sox, Senators and Tigers. Never a long-ball threat — the former pitcher only hit 37 homers in 9,140 times at bat — the left-handed hitting Cramer had an impressive .296 lifetime BA. Hits were somewhat harder to come by in his rare pinch-hitting appearances as he was 21-for-84 for a .250 average. He left the majors at the age of 40 following the 1948 campaign.

Eight seasons after leading the National League in pinch-hit at-bats and hits, Johnny McCarthy, back with the Giants following two seasons with the Braves, repeated as the leader in both categories with 45 and 13 respectively. At 38, it was to be McCarthy's last year in the big leagues.

Left-handed hitting outfielder Pete Reiser, who broke in with the Dodgers in 1940 as a much-heralded five-tool player, mostly pinch-hit for Brooklyn in 1948 and led the NL in batting average off the bench with 10-out-of-21 for a remarkable .476. The St. Louis-bred Reiser, who had a series of accidental injuries crashing into walls while fielding his position, was left weakened by the altercations and never rose to the levels expected of him. The 5' 11", 185-pounder was traded to the Braves in 1949 and after two years in Boston he played for one year each in Pittsburgh and in Cleveland. As a pinch-hitter, he hit .262 with 32 hits in 122 at-bats. Overall he batted .295 for his injury-shortened career, retiring as a player after 10 frustrating years. He spent a number of years as a coach in the majors, primarily working for his old Dodgers manager, Leo Durocher. He died in Palm Springs, California, in 1981 at the age of 62.

Once again, it was the Browns' Joe Schultz, Jr. who led the American League in pinch-hit at-bats in 1948 with 37. Hal Peck of Big Bend, Wisconsin, a left-handed hitting outfielder with the Indians, had the most hits with nine. Sherry Robertson, a utility player for the Senators, went 7-for-16 for a league-leading .438 average. The 5' 11", 175-pound Peck had a one-game trial with the Dodgers in 1943 but a hunting accident left him with the loss of part of a foot, which curtailed his career. He played for the Athletics during World War II before joining Cleveland in 1947. For his seven-year career as a pinch-swinger, he batted .274 via 23 hits in 84 appearances, close to his overall .279 lifetime BA. He passed away in 1995 at the age of 78.

The left-handed hitting Roberston, a native of Montreal, had the added distinction of being a nephew of Senators' owner Clark Griffith. After nine years in Washington, he was dealt to the Athletics in 1952, his final season in the big leagues. While he hit just under .200 as a pinch-hitter, his overall lifetime BA was not much better at .230. From 1953 on, he worked in the Senators' front office and served as their farm director from 1958 to 1970. He died in Houghton, South Dakota, on October 23, 1970, at the age of 51.

Don Mueller, a left-handed hitting outfielder from St. Louis with next to no speed was in his second season with the Giants in 1949. He led the National League in pinch-hit at-bats with 42 that year but only came up with a hit on seven of those occasions for a scrawny .167 BA. The 6-foot, 185-pound Mueller would go on to become a regular with the Giants from 1950 to 1957, until traded to the White Sox for the 1958 campaign.

He was known as "Mandrake the Magician" during his career as many of his hits seemed to find holes in the infield and outfield. Mueller's father, Walter, had played for the Pirates from 1922 to 1926. Don Mueller was a .lifetime 296 hitter overall and his 44 hits in 157 pinch-hit at-bats gave him a laudable .277 average.

The NL leader in pinch-hits with 13 in 1949 — his last in the majors — was left-handed hitting outfielder Fred "Dixie" Walker. Then with the Pirates, the 6' 1", 175-pounder had been reduced to being only a part-time player in Pittsburgh. The brother of the 1947 batting champion, Harry "The Hat" Walker, Dixie was the most popular player in Brooklyn during his eight-year tenure there from 1940 to 1947, known as "The People's Cherce." The Walkers's father, also known as "Dixie" pitched for the

Senators from 1909 to 1912, while their uncle, Ernie, played for the Browns from 1913 to 1915.

After just two seasons in the "Smoky City," as Pittsburgh was then called, Dixie Walker quit the game after a successful 18-year career at the age of 39. As a pinch-hitter, the Georgian hit a dependable .271 off 39 hits in 143 tries. Overall he was even better: a lifetime .306 batter. He passed away in Birmingham, Alabama, in 1982 at the age of 71.

Veteran Jimmy Bloodworth, a utility infielder with the Reds, had the best pinch-hitting average by far in the NL in 1949 with eight hits in 15 at-bats for a .433 mark. The right-handed Bloodworth, a native of Tallahassee, Florida, bounced around both leagues in an 11-year career that included stints with the Senators, Tigers, Pirates, Reds and Phillies. A lifetime .248 hitter, the 5' 11", 180-pounder, was significantly more accomplished as a pinch-hitter with his 17-for-53 producing an excellent .321 BA. Bloodworth was 85 years old when he died in Apalachicola, Florida, on August 17, 2002.

Little-known outfielder Mizell "Whitey" Platt of the Browns had the most pinch-hit at-bats in the American League in 1949 with 34. However, the 6' 1½", 190-pounder only hit safely seven times that season for a rather inferior .206 average. The right-handed Platt, a West Palm Beach, Florida native, was a batboy as a youngster for the Browns when the club trained in the springtime in his home town. He played with the Cubs and White Sox as well as the Browns in his brief five-year career. Platt batted .255 overall, much better than his .229 average as a pinch-swinger with 16 hits in 70 at-bats. He passed away in West Palm Beach on July 27, 1970, at the age of 49.

Buddy Lewis, who spent his entire 11-year career with the Senators, led the AL in both pinch-hits and average with 9-for-24 in 1949 for a gaudy .375 average. The left-handed hitting outfielder-third baseman from Gastonia, North Carolina, was a steady player who compiled an above-average .297 lifetime BA. He was only 18 years old when he played his first game in the big leagues in 1935.

Lewis was one of a number of players who had to sacrifice their peak years to serve in the military. Before World War II, he enjoyed three seasons in which he batted over .300. After returning from the war, he hit .292 in 1946, had an off-year in 1947 and missed all of 1948 due to an injury. When he failed to regain his earlier form in a 1949 comeback attempt, he retired at the age of 33. Although not called upon to pinch-hit that often during his career, Lewis did the job when asked, producing 16 hits in 48 at-bats for a superior .333 average.

8

1950-1959:
One Extreme—Johnny Mize—
to Another—Eddie Gaedel

Thanks in no small measure to Yankees manager Casey Stengel's platooning methodology — such as interchanging the left-handed hitting Gene Woodling with the right-handed hitting Hank Bauer — pinch-hitting began to expand as a strategic weapon in the 1950s. The increasing use of relief pitchers was also becoming more and more prominent in the game. Consequently, good-field/no-hit types began to get more playing time as teams' offenses began to slip. And switch hitters like Elmer Valo and Dave Philley were used more often off the bench as well.

Eddie Kazak (born Tkaczuk), a 6-foot, 175-pound backup third baseman for the Cardinals, led the National League in pinch-hit at-bats during his all-too-brief career with 42 in 1950. His 10-hit output was only good for a .240 batting average. It was still a tad better than his five-year big league pinch-hitting mark of .220, which came off 13 safeties in 59 at-bats. Kazak's average as an emergency batter represented 53 points less than his overall .273 BA. He was out of the majors two years, ending his career in Cincinnati after being traded for Dick Sisler and Virgil Stallcup.

Left-handed hitting outfielder Dick Whitman, whom the Dodgers had given up on after four uneventful seasons in Brooklyn, was the leader in pinch-hits with a new team in 1950. The 5' 11", 170-pounder, who hailed from Woodburn, Oregon, had been sold to the Phillies over the winter and set the pace in the NL with 12 hits as a substitute batter. In 39 at-bats, he recorded a fine .308 BA for the season.

Whitman helped his team — known as the "Whiz Kids" because of their collective relative youth — reach the World Series against the defending champion Yankees. He pinch-hit in three of the four games, going hitless with a walk in three games in New York's sweep. Whitman, like Kazak, was also done in the major leagues two years later. For his career as a pinch-hitter, he did very well: 26-for-91 for .286, much better than his lifetime .259 overall BA.

The 1950 NL's top pinch-hitter in average that season was utility infielder Pete Castiglione of the Pirates with 7-for-22 gaining him a solid .318 mark. The Greenwich, Connecticut product was a versatile athlete who played every position in the infield and some outfield as well. However, the 5' 11", 175-pounder displayed limited power and could not hit consistently enough to justify a starting spot with the ballclub. A capable pinch-hitter in his eight-year major league career, Castiglione was well-above average in the pinch with 16-for-54 earning him a strong .299 average that was considerably better than his overall lifetime .255 BA.

The American League leader in 1950 in every major pinch-hit category was Sacramento's Gordon Goldsberry of the White Sox. His 12-for-39 totals produced a meaningful .308 BA. Traded to the Browns for the 1952 season as part of a multi-player deal, the left-handed hitting first sacker was out of baseball after that year at the age of 25. For his four years in the majors, Goldsberry registered 14 hits in 52 pinch-hit at-bats for a more-than-adequate .270 mark, well above his .241 overall average. Remaining in Chicago after his playing days, he later became the Cubs director of minor leagues and scouting. Goldsberry died on February 23, 1966, in Lake Forest, California, at the age of 68.

In 1951, two former Chicago teammates— 36-year-old Bill "Swish" Nicholson and 35-year-old Phil Cavaretta — set the tone for substitute batters in the National League. Nicholson, an outfielder with outstanding power who left the Cubs in 1948 after 10 years in Chicago, was now with the Phillies, where he was to spend the final five seasons of his career. A 6-foot, 205-pound left-handed hitter from Chestertown, Maryland, Nicholson led the NL in pinch-hit at-bats with 36 that year. His 11 hits gave him a nifty .306 average. He was extremely tough to double up, hitting into double plays only once in every 90.7 times at bat.

Nicholson picked up his nickname from the fans in Brooklyn who would shout "Swish" whenever he took one of his patented swings. The two-time home run champion was once ordered to be passed intentionally with the bases loaded by manager Mel Ott of the Giants. The action took place in the second game of a doubleheader after Nicholson had already hit three home runs. The Giants led, 12-9 at the time and eventually won it, 12-10. As a pinch-hitter during his career, he collected 37 hits in 174 at-bats, including eight home runs. His .212 mark as a substitute batter was considerably less than his .268 average overall. Nicholson passed away in his hometown of Chestertown, Maryland, on March 8, 1996 at the age of 81.

Cavaretta was nearing the end of his 20-year stint with the Cubs in 1950. No longer the team's starting first baseman, he led the NL in pinch-hit base hits and average with 12-out-of-33 for an outstanding .363 average. The Chicago-born Cavaretta, who had been a schoolboy pitcher for Lane Tech there, served all of his time in the majors in the "Windy City." His tenure included two years on the south side with the White Sox, where he ended his career in 1955. He had begun as the starting first baseman for the National League champion 1935 Cubs at the age of 18. As good a hitter as he was overall with an excellent .293 lifetime average, he only managed to hit .230 in the pinch by virtue of hitting safely only 49 times in 209 official at-bats.

From 1951 to 1953, Cavaretta served as the Cubs' player-manager. He was fired in the 1954 spring training season when he honestly predicted a second-division finish for his club. (The Cubs didn't disappoint with a seventh-place finish under Stan Hack.) He later managed extensively in the minor leagues, and coached and scouted for the Tigers before he became a batting instructor in the Mets' organization.

Bobby Addis, a 6-foot, 175-pound reserve outfielder for the Braves, tied Cavaretta in pinch-hit base hits in 1951 with 12. With three more at-bats than Cavaretta, the left-handed hitter with next to no power posted a substantial .333 BA. The Mineral, Ohio native later played with the Reds, Cubs and Pirates in his brief four-year career before leaving the game in 1953 after only 15 at-bats that season. He was just 28 at the time. As a pinch-hitter, Addis recorded a respectable .261 average with 18 hits in 69 at-bats, some 20 points under his .281 lifetime BA.

The American League's pinch-hitting pace-setters in 1951 were Charlie "King Kong" Keller of the Tigers, who had the most at-bats (38), and Johnny "The Big Cat" Mize of the Yankees, and Bud Stewart and Floyd Baker of the White Sox, who each tied Keller with nine pinch-hits. Mize posted the season's best average by far with his 9-for-19 meriting a .474 mark.

The left-handed hitting 5' 10", 185-pound Keller had played alongside Joe DiMaggio for 10 years but was displaced as the club's starting left-fielder after suffering through a series of chronic back ailments. The

Johnny Mize off the bench helped the Yankees win consecutive world championships from 1949 to 1953. (Courtesy of National Baseball Hall of Fame Library,
Cooperstown, N.Y.)

Middletown, Maryland-born Keller was later brought back in 1952 for a final appearance in New York. As a pinch-hitter, he produced only 25 hits in 123 at-bats, good only for a scanty .203 BA, well under his overall .286 average. Keller died in Frederick, Maryland, on May 23, 1990, at the age of 73.

Mize, considered washed up by the Giants, came over to the Yankees during the 1949 season just before the trading deadline for $40,000. He proceeded to carve out a new career as one of the most productive and feared pinch-hitters in baseball history. The future Hall of Famer played an occasional first base for the Bronx Bombers, but his major occupation was to be Casey Stengel's first man off the bench. The left-handed hitter from Democrat, Georgia contributed mightily to the team's five consecutive world championships during his tenure with them.

The 6' 4", 215-pound Mize began to pay dividends for the Yankees almost immediately. In the 1949 World Series against the Dodgers, he got a key pinch-hit in Game Three that helped to defeat Brooklyn, 4-3. He was sent up to bat for Cliff Mapes in the top half of the ninth inning with the bases loaded, one out and the score tied. Mize singled to center driving in two critical runs, after which Jerry Coleman drove in another. Although the Dodgers scored a couple of runs in the bottom of the ninth, they still fell one run short.

Mize's heroics in the 1952 Series helped the Yankees defeat the Dodgers once again in a seven-game set. In Game Three, which the Dodgers won, 5-3, he face southpaw Preacher Roe in the ninth inning. Roe, who had replaced Tom Gorman, served up a pitch that Mize belted into the right-field seats at Yankee Stadium. It was the first pinch-hit home run in a World Series game since Yogi Berra's five years earlier off Ralph Branca. At the age of 39 and nearing the end of his illustrious career, Mize delivered two more homers in that Series and batted .400 to help the Yankees win it all.

Mize nearly ended his big league career before it began in 1935 when he had successful surgery to correct an upper-leg bone spur. The famed "Surgeon General of Baseball," Dr. Robert Hyland performed the operation that saved Mize's career. Mize is the only man in the history of the game to hit three home runs in a game six times. He also homered twice in games 30 times and hit seven pinch-hit homers. He had an extraordinary eye for the strike zone, witness his striking out only 524 times in 1,884 regular season games while hitting 359 home runs. And he had the distinction at the time he called it quits of having hit home runs in every one of the 15 ball parks in which he had played.

Mize had a book on all of the pitchers he faced and was admired as much for his graceful well-balanced style of hitting as he was for his considerable strength. As a pinch-hitter, he came to bat 187 times during his career and rapped out 53 hits for a steady .283 BA. Overall, he had 2,011 hits for a .312 average.

A former Cardinals teammate said of Mize: "Did you ever see a pitcher knock him down at the plate? Remember how he reacted when brushed back? He'd just lean back on his left foot, bend his back and let the pitch go by. Then he'd lean back into the batter's box and resume his stance, as graceful as a big cat."[1] Mize passed away in Demorest, Georgia, on June 2, 1993, at the age of 80.

Baker, a left-handed hitting utility infielder, began his 13-year major league career with the Browns in 1943. A year later he got to play in the 1944 World Series for St. Louis against the Cardinals, the only one in which the Browns ever participated. He pinch-hit twice and fanned both times. The Luray, Virginia native, who was never a regular in the big leagues, turned down a college football scholarship to play baseball. After his playing days with the Browns came to an end, Baker suited up for the Senators, Red Sox and Phillies, as well as the White Sox, spending the major portion of his 13-year career in Chicago. The 5' 9", 160-pound Baker collected 36 hits in 173 pinch-hit at-bats, only good for a .208 average, well below his .251 overall lifetime average. He collected just one home run in the course of 2,280 big league at-bats. Stewart, the former National Leaguer, was a favorite of manager Paul Richards during his four-years with the White Sox. In his nine seasons in the big time, he also played for the Pirates, Yankees and Senators. His 49 hits in 209 pinch-hit at-bats only gave Stewart a .234 career mark, well under his .268 overall average.

One of the most bizarre publicity stunts in the history of baseball took place during the 1951 season and it involved a pinch-hitter of sorts. Browns owner Bill Veeck, never one to shy away from a promotion that might bring more fans into the ball park, was the architect. On August 18, 1951, at Sportsman's Park in St. Louis, a 3' 7", 65-pound midget named Eddie Gaedel jumped out of a seven-foot birthday cake between games of a Browns-Tigers twinbill. The event was cooked up to coincide with the 50th anniversary of the ballclub and the American League, as well as the team's radio sponsor, the Falstaff Brewing Company.

Gaedel, a stage performer, wore a Browns uniform with the number ⅛ and tiny slippers that were curled up at each end like elves' shoes. In the bottom of the first inning, Browns manager Zach Taylor sent Gaedel up to home plate to pinch-hit for right fielder Frank Saucier. Veeck had told the pixie-like right-handed batter to crouch low and not swing his toy-like bat. Detroit manager Red Rolfe lodged an immediate protest but to no avail as Taylor showed umpire Ed Hurley a legitimate contract that had been filed with the league.

Gaedel's strike zone measured about 1½" and Tiger left-hander Bob Cain, who was doubled up with laughter, promptly walked him on four pitches. Outfielder Jim Delsing was sent in to run for Gaedel and the crowd of 18,369 fans rose as one to give the midget a standing ovation. The Browns eventually lost the game, 6-2.

Furious with the stunt, American League President Will Harridge tried to get Gaedel's name omitted from the record books but the attempt also failed. Gaedel was presented with a $100 appearance fee and a $1 million insurance policy. Two days later, Gaedel was banned from any future game appearances by Major League Baseball.

He was used in later promotions by Veeck, including one in 1959 when he owned the White Sox in which Gaedel and three other midgets were dressed as spacemen and landed by helicopter onto the infield at Comiskey Park in Chicago. The quartet took both Luis Aparicio and Nellie Fox as "prisoners" with ray guns with Gaedel reportedly telling them: "I don't want to be taken to your leader; I already know him."[2] The midget died of a heart attack in Chicago in 1961 at the age of 36 following a street mugging.

George "Teddy" Wilson, who divided his time between the White Sox and the Giants in his rookie year of 1952, came to bat 48 times a pinch-hitter to lead the National League in that department. Wilson, a left-handed hitting outfielder from Cherryville, North Carolina, lasted but three seasons in the big leagues. As a member of the Yankees, he batted once in the 1956 World Series against the Dodgers as a pinch-hitter and struck out. The 6' 1½", 160-pounder was only able to deliver 21 pinch-hits in 104 at-bats for a poor .202 average, but still a mite better than his .191 overall BA. He died in Gastonia, North Carolina, on October 29, 1974, at the age of 49.

The story in the NL in pinch-hitting for 1952 was really Harry "Peanuts" Lowrey of the Cardinals, who had the most pinch-hits and the best average with his 14-for-27 meriting a powerful .518 BA. The right-handed hitting outfielder, who also played some infield, had spent the first seven years of his career with the Cubs and even played in the 1945 World Series against the Tigers. After being traded to Cincinnati in 1949 for Frank Baumholtz and Hank Sauer, the 5' 8½", 170-pounder played poorly there and was eventually shipped to St. Louis in 1951 where he hit a career high .303.

It was in pinch-hitting though that Lowrey found his real niche. He repeated in 1953 when he again paced the league in hits, with 22, and led the NL in appearances with 59. Those at-bats represented the most since Sam Leslie's record 72 in 1932. (The Giants' Bobby Hofman's 13-for-34 for .382 was the NL's best pinch-hitting average in 1953.) When he retired after the 1955 season as a member of the Phillies, Lowrey had rapped out 62 pinch-hits in 230 at-bats during his career as a pinch-swinger for an above-average .270 mark, amazingly close to his overall .273 lifetime BA.

Lowrey's nickname stemmed from the fact that his grandfather described him as "no bigger than a peanut" when he was born."[3] As a youngster in Culver City, California, where many movie studios were located, Lowrey performed in child bit parts in silent films with such actresses as Thelma Todd. He also had a speaking part in "The Winning Team," a movie about Hall of Fame pitcher Grover Cleveland Alexander that starred a future president of the United States—Ronald Reagan. Lowrey passed away in Inglewood, California on July 2, 1986, at the age of 67.

Bobby Hofman, who spent his entire seven-year career with the Giants, was a right-handed hitting utility infielder who also caught on occasion. The 5' 10", 160-pound St. Louis native had some pop in his bat as evidenced by the nine home runs he slugged as a substitute batter. Overall as a pinch-swinger, Hofman garnered 38 hits in 147 times up for a fairly consistent .272 BA that was considerably better than his overall .248 average. He later coached for the Oakland A's and was also used by owner Charles Finley as the club's traveling secretary. Hofman died on April 15, 1994 in Chesterfield, Missouri, at the age of 68.

Over in the American League in 1953, Johnny Mize continued to lead the way among pinch-hitters in the Junior Circuit. "The Big Cat" and his 61 pinch-hit at-bats were the most in the league since Bill Rumler's record-setting 71 in 1917. Mize also banged out the most base hits—19—while Johnny Pesky of the Tigers, was tops in average that year with his 13-for-30 producing an impressive .433 mark.

Pesky, the former Red Sox shortstop who was born John Michael Paveskovich, was shifted to both second and third base later in his career. The 5' 9", 168-pound left-handed hitter was traded from Detroit to the Senators early in 1954. It was in Washington that he completed a 10-year turn in the big leagues, not including three years out for military service in World War II. A contact hitter, he rarely struck out—only 218 times in 4,745 times at-bat—and never more than 36 in a single season. Although the Portland, Oregon native was a lifetime .307 hitter, he had but 21 hits in his 86 pinch-hit at-bats for a somewhat inconsistent .244 average.

The 1954 season produced some major heroics in pinch-hitting in the National League. First off, reserve outfielder Joe "Cobra" Frazier of the

Cardinals came to bat 62 times as a substitute batter, the highest number recorded in the Senior Circuit since Sam Leslie's record 72 in 1932. His league-leading 20 hits as a pinch-swinger gave him a productive .323 average as well. Although Frazier had played briefly for the Indians in 1947, the left-handed hitting Liberty, North Carolina product was still considered a rookie. The 6-foot, 180-pounder played some later with the Reds and Orioles but was gone for good from the majors as a player after the 1956 season with only four years in the big leagues behind him. As a pinch-hitter, Frazier was 33-for-149 for a .221 average, 20 points below his .241 overall mark. He managed the Mets for the entire 1976 campaign and was fired 45 games into the next season.

The biggest pinch-hitting noise in 1954 came off the bat of Dusty Rhodes of the Giants, who amassed 15 pinch-hits in 45 at-bats for a .333 BA during the Giants' pennant-winning season. The 6-foot, 178-pound Rhodes saved his best for the World Series when the underdog Giants swept the Indians in four straight. The Tribe had won more games than any other team in history that year — 111 — thanks in major part to a formidable starting pitching staff comprised of Bob Lemon, Early Wynn, Art Houtteman and Mike Garcia.

Rhodes's performance in the Fall Classic is the stuff of which legends are made. In the first game at the Polo Grounds in New York, the left-handed hitting Alabama native was called upon in the bottom of the tenth inning with the score tied and two on to face the future Hall of Famer, Lemon. The first pitch was a slow curve just above Dusty's belt. Rhodes swung and delivered a lazy fly ball down the right-field line. The Indian's right-fielder, Dave Pope, watched helplessly as the ball carried into the stands to give the Giants the win, 5-2.

The next day, Giants manager Leo Durocher sent Rhodes up to hit for Monte Irvin in the fifth inning with his team trailing, 1-0. Another future Hall of Famer, Early Wynn, was on the mound for Cleveland. This time Rhodes cracked one of Wynn's sliders into center field for a single to tie the game. He stayed in the game and then homered off one of Wynn's knuckleballs in the seventh for an insurance run as the Giants won, 3-1.

Rhodes' pinch-hit single off a Garcia fastball in the third inning of Game Three in Cleveland — he was again batting for Monte Irvin — drove in the second and third runs in a game the New Yorkers won, 6-2. All told, Rhodes was 4-for-6 with two home runs and seven RBI in the sweep. His three hits as a pinch-hitter duplicated the record set by the Yankees' Bobby Brown in the 1947 World Series against the Dodgers.

After the third game of the 1954 series, sportswriter Red Smith wrote that it might not be necessary to play the fourth game: "There's talk of calling it off in order that James Lamar Rhodes of Rock Hill, South Carolina may give an exhibition of walking on water."[4]

Before that fourth game, Rhodes was asked if he ever worried when called upon to pinch-hit. "Guv'nor," Dusty responded, "in those spots, it's the pitcher that does the worryin.'"[5] His manager, Leo Durocher, had this to say about him: "Rhodes thought he could hit anybody living and he did — that one year. I always tried to use him in the right spot, where they couldn't walk him. But I didn't put him in. He put himself in. When the number seven, eight or nine men were due to hit, he'd have his jacket off and he'd be taking his practice swings. Then if we'd get a man on base he'd come over, spitting tobacco juice and saying, 'Hey, Skip. Me? Now?'"[6]

Dusty was a cartoon character of himself who did nearly nothing in his spare time. "I always heard it was tough making a go of a marriage if both parties worked," he once said, "so I quit my job."[7] During the off-season, he would get his wife up and off to work. "Then I'd go down to the pool hall."[8]

Rhodes was able to keep up this next-to-nothing tempo from one morning to the next indefinitely. When he played for former big league pitcher Charley Root in the minor leagues, the manager observed Dusty's post-game activities for a while and finally gave him an ultimatum of sorts: "Kid, if you're going to stay in baseball, you'll have to cut your drinking by 50 percent."[9] A few nights later, it became apparent to Root that Rhodes had not taken the admonishment quite seriously enough. "This is your last warning," Rood declared. "I told you you're going to have to cut your drinking in half."

"But I have," the player contended. "I've eliminated the chasers."[10] After the World Series, Rhodes had become something of a celebrity but he decided that he would reject any endorsements or accept TV show or banquet appearances. "But you must have some respect for money," one agent told him. "Take what you can get! You don't want to be broke when you leave baseball."[11]

Dusty Rhodes the philosopher replied: "Well, I was broke when I started. So it ain't gonna be no come-down."[12]

An indifferent outfielder, Rhodes enjoyed a good year in 1955 in which he hit .305 but his run production, especially home runs, began to tail off and by 1958 he was back in the minor leagues. He returned to the majors in 1959, the Giants' first season in San Francisco, but he only managed to hit a wretched .188 without a single homer. Rhodes's 55 hits in 260 pinch-hit at-bats earned him a surprisingly low .212 regular season average, over 40 points lower than his .253 overall BA. He was done following the 1959 season, but for that one year, Dusty Rhodes did it all.

A journeyman first baseman, Eddie Robinson, who played for the Indians, Senators, White Sox, Athletics (in both Philadelphia and Kansas City), Yankees and Orioles, had the most pinch-hitting at-bats and hits in the American League in 1954. His 49 times up and 15 hits were good enough for a .306 average. A left-handed power hitter from Paris, Texas, the 6' 2½", 210-pounder developed into an excellent replacement for the departed Johnny Mize in New York. He became one of Casey Stengel's super subs while playing an occasional first base, just as Mize had done for the Yankees. Robinson played for 13 years compiling a lifetime .268 average, his 30 base hits as a pinch-swinger in 156 at-bats only gave him a shaky .192 BA.

Two other Yankee pinch-hitters, Bob Cerv and Enos Slaughter, tied for the AL lead that year with 11 hits each. Cerv's 33 at-bats vs. Slaughter's 31 gave the latter the nod as the league's best in average at .333.

Cerv, a right-handed hitting slugging outfielder from Weston, Nebraska, later played for the Kansas City Athletics, Los Angeles Angels and Houston Astros. Casey Stengel told Cerv about his trade in this fashion: "Nobody knows this but one of us has just been traded to Kansas City."[13] Only he and Stengel were in the room at the time.

Never a regular, the 6-foot, 200-pound Cerv came off the bench often in his 12-year career compiling a .255 BA as a pinch-hitter by virtue of 55 hits in 213 official at-bats. Overall, he had a .276 lifetime average. In three World Series, he batted .258 overall, but he went 1-for-1 off the bench in each Series in 1955, 1956 and 1960.

The 5' 9½", 180-pound Slaughter began his career with the Cardinals in 1938 and, with time out for military service, played in St. Louis for 13 seasons. He will always be remembered for catching Johnny Pesky of the Red Sox off guard and scoring the winning run from first base on a single in the seventh and deciding game of the 1946 World Series.

Bill Taylor of the Giants, a left-handed hitting outfielder from Chapman, Alabama, was the National League leader in pinch-hit at-bats in 1955 with no less than 60. He was able to deliver 15 hits in those appearances for a moderate .250 average. The 6' 1", 185-pounder, who later played for the Tigers during his five-year career, was out of baseball after the 1958 season. All told, Taylor produced 29 base hits in 121 pinch-hit at-bats for a .240 average, fairly close to his lifetime .237 BA.

Frank Baumholtz, a former rookie of the year candidate for the Reds in 1947, also had 15 pinch-hits to tie Taylor in 1955, but he did it in only 37 at-bats to give him the NL's best average by far at a healthy .405. The 5' 10½", 175-pound Baumholtz was traded with Hank Sauer to the Cubs for Peanuts Lowrey and Harry Walker in the middle of the 1949 campaign.

An outstanding athlete who also played basketball professionally, the left-handed hitting outfielder from Midvale, Ohio was one of the better pinch-hitters during his 10 seasons in the majors. His 47 hits in 153 at-bats were good for an abundant .320 career BA as a substitute batter. Baumholtz compiled an equally impressive .290 average overall. He passed away in Winter Springs, Florida, on December 14, 1997, at the age of 79.

Dale Mitchell, a former outfield regular with the Indians for seven years, was a bench player for them in 1955. He made his mark as a fine pinch-hitter and led his league in appearances with 45. His 13 pinch-hits that season earned him a solid .288 average. Enos Slaughter, who played with both the Yankees and the Kansas City A's that season, had the most hits with 16, while Elmer Valo, also with the A's, had the best BA with 14 hits in 31 at-bats earning him a magnificent .456 average.

Mitchell, a career .312 hitter, hailed from Colony, Oklahoma. As he approached the end of his time in the majors, the 6-foot, 195-pounder played part of his last season with the Dodgers. He had the dubious distinction of taking the last strike for the final out in Don Larsen's historic perfect World Series game at Yankee Stadium on October 8, 1956. Until the day he died, Mitchell said the pitch was out of the strike zone. But there was probably no way long-time NL umpire Babe Pinelli, who was officiating his last game behind the plate, was going to call it a ball at that juncture. Mitchell passed away in Tulsa on January 5, 1987, at the age of 65.

The Hall of Fame-bound Slaughter played in the big leagues for 19 seasons and in 1955 was a backup outfielder and pinch-hitter. A tobacco farmer from Roxboro, North Carolina, the left-handed hitter hit .300 on the nose for his career and got to play in five World Series for the Cardinals and the Yankees. As a regular, Slaughter combined extra-base power to all fields with superb fielding skills that included a deadly arm. He batted over .300 a total of 10 times and was elected to the Hall of Fame in 1985.

Among Hall of Famers who pinch-hit at least 85 times in their careers, Slaughter ranks among the lowest in average at .252 based on 77 hits in 306 at-bats. Yet his single season mark of .381 with 16-for-42 in 1955 is one of the best ever for Hall of Famers who had at least 10 pinch-hits in one year. Slaughter ranks ninth on that particular list. By the same token, his 2-for-20 with the 1938 Cardinals is among the lowest for Hall of Famers with at least 15 pinch-hit at-bats in one season. He passed away in Durham, North Carolina on August 12, 2002 at the age of 86.

Elmer Valo, who was born in Czechoslovakia, could have easily been dubbed the pinch-hitting "king" of walks. He summed up his role this way: "There are times when all a pinch-hitter has to do is to get a pass. In that sort of situation, the trick is to walk and forget your temptation to go for a long hit."[14] He received a record 91 walks as a pinch-hitter during his career while amazingly collecting an almost similar number of hits (900.

A left-handed hitting outfielder who constantly hustled, Valo was renowned for his fearless style of play. He spent his first 13 years in the majors with the A's in Philadelphia and moved with them when they relocated to Kansas City in 1955. The 5' 11", 190-pounder played the remainder of his 20-year career in the big leagues with the Phillies, Dodgers, Indians, Yankees, Senators, and Twins.

Bob "Dog" Skinner took over as the starting first baseman for the Pirates in his rookie year of 1954. He moved to the outfield the following season and stayed there for the majority of his 12-year career, which included being the starting left-fielder for the 1958 NL All-Star team. The 6' 4", 190-pounder from La Jolla, California was called upon to pinch-hit often and in 1956 he came up as a substitute batter 54 times to lead the league, even though he was only able to come up with nine hits for a meager .166 average. His last 45 at-bats in the majors in 1966 came as an emergency hitter and his seven hits only produced an equally ineffective .156 BA.

Overall as a pinch-hitter, the left-handed hitting Skinner came up with 69 hits in 274 times at-bat for a better-than-most .252 average, but still 25 points lower than his .277 lifetime mark. He later managed both the Phillies and the Padres. His son, Joel, who was a catcher in the big leagues with the White Sox and the Yankees from 1983 to 1991, also became a major league manager for the Indians in 2002.

Baumholtz again was the NL's tops in pinch-hit safeties with 14 in 1956 while Ed Bailey, the starting catcher for the Reds, easily had the best pinch-hitting average with eight hits in just 13 at-bats for an outstanding .538 average. A left-handed hitter with good power, the 6' 2", 200-pound Bailey played for 14 years in the big leagues. The Strawberry Plains, Tennessee product stayed with the Reds for eight years and then played parts of his remaining six years with the Giants, Braves, Cubs and Angels. As a pinch-hitter, he collected 37 hits, including eight home runs, two of them grand slams. Bailey's 150 at-bats as an emergency batsman merited a .247 average, somewhat below his .256 overall mark. No less a hitting authority than Stan Musial once opined that Bailey, who wound up hitting 155 home runs, could have hit the ball out of any ballpark he played in if he just met the ball and stopped trying to pull everything.

A tiny young outfielder with the Senators, Ernie Oravetz, set the pace in the American League in 1956 pinch-hit at-bats with 49. The 5' 4", 145-pounder only hit safely in 11 of those appearances for a .244 average and was out of the majors after the season ended. The Johnstown, Pennsylvania native had just two years to show for his big league career in which he produced but 17 hits in 84 pinch-hit at-bats for a slight .202 BA, well below his .263 overall average.

Outfielder Ron "The Round Man" Northey, with the White Sox in 1956 after nine years in the Senior Circuit, enjoyed his best year ever as a pinch-hitter. He led the AL in hits and average with 15-out-of-39 for a robust .385 BA, which included driving in the winning run in the late innings of no less than eight games. That same year Mickey Mantle won the Triple Crown in the AL and only drove in the winning run in nine games for the Yankees. Northey, who was notorious for never swinging at the first pitch, delivered 13 of his hits with two strikes on him.

A chubby left-handed slugging outfielder from Mahanoy City, Pennsylvania, the 5' 10", 195-pounder connected for nine pinch-hit home runs that year, three of them grand slams, to establish the major league record that was tied in 1975 by Willie McCovey. In his career, Northey banged out 59 hits in 214 pinch-hit at-bats for a dependable .280 average, two points above his overall career BA of .278.

One year Northey spent part of the season contemplating how pitchers worked on the first ball they threw. He discovered that in ten times at bat as a pinch-swinger, the first pitch was never a strike. Northey also concluded that he could determine the speed and turn of the ball as it went by him. It was his belief that the pitcher made his best effort on the very first pitch he threw. He determined that as the count increased and the pressure grew on each succeeding pitch, the pitcher would come back to that same pitch when it meant the most. "And that was the pitch I was ready to hit," he said.[15]

Jim "Dutch" Bolger of the Cubs led the way in the National League in 1957 with 17 hits and 48 at-bats for a very productive .355 BA as an emergency batsman. A right-handed outfielder who had started his big league career in his hometown of Cincinnati, the 6' 2", 180-pounder was never given much of chance by the Reds in parts of the three seasons he spent there. He was traded to the Cubs at the beginning of the 1955 season where he played a good deal more but not enough to become anything but a bat off the bench. He played very little with both the Indians and the Phillies in 1959 and was gone from the majors after that season following seven unexceptional years. As a pinch-hitter he came to bat 134 times and delivered 32 hits for a .241 BA, a bit better than his .229 overall average.

The much-traveled Pete Whisenant, with the Reds in 1957, led the NL in pinch-hitting average with 8-for-20 for an even .400. What made this all the more remarkable was that five of his eight hits were home runs—

three of them off a pretty fair country pitcher named Wilmer "Vinegar Bend" Mizell of the Cardinals. A reserve outfielder who played with seven different teams during his eight years in the majors, the right-handed hitting native of Asheville, North Carolina never batted over .239 in any season, or hit more than the 11 home runs he hit in 1956 and again in 1958. As a pinch-swinger, Whisenant was called upon officially 124 times and tallied but 26 hits for a meager .209 BA, as opposed to a .224 mark overall. Whisenant died on March 22, 1996, in Port Charlotte, Florida, at the age of 66.

Over in the American League, it was Havana Cuba's Julio Becquer of Washington who led in pinch-hit at-bats and hits with 65 and 18, respectively, in 1957. Those 65 at-bats for the left-handed backup first sacker established a new record for the AL that would stand for another decade. He hit .277 off the bench, as opposed to .226 overall. Two years later, also with the Senators, the 5' 11½", 178-pounder again led the league in both pinch-hit at-bats and hits with 56 and 12 respectively for a thin .214 mark.

One of Becquer's pinch-hits that year proved disastrous for pitcher Bob Turley of the Yankees. In the second game of a doubleheader played in Washington's old Griffith Stadium, the fireballing Turley had a no-hitter going into the ninth inning when Becquer lofted a pop fly single to spoil it. All in all, Becquer banged out 63 pinch-hits in 256 at-bats during his seven years in the majors for a rather inconsequential .209 BA. Overall his lifetime average was decidedly better at .244.

The 1957 World Series between the Yankees and the Braves produced a rather unusual turn of events involving a pinch-hitter. In a career plagued by continuous back problems, Vernal "Nippy" Jones, was at the time a backup first baseman to Milwaukee's Frank Torre. In what would be his last appearance in a major league game, Jones was sent up to pinch-hit in the tenth inning of Game Four with the Yankees ahead, 5-4. After appearing to have avoided a wild pitch, Jones convinced the plate umpire that the ball had struck his foot by pointing to a smudge of polish on the ball from his spiked shoe. Jones was awarded first base and the Braves went on to score three times to win the game. The Braves won the Series in seven games. Jones died in Sacramento on October 3, 1995, at the age of 69.

Chuck Tanner, who occasionally played the outfield for four different clubs in his eight-year playing career, topped the National League in pinch-hit at-bats in 1958 with 53 for the Cubs. The 6-foot, 185-pound Tanner's 12 hits were only good enough for a .236 BA off the bench. The left-handed hitting New Castle, Pennsylvania native never achieved immortality as a player but was a very successful manager later for the White Sox, Oakland A's, Pirates and Braves. In fact, he piloted the "We Are Family" Pirates to a dramatic seven-game World Series win over the heavily favored Orioles in 1979. His career totals as a pinch-hitter show 38 hits in 174 official appearances for a far-from-great .212 average, well below his lifetime .261 average overall.

The NL pinch-hit leader in base hits in 1958 was outfielder Dave Philley of the Phillies with 18. The Paris, Texas native's 18-out-of-44 for an extraordinary .409 average was just a dash below the league's best pinch-hitting BA. Amazingly, he had hits in eight at-bats as a pinch-swinger during that season. Philley increased the record to nine in a row when he rapped out a base knock in his first pinch-hit at-bats in the following year.

"The funny thing about my streak," the 6-foot, 188-pound Philley said later, "was that I wasn't even sure if it had been broken. I got my ninth straight in April of the following season, but on my tenth pinch-hitting trip, I hit a sacrifice fly with the bases loaded against Cincinnati. It took awhile for them to determine whether that counted as an official at-bat. But it was decided that my streak had been stopped."[16]

Bob Bowman, also of the Phillies, had the league's best average in 1958 with his 13-for-31 registering an extremely effective .420 BA. The 6' 1", 195-pound Bowman, a right-handed hitting outfielder from Laytonville, California with movie star looks, played his entire five-year big league career in Philadelphia. Despite his lifetime .249 average overall, he batted .267 as a pinch-swinger with 21 hits in 79 at-bats. He possessed a strong arm and tried pitching for awhile but was gone from the big leagues after 1959 at the age of 28.

The American League's pace-setters in 1958 once again included the venerable Enos Slaughter of the Yankees with 47 times at-bat while slugging outfielder Gus "Ozark Ike" Zernial of the Tigers, had the most hits and best BA with 15-of-38 for an exceptional .399 BA.

Zernial drew his nickname from former manager Fred Haney, who was broadcasting games for the old Hollywood Stars of the Pacific Coast League when Zernial played there. At the age of 35 in 1958, the Beaumont, Texas-born Zernial was getting close to retirement. He had just come over to the Tigers after turns with the White Sox and A's (in both Philadelphia and Kansas City) beginning in 1949.

A 6' 2½", 210-pound free swinger who led the American League in strikeouts twice, the right-handed hitting Zernial left baseball after the 1959 season when he appeared in just 60 games for Detroit. A career .265 batter, he had 47 hits in 178 pinch-hit swings for an above average .264 BA. Following his retirement, Zernial became a radio and television sportscaster in Fresno, California.

In 1959, one of the greatest home run hitters ever among pinch-hitters, George Crowe, then a reserve first baseman for the Reds, began his assault on the all-time records. The left-handed hitting Crowe, who hailed from Whiteland, Indiana, led the National League that season in both at-bats and hits with 63 and 17 respectively. A former Negro Leaguer and pro basketball player in the National Basketball League, the 6' 2", 210-pound Crowe had been the Reds' regular first baseman and an All-Star before being dealt to the Cardinals after the 1958 season. St. Louis already had a first baseman named Stan Musial, so Crowe had to be content to come off the bench.

Left-handed hitting outfielder Irv Noren, who split time between the Cardinals and Cubs, had the NL's best average with 12-for-29 and a powerful .414 mark in 1959. Noren, a 6-foot, 185-pounder from Jamestown, New York, was a former Yankees outfielder who had played in three World Series with the Bronx Bombers. Despite his fine year in 1959 as a pinch-swinger, throughout his career he was only 52-for-230 for a .229 average as an emergency batsman. His overall lifetime average was a decent .275.

One of the more interesting sidelights to the 1959 season in the National League was the pinch-hitting exploits of Chuck Essegian, an outfielder with the Los Angeles Dodgers. A Boston native who played in the 1952 Rose Bowl for Stanford, Essegian is one of only two players to hit two pinch-hit home runs in one World Series. Ironically when the Dodgers arrived in Chicago to face the White Sox, there was no locker for him in the visitors' clubhouse of old Comiskey Park. He was forced to change in a corner of the room.

After losing the first game, the Dodgers were behind 2-1 in Game Two with two out in the seventh inning. Manager Walter Alston called on Essegian to bat for pitcher Johnny Podres. He had struck out as a pinch-hitter in the first game but this time he belted one out of the park off Bob Shaw to tie the score. The Dodgers went on to win, 4-3.

In the sixth and final game of the series won by the Dodgers, the right-handed Essegian hit another one when he batted for Duke Snider in the ninth inning. Although his team was safely ahead at the time, his solo shot off Ray Moore proved to be a fitting climax in the Dodgers' easy 9-3 triumph. The 5' 11", 202-pounder repeated the feat on Opening Day of the 1960 season by hitting one out in the 11th inning to beat the Cubs before a regular season record home crowd of 67,550 at the Los Angeles Coliseum. The home run represented Essegian's third straight as a pinch-hitter.

During his six-year big league career, Essegian played in only 404 games for eight different ball clubs. A lifetime .255 batter, he connected for 33 base hits in 142 at-bats as an emergency batsman during the regular season compiling a not-so-scintillating .232 average.

Julio Becquer set the pace in the American League in 1959 with both the most pinch-hit at-bats with 56 and hits with 12. However, it was the veteran left-handed hitting Gene "Old Faithful" Woodling of the Orioles, whose remarkable 10-for-18 for a sparkling .556 average represented the league's best BA. Woodling, the long-time Yankee from Akron, Ohio, had played in five consecutive world championships with them. He was famed for being able to run, throw and hit when it counted most. He was then 37 and while he continued to play fairly often, he was no longer considered a regular.

The 5' 9½", 195-pounder found himself in Washington in 1961, and later became a member of the original Mets in 1962 under his old Yankees manager, Casey Stengel, who considered him the best left-fielder he ever managed. It would prove to be Woodling's last season in the big leagues. As a pinch-swinger his 65 hits in 234 at-bats during his 17-year career garnered him a .278 average, fairly close to his steady lifetime BA of .284. He died in 2001 at the age of 79.

9

1960-1969:
Smoky Burgess and Jerry Lynch
Make It an Art Form

By the time the 1960s rolled around, managers were starting to use pinch-hitters regularly. From the seven or so substitute batters that had been employed throughout the entire 1892 major league season, midway through this new decade over 4,000 hitters were now being called off the bench to hit in the pinch each year.

The leading pinch-hitters in the National League in 1960 were destined to become not only the best in the business for the decade but among the very best of all-time. Gerald Thomas "Jerry" Lynch spent three mediocre seasons with the Pirates that included a very poor 9-for-49, or .184 pinch-hitting average. The left-handed hitter from Bay City, Michigan had been picked up by the Reds in 1957 after being out almost the entire previous year due to illness. At first Cincinnati used him as a reserve outfielder but began to like him better off the bench as a pinch-hitter. Lynch did not disappoint. He had 66 pinch-swings in 1960 and hit safely 19 times for a .sparkling .317 BA.

The other budding legend, Forrest "Smoky" Burgess, a burly 5' 8½", 185-pound catcher for the Pirates, had the league's best average that season with nine hits in 20 at-bats producing a whopping .450 BA. The left-handed hitting Burgess, a native of Caroleen, North Carolina, had broken in with the Cubs back in 1949. He was subsequently dealt away to the Phillies in 1951 who in turn traded him to the Reds early in 1955. The

At his retirement in 1966, Jerry Lynch held the big league mark for career pinch-hit home runs with 18. (Courtesy of National Baseball Hall of Fame Library, Cooperstown, N.Y.)

Pirates wanted him primarily as a backstop when they obtained him in 1959. He was short and squat and possessed excellent catching skills. In Pittsburgh he shared duties with Hal Smith.

When Jerry Lynch was signed by the Pirates, Branch Rickey, then the team's president, tried to make him a slugging catcher, but after being spiked in the neck by an incoming base runner, he was left with a pint of blood less and a sore arm. While serving in the U.S. Army, they tried to make a football player out of him and the slender 6' 1", 185-pounder almost got himself killed. And Pirates teammate Dick Groat, a great basketball player, tried to make Lynch one also; all Lynch got for his trouble were lumps in the head.

After being drafted by the Reds, manager Birdie Tebbetts phoned Lynch and told him: "Now that I got you, what am I gonna do with you?"[1] In spring training, he joined George Crowe, Bobby Thurman and Pete Whisenant as the pinch-hitting corps of the Reds. Three seasons later, they were calling Lynch "Mr. Wonderful" when he led the NL in at bats and hits off the bench.

One of the no-nos of being a professional pinch-hitter is never — well, almost never — take a called third strike. Jerry Lynch once went two years without being called out on strikes. When he did, he questioned the umpire's judgment in a manner that got him excused for the rest of the game.

Lynch always dreaded hitting against rookie pitchers, preferring to test his mettle against the veterans. "Hitting against a guy who's been around, you have an idea what his best pitch is and that's what you've got to hit in a jam," he once explained.[2] When he retired after the 1966 season, Jerry Lynch had the distinction of hitting the most home runs as a pinch-hitter up to that time — 18 — and hitting safely 19 times in a row over two seasons as an emergency batter. He also ranked second on the all-time pinch-hit list behind Smoky Burgess with 116. Lynch came to bat 447 times as a substitute batter while attaining a .260 average. Overall, he hit .277 for his career total 1,184 at-bats.

Smoky Burgess was always aware of what was being demanded of him in a particular situation. One time a base hit may have been required while another time, the direction in which the ball was hit was what was uppermost. His nickname was derived from his lack of speed on the base paths.

Burgess always stood close to the plate because he wanted to make certain he could hit and control the outside pitch. Since this approach annoyed many pitchers, then and now, Smoky was constantly driven off the dish by inside pitches. This strategy never bothered Burgess since he

Smoky Burgess's 145 career pinch-hits was the major league record from 1967 to 1979. (Courtesy of National Baseball Hall of Fame Library, Cooperstown, N.Y.)

calculated that he was up there to get on base anyway he could, even if it meant getting hit by a pitch.

Once a pitcher named John Buzhardt, who later became a teammate, threw at him five consecutive times. The first one was not quite at him, going behind his head and hitting his bat for a foul ball. "He finally hit me with the fifth pitch," said Burgess.[3] Smoky figured the orders came from the manager anyway. "We'd just gotten two home runs off him," Smoky explained.[4] He always readily accepted the risk in order to achieve what he wanted and that was to be in a position to swing at every pitch, no matter where it was.

Early in his career, Burgess had the most trouble with left-hander Dave Koslo of the Giants, even though he preferred hitting against southpaws. "I always rated Sandy Koufax and Robin Roberts as the best pitchers I hit against, but I managed to get my share of hits against Roberts," Burgess said when he was a minor league instructor for the Braves in 1978. "Roberts threw hard and was always around the plate."[5]

Unlike some pinch-hitters such as Ron Northey, Burgess was always ready to swing, especially at the first pitch. "I don't have to go through a lot of exercises to get warmed up," he was quoted as saying. "I'm lucky I can come off the bench and swing the bat hard on the first pitch."[6] Later in his career when he tied the record for pinch-hits—114 at the time—it was on the first pitch, and even the hit that set the new mark was also on the first pitch. When he retired in 1967, he had accumulated 144 pinch-hits, a record that lasted until Manny Mota broke it in 1979. In the 507 times that he came to the plate as a pinch-hitter, Burgess hit a record 27 doubles and established the all-time mark for runs batted in with 142. He hit 16 pinch-hit homers— Lynch topped him by two— and his lifetime BA was a very efficient .288, close to his .295 overall lifetime average. Although the portly Burgess was credited with 33 lifetime triples, nary a one came as a substitute batter.

The teetotaling Burgess would think no more of taking a third strike than a drink. His high school coach, a man named Forrest Hunt, had taught him to always be aggressive. "You can't hit with the bat on your shoulder. The worst thing that can happen to you is to take a third strike. Don't get cheated," Coach Hunt told his pupil.[7] Smoky's attitude was always to be ready to swing at anything, no matter where it was, even if it was not in the strike zone. "Any ball I can get a good part of the bat on is a good ball to hit," he said. "Ninety percent of the hitters will get as many hits on balls as they do on strikes."[8] He got his bat on the ball, too, striking out just 270 times in 4,471 at-bats; he walked 477 times in his career.

Burgess suffered from ulcers throughout his playing days. A year after his retirement in 1967, he underwent surgery for the condition and got down to a svelte —for him — 200 pounds, enabling him to enjoy for most of the remaining years of his life. He passed away in Asheville, North Carolina, on September 15, 1991, at the age of 64.

The leading pinch-swingers in the American League in 1960 were Bob Hale of the Indians and Vic Wertz, then a member of the Red Sox. The left-handed hitting Hale, a 5' 10", 195-pound Sarasota, Florida native, had the most at bats, 63, and greatest number of hits, 19 (a club record) for a .302 average. Wertz, also a left-handed batter who hailed from York, Pennsylvania, had the AL's best pinch-hitting BA with a .556 mark, coming off 10 hits in 18 at-bats.

Hale, who was listed on the roster as a first baseman, played little there because he could not field with any dexterity. During his career, over 40 percent of his at-bats came as a substitute batter. He always had confidence in his hitting and so did manager Paul Richards, who had him at Baltimore during his first five years in the big leagues. Richards told him: "If you hit .250 as a pinch-hitter, you're doing a good job."[9]

Under Cleveland manager Jimmy Dykes, Hale hit .300 but only had seven at-bats as a first baseman in five games in 1960. Dykes, like Richards, loved having Hale come off the bench and his streak of five straight pinch-hits that year tied an AL record previously set by Johnny Mize. "I was living on cloud nine when I made those five straight hits," Hale said at the time.[10]

Hale was the type of player who left the dugout swinging the bat. "I hate to strike out," he declared, "and I seldom do. I just hit the ball where it's pitched. As a pinch-hitter you only get one crack and you should at least wait for your ball. A pinch-hitter has his ups and downs like anyone, only he doesn't get a chance to come back as soon. You have to be lucky as a pinch-hitter."[11]

Hale completed the 1960 season one base hit shy of Ed Coleman's AL record of 20 in a single season, which the former St. Louis Browns' outfielder had set in 1936. He acknowledged that sitting on the Yankees' bench in 1961 was an education as he had never been on a ball club with such depth. "Before, wherever I went I was the Number One pinch-hitter," he stated at the time. "With the Yankees, I was Number Four."[12] Johnny Blanchard, Bob Cerv and Hector Lopez all ranked ahead of him. He marveled at the team's generosity. "I pinch-hit seven times and they still voted me two-thirds of a Series share," he said.[13]

Hale only played for seven years in the majors, leaving on top after finishing the season with the 1961 world champion Yankees. He was only 28 when he departed from the big leagues. As a pinch-swinger, he stroked 62 hits in 249 at-bats for a .265 BA, slightly lower than his overall .273 average.

Wertz, in his 14th season in the major leagues in 1960, is best remembered for the long drive to the deepest part of the Polo Grounds that Willie Mays caught over his shoulder during the 1954 World Series between the Indians and the Giants. Once a regular outfielder-first baseman for the Tigers, Browns and Indians, the 6-foot, 186-pounder had come to the Red Sox from Cleveland prior to the 1959 season with Gary Geiger for Jimmy Piersall. One of his hits as a pinch-hitter in 1960 was a grand slam home run, the second of his career which tied Bill Skowron of the Yankees, who held the record at the time. He also tied both Hale and Mize in 1960 by hitting safely on five consecutive at-bats as a pinch-hitter. Wertz batted .250 as a substitute batter with 62 hits in 248 at-bats, well below his overall .277 mark. He died in Detroit on July 7, 1983, at the age of 68.

Elmer Valo, who spent the 1960 season partly with both the Senators and the Yankees, only hit .239 as an emergency batsman that year. However, what set the 5' 11", 190-pound left-handed hitter apart from everyone else was the fact that he drew 18 walks as a pinch-hitter to set the all-time single season major league record. He was 39 years old when he established the record. Valo also set the career record for free passes as a substitute batter — 91 — a figure that almost parallels his 90 hits in the pinch.

He spent the last four years of his 20-year-career as a pinch-hitter and in 1961, his last year in the big leagues, he had played longer than anyone active at the time except Stan Musial and Early Wynn. His numbers as a substitute batter are deceptive because of his almost unique ability to draw bases on balls: 90 base hits in 386 appearances for a seemingly poor .233 average and considerably less than his .282 overall career BA. However, when combined with his 91 free passes, his on-base percentage as a pinch-hitter was close to .500. Valo passed away in Palmerton, Pennsylvania, on July 19, 1998, at the age of 77.

The year 1961 proved to be Jerry Lynch's best season ever as a pinch-hitter. For the second year in a row, he corralled 19 pinch-hits to lead the National League in that department. And getting them in only 47 times up gave him the pinch-hit batting title as well with a nifty .405. His 25 runs batted in tied the major league pinch-hit record that had been set back in 1943 by Joe Cronin. No one has come along to break it yet.

Bob "Butch" Will of the Cubs had the most pinch-hit at-bats in the NL in 1961 with 52. The left-handed hitting Berwyn, Illinois product had been a regular in the outfield for Chicago the year before but usually only came off the bench in 1961. The 5' 10½", 175-pounder played for two more years, all with the Cubs, his last one coming in 1963 for a total of six big league seasons. He was 32 at the time. In his brief time in the majors, Will had but 46 hits in 199 pinch-hit at-bats for an inconsistent .231 mark, but fairly close to his overall .247 career average.

Switch-hitting Dave Philley, in the American League in 1961, set a new league record with 72 pinch-hit at-bats and a new major league record for base hits with 24. Philley broke Bill Rumler's single season record of 71 at-bats in the AL, which had stood since 1917. And his 24 hits established a new mark for pinch-hitters which was tied nine years later by Vic Davallilo.

Philley got his record-breaking hit by way of a swinging bunt along the third base line in a game his Orioles played against the Twins on August 23, 1961 at Metropolitan Stadium. Today it ranks fourth on the all-time single season pinch-hitting records list.

When he played regularly, Philley was noted for his good speed and fine arm which contributed to his leading all AL outfielders in assists in three different seasons. In 1960 he had worn the uniforms of three different teams: the Phillies, Giants and Orioles. He played the entire year in Baltimore in 1962 before being sold to the Red Sox for the following season, his eighteenth and last in the majors. His 93 base hits in 311 pinch-hit at-bats were good enough for a exceptional .299 BA. That average ranked only a point under Bob Fothergill's .300 as a pinch-hitter but Philley accomplished his average in 58 more at-bats.

Despite Philley's record-breaking season, it was the Indians' Don Dillard who led the AL in pinch-hitting BA in 1961 with 15-for-35 for a resounding .430 mark. An outfielder by trade, the left-handed hitting Greenville, South Carolina product, played another year for the Indians before being traded to the Braves in 1963. The 6' 1", 200-pounder lasted but one more season in Milwaukee and was gone from the majors at 28 after the 1963 campaign. His 40 hits in 149 pinch-hit at-bats were good for a respectable .270 career BA and much higher than his overall .244 average.

Johnny Blanchard, a Minneapolis native, never set the world on fire with his pinch-hitting chores during the regular season. In fact, his 29-for-177 warranted a rather pathetic .166 lifetime BA as a substitute batter. But when it came to the World Series, the Yankees' third-string catcher — behind Yogi Berra and Elston Howard — still holds the mark for the most appearances in Series games by an emergency batsman with 10.

One of his three post-season pinch-hits took place in the third game of the 1961 Series against the Reds. Blanchard's dramatic two-out pinch-hit homer in the top half of the eighth inning off Bob Purkey tied the score and set the stage for Roger Maris's equally dramatic ninth inning blast (also off Purkey) which won it, 3-2. The 6' 1", 193-pounder played in the majors for eight years, leaving the game after the 1965 season when he played for three different teams — the Yankees, Kansas City A's and Milwaukee Braves. He was 32 at the time.

Earl Torgeson, who finished up his 15-year career as a player-coach for the Yankees in 1961, was first and foremost a "pinch looker," meaning that he would almost always wait out the pitcher while looking for a base on balls, was ideally suited as a rally starter and would often be sent up to lead off an inning. He was dubbed "The Earl of Snohomish," as was Hall of Famer Earl Averill before him, who hailed from the same town in Washington state.

Early in 1949, Torgeson experienced a severe injury to his left shoulder while trying to break up a double play. The injury, which sidelined him for the remainder of the season, handicapped him throughout the remainder of his career. Overall as a pinch-swinger, Torgeson hit .262 with 55 hits in 210 at-bats, almost equal to his .265 lifetime BA. Torgeson was 66 when he passed away on November 8, 1990, in Everett, Washington.

Future Hall of Famer Albert "Red" Schoendienst of the Cardinals was the National League's leader in pinch-hit at-bats with 72 and base hits with 22 for a .306 BA in 1962. The 6-foot, 170-pounder's 72 at-bats tied him for the major league record with Sam Leslie who had set the mark back in 1932. Red, who hailed from Germantown, Illinois, played in the big leagues for 19 years until he was 40, 14 of those years spent with the Cardinals. A bout with tuberculosis put him on the shelf for most of the 1959 season but he recovered fully and played on to 1963.

Schoendienst also managed the team for 12 consecutive years beginning in 1965, the longest managerial tenure in club history. His teams won both the 1967 and 1968 NL pennants and the World Series against the Red Sox in 1967.

Careerwise, the switch-hitting Schoendienst delivered 56 hits in 185 pinch-hit at-bats for a very steady .303 BA, even better than his .289 average overall. Among Hall of Famers—he was inducted in 1980—he ranks seventh on the all-time list as a pinch-swinger.

The NL leader in pinch-hitting for average in 1962 was right-handed hitting Lee Walls of the Dodgers, whose 13 hits in 27 at bats gained him an incredible .482 BA that year. Walls, a 6' 2", 205-pounder out of San Diego, had been the batboy for the Padres in the mid-1940s when they were in the Pacific Coast League. He spent 10 years in the big leagues and played for five different teams. Walls was nicknamed "Captain Midnight" because of his oversized wire-rimmed eyeglasses.

A one-time regular outfielder for Pittsburgh where he debuted in 1952 at the age of 19, Los Angeles was his last stop in the big leagues. He played some third and first base, and even caught in one game during his somewhat checkered career. He was gone from the big leagues after the 1964 season at age 31. As an emergency batsman, Walls was 46-for-183 for a .251 BA, somewhat under his overall .262 mark. He died in Los Angeles on October 11, 1993, at the age of 60.

Over in the American League a reserve outfielder named Joe Hicks of the Senators had the most pinch-hit at-bats in 1962 with 61 but he only had nine hits to show for his efforts for a rather negligible .147 average. The left-handed hitting Ivy, Virginia native played in the majors for only five years seeing time also with the White Sox and Mets. Over half (102) of his 212 career at-bats were in a pinch-hitting role, but he could only come through with 20 safeties altogether for a .199 average, even lower than his .221 BA overall.

Vic Wertz, back with the Tigers with whom he had started out in 1947, led the AL in pinch-hit base hits with 17 in 1962, while Dick Williams' 13-for-31 represented the league's best average at a resounding .420. Never a regular, the 6-foot, 190-pound Williams, back with the Orioles for a second time, was a handy utility infielder-outfielder who had been with the Dodgers, Indians and Kansas City A's before rejoining Baltimore. The right-handed hitter hailed from St. Louis and went on to become an extremely successful major league manager with the Red Sox, A's, Angels, Padres and Mariners. He guided Boston, Oakland and San Diego to the World Series.

Few names in baseball history have brought more attention to a player than John Kennedy, not the late president but the player, especially in the 1960s, and especially in Washington. John Edward Kennedy the ballplayer ironically shared the same birth date as John Fitzgerald Kennedy — May 29. A three-sport athlete at Harper High School in Chicago, the 6-foot, 185-pound Kennedy was an infielder who could play any position on the infield except first. He was just not a very good hitter on a day-to-day basis, witness his lifetime .223 BA.

On September 5, 1962, he became only the ninth player in AL history to hit a home run in his first major league at-bat. It was an inside-the-parker for the Senators and, more importantly, he did it as a pinch-hitter. The right-handed hitting Kennedy survived 12 seasons in the big leagues with stops in Los Angeles with the Dodgers, in New York with the Yankees, in Seattle with the Pilots (later Brewers) and in Boston with the Red Sox. Overall his pinch-hitting left much to be desired as he made but six hits in 39 times at bat during his career for a nearly invisible .151 average.

The amount of at-bats by the leading pinch-hit specialists in the National League took a severe dip in 1963, Matty Alou of the Giants was at the top of the list with only 45 — quite a comedown from Red Schoendienst's 72 in the previous year. Alou only had nine hits for a mere .200 BA. In only his fourth year in the big leagues and not yet a regular, the left-handed hitting outfielder from the Dominican Republic had his best years still ahead of him. He was the best hitter for average as well as the fastest and smallest among the three big league Alou brothers. Pinch-hitting, of course, would never be Matty Alou's strong suit as his 46 base hits in 219 at-bats only bore him a shallow mark of .210 while his overall lifetime BA was a spiffy .307. When he won the 1966 NL batting title with an average of .338, his brother Felipe finished second at .327. It marked the first time in history that brothers finished first and second in a league batting race. Matty, Felipe and Jesus Alou combined to play 47 seasons in the big leagues.

The player with the most pinch-hit safeties in the NL during 1963 was a second-year player named Merritt Ranew of the Cubs. A backup catcher from Albany, Georgia, the left-handed hitting Ranew got 17 hits in 41 at-bats for a .415 average. Ranew was with a different team every year during his five-year major league career: the Astros, Cubs, Braves, Angels and Pilots. He was never able to duplicate the success he enjoyed as pinch-hitter in 1963, though, finishing up with only 28 hits in 115 pinch-hit at bats for .243, but close to his overall .247 BA.

Charlie James of the Cardinals had the best pinch-hitting average in the NL in 1963 with 10 base knocks in 18 appearances for a .556 average.

A 6' 1", 195-pound reserve outfielder with very little power, he batted right-handed and played for five years in his hometown of St. Louis. Prior to the 1965 season, he was traded to the Reds with Roger Craig for pitcher Bob Purkey. He played only one year in Cincinnati leaving the game for good at 28. Overall, he was an effective pinch-hitter, going 30 for 108 for a superior .280 mark and much better than his .255 career mark. He was hitless in three pinch-hit at bats against the Yankees in the 1964 World Series, which the Cardinals won in seven games.

After 13 years in the American League, Roy "Squirrel" Sievers, was traded by the White Sox to the Phillies for pitcher John Buzhardt and third baseman Charley Smith prior to the 1962 season. Now almost exclusively a first baseman following many years in the outfield for the Browns, Senators and White Sox, the St. Louis product was a right-handed hitter known for his "sweet swing." The term is usually associated with left-handed batters who take a short back swing before whipping the club around gracefully in a flawless arc. He got his nickname as a youngster playing basketball and hanging around the "cage."

On May 26, 1963, the 6' 1", 195-pound Sievers tied a record that only Jimmie Foxx had held until then when he hit a pinch-hit grand slam home run. With that poke, he and Foxx became the only two players in major league history to accomplish the feat in both leagues. (Ironically, both Foxx and Sievers hit their NL slams as Phillies.) Overall, Sievers hit 318 home runs during his major league career.

A favorite of then-Vice President Richard Nixon, Sievers went back to Washington in the middle of 1964 and ended his 17-year career there in the following season. He was 39 years old. As a pinch-hitter, Sievers only batted .201 with 31 hits in 154 at-bats, significantly less than his .267 overall mark.

Bob Sadowski, a utility infielder for the Angels, had the most pinch-hit at-bats in the American League in 1963 with 50. His 12 hits were behind the 16 registered by Dick Williams, then with the Red Sox. George "Glider" Alusik had the league-best BA with 9-for-19 for a huge .477 BA. The left-handed hitting Sadowski, like Charlie James, was also from St. Louis. The 6-foot, 190-pounder broke in with the Cardinals in 1960 and played for the Phillies in 1961 and the White Sox in 1962 before heading to Los Angeles. He was the younger brother of Eddie Sadowski, a backup catcher for the Red Sox, Angels and Braves in the 1960s. Bob played only four years in the majors accumulating a rather modest pinch-hitting record of 22 hits in 97 at-bats for a .230 BA, but close to his overall .222 average.

The 6' 3½", 175-pound Alusik, also known as "Turk," was born in Ashley, Pennsylvania. He started his somewhat brief career with the Tigers in 1958 and his chances of breaking into the Rocky Colavito-Bill Bruton-Al Kaline outfield were both slim and none. He wound up with the Kansas City A's in 1962, where he posted his league-leading best pinch-hitting average in the following year. Another outfielder who failed to display enough power to stay very long in the majors, the right-handed hitting Alusik played for five years, leaving after the 1964 season at the age of 29. More often than not, he was used as a pinch-hitter with 110 of 298 his big league at-bats coming off the bench. He had 28 hits as a substitute batter for a not-too-shabby .255 lifetime BA, and very consistent with his overall .256 average.

Charles "Cap" Peterson of the San Francisco Giants was the pace-setter in the National League in pinch-hit at-bats in 1964 with 55. Ty Cline of the Milwaukee Braves had a memorable year, going 14-for-39 to lead the NL in hits and average at .360.

Peterson, a right-handed hitting reserve outfielder from Tacoma, Washington, was signed for a reported $64,000 bonus as a shortstop. However, he was unable to crack the lineup as a starter and was relegated to bench play throughout most of his career. The 6' 4", 195-pounder's lifetime average as a substitute batter was only .192 with only 46 hits 240 plate appearances. He later played for the Senators and the Indians in the American League where he finished his career in 1969 at the age of 27. He passed away in his hometown of Tacoma in 1980 at the relatively young age of 38.

The left-handed hitting Ty Cline, from Hampton, South Carolina, played for seven different clubs during his 12 years in the big leagues. Like Peterson, the 6' ½", 170-pounder was a reserve outfielder throughout most of his career and was never able to fill a regular slot due to a lack of power. The former Clemson All-American only hit six home runs in 892 at-bats. In 266 appearances as a substitute batter, he recorded 60 base hits for a weak .230 BA, but not much lower than his overall .238 BA.

Cline played an important role as a pinch-hitter in the 1970 National League Championship Series against the Pirates. In the third and final game which resulted in a sweep for the Reds, he drew a walk in the bottom half of the eighth inning and came home to score the tie-breaking run after successive singles by Pete Rose and Bobby Tolan. He also got a hit in three at-bats in the World Series that year in the Reds' losing effort against the Orioles. Cline retired from baseball after the next season at the age of 32.

The Cardinals' Carl Warwick's 11-out-of-43 for .256 as a pinch-hitter in the regular season was not earth-shattering, but the part-time outfielder hit safely three times in four attempts in the 1964 World Series. In fact, with his team trailing the Yankees, 4-2, in the opening game, his pinch-single in the bottom of the sixth gave his team the go-ahead run. The Cardinals eventually won the game, 9-5.

Warwick, a right-handed hitter from Dallas, played with five different teams in both leagues during his brief six-year career. The 5' 10", 170-pounder was gone from baseball after the 1966 season at the age of 29. His 27 hits in 122 pinch-hit at-bats gained him only a .221 BA, well under his overall .248 mark.

Omaha's Bob Johnson, a journeyman utility infielder with the Orioles, led the American League in pinch-hit at-bats with 45 and base hits with 15 in 1964 for a fine .333 average. The best pinch-hitter in the AL for average that season, though, was another well-traveled player, "Wonderful" Willie Smith, a reserve outfielder with the Los Angeles Angels. He produced ten base hits in 23 at-bats for a marvelous .399 average.

During his 11-year major league career, the right-handed hitting Johnson appeared in over 100 games only once. The 5' 10", 175-pounder broke in with the Kansas City A's in 1960 and subsequently wore the uniforms of the Senators, Orioles, Mets, Reds, Braves, Cardinals and Oakland A's. As a pinch-hitter, he did fairly well as his lifetime production of 66 hits in 243 appearances earned him an efficient .272 average, the same overall average he attained in 874 lifetime at-bats.

Willie Smith, a former amateur boxer out of Anniston, Alabama, actually reached the big leagues as a pitcher for the Tigers in 1963. Smith got his nickname when he was with Syracuse of the International League that year by hitting .380 and winding up 14-2 as a pitcher. The following year found Wonderful Willie in Los Angeles, where he pitched in 15 games for the Angels but was converted into an outfielder while leading the league in pinch-hitting average. On June 4 of that year in a game at Cleveland, Smith pinch-hit, played the outfield and relieved in the eighth inning.

Later in his career, he donned the uniforms of the Indians, Cubs and Reds but could not find a regular spot in the lineup, eventually winding up as a backup first baseman for the Reds. About a third of his major league at-bats were as a pinch-hitter, and his 54 hits in 239 at-bats were only good enough for a .226 average, well under his career .248 BA. He is the only African-American baseball player in major league history to appear in at least 20 games as a pitcher and 20 as a fielder. He left baseball after nine seasons following the 1971 campaign at the age of 32.

Smoky Burgess, who had come over to the White Sox from the Pirates late in the 1964 season on waivers, made his first appearance as a pinch-hitter a memorable one. He hit a home run off Detroit's Dave Wickersham to tie a crucial stretch-drive game.

Jesse Gonder, who split the 1965 season between the Mets and the

Braves, was the National League leader in pinch-hit at-bats with 52 that year, but his 13 hits only earned him a .248 BA. Bob Skinner, then with Cardinals, had the most hits in the NL with 15 while the best average that year belonged to his teammate, Gene Freese, who had nine hits in 24 at-bats for an exquisite .376. Traded in mid-season to the White Sox, Freese went 3-for-9 as a pinch-swinger in the AL to continue his excellent season in the pinch.

The 5' 10", 180-pound Gonder, a backup catcher with defensive deficiencies, broke in with the Yankees in 1960. He had been sent to the Reds in 1962 and then to the Mets the following season. Never much of a long ball threat, the left-handed hitting Monticello, Arkansas native was used mostly off the bench. His .233 career mark as a pinch-hitter (39-for-167) is some 18 points below his career .251 average. Gonder later saw service with the Pirates. After eight years he was gone from the big leagues after 1967 at the age of 31.

Skinner, who had the most National League pinch-hit at-bats nine years earlier as a Pirate, now made his mark with the most hits in the 1965 season. A year earlier, he had two base hits in three at-bats and an RBI in the 1964 World Series as a pinch-hitter against the Yankees.

In 1966, all 45 of his at-bats were as a substitute batter. He only hit safely seven times and left the majors for good at the age of 37 after his twelfth season. On the all-time list of pinch-swingers, Skinner's 69 hits place him at No. 13. He hit .252 as a substitute batter in 274 appearances as compared to .277 overall in 4,318 at-bats.

Gene Freese and his older brother, George, both played third base and one year—1955—were on the Pirates together. They actually shared the position until George was let go after the season ended. Gene was very shaky in the field but could hit with power. After suffering a broken ankle early in 1962, the right-handed hitter from Wheeling, West Virginia was never the same and lost his everyday status. Consequently, the 5' 11", 175-pounder was relegated to backing up regulars with the Pirates, White Sox and, finally, the Astros, where he finished his 12-year career in 1966. The right-handed hitting Gene Freese ranks high on the list of all-time leaders in pinch-hit home runs with nine, including two in consecutive appearances in 1959. Throughout his career, he accumulated 45 hits in 206 pinch-hit swings for a less-than-steady .218 average, as opposed to his overall lifetime BA of .254.

Smoky Burgess, who had been waived out of the National League to the Chicago White Sox late in 1964 picked up right where he left off in the American League. He had the most pinch-hit at-bats (65) and the most hits (20) as a substitute batter in 1965 in the AL. However, it was Tim

Talton, a reserve catcher for the Kansas City A's, who had the best average with his 10-for-25 for a fabulous .400 mark.

Talton, a left-handed hitter from Pikeville, North Carolina, must have tired of backing up Phil Roof, since he only lasted two years in the majors. The 6' 3", 200-pounder was gone from the majors after the next season at the age of 28. His record as a pinch-hitter in his all-too-brief career was very good though as he delivered 19 times in 57 pinch-swings for a nifty .333 BA. His overall average was excellent as well at .295, with nearly half of his times at bat coming off the bench.

Jerry Lynch, back with his original club, the Pirates, tied with Doug Clemens of the Phillies with 49 pinch-hit at-bats in the National League in 1966. For Lynch it was his 13th and final season in the big leagues, and while he had so many times at the plate that year, he only had 10 base hits for a rather puny .204 BA. He was 36 at the time.

Clemens, a rarely used outfielder out of Leesport, Pennsylvania, had been with the Cardinals and Cubs before being traded to Philadelphia for Wes Covington. The 6-foot, 180-pound left-handed Clemens fared only slightly better than Lynch as he hit safely 12 times in his 49 at bats for a .245 BA. During his career, Clemens had 41 hits in 179 pinch-hit times at bat, only good for a .239 average, but better than his overall .229 BA.

Chuck Hiller of the Mets was the NL leader in pinch-hit base hits in 1966 with 15 while Manny Mota, soon to become one of the greatest pinch-hitters of all time, had the best average with 10-for-26 for a scintillating .379.

Hiller, a left-handed hitting second baseman from Johnsburg, Illinois, had broken in with the Giants in 1961 and played 161 games for them the following season, including all seven World Series games against the Yankees as well. Hiller became the first NL player to hit a grand slam home run in a World Series when he connected off Marshall Bridges in the seventh inning of San Francisco's 7–3 Game Four victory over the Yankees on October 8, 1962. His career tailed off after that and he became a backup with the Giants as well as the Mets, Phillies and Pirates. The 5' 11", 170-pounder's eight-year career ended after the 1968 campaign when he was 34. Despite his 15 pinch-hits in 1966, he only amassed 19 more hits as a pinch-hitter in 109 other at-bats. Overall, Hiller's 38 pinch-hits in 154 at-bats earned him a .247 BA, just a few points better than his .243 career average.

Mota, who emigrated from the Dominican Republic, was destined to become the prototypical pinch-hitter against whom all other substitute batters would be measured. An outfielder by trade, the 5' 10", 160-pounder was a rookie with the Giants in 1962. He had the ability to also fill in at first, second and third and even caught a game in 1964 when he was with the Pirates. San Francisco traded him to Houston in the off-season but he never played for the club. He was shipped to Pittsburgh just before the 1963 season began and remained with the Pirates for six years. After 31 games with expansion Montreal in 1969, he was traded to the Dodgers with Maury Wills for Ron Fairly and Paul Popovich. It was in Los Angeles for the next 13 years where he would make the greatest impact on the art of pinch-hitting that been known up to then.

Over in the American League in 1966, the most pinch-hit at-bats were accumulated for the second year in a row by the veteran Smoky Burgess of the White Sox. Smoky had the most pinch-hits that year — 20 — to tie Ed Coleman's league record that was set in 1936. Fred "Wingy" Whitfield of the Indians, with 9-for-18, easily had a league-best average at .500. Whitfield, a first baseman from Vandiver, Alabama, picked up his nickname because of the way he threw. He broke in with the Cardinals in 1962, but with Bill White firmly ensconced at first, the 6' 1", 190-pound Whitfield was sent packing to Cleveland.

Whitfield was a semi-regular with the Indians for the next five years and, while he hit 93 homers for them, was eventually shipped off to the Reds who kept him for two years before unloading him to Montreal. As a pinch-hitter, the dangerous left-handed hitting Whitfeld was 56-for-225 for a modest .250, a bit under his overall lifetime average of .253. He played for nine seasons in the majors, leaving in 1970 at the age of 32.

Doug Clemens of the Phillies, who had tied Jerry Lynch of the Pirates for the most pinch-hit at-bats in 1966 in the National League, claimed the prize for himself in 1967 with 54. However, the most base hits by a substitute batter in the NL that season was shared by Bob Johnson of the Mets, who had come over early that year from the Orioles, and a newcomer, Manny Jiminez of the Pirates. Both men had 12 hits off the bench, but Johnson got his in 31 at-bats so his .390 average was much better than Jiminez's who had 11 more ABs for a .299 BA.

The 6' 1", 185-pound Jiminez was another ex-American Leaguer who had played for four years in Kansas City before coming to Pittsburgh. A left-handed hitting outfielder who had actually started for the A's in his rookie season of 1962, he became a pinch-hitter almost exclusively as the years wore on. The Dominican Republic emigree was dealt to the Cubs in 1969, the finale of seven years in the big leagues. He was 30 when he played his final major league game. His 41 hits in 176 pinch-hit at-bats (.233) was well under his .272 overall BA.

For the third consecutive year since entering the American League, Smoky Burgess of the White Sox led the Junior Circuit in pinch-hit at-bats with 60 in 1967. The rotund left-handed hitter, once a very fine catcher, no longer got behind the plate. He caught nary a single pitch in his final playing year, the 18th in a distinguished career. Perhaps the reason it was his last year in the big time was the fact that he only came off the bench to hit safely on eight occasions for an undistinguished .133 BA. When he was done, though, Smoky Burgess had more base hits (145) and at-bats (507) than any other pinch-hitter in history.

Burgess said his pinch-hit home run off Sam Jones of the Cubs with two games left in the 1956 season was his favorite moment. That round tripper was needed for his Reds to equal the Giants' 221 home runs, which up until time was the major league record. According to Burgess, manager Birdie Tebbetts sent Smoky up to hit for Roy McMillan with the following instructions: "Make it a home run or nothing."[14]

Gordy Coleman, a nine-year veteran who ended his career at the end of the 1967 season, did so as the all-time leader in pinch-hitting average for players with a minimum of 100 at-bats. A 6' 3", 210-pound former Duke football player, Coleman broke in with Cleveland in 1959 as a first baseman. Traded that off-season to the Reds with Billy Martin and Cal McLish for Johnny Temple, Coleman played a key role in Cincinnati's drive to the NL pennant in 1961 with 26 home runs and a .287 BA in 150 games. Two seasons later he was displaced as the starter by Deron Johnson and relegated to the role of a backup and pinch-hitter. While his overall average of .273 was better than most, his 40 pinch-hits in 120 at-bats merited him a .333 mark and the best ever for a player with over 100 pinch-swings. Coleman passed way in Cincinnati on March 12, 1994, at the age of 59.

Tied for the AL lead in 1967 for the most pinch-hit safeties with 13 apiece were Dalton Jones of the Red Sox and Rich Reese of the Twins, both of whose teams were locked in a season-long battle for the pennant.

Jones was a left-handed hitting utility infielder who came out of McComb, Mississippi. A prep school athlete who excelled in both baseball and basketball, the 6' 1", 180-pounder signed with the Red Sox in 1961 for a $60,000 bonus and played in Boston for six years before going off to Detroit. The former LSU star also played some outfield in his three seasons there.

Although labeled a "can't miss" prospect, Jones never lived up to expectations. Once as a member of the Tigers, he hit a grand slam home run but passed teammate Don Wert and was only credited with a single. Jones played part of his final major league season with the Texas Rangers in 1972. He hit .261 as a pinch-hitter lifetime with 81 hits in 310 at-bats. More than one third of his major league at bats came off the bench. Overall, he batted .235, much less than in his role as a pinch-hitter.

Reese played most of his 10 seasons in the big leagues with the Twins as a slick fielding first baseman and outfielder. Left-handed all the way, the Leipsic, Ohio-born Reese had a reputation for being a bit of a playboy but he played 866 major league games, all of them with Minnesota except for 59 games with Detroit in his final season of 1972. His .253 career average was the same as his mark as a pinch-hitter (44-for-174). He had three pinch-hit grand slams.

It was Reese's teammate, infielder-outfielder Frank Kostro who was the AL's leader in pinch-hitting average with 9-for-23 at a glittering .390 BA. The 6' 2", 190-pound Kostro had played briefly with the Tigers and Angels before finding his way to the Twins in 1964. He rarely started games and possessed little power. The right-handed hitter out of Windber, Pennsylvania played in the big leagues for seven years, amassing but 34 hits in 142 pinch-hit swings for .239 as compared to his lifetime .244 average overall. He was out of the big leagues after the 1969 season at the age of 32.

Manny Jiminez of the Pirates had the most pinch-hit at-bats in the National League in 1968 with 53. The former Indian, Fred "Wingy" Whitfield, who had been traded to the Reds for Tommy Harper, led the league in hits as a substitute batter with 11 although it took him 46 at-bats to do it.

Julio Gotay, with the Astros in 1968, had the league's best average with 8-of-25 for .320. Extremely superstitious—he even feared touching the cross—the right-handed hitter spent only one year in the majors as a starter (in 1962 as the Cardinals' shortstop). His time in the big leagues cut short by several trips to the minors, Gotay also played for the Pirates and Angels before coming to Houston in 1966.

The 6-foot, 180-pound native of Fajardo, Puerto Rico had virtually no power and wound up his 10-year career in 1969 at the age of 30 mainly coming off the bench. His 25 hits in 90 pinch-hit at-bats produced an efficient .277 career mark as opposed to his lifetime .260 BA.

Leon "Daddy Wags" Wagner, who had been traded from the Indians to the White Sox during the 1968 season, led the American League in pinch-hit at-bats that year with 46. An outfielder with considerable power despite gripping the bat with his hands apart, the left-handed hitting 6' 1", 195-pound Wagner came from Chattanooga, Tennessee. A professional actor who appeared in the movie, "Bingo Long's Traveling All-Stars," he was always well-dressed. He also owned a clothing store whose slogan was "Buy Your Rags at Daddy Wags."

Wagner, who had started his career with the Cardinals, was traded to the Angels before the 1961 campaign after three so-so seasons in St. Louis.

He was a regular in Anaheim for three years, and later for four more in Cleveland. Nearing the end of his career in 1968, he found himself on the bench in Chicago and ultimately out of baseball after spending the 1969 season with the Giants. His 46 hits in 196 pinch-hitting at-bats only yielded him a .235 lifetime BA, well short of his overall .272 average in which he pounded out 211 home runs during his 12 seasons in the big leagues.

The top hit-maker and batting averages among emergency batsmen in the AL in 1968 was one William "Gates" Brown, who spent his entire 13-year big league career with the Tigers. An outstanding high school running back, the Crestline, Ohio product delivered 18 base hits in 39 appearances for a superb .462 mark. Although listed as an outfielder, he never played there much mostly due a weak arm. A powerful left-handed hitter with astonishing speed, Brown never knew why his mother called him Gates, but he preferred it to Billy.

The 5' 11", 220-pound Brown was sent up to pinch-hit in first major league at-bat on June 6, 1963 and delivered a home run. He collected a total of 107 career pinch-hits, placing him fifth on the all-time list when he quit the game after the 1975 season. He also banged out 16 pinch-hit home runs to rank high on that select list as well. Overall he batted .258 as a pinch-swinger in 414 times up, almost the same average as his career .258 BA in 2,262 at-bats.

A player getting close to the end of his career in 1969, Fred Whitfield of the Reds, was the top man in pinch-hit at-bats in the National League with 51, but he was only able to hit safely eight times for a .157 BA. He was out of the majors the following year at the age of 32, after only playing in only four games with the Montreal Expos. Whitfield's 56 pinch-hits in 225 at-bats was good for a .249 average, close to his overall .253.

Leading the Senior Circuit in pinch-hit base hits and average in 1968 was Jose Pagan of the Pirates. His 19-for-42 produced a fantastic .452 mark. The right-handed batter's 19 hits were only three behind Red Schoendienst's league record of 22. The 5' 9", 160-pound Pagan was the former starting shortstop of the Giants who had played in 164 games in 1962 and even hit .368 in the World Series loss in seven games to the Yankees. A native of Barceloneta, Puerto Rico, Pagan was obtained from San Francisco early in 1965 in a trade for Dick Schofield and began a new career in Pittsburgh as a pinch-hitter and utility infielder.

On August 12, 1969, Pagan tied the major league record for consecutive pinch-hit home runs when he hit his second in a row against his former team at Candlestick Park. He played in the majors for 15 years and accumulated 56 hits in 207 at-bats as a substitute batter for a noteworthy .271 average, much better than his overall .250 mark. He is remembered for driving in the deciding run in the seventh game of the 1971 World Series that gave the Pirates the championship over the Orioles. Released after the 1972 season, Pittsburgh offered him a chance to manage in the minors but he declined, preferring to play in the big leagues. He played his final season in Philadelphia in 1973.

Richie Scheinblum of the Indians was the American League leader in pinch-hit at-bats in 1969 with 54, and his 14 hits combined to give him a .249 average. A New York City native, the right-handed hitting Scheinblum was a notoriously slow starter. Labeled as a perennial prospect, he played a little outfield for the Indians and later with the Senators, Royals, Angels and Cardinals. The 6' 1", 180-pounder played for eight years in the majors, finishing up in 1974 at the age of 32 when he played for three different teams that season. His 35 hits in 134 pinch-hit at-bats for a .261 average neatly corresponded to his .263 overall BA.

Pete Ward, who had taken over Smoky Burgess's role as the first man off the bench for the White Sox in 1969, led the AL in both pinch-hit base hits and average with 17-for-46 for a sizeable .370 BA. For his career, he batted .280 off the bench (35-for-125) and .254 overall.

The Montreal-born Ward, the son of former NHL star Jimmy Ward, had been the starting third baseman for the White Sox after they obtained him from Baltimore in a big trade early in 1963. He came to Chicago with eventual Cooperstown inductee Hoyt Wilhelm, Ron Hansen and Dave Nicholson for future Hall of Famer Luis Aparicio and Al Smith.

Ward's batting stance was somewhat strange — crouching with his rear foot pointed at the plate and his front foot pointed at the pitcher, coupled with a big uppercut. He admitted: "I got a real silly stance. Fundamentally I got a bad swing."[15] But pitcher Dean Chance once called him the league's toughest clutch hitter. Although the left-handed hitting Ward could hit for power, injuries slowed his progress and he failed to maintain the consistency needed to remain a regular.

10

1970-1979: Manny Mota, Jose Morales and the Designated Hitter Emerge

While lowering the mound and shrinking the strike zone in 1969 may have helped to give major league baseball a much-needed shot in the arm offensively, it did little or nothing to bring about any changes in pinch-hitting. There were, however, subtle shifts in the way the game was played. The increased use of relievers, the installation of artificial turf in the new stadiums and the emphasis on team speed all helped to create a better balance between hitters and pitchers. The result was an improvement in batting averages, home runs and base stealing, along with more strikeouts.

Socially the game was changing. Fewer African-Americans were attracted to baseball but rather many were opting to enter the ranks of professional basketball and football. This has become even more evident from 1975 to the present day.

The same period also saw a rapid increase in Latin Americans and American players of Hispanic origin. This surge was reflected in the top pinch-hitters of the 1970s as players like Vic Davalillo, Manny Mota, Jose Morales and Winston Llenas came into prominence as substitute batters.

Davalillo, a Venezuelan who had been the starting centerfielder for the Indians for nearly five years in the 1960s, came to the Cardinals in the middle of the 1969 season. The 5' 7", 150-pounder had spent parts of the previous two seasons with both the Indians and the Angels. In 1970, he led the National League in pinch-hit at-bats with 73 to break Sam Leslie's record of 72 which had stood since 1932. More importantly, Davalillo's 24 pinch-hits tied Dave Philley's major league record established nine years earlier. And for good measure, he smacked a record eight doubles, tied Ham Hyatt's long-standing record of three triples in one season and logged 41 total bases for yet another big league record. None of those three records have been duplicated or exceeded.

Originally a pitcher and a former Gold Glover in 1964, the Indians believed that Davalillo had lost much of his range and that his skills as a base stealer were also beginning to erode. The Tribe tried him as an emergency batter in 1966 and 1967, but his seven hits in 38 at-bats produced a lowly .181 mark. Cleveland dealt Davalillo to the Angels during the 1968 season. The change of scenery to St. Louis the following year appeared to work wonders. He hit .329 off the bench in 1970, and .311 overall in 111 games. He went on to play for the Pirates, A's and Dodgers during his 16-year career but was never able to duplicate his 1970 exploits.

An oddity with respect to scoring took place in a game in which Davalillo was sent up to pinch-hit during the course of a big inning. He got a base hit his first time up in the inning and also delivered a second one later in the same inning. However, he was not given credit for the second pinch-hit because, in the eyes of the official scorer, he was batting for himself. This ruling was made applicable to both leagues at the time but since then any second at-bat and/or hit is considered to be a pinch-hit appearance or hit.

Davalillio had one shining moment for the Dodgers in the 1977 League Championship Series against the Phillies. In Game Three with the series tied at one game each, the Dodgers trailed 5-3 with two out in the top of the ninth. Davalillo—aged 38 at the time—was sent up to pinch-hit and he beat out a two-strike drag bunt. Another pinch-hitter, Manny Mota, followed with a long double leading to a three-run rally that gave the Dodgers a 6-5 victory. Los Angeles clinched the series the following day. He batted .545 in eight career LCS games and .200 in 14 World Series games.

Davalillo's 95 hits as an emergency batsman placed him sixth all-time when he left the big leagues after the 1980 season at the age of 44. It took him 360 at-bats to get those safeties for a .261 average as a pinch-swinger, somewhat under his .279 overall lifetime BA.

Expo Jim Fairey, a left-handed hitting outfielder from Orangeburg, South Carolina, actually had a better average than Davalillio in 1970 with 14 hits in only 37 at-bats for a healthy .380 mark. The 5' 10", 190-pound Fairey was stereotyped as a left-handed bat off the bench after homering as a pinch-hitter for the Dodgers in 1968. He divided time between Los

Angeles and Montreal during his six years in the majors leaving the game following the 1973 season at the age of 29. Fairey compiled 47 hits in 185 at-bats for a .254 mark as an emergency batsman, well above his .235 BA overall.

Over in the American League in 1970, Tito Francona, in his 15th and final year in the big leagues, was the leader in both pinch-hit at-bats. His 15-for-59 produced a decent .254 average. It was Dalton Jones though, then with the Tigers, whose 11-for-29 off the bench earned him a wonderful .380 average.

Francona, a left-handed hitter from Aliquippa, Pennsylvania, had started out his major league career with the Orioles 14 seasons earlier. A 5' 11", 190-pound outfielder-first baseman with decent power, he became a kind of "super-sub," drifting around both leagues to play for the White Sox, Indians, Cardinals, Braves, Phillies, A's and Brewers. His last year in the big leagues was divided between the latter two clubs. Francona's 81 hits in 365 at-bats as a substitute batter were only good for a .222 lifetime average, considerably under his overall .272 BA. His son, Terry, had a similar career as a bench player for the Expos, Cubs, Reds, Indians and Brewers. He managed the Phillies in the late 1990s.

The greatest number of pinch-hit at-bats in the National League in 1971 was shared by Jimmy Stewart of the Reds and Bob Burda of the Cardinals, each with 48, the lowest figure since Matty Alou's 45 in 1963. While the 5' 11", 174-pound Burda hit safely 14 times for a .290 mark, Stewart could only muster 11 base hits for a .239 average. Burda, a left-handed hitter, was playing in his home town of St. Louis for the second time around; his career started out there in 1962. He went on to play for the Giants and Braves before being dealt back to the Cardinals. An outfielder-first baseman who rarely started at either position, he ended his seven-year career with the Red Sox in 1972. As a pinch-hitter, his 37 hits in 175 at-bats only merited a .211 BA, compared to an equally mediocre .224 overall average.

Stewart, a switch-hitter from Opelika, Alabama, who played every infield position as well as the outfield, began his 10-year big league stint with the Cubs in 1963. The 6-foot, 165-pounder went from the North Side of Chicago to the South Side in 1967. He played briefly for the White Sox before being sent down to the minors in 1968. He came back to the majors with the Reds in 1969 and remained with Cincinnati until 1972, when the Astros picked him up. He was used infrequently during his two years in Houston and left the majors for good after 1973 at the age of 34. His 71 hits in 330 pinch-hit at-bats produced a meager .212 average, not that far removed from his .237 overall BA.

Willie Crawford, a left-handed hitting outfielder who was signed out of high school by the Dodgers for $100,000, had the NL's best pinch-hitting average in 1972 with a Herculean .421, based on 8-for-19 output. The 6' 1", 197-pound Crawford, a native of Los Angeles, began his major league career in his home town in 1964 at the age of 17. A 9.6-second sprinter in the 100-yard dash, he was only 19 when he delivered a pinch-hit single off Jim "Mudcat" Grant in the 1965 World Series. Crawford played in LA for 12 consecutive years before going to the Cardinals in 1976 and to the Astros and A's the following year to complete his 14-year big league career.

As a pinch-hitter, Crawford was not called upon often — only 173 times in 3,455 major league at-bats. He delivered 39 pinch-hits for a .235 average, well below his .268 overall average.

Gomer Hodge, a 27-year-old rookie with the Indians, led the American League in pinch-hit at-bats in 1971 with 68, the most since Julio Becquer's 65 in 1957. The switch-hitting infielder from Rutherfordton, North Carolina also topped the AL in pinch-hits that season with 16 for a wanting .235, but still a lot better than his .205 overall average. Hodge only came to the plate officially 80 times that year — and only eight appearances in the field — in his only season in the big leagues.

Rich McKinney, a utility infielder-outfielder for the White Sox, had the best pinch-hitting average in the AL in 1971 with 11-for-19 to post an out-of-sight .579 mark. A right-handed hitter out of Piqua, Ohio, he was traded to the Yankees for pitcher Stan Bahnsen the following season and spent that entire year in New York. That same winter, the 5' 11", 185-pounder was sent to Oakland with Rob Gardner for Matty Alou. Only 80 of his 341 major league at-bats were as a pinch-hitter and he hit safely only 20 times for a .227 average, slightly lower than his overall .225 lifetime mark in seven seasons.

In 1972, Jim Fairey, now back with the Dodgers after three inconsistent seasons in Montreal with the Expos, led the National League in pinch-hit at-bats with 55. However, he only collected 10 hits for a woeful .181 BA, a far cry from the .380 he hit to lead the NL in 1970. Jim Howarth, a seldom used outfielder for the Giants, had 13 pinch-hit base hits to lead the NL in that category while Manny Mota's 10-for-25 for .400 was the best average for a substitute batter that season.

Howarth, a left-handed hitter from Biloxi, Mississippi, only played in the majors for four years, all with the Giants. Almost half of the 5' 11", 175-pounder's lifetime at-bats came as a pinch-hitter. In 1972, he hit safely 19 times in 70 pinch-hit appearances for a .271 BA, well above his .217 lifetime average overall. He was gone from the big leagues at the age of 27 early in 1974 after going hitless in four pinch-hit attempts.

Steve Hovley, an outfielder for the Royals, led the American League in pinch-hit at-bats in 1972 with only 37, the lowest total since Mizell Platt's 34 in 1949. Al Kaline, getting close to the end of his Hall of Fame career with the Tigers, tied Felipe Alou, then with the Yankees, for the most pinch-hits with 10. Kaline had the best average, though, as he got his hits in only 24 at-bats for a .417 average while it took Alou 29 at-bats to attain a not-too-shabby.341 mark.

The 5' 10", 188-pound Hovley, a Stanford graduate with good speed, was only able to garner nine hits in his league-leading 37 at-bats for an inconsistent .243 average. A line drive hitter, he began his career with the Seattle Pilots and moved with the franchise when it moved to Milwaukee to become the Brewers. He later played for the A's and Royals. A native of Ventura, California, he only hit safely 21 times in 98 pinch-hit at-bats for a dwarfish .214 BA as opposed to a much better .258 overall average. He was gone from the majors after 1973 at the age of 29.

The Baltimore-bred Kaline had one of the highest batting averages as a pinch-hitter for Hall of Famers with a minimum of 20 at-bats. The right-handed hitter is credited with 37 hits in 115 at-bats for an excellent .322 mark to rank fourth behind such hitting machines as Tris Speaker, Rod Carew and Frank Robinson. He was rarely asked to pinch-hit as evidenced by the fact that he had only 115 official at-bats as a substitute batter compared to his 10,116 at bats overall in his 22-year career. He was elected to the Hall of Fame in 1980 and later turned to broadcasting for the Tigers.

Felipe Alou was the oldest of three major league brothers from the Dominican Republic. While Felipe and Jesus hit right-handed, Matty was left-handed all the way.

Felipe, who had the most power of the three, played in the majors for 17 years, leaving the game after 1974 at 39. A regular for most of his playing career, he only pinch-hit 174 times out of 7,339 official career at-bats. His 46 hits as an emergency batsman merited him a .264 BA, well under his lifetime .286 overall mark. After his playing career concluded, he became a coach and had a long and distinguished tenure as manager of the Expos.

As the 1970s rolled on, it was evident that major league baseball's popularity was being increasingly diminished by other professional sports, particularly basketball and football. The American League was especially hurt by a growing lack of offense given credence by the continuing plight of the Yankees. The Bronx Bombers, once baseball's main attraction and now just another ballclub, contributed mightily to a marked decrease in fan interest and, most important of all, attendance.

While both leagues were offered the opportunity by Major League Baseball to adopt the new designated hitter rule, the National League opposed it vehemently, claiming it would destroy the purity of the game. The American League, which had been most damaged by the continuing lack of fan support, embraced it with open arms. The AL saw it as a means of increasing offense by taking the bat out of the pitcher's hands and turning it over to a position player. The feeling persisted that position players were professional hitters and more likely to add punch to a team's lineup rather than subtract from it.

The DH was actually the ultimate pinch-hitter, a player who would ride the bench anyhow, perhaps because of defensive shortcomings, or frailty or age. Now he would become a threat to opposing pitchers not once in a game but three or four or more times. What effect the new rule would have on team strategy, and particularly as pinch-hitters had been employed, remained to be seen.

In the National League in 1973, for obvious reasons, pinch-hitters continued to be used as always. Utility infielder Ken Boswell of the Mets set the pace in times at bat with 51. Mike Rogodzinski, a rookie outfielder for the Phillies had the most hits—16—while Frank Tepedino, a first baseman with the Braves, had the best average with 9-for-24 for a solid .375 mark.

The left-handed hitting Boswell, who hailed from Austin, Texas, was in his seventh year with the Mets. Once a highly touted second baseman, who in 1970 made just two errors in 450 chances for a remarkable .996 fielding average, the 6-foot, 170-pounder did not commit an error in 85 straight games. Throughout his 11-year career he produced 66 hits in 284 pinch-hitting appearances for a .232 BA, under his .248 overall lifetime mark. However, he tied a record that only a handful of players hold when he was a perfect 3-for-3 in the 1973 World Series against the A's. Boswell left the big leagues after 1977 at the age of 31 after three unproductive seasons in Houston.

Rogodzinski, a product of Evanston, Illinois, only played in the majors for three years with 73 of his 114 at-bats coming as a pinch-hitter. His 21 hits as an emergency batsman produced a .288 BA, considerably higher than his .219 overall average. Since he was only able to come up with four other hits in his 41 other at-bats, he was gone from the big leagues after the 1975 season at the age of 27.

The Yankees had high hopes for Brooklyn's Frank Tepedino when they first signed him in 1967. Unable to find a regular spot for the left-handed hitter, the New York club moved him to Milwaukee in 1971 along with Bobby Mitchell in a trade for Danny Walton. He came back to the Yankees for the proverbial cup of coffee in 1972 but was 0-for-8, all as a substitute batter. The Yankees subsequently packaged him with Wayne

Nordhagen, Al Closter and Dave Cheadle in a deal for Atlanta's Pat Dobson. Tepedino turned into a dependable pinch-hitter for the Braves in 1973, but his production fell off severely in the next two years. Tepedino was gone from the majors following the 1975 campaign after eight unfulfilled years. His 26 hits in 117 pinch-hitting appearances were only good for a .222 BA, or 19 points below his overall lifetime average.

Hal Breeden, a backup first baseman for the Expos, inserted himself in the record books on July 13, 1973 when he became only the second player in major league history to deliver pinch-hit home runs in both ends of a doubleheader. The 6' 2", 200-pound right-hand hitter from Albany, Georgia, thus tied the mark that the Hall of Famer Joe Cronin had established 30 years before. Breeden, whose older brother, Danny, had played for the Cubs and Reds earlier, was a lifetime .243 batter in his five-year big league career. As a substitute batter, he produced 26 hits in 111 at-bats for a .234 average.

The AL leader in both pinch-hits and pinch-hit at-bats in 1973 was Winston Llenas of the Angels. The 5' 10", 165-pound Dominican collected 16 hits in 56 times up for a creditable .269 BA. Llenas had interrupted his career as the one of the greatest third basemen in the history of the Mexican League to spend six seasons in Anaheim, primarily as a substitute batter.

During his tenure in the United States, he batted only .230 overall with but three homers in 531 at-bats. As a pinch-swinger, he was 44-for-174 and a fairly respectable .253 average. He returned to the Mexican League after the 1975 campaign at the age of 32 and played there for seven more years, including three .300 seasons.

Gail Hopkins, a reserve first baseman for the Royals, set the pace in batting average for pinch-hitters in the AL in 1973 with 7-for-19 for an excellent .368 BA. A native of Tulsa, the left-handed hitter broke in with the White Sox in 1968 and played there for three years before being traded to Kansas City prior to the 1971 season. A contact hitter who rarely struck out — only 83 times in 1,219 major league at-bats— the 5' 10", 195-pounder had been signed originally as a catcher. For his seven-year career, Hopkins batted .266 overall, exactly the same average as his 42 hits in 158 pinch-hit at-bats produced. After being sold to the Dodgers in 1974, he played in Los Angeles for a year, leaving the big leagues at the end of that season at the age of 31 to pursue a medical career.

Former Oriole Terry Crowley, in his first year in the National League with the Reds in 1974, led the Senior Circuit in pinch-hit at-bats that year with 52 while Ed Kranepool of the Mets and Tony Taylor of the Phillies had the most hits with 17 apiece. Kranepool, however, got his in only 35 at-bats for a scintillating .486 mark to set a new single-season record for average by a substitute batter with 30 or more at-bats. Taylor's hits came as a result of 46 at-bats for a very fine .370 average.

Crowley, who hailed from Staten Island, New York, was known to his teammates as the "King of Swing." The left-handed hitter began his major league career in 1969 with the Orioles. The 6-foot, 180-pounder was an outfielder by trade but saw action mostly as a pinch-hitter. He later became a designated hitter when he returned to Baltimore in 1977 after almost three seasons in the NL with the Reds and the Braves.

He hit .342 as a substitute batter in 1978 coming off a 13-for-38 season, and .317 in 1979 with 11-for-39. When he retired in 1983 after 15 years in the big leagues, the 36-year-old veteran was ranked sixth on the all-time list in pinch-hits with 108, and at-bats with 419 for a .258 BA, slightly better than his overall .250 average.

The left-handed hitting Kranepool joined the Mets in 1962 as a 17-year-old rookie in the first year of the club's existence. Signed for an estimated $80,000, he took his first plane ride to join his new team in Los Angeles. He also bought his first car and moved his mother from a crowded Bronx apartment to a comfortable home in the suburbs.

Manager Casey Stengel said of Kranepool when he joined the ball club: "He's only 17 but runs like he's 30."[1] The 6' 3", 205-pounder became the team's regular first baseman for several years. However, his career did not develop the way all parties thought it should have. When he was sent to the minors in 1970, Kranepool thought seriously about quitting the game. The New York City native had a good year the following season but his baseball life really took off when he became a pinch-hitter almost exclusively late in his career.

From 1974 through 1978, Kranepool hit a remarkable .396 as a pinch-hitter for the Mets. In his 18 years in the majors, all with the Mets, he delivered 90 pinch-hits in 325 times up for a .268 average, several points above his overall .261 mark. When he retired after the 1979 season at the age of 35, he was the Mets' all-time leader in eight different offensive categories. "Steady Eddie" was the last original Met playing in the major leagues. Proving that there is life after baseball, he went on to become a successful restaurateur and stock broker.

Taylor, a Cuban who could play every position in the infield and some outfield, was a starter for the Cubs and Phillies for 14 of his 19 years in the big leagues. In Philadelphia he was a fan favorite, but the 5' 9", 170-pounder also played for the Tigers in 1972 and 1973. He helped Detroit win a division title in his first year there, and played in the only post-season games of his career.

A right-handed hitter with good speed, Taylor stole 234 bases, including six of home for the Phillies—enough to rank second on their all-time list. As a pinch-hitter, he came to bat 245 times in his career and hit safely on 63 occasions for a fairly good .257 mark, just a few points below his lifetime .261 batting average. He stopped playing after the 1976 season at the age of 41 but remained in the game as a coach.

Gates Brown of the Tigers led the American League in pinch-hit at-bats in 1974 with 53 as well as in base hits (16) for a consistently good .302 average. He had been the club's regular right-handed DH in the first year the rule went into effect but was now relegated mostly to pinch-swinging. The following year, 1975, was his last in majors. He was 35 at the time.

Bob Hansen, a rookie DH-first baseman for the Brewers, had the best BA in the AL for a pinch-hitter in 1974 with 14-for-35 and a solid .400 BA. A left-handed hitter from Boston, exactly half of the 82 at-bats in his brief career were as an emergency batsman. All told, the 6-foot, 195-pounder collected 15 hits in 41 at-bats as a pinch-swinger for an excellent .366 average and considerably better than his .242 BA overall. Still, he was gone from the majors after only two seasons at the age of 28.

Although many observers failed to notice it at the time, 1974 represented a momentous change of direction in the career of Manny Mota. In his eleventh season in the majors in Los Angeles, who had acquired him from the Expos in 1969, the Dodgers decided it was time to make the Dominican a regular pinch-hitter. His lack of power and deficiencies in the field appeared to have finally done him in as a starting position player. The Dodgers were loaded with excellent young players and Manny, at 36, was still able to wield a potent bat.

Mota started a streak of sorts that season with 10 or more pinch-hits for six straight years. For his career, 250 of his final 309 at-bats came as a substitute batter. At his retirement following the 1982 season, he had registered a marvelous .297 BA in the pinch. Overall, his .315 average based on over 1,800 at bats as a Dodger is among the best in franchise history.

As a boy in the Dominican Republic, Manny Mota, like most of the kids with whom he grew up, was impoverished. Youngsters made their own baseballs from lemons they picked from trees and wrapped in paper and string. Mota never forgot his roots and as a major leaguer established and promoted the Manny Mota Little Leagues in his home country. At Christmas time, he would buy dozens of bats and balls and drive around the area personally distributing them to the children. Eligibility was based upon the children's' regular church attendance and obeying their parents.

In 1975, Tony Taylor of the Phillies led the National League in pinch-hit at-bats with 54, though he only had 12 hits for a weak .222 BA. Jose

Jose Morales held the major league record for pinch-hits in a season for 19 years.

Morales, a utility player for the Expos, had the most base hits (15) as a pinch-hitter that season, which he accomplished in 51 at-bats for a nifty .294 average. However, Rod Galbraith and Jay Johnstone of the Phillies tied for the NL's best pinch-hitting BA with 10-for-25 and a tremendous .400 average.

Morales, a right-handed hitting utility player from the Virgin Islands, started out as a catcher in the minors. But the 5′ 11″ 187-pounder led four different leagues in errors which delayed his entry into the big leagues for nearly 10 years. He came up to Oakland in 1973 at the advanced age of 29 but only played in six games for the A's before being sold to Montreal. The Expos learned that what Morales could do, was hit.

Morales led the NL and AL in pinch-hits twice each and was a league leader in pinch-hit at-bats three times before he hung up his spikes. He seemed to find his niche later with both the Twins and the Orioles in the American League, where he could be used as a designated hitter. Early in 1982, he was traded to the Dodgers and eventually replaced major league baseball's all-time pinch-hit champion, Manny Mota, as the club's principal substitute batter.

"For me, pinch-hitting is not difficult," Morales remarked during his time in Los Angeles. "Each individual in the major leagues should know what he's capable of doing. After one year in Montreal, I did it (pinch-hit), and I knew then I was going to be used as a pinch-hitter.

"I worked at it. It's like a singles hitter trying to hit home runs. You end up fooling only yourself. It's got to be because you're realistic with yourself. I started out as a catcher, but I work as a hitter. I take pride in it. When I can't pay my bills, then I'll worry about it."[2]

Having Mota near him as a coach was very helpful to Morales. "We sit down and discuss a lot of things," he said. "We talk about hitters and situations. I admire him as a good pinch-hitter who's done a lot to help me. I do pattern myself after his style. I feel if I do my job, the way I'm expected to, nature will take its course."[3]

It was Morales's contention that pinch-hitting was part luck, part skill and definitely part experience. "You have to be thinking something when you go up there," he claimed. "You have to have a plan. You can't go up there cold. I get frustrated when I go up there and don't do what I should. I have so much confidence. I know I'm going to get a hit … until he gets me out."[4]

Johnstone was a left-handed hitting outfielder who played for eight different clubs in a 20-year career. The Manchester, Connecticut native was considered somewhat of a free spirit, but his pinch-hitting kept him in the game until 1985. His 404 at-bats as a pinch-hitter were good enough for tenth on the all-time list when he retired, but he was only able to hit safely 92 times for a rather paltry .228 average, well under his .267 overall mark. After leaving the big leagues as a player, Johnstone dabbled in both broadcasting and coaching at the major league level.

Over in the American League in 1975, Graham, North Carolina's Jim Holt, an infielder-outfielder for the A's, had the most at bats—43—and tied Walt "No-Neck" Williams of the Yankees for the most base hits with 10. Williams's hits came in 31 at-bats for a fine .322 average, while Holt's 43 at-bats only merited a .233 BA. The leader in batting average was Doug Griffin of the Red Sox, whose eight hits in 16 at-bats were good for a .500 BA.

Holt, a left-handed hitting outfielder with next to no clout, had come up with the Twins in 1968. The 6-foot, 180-pounder, who had served in the Vietnam War, stayed in the Twin Cities for most of seven seasons before being swapped to the A's for Pat Barco late in 1974. He had no success whatsoever with either club as a pinch-hitter going nothing-for-24 that year. Although he led the AL in pinch-hit at-bats in 1975, Holt was out of the majors at the age of 32 in the following year after only four games and seven at-bats. A veteran of three division champions, he went 2-for-3 with two RBI in Oakland's 1974 World Series win. Holt's 32 hits in 144 regular season pinch-hit at-bats only earned him a .222 BA, well under his overall .265 average.

Williams, who came to the majors by way of Brownwood, Texas, occasionally played the outfield for the Astros, White Sox, Indians and Yankees. New York had obtained him in 1974 in a three-way trade with Detroit and Cleveland. The right-handed hitter's 52 hits in 226 pinch-hit at-bats were only good enough for a .230 mark and much lower than his .270 average overall. After 10 years in the big leagues, he left the majors for good after 1975 at the age of 32.

Griffin, a right-handed hitting second baseman from South Gate, California, came up with the Angels in 1970. After one season in Anaheim, the 6-foot, 160-pounder was part of a six-player deal that sent Tony Conigliaro to the Angels. He became Boston's regular second baseman in 1972 but eventually lost his job to Denny Doyle. As his usefulness to the club decreased, he continued on in Boston until 1977, never to return to the big leagues after the age of 30. Outside of his league-leading average as a pinch-hitter in 1975, he was used infrequently thereafter as a substitute batter. As a pinch-hitter, his 9-for-24 career mark was a smart .375 and well beyond his overall .245 career average.

The 1975 World Series featuring the Reds and the Red Sox, was one of the most exciting ever played and is credited with driving interest in major league baseball to new heights. It is also significant in the history of pinch-hitting as one in which a record-tying two home runs were hit by Bernie Carbo. Cincinnati, picking in baseball's first draft in 1965, selected Carbo first, ahead of Johnny Bench. A salary dispute following his selection as the NL's Rookie of the Year and a poor sophomore season led to a trade to St. Louis. Carbo was dealt to the Red Sox with Rick Wise for Reggie Smith and Ken Tatum after the 1973 season. When he wasn't playing the outfield or DH-ing, the Detroit-born Carbo would pinch-hit.

In the drama-filled 1975 World Series against his former team, the 5' 11", 173-pound Carbo's first home run came in Cincinnati in Game Three, won by the Reds, 6-5. His pinch-hit home run was one of six hit by both clubs to set a new Series record. But, it was Carbo's second pinch-hit home run that became legend.

It came in the eighth inning of that historic Game Six in Boston. His two-strike three-run blast off Rawly Eastwick tied the score. The game was eventually won by Carlton Fisk's dramatic homer in the bottom of the twelfth to give the Red Sox a 7-6 win to knot the series at three games each.

The Reds won it all the next day, 4-3, for their first world title in 35 years. All in all, Carbo was no great shakes as a pinch-hitter in the regular season, going 36-for-159 for a somewhat smallish .226 average and considerably below his .264 overall BA. He played for a total of 12 years in the majors, finishing up in Pittsburgh in 1980 at the age of 33.

Jose Morales of the Expos, who just a year earlier had led the National League in pinch-hit base hits, firmly established himself as one of the best substitute batters ever in 1976 by setting new records in both at-bats and base hits. He shattered the previous pinch-hit at-bat record of 72 shared by Sam Leslie and Red Schoendienst by officially coming to bat 78 times. And he broke Schoendienst's single season base hit mark of 22 by hitting safely 25 times for a substantial .320 average. Morales had three timely home runs and five doubles in 1976 to pile up 39 total bases, close to Lynch's 40 in 1961 and Davalillo's record 41 in 1970.

It was a left-handed hitting rookie outfielder for the Mets, Bruce Boisclair, who was the NL leader in batting average for pinch-hitters in 1976. His extremely productive .556 mark came via 12 hits in 21 at-bats. The Putnam, Connecticut native could not break into the New York club's starting outfield that included veterans John Milner, Del Unser and Dave Kingman. The 6' 2", 185-pounder played three more seasons for the Mets before departing the big leagues at only the age of 27. As a pinch-hitter, he hit safely 38 times in 133 attempts for a very effective .286 BA, better than his career .263 average. He batted with his feet far apart and did not stride; consequently he displayed almost no power as only 63 of his 241 hits were for extra bases. After the 1979 campaign, a broken wrist and a lowly .184 BA hastened his departure from the big leagues.

It was apparent that the designated hitter rule in the American League was having a deleterious effect on pinch-hitters in that circuit. Since its adoption by the AL in 1973, pinch-hit at-bat leaders had recorded totals of 56, 53 and 43 respectively. Now Ben Oglivie of the Tigers set the pace in 1976 with only 38, the lowest figure since Mizell Platt's 34 in 1948. And the nine hits that Oglivie and Ken McMullen of the A's each registered to lead all pinch-hitters that season in the AL was the lowest figure in 25 years. Tommy Davis, who split the season with both the Angels and the Orioles, led the AL in pinch-hitting average at .381 (8-for-21).

Oglivie was a lean, left-handed hitting occasional outfielder and designated hitter in 1976. A native of Colon, Panama, the 6' 2", 160-pounder started out with the Red Sox in 1971 and was traded to the Tigers in the winter of 1973 for second baseman Dick McAuliffe. He remained in Detroit until being swapped to the Brewers for Rich Folkers and Jim Slaton before the 1978 season.

Pinch-hitting was not something the strong-wristed Oglivie thrived on, as his lifetime mark of .259 coming via 42 hits in 162 times up will attest.

A career .273 hitter, Oglivie excelled as an everyday player in Milwaukee. He had good power, thumping 235 round-trippers in 1,615 regular season at-bats. Oglivie tied with Reggie Jackson for the home run crown in the American League in 1980 with 41. He completed his 16-year big league career in 1986 at the age of 37 after nine years in Milwaukee. Oglivie played in Japan before returning to the United States and signing a minor league contract with the Brewers in 1989.

McMullen, a product of Oxnard, California, was a well-traveled right-handed hitting infielder. He started out with the Dodgers at the age of 20 in 1962 after receiving an estimated $60,000 signing bonus. Los Angeles moved Jim Gilliam from third base to second base to give McMullen a shot at the hot corner but the experiment failed when McMullen did not hit. He was shipped to the Senators after the 1964 campaign as part of a multi-player deal.

In Washington, manager Gil Hodges installed him as the club's regular third baseman, a position he held for five years. With Ted Williams at the helm in 1970 and Hodges in New York managing the Mets, McMullen was sent packing to the Angels right after the season began for Aurelio Rodriguez and Rick Reinhardt.

After starting at third base for California for a couple of seasons,

McMullen was traded back to his original team, the Dodgers, for the 1973 campaign. He moved on to Oakland in 1976 and then to Milwaukee, where he spent his final season in the big leagues in 1977.

McMullen was only a part-time player during the last five years of his career. After 16 years in the majors, he concluded his time in the majors in 1977 at the age of 35 as a part-time designated hitter and utility infielder. His 41 base hits in 176 at-bats as a pinch-hitter only earned him a .233 BA, under his .248 career average.

Tommy Davis, whose big league career began as far back as 1959 as a right-handed hitting phenom for the Dodgers, was an outstanding athlete. He was a basketball teammate of Lenny Wilkins in high school. The 6' 2", 195-pounder had some great seasons as a regular in the outfield and at third base in Los Angeles, including leading the National League in batting for two consecutive years: 1962 and 1963. After a couple of injury-plagued years, he was sent to the Mets with Derrell Griffith for Jim Hickman and Ron Hunt prior to the 1967 season. The Brooklyn native had a fine year in New York hitting .302 but found himself leaving for the White Sox right after the season ended in a trade for Tommy Agee and Al Weis, which helped the Mets win it all in 1969.

During the next eight years, Davis was traded seven times, seeing action with the Pilots, Astros, A's, Cubs, Orioles, Angels and Royals. Most of his time in the AL was spent as a designated hitter and he turned out to be one of the best during the early years of the DH rule. After 18 big league seasons, he left the majors in 1976 at the age of 37. As a career pinch-hitter, he was as capable as he had ever been, hitting .320 in the pinch with 63 hits in 197 at-bats, even better than his fine .294 lifetime BA.

Another Brooklyn-born product, Lee Mazzilli, was a first-round draft choice of the Mets in 1973. He broke into the majors with a bang when he hit a three-run pinch-hit homer off Darold Knowles of the Cubs in September of 1976 in only his second big league at-bat. The son of pro welterweight boxer, Liberio Mazzilli, he spent the first part of his 12-year career was spent as a starter. The swarthy 6' 1", 180-pound switch-hitting outfielder had several milestones as a pinch-swinger. He was the hero of the 1979 All-Star Game in Seattle, when he pinch-hit a home run to tie the game in the eighth inning, and later walked with the bases loaded in the ninth to drive in the winning run for the National League. He later was a key player off the bench for the 1986 world champion Mets.

A former halfback at Ball State University, Merv Rettenmund had been drafted by the Dallas Cowboys but opted for baseball. Platooned in the outfields of the Orioles and Reds, the right-handed hitter from Flint, Michigan, was a veteran of four World Series by the time he arrived in San

Diego in 1977. The 5' 11", 190-pound Padre led the NL in pinch-hit at-bats with 67 and base hits with 21 for a solid .313 BA. His 21 hits had been surpassed by only five players in history at the time. He played for the Angels from 1978 to 1980 leaving the majors at age 37. Rettenmund's 66 career pinch-hits in 241 at-bats merited him a well-above average .274 lifetime mark, nearly the same as his .271 overall BA.

When utility infielder Lee Lacy of the Dodgers smacked a home run against the Pirates in Dodger Stadium on May 17, 1978, he accomplished something that no one in major league history had done up to that point — hit three consecutive pinch-hit home runs. Although never known for his pinch-hitting prowess, the Longview, Texas product had hit two others as an emergency batsman prior to that game — one on May 2 at Chicago and another on May 6 at Pittsburgh. In fact, he hit two others that season to give him a total of five for the year.

Never considered much of a long ball threat, the right-handed hitting Lacy only managed 91 home runs in his 4,549 major league at-bats. The 6' 1", 175-pounder went on to play for both the Pirates and the Orioles, staying on in the game until the 1987 season. He appeared in three League Championship Series and World Series for the Dodgers, and in the 1979 World Series for the "We Are Family" Pirates, who finally got him a world championship ring. As a regular season pinch-hitter, he collected 65 hits in 252 at-bats for a .258 BA, markedly below his fine .286 overall average. Lacy was 1-for-3 as a pinch-swinger in LCS play and 2-for-6 in WS action. He was 39 when he departed the big leagues.

Another player who made his mark as a pinch-hitter in the National League in 1978 was Mike Ivie, then in his first year with the Giants. A former first-round draft choice of the Padres in 1970 as a catcher, the 6' 3", 205-pound Atlanta product hated catching. He was subsequently tried at third, first and in the outfield by San Diego. On one occasion in 1977, when Ivie was switched back to third base — he had played there in 1975 but preferred first — he jumped the club for a few days. The Padres, tiring of his attitude, finally dealt him to San Francisco in exchange for Derrell Thomas, another problem child.

The right-handed hitting Ivie seemed to find his niche as a pinch-hitter in the Bay Area in 1978 by going 12-for-31 for an excellent .387 mark. That same year he tied a major league record by uncorking two grand slam home runs in the pinch. The record had been set earlier that same year by Davey Johnson of the Phillies. Ivie later played for Houston and Detroit. As a pinch-hitter, Ivie's 35-for-120 earned him a .292 lifetime mark, well above his .269 overall average. He was through with major league baseball after the 1983 season at the age of 31, never quite fulfilling his promise.

Ivie was once described as a "$40-million airport with a $30 control tower."[5]

Following the 1977 season, the Expos sold Jose Morales to the Twins where he was used as both a pinch-hitter and a DH. In 1978 he had the most pinch-hit at-bats in the American League (46) and hits (14) for a solid .305 BA. The following year, his 42 pinch-hit at-bats led the AL, but his hit production fell off to just nine for a .214 BA.

A former starting outfielder for the Senators, Indians, Phillies and Mets, left-handed hitting Del Unser replaced Jose Morales as the top man off the bench for the Expos in 1977. Unser had been obtained in a 1976 trade with the Mets along with Wayne Garrett for Pepe Mangual and Jim Dwyer. The Decatur, Illinois native was not successful at first, going seven-for-58 for a mere .121 BA in his two seasons in Montreal, but he excelled in the role when he returned to Philadelphia in 1979. Unser batted .304 with 14 hits in 46 at-bats as a substitute batter. The former 1968 AL Rookie of the Year even tied Lee Lacy's record by homering in three straight pinch-hit at-bats that season on June 30, July 5 and July 10.

Mike Lum, a left-handed hitting first baseman-outfielder, started out with the Braves in 1967 and remained with them for nine inconsistent seasons before being traded to the Reds. After three equally unproductive years in Cincinnati, the Braves re-signed the Honolulu native as a free agent. The 6-foot, 180-pounder led the NL with 17 pinch-hits in 52 at-bats for a lofty .327 BA in 1979. Two of those hits were consecutive home runs hit on September 4 and 5.

Lum appeared as a pinch-hitter in the 1969 LCS for the Braves, going 1-for-1. He was hitless in his only turn at-bat in the 1976 LCS for the Reds. As a regular season pinch-hitter, Lum had 103 base hits in 418 attempts for a .246 mark, just a shade under his overall .247 average. He left baseball in 1981 at the age of 36.

Tom Hutton, a Los Angeles native, started playing in his hometown for the Dodgers in 1966. A first baseman-outfielder, he was sent back to the minors the following season and not brought back until 1969. The 5' 11", 180-pounder played sparingly before being sent to the Phillies for Larry Hisle. He spent seven years in Philadelphia where he hit three game-winning pinch-hit homers during his tenure there. Hutton was an excellent fielder who was often sent into ball games in the late innings for defensive purposes. As a hitter, he owned Hall of Fame Pitcher Tom Seaver, hitting .700 against him for his career.

Hutton later played in Toronto and Montreal, finishing up his career with the Expos in 1981 at the age of 35. He had 79 hits in 294 appearances as a pinch-hitter for a fairly good .269 lifetime BA and considerably better than his .248 mark overall. A brother-in-law of pitcher Dick Ruthven, Hutton played guitar professionally in Las Vegas and went on to become a major league broadcaster.

Trenton, New Jersey's Steve Braun was an infielder-outfielder who made a huge jump from Class A to the majors for the Twins in 1971. Unable to find a regular spot in the starting lineup after six seasons in Minnesota, he became a member of both the Mariners and Royals in 1977. With the Royals and later the Cardinals, the left-handed hitter developed into one of the best pinch-hitters in the game. The 5' 10", 180-pounder's 113 hits placed him sixth on the all-time list at the time of his retirement. All in all, he came to bat 402 times as a substitute batter to earn a .281 lifetime mark, compared to his overall .271 BA overall. Fittingly, his final at-bat in the major leagues came as a pinch-hitter for the Cardinals in the 1985 World Series.

11

1980-1989:
Del Unser, Cliff Johnson
and Greg Gross Dominate

While Jose Morales of the Twins was 36 years of age at the start of the decade and getting closer to the end of the line, the pinch-hitter extraordinaire continued to do what he did best in 1980. He led the American League in pinch-hits with 13 in 36 at-bats for an excellent .361 average. And as might have been expected, Minnesota began to use him more and more as a designated hitter.

Morales signed on as a free agent with the Orioles for 1981 but was employed infrequently in Baltimore as both a DH and a pinch-hitter. Traded to the Dodgers early in 1982 to replace the once unexpendable Manny Mota, his pinch-hit production continued to tail off during his last three seasons in the game. He delivered 24 hits in 92 at-bats as a Dodger to produce what for him was a negligible .261 BA.

Morales was 40 when his distinguished 12-year major league career ended after the 1984 season. He led his league three times in substitute at-bats and four times in pinch-hits. He ranks fifth all-time with 123 pinch-hits. In 445 emergency at-bats he batted an above-average .276 BA, or 11 points under his even better .287 overall mark.

Kurt Bevacqua, a right-handed hitting utility infielder-outfielder from Miami Beach, came up to the big leagues with the Indians in 1971. The 6-foot, 180-pounder remained in the majors for 15 years without ever playing more than 64 games at any one position in a single season. Nonetheless, he was used a pinch-hitter 307 times during his big league career and racked up 82 hits for a .267 BA. In fact, his lifetime average as a pinch-hitter was substantially better than his overall average of .236.

As a member of the Padres and Pirates in 1980, Bevacqua led the National League with 17 pinch-hits and 56 emergency at-bats for a solid .304 mark. Nicknamed "Dirty" because of his aggressive, diving, hard-sliding style, he played for six different teams in both leagues. The Padres used him as their DH against the Tigers in 1984 World Series and he delivered a game-winning home run in Game Two—the only game won by San Diego. He walloped another one in Game Five but to no avail as Detroit prevailed and took the championship with a victory in that game. He led all San Diego regulars in the Series with four RBI, four runs, two homers, and a .412 average.

Del Unser of the Phillies was a star not only in the regular season of 1980 but also in both the League Championship Series and World Series that year. First of all, his 12-for-38 as a substitute batter in the regular season earned him a fine .316 BA. Then in the decisive Game Five of the LCS against Houston, he went 2-for-2, appearing as a pinch-hitter and staying in the game. Overall he drove in a run and scored twice, including the game winner on Garry Maddox's double in the tenth inning as the Phillies beat the Astros, 8-7, to take the series.

Unser's first hit in Game Five came off Ken Forsch, a right-hander who had just struck out future Hall of Famer Mike Schmidt. Unser knew Forsch had a good sinker that broke away from left-handers. He was looking for a pitch on the outside part of the plate when Forsch came in on him. Unser managed to get enough of his bat on the ball to hit a liner to right-center to drive in the tying run. In the tenth, Unser faced Frank Lacorte even though Dave Smith, a pitcher Unser said he could not hit with a canoe paddle, was warming up for the Astros. Houston stayed with Lacorte and Unser rapped a double down the first-base line. The run Unser scored later gave the Phillies their first pennant in 30 years.

In Game Two of the World Series and the Phillies trailing 4-2 in the bottom of the eighth, Unser went up against the Royals' ace reliever Dan Quisenberry. He knew that although the side-arming Quisenberry had great movement on his ball, he was short on velocity. Unser got hold of a pitch and ripped it into left-centerfield for a double that helped spark a four-run rally and a come-from-behind 6-4 victory.

In Game Five, Unser's fourth clutch post-season hit came in the top half of the ninth inning. With the Royals up 2-1 and threatening to take a 3-2 lead, Schmidt led off with a single. Unser came up "looking to do the same thing (as in Game 1), drive it to the left side, hoping to be on time for the change-up."[1] Quisenberry threw him a pitch ("probably a change-up that he took something off of")[2] and Unser smoked it down the first-base line for a double, scoring Schmidt with the tying run. Manny Trillo followed with a run-scoring single that plated Unser with the winning run. Momentum swung back to the Phillies, who won the next game behind Steve Carlton and Tug McGraw for the first world championship in franchise history.

Del Unser, whose dad, Al, had been a big league catcher for the Tigers and Reds in the 1940s, completed his 15-year stay in the majors in 1982 at the age of 37. On the surface, his 54 hits in 264 regular season at-bats produced only a .205 average that was 53 points less than his overall BA. Nonetheless, his 1980 regular season, LCS and World Series performances in the clutch–2-for-5 against Houston and 3-for-6 vs. Kansas City–were good enough to help his team win its only world title.

Terry Crowley, in his second tour of duty with the Orioles in 1980, had his best year as pinch-hitter ever that season. His 37 substitute at-bats led the American League and his 11 base hits he compiled to go along with them earned Crowley a league-leading .297 average. The highlight of his career as a pinch-hitter took place on August 8, 1982, when he connected for a grand slam against the Royals to give the Orioles a 10-6 victory. After leaving the majors as a player at the age of 36 following the 1983 season, Crowley worked as a major and minor league hitting instructor.

The 1981 season was marred by a crippling strike, the worst in the history of the major leagues. It started on June 11 and ended at the end of July. The 50 strike days wiped out roughly a third of the season's schedule. Commissioner Bowie Kuhn devised a split-season campaign under which the teams leading their divisions on June 11 would meet the winners of the second half, although winners of the first half were ineligible to repeat as champions. The result was some lackadaisical play on the part of three first-half winners and attendance fell in the second half of the season, which sportswriter Red Smith called "the dishonest season."[3]

Bob "Molly" Molinaro, a quick 6-foot, 185-pound outfielder by trade, broke in with the Tigers late in 1975. In the off-season, the Newark, New Jersey native took a job as a blackjack dealer in Las Vegas and seriously considered leaving the game. Unable to win a starting spot in the following season, Molinaro was sent back to the minors. When he returned to the majors in 1977, Detroit sold him to the White Sox.

After spending 1979 in Baltimore, Molinaro was sold back to the White Sox. His 9-for-35 as a substitute batter in 1981 (.257) led the American League in at-bats and hits. He joined the National League in 1982 when the south side Sox waived him across town to the Cubs on the north side of the Windy City. Later that same year he was sold to the Phillies. Between both clubs he led the NL in pinch-hit at-bats with 67. However, he was only able to muster 14 hits for a poor .209 mark. The following year the Phillies sent him back to Detroit, but his 2-for-20 in the pinch hastened his demise after eight frustrating seasons in the big leagues. His 37 hits in 160 pinch-hitting appearances earned Molinaro just a .231 average, over 30 points less than his .264 lifetime BA.

Jay Johnstone, who was with the Dodgers in 1981—his seventh club in 16 seasons—had a big pinch-hit home run for Los Angeles in Game Four of the World Series against one of his former teams, the Yankees. The Dodgers trailed in the Series two games-to-one and 6-3 in the game in the bottom of the sixth when Johnstone was sent up to pinch-hit. He smacked a two-run homer to help ignite a Dodgers' rally. LA eventually won, 8-7, and captured both remaining contests to defeat the New Yorkers in six games.

Jerry Hairston, Sr., carried on a tradition that still exists when he was signed by his father, Sam, a scout for the White Sox in 1970. Sam, a catcher, was the first African-American to play for the White Sox in 1951. His other son, John, played briefly for the Cubs in 1969. Jerry Hairston, Jr. was an infielder with the Baltimore Orioles in 2002.

Jerry, Sr., a switch-hitting outfielder whose defensive prowess was generally considered a hindrance by big league standards, was sold to the Pirates in 1977 after four sub-par years in Chicago. The 5' 10", 170-pound Birmingham, Alabama product then drifted into the Mexican League and worked his way back to the majors in 1981, once again with the White Sox.

Hairston may never have been rediscovered had it not been for the 1981 strike. While scouting pitchers in Mexico during the work stoppage, White Sox manager Tony LaRussa kept seeing him make all the right moves both offensively and defensively and signed him. Hairston led the American League in pinch-hit at-bats for four consecutive years starting in 1982, and in pinch-hits from 1983 to 1985. "Deep down inside, I want to start and get my four swings," Hairston said at the time, "but I'm not going to break into the lineup ... My role is pinch-hitting and I accept it."[4]

On April 15, 1983, Hairston's two-out, ninth inning pinch-hit ended a perfect game bid by Milt Wilcox of Detroit. It marked only the third time in history that a perfect game was stopped with one out remaining. When he was released in 1988 at the age of 35 after 12 seasons in the majors, his 93 career pinch-hits put him a tie for thirteenth place all-time. In 358 pinch-hit at-bats his BA was a respectable .260, almost equal to his .258 average overall. Hairston even made a cameo appearance with the White Sox in 1989 to pick up his 94th pinch-hit safety.

Bill Stein, a right-handed hitter who started at third base for the Mariners in their inaugural 1977 season, spent most of a 14-year career in the majors as a utility infielder-outfielder and occasional designated hitter. The 5' 10", 170-pound Battle Creek, Michigan native broke in with the Cardinals in 1972 and remained with them until the end of the following season. He joined the White Sox in 1974 and played the remainder of his career in the American League, finishing his playing days in Texas.

In 1981, Stein set an AL record with seven straight pinch-hits. His record-setting pinch-hit came on May 24, 1981, in a home game against the Twins. With the bases loaded and two out in a tie game, Rangers manager Don Zimmer called on Stein to pinch-hit. His line-drive single up the middle off Doug Corbett won the game, 3–2.

Stein claimed that he had blotted out from his mind the thought of breaking the record when he stepped up to the plate. "Once I got into the box the only thing I thought about was hitting the ball hard," he said.[5] Zimmer, a .242 career pinch-hitter himself, summed up Stein's capabilities as a pinch-hitter: "The number one thing that makes him effective in that situation is that he goes up there slashing. A lot of guys sit on the bench for a week or two weeks and when they get up there they just can't pull the trigger. Stein goes after the first thing that is in the strike zone."[6]

The former All-American shortstop from Southern Illinois University wound up leading the league in pinch-hits with a total of nine in 1981. Stein repeated as the league's top pinch-hitter the following year with 12 hits. And his 12-for-34 that season merited him a formidable .353 BA. Stein pinch hit 175 times in his career and his 48 safeties earned him a productive .274 BA, seven points in excess of his overall .267 mark. He was gone from the majors after the 1985 season at the age of 38.

After spending the first 13 years of his 23-year career in the National League as a starting outfielder, Daniel "Rusty" Staub became a designated hitter for the major portion of five seasons in the American League. The 6' 2", 190-pounder had rarely pinch-hit—only 59 times—but once the New York Mets got him back in 1981, the left-handed hitting New Orleans native became the club's top man off the bench. He tied major league records in 1983 for consecutive pinch-hits—eight (with Dave Philley)—and runs batted in—25 (with Joe Cronin and Jerry Lynch). He also had a record 81 pinch-hit at-bats and 94 appearances which, all in all, earned him a marvelous .296 BA. His 24 safeties that year place him in a tie with Philley and Vic Davalillo for second place at the time on the list of all-time pinch-hits in a single season. Staub was also the only player in history to play for four different major league ball clubs and connect for over 500 hits and play in more than 500 games for each team.

"What I did was unusual," says Staub. "Most players can't play regularly for 19 years and then the last four years pinch-hit. It's because you're used to being in the game and you can't stand the down time."[7]

Rick Miller spent the first seven years of his 15-year career with the Red Sox trying to win a starting outfield position behind the likes of Carl Yastrzemski, Dwight Evans, Jim Rice and Fred Lynn. After marrying Carlton Fisk's sister and playing out his option in 1977, the Grand Rapids, Michigan product signed with the Angels and played fairly regularly in California for the next three seasons.

Returning to Boston in 1981 as part of a multi-player trade, the 6-foot, 175-pound Miller became the club's top left-handed pinch-hitter during the 1983 to 1985 seasons. Although he never led the league in any one category as a substitute batter, his 40 hits in 130 at-bats in his second tour with the Red Sox earned him an excellent .309 average off the bench. For his career, Miller hit safely on 54 occasions in 189 pinch-hit appearances for a substantial .285 mark, well above his .269 lifetime BA. Miller was 37 when he left the majors after the 1985 campaign.

Tito Landrum, a right-handed hitting backup outfielder from Joplin, Missouri started out in the majors with the Cardinals in 1980. Always in the best of condition, he was traded to the Orioles for Floyd Rayford during the 1983 season. His unanticipated home run in the tenth inning of Game Four of the 1983 ALCS against the White Sox broke a scoreless tie and clinched the series for Baltimore. The 5' 11", 175-pounder only hit 13 homers in 995 at-bats during his eight-year career.

Landrum returned to the Cardinals in 1984 and led the National League in pinch-hitting for average that year with 9-for-23 and a superb .391 BA. He repeated in 1985 with 8-out-of-24 for .333. He also homered in Game Four of the 1985 World Series against the Royals in a game won by St. Louis, 3-0. For his big league career, Landrum delivered 40 pinch-hits in 154 at bats for a .260 BA, nine points above his .249 lifetime average. He retired following the 1988 campaign at the age of 33.

Max Venable, a left-handed hitting outfielder from Phoenix, came up to the big leagues with the Giants in 1979. The 5' 10", 185-pounder never had more than 228 at-bats in a single season during his nine-year career and only hit 11 home runs. After five years in San Francisco, he was swapped to the Expos with Andy McGaffigan for Al Oliver. He had his best year in Cincinnati in 1984 after being traded for Skeeter Barnes. Venable's 13 hits in 35 at-bats were good for an imposing .371 average. When he left the majors in 1987 at the age of 30, he had delivered 57 hits in 233 pinch-hitting appearances for a .245 mark, slightly better than his .241 lifetime average.

Dane Iorg, a backup outfielder-first baseman for most of his 10-year big league career, excelled as a substitute batter in the post-season. A contact hitter with neither power nor speed, the Eureka, California product came up with the Phillies in 1972 but quickly found himself traded in mid-season to the Cardinals with Tom Underwood and Rick Bossetti for Bake McBride and Steve Waterbury. When the Cardinals reached the 1982 World Series against the Brewers, the 6-foot, 180-pound Iorg was used as a DH and hit a thunderous .529 in that role.

Later when Iorg—the brother of long-time Blue Jays' infielder/out-fielder, Garth—played for the Royals in the 1985 World Series against the Cardinals, he came back to haunt his old team by cracking out a two-run pinch-hit single in the bottom of the ninth inning of Game Six to win it, 2-1. The game–and the Series–had been kept alive by a controversial call at first on an infield hit by another pinch-hitter, Jorge Orta. That victory forced the series into a seventh game. The Royals won it all the next day, 11-0, behind Bret Saberhagen.

Overall, Iorg's 69 hits in 287 pinch-hit at-bats during the regular season were only good for a .240 mark, well under his .276 lifetime average, but his histrionics in the post-season enabled two Missouri teams to win classic seven-game world championships.

A speedy switch-hitter with occasional power, Jerry Mumphrey was a defensive liability as an outfielder. He began his big league career with the Cardinals in 1974. After his first 12 years as a regular with St. Louis, San Diego, the Yankees and Houston, the 6' 2", 185-pounder became a part-time player and accomplished pinch-hitter for the Cubs during his last three years in the majors. He was 10-for-29 for a marvelous .345 BA in 1986 and 12-out-of-35 for an equally superior .343 mark in 1987. He was released after the 1988 campaign at the age of 36 after only hitting .136, including 5-for-50 (.100) off the bench. After 14 years in the majors, Mumphrey logged 55 pinch hits in only 207 at-bats for a .266 average. Mumphrey had a .289 mark overall.

A strong-armed reserve outfielder for most of his 14 years in the majors, Joel Youngblood actually started for the Mets in right field in 1979 and 1980. However, as the time wore on, the Houston native developed into one of the game's more reliable right-handed pinch-hitters, increasing his longevity in the big leagues.

One day in 1982, the 6-foot, 180-pounder was involved in one of the oddest happenings in baseball history. He became the first major league player to collect hits for two different teams on the same day. He singled for the Mets against the Cubs in the afternoon and was traded to the Expos right after the game. He immediately flew to Philadelphia in time to pinch-hit a single for Montreal against the Phillies that evening.

After being traded to the Giants for the 1983 season, Youngblood led the National League in errors as a third baseman with 36 in the following year and was relegated to reserve status in 1985. Thereafter he banged out 16, 13 and 15 pinch-hits respectively from 1986 to 1988 to rank among the NL's elite emergency batsmen at the time.

Cliff "Heathcliff" Johnson, who was destined to break Jerry Lynch's all-time pinch-hit home run record in the 1980s, came up with the Astros in 1972. When it became evident that the San Antonio native did not have the tools necessary to be the club's everyday catcher, he was tried at first base and in the outfield. Although his defensive shortcomings prevented him from laying claim to a starting spot, his powerful bat kept him around for some 15 years. He was used as DH 744 times.

Five of the 20 pinch-hit home runs that the 6' 4", 215-pound Johnson belted came in 1974, his first full season in Houston. While he was never consistent throughout his career as a pinch-hitter, that particular season turned out to be his best. He collected 13 pinch-hits in 38 at-bats that year to post a sparkling .342 BA. His bat often sailed across the infield when he swung at a pitch and missed.

The only season in which Johnson came close to that pinnacle was in 1983 as a member of the Blue Jays. That year he produced 11 hits in 34 at-bats to gain a .321 average. All told though his lifetime numbers as a pinch-hitter were not terribly impressive — 68 hits in 277 pinch-hit appearances, good for only a .245 average–besides the Astros, he played in 65 games for the 1980 Cubs–and somewhat under his .258 average overall.

A smart, patient hitter who was not very successful in the National League, Johnson's best years came in the American League for the Yankees, A's, Indians, Rangers and Blue Jays. He was always a threat for the long bomb. Lynch's record of 18 home runs as a substitute batter had stood for many years until Johnson broke it on August 5, 1984. In the eighth inning of a game against the Orioles, the Blue Jays rode his record-breaking 19th pinch-hit home run to a 4-3 win. Johnson's 20th pinch-hit round-tripper came the following season — his last in the majors— and remains the record.

Another San Antonio product, Danny Heep, also came up to the majors with Houston. The left-handed hitting reserve outfielder-first baseman made his debut with the Astros in 1979. After four inconsistent seasons, the 5' 11", 185-pounder was traded to the Mets in the winter of 1983 for Mike Scott. In his first year in New York, Heep smacked four pinch-hit home runs to lead the majors and establish a Mets team record. In the club's world championship season of 1986, Heep was the club's top pinch-hitter with 9-out-of-30 for a solid .300 BA. He also saw action in the WS against the Red Sox as a designated hitter. He was hitless as a DH, but singled in his only pinch-hit at-bat.

Lee Mazzilli also had a key role off the bench for the '86 Mets. In 1985, while with Pittsburgh, he led all National League pinch-hitters in plate appearances with 72 and batted .286 while posting a .437 on-base percentage in that role. When he was released by the Pirates in 1986, he was reacquired by the Mets in time for their pennant drive. The Brooklyn-born Maz, an All-Star center fielder with the Mets in 1979, played in 39 games as a part-timer in 1986.

Mazzilli set a League Championship Series record with five pinch-hit appearances that year for the Mets against Houston. He led off the eighth inning of Game Six of the World Series with a pinch-hit single off Boston's Calvin Schiraldi and

Cliff Johnson holds the all-time career record for home runs as a pinch-hitter with 20. (Courtesy of National Baseball Hall of Fame Library, Cooperstown, N.Y.)

scored the tying run in the Mets' improbable win in extra innings. In Game Seven he again started a game-tying rally with a single, this time from the right side. The Mets went on to take the Series with an 8-5 win. He continued his pinch-hitting success the following year when he led the NL with 17 pinch-hits in 55 at-bats, good for a mighty .309 BA.

Randy Bush, a left-handed hitting outfielder-DH with good power, played his entire six-year career with the Twins. The Denver product came to Minnesota in 1982 and in his rookie year tied an American League record with two consecutive pinch-hit home runs. Despite never having over 400 at-bats in a single season, the 6' 1", 190-pounder hit double figures in homers in five of his six years in the big leagues.

Still another player who broke in with the Astros and became one of the game's best pinch-hitters was outfielder Greg Gross. The York, Pennsylvania-born left-handed hitter was an excellent contact hitter who seldom struck out. He was *The Sporting News* Rookie of the Year in 1974 when he hit .314 with eight triples. A weak arm, little speed and even less power resulted in less playing time as a starter. After four seasons in Houston and two more with the Cubs, he was traded to Philadelphia with Dave Rader in the spring of 1979 for Barry Foote, Ted Sizemore, Jerry Martin, Derek Botelho and a minor leaguer.

Gross led the National League in pinch-hits with 19 in 1982. His single up the middle off the Mets' Ed Lynch on October 3 moved him ahead of Rene Monteagudo (1945) and Dave Philley (1958) for the Phils' club record. Coupled with his 53 appearances, he also registered a league-leading .358 BA. Gross had double-digit pinch-hit totals in 1984 and 1986 with 13 each year and in 1987 he collected 15 hits. Through 1988, he was the third leading pinch-hitter in major league history with 136 hits. One of those hits was a leadoff triple in the eighth inning of a game played on June 28, 1987, to break up Ron Darling's no-hitter and spark the first of two rallies that resulted in a 5-4 Phillies win over the Mets. When he retired in 1989, his 143 career pinch-hits placed him third all-time behind Manny Mota and Smoky Burgess.

Perhaps the most spectacular home run ever hit by a pinch-hitter took place at Dodger Stadium in Game One of the 1988 World Series. Kirk Gibson, suffering from a painful leg injury, was not expected to play at all in the Series but Los Angeles manager Tom Lasorda had the veteran outfielder on the team's roster anyhow. The 6' 3", 215-pound native of Pontiac, Michigan had been an All-American in both football and baseball at Michigan State University. Known for his intensity, Gibson had signed on as a free agent with the Dodgers prior to the 1988 season after nine years with the Tigers, which included the 1984 world championship.

The Dodgers were down 4-3 in the bottom of the ninth with Mike Davis on base and the A's stellar reliever, Dennis Eckersley, on the mound. An incredulous roar emanated from the home crowd as Gibson hobbled out of the Dodgers dugout, bat in hand, as a substitute batter. Wincing on every pitch, he fouled off four pitches before Eckersley served him up a slider that Gibson deposited into the right field seats to win the game, 5-4. The videotape of Gibson limping around the bases pumping his fists into the night air is often shown on broadcasts featuring great moments in sports history. The homer evoked a now-famous call by the late Hall of Fame broadcaster Jack Buck: "I don't believe what I just saw!"[8]

His blast was the first walk-off home run in a series game since Carlton

Fisk's in Game Six of the 1975 Fall Classic. Gibson's heroic at-bat was the only appearance he made in the 1988 World Series. Spurred by his dramatic clout, and blessed with great pitching, the Dodgers went on to win the world championship in only five games.

12

1990–2002:
Lenny Harris, John Vander Wal and Dave Hansen Carry On

While the use of pinch-hitters continued to lessen in the American League in the 1990s because of the designated hitter rule, their contributions to the success of many teams in both leagues remained undeniable. Three players—all from the National League—emerged in this decade to take their rightful places among the elite in baseball history.

Lenny Harris of the Mets, became the game's most prolific career pinch-hitter when he smacked hit No. 151 in 2001 to surpass his old Dodgers coach, Manny Mota. John Vander Wal, then with the Colorado Rockies, produced the highest number of base hits in a single season when he recorded 28 in 1995 to break Jose Morales's mark of 25 set in 1976. And Dave Hansen of the Dodgers, tutored by Manny Mota, set the single season record for the most pinch-hit home runs when he slammed seven in 2000 to break Johnny Frederick's 68-year-old mark of six.

It was not until the final three-game series with the Expos in 2001 before the 5' 10", 220-pound Harris was able to first tie Mota on a cold October night in a meaningless game. He broke the record the following evening with his club out of the NL pennant race.

Harris, a vexing low-ball left-handed hitter who hardly ever walks, got to know Mota when he played for the Dodgers from 1989 to 1993. "Manny was a coach and he used to tease me that I would never break his record," Harris said. "He used to say he was the greatest. He even wore a chain with the number '150' on it. I know he's happy for me, though."[1]

Harris learned the lessons he now applies to pinch-hitting from his former manager, Pete Rose, in his early days with the Reds. He credits Rose with teaching him how important it is to not just go up to the plate and swing away.

"Pete told me I have the ability to play at this level, stay in shape, always hustle, be ready to do what you can," says Harris. "So hearing that from a legend like Pete Rose made me feel good, that I had a chance. After one particular at-bat, he came to me and said, 'Did you know what the pitcher was going to throw you?' And I didn't. I realized then what I wanted to be like. I want to be the guy who watches the game, learns from it, sees what the pitchers are throwing to other guys, then be able to know a little bit about what might be coming, and what I can do with that pitch."[2]

In 2001, the Miami, Florida-born Harris began his fourteenth season in the big leagues as No. 4 on the all-time pinch-hit list with 130, behind Mota and his 150, Smoky Burgess at 145, and Greg Gross at 143. He passed Gross and Burgess and set his sights on the big prize. He understood that the task of hitting safely or just reaching base was a formidable one since the situation is usually tension-filled with the game almost always on the line. Unlike a closer, a pinch-hitter doesn't get the chance to work out of trouble. Three strikes and he is history. No matter what the situation may have been though, Harris loved it.

Harris's manager with the Mets, Bobby Valentine, understood full well the pressure of pinch-hitting and was Lenny's biggest booster. "It's like a high jumper who understands that he has to give that one effort at the moment," said Valentine. "He doesn't have another shot. I have to clear the bar now, and that's what a pinch-hitter does. He doesn't really have a second opportunity."[3]

As with most pinch-hitters, Harris never wanted to be one. "I always thought it was the worst thing you can do in baseball," he declared. "But in Los Angeles, Tommy Lasorda didn't start me for awhile and so I had a chance to get some pinch-hitting opportunities, and I wound up getting some base hits. So that label stuck with me. 'He's a guy who can get a hit off the bench.' So it hurt me and helped me."[4]

The key to successful pinch-hitting is preparation. "I watch a lot of video," says Harris. "The veteran relievers, I kind of know what they might throw. But with the young guys, I really have to watch them. I have to watch what they throw, when they'll throw a certain pitch in a count and what their out pitch is."[5]

When Harris stroked his record-breaking hit off Carl Pavano of the

Expos on October 6, 2001 at New York's Shea Stadium, the home crowd of 15,025 roared its approval. Even the bullpen emptied and the coaches joined in as the game was delayed for several minutes. Some might consider such demonstrations absurd but the emotion was genuine only because the accomplishment was an event deserving to be celebrated. Harris continued to ply his trade with his sixth team, the Milwaukee Brewers after a big three-way multi-player deal on January 21, 2002. He became the first player to have four straight seasons with 15 or more pinch-hits, knocking out 22 in 2002.

"I still can't believe it," Harris said regarding the record. "It's like a dream."[6] He was given first base and a large bottle of champagne. "Nothing's going to top this," he added, "knowing you're the best ever."[7] Harris established a new major league record with 83 pinch-hit at-bats in a single season, while compiling 21 hits for a .253 BA, and eight RBIs. He finished 2002 with a career .268 average as a pinch-hitter with 173 hits, 66 RBI and 50 walks in 646 at-bats.

Another player who claimed to detest the job of pinch-hitting was Grand Rapids, Michigan's John Vander Wal. Yet the sometime outfielder-first baseman broke Jose Morales's single-season pinch-hitting record of 25 by recording 28 pinch-hits of his own in 1995. And the 6' 2", 197-pounder did it in a strike-shortened season, making it all the more remarkable.

Vander Wal stood in seventh place on the all-time pinch-hitting list with 119 safeties through 2002. The left-handed swinger hit the ball hard and possessed good power to the opposite field. He ranked behind only Cliff Johnson and Jerry Lynch with 17 pinch-hit homeruns.

"It's tough mentally," he said. "You look at the starting players, they're getting four at-bats a game. You're pinch-hitting, not playing and you may get four at-bats a week. That's a big difference. I mean, a *big* difference trying to feel comfortable at the plate."[8]

Vander Wal was proud of his single season pinch-hitting record, to a point. "It also shows I wasn't playing a lot. It is bittersweet. I'm thankful for the accomplishment, but I want to play."[9]

Vander Wal's most memorable pinch-hit took place in the 1998 play-offs when he was with the Padres. His two-run triple in the bottom of the eighth inning gave San Diego a 4-1 lead in the fourth game and they went on to beat Houston to reach the LCS and, ultimately, the World Series.

Like Lenny Harris, John Vander Wal wore his sixth uniform in 2002, the Yankee pinstripes. Vander Wal was dealt to New York from the Giants for reliever Jay Witasick. In a break from the standard pinch-hitting career path, Vander Wal has received more regular playing time late in his career.

His pinch-hitting actually suffered because of it; from 1999 to 2002, he pinch-hit just 50 times total with 11 hits.

The third member of this select triumvirate was third baseman-first baseman Dave Hansen of the Los Angeles Dodgers. A second round draft pick of the Dodgers in 1986, the Long Beach, California product played with the big club from 1992 to 1996 before spending the 1997 season with the Cubs. After going to Japan for a year, he returned to Los Angeles for the 1999 campaign.

Like Harris and Vander Wal, Hansen also longed to be an everyday player. "But the reality is, as a role player today, you have to prepare yourself for one at-bat every so often," said Hansen. "It's

John Vander Wal's single season record of 28 pinch-hits took place in a strike-shortened 1995. (Courtesy of National Baseball Hall of Fame Library, Cooperstown, N.Y.)

totally different than playing every day, where you get into the flow of the game more, you can take a few more pitches, all that stuff. As a pinch-hitter you have to be prepared for who you might face in that game, when you might be used."[10]

Since the Dodgers moved from Brooklyn to Los Angeles after the 1957 season, Mota and Hansen led the team in pinch-hits a record five times. Len Gabrielson ranked behind them with three while Mickey Hatcher, Lee Walls, Wally Moon, Al Ferrara and Jay Johnstone were tied with two seasons apiece.

"I don't think kids are groomed to be pinch-hitters," continued Hansen. "I think I learned to be a pinch-hitter over the years. Luckily, Manny has been with me. I picked his brain. Mickey Hatcher was here. I had guys who knew what they were doing ... Manny had to learn by himself, but he had some years under his belt. Back then, that was more of an advantage. He was mentally able to make the transfer and had the confidence already to do it. A young guy is living and dying on one at-bat."[11]

Through 2002, Hansen was tied for fifth with George Crowe for the most career pinch-hit home runs with 14. He surpassed Vander Wal on the all-time pinch-hit list and stands alone in sixth place with 120.

Hansen claims his approach never differs. It is his contention that the home run record he set in 2000 represented "seven pinch-hit surprises."[12]

Hansen credits Mota's instructions and counseling with his apparent success. "I know somebody else has done it before me. Manny has laid the path, I'm just following in his footsteps. If I can do a little bit of that, I'll be OK."[13]

Hansen considers all pinch-hits equally special. "The record-breaking home run was neat. But ... that was not my favorite. The one that stands out for me is the (game-winning) grand slam against the Giants in 1993. It was 0-0 with two outs in the ninth and bases loaded. And the guy (Mike Jackson) looking very mean on the mound. I remember closing my eyes, taking a deep breath and saying, 'I see myself as a success.' "[14]

To Dave Hansen, pinch-hitting is an arduous task because "you are not in there all the time and you still have to be prepared every day. It's not exciting for regular fans to watch pinch-hitters because they don't see them enough. The regular fans are not deep into the game. The guys who realize it more are the guys in the locker room."[15]

While some teams can point to one key player and, possibly, two that they count on to deliver in the clutch, the 2001 world champion Arizona Diamondbacks had as many as five. The list was headed by David Dellucci, a 5' 10", 198-pound outfielder by trade. Faced with the almost impossible chore of trying to break into an outfield consisting of Luis Gonzalez, Steve Finley and Reggie Sanders, Dellucci did the next best thing—he became a force off the bench. In 2000, he was one of the NL's top pinch-swingers by batting a terrific .356 with 16 runs scored and 16 RBI, both club records.

Going into the 2001 season, Dellucci, who hails from Baton Rouge, Louisiana, set some goals for himself. One of them was to hit one pinch-hit home run. "And I didn't think I was going to get it—that's so hard," he said. "You're not loose, and to get a ball in the air, goodness, that's pretty tough to do. Next thing you know I look up and I've got five pinch-hit home runs, I'm very proud of what I've done. I think I'm starting to learn how to do it and I'm feeling great at the plate."[16]

Together with Erubiel Durazo, who also hit five pinch-hit home runs in 2001, the pair were only two shy of Dave Hansen's major league record of seven accomplished the year before. Called up in 1999, Durazo, a Hermosillo, Mexico native, was penciled in as a pinch-hitter and potential backup outfielder for the D-Backs. However, his red-hot hitting enabled him to earn most of the playing time at first base supplanting Greg Colbrunn and the highly-touted Travis Lee.

However, a wrist injury in 2000 limited the 6' 3", 240-pounder's playing time considerably, as Durazo endured two operations and three trips to the disabled list. In the off-season, the club signed the veteran first baseman Mark Grace. Durazo and Colbrunn joined Dellucci, Midre Cummings and Danny Bautista on the D-Backs bench to form one of baseball's most potent pinch-hitting corps in 2001.

Durazo's batting strengths lay in his ability to hit with power to all fields and judge the strike zone. Being able take close pitches for balls, Durazo developed a good strikeout-walk ratio, so critical for a pinch-hitter. He turned well on inside pitches while remaining capable of hitting the ball hard to left-center and even straightaway left field.

A journeyman first sacker, Fontana, California's Colbrunn had been in the NL since 1992 when he joined the Expos. He was also victimized by injuries during his first three years in the big leagues. He was later waived to the Florida Marlins, where he played regularly for a couple of seasons. He moved on to the Twins in 1997 and played in both Atlanta and Colorado.

Colbrunn was picked up by Arizona via the free agent route for 1999 and immediately became one of the top pinch-hitters in the game, batting .375 as an emergency batsman. He started at first base through much of 2000, hitting .313 with 15 home runs but the D-Backs couldn't resist bringing in Grace.

Colbrunn remained an important part of the club's bench strength as he was not only an effective pinch-swinger but could fill in at first or third base or in the outfield and even as an emergency catcher. An aggressive hitter who almost always gets the barrel of the bat on the ball, Colbrunn also demonstrated that he can take a free pass when being pitched around. He also has a proclivity for getting hit by pitches. In 1999, he was hit by pitches on three consecutive at-bats, and in 2000, he was hit four times in four consecutive games.

The left-handed hitting Cummings was the fourth member of the D-Backs' pinch-hitting corps. Signed by Arizona as a free agent before the 2001 season to complement the right-handed hitting Colbrunn, he had seen service with Pittsburgh, Philadelphia, Boston and Minnesota before checking in at Phoenix.

A native of St. Croix, Virgin Islands, Cummings was coming off a banner pinch-hitting year in the American League in 2000 when he led the circuit in hits with 15, in total bases with 18, in doubles with three, and RBI with 12. The 6-foot, 195-pounder's .319 BA was seventh among AL pinch-hitters with more than 20 at-bats.

Danny Bautista, a right-handed hitting reserve outfielder from the Dominican Republic, rounded out the D-Backs' deep bench in their 2001 championship season. Although the 5' 11", 204-pounder lacked power, he hit the ball hard. Another of the many free swingers in the big leagues these days, walks come few and far between for Bautista. Nevertheless, he leads all National League pinch-hitters in career average among all with over 93 appearances by virtue of a .325 BA resulting from 38 hits in 117 at-bats. He ranked seventh among NL pinch-hitters in 2001 with a .350 BA based on his 14 hits in 40 at bats.

Fountain Valley, California's Craig Wilson, a reserve rookie first base-man for the Pirates, tied Dave Hansen's single season home run record with seven in 2001. His manager, Lloyd McClendon, who as a player once made a living out of pinch-hitting, couldn't believe it. "What this kid has done is phenomenal," said McClendon. "I've never seen anything like it. I hope nobody tells him how difficult it is."[17]

The right-handed hitting Wilson, who can also catch, play first and the outfield, has a short, compact swing and doesn't offer at bad breaking balls. The 6' 2", 217-pounder also looked to John Vander Wal for advice when the two were teammates in Pittsburgh. "What he has done is awesome," said Vander Wal, a record-setter himself. "It's a tough thing to do. Pinch-hitting is tougher than playing everyday."[18]

After going 10-for-34 (.294) off the bench in 2001, Wilson did play more regularly in 2002. He batted .264 with 16 home runs in 131 games in 2002, with just 16 pinch-hit at-bats—and two hits. Although cut loose from the Angels early in 2001, right-handed hitting Glenallen Hill had already established himself as one of the top pinch-hitters in the game. Tied for sixth all-time with 13 pinch-hit home runs, the Santa Cruz, California native had power to all fields and could hit mistake pitches unmercifully. He was one of the most productive players off the bench for the world champion Yankees in 2000. Acquired from the Cubs that season on July 21, Hill hit 16 home runs in 132 at bats for the Yankees. All told, he hit 27 home runs in 300 at-bats, including three homers in 31 pinch-hit at-bats.

A young player who has literally transformed himself into an every-day player for the Texas Rangers on the strength of his pinch-hitting is outfielder Frank Catalanotto. The left-handed hitting Smithtown, New York product finished in a tie for second with Russ Johnson of Tampa Bay among

American League pinch-hitters in 2001 with a .333 BA by virtue of six hits in 18 at bats. The veteran Tony Fernandez of the Blue Jays led the AL with a hefty .406 mark coming via a league-leading 13 hits in 32 appearances.

Catalanotto, who began his career with three years in Detroit, developed a sixth sense about using the opposite field and had an ability to drive the ball in the gaps. He also improved tremendously at pulling pitches. The 5' 11", 195-pound Catalanotto probably would not have been noticed had it been for his performances off the bench. In 114 career pinch-hit at-bats, Catalanotto had 33 hits (.289) with two home runs and 18 RBI, including 14 free passes.

Russ Johnson of the Devil Rays, a right-handed hitting third baseman from Dave Hansen's home town of Baton Rouge, Louisiana, possesses a good batting eye, decent power and some speed.

Tampa Bay acquired the 5' 10", 180-pounder from Houston in May of 2000, and he was 5-for-15 with four RBI and five walks in 2001 as the team's top man off the bench. Despite suffering through severe depression during the 2002 season, Johnson still had good numbers off the bench with a .277 average via 26 hits in 95 career at-bats, including 13 RBI, one home run and 11 walks.

Alex Arias, a right-handed hitting utility infielder from New York City, finished 2002 with a lifetime mark of .322 as a pinch-hitter. A former member of the 1997 world champion Florida Marlins, the 6' 3", 202-pounder also played for the Cubs, Phillies, and Padres. He was later released by San Diego and signed to a minor league contract by the Yankees in 2002. He went hitless in six at-bats with New York.

A contact spray hitter with not much power or speed, Arias nonetheless works the counts and gets enough one-base knocks and walks to be a valuable role player for any team. Of his 66 lifetime pinch-hits— he was fifth behind active players Harris, Vander Wal, Hansen and Mark Sweeney — only 17 were for extra bases. He also had drawn 20 bases on balls and driven in 35 runs during his 205 career official at-bats.

Outfielder Wilton Guerrero, the older brother of the Expos' Vladimir, compiled 58 base hits in 210 career pinch-hit times at-bat, including 22 RBI and 14 walks, but nary a home run. In fact, the Dominican only hit 11 in his entire seven-year career which began in Los Angeles in 1996, and has included two stops each in Montreal and Cincinnati. The 6-foot, 175-pound Guerrero hit .308 as a pinch-hitter for the Reds in 2001 as he was 8-for-26 with one double and two RBI. A 2002 mid-season trade reunited Wilton with his brother Vladimir in Montreal, but it couldn't improve a dismal 11-for-56 season off the bench that lowered his career emergency average from .305 to .276.

Orlando Merced, an Astros outfielder-first baseman, who broke in with the Pirates in 1990 and played with them up until 1996, has been with six different teams since then. A disciplined hitter with good concentration at the plate, the 6' 1", 195-pounder also has never proven to be a home run threat. Nonetheless, the left-handed batter — who began his career as a switch hitter — managed to be a very productive pinch-swinger. The San Juan, Puerto Rico product's 70 hits placed him fifth behind Harris, Vander Wal, Hansen and Sweeney careerwise among active pinch-hitters. Merced had also drawn 41 walks, hit 10 homers and driven in an impressive number of runs, 62, as a substitute batter.

Marvin Benard, who has spent his entire eight-year major league career with the Giants, finished the 2002 season with a .267 career pinch-hit BA. Of his 48 hits in 180 at-bats, only 13 were for extra bases but he was still able to knock in 28 runs.

Benard, a native of Nicaragua and an outfielder by trade, was a distant 50th round draft choice of the Giants in 1992. After starting out with them as a platoon player, the 5' 9", 185-pounder took over as the club's starting center fielder in 1999. A slashing hitter who can generate some alley power, Benard can turn on inside pitches for extra bases. He is an outstanding bunter who in 2000 ranked sixth in the NL by putting 26 bunts in play.

Reserve outfielder Orlando Palmeiro of the Anaheim Angels has delivered 37 hits in 132 at-bats (.280), including one homer, eight RBI and 12 walks in his pinch-hitting career. A native of Hoboken, New Jersey, he is a scrappy, line-drive hitter who is also an intelligent base runner.

The 5' 11", 180-pound Palmeiro has the ability to take extra bases by his hustle and can steal a base occasionally as well. He is also known for his bunting ability and getting his bat on the ball, so necessary in becoming an effective pinch-hitter.

Keith Lockhart of the Braves, has amassed solid pinch-hitting numbers in nine big league seasons. The 2001 campaign was his best off the bench, hitting .326 on the strength of his 15 hits in 46 at-bats, including a homer, six RBI and five walks. In 300 career pinch-hit at-bats, he is a .253 hitter (76 hits), with five homers, 47 RBI, 40 walks and 34 runs. A utility infielder who broke in with the Padres in 1994 at the advanced age of 29, the 5' 10", 170-pound Whittier, California native once was the Kansas City Royals' regular second baseman until being traded to Atlanta in 1997 with Michael Tucker for Jermaine Dye and Jamie Walker.

Mark Sweeney, who was released by the Padres during the 2002 season, was a .267 career pinch-hitter. The journeyman outfielder-first baseman put time in with the Cardinals, Reds and Brewers, plus an earlier stint in San Diego since arriving in the big leagues in 1995. His 84 hits in 315 appearances put him in fourth place behind Harris, Vander Wal and Hansen. Although only 18 of his hits went for extra bases, he was able to drive in 43 runs and work his way on with 43 bases on balls.

Left-handed hitting outfielder Dave Clark had his best year as a pinch-hitter for the Cubs in 1997 with 20-for-65 and an impressive .308 BA, that included three home runs. His 22 RBI established a team season record for pinch-hitters, far exceeding the 14 set by Champ Summers in 1975. The 6' 2", 200-pound Clark, who came from Elvis Presley's home town of Tupelo, Mississippi, also came within three RBI of tying the major league single season mark of 25. When he left the major leagues after the 1998 season, Clark had 10 career pinch-hit homers.

Dave Magadan, who was relegated to pinch-hitting and as a backup to Phil Nevin at third base for the Padres in 2000, finally hung up his spikes a year later. After 16 years in the big time, the Tampa-born left-handed hitter — a cousin of Tampa Bay manager Lou Piniella — had spent the past three seasons mainly as San Diego's leading hitter off the bench. His line-drive bat made him ideal as a pinch-hitter. He also had the ability to induce walks out of pitchers so necessary to spark a late-inning rally.

"I think I could still play," Magadan claimed, "but it was becoming more difficult in the role I was in. Getting one at-bat a night against the other team's closer was like going up there in battle mode."[19] The 6' 4" 215-pound Magadan, who made his debut the night the Mets clinched the 1986 NL East title, became the Padres' minor league hitting coordinator in 2002. "They want to change the approach to hitting that our minor leaguers go out there with," he said. "Work the count, take walks without looking for them and don't be afraid of hitting with two strikes."[20]

In the 1990s, substitute batters in both the American and National Leagues contributed mightily to their teams' successes. The 1991 World Champion Minnesota Twins had the best pinch-hitting group in the game that season with a .304 average. In fact, it was a pinch-hit single by Gene Larkin that drove in the only run of the deciding seventh game against the Braves. Manager Tom Kelly of the Twins got high marks for the way in which he handled players coming off his bench that season. Scott Leius, who platooned with Mike Pagliarulo at third base, hit a sensational .440 coming off 11 hits in 25 at-bats as a pinch-hitter while Randy Bush delivered 13 hits in 34 at-bats for a fabulous .382 mark that included two homers and eight RBI.

In the tight National League West race in 1991, there was a great disparity between the Braves and Dodgers in substitute batters. The Braves' group hit .233 vs. only .180 for the Dodgers' corps, with Atlanta winning one more game — 94-93 — than Los Angeles. Manager Bobby Cox got Danny Heep, who many thought had seen better days, to go 6-for-13 as a pinch-swinger that year. While Chris Gwynn (Tony's brother) had 13 pinch-hits and 13 RBI, and rookie Dave Hansen produced 10-for-32 for .313 had good seasons, Dodgers manager Tom Lasorda's other choices left the team wanting. Stan Javier (5-for-52 and .096), Gary Carter (2-for-27 and .074) and Lenny Harris (3-for-24 and .125) did not come through nearly as much as expected. Mickey Hatcher, who was 14-for-47 for a .298 average and 10 RBI the year before off the bench, had retired. It was the start of a frustrating decade in Los Angeles.

In the 1992 World Series, the first one ever played north of the border, the Toronto Blue Jays got a critical game winning pinch-hit home run in Game Two. Ed Sprague was sent up in the ninth inning to hit against one of the game's all-time saves leaders, Jeff Reardon of the Braves. With Toronto railing 4-3 and facing with the prospect of falling behind two games to none, Sprague blasted a two-run homer off Reardon with one out to give the home team a 5-4 victory to tie the series.

"I didn't see it leave the park," said Sprague. "When I looked up, it was right in the lights. Then when I got to first, I saw Deion's (left fielder Deion Sanders) back and I put my hands in the air. I knew we had the lead."[21] The Blue Jays went on to win the series in six games that year.

Gerald Perry, a left-handed line drive hitter with outstanding speed for a first baseman, broke in with the Braves in 1983. The Savannah, Georgia native was the club's starting first baseman by 1987. However, he had recurring shoulder problems in 1988 that forced him to develop his talents as a pinch-hitter. In 1993, he led the National League with 24 hits for the Cardinals to tie Dave Philley, Vic Davalillo and Rusty Staub for second place on the all-time single-season pinch-hit list. He retired after the 1995 season at the age of 35 as the all-time leader in pinch-hits in St. Louis.

13

The Impact of
the Designated Hitter

No history of pinch-hitting would be complete without some discussion of the designated hitter rule and its effect on the game. Adopted by Major League Baseball for the 1973 season, only the American League opted for its use. The National League steadfastly opposed it from almost the moment a dialogue began to make it available as an alternative.

While many believed at the time that the designated hitter rule was something entirely new, it had been talked about for decades. Reports of discussions concerning its use took place as far back as the 1890s, almost simultaneously with the introduction of the pinch-hitting rule. Later, people like the much venerated owner-manager, Connie Mack, had begun to talk seriously about it somewhere in the middle of his 50-year reign at the helm of the Philadelphia Athletics. Mack noted that the pitcher was the poorest hitter on the team and the game would benefit from dropping him from the batting order.

Ironically, from an historical point of view, it was the National League and not the American League that first formally proposed using designated hitters in 1928. The NL's then-president John Heydler endorsed it and even brought it up for a vote at the annual major league meeting in Chicago on December 1 that year. NL owners approved it while their AL counterparts rejected it and there it remained.

It wasn't until the late 1960s and early '70s when deliberations heated up as the lack of offense was thought to be diminishing fan interest. Nine of the 12 AL teams drew under a million in attendance in 1972. Pitchers were considered by many to be "automatic" outs and were simply a bore to watch with a bat in their hands. Commissioner Bowie Kuhn thought highly of the DH concept and moved for the incorporation of what became Major League Rule 6.10(b) and the election to use it by "any league." The rule permits a hitter to be designated prior to the start of each game to bat for the starting pitcher and all other pitchers who enter the game without changing the status of the pitcher(s) in the game.

Major ramifications of the rule are that: the DH in the starting lineup must come to bat at least once unless the opposing team changes pitchers; a club does not have to designate a hitter for the pitcher but failing to do so before game time prevents the use of a DH for that game; a pinch-hitter for a DH is permitted, making him the DH while the player being replaced may not re-enter the game in any capacity; a DH can be used defensively and continue to bat in the same position in the batting order, but the pitcher must then bat in place of the substituted defensive player unless more than one substitution is made, and the manager specifies their positions in the batting order.

Since only the American League and not the National League voted to adopt the DH rule, certain stipulations had to be incorporated by Major League Baseball governing inter-league play. For example, in either the World Series or exhibition games, the rule is used or not used as is the practice of the home team. At first, the NL refused to acknowledge it at all until 1976, when it agreed to let both teams use it in alternating World Series years. That changed 10 years later when the current rule was put in place. In All-Star games, the rule is used only if both teams and both leagues so agree. Presently, the NL is the lone holdout among organized baseball leagues; minor leagues, colleges, high schools and international baseball associations have adopted the rule.

The National League and the so-called baseball purists have argued that the DH dilutes the game by reducing overall game strategy. AL managers, it has been claimed, are freed from the responsibility of making decisions regarding pinch-hitters, for instance. Then, too, they can have their pitchers stay in the game longer than perhaps they should, or so the argument goes. Billy Martin was accused of burning up his young pitching staff in Oakland by forcing them to pitch longer than perhaps they should have.

Former big league manager Jim Leyland believes this type of reasoning is exaggerated. "I think managing in the American League is much more difficult," he said. "In the National League, my situation is dictated for me. If I'm behind in the game, I've got to pinch-hit. I've got to take my pitcher out. In the American League, you have to zero in. You have to know exactly when to take them out of there. In the National League, that's done for you."[1]

Fred McGriff, who has played for many years in both leagues, disagrees on what distinguishes the NL from the AL. "I think the National League is a better league," he said. "The managers have to manage in the National League. In the American League you just make out the lineup and let 'em play. In the National League, you have to pinch-hit, double switch, that type of thing."[2]

Antagonists also point to the fact that had it not been for the DH rule, Eddie Murray may not have hit his 500th home run or gotten his 3,000th hit. Dave Winfield, a 2001 Hall of Fame inductee, might not have achieved many of his numbers had it not been for his many appearances as a DH in the latter stages of his career. By the same token, some wonder what records would have withstood the onslaughts of players like Babe Ruth, Mickey Mantle, Willie Mays and Honus Wagner, among others, had those players been permitted to prolong their careers as designated hitters.

On the other side of the coin, noted baseball scholar Bill James firmly believes that overall game strategy has not been reduced as a result of the DH rule. He analyzed sacrifice hits and the use of pinch-hitters between 1968 and 1983 and deduced that the DH rule had actually increased managerial strategy. Although his research found that in the AL the number of bunts was down 40 percent and the use of pinch-hitters had decreased by 50 percent following adoption of the DH rule, the decision to use these strategies became more intense.

"If strategy exists in the act of bunting, then the DH rule has reduced strategy," James has written. "But if strategy exists in the decision about *when* a bunt should be used, then the DH rule has increased the differences of opinion which exist about that question, and thus increased strategy ... (the research shows) that there is *more* of a difference of opinion, not less, in the American League."[3]

It is broadcaster Bob Costas's contention that "the time has come for the DH to go. The conditions that existed when it was brought into the game with the 1973 season no longer exist. In the early '70s, baseball was still recovering from an offensive famine. A batting title was won at .301 in 1968. An entire league batted .239 in the '72 season. Home run titles could be won with figures in the low 30s. In 1968, 21 percent of all games were shutouts.

"Now, a generation later, offense is way up — even approaching the point of distortion in the AL," he continues. "And it is generally conceded, even among fans who reflexively defend the DH, that the permutations of the game are more interesting in the NL. This doesn't mean a genius is needed to execute a double-switch, only that the strategy brought into the game by making the pitcher hit adds a texture and complexity worth preserving."[4]

Another argument raging against the DH rule claims AL pitchers are less careful about pitching to batters simply because they themselves don't have a turn at bat and thus avoid possible retaliation. It's called the "moral hazard" theory: designated hitters tend to raise the number of hit batters. Also proving the theory is that for every 50 times a pitcher hits a batter, the opposing pitcher is hit. Another theory is that retaliation by one team for a hit batter will most often be aimed at a power hitter.

As might be expected, the rebuttals in support of keeping the DH rule are just as fervent. Apart from not wishing to see pitchers make one feeble attempt after another at the plate, the retention of older, established position players who can still wield a mighty bat, has been a prime reason for championing the cause. Keeping hitters like Chili Davis, Harold Baines, George Brett and Paul Molitor around, among others, has been considered justification enough for retention of the rule. Earlier former NL stars like Rico Carty and Dave Parker had their careers extended in the AL long after they had left the older league.

While Orioles owner Peter Angelos has admitted that the game's strategy has been altered with the DH, he feels the gain in providing more offensive capability has been worth the loss. "That is important because baseball has a tendency to be slow-moving and unexciting," Angelos says. "This adds another dimension to the game and that's why I support it."[5] Chicago Cubs president Andy MacPhail sees it just the opposite: "I don't think our fans are the least bit interested in seeing the DH be part of the National League landscape,"[6] he says. It's been his view that when pitchers don't have to bat, the overall strategy available to managers has been minimized, a feeling shared by most traditionalists.

What then has been the impact of the designated hitter rule, if any, since its adoption? Blake Redabaugh studied both the National League and the American League for two periods: once between the years of 1968 and 1972 and then from 1973 to 1977. He found that with the exception of home runs, the American League improved significantly in all offensive categories in the five-season period following the establishment of the rule. In home runs, the average per team diminished only slightly when the designated hitter was used.

Although the National League, even without the DH, showed impressive gains in both batting average and runs batted in the same post-DH period, it was not as appreciable as the AL's increase. And while slugging percentage also rose in the NL, it was minimal. Home run productivity also slowed in the NL in the same period, but not tremendously.

Redabaugh noted in his study that he found no conspicuous differences in either league both before and after the DH rule took effect in batting averages, runs batted in, slugging percentages and home runs. But while the NL had higher averages than the AL in the five years before the DH rule, the AL surpassed the NL in the post-DH period in batting averages, runs batted in and slugging percentages.

Trends indicated that both leagues consistently either increased or decreased their slugging percentages every year. It also appeared that these trends took place in the other offensive categories as well. What this seemed to illustrate was that while both leagues operated quite independently from each other, offensive production tendencies were similar in both from one year to the other.

While conceding that the DH had assisted the AL somewhat in increasing its offensive stats, Redabaugh concluded that further study is needed to prove just how critical a role the rule adoption contributed to this turnaround. He suggested that a look at the AL's DH statistics compared to the NL's pitching statistics might illustrate just how much more production the designated hitter had over the pitcher.

While everyone seems to remember that Ron Blomberg of the New York Yankees became the first official DH in history when he batted on April 6, 1973 against the Boston Red Sox in Fenway Park, few can remember the names of the others who also were inserted that day as designated hitters. They included: Orlando Cepeda (Red Sox); Terry Crowley (Orioles); Tom McCraw (Angels); Mike Andrews (White Sox); John Ellis (Indians); Gates Brown (Tigers); Ed Kirkpatrick (Royals); Tony Oliva (Twins); Billy North (Athletics); Dave Collins (Mariners); and Ollie Brown (Brewers). Rico Carty of the Rangers was their first but they played a day later, that is on April 7, 1973. Otto Velez was the Blue Jays' first DH when they joined the AL on April 7, 1977. The previous evening, Dave Collins had served as the first designated hitter in Mariners history. The first DH for the expansion Tampa Bay Devil Rays was Paul Sorrento on March 31, 1998.

While Blomberg went into posterity as the first-ever DH, not many can recall what he did in that famous at bat. The left-handed batter faced the veteran right-hander Luis Tiant with the bases loaded and walked to drive in a run. Also on that same day, Tony Oliva of the Twins hit the first home run by a DH, in the first inning off Catfish Hunter in the Oakland Coliseum.

Other important firsts by designated hitters include Dan Driessen's at-bat as the NL's first DH in the 1976 World Series as the Reds swept the Yankees. Although he flied out in that appearance in Cincinnati, he homered in his team's Game Three win. Ironically, earlier that year, the Reds

took the baseball commissioner's office to court in an attempt to block a new rule that allowed use of a DH in alternate years in the World Series. A judge ruled against the Reds and Driessen went on to hit .357 for the Reds in the 1976 Series.

The record for the oldest DH ever is easily Orestes "Minnie" Minoso of the White Sox. At the age of 53 during the 1976 season, he recorded one hit in eight at-bats as a designated hitter. Four seasons later he returned at 57 to go hitless in two at-bats as a DH in his fifth decade in the big leagues.

Although he should not be classified as a designated hitter, Hall of Famer Al Kaline, who played his entire career with the Tigers, did in fact finish his career in that role. Needing 139 hits to reach the 3,000-hit milestone, he became a full-time DH and registered his 3,000th hit against Dave McNally of the Orioles. Kaline retired with a total of 3,007 hits and was elected to the Hall of Fame in his first year of eligibility, 1980.

A question that many seem to be grappling with now is whether the first true DH to win a batting title — Edgar Martinez of the Seattle Mariners — deserves to be seriously considered for election to the Hall of Fame once he becomes eligible. The New York City-born right-handed hitter had compiled some significant numbers following the 2002 season — a .317 lifetime BA, 273 home runs, 1,973 hits in 1,769 games and 1,100 runs batted in.

The first year he won the batting title in 1992, with a .343 mark, Martinez also led the league in doubles. That season he became only the second player to lead his league in batting while playing for a last-place team. He was still primarily a third baseman, but injuries the next two years led manager Lou Piniella to make him a full-time DH. He won his second batting title in 1995 with a .356 mark, including 121 runs, 52 doubles, 29 homers and 113 runs batted in. Between 1995 and 2000, the 5' 11", 200-pound Martinez averaged 103 runs, 42 doubles, 29 home runs and nearly 110 RBI per year. And during that time-frame, he never hit below .322 or walked fewer than 96 times.

A hitter with power to all fields, he combines an excellent knowledge of the strike zone with a bat that consistently produces line drives. Martinez, who moved to Maguayo, Puerto Rico as a boy, has few weaknesses. Opposing hurlers have attempted to throw him fastballs in on his hands, but even this tactic can have a deleterious effect on the selective Mariner.

Opposite: Edgar Martinez was baseball's first batting champion as a designated hitter in 1992, with a .343 BA. (Courtesy of National Baseball Hall of Fame Library, Cooperstown, N.Y.)

He is very patient and just waits for the pitch he wants, and when he gets it, he jumps all over it. Not only has he been a productive RBI man over the years, but he has created chances for those in the lineup behind him to also drive in runs thanks to his marvelous on-base percentage which stood at .403 after the 2002 season.

Like Martinez, Harold Baines, a veteran of 21 big league seasons, had also been a DH for the majority of his career. His numbers also bear close scrutiny for Hall of Fame consideration. A six-time AL all-star, he was one of the purest hitters of his era while recording 2,866 hits, 1,299 runs scored, 384 homers, 1,628 RBI and a .289 batting average. The sweet-swinging left-handed batter compiled almost all of his statistics from 1986 through 2001 as a DH.

A serious knee injury that forced Baines onto the disabled list in 1986 was the first of a series of problems that would afflict him from then on and lead him into the designated hitter role. He was an All-Star right fielder during his first six seasons in the majors, and only served as DH six times in his first 847 games.

Baines drove in more runs than any other DH in history. The former first overall draft pick of the Chicago White Sox in 1977 was always one of the game's best clutch players, particularly with men on base. Many believe that his employment as a DH during the last 15 years of his career should not diminish his consideration for a plaque in Cooperstown.

As has been noted earlier, the National League's initial use of designated hitters took place many years later when inter-league play began in 1997. The first regular season DH in NL history was Glenallen Hill of the Giants on June 12, 1997. Rickey Henderson of the Padres, Mike Piazza of the Dodgers and Dante Bichette of the Rockies were their respective teams' first designated hitters on the same day. A few days later, on June 16, 1997, the following NL players became the first to DH for their clubs: Keith Lockhart (Braves); Dave Clark (Cubs); Eddie Taubensee (Reds); Jim Eisenreich (Marlins); Sean Berry (Astros); Jose Vidro (Expos); Butch Huskey (Mets); Darren Daulton (Phillies); Mark Smith (Pirates); and Dimitri Young (Cardinals).

A century perhaps after it was first suggested, the National League had a designated hitter — if only for a designated period.

Appendix: All-Time Pinch-Hitting Records

REGULAR SEASON—INDIVIDUAL

Most Games, Season
- 94   Rusty Staub, NL–New York, 1983
- 81   Elmer Valo, AL–New York–Washington, 1960

Most At-Bats, Lifetime
- 646   Lenny Harris, NL–Cincinnati 1988–89, 1994–98; Los Angeles 1989–93; New York 1998, 2000–01; Colorado 1999; Arizona 1999–2000; Milwaukee 2002
- 591   Greg Gross, NL–Houston 1973–76, 1989; Chicago 1977–78; Philadelphia 1979–88

Most At-Bats, Season
- 83   Lenny Harris, NL–New York, 2001
- 72   Dave Philley, AL–Baltimore, 1961

Most Hits, League
- 173   Lenny Harris, NL, 1986–2002
- 107   Gates Brown, AL–Detroit, 1963–1975

Most Hits, Season
- 28   John Vander Wal, NL–Colorado, 1995
- 24   Dave Philley, AL–Baltimore, 1961

Most Hits, Consecutive, League

9   Dave Philley, NL–Philadelphia, September 9, 1958–April 16, 1959

Most Hits, Consecutive, Season

8   Dave Philley, NL–Philadelphia, September 9–28, 1958
    Rusty Staub, NL–New York, June 11–26(1g), 1983
7   Bill Stein, AL–Texas, April 14–May 25, 1981
    Randy Bush, AL–Minnesota, July 5–August 19, 1991

Most Home Runs, Lifetime

20   Cliff Johnson, NL–Houston, 1972–77; AL–New York, 1977–79;
      Cleveland, 1979–80; Oakland, 1981–82; Toronto, 1983–86

Most Home Runs, League

18   Jerry Lynch, NL, Pittsburgh, 1954–56, 1963–66; Cincinnati, 1957–63
16   Gates Brown, AL–Detroit, 1963–75

Most Home Runs, Season

7   Dave Hansen, NL–Los Angeles, 2000
    Craig Wilson, NL–Pittsburgh, 2001
5   Joe Cronin, AL–Boston, 1943

Most Home Runs, Consecutive At-Bats

3   Lee Lacy, NL–Los Angeles, May 2, 6, 17, 1978
    Del Unser, NL–Philadelphia, June 30, July 5, 10, 1979
2   Ray Caldwell, AL–New York, June 10–11, 1915
    Joe Cronin, AL–Boston, June 17 (2 games), 1943
    Charlie Keller, AL–New York, September 12, 14
    Del Wilber, AL–Boston, May 6, 10, 1953
    Johnny Blanchard, AL–New York, July 21, 22, 1961
    Chuck Schilling, AL–Boston, April 30, May 1, 1965
    Ray Barker, AL–New York, June 20, 22, 1965
    Curt Motton, AL–Baltimore, May 15, 17, 1968
    Gates Brown, AL–Detroit, August 9, 11, 1968
    Gary Alexander, AL–Cleveland, July 5, 6, 1980
    Daryl Sconiers, AL–California, April 30, May 7, 1983
    Alex Sanchez, AL–Detroit, July 20, 23, 1985
    Rupert Jones, AL–California, June 20, 28, 1987
    Randy Bush, AL–Minnesota, July 14, 19, 1991
    Jack Howell, AL–California, May 15, 17, 1996
    Jeromy Burnitz, AL–Milwaukee, August 2, 3, 1997
    Willie Greene, AL–Toronto, June 20, 30, 1999

Most Grand Slam Home Runs, Lifetime

3   Ron Northey, NL–St. Louis, September 3, 1947; May 30, 1948;
Chicago, September, 18 , 1950
Willie McCovey, NL–San Francisco, June 12, 1960; September 10,
1965; San Diego, May 30, 1975
Rich Reese, AL–Minnesota, August 3, 1969; June 7, 1970; July 9, 1972

Most Grand Slam Home Runs, Season

2   Dave Johnson, NL–Philadelphia, April 30, June 3, 1978
Mike Ivie, NL–San Francisco, May 28, June 30, 1978
Darryl Strawberry, AL–New York, May 2, August 4, 1998

Most Walks, Lifetime

91   Elmer Valo, AL–Philadelphia/Kansas City, 1940–43, 1946–56;
Cleveland, 1959; New York, 1960; Washington/Minnesota,
1960–61; NL–Philadelphia, 1956, 1961;
Brooklyn/Los Angeles, 1957–58

Most Walks, Season

20   Matt Franco, NL–New York, 1999
18   Elmer Valo, AL–Washington, 1960

Most Runs Batted In, Season

25   Joe Cronin, AL–Boston, 1943
Jerry Lynch, NL–Cincinnati, 1961
Rusty Staub, NL–New York, 1983

REGULAR SEASON—CLUB BATTING

Most Pinch-Hitters, Game

9   NL: Los Angeles (St. Louis), September 22, 1959
Montreal (Pittsburgh), September 5 (2g), 1975
Atlanta (Montreal), September 21, 1993
8   AL: Baltimore (Chicago), May 28, 1954
Baltimore (New York), September 25, 1984
Minnesota (Seattle), September 13, 1986

Extra-Inning Game

10   AL: Oakland (Chicago), September 19, 1972 (15 inn.)
9   NL: Los Angeles (St. Louis), September 1, 1982 (13 inn.)
Los Angeles (New York), September 8, 1985 (14 inn.)
San Francisco (Los Angeles), September 28, 1986
St. Louis (Cincinnati), September 25, 1997 (14 inn.)

Most Pinch-Hitters, Both Clubs, Game

13   NL: Los Angeles (7) San Diego (6) September 25, 1986
     Atlanta (9) Montreal (4) September 21, 1993
10   AL: Baltimore (6) New York (4) April 26, 1959

Extra-Inning Game

14   NL: New York (7) Chicago (7) May 2, 1956 (17 inn.)
     Los Angeles (9) St. Louis (5) September 1, 1982 (13 inn.)
     Los Angeles (7) Atlanta (7) September 18, 1986 (12 inn.)
     San Francisco (9) Los Angeles (5) September 28, 1986 (16 inn.)
     AL: Oakland (10) Chicago (4) September 19, 1972 (15 inn.)

Most Pinch-Hitters, Doubleheader

10   AL: New York (Boston) September 6, 1954
     Baltimore (Washington) April 19, 1959
     NL: St. Louis (Chicago) May 11, 1958
     St. Louis (Pittsburgh) July 13, 1958
     San Francisco (Arizona) September 23, 2000

Extra-Innings

15   NL: Montreal (Pittsburgh) September 5, 1975 (19 inn.)

Most Pinch-Hitters, Both Clubs, Doubleheader

15   NL: Milwaukee (8) San Francisco (7) August 30, 1964
     San Francisco (10) Arizona (5) September 23, 2000
14   AL: New York (10) Boston (4) September 6, 1954

Extra-Innings

19   NL: Montreal (15) Pittsburgh (4) September 5, 1975 (19 inn.)
17   AL: New York (9) Washington (8) August 14, 1960 (24 inn.)

Most Pinch-Hitters, Inning

6   NL: San Francisco (Pittsburgh) May 5, 1958 (9th)
    San Diego (San Francisco) September 16, 1986 (9th)
    Atlanta (Montreal) September 21, 1993 (7th)
    AL: Detroit (New York) September 5, 1971 (7th)

Most Pinch-Hitters, Both Clubs, Inning

8   AL: Chicago (5) Baltimore (3) May 18, 1957 (7th)
    NL: Philadelphia (5) St. Louis (3) April 30, 1961 (8th)
    New York (5) San Francisco (3) September 16, 1966 (9th)

Most Pinch-Hits, Game

6   NL: Brooklyn (Philadelphia) September 9, 1926
4   AL: Cleveland (Chicago) April 22, 1930

(Most Pinch-Hits, Game, cont.)

4 Philadelphia (Detroit) September 18, 1940
Detroit (Chicago) April 22, 1953
Kansas City (Detroit) September 1, 1958
New York (Cleveland) August 26, 1960 (11 inn.)
Cleveland (Boston) September 21, 1967
Oakland (Detroit) August 30, 1970
Chicago (Oakland) September 7, 1970
Texas (Kansas City) June 8, 1995
Boston (New York) September 8,1995

Most Pinch-Hits, Inning

4 NL: Chicago (Brooklyn) May 21 (2g), 1927 (9th)
Philadelphia (Pittsburgh) September 12, 1974 (8th)
AL: Philadelphia (Detroit) September 18, 1940 (9th)
Texas (Kansas City) June 8, 1995 (8th)
Boston (New York) September 8, 1995 (8th)

Most Pinch-Hit Home Runs, Game

2 NL: Philadelphia (St. Louis) June 2, 1928
St. Louis (Brooklyn) July 21, 1930
St. Louis (Cincinnati) May 12, 1951
Chicago (Philadelphia) June 9, 1954
New York (St. Louis) June 10, 1954
San Francisco (Milwaukee) June 4, 1958
Philadelphia (Pittsburgh) August 13, 1958
New York (Philadelphia) August 15, 1962 (13 inn.)
Los Angeles (Chicago) August 8, 1963 (10 inn.)
New York (Philadelphia) September 17, 1963
New York (San Francisco) August 4, 1969
Montreal (Atlanta) July 13 (1g) 1973
Chicago (Pittsburgh) September 10, 1974
Los Angeles (St. Louis) July 23, 1975
Chicago (Houston) August 23, 1975
Los Angeles (Chicago) August 27, 1982
San Francisco (San Diego) September 28, 1987
New York (San Francisco) May 4, 1991 (12 inn.)
Colorado (Los Angeles) May 6, 1995
Cincinnati (Atlanta) June 22, 1995
Houston (Chicago) September 8, 1995 (11 inn.)
Atlanta (St. Louis) July 22, 1996
New York (St. Louis) May 11, 1997

(Most Pinch-Hit Home Runs, Game, cont.)

2   Chicago (St. Louis) July 13, 1997
    Chicago (Milwaukee) September 12, 1998
    Atlanta (Montreal) May 29, 1999
    San Diego (Colorado) July 2, 1999
    AL: Cleveland (Philadelphia) May 26, 1937
    New York (Kansas City) July 23, 1955 (11 inn.)
    Baltimore (Boston) August 16, 1966 (12 inn.)
    Detroit (Boston) August 11, 1968 (14 inn.)
    Seattle (New York) August 2, 1969
    Minnesota (Detroit) July 31, 1970
    Minnesota (California) July 28 (2g), 1974
    Seattle (New York) April 27, 1979
    Chicago (Oakland) July 6 (2g) 1980
    Baltimore (Texas) May 5, 1984
    Baltimore (Cleveland) August 12, 1985
    Toronto (Detroit) June 14, 1986
    Texas (Boston) September 1, 1986
    California (Chicago) June 28, 1987
    Boston (Chicago) September 19, 1987 (10 inn.)

Most Pinch-Hit Home Runs, Both Clubs, Game
3   NL: Philadelphia (2) St. Louis (1) June 2, 1929
    St. Louis (2) Brooklyn (1) July 21, 1930
    Colorado (2) Los Angeles (1) May 6, 1995
    San Diego (2) Colorado (1) July 2, 1999
2   AL: Many Games, Last:
    Minnesota (1) Chicago (1) May 10, 1995

Most Pinch-Hit Home Runs, 2 Consecutive Games
3   NL: Montreal, July 12–13, 1973
    San Francisco, September 27–28, 1987
    Chicago, September 11–12, 1998
    AL: By many clubs

Most Pinch-Hit Home Runs, Inning
2   NL: New York (St. Louis) June 20, 1954 (6th)
    San Francisco (Milwaukee) June 4, 1958 (10th)
    Los Angeles (Chicago) August 8, 1963 (5th)
    Los Angeles (St. Louis) July 23, 1975 (9th)
    New York (San Francisco) May 4, 1991 (9th)
    Cincinnati (Atlanta) June 22, 1995 (8th)

(Most Pinch-Hit Home Runs, Inning, cont.)

2   New York (St. Louis) May 11, 1997 (9th)
    Atlanta (Montreal) May 25, 1999
    San Diego (Colorado) July 2, 1999
    AL: New York (Kansas City) July 23, 1955 (9th)
    Baltimore (Boston) August 26, 1966 (9th)
    Seattle (New York) April 27, 1979 (8th)
    Minnesota (Oakland) May 16, 1983 (9th)
    Baltimore (Cleveland) August 12, 1985 (9th)
    Texas (Boston) September 1, 1986 (9th)
    Boston (Chicago) September 19, 1997 (9th)

Most Grand Slam Home Runs, Game

1   By many clubs

Most Grand Slam Home Runs, Both Clubs, Game

2   NL: Boston (1) New York (1) May 26, 1929
1   AL: By many clubs

Most Walks, Inning

3   NL: Pittsburgh (Philadelphia) June 3, 1911 (9th)
    Brooklyn (New York) April 22, 1922 (7th)
    Boston (Brooklyn) June 2, 1932 (9th)
    Chicago (Philadelphia) July 29, 1947 (7th)
    St. Louis (New York) May 6, 1994 (9th)
    New York (Colorado) May 18, 1997 (8th)
    Philadelphia (Pittsburgh) July 18, 1997
    AL: Baltimore (Washington) April 22, 1955 (7th)
    Washington (Boston) May 14, 1961 (9th)
    Seattle (Boston) June 2, 1995 (9th)
    Texas (Arizona) July 15, 1999 (9th)

Most Strikeouts, Game

5   AL: Detroit (New York) September 8, 1979
    NL: Chicago (Cincinnati) May 22, 1990 (16 inn.)
    Cincinnati (San Francisco) September 20, 2000

Most Strikeouts, Both Clubs, Game

5   AL: New York (4) Boston (1) July 4, 1955
    Washington (4) Cleveland (1) May 1, 1957
    Detroit (4) Cleveland (1) August 4, 1967
    Detroit (5) New York (0) September 8, 1979
    NL: Los Angeles (3) Cincinnati (2) September 16, 1990

(Most Strikeouts, Both Clubs, Game, cont.)

  5 New York (3) San Francisco (2) August 19, 1996
      Philadelphia (3) Cincinnati (2) April 26, 1997
      Houston (4) New York (1) August 30, 1999
      Cincinnati (5) San Francisco (0) September 20, 2000

Extra-Inning Game

  7 NL: Chicago (5) Cincinnati (2) May 22, 1990 (16 inn.)

Most Strikeouts, Inning

  3 By many clubs. Last:
      NL: Cincinnati (San Francisco) September 20, 2000 (8th)
      AL: Kansas City (Detroit) July 9, 1995 (7th)

WORLD SERIES—INDIVIDUAL BATTING

Most Games, Lifetime

 12 Luis Polonia, AL: Oakland 1988, New York 2000; NL: Atlanta 1995–96

Most Games, One Series

  6 Luis Polonia, NL: Atlanta 1996

Most At-Bats, Lifetime

 11 Luis Polonia, AL: Oakland 1988, New York 2000; NL: Atlanta 1995–96

Most At-Bats, Inning

  2 George Burns, AL: Philadelphia, October 12, 1929 (7th)

Most Hits, Lifetime

  3 Ken O'Dea, NL: Chicago 1935, St. Louis 1942–1944
      Bobby Brown, AL: New York 1947
      Johnny Mize, AL: New York 1949–52
      Dusty Rhodes, NL: New York 1954
      Carl Furillo, NL: Brooklyn 1947, Los Angeles 1959
      Bob Cerv, AL: New York 1955–56, 1960
      Johnny Blanchard, AL: New York 1960–61, 1964
      Carl Warwick, NL: St. Louis 1964
      Gonzalo Marquez, AL: Oakland 1972
      Ken Boswell, NL: New York 1973

Most Hits, One Series

3   Bobby Brown, AL: New York, 1947
    Dusty Rhodes, NL: New York 1954
    Carl Warwick, NL: St. Louis 1964
    Gonzalo Marquez, AL: Oakland 1972
    Ken Boswell, NL: New York 1973

Most Total Bases, One Series

8   Chuck Essegian, NL: Los Angeles 1959
    Bernie Carbo, AL: Boston 1975

Most Home Runs, Lifetime

2   Chuck Essegian, NL: Los Angeles October 2 (7th) 8 (9th) 1959
    Bernie Carbo, AL: Boston October 14 (7th) 21 (8th) 1975

1   Yogi Berra, AL: New York October 2, 1947 (7th)
    Johnny Mize, AL: New York October 3, 1952 (9th)
    George Shuba, NL: Brooklyn September 30, 1953 (6th)
    Dusty Rhodes, NL: New York September 29, 1954 (10th)
    Hank Majeski, AL: Cleveland October 2, 1954 (5th)
    Bob Cerv, AL: New York October 2, 1955 (7th)
    Elston Howard, AL: New York October 5, 1960 (9th)
    Johnny Blanchard, AL: New York October 7, 1961 (8th)
    Jay Johnstone, NL: Los Angeles October 24, 1981 (6th)
    Kirk Gibson, NL: Los Angeles October 15, 1988 (9th)
    Bill Bathe, NL: San Francisco October 27, 1989 (9th)
    Chili Davis, AL: Minnesota October 22, 1991 (8th)
    Ed Sprague, AL: Toronto October 18, 1992 (9th)
    Jim Leyritz, AL: New York October 27, 1999 (8th)

Most Runs Batted In, Series

6   Dusty Rhodes, NL: New York 1954

Most Runs Batted In, Game

3   Dusty Rhodes, NL: New York September 29, 1954
    Hank Majeski, AL: Cleveland October 2, 1954
    Bernie Carbo, AL: Boston October 21, 1975
    Bill Bathe, NL: San Francisco October 27, 1989

Most Walks, One Series

3   Bernie Tate, AL: Washington 1924

Most Strikeouts, One Series

3   Gabby Hartnett, NL: Chicago 1929
    Rollie Helmsley, NL: Chicago 1932

(Most Strikeouts, One Series, cont.)

3   Otto Velez, AL: New York 1976
    Luis Polonia, NL: Atlanta 1996

WORLD SERIES—CLUB BATTING

Most Pinch-Hitters

23 AL: Baltimore (Pittsburgh) 1979 (7 Games)
16 AL: Cleveland (New York)1954 (4 Games)
15 NL: Cincinnati (New York) 1961 (5 Games)
14 NL: Los Angeles (New York) 1981 (6 Games)

Most Pinch-Hitters, Both Clubs

37 AL: Minnesota (Atlanta) 1991 (7 Games)
24 NL: Los Angeles (New York) 1981 (6 Games)
23 AL: Baltimore (Philadelphia) 1983 (5 Games)
19 AL: Cleveland (New York) 1954 (4 Games)

Fewest Pinch-Hitters

0   AL: New York (Cincinnati) 1939 (4 Games)
    AL: Baltimore (Los Angeles) 1966 (4 Games)
    NL: Cincinnati (New York) 1976 (4 Games)
    AL: Philadelphia (Chicago) 1910 (5 Games)
    AL: Philadelphia (New York) 1913 (5 Games)
    AL: Philadelphia (New York) 1911 (6 Games)
2   AL: Milwaukee (St. Louis) 1982 (7 Games)

Fewest Pinch-Hitters, Both Clubs

2   NL: New York (Philadelphia) 1905 (5 Games)
3   NL: Boston (Philadelphia) 1914 (4 Games)
    NL: Cincinnati (New York) 1939 (4 Games)
4   NL: New York (Philadelphia) 1911 (6 Games)
8   AL: Detroit (Pittsburgh) 1909 (7 Games)

Most Pinch-Hitters, Game

6   NL: Los Angeles (Chicago) October 6, 1959

Extra-Inning Game

8   AL: Minnesota (Atlanta) October 22, 1991 (12 inn.)

Most Pinch-Hitters, Both Clubs, Game

8   AL: Baltimore (4) Philadelphia (4) October 15, 1983
    AL: Oakland (5) New York (3) October 14, 1973

(Most Pinch-Hitters, Both Clubs, Game, cont.)

Extra-Inning Game

12   AL: Minnesota (8) Atlanta (4) October 22, 1991 (12 inn.)

Most Pinch-Hitters, Inning

4   NL: New York (Oakland) October 13, 1973 (9th)
      AL: Baltimore (Philadelphia) October 15, 1983 (6th)
      AL: Kansas City (St. Louis) October 26, 1985 (9th)
      AL: Minnesota (St. Louis) October 22, 1987 (9th)
      NL: San Diego (New York) October 18, 1998 (9th)
      NL: New York (New York) October 25, 2000

Most Pinch-Hits, Series

6   AL: New York (Brooklyn) 1947 (7 Games)
      AL: New York (Pittsburgh) 1960 (7 Games)
      AL: Oakland (Cincinnati) 1972 (7 Games)
      AL: Baltimore (Pittsburgh) 1979 (7 Games)

Most Pinch-Hits, Both Clubs, Series

11   AL: New York (6) Brooklyn (5) 1947 (7 Games)

Most Pinch-Hits, Game

3   By many

Most Pinch-Hits, Inning

3   AL: Oakland (Cincinnati) October 19, 1972 (9th)
      NL: San Diego (New York) October 18, 1998 (8th)

Most Pinch-Hit Home Runs

6   AL: New York 1947, 1952, 1955, 1960–61, 1999
5   NL: Brooklyn/Los Angeles 1953, 1959 (2)1981, 1988

Most Pinch-Hit Home Runs, Both Clubs

2   NL: Los Angeles (Chicago) 1959 (6 Games)
      AL: Boston (Cincinnati) 1975 (7 Games)

Most Pinch-Hit Home Runs, Both Clubs, One Series

2   AL: Cleveland (1) New York (1) 1954
      NL: Los Angeles (2) Chicago (0) 1959
      AL: Boston (2) Cincinnati (0) 1975

Most Pinch-Hit Walks, Inning

2   AL: New York (New York) October 15, 1923 (8th)
      AL: Baltimore (Philadelphia) October 15, 1983 (6th)
      AL: New York (Atlanta) October 23, 1999 (8th)

Most Pinch-Hit Strikeouts, Game
    4   AL: St. Louis (St. Louis) October 8, 1944
         AL: St. Louis (St. Louis) October 9, 1944

Most Pinch-Hit Strikeouts, Inning
    3   AL: St. Louis (St. Louis) October 9, 1944 (9th)

ALL-STAR GAMES—CLUB BATTING

Most Pinch-Hitters, 9 Innings
    8   National League, July 9, 1935

Most Pinch-Hitters, Both Clubs, 9 Innings
   11 National League (7) American League (4) July 24, 1973
       National League (7) American League (4) August 9, 1981
       National League (6) American League (5) July 11, 1967 (15 inn.)

Fewest Pinch-Hitters, Game
    0   American League, July 8, 1935
       National League, July 9, 1940
       American League, July 8, 1980

ALL-STAR GAMES—INDIVIDUAL BATTING

Most Hits, Career
    3   NL: Stan Musial

Most Pinch-Hit Home Runs
    1   NL: Mickey Owen, July 6, 1942
       NL: Gus Bell, July 13, 1954
       AL: Larry Doby, July 14, 1954
       NL: Willie Mays, July 10, 1956
       NL: Stan Musial, July 13, 1960
       AL: Harmon Killebrew, July 11, 1961
       NL: George Altman, July 11, 1961
       AL: Pete Runnels, July 30, 1962
       AL: Reggie Jackson, July 13, 1971
       AL: Cookie Rojas, July 25, 1972
       NL: Willie Davis, July 24, 1973
       AL: Carl Yastrzemski, July 15, 1975
       NL: Lee Mazzilli, July 17, 1979
       AL: Frank White, July 15, 1986
       NL: Fred McGriff, July 12, 1994
       NL: Jeff Conine, July 11, 1995

Notes

Introduction

1. Tim McCarver and Dan Gutman, *The Way Baseball Works*, Simon & Schuster, 1996, 111.

Chapter 1. The Makeup of an Effective Pinch-Hitter

1. Lane, F.C., *Batting*, Society for American Baseball Research, 2001, 89.
2. *Ibid*, 90
3. *Ibid*, 90.
4. *Ibid*, 90.
5. *Ibid*, 90.
6. *Saturday Evening Post*, July 28, 1962.
7. *Ibid*.
8. *Pittsburgh Post-Gazette*, May 7, 2000.
9. *Sport*, May, 1962.
10. *Ibid*.
11. *Saturday Evening Post*, July 28, 1962.
12. *Sports Illustrated*, May 28, 1962.
13. *Pacific Stars and Stripes*, August 3, 1953.
14. *Ibid*.

15. *Milwaukee Journal-Sentinel*, March 2, 2000.
16. *Saturday Evening Post*, July 28, 1962.
17. *Baseball Digest*, January, 1977.
18. *Sports Illustrated*, May 28, 1962.
19. *Saturday Evening Post*, July 28, 1962.
20. *The Sporting News*, July 25, 1983.
21. *Ibid*.
22. *Sports Illustrated*, May 28, 1962.
23. *The Sporting News*, September 27, 1980.
24. *Baseball Digest*, September, 1979.
25. *Major League Baseball News*, July 14, 2001.
26. *Ibid*.
27. *Sports Illustrated*, May 28, 1962.
28. *Baseball Digest*, June, 2001.
29. *Sport*, September, 1959.
30. *Sports Illustrated*, June 6, 1955.
31. *Ibid*.
32. *Ibid*.
33. *Ibid*.
34. *Sports Illustrated*, May 28, 1962.
35. *Ibid*.
36. *Ibid*.

191

37. *The Sporting News*, July 22, 1978.
38. *Ibid.*
39. *Ibid.*
40. *Ibid.*
41. *Major League Baseball News*, October 3, 2001.
42. *Ibid.*
43. *The Sporting News*, June 24, 1978.
44. *Ibid.*
45. *Ibid.*

Chapter 2. 1876–1899:
The Pinch-Hitting Pioneers

1. *Baseball Research Journal*, 1990.
2. *USA TODAY Baseball Weekly*, April 29–May 5, 1992.
3. *Ibid.*
4. *Total Baseball*, 2nd ed., 1991.
5. *Saturday Evening Post*, June 3, 1944.
6. *The Sporting News*, December 31, 1958.
7. *Ibid.*
8. *Total Baseball*, 2nd ed., 1991.
9. *Ibid.*

Chapter 5. 1920–1929:
Cy Williams Starts
Setting Home Run Records

1. *Baseball Digest*, February, 1962.
2. *Ibid.*
3. *Baseball Research Journal*, 1990.
4. Bill James, *The New Bill James Historical Baseball Abstract*, Free Press, 2001, 445.

Chapter 7. 1940–1949:
None Better Than a Couple of
Joes Named Cronin and Schultz

1. *The New York Times Magazine*, August 14, 1966.

Chapter 8. 1950–1959:
One Extreme — Johnny Mize —
to Another — Eddie Gaedel

1. *The Baseball Online Library*, CBS SportsLine, June 4, 2001.
2. *Ibid.*
3. *Ibid.*
4. *Time*, October 11, 1954.
5. *The New York Times Magazine*, August 14, 1966.
6. *Ibid.*
7. *Ibid.*
8. *Ibid.*
9. *Ibid.*
10. *Ibid.*
11. *Ibid.*
12. *Ibid.*
13. *The Baseball Online Library*, CBS SportsLine, May 1, 2002.
14. *Baseball Research Journal*, 1990.
15. *The New York Times Magazine*, August 14, 1966.
16. *The Sporting News*, July 25, 1983.

Chapter 9. 1960–1969:
Smoky Burgess and Jerry Lynch
Make It an Art Form

1. *Sport*, March, 1962.
2. *Ibid.*
3. *The New York Times Magazine*, August 14, 1966.
4. *Ibid.*
5. *The Sporting News*, April 29, 1978.
6. *The New York Times Magazine*, August 14, 1966.
7. *Ibid.*
8. *Ibid.*
9. *Sport*, May, 1962.
10. *Ibid.*
11. *Ibid.*
12. *Saturday Evening Post*, July 28, 1962.
13. *Ibid.*

14. Gene Karst and Martin J. Jones, Jr., *Who's Who in Professional Baseball*, Arlington House, 1973, 118.
15. *The Baseball Online Library*, CBS SportsLine, March 23, 2002.

Chapter 10. 1970–1979: Manny Mota, Jose Morales and the Designated Hitter Emerge

1. *The Baseball Online Library*, CBS SportsLine, June 4, 2001
2. *The Sporting News*, May 9, 1983.
3. *Ibid.*
4. *Ibid.*
5. *Ibid.*

Chapter 11. 1980–1989: Del Unser, Cliff Johnson and Greg Gross Dominate

1. *Baseball Digest*, October, 2000.
2. *Ibid.*
3. *Ibid.*
4. *The Sporting News*, January 9, 1984.
5. *Baseball Digest*, April, 1982.
6. *Ibid.*
7. *The Sporting News*, July 25, 1983.
8. *CBS Television Sports*, October 15, 1988.

Chapter 12. 1990–2002: Harris, Vander Wal and Hansen Carry On

1. *Metscorner.com*, November 16, 2001.

2. *Ibid.*
3. *Ibid.*
4. *Ibid.*
5. *Ibid.*
6. *Sports Illustrated*, October 6, 2001.
7. *Ibid.*
8. *Pittsburgh Post-Gazette*, May 7, 2000.
9. *Ibid.*
10. *Major League Baseball News*, June 11, 2001.
11. *Ibid.*
12. *Ibid.*
13. *Ibid.*
14. *Ibid.*
15. *Ibid.*
16. *Major League Baseball News*, September 3, 2001.
17. *Pittsburgh Post-Gazette*, July 20, 2001.
18. *Ibid.*
19. *ESPN.com Players Profile*, January 31, 2002.
20. *Ibid.*
21. *Ibid.*

Chapter 13. The Impact of the Designated Hitter

1. *Athens Daily News*, October 26, 1997.
2. *Tampa Bay.rr.com*, August 21, 2001.
3. Bill James, *The New Bill James Historical Baseball Abstract*, Free Press, 2001.
4. *The Sporting News*, September 25, 1997.
5. *Baseball Weekly*, August 21, 2001.
6. *Ibid.*

Bibliography

Biederman, Les. "Pinch-Hit King Burgess Drools Over DH." *The Sporting News*, April 1978.

_____. "These Are the Best Pinch-Hitters of All Time." *Baseball Digest*, May 1978.

Bodley, Hal. "Gross Sets Mark for Pinch-Hits." *The Sporting News*, October 18, 1982.

Bouchette, Ed. "John Vander Wal Is a Hit in a Pinch." *Pittsburgh Post-Gazette*, May 7, 2000.

Caroules, Jon. "Tug McGraw and Del Unser Played Vital Roles in Phillies' Title Run." Century Publishing, 2000.

CBS SportsLine. *The Online Baseball Library*. 2001-2002.

Collier, Phil. "Rettenmund Earns Praise as Padre in a Pinch." *The Sporting News*, June 11, 1977.

Cope, Myron. "Mr. Wonderful." *Sport*, March 1962.

Davids, L. Robert. *New Records for Pinch-Hitters*. SABR, 1977.

_____. *The Pinch-Hitters*. Total Baseball, Second Edition, Warner Books, 1991.

Drebinger, John. "Pinch-Hitters." *Baseball Magazine*, June 1944.

Durslag, Mel. "Mota … The Epitome of Patience." *The Sporting News*, September 27, 1980.

Fowler, Bob. "Morales Is Mighty Tough as Twins' Pinch-Swinger." *The Sporting News*, June 24, 1978.

Furlong, William Barry. "The Fine Art of Pinch-Hitting: How Specialized Can You Get?" *New York Times Magazine*, August 14, 1966.

Galloway, Randy. "Stein Way as Pinch-Hitter Like Music to Ranger Ears." *The Sporting News*, June 13, 1981.

Gelman, Steve. "Advice to Pinch-Hitters." *Sport*, September 1959.

Goddard, Joe. "Sox Feel Hairston Will Do in a Pinch." *The Sporting News*, January 9, 1984.

Graham, Frank. "Johnny Mize" *Baseball Extra*, A.S. Barnes, 1954.

Hannon, John T., Jr. "Ham Hyatt and the Development of Pinch-Hitting." *Baseball Research Journal*, SABR 1995.

Holtzman, Jerome. "Hitters in Waiting." *Saturday Evening Post*, July 28, 1962.

_____. "Just a Pinch." MLB.com, November 28, 2000.

Horn, Huston. "They Also Serve Who Only Sit Around." *Sports Illustrated*, May 28, 1962.

James, Bill. *The Bill James Guide to Baseball Managers from 1870 to Today*. Scribner, 1997.

_____. *The New Bill James Historical Baseball Abstract*. Free Press, 2001.

Karst, Gene, and Martin J. Jones, Jr. *Who's Who in Professional Baseball*. Arlington House, 1973.

Kermisch, Al. "Del Unser Becomes Pinch-Homer Specialist." *Baseball Research Journal*, SABR 1980.

_____. "Paschal Batted for Babe Ruth and Lou Gehrig." *Baseball Research Journal*, SABR 1995.

_____. "Pinch-Hitters for Superstars." *Baseball Research Journal*, SABR 1994.

Lane, F.C. *Batting*. Society for American Baseball Research, 2001.

Larson, Bill. "In a Pinch." MLB.com, June 11, 2001.

Lewis, Allen. "How Hall of Fame Players Performed as Pinch-Hitters." *Baseball Digest*, June 1992.

Leyden, John G. "Pinch-Hitting Role Celebrates Its Centennial." *USA Today Baseball Weekly*, April 29, 1992.

Light, Jonathan Fraser. *The Cultural Encyclopedia of Baseball*. McFarland, 1997.

Madden, Bill "Pinch-Hit Master Philley Tutored Rusty Staub." *The Sporting News*, July 25, 1983.

Mann, Arthur. "Does Pinch-Hitting Pay?" *Baseball Magazine*, April 1944.

_____. "First Pinch-Hitter." *Saturday Evening Post*, June 3, 1944.

McCarver, Tim, and Dan Gutman. *The Way Baseball Works*. Simon & Schuster, 1996.

McCoy, Bob. "The Head of the Class." *The Sporting News*, August 2, 1980.

Mockler, Stan. "Lowrey Clouts Ball in Clutch to Aid Cardinals' Campaign." *Pacific Stars and Stripes*. August 3, 1953.

Noll, Gene. "Pinch-Hitting Pitchers." *Baseball Research Journal*, SABR, 1995.

O'Brien, Jim. "Manny Mota, Baseball's Premier Pinch-Hitter." *Baseball Digest*, September 1979.

Olson, Drew. "In a Pinch: Preparation Main Ingredient for Bench." *Milwaukee Journal Sentinel*, March 2, 2000.

Pepe, Phil. "In the Pinch, Mets Turn to Kranepool." *The Sporting News*, July 22, 1978.

Pickard, Chuck. "Let's Hear It for a Little Known Record Holder." *Baseball Digest*, April 1982.

Quimby, Allen H. "An Afternoon with Red Lucas." *Baseball Research Journal*, SABR, 1981.

Rathgeber, Bob. "The Great Pinch-Hitting Pitcher: Red Lucas." The Cincinnati Reds Scrapbook, 1982.

Rausch, Gary. *Batting Around with David Dellucci.* arizonadiamondbacks.com, September 3, 2001.

Reichler, Joe. *In a Pinch, The World Series: A 75th Anniversary,* Simon & Schuster, 1978.

_____, editor. *The Baseball Encyclopedia.* Baseball Register, 1988.

Richards, Paul. "Inside Baseball." *Sports Illustrated*, June 6, 1955.

Ritter, Lawrence. *The Story of Baseball.* William Morrow, 1983.

Shatzkin, Mike, editor. *The Ballplayers.* William Morrow, 1990.

Simons, Herbert. "They Pinch-Hit for the Greats!" *Baseball Digest*, February 1962.

Siwoff, Seymour, editor. *The Book of Baseball Records.* Elias Sports Bureau, Inc., 2001.

Sparks, Barry. "These Hall of Fame Players Flopped as Pinch-Hitters." *Baseball Digest*, July 1985.

Spoelstra, Watson. "Wild-Card Pinch-Hitter? It Suits Gates." *The Sporting News*, January 11, 1969.

Stainback, Barry. "Bob Hale: Pinch-Hitting Specialist." *Sport*, May 1962.

Tattersall, John C. "Philley's 23rd Pinch-Hit Sets Major Record." *The Sporting News*, September 6, 1961.

Vass, George. "These Are the Game's Five Greatest Pinch-Hitters." *Baseball Digest*, January 1976.

Verrell, Gordon. "Dodgers' Morales a Pinch-Hit Expert." *The Sporting News*, May 9, 1983.

_____. "Lacy Misses Record, But He'll Do in a Pinch." *The Sporting News*, June 10, 1978.

Index